Lecture Notes in Computer Science 12235

More information about this series at http://www.springer.com/series/7408

António Casimiro · Frank Ortmeier ·
Erwin Schoitsch · Friedemann Bitsch ·
Pedro Ferreira (Eds.)

Computer Safety, Reliability, and Security

SAFECOMP 2020 Workshops

DECSoS 2020, DepDevOps 2020, USDAI 2020, and WAISE 2020
Lisbon, Portugal, September 15, 2020
Proceedings

 Springer

Editors
António Casimiro (iD)
University of Lisbon
Lisbon, Portugal

Erwin Schoitsch (iD)
Austrian Institute of Technology
Vienna, Austria

Pedro Ferreira (iD)
University of Lisbon
Lisbon, Portugal

Frank Ortmeier (iD)
Otto-von-Guericke University
Magdeburg, Germany

Friedemann Bitsch (iD)
Thales Deutschland GmbH
Ditzingen, Germany

ISSN 0302-9743   ISSN 1611-3349 (electronic)
Lecture Notes in Computer Science
ISBN 978-3-030-55582-5   ISBN 978-3-030-55583-2 (eBook)
https://doi.org/10.1007/978-3-030-55583-2

LNCS Sublibrary: SL2 – Programming and Software Engineering

This Springer imprint is published by the registered company Springer Nature Switzerland AG
The registered company address is: Gewerbestrasse 11, 6330 Cham, Switzerland

Preface

The SAFECOMP workshop day has for many years preceded the SAFECOMP conference, attracting additional participants. The SAFECOMP workshops have become more attractive since they started generating their own proceedings in the Springer LNCS series (Springer LNCS vol. 12235, the book in your hands; the main conference proceedings are LNCS 12234). This meant adhering to Springer's guidelines, i.e., the respective International Program Committee of each workshop had to make sure that at least three independent reviewers reviewed the papers carefully. The selection criteria were different from those for the main conference since authors were encouraged to submit workshop papers, i.e., on work in progress and potentially controversial topics. In total, 30 regular papers (out of 45) were accepted. One invited paper was added (in the DECSoS workshop), and all workshops included an introduction written by the chairs.

Two of the four workshops are sequels to earlier workshops, two are new in topics and Organizing Committees:

- DECSoS 2020 – 15th Workshop on Dependable Smart Embedded and Cyber-Physical Systems and Systems-of-Systems, chaired by Erwin Schoitsch and Amund Skavhaug, and supported by ERCIM, EWICS, and ARTEMIS/ECSEL projects.
- WAISE 2020 – Third International Workshop on Artificial Intelligence Safety Engineering, chaired by Orlando Avila-García, Mauricio Castillo-Effen, Chih-Hong Cheng, Zakaria Chihani, and Simos Gerasimou.
- DepDevOps 2020 – First International Workshop on Dependable Development-Operation Continuum Methods for Dependable Cyber-Physical Systems, chaired by Haris Isakovic, Miren Illarramendi, Aitor Arrieta, and Irune Agirre.
- USDAI 2020 – First International Workshop on Underpinnings for Safe Distributed AI, chaired by Morten Larsen and Alexandru Uta.

The workshops provide a truly international platform for academia and industry.

It has been a pleasure to work with the SAFECOMP chair Antonio Casimiro, with the publication chairs, Friedemann Bitsch and Pedro Ferreira, the workshop chairs, Program Committees, and the authors. Particular thanks goes to all partners who reorganized SAFECOMP 2020 and all workshops as an online event in hard times because of the COVID-19 crisis. Thank you all for your good cooperation and excellent work!

September 2020   Erwin Schoitsch

Organization

Committees

EWICS TC7 Chair

Francesca Saglietti   University of Erlangen-Nuremberg, Germany

General Chair

António Casimiro   University of Lisbon, Portugal

Program Co-chairs

António Casimiro   University of Lisbon, Portugal
Frank Ortmeier   Otto-von-Guericke University, Germany

General Workshop Chair

Erwin Schoitsch   AIT Austrian Institute of Technology, Austria

Publication Chairs

Friedemann Bitsch   Thales Deutschland GmbH, Germany
Pedro Ferreira   University of Lisbon, Portugal

Position Papers Chair

Jérémie Guiochet   University of Toulouse III, France

Publicity Chair

Bernardo Ferreira   University of Lisbon, Portugal

Local Organizing Committee

António Casimiro   University of Lisbon, Portugal
Pedro Ferreira   University of Lisbon, Portugal
Ibéria Medeiros   University of Lisbon, Portugal

Workshop Chairs

DECSoS 2020

Erwin Schoitsch   AIT Austrian Institute of Technology, Austria
Amund Skavhaug   NTNU, Norway

DepDevOps 2020

Haris Isakovic	TU Wien, Austria
Miren Illarramendi	Mondragon University, Spain
Aitor Arrieta	Mondragon University, Spain
Irune Agirre	IKERLAN, Spain

USDAI 2020

Morten Larsen	AnyWi Technologies, The Netherlands
Alexandru Uta	Leiden Institute of Advanced Computer Science, The Netherlands

WAISE 2020

Orlando Avila-García	Atos, Spain
Mauricio Castillo-Effen	Lockheed Martin, USA
Chih-Hong Cheng	DENSO, Germany
Zakaria Chihani	CEA LIST, France
Simos Gerasimou	University of York, UK

Gold Sponsor

Intel

Silver Sponsor

Edge Case Research

EDGE CASE RESEARCH

Supporting Institutions

European Workshop on Industrial
Computer Systems – Reliability, Safety
and Security

Faculdade de Ciências da
Universidade de Lisboa

LASIGE Research Unit

AG Software Engineering,
Otto-von-Guericke-Universität Magdeburg

Austrian Institute of Technology

Thales Deutschland GmbH

Lecture Notes in Computer
Science (LNCS), Springer Science +
Business Media

European Network of Clubs for
Reliability and Safety
of Software-Intensive Systems

German Computer Society

Informationstechnische Gesellschaft

Electronic Components and Systems
for European Leadership - Austria

ARTEMIS Industry Association

Verband österreichischer
Software Industrie

Austrian Computer Society

European Research Consortium
for Informatics and Mathematics

Contents

**15th International Workshop on Dependable Smart
Cyber-Physical Systems and Systems-of-Systems (DECSoS 2020)**

Supervisory Control Theory in System Safety Analysis   9
  Yuvaraj Selvaraj, Zhennan Fei, and Martin Fabian

A Method to Support the Accountability of Safety Cases by Integrating
Safety Analysis and Model-Based Design 23
  Nobuaki Tanaka, Hisashi Yomiya, and Kiyoshi Ogawa

Collecting and Classifying Security and Privacy Design Patterns
for Connected Vehicles: SECREDAS Approach 36
  Nadja Marko, Alexandr Vasenev, and Christoph Striecks

Safety and Security Interference Analysis in the Design Stage 54
  *Jabier Martinez, Jean Godot, Alejandra Ruiz, Abel Balbis,
  and Ricardo Ruiz Nolasco*

Formalising the Impact of Security Attacks on IoT Safety 69
  Ehsan Poorhadi, Elena Troubitysna, and György Dan

Assurance Case Patterns for Cyber-Physical Systems
with Deep Neural Networks 82
  *Ramneet Kaur, Radoslav Ivanov, Matthew Cleaveland, Oleg Sokolsky,
  and Insup Lee*

Safety-Critical Software Development in C++. 98
  *Daniel Kästner, Christoph Cullmann, Gernot Gebhard, Sebastian Hahn,
  Thomas Karos, Laurent Mauborgne, Stephan Wilhelm,
  and Christian Ferdinand*

An Instruction Filter for Time-Predictable Code Execution
on Standard Processors 111
  Michael Platzer and Peter Puschner

ISO/SAE DIS 21434 Automotive Cybersecurity Standard - In a Nutshell. . . . 123
  *Georg Macher, Christoph Schmittner, Omar Veledar,
  and Eugen Brenner*

WiCAR - Simulating Towards the Wireless Car 136
  *Harrison Kurunathan, Ricardo Severino, Ênio Filho,
  and Eduardo Tovar*

Automated Right of Way for Emergency Vehicles in C-ITS:
An Analysis of Cyber-Security Risks.   148
  Lucie Langer, Arndt Bonitz, Christoph Schmittner, and Stefan Ruehrup

Integrity Checking of Railway Interlocking Firmware   161
  Ronny Bäckman, Ian Oliver, and Gabriela Limonta

LoRaWAN with HSM as a Security Improvement
for Agriculture Applications.   176
  Reinhard Kloibhofer, Erwin Kristen, and Luca Davoli

1st International Workshop on Dependable Development-Operation Continuum Methods for Dependable Cyber-Physical System (DepDevOps 2020)

Multilevel Runtime Security and Safety Monitoring for Cyber Physical
Systems Using Model-Based Engineering.   193
  Smitha Gautham, Athira V. Jayakumar, and Carl Elks

Towards a DevOps Approach in Cyber Physical Production Systems Using
Digital Twins   205
  Miriam Ugarte Querejeta, Leire Etxeberria, and Goiuria Sagardui

Leveraging Semi-formal Approaches for DepDevOps   217
  Wanja Zaeske and Umut Durak

1st International Workshop on Underpinnings for Safe Distributed Artificial Intelligence (USDAI 2020)

Towards Building Data Trust and Transparency in Data-Driven
Business Applications   229
  Annanda Rath, Wim Codenie, and Anna Hristoskova

Distributed AI for Special-Purpose Vehicles.   243
  *Kevin Van Vaerenbergh, Henrique Cabral, Pierre Dagnely,
  and Tom Tourwé*

Cynefin Framework, DevOps and Secure IoT: Understanding the Nature
of IoT Systems and Exploring Where in the DevOps Cycle Easy Gains Can
Be Made to Increase Their Security.   255
  Franklin Selgert

Creating It from SCRATCh: A Practical Approach for Enhancing
the Security of IoT-Systems in a DevOps-Enabled Software
Development Environment   266
    Simon D. Duque Anton, Daniel Fraunholz, Daniel Krohmer,
    Daniel Reti, Hans D. Schotten, Franklin Selgert, Marcell Marosvölgyi,
    Morten Larsen, Krishna Sudhakar, Tobias Koch, Till Witt,
    and Cédric Bassem

**3rd International Workshop on Artificial Intelligence Safety
Engineering (WAISE 2020)**

Revisiting Neuron Coverage and Its Application to Test Generation   289
    Stephanie Abrecht, Maram Akila, Sujan Sai Gannamaneni,
    Konrad Groh, Christian Heinzemann, Sebastian Houben,
    and Matthias Woehrle

A Principal Component Analysis Approach for Embedding Local
Symmetries into Deep Learning Algorithms   302
    Pierre-Yves Lagrave

A Framework for Building Uncertainty Wrappers for AI/ML-Based
Data-Driven Components   315
    Michael Kläs and Lisa Jöckel

Rule-Based Safety Evidence for Neural Networks   328
    Tewodros A. Beyene and Amit Sahu

Safety Concerns and Mitigation Approaches Regarding the Use of Deep
Learning in Safety-Critical Perception Tasks   336
    Oliver Willers, Sebastian Sudholt, Shervin Raafatnia,
    and Stephanie Abrecht

Positive Trust Balance for Self-driving Car Deployment   351
    Philip Koopman and Michael Wagner

Integration of Formal Safety Models on System Level Using the Example
of Responsibility Sensitive Safety and CARLA Driving Simulator   358
    Bernd Gassmann, Frederik Pasch, Fabian Oboril,
    and Kay-Ulrich Scholl

A Safety Case Pattern for Systems with Machine Learning Components   370
    Ernest Wozniak, Carmen Cârlan, Esra Acar-Celik, and Henrik J. Putzer

Structuring the Safety Argumentation for Deep Neural Network Based
Perception in Automotive Applications   383
    Gesina Schwalbe, Bernhard Knie, Timo Sämann, Timo Dobberphul,
    Lydia Gauerhof, Shervin Raafatnia, and Vittorio Rocco

An Assurance Case Pattern for the Interpretability of Machine Learning
in Safety-Critical Systems   395
    Francis Rhys Ward and Ibrahim Habli

A Structured Argument for Assuring Safety of the Intended
Functionality (SOTIF)   408
    John Birch, David Blackburn, John Botham, Ibrahim Habli,
    David Higham, Helen Monkhouse, Gareth Price, Norina Ratiu,
    and Roger Rivett

Author Index   415

15th International Workshop on Dependable Smart Cyber-Physical Systems and Systems-of-Systems (DECSoS 2020)

15th International Workshop on Dependable Smart Cyber-Physical Systems and Systems-of-Systems (DECSoS 2020)

European Research and Innovation Projects in the Field of Dependable Cyber-Physical Systems and Systems-of-Systems
(supported by EWICS TC7, ERCIM and ARTEMIS/ECSEL projects)

Erwin Schoitsch[1] and Amund Skavhaug[2]

[1] Center for Digital Safety & Security,
AIT Austrian Institute of Technology GmbH, Vienna, Austria
Erwin.Schoitsch@ait.ac.at
[2] Department of Mechanical and Industrial Engineering,
NTNU (The Norwegian University of Science and Technology),
Trondheim, Norway
Amund.Skavhaug@ntnu.no

1 Introduction

The DECSoS workshop at SAFECOMP follows already its own tradition since 2006. In the past, it focussed on the conventional type of "dependable embedded systems", covering all dependability aspects as defined by Avizienis, Lapries, Kopetz, Voges and others in IFIP WG 10.4. To put more emphasis on the relationship to physics, mechatronics and the notion of interaction with an unpredictable environment, massive deployment and highly interconnected systems of different type, the terminology changed to "cyber-physical systems" (CPS) and "Systems-of-Systems" (SoS). The new megatrend IoT ("Internet of Things") as super-infrastructure for CPS as things added a new dimension with enormous challenges. "Intelligence" as a new ability of systems and components leads to a new paradigm, "Smart Systems". Collaboration and co-operation of these systems with each other and humans, and the interplay of safety, cybersecurity, privacy, and reliability, together with cognitive decision making, are leading to new challenges in verification, validation and certification/qualification, as these systems operate in an unpredictable environment and are open, adaptive and even (partly) autonomous. Examples are e.g. the smart power grid, highly automated transport systems, advanced manufacturing systems ("Industry 4.0"), mobile co-operating autonomous vehicles and robotic systems, smart health care, and smart buildings up to smart cities.

Society depends more and more on CPS and SoS - thus it is important to consider trustworthiness (dependability (safety, reliability, availability, security, maintainability, etc.), privacy, resilience, robustness and sustainability, together with ethical aspects in a holistic manner. These are targeted research areas in Horizon 2020 and public-private partnerships such as the ECSEL JU (Joint Undertaking) (Electronic Components and

Systems for European Leadership), which integrated the former ARTEMIS (Advanced Research and Technology for Embedded Intelligent Systems), ENIAC and EPoSS efforts as "private partners". The public part are the EC and the national public authorities of the participating member states. Funding comes from the EC and the national public authorities ("tri-partite funding": EC, member states, project partners). Besides ECSEL, other JTIs (Joint Technology Initiatives), who organize their own research & innovation agenda and manage their work as separate legal entities according to Article 187 of the Lisbon Treaty, are: Innovative Medicines Initiative (IMI), Fuel Cells and Hydrogen (FCH), Clean Sky, Bio-Based Industries, Shift2Rail, Single European Sky Air Traffic Management Research (SESAR).

Besides these Joint Undertakings there are many other so-called contractual PPPs, where funding is completely from the EC (via the Horizon 2020 program), but the work program and strategy are developed together with a private partner association, e.g. Robotics cPPP SPARC with euRobotics as private partner. Others are e.g. Factories of the Future (FoF), Energy-efficient Buildings (EeB), Sustainable Process Industry (SPIRE), European Green Vehicles Initiative (EGVI), Photonics, High Performance Computing (HPC), Advanced 5G Networks for the Future Internet (5G), the Big Data Value PPP and the cPPP for Cybersecurity Industrial Research and Innovation.

The period of Horizon 2020 Programme and the current PPPs ends with the current EU budget period. The landscape of PPPs will be updated in the context of the next EC Research Programme "HORIZON Europe" (2021-2027), where re-organized JUs are planned (e.g. ECS-KDT (Electronic Components and Systems, Key Digital Technologies) for ECSEL, including additional key themes like photonics and software, advanced computing technologies, biosensors and flexible electronics), besides new PPPs. Due to the COVID-19 crises and other negotiations within the EC, the new Programmes are delayed at the time of the writing of this text, and in any case need approval of the European Parliament to become effective.

2 ECSEL: The European Cyber-Physical Systems Initiative

Some ECSEL Projects which have "co-hosted" the Workshop, in supporting partners by funding the research, have been finished this year before Summer (see reports in last year's Springer Safecomp 2019 Workshop Proceedings, LNCS 11699). This year, mainly H2020/ECSEL projects and a few nationally funded projects are "co-hosting" the DECSOS Workshop via contributions from supported partners:

- AQUAS ("Aggregated Quality Assurance for Systems", (https://aquas-project.eu/),
- SECREDAS ("Product Security for Cross Domain Reliable Dependable Automated Systems"), (https://www.ecsel.eu/projects/secredas), contributing to ECSEL Lighthouse Cluster "Mobility.E").
- AFarCloud ("Aggregated Farming in the Cloud") (http://www.afarcloud.eu/), member of the ECSEL Lighthouse cluster Industry4.E.
- DRIVES project, ERASMUS Programme of the EC.

- Air Force Research Laboratory and the Defense Advanced Research Projects Agency (DARPA), US.
- EVE (KIRAS Programme) and COMET K2 Competence Centers (Austria).
- National funding programmes from Sweden (VINNOVA), Portugal, Japan.

Results of these projects are partially reported in presentations at the DECSoS-Workshop. Some presentations refer to work done within companies or institutes, not referring to particular public project funding.

Other important ECSEL projects in the context of DECSOS are the two large ECSEL "Lighthouse" projects for Mobility.E and for Industry4.E, which aim at providing synergies by cooperation with a group of related European projects in their area of interest:

- AutoDrive ("Advancing fail-aware, fail-safe, and fail-operational electronic components, systems, and architectures for fully automated driving to make future mobility safer, affordable, and end-user acceptable"), (https://autodrive-project.eu/), (leading project of the ECSEL Lighthouse Cluster "Mobility.E").
- Productive 4.0 ("Electronics and ICT as enabler for digital industry and optimized supply chain management covering the entire product lifecycle"), (https://productive40.eu/), (Leading project of the ECSEL Lighthouse Cluster "Industry4.E").
- ARROWHEAD Tools (European investment in digitalization and automation solutions for the European industry, which will close the tools' gaps; https://arrowhead.eu/arrowheadtools), close cooperation with Productive4.0 and member of the Lighthouse cluster Industry4.E.
- iDev40 ("Integrated Development 4.0", https://www.ecsel.eu/projects/idev40), contributing to ECSEL Lighthouse Cluster "Industry4.E.

New H2020/ECSEL projects which started this or second half of last year, and may be reported about next year at this workshop or SAFECOMP 2021, are e.g.

- Comp4Drones (Framework of key enabling technologies for safe and autonomous drones' applications, https://artemis-ia.eu/project/180-COMP4DRONES.html; started October 2019).

Short descriptions of the projects, partners, structure and technical goals and objectives are described on the project and the ECSEL websites, see also the Acknowledgement at the end of this introduction and https://www.ecsel.eu/projects.

3 This Year's Workshop

The workshop DECSoS 2020 provides some insight into an interesting set of topics to enable fruitful discussions. The mixture of topics is hopefully well balanced, with a certain focus on multi-concern assurance issues (cybersecurity & safety, plus privacy, co-engineering), on safety and security analysis, and on critical systems development, validation and applications. Presentations are mainly based on ECSEL, Horizon 2020, and nationally funded projects mentioned above, and on industrial developments of partners' companies and universities. In the following explanations the projects are mentioned, which at least partially funded the work presented.

The session starts with an introduction and overview to the DECSOS Workshop, setting the European Research and Innovation scene.

The first session on **Model-based Safety Analysis** comprises two presentations:

(1) Supervisory Control Theory in System Safety Analysis, *by Yuvaraj Selvaraj, Zhennan Fei and Martin Fabian.*
    The paper presents a model-based approach to overcome the limitations of standard FTA using Supervisory Control Theory (project Automatically Assessing Correctness of Autonomous Vehicles (Auto-CAV), FFI/VINNOVA, Sweden).

(2) A method to support the accountability of safety cases by integrating safety analysis and model-based design, *by Nobuaki Tanaka, Hisashi Yomiya and Kiyoshi Ogawa.*
    Based on FTA and FMEA analysis results and SysML diagrams, the method described allows to visualize a hybrid failure chain to understand better the artefacts of safety analysis.

The second session covers **Safety/Security/Privacy Systems Co-Engineering** with three papers:

(1) Collecting and Classifying Security and Privacy Design Patterns for Connected Vehicles, *by Nadja Marko, Alexandr Vasenev and Christoph Striecks (invited).*
    To provide modular and reusable designs to solve, security, safety and privacy issues in highly automated systems (particularly automotive), solutions are collected as design patterns (ECSEL project SECREDAS)

(2) Safety and Security Interference Analysis in the Design Stage, *by Jabier Martinez, Jean Godot, Alejandra Ruiz, Abel Balbis and Ricardo Ruiz Nolasco.*
    Safety and security co-analysis as part of co-engineering is enriched in the design stage to provide capabilities for interference analysis, discussed in context of two use cases (ECSEL project AQUAS).

(3) Formalising the Impact of Security Attacks on IoT Safety, *by Ehsan Poorhadi, Elena Troubitsyna and György Dan.*
    Connected safety critical systems are susceptible to attacks. Using the Event-B framework, the impact of security attacks on safety is formalized (supported by Trafikverket, Sweden).

The third session is dedicated to **Critical System Development and Validation:**

(1) Assurance case patterns for cyber-physical systems with deep neural networks, *by Ramneet Kaur, Radoslav Ivanov, Matthew Cleaveland, Oleg Sokolsky and Insup Lee.*
    The paper shows that an assurance case can be used to argue about DNN based systems in two autonomous driving scenarios (DARPA project).

(2) Safety-Critical Software Development in C++, *by Daniel Kästner, Christoph Cullmann, Gernot Gebhard, Sebastian Hahn, Thomas Karos, Laurent Mauborgne, Stephan Wilhelm and Christian Ferdinand.*

Inherent complexity of C++ as object-oriented language has severe implications for testability, performance and other relevant properties for safety critical systems, including tool diversity and qualification. Requirements of different safety standards are addressed.

(3) An Instruction Filter for Time-Predictable Code Execution on Standard Processors, *by Michael Platzer and Peter Puschner.*
The paper presents a novel approach that adds support for fully predicated execution to existing processor cores to facilitate timing analysis with a single path filter, implemented on LEON3 and IBEX processors.

The last session **"Applications' Assurance of Security and Integrity"** includes two application-oriented papers coverin two particular aspects of safety and security checking and improvement in railway interlocking and in agricultural automation:

(1) Integrity Checking of Railway Interlocking Firmware, *by Ronny Backmann, Ian Oliver and Gabriela Limonta.*
Trusted systems are often assured by use of core and hardware roots of trust, which is not familiar and used in Health- and Railway domains. The authors constructed a simulation environment to provide a safe means for exploring trust and integrity attacks in these domains (ECSEL project SECREDAS).

(2) LoRaWAN with HSM (Hardware Secure Module) as a Security Improvement for Agriculture Applications, *by Reinhard Kloibhofer, Erwin Kristen and Luca Davoli.*
Digital transformation in the agricultural domain requires continuously monitoring environmental data and recording of all work parameters which are used for decision making and in-time missions. To guarantee data security and protection of sensor nodes, a security improvement concept around LoRaWAN communication using a HSM is presented (ECSEL project AFarCloud).

As chairpersons of the workshop, we want to thank all authors and contributors who submitted their work, Friedemann Bitsch and Pedro Ferreira, the SAFECOMP Publication Chairs, and the members of the International Program Committee who enabled a fair evaluation through reviews and considerable improvements in many cases. We want to express our thanks to the SAFECOMP organizers, and their chairperson Antonio Casimiro, who provided us the opportunity to organize the workshop at SAFECOMP 2020 as an on-line event, despite the CoVID-19 crises, which did not allow an international conference Face-to-Face in Lisbon, because of the still possible travel restrictions being a high financial risk. Particularly we want to thank the EC and national public funding authorities who made the work in the research projects possible. We do not want to forget the continued support of our companies and organizations, of ERCIM, the European Research Consortium for Informatics and Mathematics with its Working Group on Dependable Embedded Software-intensive Systems, and EWICS, the creator and main sponsor of SAFECOMP, with its working groups, who always helped us to learn from their networks.

We hope that all participants will benefit from the workshop, enjoy the conference and will join us again in the future!

Erwin Schoitsch
Amund Skavhaug

Acknowledgements. Part of the work presented in the workshop received funding from the EC (H2020/ECSEL Joint Undertaking) and the partners National Funding Authorities ("tri-partite") through the projects AQUAS (737475), Productive4.0 (737459), AutoDrive (737469), SECREDAS (783119), iDev40 (783163), AfarCloud (783221), Comp4Drones (826610) and ARROWHEAD Tools (826452). Other EC funded projects are e.g. in the ERASMUS Program (DRIVES project, 591988-EPP-1-2017-1-CZ-EPPKA2-SSA-B). Some projects received national funding, e.g. FFI/VINNOVA (2017-05519) in Sweden, COMET K2 Program and KIRAS Program (project EVE) (Austria), DARPA (USA, FA8750-18-C-090), FT/MCTES (Portugal, UIDB/04234/2020), and other national organizations (Trafikverket Sweden, Nagoya City Japan).

International Program Committee 2020

Friedemann Bitsch	Thales Transportation Systems GmbH (DE)
Jens Braband	Siemens AG (DE)
Bettina Buth	HAW Hamburg (DE)
Aida Causevic	Mälardalen University (SE) (subreviewer)
Gerhard Chroust	Johannes Kepler University Linz (AT)
Peter Daniel	EWICS TC7 (UK)
Pedro Ferreira	University of Lisbon (PT)
Francesco Flammini (IT)	Ansaldo; University "Federico II" of Naples (IT)
Barbara Gallina	Mälardalen University (SE)
Thomas Gruber	AIT Austrian Institute of Technology (AT)
Hans Hansson	Mälardalen University (SE)
Denis Hatebur	University Duisburg-Essen (DE)
Maritta Heisel	University of Duisburg-Essen (DE)
Miren Illarramendi Rezabal	Modragon University (ES)
Haris Isakovic	Vienna University of Technology (AT)
Willibald Krenn	AIT Austrian Institute of Technology (AT)
Dejan Nickovic	AIT Austrian Institute of Technology (AT)
Thomas Pfeiffenberger	Salzburg Research (AT)
Peter Puschner	Vienna University of Technology (AT)
Francesca Saglietti	University of Erlangen-Nuremberg (DE)
Christoph Schmittner	AIT Austrian Institute of Technology (AT)
Christoph Schmitz	Zühlke Engineering AG (CH)
Daniel Schneider	Fraunhofer IESE, Kaiserslautern (DE)
Erwin Schoitsch	AIT Austrian Institute of Technology (AT)
Rolf Schumacher	Schumacher Engineering (DE)
Lijun Shan	Internet of Trust (FR)
Amund Skavhaug	NTNU Trondheim (NO)
Lorenzo Strigini	City University London (UK)
Mark-Alexander Sujan	University of Warwick (UK)
Andrzej Wardzinski	Gdansk university of Technology (PL)

Supervisory Control Theory in System Safety Analysis

Yuvaraj Selvaraj[1,2(✉)], Zhennan Fei[1], and Martin Fabian[2]

[1] Zenuity AB, Gothenburg, Sweden
{yuvaraj.selvaraj,zhennan.fei}@zenuity.com
[2] Chalmers University of Technology, Gothenburg, Sweden
fabian@chalmers.se

Abstract. Development of safety critical systems requires a risk management strategy to identify and analyse hazards, and apply necessary actions to eliminate or control them as malfunctions could be catastrophic. Fault Tree Analysis (FTA) is one of the most widely used methods for safety analysis in industrial use. However, the standard FTA is manual, informal, and limited to static analysis of systems. In this paper, we present preliminary results from a model-based approach to address these limitations using Supervisory Control Theory. Taking an example from the Fault Tree Handbook, we present a systematic approach to incrementally obtain formal models from a fault tree and verify them in the tool Supremica. We present a method to calculate minimal cut sets using our approach. These compositional techniques could potentially be very beneficial in the safety analysis of highly complex safety critical systems, where several components interact to solve different tasks.

Keywords: Fault tree analysis · Supervisory control theory · Formal methods · System safety · Autonomous driving

1 Introduction

Software development in safety critical systems necessitates a risk management strategy to identify and analyse risks, and to apply the necessary actions to eliminate or control them. The objective of safety analyses, performed during various development phases, is to ensure that the risk of safety violations due to the occurrence of different faults is sufficiently low.

Fault Tree Analysis, FTA [16], is one of the most common methods for safety analysis in various industries. While standard fault trees are simple and informative, they are not free from limitations [3]. Standard FTA is primarily a manual process based on an informal model, i.e., the process relies on the system analysts and domain experts to systematically think about all risks and their possible causes. The lack of formal semantics makes it difficult to verify the correctness of

Supported by FFI, VINNOVA under grant number 2017-05519, *Automatically Assessing Correctness of Autonomous Vehicles–Auto-CAV*.

A. Casimiro et al. (Eds.): SAFECOMP 2020 Workshops, LNCS 12235, pp. 9–22, 2020.
https://doi.org/10.1007/978-3-030-55583-2_1

the safety analysis, especially for rapidly evolving industries like the autonomous driving industry where new edge cases are continuously identified. In complex industrial software controlled systems, safety models must capture many possible interactions between system components, where different interleavings of failure events can either result in a failure or operational state. Standard fault trees are not suitable for modelling temporal, sequential and state dependencies of events. Another notable shortcoming with standard FTA for large and complex systems is the need for safety analyses to be intuitive and compositional. This is crucial in projects where the system of interest comprises interacting sub-systems, possibly delivered by different teams or suppliers.

Though several limitations exist, FTA is one of the widely used safety analysis methods. Different extensions to standard fault trees [10] have been proposed to address some of the limitations. Research on using formal logic in FTA [2,15,17] address the limitation of informal and manual FTA process. Extensions like dynamic fault trees [1], state-event fault trees [4], and temporal fault trees [8] address inability of standard fault trees to model dynamic behaviour. The most widely used extension to include temporal sequence information is dynamic fault trees [1,10]. Over the years, research on the development of model-based dependability analysis (MBDA) [12] techniques have enabled automated dependability analysis. In [12], such emerging MBDA techniques are classified into two paradigms. The first paradigm, termed failure logic synthesis and analysis focuses on automatic construction of failure analyses and the second paradigm, termed behavioural fault simulation focuses on formal verification based techniques. Despite this research, challenges remain in addressing the limitations with standard fault trees and safety analysis [10,12]. Thus any progress in addressing these limitations is helpful. The preliminary results presented in this paper is part of an ongoing endeavour to address the aforementioned limitations by a model-based approach based on Supervisory Control Theory (SCT) [9].

The formal models used in the SCT framework can describe dynamic behaviour, which is often needed to analyse modern and complex safety critical systems. The compositional abstraction based algorithms used in SCT allow automated synthesis and verification of safety models for large and complex systems. These features of the SCT framework makes it possible to define a complete model-based safety analysis approach with automated analysis. To ensure sufficient detail of explanation and some degree of familiarity, we do not present a complex example in this paper; instead we describe our approach using a rather simple example from the *Fault Tree Handbook* [16].

We make three main contributions in this paper. First, we address the issue of informal description of standard fault tree analysis by presenting a systematic approach to incrementally obtain formal models from a fault tree. Second, we present a method to analyse the fault trees using the SCT tool *Supremica* [5]. Finally, we present a method to calculate minimal cut sets using our approach. An advantage of our work is the compositional approach to modelling and verification that is beneficial in reasoning about large fault trees for highly complex systems. To the best of our knowledge, SCT has not previously been used in the context of fault tree analysis.

The paper begins with a brief introduction to FTA and SCT in Sect. 2 and Sect. 3, respectively. Section 4 discusses modelling and analysis in *Supremica* with an example from the *Fault Tree Handbook* [16]. The paper is concluded with a brief discussion on future extensions in Sect. 5. Our work is successfully integrated with a model-based systems engineering tool [14], that is widely used in the automotive industry.

2   Fault Tree Analysis

Fault Tree Analysis (FTA) [16] is a top-down deductive safety analysis technique, where an undesired safety-critical failure of a system is specified, and then analysed in the context of its operational environment to find all possible ways in which the specified failure can occur.

A fault tree is a graphical model of various combinations of faults that cause the safety critical failure, represented as a top level failure event at the root of the fault tree. From this root event, the fault tree is constructed from a predefined set of symbols [16], which results in a set of combinations of component failures that can cause the top level failure. Note that the fault tree is not a model of all possible causes for system failure, but given a particular failure it depicts the possible combinations of basic component failures that lead to this failure. Since FTA is primarily a manual process, the exhaustiveness of the analysis is left to the assessment of the analyst.

Although several extensions of fault trees have been proposed [10], in this paper we limit ourselves to the symbols described in the *Fault Tree Handbook* [16]. Broadly, the nodes in the fault tree can be classified into three types: *events*, *gates*, and *transfer symbols* [16].

2.1   Pressure Tank System

The pressure tank system [16] in Fig. 1 describes a control system to regulate a pump-motor that pumps fluid into the tank. Initially the system is considered to be dormant and de-energized: switch S1 open, relays K1 and K2 open, and the timer relay closed. The tank is assumed to be empty in this state and therefore the pressure switch S is closed. It is also assumed that it takes 60 s to pressurize the tank, and an outlet valve, which is not a pressure relief valve, is used to drain the tank.

System operation is started by pressing switch S1. This closes and latches relay K1, and subsequently relay K2 to start the pump. When threshold pressure is reached, the pressure switch opens, causing K2 to open, and consequently the pump motor to cease operation. The timer allows emergency shut-down in case the pressure switch fails. Initially, the timer relay is closed and power is applied to the timer as soon as K1 closes. If the clock in the timer registers 60 s of continuous power, the timer relay opens and latches, thereby causing a system

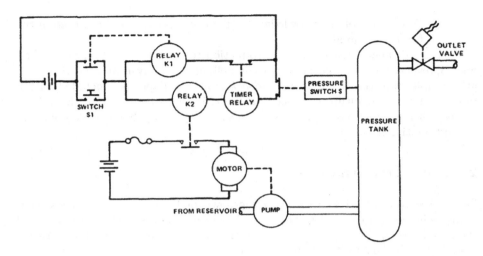

Fig. 1. Pressure tank system from [16], page VIII-1

shut-down. In normal operation, when pressure switch S opens, the timer resets to 0 s. When the tank is empty, the pressure switch closes, and the cycle can be repeated.

Figure 2 shows the basic fault tree from [16] (page VIII-13) for the pressure tank system. Here, the hazard 'rupture of pressure tank after start of pumping' is analysed and is represented by the top level failure event, E1. The basic events denoted by circles represent the respective component failures and form the leaves of the tree. The intermediate events, which are fault events that occur due to one or more antecedent causes are denoted by rectangles. The process of obtaining the fault tree following a top down analysis is out of scope of this paper; we assume a FT is given. A complete description of the example and the fault tree can be found in [16].

3 Supervisory Control Theory

The Supervisory Control Theory (SCT) [9] provides a framework to model, synthesize and verify control functions for *discrete event systems* (DES), which are dynamic systems characterised by the evolution of events causing the system to transit from one discrete state to another. Given a model of the system to control, a *plant*, and a *specification* describing the desired controlled behaviour, the SCT provides methods to synthesise a *supervisor* that dynamically interacts with the plant in a closed-loop, and restricts the event generation of the plant such that the specification is satisfied. The supervisor thus ensures a safe control of the plant by restricting the execution of certain events. However, only events that are *controllable* can be restricted by the supervisor, while events that are *uncontrollable* cannot be restricted. A dual problem that is of interest here, is

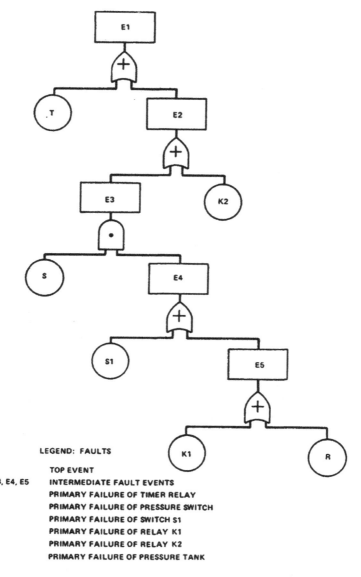

Fig. 2. Fault tree for pressure tank system in Fig. 1 from [16], page VIII-13

to given a model of a (controlled) plant and a specification, *verify* whether the specification is fulfilled or not. So, in this paper we use ideas from SCT to formally verify properties of the plant model, and do not focus on the synthesis of supervisors.

To model a fault tree as a DES, we use Extended Finite State Machines (EFSM) [13], which are finite state machines extended with bounded discrete *variables*, *guards* that are logical expressions over variables, and *actions* that assign values to variables on transitions.

Definition 1. *An Extended Finite State Machine (EFSM) is a tuple $E = \langle \Sigma, V, L, \rightarrow, l^i, L^m \rangle$, where Σ is a finite set of events, V is a finite set of bounded discrete variables, L is a finite set of locations, $\rightarrow \subseteq L \times \Sigma \times G \times A \times L$ is the conditional transition relation, where G and A are the respective sets of guards and actions, $l^i \in L$ is the initial location, and $L^m \subseteq L$ is the set of marked locations.*

A state in an EFSM is given by its current location together with the current values of the variables. The expression $l_0 \xrightarrow{\sigma:[g]a} l_1$ denotes a transition from location l_0 to l_1 labelled by event $\sigma \in \Sigma$, with guard $g \in G$, and action $a \in A$. The transition is enabled when g evaluates to *true*, and on its occurrence, the current location of the EFSM changes from l_0 to l_1, while a updates some of the values of the variables $v \in V$. EFSMs interact through shared events by *synchronous composition*, denoted $\mathcal{A}_1 \| \mathcal{A}_2$ for two interacting EFSM models, $\mathcal{A}_1$ and $\mathcal{A}_2$. In synchronous composition, shared events occur simultaneously in all interacting EFSMs, or not at all, while non-shared events occur independently. Transitions on shared events with mutually exclusive guards, or conflicting actions will never occur [13]. In an EFSM, *active events* are the events that label some transition, while *blocked events* do not label any transition. In the synchronous composition of two EFSMs, the blocked events of the synchronised EFSM, is the union of the blocked events of the synchronised EFSMs. That is, transitions in one EFSM labelled by events blocked by the other EFSM, will be removed.

3.1   Nonblocking Verification

Given a set of EFSMs $\mathcal{A} = \{\mathcal{A}_1, \dots, \mathcal{A}_n\}$, the *nonblocking* property guarantees that some marked state can always be reached from any reachable state in the synchronous composition over all the components $\mathcal{A}_i$. While the monolithic approach to nonblocking verification is explicit, it is limited by the combinatorial state-space explosion. The *abstraction-based compositional verification* [7] has shown remarkable efficiency to handle systems of industrial complexity. This approach employs *conflict-preserving abstractions* to iteratively remove redundancy and keeps the abstracted system size manageable. *Supremica* [6], a tool for modelling and analysis of DES models, implements the abstraction-based compositional algorithms (and others) for verification of EFSMs.

4   FTA in Supremica

In this section, we describe how the fault tree in Fig. 2 is modelled into a number of *plant* EFSMs. We demonstrate how the model can be validated by verifying typical *specifications* in *Supremica*. This section also includes a brief discussion about computing minimal cut sets using our approach. Both *Supremica* and the models of this section are available online[1].

4.1 Modelling

To make the best use of compositionality, we incrementally model different failure events in a modular way. Given a fault tree, we first model the lowest level and gradually proceed towards the top level event. For the higher levels, we only consider the intermediate fault events from the lower levels and hide all other inner details.

Consider the lowest level of the fault tree in Fig. 2. It consists of two basic events as inputs to the lowest OR gate leading to the intermediate fault event, E5. This forms the first level in our modelling hierarchy. Fault event E5 can occur either due to a primary failure of K1 or a primary failure of R. This behaviour is modelled in the EFSM as shown in Fig. 3a. The two events $K1$ and R denote the corresponding primary failures and when either occurs, the EFSM transits from its initial location, A_0^i to location E_5[2].

With E5 modelled, we proceed to the next level, the intermediate fault event E4. From Fig. 2, we see that this can occur either due to a primary failure of switch S1 or due to the occurrence of E5. This gives us a total of 7 possible combinations that lead to E4. However, since we have modelled the analysis for E5 as an EFSM on the previous level, we can use guards to capture this, and model E4 with just 2 events as shown in Fig. 3b. The guard condition on the event $E5$ ensures that the event is enabled only in a situation where the EFSM in Fig. 3a is in location E_5. Here, the guard $[A_0 == E_5]$ represents that the current location of the EFSM A_0 in Fig. 3a, is E_5.

(a) EFSM modelling E5   (b) EFSM modelling E4

Fig. 3. EFSMs for intermediate failure events, E4 and E5 of the fault tree

The next level in our modular hierarchy is the output event of the only AND gate in the fault tree, E3. The two inputs to the AND gate correspond to the primary failure of the pressure switch S and the analysis resulting from the intermediate fault E4. Figure 4 shows the model for this fault event E3. Since the order of events do not matter in an AND gate, there are two possible ways to reach the failure state as shown in Fig. 4.

---

[1] https://supremica.org https://github.com/yuvrajselvam/FTA_SCT.

[2] In this paper, for a fault Ex in the FT, Ex denotes the corresponding event in the EFSM and E_x denotes the location reached due to the occurrence of the fault.

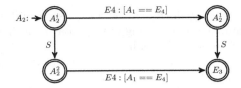

Fig. 4. EFSM, A_2 for the intermediate failure event E3

The final two levels of the fault tree corresponding to fault events E2 and E1 consist of OR gates and are modelled as already shown, see Fig. 5. Note that in the plant models, the only unmarked location is the initial location in Fig. 5b, and therefore in the synchronised plant model, which gives the complete fault tree, the marked locations correspond to the top level failure event E1.

(a) EFSM modelling E2   (b) EFSM modelling E1

Fig. 5. EFSM for intermediate failure events, E2 and E1 of the fault tree

For special cases of AND gates, like INHIBIT and PRIORITY-AND, the models look slightly different. For an INHIBIT gate, where the output is determined by a single input together with some qualifying condition, we can use a single event label together with the qualifying condition as a guard to model the transition to the failure state. For a PRIORITY-AND gate, where the output occurs only if all inputs occur in a specified ordered sequence, we can model the specified sequence as a path from the initial state to the failure state. For example if failure event E3 is at the output of a PRIORITY-AND with the order specified as E4 before S, then we only have the path $A_2^i \rightarrow A_2^1 \rightarrow E_3$ in Fig. 4 as the corresponding EFSM. This makes it possible to use EFSMs to model sequential dependencies as required by the PRIORITY-AND gate.

The distinction between inclusive and exclusive-OR gates can be ignored in the fault tree analysis when dealing with independent, low probability component failures (see [16], page VII-7). Therefore we do not introduce special approaches to differentiate them in our method. If a distinction is truly needed, additional guards and transitions can be introduced on the model.

Algorithm 1 presents a systematic method to construct EFSMs in a modular way from a given fault tree. Note that the algorithm includes modelling of two types of gates only, AND and OR. However, it can be extended to include other types of gates like INHIBIT and PRIORITY-AND as discussed above.

In Algorithm 1, lines 9–18 describe the modelling of OR gates and lines 19–30 describe AND gates. The addition of guards on the transitions mentioned in lines 16 and 28 describe the use of EFSM variables in guard conditions as shown in Fig. 3b for the OR gate, and in Fig. 4 for the AND gate, respectively.

4.2 Verification

In software controlled complex systems, safety analysis plays a significant role in formulating the safety requirements for the subsequent system design. Establishing confidence in the fault tree analysis is typically done manually. This is a shortcoming as it is error prone and even intractable for large and complex systems. An automated analysis method is very beneficial in providing sufficient verification evidence for the safety analysis phase. In this section, we present how typical specifications are modelled and verified using nonblocking verification algorithms in *Supremica*.

When system operation is started in the pressure tank in Fig. 1, the pump starts filling fluid into the tank. When the tank is full and the threshold pressure is reached, pressure switch S opens, causing K2 to open, and consequently the pump to stop. K2 failing to open would result in continuous pumping beyond the threshold and may result in the rupture of the tank. Therefore K2 is critical for safe operation and a primary failure of K2 may result in the top level failure event E1. Ideally, this behaviour should be captured in our FTA and we can verify this. Figure 6a shows the EFSM modelling this specification. $K2$ is the only active event in this EFSM and the other basic events in the fault tree are blocked. Recall that transitions labelled by blocked events are removed in the synchronous composition of the specification and the plant models. Therefore, by blocking all basic events but $K2$, we ensure that $K2$ is included in the marked language of the EFSM whereas other basic events are not. A nonblocking verification performed on the synchronised model of this specification together with the plant models, shows that the system is nonblocking, thereby verifying that a primary failure of K2 is sufficient to cause rupture of the tank, the failure event E1.

On the other hand, since we have the timer relay as a backup in the system, only a failure of the pressure switch, S, should not lead to tank rupture. We can model this as a specification shown in Fig. 6b. Since we are only interested in the primary failure of pressure switch S, we block the remaining basic events in the fault tree. A nonblocking verification of this specification synchronised with the plant model results in a blocking state, thereby verifying that only S occurring will not result in the top level failure event E1. However, if we also include the failure of the timer relay R, we get the specification as shown in Fig. 7. With this specification, we can verify that the system is indeed nonblocking, i.e., a failure of both components S and R will lead to the top level failure event E1. Specifications to model the remaining causes leading to the top level event and/or the intermediate events are done in a similar way as in Figs. 6 and 7.

Algorithm 1: Modular fault tree modelling

Input: Fault Tree, FT
Output: EFSM set corresponding to the fault tree, FT

Initialisation   1
   | declare basic events set, BE   2
   | declare variables, Q, curr_node, child   3
add **root** (FT) to Q // queue, Q contains elements to be processed   4
BE:= **getBasicEvents** (FT)   5
while $Q \neq \emptyset$ **do**   6
   | curr_node:= **pop** (Q) // get the oldest element in queue   7
   | gate:= **getGate** (curr_node) // retrieve connecting gate of node   8
   | **if** gate is OR **then**   9
     | create initial and terminal locations, l_0 and l_n 10
     | **foreach** child $\in$ **getChildren** (gate) **do**   11
       | **if** child $\in$ BE **then** // child is a basic event   12
         | **addTransition**(l_0, l_n, child)   13
       | **else** // child is an intermediate event   14
         | **addTransition**(l_0, l_n, child)   15
         | add guards using automaton variables on the respective transitions   16
         | add child to Q   17
     | **markLocations**(curr_node, **root** (FT))   18
   | **else** // node is an AND gate   19
     | create initial and terminal locations, l_0 and l_n 20
     | children:= **getChildren** (gate)   21
     | create a set of strings, $\mathbb{S}$, by permutation over children   22
     | // each string is a path from l_0 to l_n
     | **foreach** *string* $\in \mathbb{S}$ **do**   23
       | create transitions and locations correspondingly   24
       | obtain the set of events, $\mathbb{E}$ 25
       | **foreach** event $\in \mathbb{E}$ **do**   26
         | **if** event $\notin$ BE **then** // it is intermediate event   27
           | add guards using automaton variables on respective transitions   28
           | add event to Q   29
     | **markLocations**(curr_node, **root** (FT))   30

function markLocations(curr_node, **root** (FT))   31
   | **if** curr_node == **root** (FT) **then**   32
     | mark the terminal location, l_n 33
   | **else**   34
     | mark all locations   35

function addTransition(l_a,l_b,*event*)   36
   | add transition between l_a and l_b 37
   | label transition with *event*   38

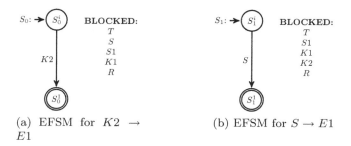

(a) EFSM for $K2 \rightarrow E1$

(b) EFSM for $S \rightarrow E1$

Fig. 6. EFSM for specifications

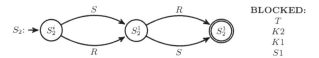

Fig. 7. EFSM for specification $S \wedge R \rightarrow E1$

The type of specifications that we have seen so far are modelled to check whether certain basic events or combinations of events lead to a failure event. Given such a specification, SP, and fault tree, FT, Algorithm 2 presents how EFSM models can be obtained from them.

4.3   Minimal Cut Sets

Our approach is not only useful for verification but also in calculating minimal cut sets, one of the most prominent qualitative analysis techniques of standard fault trees. A *cut set* is a set of component failure events that together lead to the top level failure. Formally, a minimal cut set is a *smallest* combination of component failures which, if they all occur, lead to the top level failure event. It is smallest in the sense that all failures are needed for the top level event to occur and if one of them in a cut set does not occur, then the top event will not occur by that set. For example, the minimal cut sets for the pressure tank system are {T}, {K2}, {S, S1}, {S, K1}, {S, R}.

In our modelling approach presented in Sect. 4.1, the marked locations in the composed model correspond to the top level failure event. This makes it possible to use the marked language of the plant EFSM to calculate the minimal cut sets. In our case, a cut set is a set of events that lead to marked locations corresponding to the top level failure event. Calculating minimal cut sets is then done by finding the shortest paths in the synchronised plant EFSM from the initial location to the marked locations, a task typically solved by variants of breadth-first search algorithms. Algorithm 3 presents one such method to calculate minimal cut sets by exploiting the marked language of the synchronised EFSM. Lines 11–13 of

---

Algorithm 2: Modelling specifications

Input: Fault Tree, FT and Specification, SP
Output: EFSM modelling the specification
Initialisation   1
 declare basic events set, BE   2
 declare active events set, AE   3
 declare blocked events set, BLOCKED   4

BE:= getBasicEvents (FT)   5
AE:= getBasicEvents (SP)   6
create locations $l_0, l_1, ..., l_N$ with $N = |AE|$ 7
make l_0 the initial location   8
make l_N the single marked location   9
for every pair (l_{i-1}, l_i) with $i \in \{1, 2, ..., N\}$ create N transitions   10
label each transition uniquely from $\sigma \in$ AE   11
add blocked events, BLOCKED:= BE \ AE   12

---

the algorithm adds the basic events that can reach the marked location in the synchronised EFSM to the output set. Lines 14 and 15 ensure that the same events are not repeated.

Algorithm 3: Computation of Minimal Cut Sets

Input: $EFSM_1, ..., EFSM_n$ modelling the considered FT
Output: Set of minimal cut sets, S
Initialisation   1
 declare variable Q as queue with states to be processed   2
 declare synchronised EFSM A as $EFSM_1 \,||\, ... \,||\, EFSM_n$ 3
 declare basic event set, BE   4
 declare blocked events set, BLOCKED   5

BE := getBasicEvents(A)   6
while $\exists e \in \{\sigma \mid \exists s' \text{ s.t. } (s_i, \sigma, s') \in \rightarrow_A \wedge \sigma \in BE\}$ **do**   7
 Q.put(s_i) // Enqueue the initial state s_i 8
 while $Q \neq \emptyset$ **do**   9
  s := Q.get() // Dequeue state s from Q   10
  if $\exists s', \exists \sigma$ s.t. $(s, \sigma, s') \in \rightarrow_A \wedge$ isMarked(s') **then**   11
   // Retrieve basic events labelling transitions from s_i to s
   Σ_c := getEvents$(s_i, s') \cap$ BE   12
   // Σ_c is one minimal cut set, insert it into S
   S.put(Σ_c) 13
   create a single location (marked) $EFSM_{sp}$ with BLOCKED := Σ_c 14
   // Update A by blocking all basic events in Σ_c
   A := A $||$ $EFSM_{sp}$ 15
   break   16
  else   17
   forall the s' s.t. $(s, \sigma, s') \in \rightarrow_A$ **do** Q.put(s') 18

---

5   Conclusion

We have shown how fault tree analysis can be formalised to be automatically analysed by modelling techniques from Supervisory Control Theory (SCT) using the tool *Supremica*. We present a systematic approach to incrementally obtain formal models from a given standard fault tree, as summarised in Algorithm 1. Algorithm 2 describes a method to automatically generate specifications for given properties of the fault tree, so that these properties can be verified using non-blocking verification. Finally, Algorithm 3 presented a method to automatically calculate minimal cut sets from the generated models.

Though our modelling approach can model complex systems with redundant architectures and dynamic dependencies, we here limit ourselves to the standard symbols described in the *Fault Tree Handbook*. Our approach can indeed be extended to use *dynamic* gates. The formal model obtained from the approach discussed in this paper, considers only the fault behaviour of the system as described by a given fault tree and nothing else. While we verify certain properties on the model to establish confidence in the system, we do not focus on correctness of the construction of the fault tree in the context of the system's operational environment. In a behavioural approach, we would formally model the complete behaviour of the system, i.e., including the nominal operational behaviour and not only the fault behaviour. This presents a wide range of possibilities. One possible extension is to adopt a formal approach similar to model checking [15]. Another notable extension of our work is to use the behavioural system models and the supervisor synthesis framework provided by SCT to automatically synthesize the fault behaviour. This falls in line with the model-based dependability analysis [12] approach for safety analysis. In such extensions, the system model becomes the plant models and the work in this paper can then be used to obtain formal specifications from a given fault tree. This approach makes it possible to use such formal models in several stages of a model-based design process. The state based models that are created can be re-used during the development of the software programs in the later stages. The work presented in this paper can provide a solid basis for possible extensions in those areas.

A primary motivation for this work is our current focus on formal verification of autonomous driving systems where SCT and *Supremica* have been used to verify software for autonomous driving systems [11]. We believe our work in this paper will strongly encourage the application of SCT and *Supremica* in different stages of safety critical software development starting from safety analysis in the early stages to synthesis and verification of the software in the end stages. Our work in this paper is successfully integrated with a model-based systems engineering tool [14], that is widely used in the automotive industry.

References

1. Dugan, J.B., Bavuso, S.J., Boyd, M.A.: Dynamic fault-tree models for fault-tolerant computer systems. IEEE Trans. Reliab. **41**(3), 363–377 (1992)

2. Hansen, K.M., Ravn, A.P., Stavridou, V.: From safety analysis to software requirements. IEEE Trans. Softw. Eng. **24**(7), 573–584 (1998)
3. Kabir, S.: An overview of fault tree analysis and its application in model based dependability analysis. Expert Syst. Appl. **77**, 114–135 (2017)
4. Kaiser, B., Gramlich, C., Förster, M.: State/event fault trees–a safety analysis model for software-controlled systems. Reliab. Eng. Syst. Saf. **92**(11), 1521–1537 (2007)
5. Malik, R.: Programming a fast explicit conflict checker. In: 2016 13th International Workshop on Discrete Event Systems (WODES), pp. 438–443. IEEE (2016)
6. Malik, R., Akesson, K., Flordal, H., Fabian, M.: Supremica-an efficient tool for large-scale discrete event systems. IFAC-PapersOnLine **50**(1), 5794–5799 (2017). https://doi.org/10.1016/j.ifacol.2017.08.427
7. Mohajerani, S., Malik, R., Fabian, M.: A framework for compositional nonblocking verification of extended finite-state machines. Discrete Event Dyn. Syst. **26**(1), 33–84 (2015). https://doi.org/10.1007/s10626-015-0217-y
8. Palshikar, G.K.: Temporal fault trees. Inf. Softw. Technol. **44**(3), 137–150 (2002)
9. Ramadge, P.J., Wonham, W.M.: Supervisory control of a class of discrete event processes. SIAM J. Control Optim. **25**(1), 206–230 (1987)
10. Ruijters, E., Stoelinga, M.: Fault tree analysis: a survey of the state-of-the-art in modeling, analysis and tools. Comput. Sci. Rev. **15**, 29–62 (2015)
11. Selvaraj, Y., Ahrendt, W., Fabian, M.: Verification of decision making software in an autonomous vehicle: an industrial case study. In: Larsen, K.G., Willemse, T. (eds.) Formal Methods for Industrial Critical Systems, pp. 143–159. Springer International Publishing, Cham (2019). https://doi.org/10.1007/978-3-030-27008-7_9
12. Sharvia, S., Kabir, S., Walker, M., Papadopoulos, Y.: Model-based dependability analysis: state-of-the-art, challenges, and future outlook. In: Software Quality Assurance, pp. 251–278. Elsevier (2016)
13. Skoldstam, M., Akesson, K., Fabian, M.: Modeling of discrete event systems using finite automata with variables. In: 2007 46th IEEE Conference on Decision and Control, pp. 3387–3392. IEEE (2007)
14. SYSTEMITE: Systemweaver. https://www.systemweaver.se/. Accessed 09 May 2020
15. Thums, A., Schellhorn, G.: Model checking FTA. In: Araki, K., Gnesi, S., Mandrioli, D. (eds.) FME 2003. LNCS, vol. 2805, pp. 739–757. Springer, Heidelberg (2003). https://doi.org/10.1007/978-3-540-45236-2_40
16. Vesely, W.E., Goldberg, F.F., Roberts, N.H., Haasl, D.F.: Fault tree handbook. Technical report, Nuclear Regulatory Commission Washington DC (1981)
17. Xiang, J., Ogata, K., Futatsugi, K.: Formal fault tree analysis of state transition systems. In: Fifth International Conference on Quality Software (QSIC 2005), pp. 124–131. IEEE (2005)

A Method to Support the Accountability of Safety Cases by Integrating Safety Analysis and Model-Based Design

Nobuaki Tanaka[1]([✉]), Hisashi Yomiya[2], and Kiyoshi Ogawa[3]

[1] GAIO TECHNOLOGY Co., Ltd., Higashi-Shinagawa 2-2-4, Shinagawa, Tokyo, Japan
tanaka.n@gaio.co.jp
[2] Toshiba Corporation, Komukai-Toshiba-Cho 1, Kawasaki, Kanagawa, Japan
hisashi.yomiya@toshiba.co.jp
[3] Nagoya City Industrial Research Institute, Rokuban 3-4-11, Atsuta-Ku, Nagoya, Aichi, Japan
nagoya.kaizen@gmail.com

Abstract. In this paper, we describe a method of visualizing the behavior of systems' failures in order to improve the explanatory ability of safety analysis artifacts. Increasingly complex in-vehicle systems are making traditional safety analysis artifacts more difficult for reviewers to understand. One of the requirements for improvement is to provide more understandable explanations of failure behaviors. The AIAG/VDA FMEA (Failure Mode and Effect Analysis) handbook, published in 2019, introduced the FMEA-MSR (Supplemental FMEA for Monitoring and System Response) to explicitly describe the behavior of failures called the Hybrid Failure Chain (e.g., chain of failure mode, failure cause, monitoring, system response, and failure effects). For more precise explanations of the safety analysis artifacts, we propose a method to integrate and visualize failure behaviors into architectural design diagrams using SysML. Based on FTA (Fault Tree Analysis) and FMEA results, along with SysML diagrams (e.g., internal block diagrams), the proposed method imports represent FMEA and FTA data graphically as Hybrid Failure Chains with a system model to improve information cohesion in the safety analysis artifact. We found that the proposed method facilitates the discovery or recognition of flaws and omissions in the fault model.

Keywords: MBSA (Model-Based Safety Analysis) · MBSE (Model-Based Systems Engineering) · FTA · FMEA · Hybrid Failure Chain · Safety analysis · SysML

1 Introduction

The automotive industry is introducing MBSE to address the increasing complexity of in-vehicle systems and functional safety standards for safety accountability. Those changes have also affected safety analysis as seen in the AIAG/VDA FMEA handbook published in 2019. A significant feature of AIAG/VDA FMEA is the analysis of safety mechanisms, titled FMEA-MSR (Supplemental FMEA for Monitoring and System Response).

© Springer Nature Switzerland AG 2020
A. Casimiro et al. (Eds.): SAFECOMP 2020 Workshops, LNCS 12235, pp. 23–35, 2020.
https://doi.org/10.1007/978-3-030-55583-2_2

FMEA-MSR enhances the analysis target, from the effects and causes of failure to Hybrid Failure Chains, which contain the normal responses of safety mechanisms.

On the other hand, traditional safety analysis artifacts (such as FMEA sheet, FT chart) are not able to fully explain the complex behavior of the failures and safety mechanisms [1]. We think MBSA is a methodology that can effectively solve this problem by applying modeling technology to safety analysis. The Object Management Group (OMG) recognizes the importance of safety and reliability in their standards and is developing a profile for safety and reliability for SysML [2].

In this paper, we propose a method to utilize MBSA with an activity model to improve the visibility of failures' behavior. We expect that the similarity of the structures of the activity model, the Hybrid Failure Chain, and the system model can enhance the visibility and facilitate the discovery of the defects and omissions in the safety analysis results. The method builds the Hybrid Failure Chain from FTA and FMEA analysis results and places their components on SysML diagrams (for example, internal block diagrams) to increase the cohesion of the information in the safety analysis.

The FTA and FMEA results should be consistent and in sync, but in reality, they may be inconsistent or out of sync, because they may be created by different teams with different goals. The method described in this paper aims to facilitate the understanding of such inconsistencies by the visualization.

The remainder of this paper is structured as follows: Sect. 2 handles related work. In Sects. 3 and 4, we introduce our proposal for the notation of the fault model and visualization techniques. Section 5 presents a case study. Section 6 presents an evaluation of the proposed visualization method. In Sect. 7, we describe our considerations and future work. We provide a conclusion about our current work and the planned future work in Sect. 8.

2 Related Work

2.1 MBSA

Joshi et al. [3] proposed a method for describing the behavior of failures in the MATLAB/Simulink models. The analysis is fully automated and based on the description of failure's behavior, but the author states that this technique is not scalable because it requires an enormous effort to specify the behavior of a practical system's failures completely.

Aizpurua et al. [1] analyzed the problems of traditional safety analysis and MBSA, stating that the advantage of MBSA is limited, but managing all safety analysis results as a model facilitates consistency in the artifact. The paper proposes an efficient process that combines automatic consistency checking with MBSA and manual safety analysis.

HiP-HOPS [4] is a safety analysis method that integrates results from FFA (Functional Failure Analysis), IF-FMEA (Interface-Focused FMEA), and FMEA for each component in order to assemble the safety analysis result of the whole system. HiP-HOPS analyzes the behavior of interfaces using IF-FMEA with the formal expression and combines the results of FFA and FMEA to assemble an overall analysis results according to the results of IF-FMEA. HiP-HOPS is a comprehensive methodology of safety analysis, but it does not provide visualization for all the relevant information in one diagram.

Nordmann et al. [5] proposed a method to create component fault trees (CFT) by performing a safety analysis for each component and building a fault tree for the entire system. This method constructs the CFT by combining the results of each component's FTA according to the semantics strictly described by the internal block and activity diagrams of SysML. Thus, analysts and reviewers may miss any failure propagation or cause that crosses component boundaries along with links that are not explicit in the SysML model.

Clegg et al. [6] proposed a supplemental fault model notation for SysML that adopts the fault tree model for the fault model. This method combines the fault model with the system model, but the paper does not describe the integration of the system model and the fault model in one diagram.

Tim Gonschorek [7] proposed a modeling language named SafeDeML that combines the fault model with the system model, but no description expresses both models in one diagram, as in [6].

2.2 Standards: AIAG/VDA FMEA Handbook and OMG

The AIAG/VDA FMEA handbook [8] introduced FMEA-MSR (Supplemental FMEA for Monitoring and System Response). Conventional DFMEA analyzes the failure chain, which is the chain between the cause and effect of failure mode. Additionally, FMEA-MSR analyzes the Hybrid Failure Chain, which is a chain of failure mode, monitoring, and system response. Monitoring involves checking for the failure cause or failure mode, system response deals with the monitored failure, and mitigated failure effect is the result of the handling of the failure (Fig. 1).

Geoffrey Biggs et al. [2] indicate that the standardization group in OMG will incorporate FTA and FMEA into the Safety and Reliability Analysis Profile. The diagrams in the paper refer to the fault model as the fault tree model; they do not express the Hybrid Failure Chain.

2.3 Consideration for Related Works

MBSA is an active research area, but based on our survey, it does not focus on improving explanations of the behavior of failures. We propose integrating the fault model and system model into one diagram to improve the cohesion of the safety analysis results. We adopt the activity model to better comprehend the graphical representation of fault models. System behavior at the time of failure can be easily understood by illustrating the occurrence, detection, response of failures, and system design as an activity model in a single diagram.

The explanation here refers to a correct communication, to the reviewer, of the analyst's idea of how the system will behave during a failure.

3 Structure of the Diagram to Describe Fault Models

We designed a metamodel of the system model and fault models as a basis for our visualization method, as shown in Fig. 2.

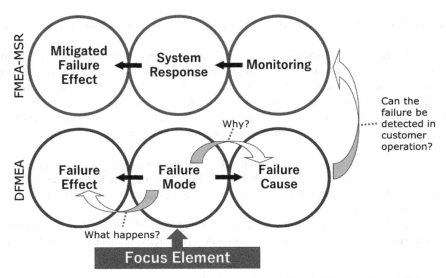

Fig. 1. Theoretical failure chain model DFMEA and FMEA-MSR (AIAG&VDA FMEA Handbook, 2019 [8])

3.1 Notation Requirement

To improve the explanatory ability of the notation, we defined the requirements below.

- **Higher cohesion of safety analysis results in one diagram**: Safety analysis artifacts should aggregate the contents into a single figure to facilitate the intuitive understanding of the associations between elements.
- **Adopting the activity model to visualize the Hybrid Failure Chain**: The fault model should adopt the activity model to improve its compatibility with the system model's structure. The fault tree model adopted in citations 3, 5, and 6 is suitable for the derivation of minimal cut sets and for calculating failure rates, but the activity model is ideal for visualizing the behavior of failures and safety mechanisms.
- **Expression of horizontal propagation**: Horizontal propagation is the transmission of a failure from a child element in one parent element to another child element. The notation should provide a model of horizontal propagation that expresses failure propagation between components. The fault tree model is suitable for representing a hierarchical structure of failures but is not convenient for showing the propagation of the failures between components. Therefore, developers sometimes omit horizontal propagations of failures in FT charts for concision. We think reviewers of current complex safety-critical devices need to understand horizontal propagations and visualizing horizontal propagations will improve the understandability of diagrams.

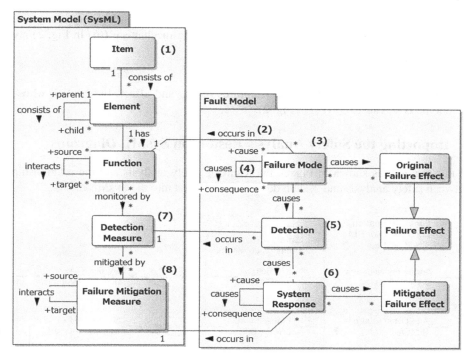

Fig. 2. The metamodel of the notation (UML class diagram)

3.2 The Metamodel of the Notation

We derived the design of the metamodel of the system model and fault model from the requirements described in the previous section as follows.

Expression of the System Model
From experience in [9], we adopted SysML to represent the system model to increase the affinity between artifacts of safety analysis and MBSE. Figure 2 shows the logical structure of the system model comprising items, elements, and functions ((1) in Fig. 2). The proposed method allows the use of any SysML diagram and element if the diagram or element is adequate for the expression of safety design. The system model also includes measures to detect the failure ((7) in Fig. 2: Detection Measure) and to mitigate its effect ((8) in Fig. 2: Failure Mitigation Measure).

Expression of the Fault Model
The fault model includes failure modes, detection of failure, system response, and failure effect to describe failures' behaviors ((3), (5), and (6) in Fig. 2).

Relationship Between the System Model and the Fault Model
The metamodel provides a relationship between function and failure mode to express their relationship ((2) in Fig. 2). Similarly, the relationship between detection of failure

and the failure detection mechanism ((5) in Fig. 2), and the relationship between system response (handling of failure) and the failure handling mechanism ((6) in Fig. 2) are associated.

Propagation of Failures

We represent the relationship between failures (cause and effect) by the link whose stereotype is ≪ causes ≫ ((4) in Fig. 2).

4   Importing the Safety Analysis Results on SysML Diagrams

In this method, as shown in Fig. 3, the result of safety analysis and the relationship between safety analysis and system design are imported into the SysML model.

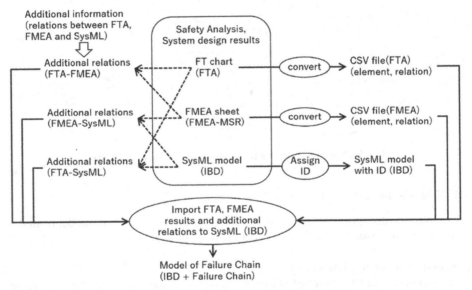

Fig. 3. Procedure and data for importing safety analysis results

4.1   Correspondence Between Elements of Different Artifacts

We assume that the components of different safety analysis results and system designs correspond, as shown in Table 1, and that the analyst must provide the relationship between those components in each artifact. We assume that events in FTA and Failure Modes in FMEA may correspond one-to-many rather than one-to-one; this is because the FTA analysis results may have a coarser granularity and a higher level of abstraction than the FMEA results.

In Table 1, we separated the events from the elements (including the function for which the failure occurred). We only listed events in the FTA column because FT charts only express events and their relationships.

Table 1. Correspondence between system design and safety analysis results (when using IBD)

SysML(IBD)	FMEA	FTA
Part property or block	Element	(None)
Part property	Function	(None)
(None)	Failure mode	Event
(None)	Failure effect	Event
(None)	Detection	Event (lack of detection)
Part property	Detection measure	(None)
(None)	System response	Event (lack of system response)
Part property	Mitigation measure	(None)

4.2 Assumptions for FTA Results and Conversion of the Fault Tree Model

The FT charts of redundant systems have a similar shape. The system's failure behavior is represented by connecting the failures of multiple redundant elements with AND gates. However, other detection mechanisms, such as sanity checks, are not commonly represented.

Therefore, we defined the following rules for representing the behavior of fault-detection and fault-handling mechanisms (system responses), such as sanity checks, in FT charts, and associated them with FMEA and SysML components in standard-style FT charts that adhere to these strict limitations.

- FT charts consist of failure events and logic gates. In our method, the FT chart is configured to violate the safety objective only when a failure event coincides with a failure of the safety mechanism (lack of protection).
- An FT chart expresses a safety mechanism failure (lack of protection) by a logical sum (OR gate) of a lack of failure detections and a lack of System Response (lack of failure handling).
- The events in FT charts have IDs that have prefixes according to event types, such as a lack of failure detection or a lack of failure handling. We identify event types by the prefixes.
- If the relationship between elements in FTA, FMEA, and SysML is available from the traceability management tool, we can utilize the data to build the relations in the model. If the relationship is not available, the analyst must provide the relationship as data or by graphical operation on the SysML modeling tool after importing the safety analysis results.

Our method adopts the activity model for the fault model. Still, the FT diagram is based on the fault tree model, so this method converts the fault tree model to the activity model, as shown in Fig. 4, under the assumption described in this section.

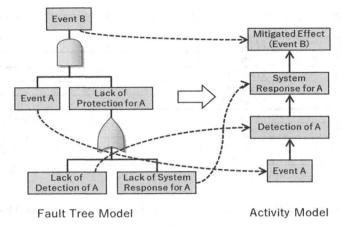

Fault Tree Model   Activity Model

Fig. 4. Conversion from the fault tree model to the activity model

5 Case Study

We conducted a safety analysis for a simple control system shown in Fig. 5 and visualized the result using the method described in this paper.

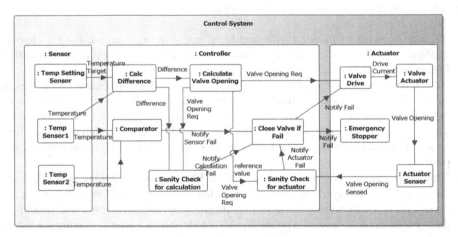

Fig. 5. Target system

Since this method assumes that safety analysis will be performed based on existing SysML models, we created the diagram as an ordinary IBD (internal block diagram). To represent the relationship between the FTA/FMEA components and the SysML components, we attached IDs as the Tagged Value to the IBD components.

The system design was analyzed based on FMEA-MSR in the AIAG/VDA FMEA handbook. After the analysis, we exported Monitor, System Response, Function, Failure Mode, Failure Effect, and their relationships from the FMEA sheet as CSV files.

We conducted FTA under the strict restriction mentioned earlier. Also, as in the case of SysML data, we assigned IDs to events and logic gates to manage the relationship with SysML and FMEA results. FTA results are exported as CSV files.

In the case study, the analyst created additional tabular data to provide the relationship between the FTA, FMEA, and SysML elements.

In the results of Step 5 (risk analysis) and Step 6 (optimization) of FMEA-MSR (Table 2), it is necessary to give occurrence points separately for the following components:

- Diagnostic Monitoring
- System Response
- Most Severe Failure Effect after System Response.

The occurrence points of other events (elements, functions, and failure modes) in FMEA-MSR are specified in the structural analysis (Step 2), functional analysis (Step 3), and failure analysis (Step 4) in each hierarchy structure of those steps. Monitoring, system response, and failure effect can occur in a component that is separate from its function and failure mode. Therefore, the analyst or the designer needs to explicitly indicate the occurrence points.

Table 2. Components that need to be explicitly given where they occur

Diag ID	Diagnostic monitoring action	SysResp ID	System response	FE ID	Most severe failure effect after system response
DET-1	Comparator	STR-1	Close valve	FEF-1	Valve closed
DET-2	Sanity check for calculation	STR-1	Close valve	FEF-1	Valve closed
DET-3	Sanity check for actuator	STR-1	Close valve	FEF-1	Valve closed

After importing the FTA and FMEA data (CSV files) into the SysML model, the reviewer places Hybrid Failure Chains (propagations of failures' effects) on top of the IBD. Since it is not practical to display many Hybrid Failure Chains in a system on one diagram, the reviewer draws multiple diagrams, and each contains Hybrid Failure Chains corresponding to the failure mode to be reviewed. The reviewer specifies the function and failure mode to be reviewed on the diagram, and the tool recursively extracts the failure effects that occur due to the effect of the failure mode and draws it on the IBD.

6   Effect of the Visualization

To obtain a comprehensive understanding of the method's effect, we examined how this visualization method facilitates the discovery of mistakes in the analysis results.

Figure 6 illustrates the results of an intentionally mistaken analysis. "Valve opening request sticks to zero" is a failure mode of the function "valve opening calculation." The analyst erroneously determined that this fault was detected by "Detect deviation." This failure cannot be detected by "sanity check for actuator" because it causes the same deviation in the valve-opening request sent to the "sanity check for actuator." There could be a safety violation of the system if reviewers overlook this error and no safety measures are taken against the failure of the valve-opening calculation.

If a reviewer sees the phrase "detect deviation" in the FMEA sheet, he or she may mistakenly believe that the results of this analysis are correct. On the other hand, if the reviewers look at Fig. 6, they can understand how the "sanity check" compares the valve opening request with the valve opening detected by the sensor on the diagram, so it is easier to find mistakes there than on the FMEA sheet.

Figures 7 and 8 show examples of the propagation of failures in a simplified or a detailed safety analysis result (Figs. 7 and 8, respectively).

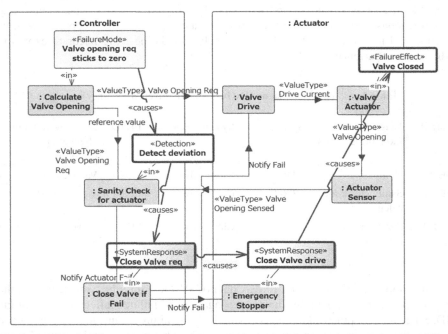

Fig. 6. Result of an intentionally mistaken analysis to explain the mismatch between failure occurrence and failure detection.

Figure 7 shows the result of FMEA-MSR, omitting horizontal propagation for simplicity, and the only direct relationship is drawn between the failure mode "no drive current," at the top center, and the detection, "detect deviation from reference." The reviewers can see the relationships between failure modes and safety mechanisms in one diagram, which makes it easier to discover mismatches between the two.

Figure 8 shows a more detailed relationship in the horizontal propagation, using detailed information from the FTA results. Reviewers can understand the failure's behavior from this diagram. On the other hand, the analysis results that express the detailed horizontal propagation are more complex than ordinary artifacts and, thus, can be impractical. Our method visualizes the level of simplification or omission in the safety analysis results and facilitates the analyst or reviewer's judgment about the appropriateness of the level.

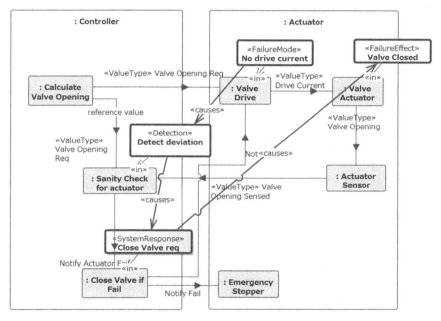

Fig. 7. Fault model with simplified or omitted fault propagation

7 Future Work

7.1 Effectiveness When Applied to a Larger System

In our approach, the entire fault model is represented by many diagrams, each representing the effects of a single failure. In the small-scale case study, the failure propagations are simple, and visualization is practical, but we should investigate the model's practicality in cases with a large number of failures.

7.2 Improvement for the Entire Safety Analysis Work

We focused on improving review activities through the growth of the visibility of safety analysis artifacts by FTA and FMEA. However, we think the benefit of the notation

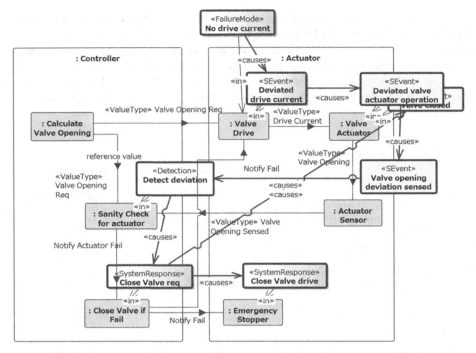

Fig. 8. Fault model without simplification or omission of propagation of faults

and functionality described in this paper can improve other activities in safety analysis. We should investigate how using the fault model within the SysML modeling tool can facilitate the work compared with traditional safety analysis work.

7.3 Completeness of Correspondence Between Safety Analysis Artifacts

We modeled the results of FTA and FMEA by relating their components, but since FTA and FMEA have different purposes and intentions, those components are not consistent and synchronized during development. At the beginning of this study, we decided to correlate and visualize the existing results of established safety analysis methods. However, in order to utilize multiple safety analysis methods in combination with modeling, the cooperation method between the safety analysis methods should be examined.

8 Conclusion

In this paper, we proposed a method to visualize the propagation of failures using an activity model and a diagram that integrates the results of FTA and FMEA and the functional block diagram of SysML. Based on the analysis of the effect of the proposed method, we found that the method facilitates understanding of flaws and omissions of safety analysis results.

The result of this study shows that the visualization of the behavior of failures included in the results of the traditional safety analysis and expression of the fault model by the activity model is effective in improving safety analysis.

References

1. Aizpurua, J.I., Muxika, E.: Model-based design of dependable systems: limitations and evolution of analysis and verification approaches. Int. J. Adv. Secur. **6**(1–2), 12–31 (2013)
2. Biggs, G., Juknevicius, T., Armonas, A., Post, K.: Integrating safety and reliability analysis into MBSE: overview of the new proposed OMG standard. In: INCOSE International Symposium, vol. 28, pp. 1322–1336, July 2018
3. Joshi, A., Miller, S.P., Whalen, M., Heimdahl, M.P.E.: A proposal for model-based safety analysis. In: The 24th Digital Avionics Systems Conference, Washington, D.C., October 2005
4. Papadopoulos, Y., McDermid, J.A.: Hierarchically performed hazard origin and propagation studies. In: Felici, M., Kanoun, K. (eds.) SAFECOMP 1999. LNCS, vol. 1698, pp. 139–152. Springer, Heidelberg (1999). https://doi.org/10.1007/3-540-48249-0_13
5. Nordmann, A., Munk, P.: Lessons learned from model-based safety assessment with SysML and component fault trees. In: MODELS 2018, 14–19 October 2018, Copenhagen, Denmark (2018)
6. Clegg, K., Li, M., Stamp, D., Grigg, A., McDermid, J.: A SysML profile for fault trees— linking safety models to system design. In: Romanovsky, A., Troubitsyna, E., Bitsch, F. (eds.) SAFECOMP 2019. LNCS, vol. 11698, pp. 85–93. Springer, Cham (2019). https://doi.org/10.1007/978-3-030-26601-1_6
7. Lane, H.C., D'Mello, S.K.: Uses of physiological monitoring in intelligent learning environments: a review of research, evidence, and technologies. In: Parsons, T.D., Lin, L., Cockerham, D. (eds.) Mind, Brain and Technology. ECTII, pp. 67–86. Springer, Cham (2019). https://doi.org/10.1007/978-3-030-02631-8_5
8. AIAG and VDA: AIAG & VDA FMEA Handbook, Automotive Industry Action Group (2019)
9. Tanaka, N., Ogawa, K.: Proposal of a graphical representation of safety analysis and a tool with high affinity to design documents (in Japanese). In: Safety Engineering Symposium 2019 (2019)

Collecting and Classifying Security and Privacy Design Patterns for Connected Vehicles: SECREDAS Approach

Nadja Marko[1]([✉]), Alexandr Vasenev[2], and Christoph Striecks[3]

[1] VIRTUAL VEHICLE, Graz, Austria
nadja.marko@v2c2.at
[2] Joint Innovation Centre ESI (TNO), Eindhoven, The Netherlands
alexandr.vasenev@tno.nl
[3] AIT Austrian Institute of Technology, Vienna, Austria
christoph.striecks@ait.ac.at

Abstract. In the past several years, autonomous driving turned out to be a target for many technical players. Automated driving requires new and advanced mechanisms to provide safe functionality and the increased communication makes automated vehicles more vulnerable to attacks. Security is already well-established in some domains, such as the IT sector, and now spills over to Automotive. In order to not reinvent the wheel, existing security methods and tools can be evaluated and adapted to be applicable in other domains, such as Automotive. In the European H2020 ECSEL project SECREDAS, this approach is followed and existing methods, tools, protocols, best practices etc. are analyzed, combined and improved to be applicable in the field of connected vehicles. To provide modular and reusable designs, solutions are collected in form of design patterns. The SECREDAS design patterns describe solution templates to solve security, safety and privacy issues related to automated systems. The grouping and classification of design patterns is important to facilitate the selection process which is a challenging task and weak classification schemes can be a reason for a sparse application of security patterns, which represent a subgroup of design patterns. This work aims to assist automotive software and systems engineers in adopting and using technologies available on the market. The SECREDAS security patterns are based on existing technologies, so-called Common Technology Elements, and describe how and where to apply them in context of connected vehicles by making a reference to a generic architecture. This allows developers to easily find solutions to common problems and reduces the development effort by providing concrete, trustworthy solutions. The whole approach and classification scheme is illustrated based on one example security pattern.

Keywords: Security · Safety · Privacy · Design patterns · Automated systems · Connected vehicles

© Springer Nature Switzerland AG 2020
A. Casimiro et al. (Eds.): SAFECOMP 2020 Workshops, LNCS 12235, pp. 36–53, 2020.
https://doi.org/10.1007/978-3-030-55583-2_3

1   Introduction

At the moment, security issues are rarely considered at the initial stages of system development in Automotive. With the new software and communication functionality required to make connected cars active, security gets more and more important in the Automotive domain. With the integration of wireless communication functionality into vehicles, new security threats appear, which have to be considered in concept and design phases.

For providing security designs, security architects want to indicate which specific security mechanisms are needed not focusing on the implementation. Therefore, a set of security design patterns is needed, that define abstract security mechanisms and specify its fundamental characteristics [10]. Security patterns have been introduced around 20 years ago, inspired by design patterns [5] and are intended to be used by non-security experts. The solution is security patterns which serve as a means of bridging the gap between developers and security experts.

While these security patterns, along with security solutions, such as encryption and secure network protocols, helped to improve many software systems, the unique architecture of automotive systems require extended and adapted design strategies. In Automotive, security needs differ from traditional computing-based systems due to the specific performance constraints and requirements imposed by a vehicle's architecture and communication infrastructure [3]. Further, security vulnerabilities often have consequences to safety where security exploits can lead to hazardous consequences.

The European H2020 ECSEL project SECREDAS[1] has the objective to advance the development of autonomous systems by incorporating high security and privacy protection while preserving functional-safety and operational performance. The challenge in the project is that a lot of partners coming from different domains provide extensive knowledge that has to be collected, harmonized and made accessible. In order to efficiently provide solutions to advance existing architectures with security and privacy mechanisms, in SECREDAS, design patterns are used to describe security, privacy and safety design solutions and best practices applicable for connected vehicles. However, the focus is on security patterns, which represent the biggest subgroup of the developed design patterns and are subject to discussion in this paper. Hence, the terms design pattern and security pattern can be seen as identical in this work. The security patterns are based on existing technologies, so-called Common Technology Elements (CTEs), that provide security functions. The idea is to use well-known design solutions and existing tools and techniques rather than inventing solutions from scratch, which would be risky because of the likelihood of design and coding flaws. CTEs are for example firewalls, authentication and authorization or transport layer security (TLS). The idea of CTEs is that they are known technologies already available in the market (starting from technology readiness level (TRL) 7) that can be used and adapted to be usable in connected vehicles' archi-

---

[1] https://secredas.eu/.

tecture. So for example, a firewall can be a security pattern but software that implements this security pattern is already available at the market and we refer to those existing technologies as security-related CTEs. In that sense, one might think of the concept as "already industrialized" security patterns which extend security patterns towards the industrial regime. The usage of CTEs in vehicle architectures, where they are not frequently applied at the moment, are our security patterns. This includes also combinations of several CTEs. For example, a security pattern can describe how to use CTEs authentication, cryptographic libraries and secure elements together to secure a Vehicle-2-X (V2X) communication, or a security pattern can be an authentication protocol for authentication of mobile devices in vehicle architectures. All in all, these security patterns describe best practices, protocol and design solutions or guidelines for the application of CTEs in the context of autonomous systems. The basis for the design patterns is the broad knowledge from the numerous SECREDAS partners and existing security patterns. Over the last few years, the number of security patterns has increased considerably. Although this situation is beneficial, it is now difficult to select appropriate security patterns from the large pool of existing patterns and to understand the consequences of its application, in particular, when choosing between patterns that address the same problem [20]. Grouping design patterns is important to facilitate the selection process. A classification organizes patterns into groups of patterns that share common properties such as application domain or a particular purpose [10]. Security patterns can be grouped into many categories based on multiple classification techniques, such as life cycle phase or the problem they are attempting to solve. In SECREDAS, the design patterns are classified according to their applicability in context of connected vehicles. Hence, the classification scheme is not applicable in general but supports solution architects for connected vehicles. In order to see the applicability of design patterns, a generic reference architecture has been developed. Security patterns are linked to this generic reference architecture to see for which systems and components the design patterns can be applied. Our approach helps solution architects to select security and privacy patterns as the link to a generic technical architecture describes where they can be applied. Further, an appropriate organization scheme is needed to manage and apply the knowledge from partners coming from various domains.

This work aims to assist automotive software and systems engineers in adopting and using technologies (nearly) available on the market. We structurally depict how design patterns are related to essential elements of the complex automotive context and the logic the users might follow when selecting the patterns. In contrast to higher-level categorizations, we build on the familiarity of the intended pattern users with the automotive industry context and typical use cases of connected vehicles. To note, this familiarity is a facilitator to effectively select the patterns, but is not a pre-requisite. The paper is structured as follows. Section 2 summarizes related work regarding security patterns, their classification and security patterns in the Automotive domain. In Sect. 3, our approach is described including the concept of CTEs, the generic reference architecture and the security pattern template we use. Section 4 demonstrates the approach based on an example design pattern. Finally, Sect. 5 summarizes the actual achievements and an outlook of the next steps.

2 Related Work

2.1 Security Pattern Catalogues

Several security pattern catalogs have emerged, and the security pattern community has produced significant contributions. There are various collections of security design patterns including surveys and overviews about papers. In [11], for example, the authors describes several security patterns differentiated by structural and procedural patterns. The focus is on information security for web applications. The collection of patterns is called security patterns repository and consists of 26 patterns and 3 mini-patterns. Yoshioka et al. [21] provide a survey of approaches to security patterns including representation, classification, security pattern repositories, quality analysis and development methodology. The authors state that guidance for developers is needed for selecting the appropriate patterns. With the new requirements on privacy, also privacy design patterns have been developed the last years. Privacy can be seen as one aspect of security and also becomes important for the Automotive domain as there are many new applications in which private data has to be protected (e.g. state of health applications). There are privacy design patterns for protecting privacy [7,14], providing privacy transparency [18], and privacy design strategies and survey [9]. In [2], the authors propose a taxonomy of types of relationships that describe relationships between privacy patterns. The taxonomy is analyzed based on existing privacy patterns. Therefore, the authors provide an overview of privacy design pattern collections in their related work.

2.2 Organization of Security Patterns

A main contribution of this paper is the organization of security patterns and providing an appropriate template in the context of connected vehicles. This differs from other approaches that provide security patterns for various domains. The basis for our security patterns are existing technologies. In [5], the authors describe an approach for expressing security patterns, built on a set of reusable and well-known security building blocks. They claim that "security patterns can be improved by building them on top of recurring security building blocks". The building blocks differ from the SECREDAS CTEs (building blocks). In SECREDAS, we use existing security mechanisms (e.g. firewall), whereas in this paper the building blocks are data specific security building blocks (e.g. data types, creation of data, data storage).

Proper organization of patterns is needed for users to find the appropriate pattern for their design. One aspect of pattern organization is classification, i.e. grouping the patterns into small, correlated sets. A good classification scheme facilitates selection of appropriate patterns as users can find a pattern that solves their particular problem more easily [8]. In [20], the authors present a selection approach for security patterns based on security requirements. Their formalized approach is based on a goal-oriented requirements language and Prolog rules and finds the most suitable security patterns based on requirements. In [12], the authors survey major contributions in the field of security design patterns and assesses their quality in the context of an established classification. They authors define a set of desirable properties as well as a template for expressing them. They propose a template based on existing templates. In [10], the authors summarize different classification schemes for security patterns and propose a new classification scheme based on Microsoft organizing table integrated with performance, implementation cost and security degree. Hafiz et al. [8] describe various classification schemes, analyze them and propose an alternative pattern organization methodology based on threat model and application context. They state that "there is no proper organization of security patterns. Several schemes for organizing the patterns have been used so far, but all of these approaches fall short of successfully organizing all the security patterns [8]". In SECREDAS, we follow this proposal and organize security patterns based on the application context of system functions of connected vehicles. The system functions and its extension with security patterns is illustrated based on a reference architecture.

2.3 Security Patterns in Automotive

Security patterns are well-known in some domains; however, in Automotive and the field of connected cars security is rather new for developers and solution architects. References regarding security patterns in this domain is rare. In [1], security issues in connected cars are described. They describe that three areas can be distinguished for security threats: the in-vehicle network and communication gateway, mobile device and the cloud infrastructure. All three areas are represented in the SECREDAS technical reference architecture and are hence part of the classification scheme. In [15], the NHTSA published security best practices for modern vehicles. This includes general cybersecurity guidance for the vehicle development process and documentation (e.g. 'penetration testing and documentation', 'limit access in production devices') as well as some design and implementation best practices, e.g. 'log events' or 'control wireless interfaces'. Cheng et al. [3] summarize some security patterns and security principles applicable for Automotive and introduces two security design patterns, namely Signature based IDS and Blacklist. Further, the authors extended common fields of design pattern templates with parameters specific for Automotive. McAfee [13] published a white paper summarizing security best practices for Automotive. They summarize some practices for hardware, software, network and cloud security. Further, the security development lifecycle and supply chain security are discussed. In [6], the European Union Agency for Cybersecurity (ENISA) published a report for security practices for smart cars. This comprehensive report contains threats and attack scenarios as well as security measures and good practices, both organizational and technical, and builds a good basis for our security patterns.

3   Security Pattern Organization for Connected Vehicles

Some authors point to the lack of a good security pattern catalog and methodology as likely reasons not using security patterns [5]. Hence, the organization of security patterns and the provided information is very important. We want to assist automotive software and systems engineers in adopting and using available technologies and structurally depict how design patterns are related to essential elements of the complex automotive context and the logic the users might follow when selecting the patterns. In addition to the technical requirements, we have to consider some constraints of the project. One important requirement is the management of knowledge from various partners coming from different domains. Those partners have a wide range of knowledge, which has to be made accessible to various partners having different background. Organizing security patterns based on limited context helps to provide and to find the appropriate security patterns. To enable contextualized choices, we relate patterns to the technical contexts of connected cars. Positioning in the technical context helps to highlight the functionality that design patterns address. Further, we plan to extend the contextualization by providing also information of business and customer context.

We first collected the design patterns based on an agreed template (see Sect. 3.3). To define an appropriate categorization that splits patterns into sets, we classified patterns as a solution to a problem in a context. Therefore, the design patterns are related to a generic reference architecture for connected vehicles (cp. Sect. 3.2) to see for which systems and components the security patterns can be applied. This represents the context of the security patterns. The relation indicates the intended systems, components and communication channels that can be extended with the design pattern functionality to make those parts more secure or privacy enhanced. This categorization helps to find appropriate security patterns from the pattern catalog. As the SECREDAS security patterns differ from security patterns from related work by using existing technologies (CTEs), the security pattern also has a relation to CTEs. In SECREDAS, a design pattern describes the usage of CTEs (cp. Sect. 3.1) and the use and interaction with domain specific technical solutions. This allows developers to easily find solutions to common problems, which they can reuse and adapt to their specific needs. The linkage of design patterns with CTEs will further reduce the development effort due to the provision of concrete, trustworthy solutions, which have been already applied in an industrial context. They include for example security and privacy best practices, protocol and architecture specifications or guidelines for the application of CTEs. The connection of security design patterns, CTEs and reference architecture is shown in Fig. 1.

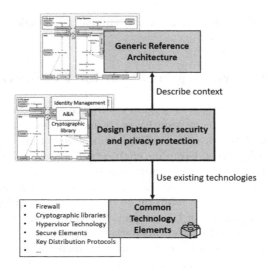

Fig. 1. Security pattern organization

3.1   Common Technology Elements

SECREDAS design patterns use building blocks that are called Common Technology Elements (CTEs). One main objective in the project is the improvement of a number of CTEs and thereby avoid redundancies and support cooperative developments between the different domains addressed. This means that technical solutions solving similar problems in the different domains are gathered, adapted and if necessary, adapted cooperatively by partners having their main expertise in different industries. We define Common Technology Elements as follows.

Common Technology Elements (CTEs) are domain independent technologies (implementations, mathematical models, specifications, processes, etc.) realized in existing systems (starting from TRL 7). Within SECREDAS, CTEs are related to safety, security, privacy protection. Examples are cryptographic libraries, hardware anchors for secure key storage, communication networks and protocols or existing security products like a firewall, trusted execution environments or blockchain. CTEs are the basis for CTE Improvements in SECREDAS.

CTE Improvements developed in SECREDAS are safety, security, privacy solutions (starting from TRL 3, mostly TRL 3–5). These solutions can be evaluations, adaptations, or enhancements of CTEs for a different application or domain.

The CTE description contains a definition of the CTE, technical aspects that are covered with the CTE, an overview about the state-of-the-art including some links to existing tools and specifications and a list of improvements that will be done during the project to be applicable for connected vehicles. An overview about the CTE structure, exemplified with CTE firewall, is shown in Fig. 2.

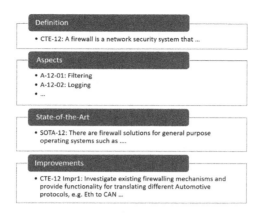

Fig. 2. CTE structure

CTEs are not limited to concrete implementations but can also contain best practices and protocol specifications. The CTEs are the starting point for the development of design patterns in SECREDAS, where design principles and best practices are combined and implementation recommendations for the correct use of CTEs are given. The available CTEs within SECREDAS and their intended fields of application will be gathered. Extensions and new developments are carried out according to the functional requirements derived from their use in the proposed design patterns. Those extensions will be constantly tracked, documented and linked to design patterns, where their application is described.

Based on the definition, design patterns are linked to CTEs and CTE improvements. The differentiation enables that design patterns can be developed based on generic and already available technologies (e.g. SSH communication protocol). These design patterns mainly describe how existing CTEs can be combined and applied in a new domain, i.e. connected vehicles. On the other hand, the linking to CTE improvements refers to design patterns that describe the application of CTE improvements developed in SECREDAS and also reflect requirements to existing CTEs.

3.2 Reference Architecture: Technology Aspect

Design patterns can be interrelated and discussed using the SECREDAS generic reference architecture, which is a type of architectural guidance to assist and constrains the instantiation of multiple architectures [16]. Relating patterns to high-level system functionalities aims to assist shared understanding of the patterns' scope and their interconnections. Empowered by the reference architecture, solution architects can make informed choices which design patterns to consider in their case. Figure 3 illustrates a technical view of the SECREDAS reference architecture. At the core of it is a vehicle that interacts with travelers (including the driver) and roadside infrastructure. Traveler(s) can have mobile devices, such as a smart phone. Roadside infrastructure consists of Road-side Units (RSU) and Cooperative Intelligent Transport Systems (C-ITS). Several communication channels can be established and used, including Vehicle-to-Vehicle (V2V), Vehicle-to-Everything (V2X), Vehicle-to-Infrastructure (V2I) and Infrastructure-to-Everything (I2X). Figure 3 also includes Other Systems that can for example correspond to the OEM infrastructure to do over-the-air updates. An example of such a system is described in [19].

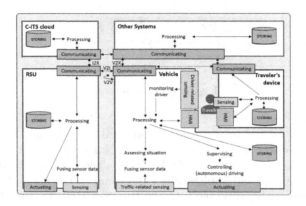

Fig. 3. Technical reference architecture C-ITS: Cooperative Intelligent Transport Systems, RSU: Road Side Unit, HMI: Human-Machine Interface

Solution architects can consider design patterns in connection to their use case and deploy needed security functionality. Figure 3 is an implementation-agnostic figure that conceptualizes the relevant high-level functionality breakdown (sensing, processing, storing, communicating). Solution architects can instantiate the technical reference architecture by reasoning along the following lines:

- In a particular case, each system can occur 0, 1, or multiple times. As an example, several external systems (Other systems), one or more vehicles and no C-ITS clouds can be included.
- A functionality can be implemented in hardware or software; in one or multiple ECUs (Electronic Control Unit).
- Storage can be differentiated as tamper-resistant or not.
- Processing can take place in secure (or not) environments.
- Vehicle's sensing can focus on: (1) the driver or (2) the outside world.

Some design patterns can benefit from an additional (but optional) functional breakdown of the generalized functionality. Figure 4 provides such support. This structure is not obligatory, as SECREDAS design patterns are not required to describe the degrees of processing or explicitly consider a high-tech product topology. (Delegated) processing can also be in one or several ECUs.

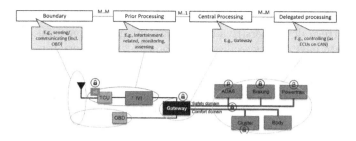

Fig. 4. Functional breakdown of in-vehicle topology OBD: On-Board Diagnostics, CAN: Controller Area Network, TCU: Telematics Control Unit, IVI: In-Vehicle Infotainment, ADAS: Advanced Driver-Assistance Systems, SE: Secure Element.

3.3 Security Design Pattern Organization

The design patterns are developed using a bottom-up and a top-down approach. The bottom-up approach uses known CTEs as a basis and creates design patterns describing their intended and most efficient application. In the top-down approach, common problems, which have to be solved in one of the domains in SECREDAS, are defined and potential technical solutions are described in form of design patterns. These design patterns can provide suggestions for new common or domain specific CTEs or improvements of existing ones, which allow their efficient implementation.

Design Pattern Definition. SECREDAS design patterns have additional properties, compared to software patterns for example, as they are tailored to project requirements in the context of connected cars. More precisely, they are defined as follows.

A design pattern is a best-practice solution template for a specific technical challenge allowing its efficient realization and verification. In SECREDAS, a design pattern has the following properties:

- *providing a generic, reusable solution template for a commonly occurring security, privacy or safety problem within a given context*
- *domain independence; it can for example include hardware and software designs as well as concepts on system level*
- *providing a concept that is related to one or more CTEs*

A design pattern is used as a guideline for

- *solving a safety, security or privacy problem (top-down approach in SECREDAS)*
- *using common technology elements (bottom-up approach in SECREDAS)*

Design Pattern Template. The design pattern template provides a guideline for design pattern developers to support describing their patterns. The elements of the template have been specified based on existing pattern templates, such as [17], and the project requirements. The project requirements makes it necessary to have a relation to the technical reference architecture and the used technologies (CTEs). It is planned to extend the template to provide further information to the design patterns by including the missing template fields proposed in [17]. These extensions are the dynamics (describing the behaviour in more detail), implementation guidelines and variants of the pattern. Further planned extensions are described in more detail in Sect. 5.

Design Pattern Name. The design pattern name should reflect the main purpose of the design pattern and should be memorable and useful as a new vocabulary for engineers doing the design.

Context. The context describes the relation of the design pattern to the technical reference architecture. In this part, the components of the architecture, which will be improved with the design pattern with regard to safety, security or privacy, are marked. Hence, the marking indicates the design pattern user which components can be improved when applying the design pattern. In Sect. 4 an example is shown. If needed, a short description about the context should be given providing more details about the environment, at which level of development the design pattern can be applied and the idea of the design pattern (e.g. definition of an advanced communication protocol or validation of data input).

Purpose. The purpose describes the intent of the pattern, i.e. what can be achieved with the application of the design pattern. It should answers questions like: What security problem is solved with this pattern or what is the motivation for applying this pattern. For example, a purpose could be improved authentication for multiple vehicles for V2X communication.

Safety/Security/Privacy. This field indicates whether the pattern is related to safety, security, and/or privacy. It should also include a description of which kind of attacks, hazards or privacy aspects can be detected, prevented and/or mitigated.

Classification. The classification indicates whether the pattern describes a concept, a system, a software or hardware solution. Examples are:

- Concept: a new architecture for safe sensor fusion
- System: adding a combination of hardware and software for authentication
- Software: application of advanced software algorithms for securing a communication
- Hardware: adding hardware to the system to protect a key

Related CTEs. In this part, the related CTEs are listed which are used when the design pattern is applied. The relation of design pattern and CTEs has already been described in more detail in the previous sections.

Preconditions. The preconditions describe all constraints and prerequisites that must be considered so that the pattern can be successfully applied. For example, the security algorithm is based on a TCP connection or the user must install an app on a phone. If these conditions are not fulfilled, the pattern is not applicable.

Design. The design shows an architectural picture of the design pattern. If applicable, the picture includes the applied CTEs and any further additional components and their relations. This is not possible for all design patterns but nevertheless, the application of the CTE should be clear.

Additional Components. Here, additional components that are needed to apply the design pattern are described.

Required CTE Improvements. The required CTE improvements refer to the CTE improvements, which have to be developed, either within the project or outside, so that the pattern can be applied correctly.

Output. The outputs after the application of the design pattern are listed. This field can be seen as post condition of the pattern usage. For example, secure V2X communication or privacy guarantee for authentication data.

Description. The description part specifies the design pattern in more detail and includes the usage of single CTEs or their combined use. With this description, it should become clear how the design pattern works (structure and behaviour). As it should be applicable in different architectures, this part should be generic, i.e. the description should be on a functional, tool independent level.

Example Application(s). Within this field, applications of the design pattern are illustrated. This can include:

– descriptions of pattern usages in different domains or applications
– specific implementations describing how the pattern is realized for a specific purpose
– descriptions of how the pattern is applied in SECREDAS

Further Comments. Further notes, comments that have not been described elsewhere.

Design Pattern Classification. In the first iteration of design pattern development, 30 design patterns for security, privacy and safety have been collected, whereat the most are related to security. One security pattern is illustrated in Sect. 4. Further examples of SECREDAS design patterns are:

– Automated Threat Detection and Vulnerability Management. This process is mostly related to the collection of incidents and the correlation to common vulnerabilities and exploits in order to execute various security tests.
– Cryptographic Erasure. This design pattern applies to data processors (Vehicle, RSUs, etc.) to enable data sanitization across distributed data storages.

- Digital Identity Management and Smart Profiling. This design pattern can be applied to RSUs. The purpose is to manage digital identities through the complete life cycle and to monitor access roles. This includes for example controlling access privileges or to integrate password management across multiple authentication resources.
- Health Data Exchange. This design pattern aims to provide reliable, secure access to accurate healthcare information about the driver to be used for fitness-to-drive check while considering privacy aspects.
- Mutual Authentication. The purpose of this security pattern is to establish robust identification and authentication processes by enabling mandatory mutual authentication for external communication channels (e.g. V2X).
- Secure Embedded Networks. The main goal is the supervision of an embedded network system from a central instance using 'access tickets' that allow flexible design of the policy environment during the whole life cycle.
- End-to-End security for Constrained Devices. The purpose is to enable resource-constrained devices to use certificate-based cryptography to secure communication, notably with external 3rd-party clouds.
- In-vehicle Network Intrusion Detection. The goal of this security pattern is to find attempts to tamper with the vehicle operation through manipulation of the in-vehicle bus.
- Virtualized Embedded System. The usage of a virtual machine monitor, or so-called hypervisor, enforces a stricter separation between individual tasks/processes, as well as the access to the underlying hardware. This design pattern improves safety and security aspects on embedded devices by using hypervisor technologies.

Based on the design pattern collection, the patterns are grouped to help pattern users to find the right pattern for their scope. The design patterns are grouped as follows:

- Vehicle connectivity. Vehicle connectivity covers design patterns that improve the external communication of vehicles and all other systems in the technical reference architecture.
- In-vehicle network. Design patterns related to in-vehicle network cover in-vehicle network including the internal communication, gateways as well as all processing and storing components.
- Sensing. Design patterns related to sensing include RSU sensing, vehicle sensing, driver-related sensing and traveler's device sensing.
- Connected systems. This group includes design patterns that focus on improving the systems connected to vehicles. These systems are RSU, C-ITS cloud, other systems and traveler's device.
- Storing. Design patterns related to storing improve storages. They can be related to a storage of one system, e.g. in-vehicle storages, or they can improve storages in general, independent of the system.
- Processing. Processing design patterns improve processing units of all systems in the technical reference architecture.

Based on this structure, design patterns can be selected. For example, if a user wants to improve the communication of a vehicle, the user can look to the vehicle connectivity design patterns. For all design pattern groups, the involved components in the technical reference architecture are marked. If a design pattern improves more than one part of the architecture, it can be assigned to several groups (e.g. vehicle connectivity and the in-vehicle network).

Having the first security pattern collection, the next steps are to harmonize the patterns, extend the template, extend the list of design pattern and improve patterns based on feedback and experiences with the application of the pattern. More information regarding the next steps is given in Sect. 5 and an example security pattern is illustrated in the next section.

4   Security Pattern: Separation of Networks

In this section, the approach described in Sect. 3 is illustrated with one security pattern. On the one hand, this should help to understand the approach and on the other hand, it can be seen what kind of design patterns are developed in SECREDAS.

Name: DP18 Separation of networks

Context: This design pattern is applicable to in-vehicle networks. It can be applied between processing components (controllers) that are connected with a bus system. Figure 5 shows that the network for 'assessing situation' and 'supervising' is separated (marked with boxes around the components).

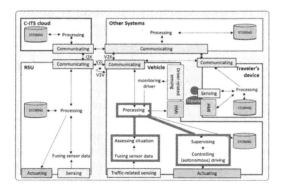

Fig. 5. Context of design pattern: separation of network

Purpose: Prevent security attacks to further components in case one component is hacked.

Safety/Security/Privacy Protection: Prevention and mitigation of security attacks. This pattern should prevent manipulation of information and denial of services attacks on critical functions (e.g. automated driving functions) in the vehicle.

Classification: Software pattern.

Related CTEs: CTE-12 Firewall.

Preconditions: This design pattern can be applied if there are several controllers connected with a bus system.

Design: The design is pictured in Fig. 6.

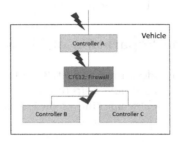

Fig. 6. Design pattern separation of network

Additional Components: No additional components needed.

Required CTE Improvements: Standard firewall mechanisms can be used. However, the firewall functions have to be implemented for the appropriate operating system and bus system. Further, real-time requirements have to be considered.

Output: Secure critical controllers (e.g. driving controller) from attacks through limitation of network access between controllers.

Description: Controllers are separated via a firewall so that no security attack is possible to the components behind the firewall. This ensures if one controller is hacked, other controllers are not automatically hacked as well (see Fig. 6). This can be applied for example for separating high level controllers, that are responsible for communication with other systems (e.g. RSU, C-ITS), and driving controllers, where an external control can have hazardous consequences.

Applied CTEs: CTE-12 Firewall: The firewall controls the data traffic and based on defined rules, data packets are accepted or not. Not allowed data access (e.g. from external sources) is prohibited.

Example Application(s): In order to secure the driving controller, in which a security exploit can have hazardous consequences, a firewall is setup before the driving controller. The firewall allows only communication from predefined sources. Hence, only registered sensors and communication devices are allowed to send messages to the driving controller. This reduces the risk that the driving controller is externally controlled by an attacker.

Further Comments: No further comments.

This security pattern shows how the design patterns are described in SECREDAS. The relation to the CTEs describes how existing technologies can be used for automated vehicles. The CTE can also be seen as variable part of the design pattern which changes over time as tools and methods are improved. In the pattern presented above, the CTE firewall is used. This CTE describes different aspects of a firewall solution to be used for secure communication to address threat detection, prevention and auditability of the on-board domain. Aspects that are covered are Packet Filtering, Packet Inspection, Logging and Intrusion Detection. There are several evaluations and improvements done for this CTE to be applicable for automated systems and specially connected vehicles. For example, shortcomings of existing firewall technologies are analyzed and possible solutions are suggested. Challenges can for example be the real-time requirement for safety related messages.

5 Conclusion

In this paper, the authors presented a work-in-progress approach for collecting security design patterns for automated systems, specially connected cars. The approach differs from other security pattern repositories in two main points. First, the context of application is limited and hence, tailored for connected vehicles. This enables to provide specialized design patterns for this context. Second, the design patterns are based on existing technologies, called CTEs. The linkage of design patterns with CTEs reduces the development effort by providing concrete, trustworthy solutions. After the first iteration, a collection of 30 security and privacy design patterns exists which will be extended until the SECREDAS project ends. Further, the template is currently reworked to provide more information about the pattern. Mainly, the tradeoff of the patterns should become more explicit and clear. It's a challenge to find an appropriate way for describing the benefits of a pattern, its liabilities and hence, its tradeoff. For describing the benefits, the provided security should be outlined by informing about the reduced threats and attack potentials. In return, the costs (e.g. implementation effort or material costs) to be expected represent the liabilities. However, we plan to extend the template with the following fields.

- Principles. Principles denote a basic guideline for designing secure systems. Security and privacy principles are part of the reference architecture and will be connected to the design patterns.
- Customer context. The customer context indicates which stakeholders can apply the pattern.
- Business architecture. The business architecture describes which types of companies (e.g. OEM or service supplier) might apply the design pattern.

- Provided security. This field describes the provided security based on several factors. It is planned that Common Criteria [4] is used for the determination of the security. Common Criteria defines five factors that have to be rated, and based on the rated values a security class can be determined.
- Reduced threats. This field should provide information about the threats that are reduced with the security pattern.
- Cost factor. The cost factor summarizes all efforts and costs that have to be considered when applying the pattern.
- Status. This field indicates the status of the design pattern realization. Is this pattern available only as concept or is also an implementation available that can be evaluated? How far is the implementation?
- Related design patterns. Here, relations to other design patterns will be described such as in [2] for privacy design patterns.
- Usage Guidelines. This field provides information about lessons learned by applying the pattern. This can also include examples for incorrect application.
- Constraints. Constraints describe existing limitations for applying this pattern. This can be timing constraints, environmental or technical constraints.

The next steps will be the definition of the new fields and the update of the patterns according to the new template. Further, new design patterns will be added to the pattern collection. The extended list of design pattern will be harmonized and feedback of the applications will be considered for improving the pattern catalog.

Acknowlegements. This work has been partially funded by EU ECSEL Project SECREDAS. This project has received funding from the European Union's Horizon 2020 research and innovation programme under grant agreement No 783119. The publication was written at VIRTUAL VEHICLE Research Center in Graz and partially funded by the COMET K2 – Competence Centers for Excellent Technologies Programme of the Federal Ministry for Transport, Innovation and Technology (bmvit), the Federal Ministry for Digital, Business and Enterprise (bmdw), the Austrian Research Promotion Agency (FFG), the Province of Styria and the Styrian Business Promotion Agency (SFG). We are also grateful to Netherlands Organization for Applied Scientific Research TNO for supporting this research.

References

1. Bécsi, T., Aradi, S., Gáspár, P.: Security issues and vulnerabilities in connected car systems. In: 2015 International Conference on Models and Technologies for Intelligent Transportation Systems (MT-ITS), pp. 477–482 (2015)
2. Caiza, J.C., Martín, Y.S., Del Alamo, J.M., Guamán, D.S.: Organizing design patterns for privacy: a taxonomy of types of relationships. In: Proceedings of the 22nd European Conference on Pattern Languages of Programs, pp. 1–11 (2017)
3. Cheng, B.H., Doherty, B., Polanco, N., Pasco, M.: Security patterns for automotive systems. In: 2019 ACM/IEEE 22nd International Conference on Model Driven Engineering Languages and Systems Companion (MODELS-C), pp. 54–63 (2019)

4. Common Criteria Working Group: Common Methodology for Information Technology Security Evaluation (2017). https://www.commoncriteriaportal.org/files/ccfiles/CEMV3.1R5.pdf, Version 3.1 Revision 5
5. van Den Berghe, A., Yskout, K., Joosen, W.: Security patterns 2.0: toward security patterns based on security building blocks. In: 2018 IEEE/ACM 1st International Workshop on Security Awareness from Design to Deployment (SEAD), pp. 45–48 (2018)
6. ENISA: ENISA good practices for security of smart cars. Report, European Union Agency for Cybersecurity (2019)
7. Hafiz, M.: A collection of privacy design patterns. In: Proceedings of the 2006 Conference on Pattern Languages of Programs, PLoP 2006, pp. 1–13. Association for Computing Machinery, New York (2006)
8. Hafiz, M., Adamczyk, P., Johnson, R.E.: Towards an organization of security patterns. https://munawarhafiz.com/research/patterns/haj07-security-patterns.pdf. Accessed 30 Jan 2020
9. Hoepman, J.-H.: Privacy design strategies. In: Cuppens-Boulahia, N., Cuppens, F., Jajodia, S., Abou El Kalam, A., Sans, T. (eds.) SEC 2014. IAICT, vol. 428, pp. 446–459. Springer, Heidelberg (2014). https://doi.org/10.1007/978-3-642-55415-5_38
10. Hudaib, A., Edinat, A.: A survey on security patterns and their classification schemes. Int. J. Sci. Eng. Res. 6, 79–90 (2019)
11. Kienzle, D.M., Elder, M.C., Tyree, D., Edwards-Hewitt, J.: Security patterns repository version 1.0. DARPA, Washington DC (2002)
12. Laverdiere, M., Mourad, A., Hanna, A., Debbabi, M.: Security design patterns: survey and evaluation. In: 2006 Canadian Conference on Electrical and Computer Engineering, pp. 1605–1608 (2006)
13. McAfee: Automotive Security Best Practices (2016). https://www.mcafee.com/enterprise/en-us/assets/white-papers/wp-automotive-security.pdf, Accessed 30 Jan 2020
14. Munawar, H.S.: A pattern language for developing privacy enhancing technologies. Softw.: Pract. Exp. 43(7), 769–787 (2013)
15. NHTSA: Cybersecurity Best Practices for Modern Vehicles. Report DOT HS 812 333, National Highway Traffic Safety Administration (2016)
16. van der Sanden, B., Vasenev, A.: Architectural guidance in automotive for privacy and security: survey and classification. In: Annual IEEE International Systems Conference (SysCon) (IEEE SysCon 2020) (2020, accepted)
17. Schumacher, M., Fernandez, E., Hybertson, D., Buschmann, F., Sommerlad, P.: Security Patterns: Integrating Security and Systems Engineering. Wiley, Hoboken (2006)
18. Siljee, J.: Privacy transparency patterns. In: Proceedings of the 20th European Conference on Pattern Languages of Programs, pp. 1–11 (2015)
19. Vasenev, A., et al.: Practical security and privacy threat analysis in the automotive domain: long term support scenario for over-the-air updates. In: Proceedings of the 5th International Conference on Vehicle Technology and Intelligent Transport Systems (VEHITS 2019), pp. 550–555 (2019)
20. Weiss, M., Mouratidis, H.: Selecting security patterns that fulfill security requirements. In: 2008 16th IEEE International Requirements Engineering Conference, pp. 169–172 (2008)
21. Yoshioka, N., Washizaki, H., Maruyama, K.: A survey on security patterns. Prog. Inform. 5(5), 35–47 (2008)

Safety and Security Interference Analysis in the Design Stage

Jabier Martinez[1]($\boxtimes$), Jean Godot[2], Alejandra Ruiz[1], Abel Balbis[3],
and Ricardo Ruiz Nolasco[4]

[1] Tecnalia, BRTA (Basque Research and Technology Alliance), Derio, Spain
{jabier.martinez,alejandra.ruiz}@tecnalia.com
[2] All4Tec, Laval, France
jean.godot@all4tec.net
[3] Thales Alenia Space, Madrid, Spain
abel.balbis@thalesaleniaspace.com
[4] RGB Medical Devices, Madrid, Spain
rruiznolasco@rgb-medical.com

Abstract. Safety and security engineering have been traditionally separated disciplines (e.g., different required knowledge and skills, terminology, standards and life-cycles) and operated in quasi-silos of knowledge and practices. However, the co-engineering of these two critical qualities of a system is being largely investigated as it promises the removal of redundant work and the detection of trade-offs in early stages of the product development life-cycle. In this work, we enrich an existing safety-security co-analysis method in the design stage providing capabilities for interference analysis. Reports on interference analyses are crucial to trigger co-engineering meetings leading to the trade-offs analyses and system refinements. We detail our automatic approach for this interference analysis, performed through fault trees generated from safety and security local analyses. We evaluate and discuss our approach from the perspective of two industrial case studies on the space and medical domains.

Keywords: Safety · Security · Co-engineering · Interference analysis · Fault tree analysis

1 Introduction

Several engineering disciplines are required to design and build the increasingly complex critical systems present in industrial settings and public infrastructures. Besides the different specialized disciplines related to designing and implementing the software and hardware parts for the functional capabilities of the system, there are experts on assuring the relevant non-functional properties. *Safety* is a non-functional property which considers the mitigation measures to avoid negative impact on humans or the environment, while *Security* is the combination of three criteria: confidentiality, the prevention of the unauthorized disclosure of

© Springer Nature Switzerland AG 2020
A. Casimiro et al. (Eds.): SAFECOMP 2020 Workshops, LNCS 12235, pp. 54–68, 2020.
https://doi.org/10.1007/978-3-030-55583-2_4

information; integrity, the prevention of the unauthorized amendment or deletion of information; and availability, the prevention of the unauthorized withholding of information [2]. Thus, safety and security experts aim to reduce those risks to acceptable values by integrating the needed barriers and measures within the components of the system. However, preventing both safety and security could cause contradictory situations [6] (e.g., the introduction of a security method could cause a time delay which is in contradiction with a safety requirement).

Security is usually needed to ensure safety (security-informed safety) [21] and therefore they are highly interrelated. However, current engineering practices reveal that they are mostly faced independently because safety and security teams have different highly specialized knowledge and skills. For instance, safety experts and security experts tackle the analysis of feared events in different ways [32]. Also, they are forced to show compliance to standards, jurisdictions, and regulations focusing only on one aspect [25] which usually impose the life-cycle, activities, methods, terminology conventions that they should follow, and the expected artefacts that they should produce.

Co-engineering safety and security is still a challenge [13,24] affecting several industrial scenarios such as medical devices, industrial automation, railway, air traffic management or space [25]. Safety and security separation led to redundant efforts [27] and, most importantly for this work, to late identification of conflicts and trade-offs in safety and security requirements [25]. The costs of not identifying issues related to safety and security concerns during early phases of the product life-cycle can be very significant.

In this work, we focus on how to support the co-engineering process in the design stage. We contribute with the integration of safety-security co-engineering within mainstream practices. Concretely, we extend an existing method for the combined analysis of safety and security by introducing an *interference analysis* approach. Interference analysis refers to techniques analysing the mutual influence and inter-links of different quality attributes [5]. Notably, there is a debate about what triggers trade-off meetings and interaction points [25]. They may either be scheduled interaction points or interaction points triggered when a sufficient critical mass of interference needs to be treated. It is the goal of our work to define how this may be identified and measured. We propose a solution to these measurements taking as input *fault trees* [14,17] automatically generated from *component local analyses* of the combined safety-security analysis. Thus, this interference analysis provides high-level reports on the interdependence of safety and security using artefacts from the combined analysis. The objective of these reports is to reveal and trigger the need of a co-engineering meeting and to visualise the evolution of the safety and security interdependence. We also contribute a qualitative evaluation of the presented approach from the perspective of two industrial pilot projects: earth observation and medical devices.

This paper is structured as follows. Section 2 introduces the case studies and Sect. 3 presents background information on relevant topics needed to better understand this work and using the case studies context. Section 4 positions our approach for the co-engineering method including the interference analysis part.

Section 5 presents the qualitative evaluation and a discussion. Finally, Sect. 6 presents the conclusions and future work.

2   Case Studies

The two case studies of this work stems from the AQUAS project (Aggregated Quality Assurance for Systems) [25] which objective is to provide a holistic app-roach to Safety/Security/Performance Co-Engineering. In the presented work, we have focused only on the design stage of two diverse domains, earth observa-tion and medical devices, that we introduce below.

Earth observation market is growing with its main application on mili-tary settings followed by usage by civilians and enterprises. Earth observation is in many cases mission-critical and the cyber-physical systems enabling these services have strong requirements on safety, security and performance, notably because of the stringent rules specified for space equipment design. In this work, a simplified version of the AQUAS space case study [25] supports the technical description. The original case study considered the more general Space multicore case, applicable to both Telecom and earth observation payloads. Most of the safety issues are related to the fact of using dual-core architectures (complex resource sharing schemes and software design). It has been simplified because of confidentiality issues but it also provides a more comprehensible presenta-tion. We focused on a subsystem which architecture is illustrated in Fig. 1. The mission-critical responsibility of this subsystem is taking pictures (`Camera` com-ponent), packaging them before the transmission (`Data packaging` component) and transmitting them to the ground station (`Transmitter` component).

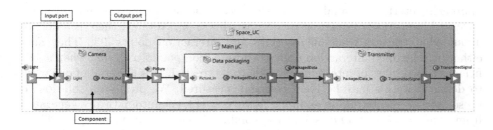

Fig. 1. Simplified system architecture of the space case study

Medical devices integrated in hospital settings and information systems have strong safety, security and performance requirements. In the AQUAS project, the development of a closed-loop controller for muscle relaxation is being investigated with respect to co-engineering challenges [25]. The device consists of a neuromuscular transmission monitor and an infusion pump system with sev-eral pumps for different patients. Because of space limitations, the architecture and more details can be found in a related publication [28].

3 Background

This section provides details on safety and security engineering (Sect. 3.1) as well as basic technical information on component local analysis (Sect. 3.3) and fault and attack trees (Sect. 3.2) for a better understanding of this work.

3.1 Safety and Security Engineering

As mentioned in the introduction, safety and security are usually separated processes. An industrial survey on safety and security aspects has shown that the lack of communication between engineering disciplines and their different focus and approaches are considered as a major issue [12]. However, some approaches exist trying to support combined analyses. In the STAMP analysis [18] both disciplines combine applying system engineering for accident cause analysis. Other proposals are, for instance, Failure Modes Vulnerabilities and Effects Analysis (FMVEA) [29], SAHARA (Security-aware Hazard Analysis and Risk Assessment) [20], or the combination of Fault Tree Analysis (FTA) [14,17,26], Stochastic Coloured Petri Net (SCPN) [11], Attack Trees Analysis (ATA) and FMVEA [35]. Besides the safety-security combined analyses in the concept, requirements [4], or risk analyses stages, other techniques are proposed for the subsequent phases. Extensive list of examples of those techniques are available [5,24] and a mapping of safety and security processes have been presented in several application domains such as medical [28] or industrial automation systems [27]. In this work, we focus on the design stage where the architecture and the components involved in the system are defined. This is a crucial stage before the actual software, hardware and communications implementation. Thus, preventing the late identification of issues that might have been avoided through co-engineering in the design stage is of high interest.

3.2 Fault Trees and Attack Trees

Fault Tree Analysis, a widely adopted practice on reliability and safety engineering [14,17,26], proposes a hierarchical structure of events, where the top event is an undesired event or system state, and the rest of the tree are events or gates describing the Boolean conditions which are sufficient to reach the top event. Traditional usage includes probability analysis to asses if the risk is under an acceptable threshold, and identification and analysis of the shortest or more probable paths to reach the top event with the objective to refine the system with the appropriate safety barriers. Besides that, diverse extensions to FTA were proposed [26]. Fault trees quickly get complex in terms of size complicating their human visualization and comprehension [19]. It is even more complicated to reason on high-level concepts (e.g., safety, security) and their interactions by just looking at the fault tree.

In the security engineering domain, a similar approach was used named attack trees [30] for modelling security threats where the top events represent an attack goal. Following the trend of safety-security co-engineering, approaches to conciliate safety-related fault trees with security attack trees are proposed [32] and industrial experiences of this mix are reported (e.g., railways domain [36]).

3.3   Component Local Analysis

In safety engineering, methods such as Failure Propagation and Transformation Notation (FPTN) [9] or Interface Focused-FMEA (IF-FMEA) [23] have been established to cope with the analysis of complex and large systems based on abstraction and decomposition. Thus, the analysis is conducted locally on components to identify and describe their failure behaviour. Technically, a component local analysis can be represented with specific equation syntax [9], table [23] or diagram [15]. The diagram solution is used in Safety Architect tool[1] with a notation based on Component Fault Trees [15] as depicted in Fig. 2. In the earth observation case study, the `Transmitter` component design, with its input and output ports (Fig. 1), is enriched with information about failure modes, feared events, and how system or local events can lead to the latter through logic expressed with Boolean gates. For instance, in the `Transmitter` component, perturbations, internal errors of the transmission, or errors from upstream components via the input port can lead to the feared event `Erroneous transmitted signal`.

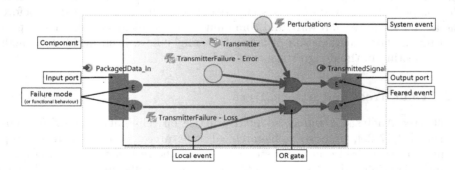

Fig. 2. Example of a safety component local analysis in Safety Architect

This local analysis is performed for single components of the system. However, given that this analysis is performed for each component in the system, the potential of components triggering feared events are captured for the whole system (i.e., the analysis span over components). Then, the enriched information introduced through the system components architecture, can be used to generate a Failure Modes and Effects Analysis (FMEA); taking as input the local

---

[1] Safety Architect: https://www.riskoversee.com/en/safety-architect-en/.

analyses of all system components, or, more importantly for this work, a global system safety analysis such as, fault trees for feared events. Generated fault trees for the whole system, gathering the local analyses, present even more challenges for visualization and comprehension given their size and the technical details included directly from the system design.

4 Enriching Safety-Security Co-analysis in the Design Stage with Interference Analysis

We propose a reusable building block for safety-security co-engineering in the design stage trying to integrate co-engineering into mainstream practices. Figure 3 is a UML activity diagram representing the enriched safety-security co-analysis approach that we propose. The parts tagged with ① and ② are advanced but established techniques dealing separately with safety and security aspects, and ③ is an advanced co-engineering technique. Then, ④ adds more co-engineering support through advanced interference analysis.

The proposed method falls within the design stage of the development life-cycle (see that the start and end UML symbols at Fig. 3 are within the design stage). The main goal is to define the system architecture with the chosen technological solutions to cover the requirements. Then, several engineering domains are involved such as hardware, software, safety, security or performance. These specialist teams for each domain receive inputs including the results of the concept phase: requirements and specification; and they are responsible for evolving the initial system architecture under design. Each of these domains work with their own processes, methods and tools, and progress in parallel during the development life-cycle (e.g., ① and ②).

As mentioned in Sect. 3.1, recent approaches propose to cross the result of different engineering domains. Our goal is to reduce the number of iterations for designing the system architecture that are usually required to tune the technical solutions and to find and solve potential trade-offs. The proposed method is dedicated to the co-engineering between safety and security domains based on a combined local analysis (③ and more explanations in Sect. 4.1). The co-engineering interference analysis is supported by an automatic tagging method applied on the fault trees and by high level reports that help to identify and set the scope of the issues to be analysed (④ and details in Sect. 4.2). Co-engineering meetings are triggered by issues or by an increase on the interference that should be discussed. These moments in the product life cycle where experts from the different disciplines met are called interaction points [25]. In case of trade-offs and where design decisions need to be made, rationale representations [7,31] (e.g., decision reports) are recommended.

The proposed method is associated with a fully integrated toolchain. Regarding tool-support, all parts are supported by Safety Architect and Cyber Architect, and we add the interference analysis with a seamless integration of the Concept-aware analysis library. The safety-security co-analysis and interference analysis are explained in details in the following sub-sections.

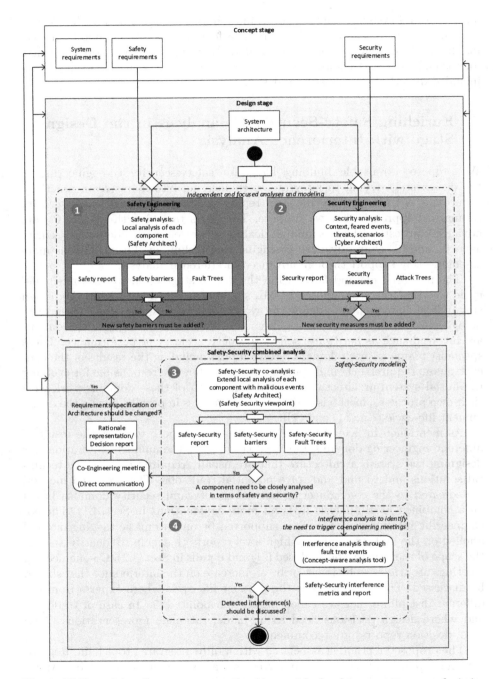

Fig. 3. UML activity diagram representing the enriched safety-security co-analysis in the design stage with interference analysis

4.1   Safety-Security Co-analysis

As described in the background Sect. 3, the safety analysis can be decomposed by local analysis of the system components to automatically generate fault trees, FMEA or reports for the whole system. Security analysis has its own concepts and methodology such as Ebios2010 [3] or ISO/IEC 27005 [1]. To propose a co-engineering method, a shared conceptual framework should be defined. Figure 4 presents the mapping proposal between safety and security concepts enabling the safety-security combined analysis (③ in Fig. 3).

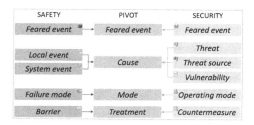

Fig. 4. Mapping between safety and security concepts

Thanks to this mapping, it is possible to bring safety elements into security analysis and vice-versa. Thus, in Safety Architect, a security threat scenario can be displayed with the component local analysis syntax. Figure 5 shows an example. In the **Transmitter** component, the external threat source of malevolent people and internal vulnerabilities and threats can led to the feared event of **Spying**.

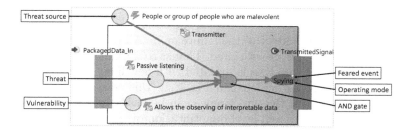

Fig. 5. Example of a security component local analysis

Then a safety-security local analysis can be conducted on each of the components that integrate safety and security concerns to represent their mutual impact. For instance, if safety engineers require a new barrier to comply with the safety goals, or conversely, the security engineers require a new countermeasure to reach the desired security level, an automatic analysis can be conducted to identify if the addition of this element could impact or interfere on other engineering domains.

In the first version of the earth observation case study, no security protection was implemented as, traditionally, with the exception of commercial telecommunications missions, security mechanisms have not been widely employed on civilian space missions. However, in recognition of increased threat, there has been a steady migration towards the integration of security services and mechanisms [33]. Then, in the case study, security engineers require to integrate an encryption module in the telecommunication space system. Thus, the previous security analysis (Fig. 5) is updated with the proposal to add a `Cipher` to protect the transmitted message as shown in Fig. 6.

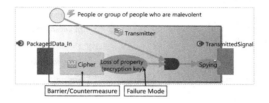

Fig. 6. Example of a security barrier in a component local analysis

The safety-security view allows to overlay, in the same local analysis, the safety and security one. Then, it is possible to analyse how the cipher module impacts the safety-related elements. One of the problems common to all forms of satellite encryption relates to signal degradation caused by different perturbations: terrestrial weather, solar and cosmic radiation or many other forms of electromagnetic noise. Depending on the encryption algorithm chosen, this situation can be particularly problematic because the entire encrypted message may be lost if even a single bit of data is out of place [34]. Then, new propagation links related to safety are added as part of the design of the solution to describe that perturbations can conduct to the failure mode Absent (A) where the feared event "Loss of the message" is associated. Thanks to the combined safety-security local analysis, the safety analysis is updated with new links involving the cipher and the perturbations, as depicted in Fig. 7. In this co-modelling step of the component local analysis, the interference can be easily identified and treated, however, we do not get system-level quantification of the interference.

4.2 Interference Analysis

From the combined safety-security local analyses, fault trees are automatically generated. This is the input for ④ in Fig. 3. The combined fault trees describe the combination of safety and security events (failure mode, vulnerability, threat) that conduct to a safety or a security feared event. Figure 8 presents an illustrative excerpt of a safety-security fault tree generated from the earth observation example. The events are annotated with `Safety` and `Security`. However, this is not

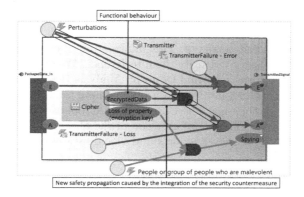

Fig. 7. Example of a safety-security component local analysis

visible in the tools. We added it for illustration purposes. In the example, because of its small size, the identification of the interference of safety and security is easy but in real projects it requires to deeply explore the generated safety-security trees which can count hundreds of events making it time-consuming or impossible to comprehend the safety-security interference.

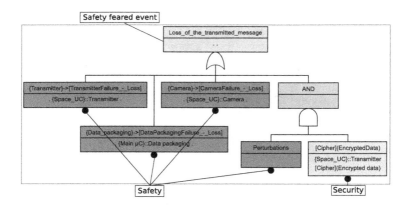

Fig. 8. Excerpt of a safety-security tree example

In the use of the CyberArchitect and SafetyArchitect tools, events belong to either safety or security concepts, we were able to export the fault tree models using Open-PSA exchange format [22] with attributes to add this information for each event. This information is seamlessly consumed by the tool named Concept-aware which takes these attributes in the events and performs a propagation mechanism of these tags. When an event is annotated with a tag (e.g., Safety), this event is a Safety-related event but, at the same time, through the propagation, *all ancestors and descendants* are events where this tag is potentially

64   J. Martinez et al.

involved. For example, `Cipher,EncryptedData` is a Security event and given that `Loss of the transmitted message` is its ancestor, Security is involved in `Loss of transmitted message`. This information of events and tags (direct and propagated) are used to identify the interference. We automatically create a formal context to perform a Formal Concept Analysis [10] (a wide-spread technique to create concept hierarchies and groups) where the objects are the events and the properties are the tags. The Concept-aware tool uses the Galatea library to perform this analysis [8]. The information of the obtained concept lattice [10] is then used to create high-level reports and visualisations.

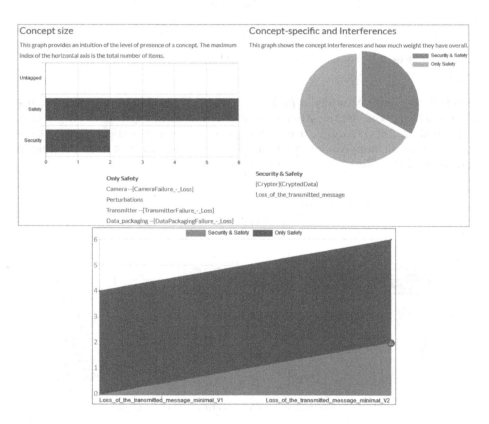

Fig. 9. Concept report and evolution report of the illustrative example

We provided a report consisting on a snapshot of the interference at a given point in time, usually the latest version of the design, and another report on the evolution of the interference given that the design evolve during the design process and also during refinements caused by issues or improvements found in later product life-cycle stages. Figure 9 shows an example of the reports generated from the illustrative example of the fault tree from Fig. 8. In the Concept size part on the left, we can observe how all events are involved in Safety and two on Security. In the right side, we can observe the level of the interference of Safety and Security in the system. In the evolution report we can compare the increase of the interference from zero to two (the latter corresponds to the latest version of the fault tree shown in Fig. 8).

5 Qualitative Evaluation and Discussion

Given the confidentiality of the case studies, we rely on a qualitative discussion of the practitioners from the industrial companies involved in the pilots. To show the characteristics of the pilots, Table 1 reports on the size of the modelled sub-systems and Table 2 the size of the generated fault trees. As mentioned in Sect. 3.2, we highlight the difficulty on visualising such large fault trees to infer interferences between safety and security concerns. The following paragraphs are based on feedback from the persons who applied the approach.

Table 1. Number of components (HW: Hardware, SW: Software) for the two pilots

Case study	HW components	SW components	Total
Earth observation	2	8	**10**
Medical devices	17	30	**47**

Table 2. Elements in the fault trees (Tmtc: Tele-Metrics to TeleCommunication)

	Feared event	Events	Gates	Total
Earth observation	Absent Tmtc out	24	67	**91**
	Erroneous Tmtc out	17	49	**66**
	Data spying	6	17	**23**
Medical devices	Erroneous drug dose rate	43	188	**231**
	Loss of integrity drug dose rate	2	16	**18**

Earth Observation Feedback: The high level reports on safety-security interference created through the proposed tool-supported process can help to make "trade-offs" decisions at the design stage, specially in large projects, where integration of complex systems and the involvement of different teams make system design decisions more difficult to be evaluated because of the lack of visibility of the fine-grained details. Figure 10 shows the evolution report for a feared event. We can observe how the design evolved taking only Safety into account and then Security was integrated creating a significant interference. The interference analysis report and the design should be analysed to check whether the elements in the interference requires a decision, an action, or introduces a trade-off. As mentioned before, the final objective of this interference analysis technique is to potentially trigger a co-engineering meeting to discuss the implications of the refinements of the design.

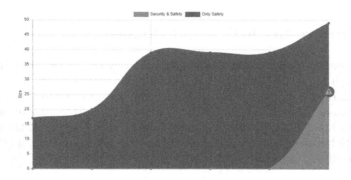

Fig. 10. Evolution report for a feared event of the earth observation case study

Medical Devices Feedback: The proposed co-engineering method is a structured method that can help refining the design and may led to improve significantly the detection of interferences between safety and security requirements at early stages of the design. This improvement will have a positive impact on the reduction of cost and time required for designing a medical device. The cybersecurity is an increasingly important factor to consider for the design of medical devices, so it is becoming highly regulated. Given the interlinks between safety and security, that we already acknowledged in the product-life cycles of RGB products [16], the proposed independent safety and security analyses followed by the combined analysis, can provide evidences that issues related to this interference were considered, and eventually, discussed and treated. As a drawback, RGB has experience on safety and security analysis using fault tree analysis, but integrating these new methods and tools can represent a significant learning curve.

6   Conclusion

We proposed a method for co-engineering in the design stage based on enriching components' local analyses and enabling interference analysis to avoid the later identification of issues and conflicts between safety and security aspects. The system-level reports on safety-security interference are possible through generated fault tree models. These high-level reports can help quantifying the interference at a given point in time as well as from the historic of changes. We used our approach in two pilot projects. As further work, we aim to provide more support for the interference analysis to rank or prioritize the interference events identified in fault tree analysis, and by supporting an integrated interference analysis approach using other artefacts such as requirements.

Acknowledgments. The research leading to this paper has received funding from the AQUAS project (H2020-ECSEL grant agreement 737475). The ECSEL Joint Undertaking receives support from the European Union's Horizon 2020 research and innovation programme. It is a collaboration between Spain, France, United Kingdom, Austria, Italy, Czech Republic and Germany.

References

1. ISO/IEC 27005:2018 - Information security risk management
2. Abdulkhaleq, A., Wagner, S., Lammering, D., Boehmert, H., Blueher, P.: Using STPA in compliance with ISO 26262 for developing a safe architecture for fully automated vehicles. In: Automotive-Safety and Security 2017, Stuttgart (2017)
3. ANSSI: Expression of Needs and Identification of Security Objectives - EBIOS Security knowledge Base (2010). https://tinyurl.com/ebios2010
4. Apvrille, L., Li, L.W.: Harmonizing safety, security and performance requirements in embedded systems. In: DATE 2019, pp. 1631–1636. IEEE (2019)
5. AQUAS project: D3: Combined Safety, Security and Performance Analysis and Assessment Techniques (2019). https://aquas-project.eu/documents/
6. Avizienis, A., Laprie, J.C., Randell, B., Landwehr, C.: Basic concepts and taxonomy of dependable and secure computing. IEEE TDSC **1**(1), 11–33 (2004)
7. Dutoit, A.H., McCall, R., Mistrik, I., Paech, B.: Rationale Management in Software Engineering. Springer, Heidelberg (2006). https://doi.org/10.1007/978-3-540-30998-7
8. Falleri, J.R.: Automatic Refactoring and Alignment of Class Models (Contributions à l'IDM : reconstruction et alignement de modèles de classes). Ph.D. thesis (2009). http://www.theses.fr/2009MON20103 and https://github.com/jrfaller/galatea
9. Fenelon, P., McDermid, J.A., Nicolson, M., Pumfrey, D.J.: Towards integrated safety analysis and design. SIGAPP Appl. Comput. Rev. **2**(1), 21–32 (1994)
10. Ganter, B., Wille, R., Franzke, C.: Formal Concept Analysis: Mathematical Foundations, 1st edn. Springer, Heidelberg (1997). https://doi.org/10.1007/978-3-642-59830-2
11. Gehlot, V., Nigro, C.: An introduction to systems modeling and simulation with colored petri nets. In: Winter Simulation Conference, pp. 104–118 (2010)
12. ARC advisory group, Kaspersky, T.M.: The state of industrial cybersecurity (2019). https://ics.kaspersky.com/media/2019_Kaspersky_ARC_ICS_report.pdf
13. Gruber, T., Schmittner, C., Matschnig, M., Fischer, B.: Co-engineering-in-the-loop. In: Gallina, B., Skavhaug, A., Schoitsch, E., Bitsch, F. (eds.) SAFECOMP 2018. LNCS, vol. 11094, pp. 151–163. Springer, Cham (2018). https://doi.org/10.1007/978-3-319-99229-7_14
14. IEC 61025: Fault Tree Analysis, 2nd edn. (2006)
15. Kaiser, B., et al.: Advances in component fault trees. In: ESREL (2018)
16. Larrucea, X., Nanclares, F., Santamaria, I., Nolasco, R.R.: Approach for enabling security across PLC phases: an industrial use case. In: Larrucea, X., Santamaria, I., O'Connor, R.V., Messnarz, R. (eds.) EuroSPI 2018. CCIS, vol. 896, pp. 354–367. Springer, Cham (2018). https://doi.org/10.1007/978-3-319-97925-0_29

17. Lee, W.S., Grosh, D.L., Tillman, F.A., Lie, C.H.: Fault tree analysis, methods, and applications - a review. IEEE Trans. Reliab. **R–34**(3), 194–203 (1985)
18. Leveson, N.G.: Engineering a Safer World: Systems Thinking Applied to Safety. The MIT Press, Cambridge (2012)
19. Maaskant, R.: Interactive visualization of fault trees (2016). https://fmt.ewi.utwente.nl/media/169.pdf
20. Macher, G., Sporer, H., Berlach, R., Armengaud, E., Kreiner, C.: Sahara: a security-aware hazard and risk analysis method. In: DATE (2015)
21. Netkachova, K., Bloomfield, R.E.: Security-informed safety. IEEE Comput. **49**(6), 98–102 (2016)
22. Open-PSA: Fault tree exchange format. https://open-psa.github.io
23. Papadopoulos, Y., McDermid, J.A.: Hierarchically performed hazard origin and propagation studies. In: Felici, M., Kanoun, K. (eds.) SAFECOMP 1999. LNCS, vol. 1698, pp. 139–152. Springer, Heidelberg (1999). https://doi.org/10.1007/3-540-48249-0_13
24. Paul, S., et al.: Recommendations for Security and Safety Co-engineering - Part A. MERGE project (2016)
25. Pomante, L., et al.: The AQUAS ECSEL Project aggregated quality assurance for systems: co-engineering inside and across the product life cycle. Microprocess. Microsyst. **69**, 54–67 (2019)
26. Ruijters, E., Stoelinga, M.: Fault tree analysis: a survey of the state-of-the-art in modeling, analysis and tools. Comput. Sci. Rev. **15**, 29–62 (2015)
27. Ruiz, A., Puelles, J., Martinez, J., Gruber, T., Matschnig, M., Fischer, B.: Preliminary safety-security co-engineering process in the industrial automation sector. In: ERTS 2020, 10th European Congress on Embedded Real Time Systems (2020)
28. Sango, M., Godot, J., Gonzalez, A., Nolasco, R.R.: Model-based system, safety and security co-engineering method and toolchain for medical devices design. In: 2019 Design of Medical Devices Conference (DMDC) (2019)
29. Schmittner, C., Gruber, T., Puschner, P., Schoitsch, E.: Security application of failure mode and effect analysis (FMEA). In: Bondavalli, A., Di Giandomenico, F. (eds.) SAFECOMP 2014. LNCS, vol. 8666, pp. 310–325. Springer, Cham (2014). https://doi.org/10.1007/978-3-319-10506-2_21
30. Schneier, B.: Attack trees. Dr. Dobb's J. **24**(12), 21–29 (1999)
31. Shipman, F.M., McCall, R.J.: Integrating different perspectives on design rationale: supporting the emergence of design rationale from design communication. AI Eng. Des. Anal. Manuf. **11**(2), 141–154 (1997)
32. Steiner, M.: Integrating Security Concerns into Safety Analysis of Embedded Systems Using Component Fault Trees. Ph.D. thesis, TU Kaiserslautern (2016)
33. The Consultative Committee for Space Data Systems: CCSDS Cryptographic Algorithms, December 2014
34. Vacca, J.R.: Computer and Information Security Handbook, 3rd edn. Morgan Kaufmann Publishers Inc., Burlington (2017)
35. Verma, S., Gruber, T., Schmittner, C., Puschner, P.: Combined approach for safety and security. In: Romanovsky, A., Troubitsyna, E., Gashi, I., Schoitsch, E., Bitsch, F. (eds.) SAFECOMP 2019. LNCS, vol. 11699, pp. 87–101. Springer, Cham (2019). https://doi.org/10.1007/978-3-030-26250-1_7
36. Yi, S., Wang, H., Ma, Y., Xie, F., Zhang, P., Di, L.: A safety-security assessment approach for communication-based train control (CBTC) systems based on the extended fault tree. In: ICCCN (2018)

Formalising the Impact of Security Attacks on IoT Safety

Ehsan Poorhadi, Elena Troubitysna$^{(\boxtimes)}$, and György Dan

KTH – Royal Institute of Technology, Stockholm, Sweden
{poorhadi,elenatro,gyuri}@kth.se

Abstract. Modern safety-critical systems become increasingly networked and interconnected. Often the communication between the system components utilises the protocols similar to the standard Internet Protocol (IP). In particular, such protocols are used for communication between smart sensors and controller. While offering advanced capabilities such as remote diagnostics and maintenance, this also make safety-critical systems susceptible to the attacks implementable against IP-based systems. In this paper, we propose an approach to specifying a generic IP-based networked control system and formalising its security properties. We use the Event-B framework to formally analyse the impact of security attacks on safety properties of the system.

Keywords: Formal modelling · Safety-critical systems · Security · Event-B · Refinement

1 Introduction

Modern safety-critical systems become increasingly open and interconnected. In particular, the use of smart sensors and Internet of Things (IoT) enable the development of systems with advanced capabilities including remote diagnostics and proactive maintenance. Often their communication rely on standard or adapted versions of the Internet Protocol (IP). Hence, such systems become susceptible to the security attacks typical for the IP-based systems.

Networked control systems and IoT rely on remote sensing and actuation in providing their functions, including the safety-critical ones. Therefore, to ensure system dependability, we need to analyse the impact of security attacks on system safety and devise the measures for protecting the system against malicious faults.

In this paper, we propose a formal approach to modelling safety-critical networked systems and analysing the impact of the security attacks on system safety. We demonstrate how to rigorously specify the behaviour of a control system relying on a generic IP protocol for the communication with remote sensors.

Supported by organization Trafikverket.

A. Casimiro et al. (Eds.): SAFECOMP 2020 Workshops, LNCS 12235, pp. 69–81, 2020.
https://doi.org/10.1007/978-3-030-55583-2_5

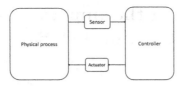

Fig. 1. Architecture of generic control system

The proposed approach supports a formal analysis of the impact of typical security attacks on the data transmitted between components. We demonstrate how to represent the results of a denial-of-service and tampering attacks by defining the corresponding system-wide invariant properties. Such an approach allows us to identify the impact that the deviations caused by the security attacks make on system safety functions.

We rely on formal modelling in Event-B [1] to systematically specify and verify both nominal and faulty system behaviour. Event-B is a rigorous approach to correct-by-construction system development by refinement. While refining the system model, we can gradually define the main stages of communication between the system components and specify the effect of security attacks.

The stepwise Event-B refinement process allows us to systematically derive the constraints and explicitly define the assumptions that should be fulfilled to guarantee system safety in the presence of attacks. The Rodin platform [2] provides an automated tool support for modelling and verification in Event-B. It automatically generates the proof obligations required for demonstrating correctness of specification and refinement and attempts to discharge them automatically. The use of an automated tool support improves scalability of formal verification and allows us to analyse the behaviour of complex networked systems. We believe that the proposed approach supports a systematic rigorous analysis of the impact of security on system safety functions.

2   A Formal Analysis of Security Properties of Networked Control Systems

2.1   Safety of a Generic Control System

In this paper, we focus on the analysis of a generic architecture of a networked control system depicted in Fig. 1. The main goal of the system is to control a certain physical process.

Without loss of generality, we assume that the state of the physical process is represented by a certain parameter s. The value of s is measured by the corresponding remote smart sensor. The sensor reading is transmitted by the communication channel connecting the sensor and controller. Based on the obtained sensor reading, the controller changes the state of the actuator, which, in its turn, affects the state of the physical process. The behaviour of the system is cyclic. At each cycle, the sensor performs the measurement of s and sends the corresponding data consisting of several packets to the controller. Based on the received data, the controller assigns a new state of the actuator. In general, the controller and actuator are also communicating over a network. However, since the behaviour of sensor-controller and controller-actuator channels are similar, we omit a detailed discussion of the latter.

Let us assume that the specification of the controller contains the operations *Setting_Actuator_high* defined as follows

$$\textbf{if } input\_s \leq low \textbf{ then } actuator := increasing$$

and similarly *Setting_Actuator_low*:

$$\textbf{if } input\_s \geq high \textbf{ then } actuator := decreasing$$

These operations of the controller change the state of the actuator according to the obtained data from the sensor. The operations are used to achieve the desired functional behaviour of the control system.

An important non-functional requirement imposed on the system is to ensure safety, i.e., guarantee that the value of the physical parameter s does not breach certain safety threshold, i.e.,

$$s \in [low\_safe, high\_safe]$$

It is clear that the required safety property can be guaranteed only if $input\_s$ is marginally different from the actual physical value of s, i.e.,

$$|s - s\_input| \leq \delta$$

where $\delta < low - low\_safe$ (we assume that $low - low\_safe = high\_safe - high$)

Now let us investigate how the security attacks can violate these conditions.

2.2 Modelling Security Attacks and Defense Against Them

In our modelling, we aim at representing the essence of the IP communication and defining the security properties as the invariant properties over the state of the input and output buffers of the communicating parties. We analyse the sensor-controller communication.

In the IP-based systems, the components communicate with each other by exchanging packets, which are assembled into the messages by the receiver. Hence, we model the communication between the sensor and controller as a packet exchange. Lets assume that a message to be sent by a sensor consists of n packets. We assume that a packet has three parts: an integer number designating the sequence number, the header containing the required networked information, and the payload. Formally, a packet is a triple:

$$(i, h, p) \in \mathbf{N} \times Header \times Payload,$$

where *Header* and *Payload* are the abstract sets containing all possible values in the header except the sequence number and payload. The following data structure models a message:

$$message \in \{1, ..., n\} \rightarrow Header \times Payload. \tag{1}$$

For simplicity, to analyse the payloads and headers separately, we define two auxiliary functions $message_1$ and $message_2$ as follows:

$$message_1 \in \{1, ..., n\} \rightarrow Header, \quad message_2 \in \{1, ..., n\} \rightarrow Payload,$$

$$\forall i. \ 1 \leq i \leq n \ \Rightarrow \ message(i) = (message_1(i), message_2(i)).$$

We assume that at each cycle the sensor and controller should first establish a connection, i.e., open and close a session. After sending a message which initiates a new session, the sensor waits for the acknowledgement from the controller. Once the acknowledgement is received, the connection is established and the sensor starts to send the packets with the measurement data. At the receiving side, the controller stores the delivered packets in its input buffer. After the predefined number of packets have been received, it assembles them into the corresponding message by relying on the sequence number of each packet.

In our work, we focus on modelling an impact of security attacks on system safety. Hence, we need to model how an attack affects the packets received by the controller. Therefore, in general, the input buffer containing the packets to be received by the controller can be different from the output buffer containing the packets to be sent by the sensor. If a message can be represented by a total function mapping the sequence number to the packet then the input buffer can be represented by a similar but partial function.

The communication channel between the sensor and the controller is susceptible to the attacks typical for the IP- based systems. Hence, the attacks can affect both the availability and integrity of the inputs received by the controller.

Next we discuss two typical types of the attacks and formally define their effect on the controller inputs.

Packet Tampering. As a result of man-in-the-middle attack, an attacker can change the payload of some packets (the sequence number and header are unchanged). If not detected, such an attack would result in the controller making the decisions regarding the actuator state based on the incorrect input. Formally, this threat can be formalized as follows:

$$message_1(i) = delivery_1(i) \ \wedge \ delivery_2(i) \neq message_2(i). \tag{2}$$

where $1 \leq i \leq n$ and *delivery* represents the packet received by the controller.

DoS Attack. As a result of DoS attack, the receiver obtains a large number of packets initiating a new connections. Eventually, it overflows the input buffer of the controller and all the consequent packets are dropped. Formally, it can be represented as follows:

$$message_1(i) \neq delivery_1(i)$$

By defining such system-wide properties, we can formally specify the impact of a security attack on the system. Hence, we obtain a formal ground for identifying the impact of the security control mechanisms as well as the effect of a security attack on safety.

Let us specify a behaviour of such widely-used security control mechanisms as a security gateway. We introduce the *Detection* function that maps each packet to a boolean value:

$$Detection : \{1, ..., n\} \times H \times P \to BOOL \qquad (3)$$

Mapping to the value $TRUE$ denotes that an attack has been detected.

Therefore, we can ensure safety in the presence of an active attacker who only tampers the payload of some packets if and only if we can prove the following security properties.

Suppose that the security gateway receives the ith packet, then the following property should hold.

$$detection(i, delivery_1(i), delivery_2(i)) = TRUE \Leftrightarrow$$
$$message_1(i) = deliveryr_1(i) \quad \wedge \quad message_2(i) \neq delivery_2(i).$$

Obviously, once the attack is detected, the controller can no longer rely on the data received from the sensor. Hence, to ensure that the system does not breach safety when an attack is detected, the specification of the controller should contain some fall-back operations. Such an operation can be, e.g., the use of the last good value received by the controller. Such a mechanism would allow the system to continue to function for a few cycles and might alleviate the impact of a security attack in case it had a short duration. However, if the attack persists the system should be shut down. Alternatively, the controller can directly put the system in a safe but non-operational state upon detection of a security attack.

In the next section, we give a brief overview of our formal modelling framework Event-B and then demonstrate how to formally specify a networked control system and its security properties in Event-B.

3 Event-B

Event-B is a state-based formal approach that promotes the correct-by-construction development paradigm and formal verification by theorem proving [1]. In Event-B, a system model is specified as an *abstract state machine*. An abstract state machine encapsulates the model state, represented as a collection of variables, and defines operations on the state, i.e., it describes the dynamic behaviour of a modelled system. The variables are strongly typed by the constraining predicates that, together with other important system properties, are defined as model *invariants*. Usually, a machine has an accompanying component, called a *context*, which includes user-defined sets, constants and their properties given as a list of model axioms.

The dynamic behaviour of the system is defined by a collection of atomic *events*. Generally, an event has the following form:

$$e \; \widehat{=} \; \textbf{any} \; a \; \textbf{where} \; G_e \; \textbf{then} \; R_e \; \textbf{end},$$

where e is the event's name, a is the list of local variables, G_e is the event *guard*), and R_e is the event action.

The guard is a state predicate that defines the conditions under which the action can be executed, i.e., when the event is *enabled*. If several events are enabled at the same time, any of them can be chosen for execution non-deterministically. If none of the events is enabled then the system deadlocks. The occurrence of events represents the observable behaviour of the system.

In general, the action of an event is a parallel composition of deterministic or non-deterministic assignments. In Event-B, this assignment is semantically defined as the next-state relation R_e. A deterministic assignment, $x := E(x, y)$, has the standard syntax and meaning. A non-deterministic assignment is denoted either as $x :\in S$, where S is a set of values, or $x :| P(x, y, x')$, where P is a predicate relating initial values of x, y to some final value of x'. As a result of such a non-deterministic assignment, x can get any value belonging to S or according to P.

Event-B employs a top-down refinement-based approach to system development. A development starts from an abstract specification that nondeterministically models most essential functional requirements. In a sequence of refinement steps, we gradually reduce nondeterminism and introduce detailed design decisions. The consistency of Event-B models, i.e., verification of well-formedness, invariant preservation as well as correctness of refinement steps, is demonstrated by proving the relevant verification theorems – proof obligations.

Proof obligations are expressed as logical sequences, ensuring that the transformation is performed in a correctness-preserving way. For instance, *invariant preservation* property for the given model invariant I_j is formulated as follows:

$$A(d, c), \; I_j(d, c, v), \; G_e(d, c, a, v), \; R_e(d, c, a, v, v') \; \vdash \; I_j(d, c, v') \qquad \text{(INV)}$$

where A are model axioms, G_e is the event guard, d are model sets, c are model constants, a are the event local variables and v, v' are the variable values before and after the event execution.

Modelling, refinement and verification in Event-B is supported by an automated tool – Rodin platform [2]. The platform provides the designers with an integrated modelling environment, supports automatic generation and proving of the necessary proof obligations. Moreover, various plug-ins created for Rodin platform allow a modeller to transform models from one representation to another. They also give access to various verification engines (theorem provers, model checkers, SMT solvers).

4 Formal Development of a Safety-Critical System with Security Consideration

In this section, we demonstrate how to formally model a communication between the sensor and controller in the presence of tampering and DoS attacks. We create a formal model of a packet tampering and DoS attack and the introduce a defense mechanism ensuring that safety can be maintained when the system is attacked.

In our model, a control cycle starts from an attempt to establish a connection between the sensor and the controller and finishes with the connection termination either with successfully completed transmission or aborted transmission due to the detected security attack.

We start by explaining how the message transfer is modelled. Since we consider an IP-based systems, to establish a connection, the sender – a smart sensor – first sends a session invitation message to the receiver – the controller. The controller replies with an acknowledgement and opens a connection. To enable modelling of a security attack, we introduce a modelling abstraction – an intermediate buffer. The intermediate buffer models a behaviour of a transmission channel. When the channel is not attacked then a packet transmitted by a receiver is stored in the intermediate buffer unchanged and consequently copied to the receiver's input buffer.

When the system is under a tampering attack, the intermediate buffer allows us to model an effect of an attack – the payload of the packet is changed in the intermediate buffer. Consequently, the receiver obtains a packet, which is different from the packet, which was sent by the sender. To model DoS attack, we use the intermediate buffer to insert packets that have never been sent by the sender. Let us observe, that such a modelling approach can also be easily adapted to model a replay attack. We introduce a similar buffer to model a communication in the reverse direction. The similar buffer is introduced to store the acknowledgements sent by the controller to the sensor.

We model this cyclic behavior as a sequence of phases.

$$... \; MSG \Rightarrow Start \Rightarrow Established \Rightarrow CPLT \; or \; SecPro \Rightarrow MSG \; ....$$

In our abstract specification, outlined in Fig. 2 the sender and receiver share the state space. Hence, the successful transmission of a packet can be represented as a simple assignment of the buffer of the sender to the buffer of the receiver.

In the abstract specification, a variable *process* models the different phases of communication.

In the phase MSG, the sensors generates a message *message* to be sent. In phase *Start*, the transmission process begins. When *process* is equal to *Established*, the sensor and controller are exchanging packets. In the abstract specification, the controller receives the whole message at once. At the end of this phase, *process* can be in phases $CPLT$ if an attack is detected or in *SecPro* otherwise.

Machine M1
Variables $message_1$, $message_2$, process, $AbsDelivery_1$, $AbsDelivery_2$.
Invariants $message_1 \in 1..n \rightarrow 1..n \wedge message_2 \in 1..n \rightarrow 1..n \wedge$
$AbsDelivery_2 \in 1..n \rightarrow 1..n \wedge AbsDelivery_1 \in 1..n \rightarrow 1..n \wedge process \in status \wedge$
$process = finish \Rightarrow (delivery_1 = message_1 \wedge delivery_2 = message_2)$
Events ...
  Sender Creates a Message $\widehat{=}$
   When $process = MSG$
   Then $message_1 :\in 1..n \rightarrow 1..n \wedge message_2 :\in 1..n \rightarrow 1..n \wedge AbsDelivery_2 := \emptyset \wedge$
  $AbsDelivery_1 := \emptyset \wedge process := star$
  Connection Establishment $\widehat{=}$
   When $process = start$
   Then $process := Established$
  Final
   When $process = Established$
   Then $process := CPLT \wedge AbsDelivery_1 := message_1 \wedge AbsDelivery_2 := message_2$
  Next Message
   When $process = CPLT \wedge process = SecPro$
   Then $process := MSG$
  Security Gateway
   When $process = Established \vee process = start$
   Then $process :\mid process' = process \vee process' = SecPro$

Fig. 2. The structure of abstract specification

In this level, we can prove the following invariant to show the message is sent successfully:

$$process = CPLT \Rightarrow AbsDelivery = message.$$

The first refinement step aims at decomposing a message into a number of packets and modelling their step-by-step transmission. We introduce a the new event *receive*, which models receiving a packet by the controller. The controller keeps track of the received packets and after all the packets have been received, composes them into a message. We define the following invariant to model the fact that for a message to be successfully received all its packets should be delivered successfully.

$$delivery = (1..(c - 1)) \lhd message$$

where $\lhd$ stands for a domain restriction.

Our next refinement step focuses on separating state spaces of the sender – the sensor – and receiver – the controller and introducing an intermediate buffer between them to model the affect of an attack. However, at this level, the sensor can still access the state of the controller, i.e., our security properties are yet not defined in an entirely distributed way.

The intermediate buffer is modeled by two variables denoted by $BufCounter$ and $BufData$.

$$BufCounter \in (0..n) \wedge BufData \in Header \times Payload.$$

We define a new event *send* to add (i.e., assign) a new packet to the intermediate buffer. Correspondingly, we refine the event *receive* to model the fact that the packets received by the controller are transmitted via a communication channel, i.e., are first stored (an modified, in case of an attack) in the intermediate buffer.

In the previous refinement step, the sensor could still read the variable of the controller. In this specification, we remove this modelling abstraction. Namely, we model the behaviour of the sensor waiting for an acknowledgment before starting to send a new packet.

To model this, we define a variable $SensorRcv$ of type Boolean. It specifies the conditions defining whether the sensor should send a new packet, i.e., has received the acknowledgement for the previously sent packet. We also introduce the intermediate buffer $AckCh$ for the controller-sensor communication and two new events modelling sending and receiving the acknowledgments. When the controller receives a packet, it changes the value of $AckCh$ to indicate that the previous packet has been delivered successfully.

At this point of the formal development, we have completed modeling the communication between the sender – the smart sensor – and a receiver – the controller. The system model is distributed, i.e., the state spaces of the communicating components are disjoint. All the invariant properties are defined over the distributed state space of the system. Now we are ready to model an effect of an attack on the system behaviour.

In the fourth refinement step, we model the attacker's behavior and security control mechanisms. To achieve this, we introduce the events tampering and injection defined as follows:

$$\textbf{tampering} \mathrel{\widehat{=}}$$
$$\textbf{when } process = Established \ \wedge \ BufCounter = c$$
$$\textbf{then } CBufData_2 :\in Payload.$$

$$\textbf{injection} \mathrel{\widehat{=}}$$
$$\textbf{when } process = Established \ \wedge \ BufCounter = c$$
$$\textbf{then } BufData2_2 :\in Payload \ \wedge \ BufData2_1 :\in Header$$
$$\wedge \ BufCounter2 := c.$$

The events become enabled after the sensor sends a new packet. The **tampering** event results in changing the payload of the packet. The payload is changed to any arbitrary value in the set $Payload$. The **injection** event results in generating an new packet that is stored in the intermediate buffer.

To model a security control mechanism, we introduce a variable $validity \in \{Checked, Nchecked\}$. The variable is modified by the controller. It models the outcome of integrity verification for the last packet stored in $delivery$, i.e., represent the fact that the packet has either passed the security verification or not. Whenever a new packet arrives to the controller side, the controller verifies its integrity, which is abstractly modelled by an event **gateway**, which assigns a new value to the variable $validity$. If the packet is valid then the variable $validity$ receives the value $Checked$ and the controller sends the corresponding acknowledgement to the sensor. If the verification fails then the system terminates the connection and $process$ becomes $SecPro$.

Now we can prove the general security property defined in Sect. 2.

$validity = Checked \Rightarrow$
$detection(c - 1, delivery_1(c - 1), delivery_2(c - 1)) = TRUE \Leftrightarrow$
$message_1(c - 1) = delivery_1(c - 1) \;\land\; message_2(c - 1) \neq delivery_2(c - 1).$

The introduction of the security protection mechanism – the secure gateway – allows us to ensure that the tampered or injected messages would not be accepted by the controller as an input. Hence, we can guarantee that the controller input would remain sufficiently close to the real physical value of the controlled parameter. Otherwise, if the secure gateway does establish message validity, i.e., the message is suspected to be tampered or injected, the controller can rely on its own fault tolerance mechanisms to ensure safety.

4.1   Discussion of Development

While modelling, we have adopted an implicit discrete model of time. Namely, we define the abstract function representing the change in the dynamics of the controlled process as well as the constraints relating the components behaviour in the successive iterations. Such an approach is based on our previous experience in modelling control systems, e.g., [11]. Such an approach allows us to define system invariant properties in relation to a particular phase of control loop execution or a communication progress. An alternative way to approach the problem of modelling time could be to rely on real-time extension of Event-B [17]. In such a way, we could also express the time-related properties of data transmission as well as define time explicitly the time-stamps of the packets.

Another abstraction, in which we relied in our modelling, is a representation of a networked architecture. In the proposed chain of refinements, we have gradually moved from modelling a centralised architecture to separating state space of communicating components. However, formally, the behaviour of the components is modelled within a single monolithic specification. To address this issue and explicitly represent each component separately, we can rely on the modularisation approach [12–14], which supports compositional reasoning and specification patterns [15].

5   Related Work and Conclusions

The problem of safety and security interactions has recently received a significant research attention. It has been recognised that there is a clear need for the approaches facilitating an integrated analysis of safety and security [4,8,9].

This issue has been addressed by several techniques demonstrating how to adapt traditional safety techniques like FMECA and fault trees to perform a security-informed safety analysis [5,8]. The techniques aim at providing the engineers with a structured way to discover and analyse security vulnerabilities that have safety implications. Since the use of such techniques facilitate a systematic analysis of failure modes and results in discovering important safety and security requirements, the proposed approaches provide a valuable input for our modelling.

There are several works that address formal analysis of safety and security requirements interactions [6,10]. Majority of these works demonstrate how to find conflicts between them. A typical scenario used to demonstrate this is a contradiction between the access control rules and safety measure. In our approach, we treat the problem of safety-security interplay at a more detailed level. Namely, we model the data transmission in an IP-based system and demonstrate how a security attack affects system behaviour on the level of packet transmission and as a result can jeopardise safety.

The distributed MILS approach [3,7] employs a number of advanced modelling techniques to create a platform for a formal architectural analysis of safety and security. The approach supports a powerful analysis of the properties of the data flow using model checking and facilitates derivation of security contracts. Since our approach enables incremental construction of complex distributed architectures, it would be interesting to combine these techniques to support an integrated safety-security analysis throughout the entire formal model-based system development.

An explicit reasoning about communication between decentralised components in Event-B has been discussed in [16]. In the similar way, the behaviour of components and data is represented via the corresponding buffers. However, this work does not consider an effect of security attacks on the transferred packets and focuses on another communication protocol.

A formal development of safety-security interplay has been carried out in a number of recent works [18–21]. In these approaches, a more high-level analysis of security impact has been undertaken. These works focus on modelling data-flow related properties as well as integration of different safety analysis techniques to identify the impact of security attacks on safety. Despite of sharing many common modelling solutions, in this paper, we focused on a different aspect – modelling of an IP-based system and analysis of the impact of the typical IP-related attacks on safety.

In this paper, we have presented a formal approach to modelling a security attacks in an IP-based system and their impact of safety. Our approach considers the detailed data transmission process between the sensor and the controller. It allowed us to explicitly model the actions of the attackers and their impact on the transmitted messages. As a result, we were able to formally demonstrate that an introduction of a security control mechanism allows us to guarantee preservation of safety.

As a future work, we are planning to continue to study different types of attacks at a detailed level and validate our approach by large-scale case studies.

References

1. Abrial, J.-R.: Modeling in Event-B. Cambridge University Press, Cambridge (2010)
2. Rodin: Event-B platform. http://www.event-b.org

3. Bytschkow, D., Quilbeuf, J., Igna, G., Ruess, H.: Distributed MILS architectural approach for secure smart grids. In: Cuellar, J. (ed.) SmartGridSec 2014. LNCS, vol. 8448, pp. 16–29. Springer, Cham (2014). https://doi.org/10.1007/978-3-319-10329-7_2

4. Young, W., Leveson, N.G.: An integrated approach to safety and security based on systems theory. Commun. ACM **57**—-**2**, 31–35 (2014)

5. Fovino, I.N., Masera, M., De Cian, A.: Integrating cyber attacks within fault trees. Rel. Eng. Syst. Saf. **94**—-**9**, 1394–1402 (2009)

6. Kriaa, S., Bouissou, M., Colin, F., Halgand, Y., Pietre-Cambacedes, L.: Safety and security interactions modeling using the BDMP formalism: case study of a pipeline. In: Bondavalli, A., Di Giandomenico, F. (eds.) SAFECOMP 2014. LNCS, vol. 8666, pp. 326–341. Springer, Cham (2014). https://doi.org/10.1007/978-3-319-10506-2_22

7. Cimatti, A., DeLong, R., Marcantonio, D., Tonetta, S.: Combining MILS with contract-based design for safety and security requirements. In: Koornneef, F., van Gulijk, C. (eds.) SAFECOMP 2015. LNCS, vol. 9338, pp. 264–276. Springer, Cham (2015). https://doi.org/10.1007/978-3-319-24249-1_23

8. Schmittner, C., Gruber, T., Puschner, P., Schoitsch, E.: Security application of failure mode and effect analysis (FMEA). In: Bondavalli, A., Di Giandomenico, F. (eds.) SAFECOMP 2014. LNCS, vol. 8666, pp. 310–325. Springer, Cham (2014). https://doi.org/10.1007/978-3-319-10506-2_21

9. Steiner, M., Liggesmeyer, P.: Combination of safety and security analysis - finding security problems that threaten the safety of a system. In: SAFECOMP 2013 - Workshop DECS-2013, HAL (2013)

10. Troubitsyna, E., Laibinis, L., Pereverzeva, I., Kuismin, T., Ilic, D., Latvala, T.: Towards security-explicit formal modelling of safety-critical systems. In: Skavhaug, A., Guiochet, J., Bitsch, F. (eds.) SAFECOMP 2016. LNCS, vol. 9922, pp. 213–225. Springer, Cham (2016). https://doi.org/10.1007/978-3-319-45477-1_17

11. Laibinis, L., Troubitsyna, E.: Refinement of fault tolerant control systems in B. In: Heisel, M., Liggesmeyer, P., Wittmann, S. (eds.) SAFECOMP 2004. LNCS, vol. 3219, pp. 254–268. Springer, Heidelberg (2004). https://doi.org/10.1007/978-3-540-30138-7_22

12. Iliasov, A., et al.: Supporting reuse in event B development: modularisation approach. In: Frappier, M., Glässer, U., Khurshid, S., Laleau, R., Reeves, S. (eds.) ABZ 2010. LNCS, vol. 5977, pp. 174–188. Springer, Heidelberg (2010). https://doi.org/10.1007/978-3-642-11811-1_14

13. Iliasov, A., et al.: Developing mode-rich satellite software by refinement in Event-B. Sci. Comput. Program. **18**(7), 884–905 (2013)

14. Iliasov, A., Troubitsyna, E., Laibinis, L., Romanovsky, A., Varpaaniemi, K., Väisänen, P., Ilic, D., Latvala, T.: Verifying mode consistency for on-board satellite software. In: Schoitsch, E. (ed.) SAFECOMP 2010. LNCS, vol. 6351, pp. 126–141. Springer, Heidelberg (2010). https://doi.org/10.1007/978-3-642-15651-9_10

15. Iliasov, A., Troubitsyna, E., Laibinis, L., Romanovsky, A.: Patterns for refinement automation. In: de Boer, F.S., Bonsangue, M.M., Hallerstede, S., Leuschel, M. (eds.) FMCO 2009. LNCS, vol. 6286, pp. 70–88. Springer, Heidelberg (2010). https://doi.org/10.1007/978-3-642-17071-3_4

16. Iliasov, A., Laibinis, L., Troubitsyna, E., Romanovsky, A.: Formal derivation of a distributed program in event B. In: Qin, S., Qiu, Z. (eds.) ICFEM 2011. LNCS, vol. 6991, pp. 420–436. Springer, Heidelberg (2011). https://doi.org/10.1007/978-3-642-24559-6_29

17. Iliasov, A., Romanovsky, A., Laibinis, L., Troubitsyna, E., Latvala, T.: Augmenting Event-B modelling with real-time verification. In: FormSERA 2012, pp. 51–57. IEEE (2012)
18. Vistbakka, I., Troubitsyna, E., Kuismin, T., Latvala, T.: Co-engineering safety and security in industrial control systems: a formal outlook. In: Romanovsky, A., Troubitsyna, E.A. (eds.) SERENE 2017. LNCS, vol. 10479, pp. 96–114. Springer, Cham (2017). https://doi.org/10.1007/978-3-319-65948-0_7
19. Vistbakka, I., Troubitsyna, E.: Towards a formal approach to analysing security of safety-critical systems. In: EDCC 2018, pp. 182–189. IEEE (2018)
20. Troubitsyna, E., Vistbakka, I.: Deriving and formalising safety and security requirements for control systems. In: Gallina, B., Skavhaug, A., Bitsch, F. (eds.) SAFECOMP 2018. LNCS, vol. 11093, pp. 107–122. Springer, Cham (2018). https://doi.org/10.1007/978-3-319-99130-6_8
21. Vistbakka, I., Troubitsyna, E.: Pattern-based formal approach to analyse security and safety of control systems. In: Papadopoulos, Y., Aslansefat, K., Katsaros, P., Bozzano, M. (eds.) IMBSA 2019. LNCS, vol. 11842, pp. 363–378. Springer, Cham (2019). https://doi.org/10.1007/978-3-030-32872-6_24

Assurance Case Patterns for Cyber-Physical Systems with Deep Neural Networks

Ramneet Kaur$^{(\boxtimes)}$, Radoslav Ivanov, Matthew Cleaveland, Oleg Sokolsky, and Insup Lee

PRECISE Center, University of Pennsylvania, Philadelphia, USA
{ramneetk,rivanov,mcleav,sokolsky,lee}@seas.upenn.edu

Abstract. With the increasing use of deep neural networks (DNNs) in the safety-critical cyber-physical systems (CPS), such as autonomous vehicles, providing guarantees about the safety properties of these systems becomes ever more important. Tools for reasoning about the safety of DNN-based systems have started to emerge. In this paper, we show that assurance cases can be used to argue about the safety of CPS with DNNs by proposing assurance case patterns that are amenable to the existing evidence generation tools for these systems. We use case studies of two different autonomous driving scenarios to illustrate the use of the proposed patterns for the construction of these assurance cases.

Keywords: DNNs · Safety-critical CPS · Safety properties · Assurance case

1 Introduction

With recent advances in machine learning, there is much interest in using deep neural networks in safety-critical cyber-physical systems (CPS), such as self-driving vehicles [5], aircraft collision avoidance [22], and medical diagnoses [10]. The black-box nature of neural networks (NNs) makes it difficult to interpret their behavior on perturbed or even unseen inputs and therefore makes it challenging to provide safety guarantees about systems with NNs. To enable the use of NNs in safety-critical CPS, it is therefore important to convincingly demonstrate that CPS with NNs (CPSNN) are acceptably safe to use.

One way to argue about the safety of CPSNN is through assurance cases [1]. Systems developed for medical, transportation, infrastructure applications, etc. that significantly impact life, property, or environment need to get the approval of an independent entity such as a regulatory body. This approval process can be viewed as the manufacturer making the case that their system meets the

This work is supported in part by the Air Force Research Laboratory and the Defense Advanced Research Projects Agency as part of the Assured Autonomy program under Contract No. FA8750-18-C-0090.

A. Casimiro et al. (Eds.): SAFECOMP 2020 Workshops, LNCS 12235, pp. 82–97, 2020.
https://doi.org/10.1007/978-3-030-55583-2_6

criteria for certification and the regulatory body assessing this case to arrive at a certification decision. An assurance case provides a structure for making this case by using arguments supported by evidence to justify the claim in a hierarchical fashion. This hierarchical structure of the assurance case with explicit claims, arguments, and evidence has favored its use in the certification process [30]. For instance, the Food and Drug Administration (FDA) changed its approval process to enable the use of assurance cases for demonstrating the safety of insulin pumps [9] and the Federal Aviation Administration (FAA) accepts assurance cases to approve the safety of aviation systems [11].

Assurance cases have been used to assure the safety of the traditional CPS (CPS without NN components) in the past [3,12,26,35]. These cases analyze the system's specification by making use of the analytical techniques (such as proofs [35]) build on model-based development [3,35], hazard mitigation [12] or both [26]. The black-box nature of NNs makes it difficult to apply these analytical techniques for reasoning about CPSNN and thus structuring their assurance case in the way they are done for the traditional CPS.

Prior work has been done on proposing assurance case patterns for the safety-critical CPSNN [7,25,28]. Some of these patterns argue about the safe functionality [25] or performance [28] of machine learning components in the CPS. Others [7] argue about the acceptance of residual risk in these systems due to the functional insufficiency of machine learning. All of these patterns are specific to the assurance of the functional requirements (or features) of machine learning components in the CPS and do not provide assurance about specifications of the entire system. Also, the challenge of coming up with a provably exhaustive list of requirements for machine learning components in CPSNN makes it difficult to extend these patterns for the assurance of CPSNN.

We propose assurance case patterns for specifications of the closed-loop behavior of CPSNN. The main challenge in building an assurance case for CPSNN is the black-box nature of NNs, which makes it difficult to generate the evidence required for the assurance of CPSNN. An assurance case built for CPSNN should be structured in a way that is amenable to generating evidence about the NN for the assurance of the larger system.

A feasible approach to generating evidence for the assurance of CPSNN is to make use of the computational tools that have been developed recently to provide formal guarantees about these systems. These tools can be broadly classified into two categories. The first analyzes the NN separately from the rest of the system. Existing tools analyzing the behavior of NNs characterize the correctness of these networks based on robustness [6,24], safety guarantees [19,23] or properties [15,17] of these networks. These tools can generate evidence for NN-specific, component-level claims in the assurance case of CPSNN. The second analyzes the closed-loop behavior of CPSNN for both verification [21,32] and falsification [14,33]. These tools can generate evidence for system-level claims made in assurance cases for CPSNN. This classification of the evidence generation tools for the assurance of CPSNN into two categories motivates us to propose two assurance case patterns for CPSNN, one for each category.

The first pattern is based on an assume/guarantee argument. The system makes an assumption about some property of the NN. This assumption leaves us with a much simpler model of the CPSNN to analyze, allowing us to scale the existing verification [8] or falsification [13,16] techniques for the CPS to the CPSNN. Arguments to guarantee the assumed property of the NN need to be made and justified separately in this pattern. These guarantees are composed with the claim about the system with the assumed property of the NN to provide assurance about the CPSNN. Tools analyzing the behavior of NNs can be used to generate evidence for the NN-specific claims made in this pattern. The second pattern is based on a holistic approach to the assurance of CPSNN. This approach relies on the analysis of the closed-loop behavior of the system and does not require a separate specification for the NN. Tools analyzing the closed-loop behavior of the CPSNN can be used to generate system-level evidence in this pattern.

To evaluate the applicability of the proposed patterns, we consider two case studies. The first case study is about the safety specification of the closed-loop system from [20]. It consists of an NN-controlled F1/10 car [2] equipped with LiDAR, running in a known hallway environment. We make use of the holistic pattern to provide assurance about this system. The second case study is about the safety specification of the closed-loop system from [14]. It consists of an autonomous car with a perception-based NN and an emergency braking system (AEBS) [31], driving on a highway with a stationary car in front of it. We make use of the assume/guarantee pattern to provide assurance about this system.

Our contributions in this paper can be summarized as follows. First, we propose two assurance case patterns based on the existing tools for generating evidence for specifications of the closed-loop behavior of the CPSNN. Second, we illustrate the applicability of the proposed patterns with the help of two case studies. Third, we discuss directions for the development of new tools for the assurance of CPSNN with the help of undeveloped claims in the case studies.

2   Background

Here, we first define the assurance case and its goal structuring notation. We then describe the model-based assurance approach of the traditional CPS. Finally, we classify the existing tools that can be used to generate evidence in the assurance case of CPSNN into two categories with examples for each category.

2.1   Assurance Case and GSN

Assurance cases provide a structure for arguing about the safety of a system by making arguments that are supported by evidence to justify the safety claims about the system in a hierarchical fashion. It is defined as a "reasoned and compelling argument, supported by a body of evidence, that a system, service or organization will operate as intended for a defined application in a defined environment" [18].

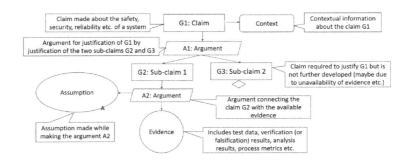

Fig. 1. An example of the hierarchical structure of assurance case made in GSN

Fig. 2. Model-based approach for the assurance of CPS (left) and CPSNN (right)

Goal Structuring Notation (GSN) [18] is the most widely used graphical notation for representing assurance cases. The principle symbols of GSN are rectangles, parallelograms, circles, ovals with an 'A' at the bottom, rounded rectangles and rectangles with a diamond at the bottom representing claim (or goal), argument (or strategy), evidence (or solution), assumption, context and undeveloped claim in the assurance case, respectively. An example of the hierarchical structure of the assurance case made in GSN is shown in Fig. 1.

Claims, arguments and evidence (CAE) is another framework used to represent assurance cases. CAE leaves arguments as black boxes, while GSN makes them explicit through strategies. We were interested in the details of arguments and that is why we chose GSN over CAE.

2.2   Model-Based Approach for the Assurance of Traditional CPS

The model-based approach of building an assurance case targets the model-based development process of real-world systems [3]. This approach has been used for building assurance cases for the traditional CPS in the past [3,35]. The use of the model-based approach for providing assurance about CPS is motivated by the fact that most of the existing evidence for these systems is based on the models of these systems [27]. Verification tools such as Flow* [8] and falsification tools such as Breach [13] and S-TALIRO [16] are some examples of the existing tools that can be used to generate evidence for the model of the traditional CPS.

The structure of the assurance case for CPS based on the model-based argument was proposed in [35]. This structure is shown in the Fig. 2. It reflects the fact that the model-based evidence for a real-system is only as useful as the

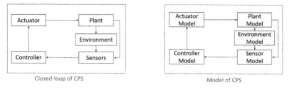

Fig. 3. Closed-loop of a traditional CPS (left) and its corresponding model (right)

model that is used to represent the system. Thus, in addition to the claim about the model of the CPS ($G2$), another claim about the validity of the model with respect to the real CPS ($G3$) needs to be made and justified.

2.3 Existing Tool-Based Evidence for the Assurance of CPSNN

The uninterpretable nature of NNs restricts the use of the traditional analytical methods to provide guarantees about CPSNN [25]. This motivates the use of computational tools based on techniques such as verification, falsification, and optimization to generate evidence about these systems. Existing tools based on these techniques that can be utilized to generate evidence for CPSNN can be classified into the following two categories.

Tools Analyzing the Component-Level Behavior of CPSNN. Work has been done in developing tools that analyze the behavior of NNs. These tools can be used to generate evidence for the NN-specific component-level claims made in the assurance case for CPSNN. Some examples of these tools are as follows. Verification tools such as Reluplex [23] and DLV(Deep Learning Verification) [19] can be used to provide evidence for the verification of the safety properties of NNs. Guarantees about the robustness of NNs can be generated with the help of the tools such as CNN-Cert [6] and POPQORN [24]. Other tools such as Sherlock [15] and LipSDP [17] can be used to assure tight bounds on the output set and global Lipschitz constant for NNs, respectively.

Tools Analyzing the System-Level Behavior of CPSNN. Verification tools for properties of the CPSNN with NN controllers have been developed recently [21,32]. System-level verification has been so far applied to only these types of CPSNN. CPSNN with perception-based NNs do not lend themselves to these verification techniques due to the high dimensionality of their input space. This has led to the development of falsification tools [14,33] for analyzing the closed-loop of CPSNN with perception-based NNs. The absence of counterexamples from these falsification techniques provides evidence of the correct behavior of CPSNN with respect to its specification.

3   Assurance Case Patterns for CPSNN

We propose two assurance case patterns for the safety specifications of CPSNN. These patterns are built on the model-based approach for assurance.

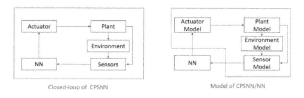

Fig. 4. An example of the closed-loop of a CPSNN (left) and the corresponding model of its CPSNN/NN composed with the NN (right)

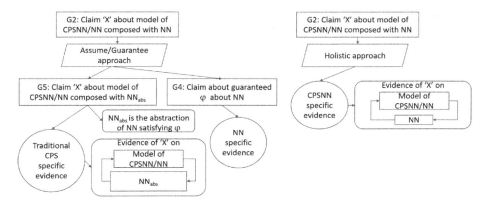

Fig. 5. Modular (left) and Holistic (right) patterns for the assurance of $G2$ in the model-based approach for CPSNN

Figure 3 shows the closed-loop structure of a traditional CPS and its corresponding model used in the model-based assurance approach for CPS [35]. The plant in this system is a physical object such as a vehicle or robot. Sensors collect information about the state of the plant and objects in the plant's environment. This sensory information is used by a controller to produce control actions, which are actuated by actuators on the plant. The model of a traditional CPS is the composition of the models of the individual components of the real-system.

The proposed patterns reflect the model-based assurance approach of the traditional CPS by modeling the sub-system of a traditional CPS present in a CPSNN. Figure 4 shows an example of the closed-loop structure of a CPSNN, where the controller in the traditional CPS is replaced by an NN in the CPSNN. We call a CPSNN without its NN components a CPSNN/NN. The model of a CPSNN/NN is equivalent to the model of the sub-system of CPS present in the CPSNN. This model is composed with the NN to close the loop in the system.

The Fig. 2 shows the model-based approach for the assurance of CPSNN. Assurance about the CPSNN is provided on the model of the CPSNN/NN composed together with the NN component via claim $G2$. Since assurance about CPSNN is provided on a system that approximates (via model) the CPSNN/NN in the CPSNN, an additional claim, $G3$, is made about the validity of this approximation.

The proposed patterns are amenable to the existing evidence generation computational tools for the assurance of the claim $G2$ in the model-based assurance approach for CPSNN. These patterns differ from each other in their approach to generate this evidence. The first pattern analyzes the NN separately from the model of the CPSNN/NN for the assurance of $G2$ and makes use of the component-level tools for the assurance of CPSNN. The second pattern analyzes the closed-loop behavior of the CPSNN/NN model composed with the NN and does not require a separate claim about the NN in the system. This pattern makes use of the system-level tools for the assurance of CPSNN. Next, we describe the two assurance case patterns as shown in Fig. 5, in detail.

3.1   Pattern 1: Modular Pattern

The first pattern is based on the assume/guarantee approach for providing assurance about the claim $G2$ in the model-based assurance approach for CPSNN. Here, an abstraction of the NN, NN_{abs}, satisfying a property φ is considered. The assurance about the claim made in $G2$ is provided on the closed-loop of the model of CPSNN/NN composed with NN_{abs}, via claim $G5$ in this pattern. This abstraction of the NN leaves us with a much simpler closed-loop model of the CPSNN/NN composed with NN_{abs} to analyze. This analysis can be performed with the existing verification or falsification techniques for the traditional CPS.

Since $G2$ is assured on the model of CPSNN/NN composed with an abstraction of the NN satisfying φ, an additional claim, $G4$, about the satisfaction of φ by the NN needs to be made separately in this pattern. Tools analyzing NNs in terms of the safety guarantees [19,23], robustness [6,24] or properties [15,17] can be used to provide evidence for the guaranteed property of the NN. We call this pattern the modular pattern because the system-level assurance is generated by composing assurance claims about the modules, CPSNN/NN and NN, of the system in this pattern.

An example of instantiation of the modular pattern is the assurance about the safe reachable set of states of a NN controlled linear time-invariant dynamical plant under bounded perturbations. Bounded models for both the plant and measurements comprise the model of the CPSNN/NN in this system. This model composed with an NN_{abs} can be used to argue about the reachable (and hence safe) state by the plant with the help of the evidence of Theorem 1 from [34]. NN_{abs} is the abstraction of the NN satisfying the property of a bounded output for a given set of bounded input. This property of the NN can be verified by the existing tools [15,17] for providing NN specific evidence in this pattern.

3.2   Pattern 2: Holistic Pattern

The second assurance case pattern for the CPSNN is based on analyzing the whole system without decomposing it down into its modules. Therefore, we call this pattern as the holistic pattern. The evidence for the claim $G2$ about the closed-loop behavior of the model of CPSNN/NN composed with NN is generated by the existing system-level tools for CPSNN [14,21,32,33] in this pattern.

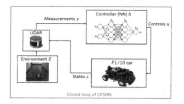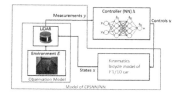

Fig. 6. Closed-loop system, S_1, of the CPSNN considered for the case study of the holistic pattern (left) and the corresponding model of its CPSNN/NN composed with the NN-controller in the system (right) [20]

An example of instantiation of this pattern is the assurance about the safe distance between two cars, where the follower car is equipped with an NN-based adaptive cruise control and a radar to measure the distance to the lead car. The dynamics model for the two cars traveling on a straight road together with the measurement model of the radar comprises the model of the CPSNN/NN, which when composed with the NN-controller can be used to argue about the safety of the system with the help of evidence generated by the verification tool from [32].

4 Case Studies

We provide case studies to illustrate the applicability of the proposed patterns.

4.1 Case Study for the Holistic Pattern

System Description and the Model of Its CPSNN/NN Composed with the NN in the System. We consider a CPS with an NN-controller from [20] for this case study. This system, S_1, is shown in Fig. 6. It consists of an autonomous F1/10 car [2] running at a constant throttle and low speed ([0, 5] m/s) in an empty hallway. The car is equipped with a LiDAR to provide distance measurements from the hallway walls. These distance measurements are fed into an NN-controller which gives front steering commands to the car, thereby controlling the heading of the car. The NN is a small fully connected network with smooth activation functions. The safety property of interest for S_1 is that the car navigates the hallway without hitting its walls.

The model of the CPSNN/NN in S_1 composed with the NN-controller in the system is shown in Fig. 6. It contains three main components. First, the behavior of the car is captured by a continuous-time dynamical system that uses a control signal generated by the NN-controller as input and contains differential equations that represent the evolution of the system state. A Kinematic bicycle model, which is known to work well for front-steering cars at low speeds [29], is

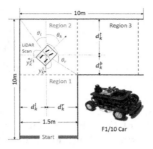

Fig. 7. Hallway divided into three regions depending on number of walls reachable by LiDAR [20]

used to represent the dynamics of the F1/10 car by the following equations:

$$\dot{x} = vcos(\theta + \beta), \; \dot{y} = vsin(\theta + \beta), \; \dot{v} = -c_a v + c_a c_m (u - c_h)$$
$$\dot{\theta} = \frac{Vcos(\beta)}{l_f + l_r} tan(\delta), \; \beta = tan^{-1}\left(\frac{l_r tan(\delta)}{l_f + l_r}\right), \tag{1}$$

where v, θ, β and (x and y) is the car's linear velocity, orientation, slip angle and position respectively. u is the throttle input, δ is the heading input. c_a is an acceleration constant, c_m is a motor constant, c_h is a hysteresis constant. l_f and l_r are the distances from the car's centroid to the front and rear, respectively.

Second, the observation model captures how measurements supplied by the LiDAR are produced, based on the heading of the car relative to the walls and its position in the hallway. The behavior of the LiDAR at turns is different from the straight sections of the hallway. To accurately capture the dynamics of measurements, the hallway is therefore divided into three regions and a measurement model of LiDAR is provided for each region, as shown in Fig. 7. The measurement model of the LiDAR scan with 1081 rays for Region 2 (other regions are special case of region 2) is as described by the following equations:

$$y_k^i = \begin{cases} d_k^r / cos(90 + \theta_k + \alpha_i) & \text{if } \theta_k + \alpha_i \leq \theta_r \\ d_k^b / cos(180 + \theta_k + \alpha_i) & \text{if } \theta_r < \theta_k + \alpha_i \leq -90 \\ d_k^t / cos(\theta_k + \alpha_i) & \text{if } -90 < \theta_k + \alpha_i \leq \theta_l \\ d_k^l / cos(90 - \theta_k - \alpha_i) & \text{if } \theta_l < \theta_k + \alpha_i, \end{cases} \tag{2}$$

where k is the sampling step, $d_k^t, d_k^b, d_k^l, d_k^r$ are distances to the four walls. $\alpha_1, .., \alpha_{1081}$ are the relative angles for rays in the LiDAR scan with respect to the car's heading. θ_l and θ_r are the relative angles to the two corners of the turn.

The third component that closes the loop is the NN-controller used in S_1 to control the heading of the car.

Existing Techniques that can be Used to Provide Assurance About the Model of CPSNN/NN in S_1 Composed with the NN in the System.
The NN used as a controller in S_1 is well suited for the closed-loop verification of NN-controlled systems, supported by recent tools [21,32]. Verisig [21] is used

here to obtain the system-level evidence in the holistic pattern. Verisig operates directly on the NNs without approximating it some other function. This allows us to compose the model of CPSNN/NN in S_1 with its NN-controller and use Verisig to verify this composition for the safety specification of S_1.

Construction of Assurance Case for S_1 Based on Holistic Pattern. The assurance case for the safety specification of S_1 based on the holistic pattern is shown in Fig. 8. The top-level assurance claim, $G1$, states that "$\forall i \in I$, $\forall t \in T_i$, the distance of the car from the hallway walls in S_1 is always greater than zero". Here, 'I' is a set of initialization positions of the car in the hallway and for some $i \in I$, 'T_i' is a set of discretized time instants spent by the car on its trajectory starting from i. $G1$ is assured on the model of the CPSNN/NN in S_1 composed with the NN-controller in the system via claim $G2$ in the assurance case. This model-based assurance approach for S_1 requires an additional claim, $G3$, about the validity of the model used to represent the CPSNN/NN in S_1. Both $G2$ and $G3$ together imply the top-level safety claim $G1$ in this case.

G2 states that "$\forall i \in I$, $\forall t \in T_i$, the distance of the car from the hallway walls in the model of CPSNN/NN in S_1 composed with the NN-controller in the system is always greater than zero". It is a reachability property that can be checked by a verification tool. Thus, this branch of the argument follows the holistic approach to generate evidence for $G2$, which comes from the verification result obtained by Verisig as shown in Fig. 8.

The argument used for the assurance of the model validation claim, $G3$, is about the choice of the individual components that make the model of CPSNN/NN in S_1. Sub-claims $G4$ and $G5$ about the accuracy of the observation and the dynamics model, respectively, together provide assurance about the accuracy of the model of the CPSNN/NN in S_1. Characteristics of the F1/10 car in S_1 (it is a front steering car and its speed lies in $[0, 5]$ m/s) makes it a suitable candidate for the kinematics bicycle model. The observation model is based on the ideal (noiseless) LiDAR operation in the known geometry of the hallway. Validating observation models is challenging in general due to the complex and uncertain behavior of the environment. This is one of the main directions for future work, as discussed in the discussion section.

4.2   Case Study for the Modular Pattern

System Description and the Model of Its CPSNN/NN Composed with the NN in the System. We consider the CPS with a perception-based NN from [14] for the case study of the modular pattern. This system, S_2, is shown in Fig. 9. It consists of an autonomous car (ego vehicle) driving on a highway through a desert with a stationary car in front of it. The vehicle is equipped with an automatic emergency braking system (AEBS) for avoiding collisions with preceding obstacles. The AEBS uses a perception-based NN and radar to get information about the preceding obstacles. It relies on the radar for obstacles at a distance less than or equal to 30 m from the vehicle. For obstacles farther than 30 m from the vehicle, the AEBS relies solely on the NN for detection. In

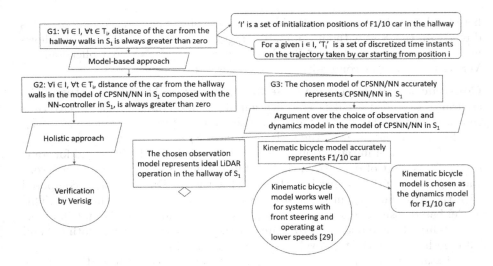

Fig. 8. Assurance case for the safety specification of S_1

Fig. 9. Closed-loop system, S_2, of the CPSNN considered for the case study of the modular pattern (left) and the corresponding model of its CPSNN/NN composed with the perception-based NN in the system (right)

the event that an obstacle is detected, the AEBS issues a full braking command to the car. The input to the NN is provided by a camera that generates RGB images of size 1000×600. The safety property of interest for this system is that no collision happens between the vehicle and the stationary car.

A general model of the CPSNN/NN in S_2 composed with the perception-based NN as shown in Fig. 9 is described as follows. It contains four components. First, the dynamics model represents the behavior of the ego vehicle on the highway. Second, a simulator captures how observations of the environment supplied by the camera and radar are produced, based on the position of the ego vehicle. Third, the AEBS algorithm used as it is. The last component is the perception-based NN in S_2 that closes the loop in the system.

Existing Techniques that can be Used to Provide Assurance About S_2. Since the input dimension for the NN in S_2 is very large, verifying S_2 for its specification is challenging. Most of the existing tools for the assurance of CPSNN with perception-based NN are based on falsification techniques [14,33]. We consider the falsification tool developed for the perception-based NN in [14] to generate the NN-specific evidence in the modular pattern for the assurance of S_2. This tool approximates the NN to a lower-dimensional input function $\tilde{f}$ and finds falsifying examples for the NN from this lower-dimensional input space. The idea is to explore only realistic modifications in the input space of the NN, instead of exploring the high-dimensional input space for finding falsifying examples for the NN. The input space of $\tilde{f}$ is analyzed to find misclassifications by $\tilde{f}$. These misclassifications are then concretized back into the input images for NN to check for misclassifications by the NN.

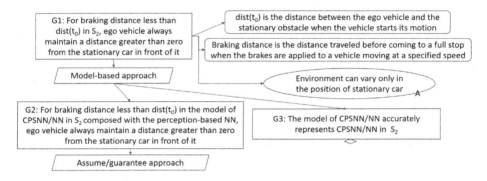

Fig. 10. Model-based approach for the assurance of S_2

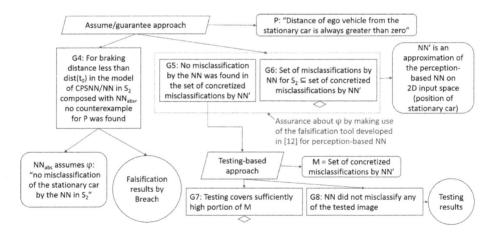

Fig. 11. Assurance of the claim $G2$ for S_2 by assume/guarantee approach

Construction of Assurance Case for S_2 Based on the Modular Pattern. The assurance case for the safety specification of S_2 based on the modular pattern is described as follows. The safety claim, $G1$, about S_2 is that "if the initialization distance between the two cars is greater than the ego vehicle's braking distance, then the vehicle always maintains a distance greater than zero from the stationary car". We assume that the environment of S_2 can vary only in the 2-dimensional position of the stationary car. As shown in Fig. 10, $G1$ is assured on the model of the CPSNN/NN in S_2 composed with the perception-based NN in the system, via claim $G2$ in the assurance case. The claim $G3$ about the accuracy of the model of CPSNN/NN in S_2, required in addition to the claim $G2$ for completing the model-based argument for the assurance of $G1$ is marked as an undeveloped claim here. It can be developed by making arguments about the choice of the individual components composing the model of CPSNN/NN in S_2 as done for the justification of the model validation claim for assurance of S_1.

Figure 11 shows the assume/guarantee assurance approach for the claim $G2$ about the model of the CPSNN/NN in S_2 composed with the perception-based NN. An abstraction of the NN, NN_{abs}, satisfying the property φ of no misclassifications of the stationary car by the network, is considered here. NN_{abs} is composed with the model of the CPSNN/NN in S_2 to provide assurance about $G2$ via falsification claim $G4$ in the assurance case. The evidence for $G4$ is generated by Breach, a falsification tool for traditional CPS.

Since $G2$ is assured on the model of CPSNN/NN composed with an abstraction of the NN satisfying φ, an additional claim about the guaranteed satisfaction of φ by the NN is required to be justified to complete the assume/guarantee argument for the assurance of $G2$. Claims $G5$ and $G6$ together provide this guarantee by making use of the falsification tool for the perception-based NNs from [14]. The NN is approximated by a 2-dimensional input function $\tilde{f}$. The input to $\tilde{f}$ is the position of the stationary car in the 2D plane.

$G5$ states that the NN does not misclassify any of the concretized images from the set S of misclassification by $\tilde{f}$. The testing-based approach is used to sample the input space of $\tilde{f}$ for finding S. A claim supported by testing argument is only as good as the coverage by testing. So, we need to argue about the sufficiency of the sampling method used to cover the input set of $\tilde{f}$, via claim $G7$ in this case. The sufficiency of the sampling methods used to generate inputs for testing either in terms of high coverage or coverage of the corner cases could be used to generate evidence for $G7$. In addition to $G7$, a claim about no misclassifications by NN on concretized images of S is required to complete the argument for the assurance of $G5$. This is done via claim $G8$ supported by testing results.

Since $G5$ is the assurance of φ on the set S of misclassifications by $\tilde{f}$, an additional claim about the set of misclassifications by the NN as a subset of concretized S needs to be made. This is done via undeveloped claim $G6$ in the assurance case. $G6$ reflects the safety of the approximation function $\tilde{f}$ for the NN. By safe approximation in the context of falsification, we mean that any element in the input space of $\tilde{f}$ lying outside its set of misclassifications is not a concretized misclassification by NN. We propose the development of techniques that can be used to generate evidence about this claim as it will enable the reduction of misclassification space of the NN and enhance the use of falsification for providing assurance about systems with high-dimensional input space of NN.

5   Discussion and Conclusion

In this paper, we proposed two model-based assurance case patterns for the safety specifications of CPSNN. These patterns are amenable to the existing tools for generating evidence for the assurance of CPSNN. We used two case studies, one for each pattern, to illustrate the applicability of the proposed patterns. We note that the two case studies are no more than illustrations and our goal is not to try and convince the reader that these systems are, in fact, safe. Therefore, we did not try to fully elaborate the arguments, nor tried to uncover assurance deficits in each of the systems. Instead, we aimed to consider development and analysis technologies available in the literature to see how suitable they would be to supply evidence for arguments following each of the patterns. These patterns are designed to help expose challenges involved with the evidence generated from the existing tools. The undeveloped claims in the case studies, for instance, attempt to formulate these challenges as requirements of new (or enhancement of existing) tools for the system-level assurance of the CPSNN. This is different from the approach proposed in a recent work [4] to identify component-level gaps in the assurance of the CPSNN.

One of the main challenges in the model-based assurance argument that needs to be addressed is the assurance about the accuracy of the observation (or simulation) model used to capture measurements (or observations) in the environment. The complex and uncertain nature of the environment makes it difficult to precisely capture it in a model. Improving the scalability of the existing system-level verification tools for CPSNN is another challenge that needs to be addressed to strengthen the evidence for the holistic pattern. Formalization of requirements for the perception-based NNs is required to help develop tools for the assurance of these NNs in the modular pattern. Addressing these challenges form one of the directions of future research for us. Another promising direction to extend this work is to extend the proposed design-time patterns with arguments to include safety monitoring and runtime adaptation tools for assurance.

References

1. Adelard: ASCAD - the Adelard Safety Case Development (ASCAD) Manual (1998)
2. F1tenth. http://f1tenth.org/
3. Ayoub, A., Kim, B.G., Lee, I., Sokolsky, O.: A safety case pattern for model-based development approach. In: Goodloe, A.E., Person, S. (eds.) NFM 2012. LNCS, vol. 7226, pp. 141–146. Springer, Heidelberg (2012). https://doi.org/10.1007/978-3-642-28891-3_14
4. Bloomfield, R., Khlaaf, H., Conmy, P.R., Fletcher, G.: Disruptive innovations and disruptive assurance: assuring machine learning and autonomy. Computer **52**(9), 82–89 (2019)
5. Bojarski, M., et al.: End to end learning for self-driving cars. arXiv preprint arXiv:1604.07316 (2016)

6. Boopathy, A., Weng, T.W., Chen, P.Y., Liu, S., Daniel, L.: CNN-Cert: an efficient framework for certifying robustness of convolutional neural networks. In: Proceedings of the AAAI Conference on Artificial Intelligence, vol. 33, pp. 3240–3247 (2019)

7. Burton, S., Gauerhof, L., Heinzemann, C.: Making the case for safety of machine learning in highly automated driving. In: Tonetta, S., Schoitsch, E., Bitsch, F. (eds.) SAFECOMP 2017. LNCS, vol. 10489, pp. 5–16. Springer, Cham (2017). https://doi.org/10.1007/978-3-319-66284-8_1

8. Chen, X., Ábrahám, E., Sankaranarayanan, S.: Flow*: an analyzer for non-linear hybrid systems. In: Sharygina, N., Veith, H. (eds.) CAV 2013. LNCS, vol. 8044, pp. 258–263. Springer, Heidelberg (2013). https://doi.org/10.1007/978-3-642-39799-8_18

9. Chen, Y., Lawford, M., Wang, H., Wassyng, A.: Insulin pump software certification. In: Gibbons, J., MacCaull, W. (eds.) FHIES 2013. LNCS, vol. 8315, pp. 87–106. Springer, Heidelberg (2014). https://doi.org/10.1007/978-3-642-53956-5_7

10. De Fauw, J., et al.: Clinically applicable deep learning for diagnosis and referral in retinal disease. Nat. Med. 24(9), 1342–1350 (2018)

11. Denney, E., Pai, G.: Safety considerations for UAS ground-based detect and avoid. In: 2016 IEEE/AIAA 35th Digital Avionics Systems Conference, pp. 1–10 (2016)

12. Denney, E., Pai, G., Habli, I.: Towards measurement of confidence in safety cases. In: 2011 International Symposium on Empirical Software Engineering and Measurement, pp. 380–383. IEEE (2011)

13. Donzé, A.: Breach, a toolbox for verification and parameter synthesis of hybrid systems. In: Touili, T., Cook, B., Jackson, P. (eds.) CAV 2010. LNCS, vol. 6174, pp. 167–170. Springer, Heidelberg (2010). https://doi.org/10.1007/978-3-642-14295-6_17

14. Dreossi, T., Donzé, A., Seshia, S.A.: Compositional falsification of cyber-physical systems with machine learning components. In: Barrett, C., Davies, M., Kahsai, T. (eds.) NFM 2017. LNCS, vol. 10227, pp. 357–372. Springer, Cham (2017). https://doi.org/10.1007/978-3-319-57288-8_26

15. Dutta, S., Chen, X., Jha, S., Sankaranarayanan, S., Tiwari, A.: Sherlock-a tool for verification of neural network feedback systems: demo abstract. In: Proceedings of the 22nd ACM International Conference on Hybrid Systems: Computation and Control, pp. 262–263 (2019)

16. Fainekos, G.E., Sankaranarayanan, S., Ueda, K., Yazarel, H.: Verification of automotive control applications using S-TaLiRo. In: 2012 American Control Conference (ACC), pp. 3567–3572. IEEE (2012)

17. Fazlyab, M., Robey, A., Hassani, H., Morari, M., Pappas, G.: Efficient and accurate estimation of Lipschitz constants for deep neural networks. In: Advances in Neural Information Processing Systems, pp. 11423–11434 (2019)

18. Group, A.C.W., et al.: Goal structuring notation community standard (2018)

19. Huang, X., Kwiatkowska, M., Wang, S., Wu, M.: Safety verification of deep neural networks. In: Majumdar, R., Kunčak, V. (eds.) CAV 2017. LNCS, vol. 10426, pp. 3–29. Springer, Cham (2017). https://doi.org/10.1007/978-3-319-63387-9_1

20. Ivanov, R., Carpenter, T.J., Weimer, J., Alur, R., Pappas, G.J., Lee, I.: Case study: verifying the safety of an autonomous racing car with a neural network controller. arXiv preprint arXiv:1910.11309 (2019)

21. Ivanov, R., Weimer, J., Alur, R., Pappas, G.J., Lee, I.: Verisig: verifying safety properties of hybrid systems with neural network controllers. In: Proceedings of the 22nd ACM International Conference on Hybrid Systems: Computation and Control, pp. 169–178. ACM (2019)

22. Julian, K.D., Kochenderfer, M.J.: Neural network guidance for UAVs. In: AIAA Guidance, Navigation, and Control Conference, p. 1743 (2017)
23. Katz, G., Barrett, C., Dill, D.L., Julian, K., Kochenderfer, M.J.: Reluplex: an efficient SMT solver for verifying deep neural networks. In: Majumdar, R., Kunčak, V. (eds.) CAV 2017. LNCS, vol. 10426, pp. 97–117. Springer, Cham (2017). https:// doi.org/10.1007/978-3-319-63387-9_5
24. Ko, C.Y., Lyu, Z., Weng, T.W., Daniel, L., Wong, N., Lin, D.: POPQORN: quantifying robustness of recurrent neural networks. arXiv preprint:1905.07387 (2019)
25. Kurd, Z., Kelly, T., Austin, J.: Developing artificial neural networks for safety critical systems. Neural Comput. Appl. **16**(1), 11–19 (2007)
26. Lin, C.L., Shen, W.: Applying safety case pattern to generate assurance cases for safety-critical systems. In: 2015 IEEE 16th International Symposium on High Assurance Systems Engineering, pp. 255–262. IEEE (2015)
27. Nicolescu, G., Mosterman, P.J.: Model-Based Design for Embedded Systems. CRC Press, Boca Raton (2009)
28. Picardi, C., Hawkins, R., Paterson, C., Habli, I.: A pattern for arguing the assurance of machine learning in medical diagnosis systems. In: Romanovsky, A., Troubitsyna, E., Bitsch, F. (eds.) SAFECOMP 2019. LNCS, vol. 11698, pp. 165–179. Springer, Cham (2019). https://doi.org/10.1007/978-3-030-26601-1_12
29. Polack, P., Altché, F., d'Andréa Novel, B., de La Fortelle, A.: The kinematic bicycle model: a consistent model for planning feasible trajectories for autonomous vehicles? In: Intelligent Vehicles Symposium (IV), pp. 812–818. IEEE (2017)
30. Rushby, J.: The interpretation and evaluation of assurance cases. Comp. Science Laboratory, SRI International, Technical report, SRI-CSL-15-01 (2015)
31. Taeyoung, L., Kyongsu, Y., Jangseop, K., Jaewan, L.: Development and evaluations of advanced emergency braking system algorithm for the commercial vehicle. In: Enhanced Safety of Vehicles Conference, ESV, pp. 11–0290 (2011)
32. Tran, H.D., Cai, F., Diego, M.L., Musau, P., Johnson, T.T., Koutsoukos, X.: Safety verification of cyber-physical systems with reinforcement learning control. ACM Trans. Embed. Comput. Syst. (TECS) **18**(5s), 1–22 (2019)
33. Tuncali, C.E., Fainekos, G., Ito, H., Kapinski, J.: Simulation-based adversarial test generation for autonomous vehicles with machine learning components. In: 2018 IEEE Intelligent Vehicles Symposium (IV), pp. 1555–1562. IEEE (2018)
34. Wang, Y.S., Weng, T.W., Daniel, L.: Verification of neural network control policy under persistent adversarial perturbation. arXiv preprint arXiv:1908.06353 (2019)
35. Weimer, J., Sokolsky, O., Bezzo, N., Lee, I.: Towards assurance cases for resilient control systems. In: 2014 IEEE International Conference on Cyber-Physical Systems, Networks, and Applications, pp. 1–6. IEEE (2014)

Safety-Critical Software Development in C++

Daniel Kästner[✉], Christoph Cullmann, Gernot Gebhard, Sebastian Hahn,
Thomas Karos, Laurent Mauborgne, Stephan Wilhelm,
and Christian Ferdinand

AbsInt GmbH., Science Park 1, 66123 Saarbrücken, Germany
kaestner@absint.com

Abstract. The choice of the programming language is a fundamental
decision to be made when defining a safety-oriented software development process. It has significant impact on code quality and performance,
but also on the achievable level of safety, the development and verification
effort, and on the cost of tool qualification. Traditionally, safety-critical
systems have been programmed in C or ADA. In recent years, also C++
has entered into the discussion. C++ enables elegant programming, but
its inherent language complexity is much higher compared to C. This has
implications for testability, structural coverage, performance, and code
analysis. Further issues to be considered are tool chain diversity, the role
of the standard library, and tool qualification for compilers, analyzers
and other development tools. This article summarizes the requirements
of different safety norms, illustrates development and verification challenges and addresses tool qualification.

1 Introduction

During the past years the size and complexity of embedded software has sharply
increased, in particular in the automotive domain. Contributing factors have
been the trend to higher levels of automation, cost reduction by shifting functionality from hardware to software, and generic interfaces imposed by standardization frameworks such as AUTOSAR (AUTomotive OpenSystem ARchitecture)
or Adaptive AUTOSAR.

A significant part of embedded software deals with safety-relevant functionality. A failure of a safety-critical system may cause high costs or even endanger
human beings. Furthermore, due to increasing connectivity requirements (cloud-
based services, device-to-device communication, over-the-air updates, etc.), more
and more security issues are arising in safety-critical software as well.

Traditionally, safety-critical software is written in C or Ada. In recent years,
also C++ is being in discussion, mainly because of its object-oriented language
and abstraction features and its compatibility with C. Object-oriented programming can enable well-encapsulated programming, but also has drawbacks, as,
e.g., a very implicit control flow structure. In the case of C++ there are also

A. Casimiro et al. (Eds.): SAFECOMP 2020 Workshops, LNCS 12235, pp. 98–110, 2020.
https://doi.org/10.1007/978-3-030-55583-2_7

other language properties which can make its use in safety applications hazardous unless the language is reduced to a safety-compatible subset and great care is taken.

Obviously, the safety of a system must be established whichever programming language is used, so safety-relevant C++ programs must satisfy the same safety and quality requirements as C or ADA programs. The selection of an appropriate programming language is a fundamental part of the definition of the software development process, and is one aspect in the definition of compliant software development life cycles and processes imposed by contemporary safety norms, including DO-178C, IEC-61508, ISO-26262, or EN-50128. That also includes the definition of appropriate coding guidelines to ensure safety-compliant use of a programming language. In addition, all relevant safety standards also require to identify potential hazards and to demonstrate that the software does not violate the relevant safety goals. The process of demonstrating that the requirements are satisfied is typically termed verification. Software tools used in such a safety process have to be appropriately qualified.

As of 2020, the discussion which C++ language features should be admitted to which extent for safety-critical software projects, is in full swing, and there is no clear consensus yet. This article attempts to give an overview: we address considerations to be taken into account when writing safety-critical C++ programs and discuss the implications of the programming language design on development, verification, analyzability, and tool qualification.

2   The C++ Language

In 1979, Bjarne Stroustrup started his work on extending the procedural programming language C with object-oriented features. Nowadays, after several revisions and extensions, C++ is a multi-paradigm language that supports not only procedural and object-oriented, but also generic as well as functional programming. Similar to C, C++ still supports low-level system programming but also appeals to high-level application programmers by offering a high degree of abstraction. The C++ language has been standardized first in 1998 by the International Organization for Standardization (ISO). Since then, it encountered revisions in 2011, 2014, and 2017, and the next revision C++2020 has been announced.

The C++ *standard library* covers useful infrastructure that is implemented in but not part of the core language itself. The language support library includes basic support for the run-time type information, dynamic memory allocation, and exception handling. The string library defines support for creating and manipulating sequences of characters while the input/output library provides utilities for communication with the outside world. The standard library defines a variety of containers to hold and manipulate data, e.g., vectors and arrays, including a standardized way of iterating these containers. The algorithm library maintains a collection of useful generic algorithm, e.g., to process containers. In later C++ versions, the standard library was significantly extended, e.g., by introducing unordered hash containers, a library for handling and using regular expressions, smart pointers, and support for multi-threading as well as atomic operations on shared data, parallel versions of many algorithm in the library, new types such as `optional` and `variant`, etc.

3   A Safety Standard's Perspective

The supplement DO-332 ("Object-Oriented Technology and Related Techniques") to DO-178C refines and extends the DO-178C objectives for usage of object-oriented technology. In particular, it lists language features of object-oriented programming that need to be taken into account when considering software safety, such as inheritance, parametric polymorphism, overloading, type conversion, exception management, and dynamic memory management. All these concepts are part of the C++ language, so these considerations immediately apply to safety-critical software development in C++. The DO-332 gives a definition of the relevant features, discusses their safety vulnerabilities and formulates dedicated verification objectives. It also lists generic issues for safety which always have to be taken into account and which might be negatively impacted by object-oriented language features. In the following we will summarize the overview of safety-relevant language features of the DO-332.

Inheritance. Classes can be considered as user-defined types, a subclass derived from a superclass then is a subtype. An important rule is that any subtype of a given type should be usable wherever the given type is required, otherwise the type system becomes unsafe. This is formally defined by the Liskov Substitution Principle (LSP): "Let $q(x)$ be a property provable about objects x of type T. Then $q(y)$ should be true for objects y of type S where S is a subtype of T". In particular that means that for all methods of a subclass which overload a superclass method the following requirements must be satisfied: preconditions may not be strengthened, postconditions may not be weakened, and invariants may not be weakened. The DO-332 requires the LSP to be demonstrated.

A derived class inherits properties from its parent class. In case the subclass may have several parent classes this is called *multiple inheritance*, otherwise *single inheritance*. With *interface inheritance*, the derived class shares only the complete signatures of the methods of its parents without the underlying implementation. With implementation inheritance, the inheriting class shares the implementation as well as the complete method signatures of the parent.

Method dispatch can be done statically based on the declared type of the object, or it can be done dynamically based on the actual type of the object. In C++ static dispatch happens on procedure calls, or when prefixing the invocation of a method m with a class type (`base_class::m()`). When a subtype of the static type redefines the method being called, the method of the static type is still called. When a method call is dynamic dispatched, the mapping of a specific implementation is performed at runtime. Each method is associated with an offset in the method table for the class of the object, so dispatching is an indirect procedure call. Vulnerabilities may be introduced by:

– Substitutability: When a method is overridden in a subclass such that it is functionally incompatible with the original definition, the LSP is violated and class substitution can cause an application to behave incorrectly.
– Method implementation inheritance: When a subclass has an additional attribute and a method which would need to update that attribute is not overwritten, a call to that method could result in an improper object state and unexpected behavior.
– Unused code: When a method of a superclass is overridden by the subclass and the superclass is not instantiated, the code will be unreachable; on the other hand, removing the method at the superclass may break its integrity.
– Dispatching: When static dispatch is used with method overriding, i.e., when the subclass overrides method m, the actual type is the subclass, and the method implementation of the superclass is invoked (`base_class::m()`), incorrect behavior, or state inconsistency might result.
– Multiple inheritance: Inheriting from two different classes with incompatible intentions may lead to unexpected behavior.

Polymorphism. Parametric polymorphism is a feature where a function takes one or several types as arguments treating the types uniformly, i.e., the function does the same kind of work independently of the type of its arguments. In C++ parametric polymorphism is realized via templates. *Ad-hoc polymorphism* means that the same function name (symbol) can be used for functions that have different implementations. In C++ ad-hoc polymorphism exists in the form of method overloading and method overriding. *Overloading (static polymorphism)* means that multiple methods have the same name but different types of arguments. Calls to overloaded methods are resolved at compile-time based on the type of call arguments. *Overriding (dynamic polymorphism)* means redefining a virtual method in a subclass. Calls to overridden methods are resolved at run-time based on the dynamic type of the object on which the call is invoked.

The parametric polymorphic operations that act on the generic data (template) may not be consistent with the substituted data. Also, source code to object code traceability is more difficult. In C++, one template class will be expanded into a different versions of the code for each type used. Overloading ambiguity occurs when a compiler performs implicit type conversions on parameters in order to select an acceptable match. This implicit type conversion could lead to an unintended method being called.

Type Conversions. 0l5A *narrowing conversion* is structural change in which the destination data element cannot fully represent the source data. A *downcast* is a change of view from supertype to subtype. A type conversion is called *implicit* if it is an automatic type conversion performed by the compiler. Although languages and compiler typically have strict implicit conversion rules, a lack of familiarity with these rules, or ignorance of the conversion taking place are often the cause of coding problems. With a narrowing type conversion, data may be lost. A downcast may result in data corruption of the object itself or its neighbors in memory, incorrect behavior, or a run-time exception being thrown.

Exception Management. Exception handling, i.e., the ability to throw exceptions within a method and to handle exceptions in calling methods, is a common feature of object-oriented languages. Exception handling is used for conditions that deviate from the normal flow of execution. When an exception is raised the execution will transfer to the nearest enclosing handler. In case of *checked exceptions* the subprogram signature lists all exceptions that can be thrown by the subprogram, and there are compile-time checks that corresponding handlers exist. *Unchecked exceptions* are not part of the subprogram signature so there can be no assurance that they will be handled.

Potential vulnerabilities include that an exception may not be handled, that either no action or inappropriate actions may be performed when the exception is caught (handled), or that operations are unexpectedly interrupted by exceptions. Exception handling can cause unexpected delays.

Dynamic Memory Management. With dynamic memory management, objects can be created on-demand during run-time. The deletion of such objects after their use is either performed explicitly using a program statement or automatically by a runtime system. The most important techniques are memory pooling, stack- and heap-based memory management. Dynamic memory allocation, typically stack and heap usage, can lead to free memory exhaustion and improper behavior can lead to memory corruption. The DO-332 lists the following potential vulnerabilities:

- Ambiguous references: An allocator returns a reference to live memory, e.g., an object that is still reachable from program code, allowing the program to use this memory in an unintended manner.
- Fragmentation starvation: An allocation request can fail due to insufficient logically contiguous free memory available.
- Deallocation starvation: An allocation request can fail due to insufficient reclamation of unreferenced memory, or lost references.
- Heap memory exhaustion: The size of the available memory could be exceeded.
- Premature deallocation: A memory fragment could be reclaimed while a live reference exists.
- Lost update and stale reference: In a system where objects are moved to avoid fragmentation of memory, e.g., an old copy might be accessed after the new copy has been created and is in use.
- Time-bound allocation or deallocation: Dynamic memory management could cause unexpected delays.

In particular for heap-based memory management, all vulnerabilities have to be addressed.

Structural Coverage. Structural coverage analysis provides evidence to which degree requirements-based testing exercised the code structure. It covers code coverage (statement coverage vs. decision coverage vs. MC/DC coverage), source code to object code traceability, control coupling and data coupling.

Object-oriented languages use control coupling to minimize data coupling by introducing control coupling via dynamic dispatching. Almost all object-oriented language features complicate determining the degree of structural coverage, inheritance, method overriding, dynamic dispatch, subprogram overriding with static dispatch and parametric polymorphism. In particular, code coverage itself does not take data and control coupling into account, e.g., covering a method in the context of the superclass or subclass alone may not exercise all possible execution conditions. To judge the extend of structural coverage reached by testing, sound static analysis can to be applied beforehand to determine class structure, inheritance hierarchy, and the maximal possible data and control coupling.

4   Coding Guidelines for C++

Many C software development projects are developed according to coding guidelines, such as MISRA C, SEI CERT C, or CWE (Common Weakness Enumeration), aiming at a programming style that improves clarity and reduces the risk of introducing bugs. In particular in safety-critical software projects, obeying suitable coding guidelines can be considered mandatory as this is strongly recommended by all current safety standards, including DO-178B/DO-178C, IEC 61508, ISO 26262, and EN 50128.

Safety norms do not enforce compliance to a particular coding guideline, but define properties to be checked by the coding standards applied. As an example, the ISO 26262 gives a list of topics to be covered by modelling and coding guidelines, including enforcement of low complexity, enforcing usage of a language subset, enforcing strong typing, and use of well-trusted design principles (cf. ISO 26262 2018, Part 6, Table 1). The language subset to be enforced should exclude, e.g., ambiguously defined language constructs, language constructs that could result in unhandled runtime errors, and language constructs known to be error-prone. Table 6 of ISO 26262:6 2018 lists some principles for software unit design that can be addressed by coding guidelines, such as having one entry and one exit point in functions, and avoiding dynamic objects/variables, multiple use of variable names, implicit type conversions, hidden data flow or control flow, and recursions. Similar requirements are imposed by IEC-61508 and DO-178C. In the following we list the most prominent C++ coding guidelines, and give a brief comparison focusing on safety-related requirements.

The MISRA C++:2008 coding guidelines [15] were released in 2008. The guidelines explicitly demand for a single point of function exit (Rule 6-6-5), ban any kind of heap memory allocation (Rule 18-4-1), require any variable to be initialized before use (Rule 8-5-1) and forbid recursion of any kind (Rule 7-5-4). Further rules impose restrictions on the use and uniqueness of entity names (including types, variables and scoping), and on the use of pointers, concerning among others (unsafe) pointer conversions, pointer arithmetic and the use of invalid pointers. Dangerous implicit type conversions are forbidden, e.g., downcasts (Rule 5-2-3) and implicit change of signedness (Rule 5-0-4). Similarly, the use of inheritance is further restricted, e.g. virtual inheritance shall be avoided in general (Rule 10-1-1) and only used if required in diamond hierarchies (Rule 10-1-2). Polymorphism in form of templates is regulated by another 10 rules addressing name lookup, instantiation and more. MISRA allows the use of exceptions, but restricts it to error handling (Rule 15-0-1) and gives further prerequisites that need to be fulfilled.

In 2018, the AUTOSAR consortium has released a set of guidelines for C++14 [1] aiming at complementing MISRA C++:2008 with respect to new language features. The guidelines cover new language features, but also relax some restrictions of MISRA C++:2008. In particular, dynamic memory allocation is allowed, though heavily restricted and bound to the use of C++'s memory management facilities (such as managed pointers). Exceptions can be used but their use is constrained by a set of 30 dedicated rules.

The Joint Strike Fighter Air Vehicle C++ Coding Standards [14] were released in 2005 and thus do not incorporate C++11 or later versions of the standard. A single point of exit per function is enforced (AV Rule 113), heap memory allocation is mostly forbidden (AV Rule 206) as well as recursion (AV Rule 119). The use of templates is restricted, e.g., tied to a dedicated code review (AV Rule 101) and exhaustive testing (AV Rule 102). The use of inheritance is also highly restricted by a set of 13 rules. The most notable difference with respect to the MISRA and AUTOSAR guidelines is that the use of exceptions is strictly forbidden (AV Rule 208), independently of the purpose.

Outside the domain of safety-critical systems many other coding guidelines have been proposed for C++. Most of them aim at reducing common weaknesses associated with certain language features and more or less strictly regulate their use. The use of exceptions is forbidden by the LLVM Coding Standards as well as the Google C++ Style Guide [5], while the SEI CERT C++ Coding Standard and C++ Core Guidelines [2] do not. Dynamic objects and resources are usually tied to the ownership concept and/or smart pointers. The Google C++ Style Guide also bans implicit conversions and restricts the use of inheritance, advocating the use of members/compositions instead where appropriate.

5   Analyzability

In this section we give an overview of static analysis as a standard verification technique recommended by all safety norms, and also summarize verification obligations that can be addressed by static analysis. However, the analyzability considerations described in the following sections also apply to other static verification techniques.

One application of static analysis is checking compliance to coding standards. Purely syntactical methods can be applied to check syntactical coding rules. Safety norms also require to demonstrate the absence of critical programming defects, such as runtime errors, stack overflows, or deadline violations. To find such defects – which to some degree can be covered by semantical coding rules –, semantics-based static analysis can be applied. Semantical analyzers can be further grouped into unsound vs. sound approaches, the essential difference being that in sound methods there are no false negatives, i.e., no defect will be missed (from the class of defects under consideration). Sound analyzers are based on a mathematically rigorous formal method for semantics-based static program analysis, called abstract interpretation [4].

Runtime errors due to undefined or unspecified behaviors of the programming language used are a particularly dangerous class of software errors. Examples are faulty pointer manipulations, numerical errors such as arithmetic overflows and division by zero, data races, and synchronization errors in concurrent software. Such errors can cause software crashes, invalidate separation mechanisms in mixed-criticality software, and are a frequent cause of errors in concurrent and multi-core applications. At the same time, these defects also constitute security vulnerabilities, and have been at the root of a multitude of cybersecurity attacks, in particular buffer overflows, dangling pointers, or race conditions [9].

In safety-critical C programs, the run-time stack (often just called "the stack") typically is the only dynamically allocated memory area. It is used during program execution to keep track of the currently active procedures and facilitate the evaluation of expressions. When the stack area is too small, a *stack overflow* occurs: memory cells from the stacks of different tasks or other memory areas are overwritten. This can cause crashes due to memory protection violations and can trigger arbitrary erroneous program behavior, if return addresses or other parts of the execution state are modified.

In real-time systems the overall correctness depends on the correct timing behavior: each real-time task has to finish before its deadline. Providing evidence that no deadlines are violated requires the worst-case execution time (WCET) of all real-time tasks to be determined.

Sound static analysis is often perceived as a technique for source code analysis at the programming language level. Run-time error analysis deals with unspecified and undefined behavior in the programming language semantics and therefore works at the source code level. However, sound static analysis can also be applied at the binary machine code level. In that case it does not compute an approximation of a programming language semantics, but an approximation of the semantics of the machine code of the microprocessor. Worst-case execution time analysis and worst-case stack usage analysis are performed at the binary level, because they have to take the instruction set and hardware architecture into account. In runtime error analysis, soundness means that the analyzer never omits to signal an error that can appear in some execution environment. In WCET and stack usage analysis soundness means that the computed WCET/stack bound holds for any possible program execution.

Nowadays, abstract interpretation-based static analyzers that can compute safe upper bounds on the maximal stack usage and on the worst-case execution time [8,10], and that can prove the absence of runtime errors and data races [11] are widely used for developing and verifying safety-critical software.

The complexity and precision of semantical analysis depends on the language semantics and the relevant language subset. For C++ code, the analyzability may be reduced due to certain language features discussed in the following.

6   C++ Challenges

All safety vulnerabilities presented in Sect. 3 are relevant for safety-critical C++ programs. In this section we revisit some of them and discuss additional topics, putting a particular focus on analyzability by static analysis tools. Differences in the impact to source- and binary-level analysis will also be discussed.

Rapid Language Evolution. Unlike in the older phases of the C++ language standardization, where more than a decade passed between two versions of the standard (e.g. C++98 to C++11), the evolution now happens at a much faster pace. The C++ standardization committee settled on a three-year cadence for new standard versions. This has led to the succession of the C++14, C++17 and soon C++20 standard. Each of the new versions of the standard incorporates both, new core language features and library extensions. Unlike other languages like C, for which new standard versions often only add minor changes, each of the C++ standard revisions is a rather large change. Compilers, analyzers and other development tools must keep up with the fast pace of this evolution.

Complex Language Frontend. Unlike the C language, the C++ language requires a highly complex frontend to support all current language features, e.g., to support template resolution. A C frontend is comparatively easy to implement and validate, and there is a plethora of different C frontends in use. In contrast, there is only a small set of frontends available that support modern C++, to our knowledge GCC/clang/MSCV/EDG. Qualifying such a frontend for safety-critical systems can be a challenge.

Compilation. Based on a formal executable semantics of C [12], the formally verified CompCert compiler has been developed. CompCert has been proven, using machine-assisted mathematical proofs, to be exempt from miscompilation issues: the executable code it produces is proved to behave exactly as specified by the semantics of the source C program [13]. The article [7] describes the qualification strategy used to successfully qualify CompCert for use in a highly critical control system from the nuclear power domain, compliant with IEC60880 and IEC61508 (SCL3). There is also a DO-178C-compliant Qualification Support Kit, that exhaustively maps the ISO C99 standard to functional tool requirements and, by a combination of formal proof and test cases, demonstrates 100% requirement coverage, which cannot be achieved for other existing compilers.

To the best of our knowledge no formal semantics for C++ has been proposed yet, which means that no comparable confidence in compiler correctness can be established.

The Standard Library. The C++ standard library provides abundant functionality. There is only a small number of library implementations available which cover the full functionality as required by the latest C++ standard.

From the perspective of the programmer, the high level of abstraction eases development and increases productivity. The underlying complexity is not apparent in the application code, but it can lead to negative effects for the analyzability of the resulting software. Many parts of currently available standard libraries hide dynamic memory allocation, creating the danger of complex allocation scenarios which are hard to analyze, and of unintentionally using dynamically allocated objects. The container parts of the standard library provide many conveniently usable data structures like associative maps (both ordered and unordered). Whereas the use is intuitive, the underlying data structures (highly dynamic pointer-based trees and hash tables) are sophisticated and make the analysis complex.

The commonly used standard libraries have not been developed according to safety standard requirements and are highly complex, e.g., the LLVM standard library consists of more than 800.000 lines of C++ code.

Library code is part of the safety-critical system and has either has to be developed with the same criticality level than the most critical component it is used in, or appropriately qualified (cf. DO-178C Sec. 12.1, ISO 26262:8).

Dynamic Memory Allocation. It is essential that for safety-critical systems adequate memory, processor and network resources are available to complete the tasks in a timely manner. Stack memory usage is well understood and can be efficiently and precisely handled by binary-level static analysis. With heap memory, the life range of an allocated object is not bound by the activity or the scope of the subprogram in which it was initially allocated. In consequence, its deallocation, in general, is not performed in the same context in which it was allocated, making its correct implementation a significantly greater problem than that of stack memory allocation and deallocation (DO-332, Sec. OO.D.2.4.2). It is necessary to determine the lifespan of each object, which is intractable, since exact lifespans depend on the data the program receives from its environment. Hence, manual allocation and reclamation of heap memory is error-prone, frequently leading to memory corruption through dangling pointers, and to memory leaks.

Dynamic heap memory allocation can also have impact on execution time, and sometimes also on the scheduling of time-critical tasks. The worst-case execution time often depends on the concrete addresses and their alignment on the target. For dynamically allocated data structures such properties are hard to derive. To the best of our knowledge, providing safe upper bounds for the time needed to allocate and free objects is an unsolved problem.

Even when the scope of dynamically allocated memory is well known, static analysis is challenging: the analysis problem becomes much harder to solve when the size of the state space cannot be precisely determined. The first difficulty is to keep the size of states representation finite (and small enough). In addition, because of approximations, the analyzer may consider more potential memory being allocated than is actually requested by the program during its executions, leading either to intractable memory consumption or further approximations on the allocated memories. Another aspect is that dynamic memory allocation makes using complex data structures, such as lists, trees or graphs, much easier for the programmer, which naturally tends to use them more. Such data structures are in themselves challenging to analyze, witnessed by the very active and abundant research on the subject of shape analysis [6].

Dynamic Polymorphism. The increased control coupling of dynamic dispatch means that the control flow is more dependent on the data flow in a program. In consequence, accurate information from data flow analysis has to be obtained to supplement control flow analysis (cf. DO-332, Sec. OO.D.2.4.1). The time needed to traverse method tables to find the correct method to invoke is relevant for WCET analysis.

The analysis is complicated by the need to determine at each dispatch point the set of methods inherited from a superclass or redefined by a subclass which might be invoked at that dispatch point. At the source level, even in case of non-perfect knowledge, the C++ type system will provide enough information to at least detect some super-set of the potentially called functions for function pointers and virtual functions. At the binary level however, identifying a virtual call site and its call targets needs additional information about the accessed object's base class type, and the called virtual member function including its signature. Determining this information typically requires debug information, and an explicit mapping from source code analysis to the binary level analysis, which, depending on the compiler optimization level, can be a challenge.

Exception Handling. C++ provides exceptions as one standard way for error handling, in addition to functions returning error codes. The C++ standard library use a mixture of exception handling and returning error codes. This renders uniform error handling difficult.

C++ exceptions are not checked by the compiler and there is no guarantee that an exception will be handled by the calling code. There is even no guarantee that throwing an exception succeeds: most C++ compilers generate code that indirectly invokes malloc in order to allocate heap memory for the exception object. If dynamic memory allocation fails, program execution is aborted by a call to `std::terminate`. An exception also may lead to unexpected program termination before reaching its handler, if the exception is raised in the scope of a destructor or in a method declared with the noexcept specifier.

Similarly to overloading, exception handling also massively increases the control coupling, as there is an additional implicit control path from every program point to all exception handlers in scope. For static analyzers this is particularly harmful, since analysis imprecision may cause additional over-approximations on calls to cleanup paths in case of an exception thrown. This, in turn, increases the complexity of the analysis and further reduces analysis precision.

At the binary code level, exceptions are hard to analyze at all, as the required stack unwinding is often handled via complex state machines that use extra information stored in debug sections (e.g., cf. [3]).

Extensions and/or modifications to the exception handling facilities of C++ are currently discussed in the C++ working group (WG21). More details can be found in [16], which proposes a model where functions have to declare that they throw a statically defined exception type by value, thereby making exception handling deterministic and avoiding dynamic or non-local overheads.

7 Summary

C++ has evolved to a complex multi-paradigm language which enables high programming productivity, in particular due to its powerful language abstractions. Object-oriented features like the C++ classes support well-structured programs, e.g., providing for encapsulation and reducing data coupling between components. However, for safety-critical programming the underlying concepts have to be well understood, since they typically have safety implications which have to be taken into account. Also, while supporting well-structured programs, the very same concepts may introduce safety defects when improperly used, cause hidden complexity in other aspects like an increased control coupling, or cause additional effort in other development stages, e.g., for achieving structural coverage. The expressiveness and complexity of the standard library constitutes a challenge for providing safety-compliant implementations, while rapid language evolution and frontend complexity represent challenges for tool chain qualification.

In this article en in DO-332, we have discussed language features which might have implications for software safety, in particular, inheritance, parametric polymorphism, overloading, type conversion, exception handling, and a higher temptation to use dynamic memory management. We also addressed C++ specific aspects, like its rapid language evolution, the central role of the standard library, and its frontend complexity. We have given an overview of the most important coding standards for C++, and shown that for some language features, in particular exceptions, there are significant differences in whether or to which extend their usage should be allowed. We discussed analyzability by static analysis tools, and showed that some language concepts can significantly increase analysis complexity and reduce the achievable confidence in the absence of defects.

References

1. AUTOSAR. Guidelines for the use of the C++14 language in critical and safety-related systems (2018)
2. Bjarne Stroustrup, H.S.: C++ Core Guidelines. https://isocpp.github.io/CppCoreGuidelines/CppCoreGuidelines. Accessed Jan 2020
3. C++ ABI for Itanium: Exception Handling. https://refspecs.linuxbase.org/abi-eh-1.21.html. Accessed Jan 2020
4. Cousot, P., Cousot, R.: Abstract interpretation: a unified lattice model for static analysis of programs by construction or approximation of fixpoints. In: 4th POPL, pp. 238–252. ACM Press, Los Angeles (1977)
5. Google C++ Style Guide. https://google.github.io/styleguide/cppguide.html. Accessed January 2020
6. Illous, H., Lemerre, M., Rival, X.: A relational shape abstract domain. In: Barrett, C., Davies, M., Kahsai, T. (eds.) NFM 2017. LNCS, vol. 10227, pp. 212–229. Springer, Cham (2017). https://doi.org/10.1007/978-3-319-57288-8_15

7. Kästner, D., et al.: CompCert: practical experience on integrating and qualifying a formally verified optimizing compiler. In ERTS2: Embedded Real Time Software and Systems, Toulouse, France, p. 2018 (2018)
8. Kästner, D., Ferdinand, C.: Proving the absence of stack overflows. In: Bondavalli, A., Di Giandomenico, F. (eds.) SAFECOMP 2014. LNCS, vol. 8666, pp. 202–213. Springer, Cham (2014). https://doi.org/10.1007/978-3-319-10506-2_14
9. Kästner, D., Mauborgne, L., Ferdinand, C.: Detecting safety- and security-relevant programming defects by sound static analysis. In: Rainer Falk, J.-C.B., Chan, S. (eds.) The Second International Conference on Cyber-Technologies and Cyber-Systems (CYBER 2017), volume 2 of IARIA Conferences, pp. 26–31. IARIA XPS Press (2017)
10. Kästner, D., Pister, M., Gebhard, G., Schlickling, M., Ferdinand, C.: Confidence in timing. In: Safecomp 2013 Workshop: Next Generation of System Assurance Approaches for Safety-Critical Systems (SASSUR), September 2013
11. Kästner, D., Schmidt, B., Schlund, M., Mauborgne, L., Wilhelm, S., Ferdinand, C.: Analyze this! sound static analysis for integration verification of large-scale automotive software. In: Proceedings of the SAE World Congress 2019 (SAE Technical Paper). SAE International (2019)
12. Krebbers, R., Leroy, X., Wiedijk, F.: Formal C semantics: CompCert and the C standard. In: Klein, G., Gamboa, R. (eds.) ITP 2014. LNCS, vol. 8558, pp. 543–548. Springer, Cham (2014). https://doi.org/10.1007/978-3-319-08970-6_36
13. Leroy, X., Blazy, S., Kästner, D., Schommer, B., Pister, M., Ferdinand, C.: CompCert - a formally verified optimizing compiler. In: ERTS: Embedded Real Time Software and Systems, 8th European Congress, Toulouse, France, p. 2016, January 2016
14. Martin, L.: Joint strike fighter air vehicle C++ coding standards for the system development and demonstration program (2005)
15. MISRA (Motor Industry Software Reliability Association) Working Group. MISRA C++:2008 Guidelines for the use of the C++ language in critical systems (2008)
16. Sutter, H.: Zero-overhead deterministic exceptions: throwing values. Technical report P0709 R0, SG14, May 2018

An Instruction Filter
for Time-Predictable Code Execution
on Standard Processors

Michael Platzer$^{(\boxtimes)}$ⓘ and Peter Puschnerⓘ

Institute of Computer Engineering, TU Wien, Vienna, Austria
michael.platzer@tuwien.ac.at, peter@vmars.tuwien.ac.at

Abstract. Dependable cyber-physical systems usually have stringent requirements on their response time, since failure to react to changes in the system state in a timely manner might lead to catastrophic consequences. It is therefore necessary to determine reliable bounds on the execution time of tasks. However, timing analysis, whether done statically using a timing model or based on measurements, struggles with the large number of possible execution paths in typical applications. The single-path code generation paradigm makes timing analysis trivial by producing programs with a single execution path. Single-path code uses predicated execution, where individual instructions are enabled or disabled based on predicates, instead of conditional control-flow branches. Most processing architectures support a limited number of predicated instructions, such as for instance a conditional move, but single-path code benefits from fully predicated execution, where every instruction is predicated. However, few architectures support full predication, thus limiting the choice of processing platforms. We present a novel approach that adds support for fully predicated execution to existing processor cores which do not natively provide it. Single-path code is generated by restructuring regular machine code and replacing conditional control-flow branches with special instructions that control the predication of subsequent code. At runtime an instruction filter interprets these predicate-defining instructions, computes and saves predicates and filters regular instructions based on the predicate state, replacing inactive instructions with a substitute that has no effect (e.g. a NOP). We are implementing this single-path filter for the LEON3 and the IBEX processors.

Keywords: Single-path · Real-time · Predictable timing

1 Introduction

In many dependable cyber-physical systems the execution of a task must complete within a time limit, otherwise the system might fail. It is therefore essential to guarantee that the task will not exceed that limit, which requires to bound its Worst-Case Execution Time (WCET). This is usually done either through Static

ⓒ Springer Nature Switzerland AG 2020
A. Casimiro et al. (Eds.): SAFECOMP 2020 Workshops, LNCS 12235, pp. 111–122, 2020.
https://doi.org/10.1007/978-3-030-55583-2_8

Timing Analysis (STA) or through measurement-based techniques, however both of these approaches struggle with the large number of execution paths in typical programs [14]. In STA every additional path requires to keep track of an ever growing number of possible hardware states thus leading to the state space explosion problem. In measurement-based approaches, exhaustively measuring the duration of every path is infeasible in practice.

Single-path code is a code generation paradigm which makes execution time bounding trivial by producing a program with a single execution trace [6]. The STA of a single-path program needs to keep track of one path only. On time-predictable hardware the execution time of single-path code is constant, hence a single measurement is enough to determine the execution time. Single-path code makes use of predicated execution to enable or disable instructions conditionally and thereby replace conditional control-flow branches with predicated instructions [1].

Since single-path code relies on predicated execution for conditional parts of a program, the target architecture must support that. Most Instruction Set Architectures (ISAs) have some form of conditional instructions besides control-flow instructions, such as for instance a *conditional move* instruction [4]. That allows to execute all traces in a conditional statement speculatively and then discard the results of all but one trace. However, this adds additional complexity to the code, in particular when a speculatively executed trace must avoid exceptions (e.g. division by zero). Therefore, in order to *efficiently* execute single-path code, the processor should support fully predicated execution, where all instructions can be enabled or disabled based on predicates.

Fully predicated execution is not a common feature in modern processor architectures [4]. The ARM ISA is notable for supporting it, by allowing every instruction to be enabled or disabled based on condition codes in the status register. The limited availability of fully predicated execution confines single-path code to those few architectures. However, these might not always be the best fit for every application, since other requirements could favor different execution platforms. In that case one option is to build a custom processor with custom ISA, as has been done by Schoeberl et al. [11], who developed the Patmos processor. Patmos supports fully predicated execution and the compiler backend written especially for it has the option to produce single-path code that has an execution time that is effectively independent of input data. Developing a purpose-built processor with a dedicated instruction set is already a daunting and complex task on itself. On top of that it requires to build a custom toolchain which can compile programs to that new instruction set.

We would like to bring the benefits of single-path code to existing architectures without the need to build a new processor and to develop a new instruction set. We also want to avoid tying single-path code generation to a specific compiler. Therefore, we apply the single-path transformation as a post-processing step to the fully compiled and linked executable file of a program. We propose a novel approach to upgrade existing processors with the ability to execute single-path code generated that way by adding an instruction filter in the instruction fetch path of the processor core. This requires minor modifications to the hardware that can easily be applied to a wide variety of processor architectures. To demonstrate the feasibility of our approach we have started to apply these changes to two processors: LEON3, a core using the SPARC v8 ISA and IBEX, which uses the RISC-V architecture.

This paper makes following contributions:

- We adapt the single-path generation algorithm of the Patmos compiler such that it can be used to convert machine code of various ISA to single-path code. Special instructions controlling the state of predicates are encoded with unused opcodes.
- We present a novel approach to add predicated execution to existing processor cores by adding an instruction filter with an internal predicate stack. The filter interprets the special instructions controlling the predicates at runtime and filters instructions fetched by the core depending on the state of these predicates.

This work is organized as follows: Sect. 2 gives a more detailed overview of the single-path paradigm, along with its advantages and drawbacks. Section 3 presents prior approaches to generating and executing single-path code. In Sect. 4 we discuss the concept and requirements of an instruction filter for the execution of single-path code and in Sect. 5 we explain details of our implementation. Section 6 describes the current state of our implementation and Sect. 7 concludes this paper.

2   Single-Path Paradigm

Although it is essential to determine the WCET of a task in critical real-time applications, actually determining a tight bound using STA remains a complex undertaking. It requires solving two problems: modelling the timing behavior of the execution platform and determining the possible execution paths of a program [14]. While the severity of the first problem depends on the temporal predictability of the hardware, the complexity of the latter increases with the number of execution paths in the software.

Measurement-based methods were proposed as an alternative to STA [10]. These are usually hybrid approaches, combining measurements with static analysis. For instance, Measurement-Based Probabilistic Timing Analysis (MBPTA) has been introduced by Wenzel et al. [13], where timing measurements are used to build a hardware timing model which complements standard STA for determining WCET bounds. While these approaches generally allow to obtain lower bounds, the accuracy of those bounds and their respective violation probabilities depends on hardware systemic effects and appropriate test coverage [3], i.e. the proportion of execution paths of which the execution time was actually measured.

The number of possible program execution paths grows exponentially with the number of control-flow alternatives, hence analysis of all paths in STA as well as measuring the execution time of all paths quickly becomes intractable. Single-path code is a code generation paradigm in which all execution traces of a program are merged into a single execution path [6], thus making timing analysis trivial. Single-path code executed on a time-predictable processor has constant execution time regardless of input data and therefore the WCET can be determined with a single measurement.

Instead of conditionally executing code blocks using branches, single-path code makes use of predicated execution to conditionally enable or disable individual instructions [1]. While the same sequence of instructions is executed by the processors every time a single-path program is run, instructions might have no effects depending on the state of predicates. These predicates capture the truth values of conditions and thus predicated instructions replace the conditional branches used in regular machine code. Loops are executed for a constant number of iterations based on a loop bound. It has been shown that every WCET-analyzable code can be converted to single-path code [9].

The drawback of single-path code is that all execution traces must be executed, which is why the execution time of single-path code is typically larger than that of regular code. However, reduced performance is traded for increased predictability. Also, the increased execution time is often lower than the WCET bound of the equivalent regular code [7].

3   Related Work

A method to transform regular code into single-path code for platforms which support partial predicated execution has first been described by Puschner et al. [8]. It makes use of the *conditional move* instruction, which is implemented in several processor architectures. Conditional code sections are always executed speculatively regardless of the truth value of the respective condition, but the results are discarded if that condition is false.

In order to achieve constant execution times with respect to input data, single-path code must be executed on time-predictable hardware. Schoeberl et al. [12] implemented the *conditional move* instruction on the time-predictable Java Optimized Processor (JOP). They demonstrated that single-path programs executed on this platform do indeed have a constant execution time regardless of input values.

Geyer et al. [2] investigated which ISA and extensions thereof are particularly suitable for the execution of single-path code both in terms of execution time and code size. In particular, they compared single-path code using partial predication, which made use of a conditional move instruction as did earlier work, with single-path code using full predication. For the latter they implemented *predicated blocks* for the SPARC v8 architecture, a form of predication where an entire block of code is predicated by specifying a condition that would apply to subsequent code with a special *predbegin* instruction. The predication remains active until an associated *predend* instruction is encountered.

While those early contributions focused on a description of the principles of single-path code, Prokesch et al. [5] analyzed single-path conversion on the

Control-Flow Graph (CFG) level of a program and introduced an algorithm to automatically generate single-path code for platforms that support fully predicated execution. Each basic block of the CFG is predicated according to the conditions that apply to it. All instructions from the original regular machine code are kept, with the exception of conditional branches, which are replaced by special instructions that modify the predicates. The algorithm also retains the topological ordering of instructions, hence all active instructions are executed in the exact same order in which they would have been executed in the equivalent regular code. The algorithm was embedded into their port of the LLVM compiler which produces code for the time-predictable processor Patmos.

Although Prokesch et al. implemented single-path transformation in the Patmos compiler, the algorithm itself works independent of the target architecture. Since it operates on the CFG of a program and does not require access to the source code, it can also be applied as a post-processing step to the executable file produced by an arbitrary compilation toolchain. We use this method to generate single-path code for various ISA, which we extend with special instructions to control the state of predicates.

4   Single-Path Extension

The goal of our work is to execute single-path code on existing processor cores. We want to take advantage of fully predicated execution to execute single-path code efficiently [4]. Since most ISA do not support full predication, we extend those with special instructions that manipulate the state of predicates. These special instructions are encoded with unused opcodes of the respective ISA.

We use the automated single-path transformation algorithm developed by Prokesch et al. [5] to convert regular machine code to single-path code. While Prokesch et al. implemented single-path generation inside their port of the LLVM compiler, we apply this transformation as a post-processing step to a fully compiled and linked executable. That way the single-path conversion is not tied to a specific compilation toolchain. The transformation rearranges the basic blocks of the CFG of a program and replaces conditional control-flow branches with special instructions that modify predicates.

Existing cores do not understand these special instructions, thus requiring some modifications. In an attempt to keep the required changes to a minimum, we design an instruction filter which interprets the special instructions controlling the predicates and implements predication for all other instructions by filtering out the inactive ones based on predicate values identified by the filter. It either passes fetched instructions to the processor or replaces them with NOP instructions (depending on the architectures there might be several instructions that have no effect, but for simplicity we refer to all of them as NOPs).

Allowing existing processor cores to execute single-path code therefore involves two steps:

1. Single-path code is generated from regular machine code by applying the method of Prokesch et al. to the executable file of a program. This single-path

code consists of restructured object code that includes special instructions for computing predicates.

2. An instruction filter is added to the processor core. At runtime, this filter interprets the special instructions of the single-path code, to compute predicates and filter instructions depending on the actual predicate states. As a result the processor receives a stream of filtered native instructions (either instructions from the object code or NOPs) at runtime.

The filter is placed on the instruction fetch path, such that all instructions pass through it as they are fetched by the core. Figure 1 shows a concept diagram of a processing platform using the filter. Instructions are only forwarded to the core if all predicates on the predicate stack are true, otherwise they are replaced by NOPs. Conditionally modifying predicates requires access to the condition codes of the processor, therefore we add an interface that routes the condition codes out of the core and into the filter. The remainder of this section discusses the requirements for such a single-path filter.

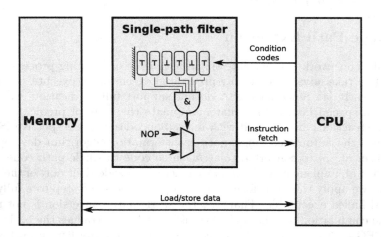

Fig. 1. Concept diagram of the single-path filter: Instructions are fetched from memory and pass through the filter, from where they are either passed on to the core or replaced by an instruction with no effects. The filter has access to the condition codes of the core, thus allowing to set predicates conditionally.

We apply the single-path conversion to the executable file of a program, after all compilation and linking steps have been completed, which has the advantage that it is not dependent on a specific compilation toolchain. That requires, however, that any additional state information necessary for the execution of the single-path code (such as for instance the predicate values) need to be saved in the filter, as saving it in memory or registers might lead to collisions with the memory or register allocation of the preceding compilation or linking steps.

The first requirement to execute single-path code generated in this manner is that the execution platform must support fully predicated execution. The single-path filter must interpret special instructions that compute predicates, manage the predicates and filter out instructions that are disabled by these predicates. Predicates capture the truth values of conditions and a new predicate is required for every condition that we encounter. Predicates expire when the execution of subsequent instructions no longer depends on the associated condition. Programming constructs that use conditions, such as conditional statements (e.g. *if-then-else* statements) or loops, can be nested, with new conditions applying on top of others. Consequently the predicates should be managed in a predicate stack. A new predicate is pushed to the stack when encountering a condition and the predicate is removed from the stack when it expires. That predicate stack must be stored in dedicated hardware in the filter, such that the predicate values are readily available to it.

Apart from fully predicated execution, another requirement is that loops require an iteration counter. In regular code the number of iterations of a loop depend on the loop condition only. However, in single-path code the loop bound dictates the number of iterations and a counter is required to count these iterations. This counter cannot be stored in memory or a register either, since we do not want to restrict the hardware resources available to the compiler. Therefore, the iteration counters for loops in single-path code also need to be stored in hardware. Loops might be nested, hence instead of a single loop counter a loop counter stack is required. A new loop counter is pushed to that stack upon entering a loop and initialized with the total iteration count. The counter is then decremented on every iteration. When the loop counter reaches 0 the loop exits and the loop counter is removed from the stack.

Finally, the single-path filter must have a dedicated return address stack for single-path functions. In regular code a function call writes the address of the call instruction to a specific register known as the *return address register*. When the function returns, it transfers control back to that address. Function calls can be conditional, for instance when they appear inside conditional statements. In single-path code, every function call is executed unconditionally, but depending on the values of predicates, all instructions of that function might be inactive and thus the function call might have no effects. This is equivalent to a function that would not have been executed in regular code. Since an inactive function does not modify any memory locations or registers, including the return address register, the return address would be lost if it were not saved elsewhere. Therefore, the return address of single-path function calls must be stored in the filter as well. Function calls are usually nested, hence a return address stack is required.

5   Filter Implementation

In order to add the ability to execute single-path code to an existing processor, we add an instruction filter with a predicate stack which computes and saves predicates triggered by special predicate-defining instructions and filters regular instructions based on the values of these predicates, by either passing them on to the core or replacing them by instructions that have no effects (NOPs). The filter also manages a loop counter stack which holds the iteration counters of loops in single-path code and a return address stack which stores the return addresses of single-path function calls. To control the behavior of the single-path filter the instruction set must be extended with special single-path instructions, which modify the state of these hardware stacks. Unused opcodes in the instruction set are used to encode these special instructions, which replace conditional control-flow branches when generating single-path code and are parsed and applied directly by the filter when fetched by the processor core.

Single-path code requires the ability to conditionally modify predicates, since the predicates are used to capture the truth value of conditions. Therefore, the instruction filter needs access to the results of comparisons in the core. On most architectures condition codes are used to capture the results of compares and to evaluate conditions. Hence, by giving the instruction filter access to these condition codes, it can evaluate conditions based on these condition codes analogously to the processor core and modify predicates accordingly.

Individual predicates are pushed to the predicate stack, where they are then modified either conditionally or unconditionally, thereby enabling and disabling the execution of subsequent instructions. Predicates are removed from the predicate stack in the reverse order than they have been added to it.

In our implementation we require that all instructions on the predicate stack are true in order to enable instructions and thereby forward them to the core. Although our hardware implementation does not differentiate between different types of predicates, we distinguish them logically based on the purpose they serve in single-path code.

1. *Function predicates:* Each function has a function predicate, which is the first predicate pushed to the predicate stack upon entering a function and conversely the last predicate popped from the stack upon leaving that function. The function predicate is initially true and changes to false when the code encounters a *return* statement. Single-path code requires that all instructions of a function are always executed, hence an early return from a function is realized by clearing the function predicate and thereby causes the filter to substitute all remaining instructions of that function by NOPs.
2. *Conditional predicates:* A conditional predicate is pushed to the stack for each conditional statement (e.g. *if-then-else* statements). The conditional predicate is initialized based on the result of a condition and remains on the stack for as long as the condition applies.
3. *Loop predicates:* Each loop has a loop predicate. Similar to a function predicate, this is the first predicate pushed to the predicate stack when entering a loop and the last predicate removed when exiting the loop. The loop predicate is true as long as the loop condition is true. Once cleared it remains false for all remaining loop iterations.
4. *Iteration predicates:* In addition to the loop predicate, every loop also has an iteration predicate. The iteration predicate is set to true at the beginning

of each loop iteration and is cleared if one iteration of the loop is aborted without exiting the loop, such as would happen when encountering a *continue* statement.

The following examples illustrate the use of predicates for conditional statements and for loops.

Figure 2 shows the C code for a simple conditional statement, along with pseudo-assembler representations of the regular version as well as of the single-path version of the machine code for that conditional. The generic operation OP_A is executed unconditionally prior to the conditional block. OP_B is executed if the condition $COND$ is true, otherwise OP_C is executed instead. Finally, OP_D comes after the conditional block and is again executed unconditionally. In regular machine code the conditional execution of either OP_B or OP_C is realized with control-flow instructions. A conditional branch moves control to the *else* label if $COND$ is false, thus executing OP_C. Otherwise OP_B is executed and then an unconditional jump brings control to the end of the conditional block. The single-path version, by contrast, does not use any control-flow instructions. Instead a new predicate is pushed to the stack and that predicate (with index 0 since it is at the top of the stack) is cleared if $COND$ is false. Hence, the predicate at the top of the stack initially corresponds to the truth value of $COND$, and therefore the operation OP_B is only enabled if $COND$ is true. Then, the value of the predicate is inverted, thereby enabling OP_C if $COND$ is false. The right column shows the state of the predicate stack depending on the truth value of $COND$ for each of the generic operations.

Figure 3 shows a similar representation for a simple loop. This time however the single-path version also contains a control-flow instruction. This is a special instruction that is used in conjunction with a loop counter, which will be replaced either by an unconditional jump to the beginning of the loop as long as the loop counter is not 0 or by a NOP to exit the loop when the loop counter reaches 0. Simultaneously, the loop counter is decremented by one every time control jumps back to the start of the loop. The loop counter is pushed to the loop counter stack and initialized with the loop bound specified in the annotation before the start of the loop. Loops use a loop predicate to capture the state of the loop condition and an iteration predicate that is replaces branches to the start of the loop. While the loop predicate at index 1 in the predicate stack is cleared once if the loop condition $COND\_A$ is false and then remains false for all remaining iterations, the iteration predicate at index 0 is conditionally cleared if $COND\_B$ is true for one loop iteration only and is reset to true for the next iteration. Both of these predicates are pushed to the predicate stack before the beginning of the loop and removed from the stack after the loop has been left.

The single-path filter substitutes the instructions fetched from memory by instructions that have no effects (NOPs) when any of the predicates on the stack is false. In order to achieve constant execution time that substitute instruction must also have the same execution time than the original instruction. Which and how many instructions are used for this purpose will therefore depend on the specific processor. On architectures that use a hard-wired zero-register (i.e.

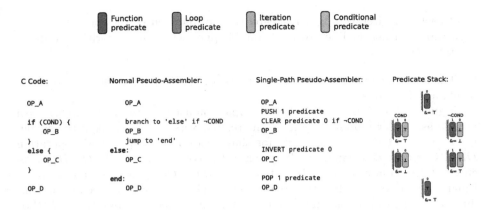

Fig. 2. Example of a conditional statement in single-path code: While regular machine code uses control-flow branches to conditionally execute code, in single-path code predicates are used instead.

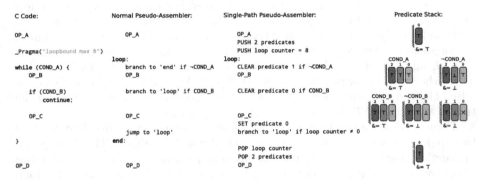

Fig. 3. Example of a loop in single-path code: The loop bound annotation is used to initialize the loop counter in single-path code and the loop is executed for a constant number of iterations. The loop predicate capturing the loop condition and the iteration predicate, which is cleared by a *continue* statement and reset at the start of each iteration, control whether the instructions are actually active.

a register that always reads as 0 and cannot be written) the destination register of an instruction can simply be replaced by that zero register, in which case the instruction does not modify any registers and thus has no effect.

6   Current Work

We are implementing the single-path generation and the instruction filter for two Reduced Instruction Set Computer (RISC) processors that are synthesized as softcores in a Field-Programmable Gate Array (FPGA):

- LEON3, a SPARC v8 processor core developed by Cobham Gaisler for safety-critical applications.
- IBEX, a RISC-V processor core developed by ETH Zürich and the non-profit organization lowRISC.

Both of these processors have a multi-stage in-order pipeline with predictable timings, thus they execute a given single-path program in constant time regardless of input values.

The single-path code is generated following the method of Prokesch et al. [5], which is applied to the fully compiled and linked executable file generated by a target-dependent version of the GNU C Compiler (GCC).

Currently our implementation allows the successful translation and execution of a set of experimental sample programs. We are working on the completion of the single-path translation and filtering, such that all WCET-analyzable programs can be transformed to single-path and executed on these two processors, and possibly extending the approach to other architectures.

7   Conclusion

We have presented a method to enable existing processor cores to efficiently execute single-path code by placing a filter in the instruction-fetch path of the core which provides predicated execution by filtering instructions depending on the values of predicates. The predicates are managed on a predicate stack in the filter and are controlled by special instructions that are interpreted by the filter itself. The condition codes of the processor are routed to the filter to allow predicates to be set conditionally.

Single-path code that can be executed by a processor that was upgraded with this filter is generated from regular machine code by applying the single-path transformation method developed by Prokesch et al. to the executable produced by a regular compilation toolchain in a post-processing step. This conversion reorders the basic blocks of the CFG of the program and replaces conditional control-flow branches with special instructions that control the state of predicates. These special instructions are parsed and interpreted by the filter.

We are implementing the single-path generation and the instruction filter for two RISC processors. Currently our implementations allow the successful execution of few simple test programs. We plan to complete the single-path filters for these two processors and potentially implement versions for more architectures. Once fully functional we will evaluate the performance of single-path code on these platforms and compare the WCET of regular code with the constant execution time of the equivalent single-path code.

References

1. Delvai, M., Huber, W., Puschner, P., Steininger, A.: Processor support for temporal predictability - the spear design example. In: 2003 Proceedings of the 15th Euromicro Conference on Real-Time Systems, pp. 169–176, July 2003

2. Geyer, C.B., Huber, B., Prokesch, D., Puschner, P.: Time-predictable code execution - instruction-set support for the single-path approach. In: 16th IEEE International Symposium on Object/Component/Service-Oriented Real-Time Distributed Computing (ISORC 2013), pp. 1–8 (2013)

3. Law, S., Bate, I.: Achieving appropriate test coverage for reliable measurement-based timing analysis. In: 2016 28th Euromicro Conference on Real-Time Systems (ECRTS), pp. 189–199, July 2016. https://doi.org/10.1109/ECRTS.2016.21

4. Mahlke, S.A., Hank, R.E., McCormick, J.E., August, D.I., Hwu, W.M.W.: A comparison of full and partial predicated execution support for ILP processors. In: Proceedings of the 22nd Annual International Symposium on Computer Architecture, ISCA 1995, pp. 138–150. Association for Computing Machinery, New York (1995). https://doi.org/10.1145/223982.225965

5. Prokesch, D., Hepp, S., Puschner, P.: A generator for time-predictable code. In: 2015 IEEE 18th International Symposium on Real-Time Distributed Computing, pp. 27–34, April 2015. https://doi.org/10.1109/ISORC.2015.40

6. Puschner, P.: The single-path approach towards WCET-analysable software. In: IEEE International Conference on Industrial Technology, vol. 2, pp. 699–704 (2003). https://doi.org/10.1109/ICIT.2003.1290740

7. Puschner, P.: Experiments with WCET-oriented programming and the single-path architecture. In: 10th IEEE International Workshop on Object-Oriented Real-Time Dependable Systems, pp. 205–210 (2005)

8. Puschner, P.: Transforming Execution-Time Boundable Code into Temporally Predictable Code, pp. 163–172. Springer, Boston (2002). https://doi.org/10.1007/978-0-387-35599-3_17

9. Puschner, P., Kirner, R., Huber, B., Prokesch, D.: Compiling for time predictability. In: Ortmeier, F., Daniel, P. (eds.) Computer Safety, Reliability, and Security, pp. 382–391. Springer, Heidelberg (2012). https://doi.org/10.1007/978-3-642-33675-1_35

10. Santinelli, L., Guet, F., Morio, J.: Revising measurement-based probabilistic timing analysis. In: 2017 IEEE Real-Time and Embedded Technology and Applications Symposium (RTAS), pp. 199–208, April 2017

11. Schoeberl, M., et al.: T-CREST: time-predictable multi-core architecture for embedded systems. J. Syst. Archit. **61**(9), 449–471 (2015). https://doi.org/10.1016/j.sysarc.2015.04.002

12. Schoeberl, M., Puschner, P., Kirner, R.: A single-path chip-multiprocessor system, vol. 5860, pp. 47–57 (2009). https://doi.org/10.1007/978-3-642-10265-3_5

13. Wenzel, I., Kirner, R., Rieder, B., Puschner, P.: Measurement-based timing analysis. Commun. Comput. Inf. Sci. **17**, 430–444 (2008). https://doi.org/10.1007/978-3-540-88479-8_30

14. Wilhelm, R., et al.: The worst-case execution-time problem-overview of methods and survey of tools. ACM Trans. Embed. Comput. Syst. **7**(3) (2008). https://doi.org/10.1145/1347375.1347389

ISO/SAE DIS 21434 Automotive Cybersecurity Standard - In a Nutshell

Georg Macher[1]($\boxtimes$), Christoph Schmittner[2], Omar Veledar[3],
and Eugen Brenner[1]

[1] Institute of Technical Informatics, Graz University of Technology, Graz, Austria
{georg.macher,brenner}@tugraz.at
[2] Austrian Institute of Technology, Vienna, Austria
christoph.schmittner@ait.ac.at
[3] AVL List GmbH, Graz, Austria
omar.veledar@avl.com

Abstract. A range of connected and automated vehicles is already available, which is intensifying the usage of connectivity features and information sharing for vehicle maintenance and traffic safety features. The resulting highly connected networking amplifies the attractiveness level for attacks on vehicles and connected infrastructure by hackers with different motivations. Hence, the newly introduced cybersecurity risks are attracting a range of mitigating strategies across the automotive field. The industry's target is to design and deliver safe and secure connected and automated vehicles. Therefore, efforts are being poured into developing an industry standard capable of tackling automotive cybersecurity issues and protecting assets. The joint working group of the standardization organizations ISO and SAE have recently established and published a draft international specification of the "ISO/SAE DIS 21434 Road Vehicles - Cybersecurity Engineering" standard.

This document delivers a review of the available draft. This work provides a position statement for discussion of available analysis methods and recommendations given in the standard. The aim is to provide a basis for industry experts and researchers for an initial review of the standard and consequently trigger discussions and suggestions of best practices and methods for application in the context of the standard.

Keywords: ISO 21434 · ISO 26262 · Automotive · Security analysis

1 Introduction

Prior to the introduction of connectivity features and automated driving functionalities, safety engineering was at the forefront of the automotive domain's priorities. Functional safety engineering methods and processes are thus becoming industry standard and a critical part of the development. Today, many connected and automated vehicles are available and connectivity features and information sharing is increasingly used for additional vehicle, maintenance and traffic safety

© Springer Nature Switzerland AG 2020
A. Casimiro et al. (Eds.): SAFECOMP 2020 Workshops, LNCS 12235, pp. 123–135, 2020.
https://doi.org/10.1007/978-3-030-55583-2_9

features. This has also increased the vulnerability of vehicle attacks by hackers with different criminal motivations and thus introduces new risks for vehicle cybersecurity.

Consequently, new challenges regarding automotive cybersecurity have emerged; these in turn require additional efforts, engineering approaches and a very specific skill-set to deal with threats, risk management, secure design, awareness, and cybersecurity measures over the whole lifecycle of the vehicle. Well aware of these facts, the automotive industry has thus been making enormous efforts in the design and production of safe and secure connected and automated vehicles. As the domain geared up for the cybersecurity challenges, it has been able to leverage a broad range of valuable experiences from many other domains, but it must nevertheless face several unique challenges.

The automotive industry has clearly recognized these requirements and therefore invested in the development of an industry standard to tackle automotive cybersecurity issues and protect their assets. The joint working group of the standardization organizations ISO and SAE has recently established a committee draft of the "ISO/SAE DIS 21434 Road Vehicles - Cybersecurity Engineering" standard [11].

From the perspective of the automotive industry, this standard achieves a common understanding of security by design in product development and along the entire supply chain.

This document is a review of the available draft. The aim of this work is to provide a position statement of the available draft, the presented analysis methods and recommendations given in the standard.

We further provide an overview of recommendations of the ISO/SAE DIS 21434 Road Vehicles - Cybersecurity Engineering standard regarding the mapping of cybersecurity processes in context of established processes. The aim of this work is to provide a basis for industry experts and especially researchers for an initial review of the standard. Based on this work we intend to trigger discussions on mapping and suggestions of best practices and methods for application in the context of the standard.

2   Established Safety and Security Frameworks

Safety and security engineering are tightly interlinked disciplines. They both focus on system-wide features and could greatly benefit from one another if adequate interactions between their processes are defined.

2.1   Safety Engineering Standards

Safety engineering is already an integral part of automotive engineering and safety standards, such as the road vehicles - functional safety norm ISO 26262 [10] and its basic norm IEC 61508 [7], are well established in the automotive industry. Safety assessment techniques, such as failure mode and effects analysis

(FMEA) [8] and fault tree analysis(FTA) [9], are also specified, standardized, and integrated in the automotive development process landscape.

IEC 61508 Ed 2.0 provides a first approach for integrating safety and security; security threats are to be considered during hazard analysis in the form of a security threat analysis. However, this threat analysis is not specified in more detail in the standard and Ed 3.0 is about to be more elaborated on security-aware safety topics.

ISO 26262 Ed 2.0, which was published at the end of 2018, includes more recommendations for the interaction between safety and security. Separate standards were published based on an initial discussion about how to deal with safety and cybersecurity in Automotive standardization, but with a description of interactions. Annex E of ISO 26262:2018 delivers additional guidance on interactions. The coordination of plans and milestones is suggested for the management, as well as field monitoring. During concept phase a focus is on the interaction between HARA and TARA and the coordination between countermeasures. In the development phase a focus is on consecutive analysis and the identification of potential impacts between the disciplines. The Annex is concluded with guidance on the interaction in the production phase.

2.2   Security Engineering Standards

The SAE J3061 [22] guideline is a predecessor of ISO/SAE 21434 and establishes a set of high-level guiding principles for cybersecurity by:

- defining a complete lifecycle process framework
- providing information on some common existing tools and methods
- supporting basic guiding principles on cybersecurity
- summarizing further standard development activities

SAE J3061 states that cybersecurity engineering requires an appropriate lifecycle process, which is defined analogous to the process framework described in ISO 26262. Further, no restrictions are given on whether to maintain separate processes for safety and security engineering with appropriate levels of interaction or to attempt direct integration of the two processes.

The guidebook also recommends an initial assessment of potential threats and an estimation of risks for systems that may be considered cybersecurity relevant or are safety-related systems, to determine whether there are cybersecurity threats that can potentially lead to safety violations. A report on the application of SAE J3061 was published [20].

While other standards, such as the IEC 62443 [1] or the ISO 27000 series [2] are not directly aimed at automotive systems, they are nevertheless relevant for the production and backend systems on automotive systems.

In [13] we reviewed the available threat analysis methods and the recommendations of the SAE J3061 guidebook regarding threat analysis and risk assessment method (TARA) in context of ISO 26262 (2011) and SAE J3061. We provided an evaluation of available analysis methods together with a review of recommended threat analysis methods. Furthermore, we investigated systematic approaches to support the identification of trust boundaries and attack vectors for the safety- and cybersecurity-related aspects of complex automotive systems also in context of ISO 26262 (2011) and SAE J3061 in [14]. In the work of [15] we proposed a structured method for integrating security and safety engineering in the existing Automotive SPICE context.

Aside from this, in [18] we presented a first overview about the ongoing development and status of ISO/SAE 21434. Our working group presented ThreatGet, a new tool for security analysis, based on threat modelling [5] and a method for evaluating risk in cybersecurity with the name RISKEE [12]. This method is based on attack graphs and the Diamond model [3] in combination with the FAIR method for assessing and calculating risk. In a comparison with these works we updated the overview to consider the ongoing development, review the current status regarding methodological guidance and give a first evaluation on integrating cybersecurity into established automotive processes.

In recent years, SafeComp workshops have started a discussion on automotive efforts taken in the context of designing and producing safe and secure connected and automated vehicles. With the focus on industry standards to tackle automotive cybersecurity issues and additional standards by European Telecommunications Standards Institute (ETSI) and International Telecommunication Union (ITU) working on security topics of connected vehicles [21]. Further activities of last year's SafeComp also focus on presenting the method gaps and a proposal towards a solution to achieve coordinated risk management by applying a quantitative security risk assessment methodology [4].

3   ISO/SAE DIS 21434

In January 2016, the first guidebook for cyber-physical vehicle systems cybersecurity, SAE J3061 [22], was issued and marked the beginning of the cooperation between ISO and SAE to collaborate on the development of a cybersecurity standard for road vehicles in September 2016. The purpose of the fist standard to be created (ISO/SAE 21434 [11]) was to (a) define a structured process to ensure cybersecure design, (b) thus reducing the potential for a successful attack and reducing the likelihood of losses, and (c) provide clear means to react to cybersecurity threats consistently across global industry.

As already mentioned, ISO/SAE DIS 21434 [11] is intended for application to road-vehicles and focuses on setting minimum criteria for automotive cybersecurity engineering. In the standard neither the specifics of cybersecurity technologies, nor solutions and remediation methods are given. Furthermore no unique requirements for autonomous vehicles or road infrastructure given. A risk-oriented approach for prioritization of actions and methodical elicitation of cybersecurity measures is encouraged.

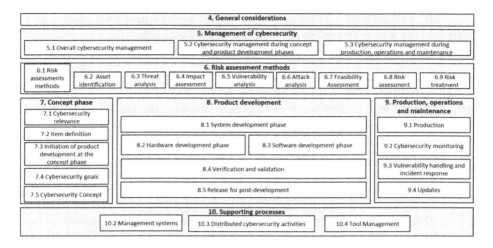

Fig. 1. Overview of the ISO/SAE DIS 21434 chapter structure [11]

3.1   ISO/SAE DIS 21434 Structure and Sections

Key principles focused by ISO/SAE DIS 21434 [11] are the cybersecurity activities in all phases of the vehicle life-cycle; ranging from design and development, production, operation and maintenance to decommissioning. In this section, the structure of the ISO/SAE DIS 21434 draft, depicted in Fig. 1, is analysed and briefly described before a more detailed description is given in the following sections of this work.

Section 1 defines the scope of the standard.

Section 2 provides normative references.

Section 3 defines abbreviated terms and definitions of terms used in the document.

Section 4 is an *informative part* describing the vehicle ecosystem, organizational cybersecurity management and the related automotive lifecycle.

Section 5 includes descriptions of organizational cybersecurity strategy, policy and objectives.

Section 6 defines risk management requirements, which includes a plan and method to determine the extent to which the road user is threatened by a potential circumstance or event.

Section 7 deals with the concept phase and defines cybersecurity goals, resulting from a threat analysis and risk assessment; as well as cybersecurity requirements definition to achieve the cybersecurity goals.

Section 8 specifies the implementation and verification of cybersecurity requirements specific to product development phase.

Section 9 is focussed on the production, operation and maintenance phases and also on specifying requirements to ensure that the cybersecurity specifications are implemented in the produced item; also covering in-field cybersecurity activities.

Section 10 describes supporting processes, including organizational processes.
Annexes are also *informative parts* describing several activities, examples and
    methods which have not been agreed to be mandatory.

Sections 1, 2, and 3 define the scope of the standard. The abbreviated terms
and definitions of terms used on the first pages of this document and are not
further detailed in this work, since already introduced in the introduction section
and because more details do not provide additional added value.

3.2   ISO/SAE DIS 21434 Section 4 - General Considerations

This section informs of the vehicle ecosystem, organizational cybersecurity management and the related automotive lifecycle. In this context, automotive cybersecurity is defined, as concerning the protection of all assets in the vehicle against
cybersecurity threats. Automotive cybersecurity thus considers (a) threats to
the vehicle or its components and (b) threats to the ecosystem that compromise
assets outside of the vehicle but utilize vulnerabilities within the vehicle. Additionally, a general organizational overview of cybersecurity management and the
cybersecurity engineering lifecycle activities is provided.

3.3   ISO/SAE DIS 21434 Section 5 - Management of Cybersecurity

The objectives of this section:

a Describing the organizational objectives regarding cybersecurity and the organizational strategy to achieve these objectives.
b The specification of organization-specific rules and processes to implement
   the organizational cybersecurity strategy.
c Assign responsibilities for cybersecurity engineering and the corresponding
   authority.
d Provision of the resources needed.
e Foster a cybersecurity culture.
f Managing the competences and awareness needed to perform the cybersecurity activities.
g Applying continuous improvement.
h The performing of an organisational cybersecurity audit.
i Managing interactions between cybersecurity processes.

Paragraph 5.1.4.7 details the interaction between cybersecurity processes and
existing processes within the organisation. This section also states that effective
communication channels between cybersecurity, functional safety, privacy and
other disciplines that are related to the achievement of cybersecurity shall be
maintained. This also includes communication between cybersecurity and functional safety engineering to exchange relevant information (e.g. threat and hazard information, violations of either cybersecurity goals or safety goals). In this
context the SAHARA method [16] was intended to have the same purpose.

Furthermore, paragraph 5.1.4.6 expresses the requirement of a cybersecurity audit, which shall be performed to independently judge whether the organizational processes achieve the process related objectives of this standard. This paragraph also states that the independence scheme can be based on Automotive SPICE, IATF 16949 in conjunction with ISO 9001, or ISO 26262.

Aside from this, general statements are given with regard to cybersecurity management during the concept phase and product development (paragraph 5.2) and during production, operation and maintenance (paragraph 5.3). This also includes tailoring of cybersecurity activities for reuse (5.2.4.2.2), system or component out of context development (5.2.4.2.3) and off-the-shelf development (5.2.4.2.4).

3.4   ISO/SAE DIS 21434 Sections 6 - Risk Assessment Methods

This section is introduced with an informative risk assessment methods introduction paragraph (6.1), which generally deals with risk assessment on organisational level, but does not specify any specific risk assessment methods or does not propose approaches to be used.

Here the work of SafeComp2016 [13] analysed some possible TARA analysis methods for their applicability in the automotive context. The work of Dobaj et al. [4] recently proposed a solution to achieve coordinated risk management by applying a quantitative security risk assessment methodology. This methodology extends established safety and security risk analysis methods with an integrated model, denoting the relationship between adversary and victim, including the capabilities and infrastructure used. This model is applied in estimating the resistance strength and threat capabilities, for determining attack probabilities and security risks. Other related works may be EVITA method [6], HEAVENS model, or the threat matrix approach. As mentioned initially, a method for evaluating risk in cybersecurity called RISKEE [12], is based on attack graphs and the Diamond model [3] in combination with the FAIR method for assessing and calculating risk. In terms of a structured threat analysis and threat modelling, the presented ThreatGet tool for security analysis [5] needs to be mentioned.

Paragraph 6.2 deals with asset identification and thus focuses on (a) assets, (b) their security properties (e.g. CIA) and (c) damage scenarios (e.g. a safety, financial, operational or financial impact) in the event of the loss of their security properties. To that end, candidate assets and potential damage scenarios are identified and an impact analysis is performed on the potential damage scenarios; here too no specific methods or approaches are suggested.

In the following paragraphs the threat analysis (6.3), impact assessment (6.4), and vulnerability analysis (6.5) are depicted. The objective of the threat analysis is to identify threats scenarios that could potentially compromise the security properties of the item. The impact assessment additionally assesses the impact or the extent of damage resultiong from a given damage scenario. The impact is defined as something that would be experienced or eventually sustained by the stakeholders (e.g. road users or businesses). While vulnerability analysis results in (a) a list of security vulnerabilities, (b) the distinguishing of flaws and weaknesses and (c) identifying the attack paths that connect these security vulnerabilities to an attack.

Paragraph 6.6 describes the objective of attack analysis, which is to develop and/ or update a set of attack paths which could be exploited to realize a threat scenario. The assessment of the exploitability of these attack paths is subject of an attack feasibility assessment (described in paragraph 6.7).

Finally, the risk assessment (paragraph 6.8) and risk treatment (6.9) deal with classification of the identified threat scenarios (based on the impact and attack feasibility) and the selection of appropriate risk treatment options.

As already mentioned, dedicated methods or specific approaches are not mentioned in this normative part, but they are mentioned in some parts of the Annex.

3.5   ISO/SAE DIS 21434 Sections 7 - Concept Phase

This section of the norm determines if the system under development is cyber-security relevant (paragraph 7.1), the item definition in cybersecurity context (7.2), and the initiation of product development at concept phase (7.3). It also includes, in alignment with the ISO 26262 approach, the definition of cybersecurity goals (7.4) and a cybersecurity concept (7.5). Here the link to the SAHARA method [16] shall be mentioned, which was one of the first methods to map the safety HARA analysis on the cybersecurity challenge.

The determination of the cybersecurity relevance of an item is not specifically mentioned, but Annex H provides a questionnaire that can be used to assess an item. The item definition and mining of cybersecurity goals is very much aligned with the safety-related approach known from ISO 26262 [10]. The cybersecurity concept consists, again as known from ISO 26262, of the cybersecurity requirements that achieve the cybersecurity goals along with their allocation at the appropriate level of architecture.

The cybersecurity concept also contains a collection of cybersecurity requirements which achieve the cybersecurity goals in implementation-independent manner.

3.6   ISO/SAE DIS 21434 Sections 8 - Product Development

This section of the standard describes the remaining product development phases. *System development* phase in paragraph 8.1, which can be linked to ISO 26262 part 4, *Hardware development* phase (paragraph 8.2), which can be linked to ISO 26262 part 5, and *Software development* phase (paragraph 8.3), which can be linked to ISO 26262 part 6. The additional paragraphs 8.4 is dealing with verification and validation and 8.5 is dealing with post-development release. In this context the work of Schmittner et al. [19] provides an FMEA application for security topics, called FMVEA.

Various different risk assessment activity types are also mentioned at various stages in the system development but these are not detailed. Three assessments are made, first at concept phase an assessment of the threats for the item and its operational environment, second at system development phase an assessment of system specification vulnerabilities that cause residual risk and third an assessment of system integration vulnerabilities that cause residual risk. The only mention, that system development shall be planned to identify methods and measures for system development and the cybersecurity activities.

Clause 8.1.4.2.2.3 mentions the following best practices of cybersecurity design:

1. principle of least privilege
2. authentication
3. authorization
4. audit
5. End-to-End security
6. architectural trust level (segregation of interfaces, defense in depth)
7. segregation of interfaces (to allow proper cyber security analysis)
8. protection of maintainability during service (test interface, OBD)
9. testability during development (test interface) and operations
10. Security-by-default (simplicity, non-obfuscation, no reliance on expert users)

Further, *system integration* shall be verified and tested by a combination of the proper methods, namely (a) requirement-based positive and negative testing, (b) interface testing, (c) penetration testing, (d) vulnerability scanning and (e) fuzz testing. For *hardware design*, the following mechanisms that ensure cybersecurity functionalities should be considered (clause 8.2.4.3.3):

- design cybersecurity domain (domain separation)
- self-protection of security functionalities
- protection against bypass of the security functionalities
- secure initialization of the security functionalities.

Further, all physical and logical interfaces of hardware elements related to cybersecurity, shall be identified by their purpose, usage and parameters. Since interfaces are a potential entry point for cybersecurity attacks and should serve as an input to the vulnerability analysis, also mentioned in [17].

For cybersecurity related *software development*, software cybersecurity requirements have to be derived from the system cybersecurity requirements and allocated to software modules. Software unit design specifications and their implementations need to be verified statically and dynamically. Therefore, secure design rules and coding guidelines, domain separation, self-protection, non-bypass characteristics, and secure initialization definition shall be considered. Paragraph 8.3.4.6.5 states design principles for software unit design and implementation at the source code level. Including also the properties of (a) correct order of execution of subprograms and functions, (b) consistency of the interfaces, (c) correctness of data flow and control flow, (d) simplicity, readability and comprehensibility, and (e) robustness, verifiability and suitability for software modification. Regarding *verification and validation* most activities are described in Annex F.

3.7   ISO/SAE DIS 21434 Sections 9 - Production, Operation and Maintenance

This section deals with production (paragraph 9.1) to ensure that the cybersecurity specifications from development are implemented in the produced item and that the implemented processes prevent the introduction of additional cybersecurity vulnerabilities. The cybersecurity monitoring (9.2), must have processes in place for gathering relevant cybersecurity information and for the reviewing of cybersecurity information. Additionally, the handling and incident response (9.3) processes present how to handle cybersecurity events and updating of basic cybersecurity requirements and capabilities are mentioned (9.4).

3.8   ISO/SAE DIS 21434 Sections 10 - Supporting Processes

The processes described in this section are for supporting the cybersecurity activities and for defining interactions, dependencies and responsibilities between customers and suppliers. Included in this are management systems (paragraph 10.2) together with distributed cybersecurity activities (10.3) describing the relation between customer and suppliers and tool management (10.4). While no standard tools for development processes mentioned, a hint is given in the direction of safety standards such as ISO 26262, IEC 61508, DO-178B is referred for tool qualification also for cybersecurity tools.

4   Review

A challenging task of the ISO/SAE 21434 committee was to create a brand new cybersecurity standard for the specifics of the automotive industry without building upon a wider variety of previous standards. While SAE J3061 was an important step forward, it was also recognized that this guidebook could not fulfil a role similar to that as was intended by ISO/SAE 21434, as in the case of ISO 26262, for the cybersecurity engineering of road-vehicles. The cybersecurity topic in the automotive context is a very new one and the ambitious plan of providing a framework that includes both the requirements for cybersecurity processes and a common language for communicating and managing cybersecurity risk among the stakeholders is aiming high. The fact that this standard does not prescribe specific technology or solutions related to cybersecurity brings additional ambiguities to the descriptions of processes and approaches.

Another stated high aim is to provide a clear means of reacting to cybersecurity threats consistently across the global industry. This is a relatively challenging target to achieve. A prominent example, is the CAL, a counterpart to the Automotive Safety Integrity Level (ASIL) from ISO 26262 during the risk assessment. The CAL should be used to define rigorous and applicable methods, but since no consensus has been found as yet on how to determine and treat such a parameter, this part has also been relegated to the Annex only. Thus, a risk-oriented approach for prioritization of actions and methodical elicitation of cybersecurity measures is encouraged, but no further added value in terms of best practices or agreed approaches is given.

In conclusion, this work is a highly creditable effort. The first common standard is both a major and an essential step in the right direction, but in the standard context it has not been possible to provide all the answers to questions related to methods, guidelines and best practices (or for those that are intended). The aim of this work is thus to share a basis for discussion and exchange between industry experts and researchers. Starting form this it will be possible to mine best practices and state-of-the-art methods for application in the context of the standard.

5   Conclusion

The joint working group of the standardization organizations ISO and SAE has recently established and published a draft of the "ISO/SAE 21434 Road Vehicles - Cybersecurity Engineering" standard. With this standard, the goal was to provide a basis for an entire uniform cybersecurity development process in the automotive industry. The relevant aspects for product definition, design, implementation and testing with this standard have been described, but no specific implementation details or best practice approaches given.

In this work we have thus highlighted the outcomes of the current draft standard and described how security standards, such as ISO/SAE 21434, are not the silver-bullet answer to applications in practice. These are often in a fragmented state, or provide descriptions at an abstract level for direct application in working environment and are not intended to provide answers to questions related to methods, guidelines and best practices.

Thus, one aim of this work is to provide a basis for industry experts and especially researchers for an initial review on the standard. The more important goal was to trigger discussions on mapping and suggestions of best practices and methods for application in the context of the standard and the domain. This work has solely provided some additional related efforts and was intended to provide a position statement for discussion, invite experts to get in contact and set/improve the state-of-the-art.

Acknowledgments. This work is supported by the *DRIVES* project. The Development and Research on Innovative Vocational Educational Skills project (*DRIVES*) is co-funded by the Erasmus+ Programme of the European Union under the agreement 591988-EPP-1-2017-1-CZ-EPPKA2-SSA-B.

References

1. IEC 62443: Industrial communication networks - network and system security
2. ISO 27000 series, information technology - security techniques
3. Caltagirone, S., Pendergast, A., Betz, C.: The diamond model of intrusion analysis. Technical report, Center for Cyber Intelligence Analysis and Threat Research Hanover Md (2013)

4. Dobaj, J., Schmittner, C., Krisper, M., Macher, G.: Towards integrated quantitative security and safety risk assessment. In: Romanovsky, A., Troubitsyna, E., Gashi, I., Schoitsch, E., Bitsch, F. (eds.) Computer Safety. Reliability, and Security, pp. 102–116. Springer, Cham (2019). https://doi.org/10.1007/978-3-030-26250-1_8
5. El Sadany, M., Schmittner, C., Kastner, W.: Assuring compliance with protection profiles with threatget. In: Romanovsky, A., Troubitsyna, E., Gashi, I., Schoitsch, E., Bitsch, F. (eds.) Computer Safety. Reliability, and Security, pp. 62–73. Springer, Cham (2019). https://doi.org/10.1007/978-3-030-26250-1_5
6. Henniger, O., Ruddle, A., Seudié, H., Weyl, B., Wolf, M., Wollinger, T.: Securing vehicular on-board IT systems: The EVITA project. In: VDI/VW Automotive Security Conference, p. 41 (2009)
7. ISO - International Organization for Standardization. IEC 61508 Functional safety of electrical/electronic/programmable electronic safety-related systems
8. ISO - International Organization for Standardization. IEC 60812 Analysis techniques for system reliability - Procedure for failure mode and effects analysis (FMEA) (2006)
9. ISO - International Organization for Standardization. IEC 61025 Fault tree analysis (FTA), December 2006
10. ISO - International Organization for Standardization. ISO 26262 Road vehicles Functional Safety Part 1–10 (2011)
11. ISO - International Organization for Standardization. ISO/SAE DIS 21434 Road Vehicles - Cybersecurity engineering (2020)
12. Krisper, M., Dobaj, J., Macher, G., Schmittner, C.: RISKEE: a risk-tree based method for assessing risk in cyber security. In: Walker, A., O'Connor, R.V., Messnarz, R. (eds.) EuroSPI 2019. CCIS, vol. 1060, pp. 45–56. Springer, Cham (2019). https://doi.org/10.1007/978-3-030-28005-5_4
13. Macher, G., Armengaud, E., Brenner, E., Kreiner, C.: A review of threat analysis and risk assessment methods in the automotive context. In: Skavhaug, A., Guiochet, J., Bitsch, F. (eds.) SAFECOMP 2016. LNCS, vol. 9922, pp. 130–141. Springer, Cham (2016). https://doi.org/10.1007/978-3-319-45477-1_11
14. Macher, G., Messnarz, R., Armengaud, A., Eric, A., Riel, A., Brenner, E., Kreiner, C.: Integrated safety and security development in the automotive domain. In: SAE Technical Paper. SAE International (2017)
15. Macher, G., Schmittner, C., Dobaj, J., Armengaud, E., Messnarz, R.: An integrated view on automotive spice, functional safety and cyber-security. In: SAE Technical Paper. SAE International, April 2020
16. Macher, G., Sporer, H., Berlach, R., Armengaud, E., Kreiner, C.: SAHARA: a security-aware hazard and risk analysis method. In: Design, Automation Test in Europe Conference Exhibition (DATE), pp. 621–624, March 2015
17. Macher, G., Sporer, H., Brenner, E., Kreiner, C., An automotive signal-layer security and trust-boundary identification approach. Procedia Comput. Sci. **109**, 490–497 (2017). 8th International Conference on Ambient Systems, Networks and Technologies, ANT-2017 and the 7th International Conference on Sustainable Energy Information Technology, SEIT 2017, 16–19 May 2017. Madeira, Portugal (2017)
18. Schmittner, C., Griessnig, G., Ma, Z.: Status of the development of ISO/SAE 21434. In: Larrucea, X., Santamaria, I., O'Connor, R.V., Messnarz, R. (eds.) Systems, Software and Services Process Improvement, vol. 896, pp. 504–513. Springer, Heidelberg (2018). https://doi.org/10.1007/978-3-319-97925-0_43

19. Schmittner, C., Gruber, T., Puschner, P., Schoitsch, E.: Security application of failure mode and effect analysis (FMEA). In: Bondavalli, A., Di Giandomenico, F. (eds.) SAFECOMP 2014. LNCS, vol. 8666, pp. 310–325. Springer, Cham (2014). https://doi.org/10.1007/978-3-319-10506-2_21
20. Schmittner, C., Ma, Z., Reyes, C., Dillinger, O., Puschner, P.: Using SAE J3061 for automotive security requirement engineering. In: Skavhaug, A., Guiochet, J., Schoitsch, E., Bitsch, F. (eds.) SAFECOMP 2016. LNCS, vol. 9923, pp. 157–170. Springer, Cham (2016). https://doi.org/10.1007/978-3-319-45480-1_13
21. Schmittner, C., Macher, G.: Automotive cybersecurity standards - relation and overview. In: Romanovsky, A., Troubitsyna, E., Gashi, I., Schoitsch, E., Bitsch, F. (eds.) Computer Safety. Reliability, and Security, pp. 153–165. Springer, Cham (2019). https://doi.org/10.1007/978-3-030-26250-1_12
22. Vehicle Electrical System Security Committee. SAE J3061 Cybersecurity Guidebook for Cyber-Physical Automotive Systems

WiCAR - Simulating Towards the Wireless Car

Harrison Kurunathan[✉], Ricardo Severino, Ênio Filho, and Eduardo Tovar

CISTER/INESC TEC and ISEP-IPP, Porto, Portugal
{hhkur,rarss,enpvf,emt}@isep.ipp.pt

Abstract. Advanced driving assistance systems (ADAS) pose stringent requirements to a system's control and communications, in terms of timeliness and reliability, hence, wireless communications have not been seriously considered a potential candidate for such deployments. However, recent developments in these technologies are supporting unprecedented levels of reliability and predictability. This can enable a new generation of ADAS systems with increased flexibility and the possibility of retrofitting older vehicles. However, to effectively test and validate these systems, there is a need for tools that can support the simulation of these complex communication infrastructures from the control and the networking perspective. This paper introduces a co-simulation framework that enables the simulation of an ADAS application scenario in these two fronts, analyzing the relationship between different vehicle dynamics and the delay required for the system to operate safely, exploring the performance limits of different wireless network configurations.

Keywords: Automotive · Safety · ADAS · Intra-vehicle communication · DSME · Robotic-network co-simulation

1 Introduction

In the past decade, Wireless Sensor Networks (WSN) have been widely adopted and supporting several innovative applications in a multitude of domains, such as in health, security, and agricultural. Nowadays, the increasing miniaturization of modern embedded systems, together with the advancements in the area of WSNs and energy harvesting, have opened up new possibilities to fit wireless communications into an unexpected series of applications. The automotive industry, has understandably been reluctant to adopt WSN, mostly pointing out its non-deterministic communication behaviour, unreliability due to interference and security issues. Therefore, wireless has been confined to some limited functionalities of infotainment systems and its adaption in critical systems has been non-existent in vehicles, although it has been already enabling a series of critical scenarios in other industrial domains.

The day-to-day automobile has gradually evolved from fully mechanical design to a fully electronically equipped modern car. The existing subsystems

© Springer Nature Switzerland AG 2020
A. Casimiro et al. (Eds.): SAFECOMP 2020 Workshops, LNCS 12235, pp. 136–147, 2020.
https://doi.org/10.1007/978-3-030-55583-2_10

of a modern car consist of several sensors and actuators that are coupled with hundreds of Electronic Control Units (ECU) that are interconnected through thick wired harnesses and communicate based on real-time communication protocols. These wired harnesses can increase the overall weight of the car resulting reduction of the performance of the vehicle in terms of fuel consumption. Thus, the excess weight of the car also can be extrapolated to an environmental issue.

Current trend, is to continue to increase the number of application modules and complexity in the vehicle, by fitting newer models with improved advanced driving assistance systems (ADAS) to increase their safety. However, this effort is not being applied to the millions of older vehicles that will continue to share the roads in the next 15 years, partially due to the tremendous complexity involved in retrofitting such vehicles. Wireless communications can potentially become an enabling technology to support such possibility, considering its flexibility and ease of deployment, by exploring the innovative plug-and-play possibilities introduced by these networked sensor networks. Ideally, additional sensing arrays could be introduced into the vehicle with minimum complexity, and without requiring complex re-wiring. However, ADAS pose stringent requirements to a system's control and communications, in terms of timeliness and reliability, and these properties must be ensured by the communications technology. The improvements to the low-power, low-rate IEEE 802.15.4 standard [1], introduced by the .e amendment, enables interesting features such as guaranteed bandwidth, deterministic delay and several other improved reliability support via the introduction of multi-channel techniques. These characteristics turn this communication technology as a prominent candidate to support wireless ADAS as well as other non-critical applications.

However, to effectively test and validate these systems, there is a need for tools that can support the simulation of these complex communication infrastructures from the control and the networking perspective, focusing on the interplay between these two dimensions. This paper introduces a co-simulation framework that enables the simulation of an ADAS application scenario in these two fronts, analyzing the relationship between vehicle dynamics, i.e. speed and braking force, and the delay required for the system to operate safely, exploring the performance limits of different network configurations of the DSME protocol.

The main contributions of this paper are as follows:

- We provide a co-simulation framework that joins a network simulator fitted with a DSME communications stack i.e. OmNet++/OpenDSME, with a robotics simulator i.e. Gazebo, that simulates the control and dynamics of a real vehicle.
- We implement a proof-of-concept Parking Assistance ADAS systems that relies on external sensors and wireless communications.
- We investigate the adequacy of the DSME MAC behavior of IEEE 802.15.4 for supporting the ADAS, and from the application perspective, we determine speed limits that guarantee the safety of the system.

2   Related Work

The research community has continuously looked into the possibility of using Wireless Sensor and Actuator Networks (WSANs) in intra-car communication. One of the foremost motivation for its implementation is to reduce the weight of the car and increase the overall performance in terms of fuel economy and reliability. Researchers in [2] investigated the design aspects of WSANs in intra-car systems and if whether they could become a viable solution to partially replace or enhance current wired measurement and control subsystems.

In [3], authors used IEEE 802.15.4 Compliant and ZigBee RF Transceivers to create a Blind Spot Information System (BLIS). BLIS systems implemented by many car manufacturers (e.g., General Motors, Ford, and Volvo) are based on costly hardware components such as cameras and radars. The proposed intra-car system in this work was non-intrusive at the same time cost-efficient. This work provided important information on the ideal location for sensors in an intra-car system, which we have adopted in our intra-car scenario depicted in Fig. 3.

Case studies such as [4] have proven that multi-hop has the potential for providing additional reliability, robustness, and energy usage improvements over existing single-hop approaches. In their study, they state that aggregating data in one or several processing centers in the vehicle is critical for the monitoring capabilities of the sensors, which are constrained by both energy and computational power. Multi-hop systems, despite its large overhead, can enhance system reliability, robust performance, and reduce communication energy. In our work, we look into a communication technology which features multi-hop and multi-channel capabilities and hence can enhance the performance of the network.

There have also been several simulation studies [5], [6] on implementing low power and low rate wireless sensor networks for intra-vehicle communications. These authors considered ZigBee to be a good candidate because of its mesh networking capabilities and low power consumption. Zigbee solves multi-path fading using Direct Sequence Spread Spectrum (DSSS) technology and interference resilience using Carrier Sense Multiple Access (CSMA). The propagation channel inside a vehicle is closed and is affected by the mechanical vibrations caused by the movement of the vehicle. Hence authors propose a simulation of the physical layer of the ZigBee network and the propagation channel inside a vehicle along with an adaptive equalizer at the receiver. Though Zigbee had mesh capabilities, determinism is not assured in such networks due to the usage of a contention-based mechanism for transmission. From our previous works [7, 8] we were able to confirm that DSME had the capability to communicate under strict time bounds and support time-critical applications. In this work, we rely on DSME which supports both a contention-based to be a possible candidate for intra-car communication systems.

3   Co-simulation Framework

Simulation of integrated application and network models can be done in diverse ways either by co-simulating with two different simulators, by expanding a network simulator with physical models [9] or by expanding the physical simulator with network model [10]. However, joining two, or more, well-proven simulators, in each particular area, can offer significant advantages. Kudelski et al. in their work [11] propose a an integrated framework to support multi-robot and network simulation. In this work the authors propose an integration of three simulators namely ARGoS [12], NS-2 and NS-3 that can be used in co-simulation scenarios. ARGoS is a ARGoS is a multi-physics robot simulator that can simulate large-scale swarms of robots of multiple variants. Similarly to the Gazebo simulator, which we use in our work, ARGoS can be extended with plugins, however, the integration of Gazebo with ROS constitutes an undeniable advantage, by providing flexibility, modularity, and easing robotics integration. NS-2 and NS-3 are legacy network simulators that can simulate a network stack. In this work the authors propose a synchronization approach between the simulators in which the number of nodes, characteristics of the equipment and simulation area a synchronized together. At every simulation step the ARGoS sends the updated robot position to the network simulator and the communication is carried our and is transferred back to the robotic simulator that the data packets are carried out. In our work, we take a similar approach by integrating Gazebo with OMNeT++++. In our case, we use the ROS sync application to handle the synchronization in our simulations as it will be shown in the next section.

BARAKA [13] is another co-simulator tool introduced by Thomas Halva Labella et al. In this work they provide a tool that is able to perform integrated simulation of communication networks using OMNeT++ and robotic aspects using Open Dynamics Engine (ODE) [14] for rigid-body physics simulation. The steps for integration in this simulation is done in two steps, they first integrate the collision/detection step loop in the OMNeT++. Then they create modules that simulate the robots and motes both in the physical aspects. Finally these modules are accessed by an agent program to control the behavior of the agents in the simulated world. The ODE loop in the OMNeT++ in this case has no connection to any other module in the simulation. In our work, for every simulation step, the simulators are synchronized in a seamless way by relying upon the ROS middleware and its topics. The flexibility of such middleware is tremendous and we use it for exchanging information between the simulators.

In this work we built a Wireless-ADAS co-simulation framework that combines the network simulation capabilities of OMNeT++/INET and the ability to emulate the vehicle physics and sensors behaviour in 3D scenarios using the Gazebo robotics simulator. This will enable us to analyze the mutual impact between the control and the networking aspects. The integration is done over the Robotics Operating System (ROS), based our previous works in [15,16] which focused on inter-vehicle communications (i.e. using ETSI ITS-G5) to enable a cooperative platooning function. A general Architecture for our framework is presented in Fig. 1. The integration of the network model is supported by the openDSME open-source framework [17] to implement the DSME protocol on top of the IEEE 802.15.4 physical layer. Two kinds of nodes are implemented in OMNeT++/INET simulation: the sensor nodes and the sink, corresponding to 8 end-devices and a PAN Coordinator respectively. In the OmNet++/INET side, the displayed outward 8 nodes (sensor nodes - IEEE 802.15.4 End Devices) correspond to the wireless radar/sonar modules implemented in the Gazebo vehicle model to achieve a 360 degree coverage of the vehicle without any blind spots. At the center of the layout, the "sink" node (IEEE 802.15.4 PAN Coordinator) is also displayed and corresponds to the Application Unit (AU) wireless interface. The AU is responsible for the ADAS system control implementation. It processes the sensor inputs and reacts accordingly, by interfacing the vehicle's steering and braking systems. To handle the synchronization between the two simulations, we developed a ROS Sync Application, which we describe next.

Synchronization Approach

OMNeT++ is an event-driven simulator and Gazebo a time-driven simulator, therefore synchronizing both simulators represented a key challenge. In order to accomplish this, a synchronization module was implemented in OMNeT++ to carry out this task, relying upon the ROS "'/Clock" topic as clock reference. The OMNeT++ synchronization module subscribes to ROS' "/Clock" topic, published at every Gazebo simulation step (i.e. every 1 ms) and proceeds to schedule a custom made OMNeT++ message for this purpose ("syncMsg") to an exact ROS time, which allows the OMNeT++ simulator engine to generate an event upon reaching that timestamp and be able to execute any other simulation process that must be run.

Data Workflow

In order to support data flowing between the Gazebo and OMNeT++ simulators, the ROS publish/subscribe middle-ware support was crucial. For each node in the OmNet++/INET simulation, there is a corresponding sensor in the Gazebo vehicle model which publishes its relevant data into a rostopic i.e. "/car1/sensors/sonar1". In the OmNet++/INET side, each node subscribes to the corresponding rostopic and prepares a message that is en-queued into the openDSME MAC layer to be transmitted to the sink node, which role is assumed by the network PAN Coordinator. OpenDSME handles the transmission and, if successful, the sink node publishes a rostopic with the sensor data that is subscribed by the AU. The AU then uses this input to feed its control loop. As for the Gazebo model, a Toyota Prius car model (visible at Fig. 1) is used as the baseline deployment for this WSN layout with 7 sonars and a radar. With this general layout architecture, different ADAS scenarios can be implemented, by changing sensors or their characteristics, the vehicle model, the track and the surrounding environment, enabling the possibility to extensively test and validate a ADAS behaviour and explore its performance limits pre-deployment.

For the upcoming ADAS, vehicles are increasingly being equipped with a wide variety of sensors, in order to get a good awareness of their surroundings. In addition, Sensors are already being deployed in current ADAS to evaluate the status of some of the vehicle components (i.e., steer, brakes) to detect stress and

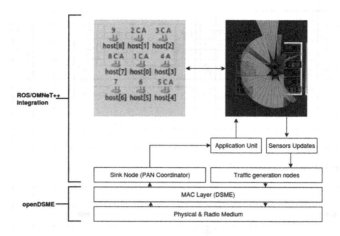

Fig. 1. Integration architecture

prevent any failure. In this framework, all these sensors, can be implemented in a vehicle model, and later be integrated into the network model as a new node that feeds data into the AU, for a integrated perspective of the system on a multitude of scenarios.

4 Network Specification

For our intra-car system, we used the DSME MAC behavior of IEEE 802.15.4e because of its deterministic capabilities. The DSME network provides deterministic communication using its beacon-enabled mode. This mode is supported by multisuperframes that may contain stacks of superframes, as shown in Fig. 2. Each superframe comprises a Contention Access Period (CAP) in which the nodes contend to access the channel and a Contention Free Period (CFP) in which the nodes send the data using Guaranteed timeslots (GTSs). It is in this period that the vehicle's sensors are accommodated, for guaranteed service.

The superframe is defined by BO, the Beacon Order which is the transmission interval of a beacon in a superframe. MO is the Multi superframe Order that represents the Enhanced Beacon interval of a multi-superframe, and SO is the Superframe Order that represents the beacon interval of a superframe. The number of superframes in a multisuperframe is given by 2^{MO-SO}. These values are conveyed to the nodes by an Enhanced Beacon (EB) at the beginning of each Multisuperframe. Reducing the values of SO and MO reduces the size of the timeslots and the number of superframes in a multi superframe duration, but also decreases the network's latency. In what follows we evaluate the relationship between such network settings and latency in the context of a ADAS application as a proof-of-concept.

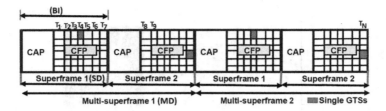

Fig. 2. DSME superframe

5   Performance Analysis

To showcase our proposal and simulation tool, we evaluate a parking lot Wireless
ADAS scenario presented in Fig. 3. When roaming inside a parking lot while
searching for a parking spot, a driver can suffer from decreased perception of
the overall environment. As his attention diverges from the driving actions into
his visual search for the parking space, his ability to respond to unexpected
situations is hindered, and may not be capable of perceiving an obstacle in time
to avoid it. In this case, we consider the obstacle as a car that suddenly exits a
parking space form the right-hand side of our vehicle. We push the requirements
of the scenario to a point in which a typical driver would be unable to stop the
car in time due to his reaction times. In this scenario, we consider the car can
be traveling up to 30 Km/h (typical maximum speed inside a parking lot) and
is fitted with an array of sensors covering a 360° field of view.

We evaluate this scenario from the two complementary perspectives. Firstly,
we take the application perspective, by varying the braking capacity of the vehicle and its speed, and then the network perspective, by varying the MO and SO
settings, and thus its worst-case delay. This is one of the greatest advantages
of our co-simulation tool, which enables a multi-dimensional assessment of an
application scenario.

5.1   Impact of Braking Force

Braking capacity is one of the common parameters in any car that deteriorates
over time. This is a result of the loss of friction in the clamping mechanism while
actuating a brake. In a 100% operational brake, the clamping load is assumed to
act on all friction surfaces equally. The loss in this force is only generated when
the wheel does not lock because the friction of a sliding wheel is much lower
than a rotating one.

In this experiment, we study the limits of this system by averaging the results
for several trials for different braking forces and calculating the maximum acceptable delay for the vehicle to operate without a crash. From the results in Fig. 4,
it is evident and expected, that the braking force and vehicle speed impose different requirements into the network delay. Decreased braking capacity or higher
speeds demand lower communication delays to avoid the crash. At 30 km/h, with

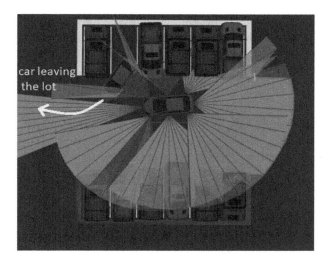

Fig. 3. Scenario taken for evaluation

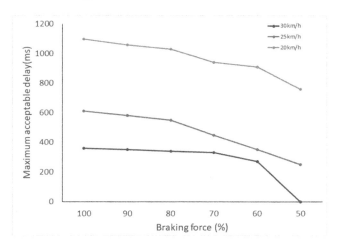

Fig. 4. Maximum acceptable delay for the braking force applied

a 50% braking capacity, the vehicle is unable to avoid hitting the car leaving the
parking space, independently of the delay. This is the point where we reach the
performance limit of the control system as dictated by vehicle dynamics.

5.2   Impact of Network Settings

We carried out several trials for these application settings, and different network MO/SO settings, to explore the performance limits of the Wireless ADAS
scenario. Figure 5 presents the communication's delay tolerances, for different

speeds (25 and 30 km/h) and braking capacities (100% to 50%), to prevent a crash, superimposed by the overall bounded delay at different network settings.

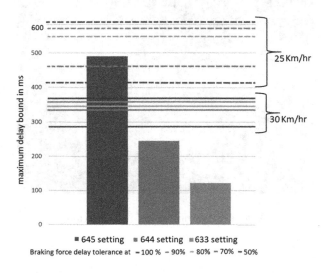

Fig. 5. Impact of static scheduling and braking force on the crash rate

As observed in Fig. 5, if the vehicle travels at 25 km/h in the parking lot, and has its braking capacity at 80%, it can still allow approximately 550 ms of delay in the ADAS communications; therefore, a (BO/SO/MO) = (6/4/5) setting suffices. This is important considering the usage of a higher MO can support the allocation of additional superframes and support additional nodes, particularly if CAP reduction is activated, increasing the scalability of the system. Thus finding this trade-of between delay and scalability, in parallel with speed and braking capacity, can lead to increased efficiency and safety. When the braking capacity reduces to 70 or 60%, the maximum acceptable delay decreases steeply and can only be met by lower MO/SO network settings. This is also the case for a speed of 30 Km/h, that even at 100% braking capacity, only (BO/SO/MO) = (6/4/4) settings or lower, can meet the imposed delay requirement of approximately 360 ms. These results show us that for those settings, at the targeted speed for our scenario of 30 km/h, our system can still guarantee the safety of the vehicle even with its braking capacity impaired by 50%.

5.3   Impact of Delay

One of the important prerequisite for the safe functioning of this scenario is the ability to adhere to a maximum speed limit of 30 Km/h. To achieve this we must be able to provide a maximum delay bound of 350 ms which is a crucial aspect for safe functioning. Hence, we must verify the determinism of the network. In the worst-case scenario, the maximum time a superframe can take to accommodate a transmission will be the size of the superframe. Hence by varying the size of the superframe, we will be able to control the latency of the network and determine definite bounds. The following experiment is carried out with (BO/MO/SO) = (6/4/4) setting with fixed static schedule. As previously mentioned, the results strictly adhere to the limit of the worst-case delay. We experience a maximum delay of 0.23 s and it is bounded as seen in Fig. 6. This also means we will be also able to operate the application at a steady speed of 30 km/h with a fixed delay using this setting.

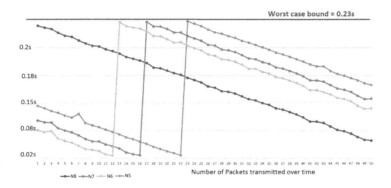

Fig. 6. Delay with Static scheduling for MO = 4 and SO = 4

The fluctuations of delay values in these static settings can be attributed to the arrival time of the packet. The packets that are served immediately with respect to its arrival result in a much lower delay. The worst-case delay is produced when the sensor data arrival happens at the end of the first superframe and gets scheduled for its adjacent superframe. One significant advantage of static scheduling is that the user has the possibility to vary the network settings and fix a steady worst-case bound based on the network prerequisite.

6   Conclusion and Future Scope

In this work we introduce a co-simulation tool that can combine both the network and the application perspectives of a realistic ADAS scenario. As a proof of concept, we provide a detailed delay analysis with the DSME network to evaluate its ability to meet the required deadlines for the control system. Furthermore, we also implemented a static scheduled network that can help in providing worst case delay deterministic bounds to ensure the safety of the system and explored it in our scenario at different speeds and braking capabilities. Preliminary results, show that the DSME network can cope with these, however, further exploration work is needed, and particularly a new more demanding scenarios with different sensors, vehicles, and speeds can and will be studied. Overall, the co-simulation framework proved to be up to the evaluation task and we are confident it will become mandatory tool to carryout a serious analysis of such networked ADAS systems.

Acknowledgements. This work was partially supported by National Funds through FCT/MCTES (Portuguese Foundation for Science and Technology), within the CISTER Research Unit (UIDB/04234/2020).

References

1. Kurunathan, H., Severino, R., Koubaa, A., Tovar, E.: IEEE 802.15. 4e in a nutshell: survey and performance evaluation. IEEE Commun. Surv. Tutorials **20**(3), 1989–2010 (2018)
2. Stamatescu, G., Popescu, D., Stamatescu, I.: Modeling for deployment techniques for intra-car wireless sensor networks. In: 2014 18th International Conference on System Theory, Control and Computing (ICSTCC), pp. 501–505. IEEE (2014)
3. Lin, J.-R., Talty, T., Tonguz, O.K.: Feasibility of safety applications based on intra-car wireless sensor networks: a case study. In: IEEE Vehicular Technology Conference (VTC Fall), pp. 1–5. IEEE (2011)
4. Hashemi, M., Si, W., Laifenfeld, M., Starobinski, D., Trachtenberg, A.: Intra-car multihop wireless sensor networking: a case study. IEEE Commun. Mag. **52**(12), 183–191 (2014)
5. Reddy, A.D.G., Ramkumar, B.: Simulation studies on zigbee network for in-vehicle wireless communications. In: 2014 International Conference on Computer Communication and Informatics, pp. 1–6. IEEE (2014)
6. Tsai, H.-M., Tonguz, O.K., Saraydar, C., Talty, T., Ames, M., Macdonald, A.: Zigbee-based intra-car wireless sensor networks: a case study. IEEE Wirel. Commun. **14**(6), 67–77 (2007)
7. Kurunathan, H., Severino, R., Koubâa, A., Tovar, E.: Worst-case bound analysis for the time-critical MAC behaviors of IEEE 802.15. 4e. In: IEEE 13th International Workshop on Factory Communication Systems (WFCS), pp. 1–9. IEEE (2017)
8. Kurunathan, H., Severino, R., Anis, K., Tovar, E.: Symphony: routing aware scheduling for DSME networks, pp. 26–31 (2020)
9. Ramos, D., Oliveira, L., Almeida, L., Moreno, U.: Network interference on cooperative mobile robots consensus. Robot 2015: Second Iberian Robotics Conference. AISC, vol. 417, pp. 651–663. Springer, Cham (2016). https://doi.org/10.1007/978-3-319-27146-0_50
10. Li, W., Zhang, X., Li, H.: Co-simulation platforms for co-design of networked control systems: an overview. Control Eng. Practice **23**, 44–56 (2014)
11. Kudelski, M., Gambardella, L.M., Di Caro, G.A.: Robonetsim: an integrated framework for multi-robot and network simulation. Robot. Auton. Syst. **61**(5), 483–496 (2013)
12. Pinciroli, C., et al.: Argos: a modular, parallel, multi-engine simulator for multi-robot systems. Swarm Intell. **6**(4), 271–295 (2012)
13. Labella, T.H., Dietrich, I., Dressler, F.: BARAKA: a hybrid simulator of SANETs. In: 2007 2nd International Conference on Communication Systems Software and Middleware, pp. 1–8. IEEE (2007)
14. Smith, R., et al.: Open dynamics engine (2005)

15. Vieira, B., Severino, R., Koubaa, A., Tovar, E.: Towards a realistic simulation framework for vehicular platooning applications. In: 22nd IEEE International Symposium on Real-Time Computing (ISORC 2019). Institute of Electrical and Electronics Engineers (2019)
16. Severino, R., Vasconcelos Filho, E., Vieira, B., Koubaa, A., Tovar, E.: COPADRIVe - a realistic simulation framework for cooperative autonomous driving applications. In: IEEE International Conference on Connected Vehicles and Expo (ICCVE) (IEEE ICCVE 2019), Graz, Austria, p. 2019, November 2019
17. Kauer, F., Köstler, M., Lübkert, T., Turau, V.: OpenDSME - a portable framework for reliable wireless sensor and actuator networks (demonstration). In: Proceedings of the 3rd International Conference on Networked Systems (NetSys 2017), March 2017

Automated Right of Way for Emergency Vehicles in C-ITS: An Analysis of Cyber-Security Risks

Lucie Langer[1]([✉]), Arndt Bonitz[1], Christoph Schmittner[1], and Stefan Ruehrup[2]

[1] Austrian Institute of Technology, Vienna 1210, Austria
{lucie.langer,arndt.bonitz,christoph.schmittner}@ait.ac.at
[2] ASFINAG, Vienna 1120, Austria
stefan.ruehrup@asfinag.at

Abstract. Cooperative Intelligent Transport Systems (C-ITS) provide comprehensive information and communication services to enable a more efficient and safe use of transport systems. Emergency vehicles can benefit from C-ITS by sending preemption requests to traffic lights or other connected road users, thus reducing their time loss when approaching an emergency. This, however, depends on a secure and reliable communication between all involved parties. Potential risks involve cyber-attacks and acts of sabotage. A major issue is the security process applied to provide C-ITS vehicles with the authorisations to exercise the right of way intended for emergency vehicles.

This paper presents results from the research project *EVE (Efficient right of way for emergency vehicles in C-ITS)*: Following the lifecycle and processes of the emergency vehicle and its on-board unit from installation to decommissioning, relevant use cases are subjected to an extended Failure Mode and Effects Analysis (FMEA) to assess inherent flaws that could be exploited by cyber-attacks. The results show that, while the technical provisions foreseen by the relevant standards in general provide strong security, detailed security management processes need to be specified.

Keywords: C-ITS · SSP · Risk analysis · FMEA · Emergency vehicle

1 Introduction

In our future transport systems vehicles will interact both with road infrastructure and with each other: Intelligent Transport Systems (ITS) are defined as "systems in which information and communication technologies are applied in the field of road transport, including infrastructure, vehicles and users, and in traffic management and mobility management, as well as for interfaces with

---

The work described in this paper was carried out as part of the project EVE funded by the Austrian Security Research Programme KIRAS.

A. Casimiro et al. (Eds.): SAFECOMP 2020 Workshops, LNCS 12235, pp. 148–160, 2020.
https://doi.org/10.1007/978-3-030-55583-2_11

other modes of transport" [18]. ITS use digital communication to exchange information about road works, hazardous locations, traffic rules etc., partially based on data provided by various sensors. Cooperative ITS (C-ITS) place additional demands on the communication equipment: "Cooperative" means that each ITS station (on-board or roadside) must be able to communicate ad hoc with other ITS stations and exchange relevant information in a trusted domain.

Currently emergency vehicles indicate the urgency of their mission by warning lights and siren. On a rescue mission they usually have the right of way, and may disregard traffic lights. However, exercising this right can be challenging for the driver, especially with dense urban traffic or multi-lane roads, and requires a significant slow-down. There are systems for traffic signal preemption that change the signal to give way to the approaching emergency vehicle. These systems are also used for public transport, and are implemented in different ways, resulting in country- or even city-specific solutions.

The Austrian research project *EVE (Efficient right of way for emergency vehicles in C-ITS)*[1] investigates how this situation could be improved by C-ITS: At signalised intersections (see Fig. 1) the emergency vehicle can send a preemption request to the traffic light controller or other connected vehicles. On a motorway, the efficiency of forming a rescue lane may be enhanced by announcing an approaching emergency vehicle. To prevent misuse, so-called Service-Specific Permissions (SSPs) limit the use of preemption requests to authorised parties.

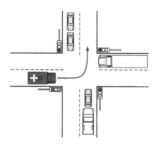

Fig. 1. Traffic signal preemption for emergency vehicles.

As C-ITS relies heavily on ad-hoc communication between the different participants, cybersecurity aspects play an important role: Tampering with C-ITS messages could, for example, cause drivers to react to fake events or follow incorrect rules, resulting in undesired or even unsafe driving behaviour. If an attacker obtains the Service-Specific Permissions reserved for emergency vehicles, he could use them for his own prioritisation or to disturb the overall traffic situation. C-ITS are therefore embedded in a comprehensive security and trust architecture to ensure the authorised use of C-ITS services. However, a high level

---

[1] https://kiras.at/en/financed-proposals/detail/d/eve-effiziente-bevorrangung-von-einsatzfahrzeugen-im-automatisierten-strassenverkehr/.

of security and safety of the target system can be ensured only by performing a comprehensive risk analysis and implementing according countermeasures.

This work presents a threat and risk analysis for prioritised emergency vehicles in C-ITS. Following the lifecycle of the emergency vehicle and its on-board unit from installation to decommissioning, relevant use cases have been subjected to an extended Failure Mode and Effects Analysis (FMEA) as part of the EVE project. The FMEA procedure and results are presented along the core use case, i.e., traffic signal preemption.

The paper is structured as follows: Sect. 2 summarises the state of the art in C-ITS, focusing on security aspects. Section 3 explains the methodology used for the risk analysis in the EVE project. Section 4 describes the risk analysis and evaluation results along the core use case of traffic signal preemption. Section 5 concludes the paper and provides an outlook on future work.

2   State of the Art

2.1   Status of C-ITS in Europe

C-ITS applications are currently being rolled out in Europe in mass production vehicles and in infrastructure deployments in several countries. The CAR-2-CAR Communication Consortium (C2C-CC) [28] has published profiles for C-ITS in vehicles based on standards and specifications from European Telecommunications Standards Institute (ETSI), European Committee for Standardization/International Organization for Standardization (CEN/ISO), Society of Automotive Engineers (SAE), and Institute of Electrical and Electronics Engineers (IEEE). For the infrastructure deployment, 18 EU Member states have joined the C-ROADS Platform which aims at cross-border harmonisation and interoperability for the roll-out C-ITS services. C-ROADS published a set of profiles that determine which ITS standards and which data elements and options should be used for the so-called Day-1 services, i.e., C-ITS services which should be available in the short term due to their expected societal benefits and technology maturity [1]. The profiles of C2C-CC and C-ROADS are coordinated to form a harmonised basis for Day-1 C-ITS services in Europe.

C-ROADS pilot deployments play an important role to launch the Europe-wide infrastructure roll-out. C-ROADS built on the experience from corridor projects, such as the Cooperative ITS Corridor between Rotterdam and Vienna [29], where the Austrian part ECo-AT [30] was characterised by a large set of use cases including road works and hazardous location warnings, as well as In-Vehicle Information (IVI) and Intersection Safety (ISS). In France, the SCOOP@F [31] project has equipped five pilot regions in France with C-ITS equipment since 2014. While most deployments target Day-1 or -1.5 use cases involving normal passenger vehicles, the specialised emergency vehicles and their specific use cases have only gained little attention.

The ITS Directive [18] provides the legal and technical framework for ITS within the European Union. It was followed by the European strategy on Cooperative Intelligent Transport Systems [5]. Based on this, the EC has initiated the

C-ITS platform in Phase I (2014–2016) [4] as a cooperative framework for developing a common European vision for the interoperable deployment of C-ITS. In Phase II (2016–2017) [6], the common vision for C-ITS was further developed towards Cooperative, Connected and Automated Mobility (CCAM).

2.2   Relevant C-ITS Services and C-ITS Security

ETSI TR 102 638 [13] defines a Basic Set of Applications (BSA) that reflect the main user needs and requirements. In the context of emergency vehicles, the following three services are important: The **Cooperative Awareness (CA) Basic Service** [11] allows road users to inform each other about their current position, velocity and other attributes. This service could be used by a vehicle to indicate its type (i.e., emergency vehicle) to other road users. The **Decentralised Environmental Notification (DEN) Basic Service** [10] supports informing road users about road hazards or abnormal traffic conditions, for example an approaching emergency vehicle or closed lanes on a motorway after an accident. Regarding infrastructure elements, [17] provides a set of services, including the **Traffic Light Control (TLC) Service** which enables the prioritisation of public transport and public safety vehicles at traffic lights.

The C-ITS **security architecture** defined in ETSI TS 102 940 and TS 102 941 [15,16] details a set of security requirements and a security (lifecycle) management system to establish the C-ITS trust model for the general communication architecture [9]. This trust model is based on a fully defined public key infrastructure (PKI), including concepts regarding Certificate Trust Lists with multiple Root Certificate Authorities and the revocation of certifications via Certificate Revocation Lists. With TS 103 097, ETSI also gives guidance on how to secure communication between road users and infrastructure elements [14]. For example, the **Service-Specific Permissions (SSPs)** transmitted as part of every ITS message ensure that only authorised ITS stations disseminate certain messages (for example, only an emergency vehicle may generate the DEN message *emergency vehicle approaching*). The PKI-based Certificate Policy [19] includes legal and technical requirements for the management of PKI certificates for C-ITS applications and all entities participating in the European C-ITS.

3   Methodology

With regard to EVE's focus on the ITS-S lifecycle and related processes, the risk analysis was performed through a process-based FMEA, which is an established method to systematically analyse each process step for potential risks, and has already been used for security analysis [23]. The attacks were classified according to the STRIDE model [22,24].

The first step of the analysis was to determine the lifecycle of the ITS station (ITS-S) from provisioning to decommissioning. Next, the processes defining each phase of the lifecycle were broken down into process steps and visualised in activity diagrams. This output was subsequently used for the process-based FMEA. Each of these steps is described in more detail in the following.

3.1   Lifecycle Definition

From a security point of view, the lifecycle of an ITS-S includes the initial configuration, enrolment, authorisation, operation[2], and end of life (see Fig. 2): The **initial configuration** of the ITS-S is done as part of the manufacturing process, and establishes information and key material in the ITS-S and the Enrolment Authority (see [16] for details). This information includes the designated *appPermissions* for the ITS-S, i.e. the C-ITS services that this ITS-S is permitted to use. For emergency vehicles, these may include sending DEN messages such as *emergency vehicle approaching* (cf. Sect. 2).

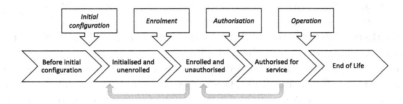

Fig. 2. ITS-S security lifecycle (cf. [16]).

In the **enrolment** phase, the initialised ITS-S requests its enrolment credential from the Enrolment Authority. For **authorisation**, the enrolled ITS-S uses this credential to request authorisation tickets from the Authorisation Authority, who checks with the Enrolment Authority whether the requested authorisations correspond to the approved *appPermissions* for that ITS-S.

During **operation**, the ITS-S communicates with other ITS-S. For each transmitted message the ITS-S uses an Authorisation Ticket to prove to the receiver that it is entitled to send that message and use the corresponding C-ITS service without revealing its identity. For the operation phase of the ITS-S lifecycle, two specific scenarios were considered for an emergency vehicle ITS-S: (i) requesting traffic signal pre-emption in urban areas (see Sect. 4) and (ii) requesting the formation of an ad-hoc emergency corridor on motorways (beyond the scope of this paper).

If the ITS-S has been compromised or has otherwise reached its **end of life**, it is passively revoked, i.e. the Enrolment Authority rejects any further authorisation requests for this ITS-S.

3.2   Process Analysis

For each of the ITS-S lifecycle phases, a process analysis was performed to identify the individual steps required to accomplish the target state. In order to ensure a structured procedure and to obtain an easily comprehensible overview of the processes, this breakdown into individual process steps was done by using

---

[2] Maintenance is not considered here.

UML activity diagrams for modelling (see Fig. 3) followed by a (textual) description of each process step. This analysis provided the basis for the subsequent process-based FMEA.

3.3 FMEA

The security analysis focuses on the processes relevant to the operation of emergency vehicles in a C-ITS environment. It is based on an extended FMEA, a structured technique that examines failure modes and effects. The aim is to identify potential weaknesses and improve the reliability, availability or safety of a system. The system or process under examination is hierarchically broken down into its basic elements and steps. Subsequently, the failure modes (i.e., error causes) of the elements are examined for causes and effects [21].

Originally, FMEA was aimed at the reliability or safety of hardware. It was later extended to cover additional topics like process analysis and security. The FMEA type used in this work is a process-based FMEA, which aims to identify possible weaknesses in production or performance processes. Since the focus is on security aspects, the FMEA method is applied in a slightly modified variant: If the failure of a component is caused by an attack, it is treated as a malfunction [27]. The main difference to the method presented in ETSI TR 102 893 "Intelligent Transport Systems (ITS); Security; Threat, Vulnerability and Risk Analysis (TVRA)" [12] is our focus on the process and lifecycle of the system which requires a different approach than the more technical system-focused approach presented in [12].

The FMEA is based on the outcomes of the process analysis (see Sect. 3.2). Each process step is analysed for potential attacks. For each attack, the potential causes and effects (or attack vectors) are listed. Control measures defined by the relevant ETSI specifications are considered as well as additional security measures that supplement or refine these provisions.

The risk assessment, i.e. determining the risk level pertaining to a certain attack vector, is based on the factors **likelihood, severity** and **detection probability**. Each factor is assigned a numerical value[3], and the product of these values gives a risk priority number (RPN), as standardised in [8]. In recent years there have been some reservations against the use of the RPN [2,3]; it is, however, a familiar concept and widely used in the automotive industry. While there are differing risk curves, depending on the multiplication or addition of the contributing values, the FMEA standard IEC 60812 [21] proposes to use multiplication for obtaining the RPN. In addition, with regard to our focus on the security of the underlying lifecycle processes, [7] supports using multiplication for RPN when assessing process-related risk.

The risk assessment was conducted by a group of experts from the EVE consortium and discussed in multiple workshops. To provide a structured assessment, two additional elements were considered: A classification of the attack

---

[3] The range is from *low* (1) to *high* (10) for severity and likelihood, and vice versa for detection probability.

according to the Microsoft STRIDE model [22,24], and an assessment of the most probable adversaries. Here, attacker profile archetypes, as defined by [26], have been used to guide the assessment. These profiles include *Basic User* (low skill, low resources, no direct aim to attack the system), *Cybercriminal* (advanced ICT skill, low skills for physical attacks, advanced tools, average financial resources), *Insider* (advanced system knowledge, access to physical properties, dedicated tools, but low financial resources), *Nation State* (high offensive skills, resources and determination, advanced tools, focus on stealth), and *Terrorist* (low offensive skills, average resources, focus on physical availability).

Since an exact assessment could not always be achieved for the three determining factors, the resulting RPN often is a number *range* rather than a single value: This is also due to the fact that severity depends strongly on the distribution of autonomous or semi-autonomous vehicles that can react automatically to falsified ITS messages and thus cause greater damage. Similar scenarios are also conceivable for likelihood and detection probability. Depending on the distribution of ITS-enabled road users, the probability of an attack and its detection increases. The resulting risk priority score nevertheless provides a good basis to point out potentially critical process steps.

4   Exemplary Use Case

This section describes the procedure and outcomes of our risk analysis for one specific use case part of the lifecycle phase *operation*: An emergency vehicle approaches an intersection with ITS-enabled traffic lights and requests signal preemption (cf. the *Emergency Vehicle Approaching* use case from the SCOOP project [20]). This use case focuses on two infrastructure services, the **Road and Lane Topology (RLT)** and **Traffic Light Maneuver (TLM)** services [17], with two main components: (i) the on-board unit (OBU) of the emergency vehicle and (ii) the road-side unit (RSU) of the traffic light installation at the intersection.

4.1   Exemplary Process Analysis

The first step is a process analysis (see Sect. 3.2) including a visual representation of all required process steps (see Fig. 3). Each process step is then described in more detail (see Table 1) to facilitate the FMEA.

4.2   Exemplary FMEA

Since presenting the full FMEA table for this example would exceed the scope of this paper, the individual results are presented in a simplified list below. For each process step, possible attack vectors are listed including a first classification according to STRIDE, followed by effects and causes (in this order), see Sect. 3.3.

– **PS-001 Drive towards intersection**: Out of scope as we only considered cyber-security attacks.

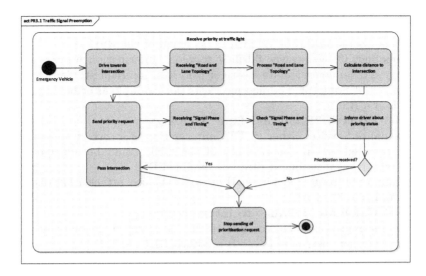

Fig. 3. UML activity diagram: traffic signal preemption for emergency vehicles.

Table 1. Process steps (PS) of the traffic signal preemption use case.

Process step	Description
PS-001 Drive towards intersection	Vehicle is approaching an intersection intending to cross it
PS-002 Receive "Road and Lane Topology"	OBU receives the road and lane topology transmitted by the RSU (Signal Phase And Timing Extended Message, SPATEM)
PS-003 Process "Road and Lane Topology"	OBU receives the topology information and checks it for correctness (authenticity)
PS-004 Calculate distance to intersection	OBU calculates distance to intersection using the topology information
PS-005 Send priority request	OBU sends priority request with Estimated Time of Arrival (ETA) to the RSU (Signal Request Extended Message, SREM)
PS-006 Receive "Signal Phase and Timing"	OBU receives "Signal Phase and Timing" of the RSU (Signal request Status Extended Message, SSEM)
PS-007 Check "Signal Phase and Timing"	OBU checks "Signal Phase and Timing" information for priority and authenticity status
PS-008 Inform driver about priority status	OBU informs driver via on-board display about status of prioritisation
PS-009 Pass intersection	Vehicle passes intersection
PS-010 Stop sending preemption request	OBU stops sending the preemption request once the intersection has been successfully crossed

- **PS-002 Receive "Road and Lane Topology"**:
  1. Denial of Service: OBU cannot receive topology information from RSU; Cause: attacker interferes with radio signal of the RSU
  2. Spoofing: OBU receives falsified topology information for the intersection and cannot calculate a correct prioritisation request; Cause: attacker sends out faulty or modified messages (for example after having compromised a RSU)
- **PS-003 Process "Road and Lane Topology"**:
  1. Denial of Service: either (i) RLT information is incorrect and cannot be distributed or (ii) the stability of the OBU could be affected; Cause: attacker has distributed (invalid) modified RLT
  2. Tampering: RLT model in OBU incorrect; Cause: attacker has distributed (valid) modified RLT
- **PS-004 Calculate distance to intersection**:
  - Tampering: Distance to intersection calculated incorrectly; Cause: attacker has distributed (valid) modified RLT
- **PS-005 Send priority request**:
  1. Denial of Service:
     (a) RSU cannot receive priority request; Cause: attacker interferes with radio signal of the OBU
     (b) RSU has incorrect arrival time, possible consequences for traffic; Cause: attacker modifies ETA on OBU side
  2. Elevation of Privilege: Vehicle is illegitimately prioritised; Cause: attacker pretends to be a vehicle on a rescue mission
- **PS-006 Receive "Signal Phase and Timing"**:
  1. Denial of Service: OBU cannot receive signal phase and timing (SPAT) information from RSU, vehicle cannot pass intersection; Cause: attacker interferes with radio signal (of the RSU)
  2. Spoofing: (i) Vehicle cannot pass intersection (ii) Vehicle attempts to pass intersection without prioritisation; Cause: attacker sends out faulty or modified SPAT information (must spoof signature)
- **PS-007 Check "Signal Phase and Timing"**:
  - Denial of Service: Could possibly affect the stability of the OBU; Cause: attacker has distributed modified RLT
- **PS-008 Inform driver about priority status**:
  - Tampering: Driver tries to pass an intersection assuming that he has been granted priority treatment; Cause: attacker modifies on-board display and shows incorrect prioritisation status (i.e., pretends that priority has been granted)
- **PS-009 Pass intersection**: Out of scope as we only considered cyber-security attacks.
- **PS-010 Stop sending of prioritisation request**:
  - Denial of Service: RSU continues to give priority, traffic disruption; Cause: attacker continues to send preemption requests

4.3 Risk Assessment and Results

Based on these attack vectors the actual risk assessment was performed by determining likelihood, severity and detection probability for each individual attack scenario (see Fig. 4 as an example for process steps PS-002, PS-003 and PS-006). The attacker profile and security measures provided for by the relevant ETSI specifications were taken into account as these can affect the individual values: For example, the use of cryptographically signed messages reduces the likelihood of a successful attack. In many cases it was difficult to pin down the individual scores to one exact number due to the lack of real-world large-scale C-ITS implementations which could provide reliable data. Therefore, number ranges were used instead (cf. Fig. 4). Risk priority scores with a particularly wide range were additionally discussed in expert workshops within the EVE consortium in order to narrow the range.

Process Step	Attacks Classification	Effects	Causes	Control & Mitigation	Attacker Profile	Likelihood	Severity	Detection Probability	RPN
PS-002 Receive Road and Lane Topology	Spoofing	OBU receives wrong topology information and fails to submit a valid preemption request	Attacker sends incorrect or modified messages (e.g., after having compromised a RSU)	Cryptographic protection of ITS messages (time stamps, signatures)	C	3-4	6-7	5-6	30-168
	Denial of Service	OBU cannot receive topology information from the RSU	Attacker jams radio signal from the RSU	n/a	T	5-6	4	3-4	36-96
PS-003 Process "Road and Lane Topology"	Denial of Service	RLT information is incorrect and cannot be distributed	Attacker has distributed (invalid) modified RLT	Cryptographic protection of ITS messages (time stamps, signatures)	C	3-4	4	3-4	36-64
		Could possibly affect the stability of the OBU			C	3-4	5-7	3-4	45-112
	Tampering	RLT model in OBU incorrect	Attacker has distributed (valid) modified RLT		C	2-4	8	3-4	54-144
PS-006 Receive Signal Phase and Timing	Denial of Service	OBU is unable to receive SPAT information from the RSU	Attacker jams RSU radio signal	n/a	T	5-6	3	7-8	104-144
	Spoofing	1. Vehicle cannot pass intersection 2. Vehicle tries to pass intersection without prioritization	Attacker sends out incorrect / modified SPAT information (must forge signature, therefore low probability of occurrence)	Cryptographic protection of ITS messages (time stamps, signatures)	C	2	4-6	5-6	40-72

Fig. 4. Analysis of process step PS-002 *Receive "Road and Lane Topology"*, PS-003 *Process "Road and Lane Topology"* and PS-006 Receive *"Signal Phase and Timing"*; Attacker Profile *C* refers to *Cybercriminal* and *T* to *Terrorist*, cf. Sect. 3.3.

The attack vectors with the highest risk priority scores of this exemplary use case apply to process steps **PS-002** (Receive "Road and Lane Topology"), **PS-003** (Process "Road and Lane Topology") and **PS-006** (Receive "Signal Phase and Timing"), see underlined values in Fig. 4: The risk posed by compromised road-side infrastructure is in general higher than the risk associated with compromised on-board units. While road infrastructure is more prone to tampering due to its easier accessibility, it is still managed by an infrastructure provider, and manipulations will probably be quickly detected. However, successful attacks may affect many other road users and therefore tend to be more severe than those targeted at on-board units of individual vehicles.

The relevant standards and guidelines suggest a number of countermeasures to minimise the risk from (cyber) threats. Additional countermeasures were defined as part of the process-based FMEA in EVE. Suggested countermeasures for the exemplary use case include system hardening of the ITS-S, i.e., removing all software components and functions that are not absolutely necessary for the ITS-S to perform its intended task. Secure software development techniques (e.g., input validation and sanitation) should be used to create the ITS-S software. Validating the achieved security level, for example through penetration tests and code reviews, can also help to ensure that the measures taken have been effectively implemented. Another countermeasure that applies specifically to the attack vector in process step PS-006 is anomaly detection for RSUs: Attacks to road-side infrastructure could be detected more efficiently by using systems that automatically report anomalies in the communication traffic between RSUs and OBUs. For example, an alarm could be triggered if no Common Awareness Messages (CAMs) from the OBUs of passing vehicles have been received by an RSU for several minutes at peak hours, possibly indicating a Denial of Service attack.

5   Conclusion and Outlook

Emergency vehicles can use the novel information and communication services provided by C-ITS to request right of way from infrastructure components or other connected road users, thus reducing the time loss when approaching an emergency. Cyber-attacks and acts of sabotage can, however, pose a significant risk to these scenarios, for example when attackers get hold of the credentials used for prioritisation. Our process-based FMEA shows that, while existing specifications and standards foresee a high level of security and reliability in general, they fall short of providing a full specification of security processes. Detailed procedures need to be defined for secure provisioning and decommissioning to ensure that unauthorised persons do not get hold of sensitive material. For Example, the Enrolment Authority must be informed in case an ITS-S has reached its end of life to prevent that it is used in an unauthorised way beyond the end of its lifecycle.

In addition, while there are standards, concrete guidance regarding security for infrastructure operators, automotive original equipment manufacturers (OEMs) and emergency fleet management organisations is still missing. One notable progress in this area is the recently published and approved Common Criteria Protection Profile for the C-ITS communication gateway in road work warning units [25]. This document provides not only guidance on the security measures the technical system should possess, it also includes Organisational Security Policies aimed at ensuring secure processes. While the Protection Profile for the C-ITS communication gateway in road work warning units has a rather restricted application area, it can provide the basis for a more general Protection Profile for C-ITS stations. Countermeasures that resulted from the process-based FMEA presented herein can be helpful when developing recommendations for such an extended Protection Profile.

References

1. C-ITS Platform Final Report, January 2016. https://ec.europa.eu/transport/sites/transport/files/themes/its/doc/c-its-platform-final-report-january-2016.pdf
2. Certa, A., Enea, M., Galante, G.M., La Fata, C.M.: An alternative to the risk priority number. ELECTRE TRI-based approach to the failure modes classification on the basis of risk parameters. Comput. Ind. Eng. **108**, 100–110 (2017)
3. Ciani, L., Guidi, G., Patrizi, G.: A critical comparison of alternative risk priority numbers in failure modes, effects, and criticality analysis. IEEE Access **7**, 92398–92409 (2019)
4. Commission, European: C-ITS Platform, Phase I. Final Report, Technical report (2016)
5. European Commission. COM 2016/766 A European strategy on Cooperative Intelligent Transport Systems, a milestone towards cooperative, connected and automated mobility (2016)
6. Commission, European: C-ITS Platform, Phase II. Final Report, Technical report (2017)
7. Bundesministerium des Innern/Bundesverwaltungsamt. Handbuch für Organisationsuntersuchungen und Personalbedarfsermittlung, February 2018
8. DIN EN ISO 13485:2010–01, Medizinprodukte – Qualitätsmanagementsysteme – Anforderungen für regulatorische Zwecke (2016)
9. ETSI EN 302 665 Intelligent Transport Systems (ITS); Communications Architecture V1.1.1. European Standard (2010)
10. ETSI EN 302 637–3 Intelligent Transport Systems (ITS); Vehicular Communications; Basic Set of Applications, Part 3: Specifications of Decentralized Environmental Notification Basic Service V1.2.1. European Standard (2014)
11. ETSI EN 302 637–2 Intelligent Transport Systems (ITS); Vehicular Communications; Basic Set of Applications, Part 2: Specifications of Cooperative Awareness Basic Service V1.4.1. European Standard (2019)
12. ETSI TR 102 893 Intelligent Transport Systems (ITS); Threat, Vulnerability and Risk Analysis (TVRA) V1.2.1. Technical Report (2017)
13. ETSI TS 102 637–1 Intelligent Transport Systems (ITS); Vehicular Communications; Basic Set of Applications; Part 1: Functional Requirements V1.1.1. Technical Specification (2010)
14. ETSI TS 103 097 Intelligent Transport Systems (ITS); Security; Security header and certificate formats V1.3.1. Technical Specification (2017)
15. ETSI TS 102 940 Intelligent Transport Systems (ITS); Security; ITS communications security architecture and security management V1.3.1. Technical Specification (2018)
16. ETSI TS 102 941 Intelligent Transport Systems (ITS); Security; Trust and Privacy Management V1.3.1. Technical Specification (2019)
17. ETSI TS 103 301 Intelligent Transport Systems (ITS); Vehicular Communications; Basic Set of Applications; Facilities layer protocols and communication requirements for infrastructure services V1.3.1. Technical Specification (2020)
18. Directive 2010/40/EU of the European Parliament and of the Council of 7: on the framework for the deployment of Intelligent Transport Systems in the field of road transport and for interfaces with other modes of transport. Official J. Eur. Union L **207**(296–308), 2010 (2010)
19. European Commission. Certificate Policy for Deployment and Operation of European Cooperative Intelligent Transport Systems (C-ITS)

20. Ministry for an Ecological, Transport Solidary Transition – Directorate General for Infrastructure, and the Sea (DGITM). C-ITS French Use Cases Catalog Functional descriptions. Technical Report
21. IEC 60812: Analysis techniques for system reliability: Procedure for failure mode and effects analysis (FMEA). International Standard (2006)
22. Kohnfelder, L., Garg, P.: The threats to our products. Microsoft Interface **33** (1999)
23. Lai, L.K.H., Chin, K.S.: Development of a failure mode and effects analysis based risk assessment tool for information security. Ind. Eng. Manag. Syst. **13**(1), 87–100 (2014)
24. Microsoft. The STRIDE Threat Model. https://docs.microsoft.com/en-us/previous-versions/commerce-server/ee823878(v=cs.20)
25. Niehöfer, B., Wagner, M., Berndt, S.: Protection Profile for a Road Works Warning Gateway v1.1. Common Criteria Protection Profile (2019)
26. Rocchetto, M., Tippenhauer, N.O.: On attacker models and profiles for cyber-physical systems. In: Askoxylakis, I., Ioannidis, S., Katsikas, S., Meadows, C. (eds.) European Symposium on Research in Computer Security, vol. 9879, pp. 427–449. Springer, Heidelberg (2016). https://doi.org/10.1007/978-3-319-45741-3_22
27. Schmittner, C., Gruber, T., Puschner, P., Schoitsch, E.: Security application of failure mode and effect analysis (FMEA). In: Bondavalli, A., Di Giandomenico, F. (eds.) SAFECOMP 2014. LNCS, vol. 8666, pp. 310–325. Springer, Cham (2014). https://doi.org/10.1007/978-3-319-10506-2_21
28. CAR 2 CAR Communication Consortium. https://www.car-2-car.org
29. Cooperative ITS Corridor. http://c-its-korridor.de/
30. ECo-AT. http://www.eco-at.info/
31. SCOOP@F Project. http://www.scoop.developpement-durable.gouv.fr/en/

Integrity Checking of Railway
Interlocking Firmware

Ronny Bäckman, Ian Oliver$^{(\boxtimes)}$, and Gabriela Limonta

Nokia Bell Labs, Espoo, Finland
{ronny.backman,ian.oliver,gabriela.limonta}@nokia-bell-labs.com

Abstract. While uses of trusted computing have concentrated on the boot process, system integrity and remote attestation of systems, little has been made on the higher use cases - particularly safety related domains - where integrity failures can have devastating consequences, eg: StuxNet and Triton. Understanding trusted systems and exploring their operation is complicated by the need for a core and hardware roots of trust, such as TPM module. This can be problematical, if not impossible to work with in some domains, such as Rail and Medicine, where such hardware is still unfamiliar. We construct a simulation environment to quickly prototype and explore trusted systems, as well as provide a safe means for exploring trust and integrity attacks in these vertical domains.

1 Introduction

The increasing use and implementation of digitalisation technologies and infrastructures enabled by the use of 5G communications, edge and far-edge computing into safety related and safety-critical verticals, such medical and rail, is inevitable. This brings an increasingly larger attack surface for a wide (and expanding) range of cybersecurity attacks. We can no longer rely upon network or device isolation as mechanisms to provide security - indeed the authors here argue that, except in some exceptional scenarios, there is no such thing as an isolated network.

The European Railway Agency (ERA) launched a study in 2018 amongst 10 countries to get an overview of the existing Command, Control and Signaling (CCS) systems. This was done to assist ERA with the deployment of European Rail Traffic Management System (ERTMS). ERTMS aims at replacing the different national train control and command systems in Europe [5,11]. The EN 50126 standard [3] specifies the CCS-systems safety and functional safety in railway applications. Key specifications are made for the development process [14]. While provision is made for maintenance, patching, update and system provisioning, implementation is left solely to the vendor or contractor that is in charge of maintenance [38]. These specifications furthermore do not touch upon the subject of platform trust, meaning integrity guarantees of hardware, firmware and software during the mentioned processes.

The Railway CCS-systems have been in the past vendor specific implementations for specific applications, components and interfaces to comply with

© Springer Nature Switzerland AG 2020
A. Casimiro et al. (Eds.): SAFECOMP 2020 Workshops, LNCS 12235, pp. 161–175, 2020.
https://doi.org/10.1007/978-3-030-55583-2_12

national specifications. This has made the systems hard to attack through from cyberspace. With new interoperability specifications in Europe and the demand to lower the cost of the old relay based systems, new standardized CCS-systems will emerge [32]. While vendors have already implemented remote maintenance on these systems, these are proprietary solutions that are protected by public key infrastructure if at all [10].

This paper is split into the following parts. We first describe the use of trusted computing technologies [28] to provide security and integrity guarantees and how this technology can be scaled up from its firmware roots into a larger scale set of trust services. We then describe how trusted computing can be utilised and investigated through the use of a simulation environment [29] and how this simulation environment can be utilised to accurately describe a railway signalling system. We then describe a simplified firmware or configuration attack upon a railway system. We then conclude with a discussion of the role of trusted computing and simulation in the railway environment and how it impacts how cybersecurity is viewed and how it can be utilised to develop sound cybersecurity procedures [15,16] with particular emphasis on the remote attestation and firmware tampering case.

2 Trusted Computing Concepts

A trusted system [1,33] can be defined as one that provides trusted execution environment (TEE) to the workload running on it *and* one where its integrity can be determined. A trusted execution environment is defined through the provisioning of one or more of the features listed below. We concentrate on the first point in this paper that a trusted system is one where the system and workload integrity can be checked and assured. Such facilities are usually integrated into processing environment and Trusted Platform Module (TPM) [6, 7].

- integrity measurement
- secure storage
- execution isolation
- authentication
- attestation
- physical location

The use cases for such mechanisms are based around integrity checking of the firmware, bootloader, operating system and application components as typically seen in systems using a TPM [2]. Other use cases relate to secure data storage, such as key management and disk encryption schemes. Further use cases such as DRM also exist though mainly in more specific areas such as found in embedded system software and mobile/telecommunications devices. In all of these cases there is an underlying reliance on a core root of trust which is provisioned typically through an initial set of measurement code and a measurement mechanism.

2.1   Platform Integrity and Boot

The x86 platform **measured boot** with legacy BIOS or UEFI is standardised by the TCG. The crucial point for establishing trust in a platform starts from the moment the platform is started. In the initial start up phase the first code to run on the platform is a process called the Core Root of Trust for Measurement (CRTM). The CRTM's purpose is to start a chain of trust, to accomplish this it needs to be able to control the environment of the platform in the initial phase.

The x86 platform boot and measurements are shown in Fig. 1. Measurements are taken during the phases of the boot, through to starting the required operating system. These measurements are written to the Platform Configuration Registers (PCRs) through a process of extension thus forming a simple Merkel Tree-like structure: $PCR_{new} := hash(PCR_{old}||new)$. The measurements are a mechanism to spot changes in the code and configuration of the firmware. Reference points need to be made of trusted states of these values by platform manufacturers, OEMs, vendors and customers.

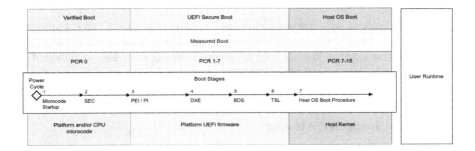

Fig. 1. Boot time measurements

2.2   Device Identity and Keys

The TPM provides key generation and storage features to provide unique keys which cannot be extracted. Incorporated in the TPM there are different seeds, which are multiple one-time programmable eFuses set during manufacturing time. These are used to create keys inside the TPM. Keys are protected in hierarchies as shown in Fig. 2 which can be locked during the manufacturing and supply-chain in a process called provisioning.

This combination of prior-provided keys can be utilised to form part of a device identity [4]. The TPM however provides two unique keys which themselves form the basis of the device's identity, these are known as the Endorsement (EK) and Attestation Keys (AK) and are used in a number of processes: the EK is effectively a root certificate and the AK - derived from this - is used in signing cryptographic measurements from the TPM.

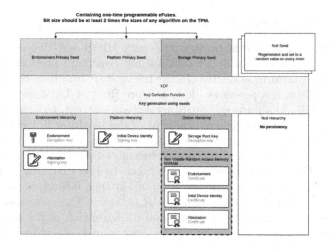

Fig. 2. Certificate and key storage for provisioning and attestation

The TPM uses an attestation structure - known as a quote - that contains a digest of one or more requested PCR measurements, certain device meta-data, the name of the signing key as well as limited nonce and user supplied data. This quote is also signed and verifiable against the TPM's specific attestation key further guaranteeing the provenance of the information.

2.3 Typical Integrity Attacks

Attacks against industrial control systems (ICS) can be described as cyber-physical attacks and they involve more layers than every day criminal attacks [9, 36]. The layers can be divided into an IT layer which is used to spread the malware, the control system layer which is used to manipulate process control and, finally, the physical layer where the actual damage is created.

Depending on the physical security of the system it can also be possible to directly target the Industrial Control System layer without touching the IT layer [37]. In railway systems the security of the control systems are not as high as in private production facilities. This makes the attack vector against the control system more compelling as has been seen with StuxNet and others [8,12,21,27].

One interesting approach to quantifying the amount of potential attacks against railway systems has been the HoneyTrain project [20][1] which has utilised a honey pot to simulate railway infrastructure [35]. While addressing a different area of security, specifically API attacks and denial of service, this approach has demonstrated clearly the amount of attacks (approximately 2.7 million individual attempts in one week in this study), the availability of attack vectors and the ease by which they might be utilised to deliver a much more destructive payload.

---

[1] https://news.sophos.com/de-de/2015/09/17/projekt-honeytrain-hackerwork/.

Combining attacks on the two lowest layers is also possible, especially if the levels are not properly secured. Tampering or substitution of sensors can provide useful outcomes when combined with tampered logic on the control level [39]. These attacks are many times possible due to lacking security protocols and procedures in these systems. Securing interconnections, cryptographic identities, configuration monitoring and signing are just a few things that always should be implemented on these systems but have not formally been used.

3   Simulation Environment

Tampering with railway signalling needs to be done in a controlled environment. We do not want real incidents to happen when testing. It is more secure, cost friendly and safer to simulate the system. When tampering with firmware on real devices there is a big risk that the system as a whole will not be recoverable. This section introduces a simulation framework that is utilised in the experimentation and attacking of the railway signalling system.

An overview of the framework can be seen in Fig. 3. Along with a management environment, each docker container corresponds to a real-World device with the addition of a set of tools to simulate the core root of trust, firmware and the measured boot process.

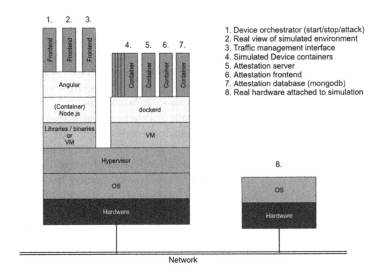

Fig. 3. Overview of simulation environment.

While providing a mechanism to develop simulated devices, it is also necessary for the simulation environment to provide two further services:

– Simulation Environment Management

– Attestation Services

The first refers to the functionality used to configure the devices and their communication (for rapid design, IP networking and MQTT message passing is used) and is utilised by the person in the role of setting up a simulation environment. The second contains the pre-built components specifically for the provisioning and remote attestation of the simulated (or real) trusted devices. These components are called by elements within the base containers automatically by the simulation environment. The remote attestation facilities would be presented to the users of the simulation as part of the cybersecurity forensics and failure detection processes.

4   Finnish Rail Traffic Management System

The Finnish rail traffic management system consists of four individual systems that work together: the interlocking, automatic train protection (JKV[2]), track vacancy monitor and the remote control system and is explained in [14].

The system uses track vacancy as the main safety criteria. A interlocking device takes the vacancy inputs and restricts traffic according to a predefined logic application. Trains are only allowed to move on tracks that are not occupied while speed is controlled by the interlocking system, partly through signalling and partly via track parameters.

There are two different methods for monitoring the track vacancy. The newer method is able to count train and carriage axles: if a carriage is broken loose from the train, the count between two sequential counters is not the same. The interlocking system will protect the track section between the counters and not let any trains pass. The older vacancy monitoring equipment depends on forming a track circuit; it can only report if the track section is occupied or not.

The interlocking system takes the inputs from the vacancy control system with the purpose to protect the railway environment by granting and prohibiting access for trains on track sections. Granting access is done by reserving track sections from the remote control system. A protective logic is implemented on the interlocking system that protects the rail environment from dangerous reservations. As an example it is not possible to reserve an already occupied track. It is not possible to reserve a soon to be occupied section, if stopping an incoming train is not possible.

Track switching is controlled by the interlocking system, so when a reservation is made and granted the track also switches to move the train to the designated endpoint. When the train moves on the reserved sections past vacancy control, track sections can be freed manually or even automatically. Track switches always try to protect the movement in a fail-safe manner, for example, if a stop signal is passed the train is routed to a free section.

The interlocking system is in charge of controlling all signals. The track side signals have three different modes *proceed, proceed 35* and *stop*[3]. These are shown

---

[2] [Automattinen] Junan Kulunvalvonta.
[3] The official Finnish terms are Aja, Aja35 and Seis.

by green, yellow/green and red lights on the physical track-side signal posts. An occupied track section is protected by a stop aspect, that section by a proceed 35 (warning) and that section by a proceed aspect. Other combinations are possible based on track speeds, train type (express vs freight), braking distances etc.

The Finnish automatic train protection system (JKV) is a second or additional signalling system that is installed on the train. It communicates with track side equipment, in this case a balise, which sends information to the train about the signalling and track information. The JKV system can react to lack of driver input and stop the train.

Safety is the sole purpose of the interlocking system, it takes the vacancy input, grants access to a remote control request if a safe passage can be routed, controls track side signals and data sent to the JKV system. Integrity of the interlocking system and the implemented logic is of high importance. When implementing an interlocking system it is tested, simulated and verified before production use. After it is put into use the interlocking integrity **is not actively monitored**.

5   Attacking the Trusted Railway Simulation

Attacking the firmware layer before the protective logic application can produce issues as described in [17,32]. Hardware initialization is done during the boot stage and this maps interfaces cards that produce outputs and take inputs from track side equipment. These inputs/outputs are in many cases analog and therefore can be directly swapped on the interlocking device. A trusted system would record the configuration measurements as cryptographic hashes of these components and write these to the TPM for subsequent remote attestation before admitting that device to the system.

For example a point device that controls the turnout of a train in a specific point could have 2 inputs and 2 outputs. The inputs tell the interlocking device where the pointing device turnout is. This is a simple analog circuit, if the circuit is closed the turnout is active. Through the outputs the turnout could be controlled. Note, this is intentionally (and maybe grossly) simplified - real systems rely upon multiple points within the interlocking to ensure functional integrity [23]; however the point here is to demonstrate a detectable misconfiguration in a digitalised system.

Swapping the input and output could - in the worst case - derail a train or cause a collision [34]. The interlocking device would believe that the turnout is connected to the correct track according to the application logic. However the input and output are swapped on firmware level, which of the application have no control of.

Firmware changes require a reboot of the device to take effect. Simulating device reboots with changes gives an opportunity to verify Traffic Management procedures so that right mitigation can be done and failed integrity can be corrected.

The mechanism for firmware updates typically requires a reboot of the system - this means that the effects of tampering can be hidden to take effect later and not directly after a reboot changes in the firmware which are measured during the measured boot are detectable and actionable once they have been reported to the attestation mechanisms. Indeed some cases of malware [26] have included secondary attacks embedded within these [13].

5.1   Attack Anatomy

An example scenario is seen in Fig. 4 which shows the user-interface to the railway management system. In the simulator this interface is provided by its own container and the track and signalling devices as well as the interlock(s) similarly by their own containers.

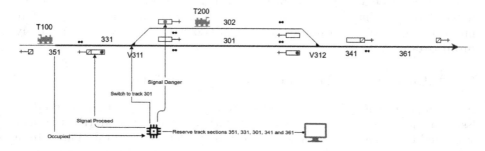

Fig. 4. Example of track section under attack

In this case we have a train (T100) approaching a switch (V311) set to enter track section (301). The signal protecting the switch (311) should display the appropriate aspect to allow the train to progress, typically a proceed or caution.

The attack upon this system - obviously relying upon digital components - is introduced by some vector as referenced earlier and need not be a direct attack against that device but also via some other attack medium. The attack here is designed to swap or misconfigure input and output signals. Figure 5 shows the input and output signals that will be mapped to each other in the attack. The delivery of the attack could further be made during normal maintenance operations [18]. The effect of swapping the input and output lines here would allow the train to cross the switch and enter the occupied section of track (302).

We introduce here three different attack triggers:

– Attacker triggers reboot after tampering.
– Passive reboot triggering waiting for maintenance reboot.
– Dynamic trigger activated a certain time after reboot.

As typical of firmware attacks, a reboot of the device is required to take effect. Either the reboot is directly triggered by the tampered firmware or we wait until a scheduled reboot is made.

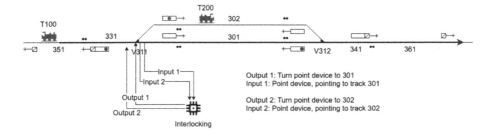

Fig. 5. Input-output signals that are flipped in the attack.

The first trigger would be activated directly after tampering the device firmware. Due to fail safe procedures, which should be monitoring for certain kinds of misconfiguration, every device connected to the interlocking device would go into fail safe mode when active signals from the device are removed. This assumes however that the particular misconfiguration is detectable and that the incorrect configurations have been properly characterised.

Although it depends upon the implementation of the interlocking device reboot, we can assume that most of the implementations would show a notice of the reboot which should trigger reattestation. As reboots are indicative of a potential reconfiguration detecting and accurately reporting on reboots and being able to provide forensics of why a reboot took place is a critical part of firmware integrity security.

From the traffic controllers perspective an interlocking device reboot would be identified, if the reboot activity is monitored. Otherwise the reboot would just show up/seem as a moment of downtime for the device. In our scenario it is possible to discover a short disruption of the interlocking device service. This can be discovered by every controlled track side device from that interlocking device to go into fail safe for the rebooting time. Depending on traffic management procedures mitigation would be done to resume normal operations.

Attacks could wait for a maintenance reboot from after which the configuration change would be in place. More advanced attacks could also do a dynamic mapping and implement a trigger for the swap to occur during normal operating hours. This makes reboot monitoring not a full covered mitigation to discover firmware tampering.

5.2 Measurement

Detecting firmware attacks depends upon the element being trustable and measuring relevant parameters. In our railway elements as we have built in the simulation we measure the firmware, the configuration of the firmware and then finally the configuration and static software (or hardware) elements that make up the configurable parts of the element. In this case we take cryptographic measurements of the input and output port configurations and these are loaded into the PCR registers on board the TPM.

In all of the above cases the TPM provides information about device reboots through monotonically increasing counters that indicate the amount of power cycles. These counters are reported as metadata during the acquisition of a device quote of its measured configuration. Further forensics are provided by the use of a 'safe' counter which provides information whether the TPM embedded in that device was cleanly shut down or not.

5.3   Mitigation

Controller software is mostly firmware that is upgraded by flashing after the device is rebooted. So firstly we will see a reboot of a device when attacked. If the devices are constantly monitored, there will be a short downtime off a device if it is rebooted. The best practice would be to attest the device as soon as possible after the reboot.

Attestation of a device can be made locally or remotely. In local attestation the device itself is responsible for checking the measurements made against locally stored known good values. This was the default mechanism used in the earlier TPM 1.2 devices which did not take into consideration larger, distributed systems. This local attestation mechanism is now largely deprecated and not used in TPM 2.0.

In the newer TPM 2.0 standard we either utilise remote attestation system and rely upon the attestation integrating with other parts of the system to report trust failures, or, we can *seal* certain information in the TPM's non-volatile RAM that can only be obtained if a correct configuration is measured. In reality both mechanisms need to be used though with more of a focus on the remote attestation occurs for reliability and relatively ease of use and configuration.

We have constructed a remote attestation and integrated that with the simulation environment for railway signalling described here. This has been adapted from an earlier system targeted towards telecommunication systems [22,29–31]. Each device reports its immutable identity (via its EK and AK keys) and its configuration to the remote attestation service. Figure 6 shows the attestation server and the basic device identity information.

Upon reboot of a device, the remote attestation server would communicate with the device and report that the device has failed the correct system measurements as shown in Fig. 7. This is achieved using the quoting mechanism described earlier. Here we can also see that the device still has a valid signature and that the quote returned by the TPM is both syntactically and semantically valid.

The remeasurement of a device may be triggered in a number of ways. Firstly the reboot might have been triggered by some other system and the attestation server notified to take measurements. The device itself may also trigger attestation by reporting explicitly its reboot. Depending upon the nature of the environment, communication and real-time properties either or both systems might be utilised.

In Fig. 7 we see that the device has failed its expected measurements test which is indicative of some change to the configuration. As we have mentioned

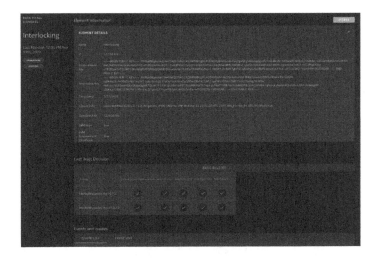

Fig. 6. Device identity

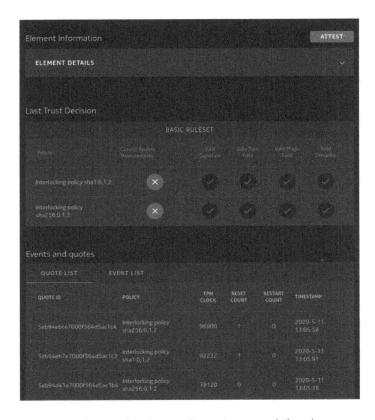

Fig. 7. Device showing configuration trust failure/error

other tests has passed successfully so we can be sure that the correct device is present.

Once we have identified a change in some measurements we proceed with the initial forensics where we examine the particular PCRs reported by the TPM as shown in Fig. 8. In this case we see that there has been a change in PCR1 which depending upon the semantics of the PCRs, at least on an x86 system, would indicate a change in the actual firmware itself.

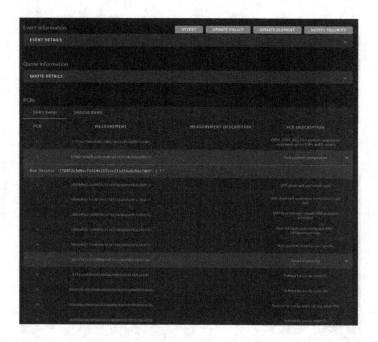

Fig. 8. TPM forensics using PCR listing

Further forensics can now start, for example examining the TPM boot logs exposed by the UEFI firmware on x86 machines. Similar mechanisms would have to be developed for other architectures, such as ARM, where this has not been standardised.

6   Conclusion

The work here has presented an attack on the integrity of a railway interlocking environment using the firmware and configuration of those systems in such a way - through simulation - that it causes changes in the measurable - in a trusted sense - aspects of the system. This allows us to safely understand the role of trusted computing in the firmware attack scenarios and develop techniques and plans to deal with such incidents.

This has been developed as the case study for a larger simulation environment for trusted systems. This provides us therefore with an educational environment where - in this case - railway signallers and control role operators can explore their reactions and develop mechanisms for the successful diagnosis and recovery.

Future work includes developing the scenarios shown in conjunction with trusted hardware and remote attestation specifically designed for safety-critical systems. It must be pointed out that dealing with trust failures is relatively novel and an unexplored area. Beyond preliminary investigations into root cause analysis there is currently no mechanism for trust failure forensics, analysis and recovery - especially in the case of safety critical systems [24].

A number of aspects have come out of this work so far which require more discussion. Firstly the response to a failure in a safety-critical system can not be a reboot/reinstall or taking that element out of usage [19]; instead a more sophisticated mechanism of managed degradation of functionality put in place. In the signalling case this might require manual intervention and imposition of procedures such as 'drive on sight.'

The real-time characteristics and data transmission restrictions also come into play. The size of a TPM quote is around 1000 bytes, but the time to generate, sign and check a quote might take a number of seconds [25]. So while the reporting of attestation information is well within specifications such as the EuroBalise data transmission specification, the real-time properties present significant problems to the obtaining of timely information. If a quote take 3 s to generate and check, then a high speed train at 300 kmh will travel approximately 250 m during that time. Even at slower speeds this might prove to be a significant obstacle especially when mitigation mechanisms need to put into place.

Finally handling of trust failures needs to be properly developed. While integration of cybersecurity procedures into normal railway signalling procedures is starting to happen, trust failure forensics and management is undeveloped. We have examined how root cause analysis can be integrated and automated with the remote attestation at least in the telecommunications server environment. Extending this into rail and other safety-critical domain use cases is ongoing.

Acknowledgements. This work has been partially funded by EU ECSEL Project SECREDAS (Grant Number: 783119).

References

1. Trusted computing platform alliance main specification. Trusted Computing Group (2002)
2. Trusted platform module library, part 1: architecture. Trusted Computing Group (2016). Version Number: Level 00 Revision 01.38
3. EN 50126–1. European Committee for Electronic Standardization (2017)
4. TCG TPM v2.0 Provisioning Guidance. Trusted Computing Group (2017). Version Number: 1.0
5. Hybrid ERTMS/ETCS Level 3. EEIG ERTMS Users Group (2018). Version Number: 1C

6. TCG PC Client Platform Firmware Profile. Trusted Computing Group (2019). Version Number: Level 00 Revision 1.04
7. TCG PC Client Platform Firmware Profile Specification. Trusted Computing Group, June 2019. Version Number: 1.04
8. Assante, M.J., Conway, T., Lee, R.M.: German steel mill cyber attack. Technical report, SANS Industrial Control Systems (2014)
9. Basnight, Z., Butts, J., Lopez Jr., J., Dube, T.: Firmware modification attacks on programmable logic controllers. Int. J. Crit. Infrastruct. Prot. **6**(2), 76–84 (2013)
10. Bastow, M.D.: Cyber security of the railway signalling & control system (2014)
11. Buurmans, K., Koopmans, M., Rijlaarsdam, R., Es, A.V., Vliet, M.V.: Feasibility study reference system ERTMS: final report, digitalisation of CCS (control command and signalling) and migration to ERTMS. Techreport, European Railway Agency (2018)
12. Falliere, N., Murchu, L.O., Chien, E.: W32.Stuxnet dossier. Technical report (2011). Volume: Version 1.4
13. Gotora, T.T., Zvarevashe, K., Nandan, P.: A survey on the security fight against ransomware and Trojans in Android. Int. J. Innov. Res. Comput. Commun. Eng. **2**(5), 4115–4123 (2014)
14. Kantamaa, V.M., Sorsimo, T.: Rautatieturvalaitteet. Otavan Kirjapaino Oy (2018)
15. Karjalainen, M., Kokkonen, T., Puuska, S.: Pedagogical aspects of cyber security exercises. In: 2019 IEEE European Symposium on Security and Privacy Workshops (EuroS&PW), pp. 103–108. IEEE (2019)
16. Kokkonen, T., Hautamäki, J., Siltanen, J., Hämäläinen, T.: Model for sharing the information of cyber security situation awareness between organizations. In: 2016 23rd International Conference on Telecommunications (ICT), pp. 1–5. IEEE (2016)
17. Konstantinou, C., Maniatakos, M.: Impact of firmware modification attacks on power systems field devices. In: 2015 IEEE International Conference on Smart Grid Communications (SmartGridComm), pp. 283–288. IEEE (2015)
18. Kour, R., Aljumaili, M., Karim, R., Tretten, P.: eMaintenance in railways: issues and challenges in cybersecurity. Proc. Inst. Mech. Eng. Part F J. Rail Rapid Transit **233**(10), 1012–1022 (2019)
19. Kour, R., Thaduri, A., Karim, R.: Railway defender kill chain to predict and detect cyber-attacks. J. Cyber Secur. Mobil. **9**(1), 47–90 (2020)
20. Kühner, H., Seider, D.: Security engineering für den schienenverkehr. In: Eisenbahn Ingenieur Kompendium, pp. 245–264 (2018)
21. Langner, R.: To kill a centrifuge. Technical report, The Langner Group (2013)
22. Hippelainen, L., Oliver, I., Lal, S.: Towards dependably detecting geolocation of cloud servers. In: 2nd International Workshop on Security of Internet of Everything, SECIOE 2017, Helsinki, Finland. IEEE, August 2017
23. Lim, H.W., Temple, W.G., Tran, B.A.N., Chen, B., Kalbarczyk, Z., Zhou, J.: Data integrity threats and countermeasures in railway spot transmission systems. ACM Trans. Cyber-Phys. Syst. **4**(1), 1–26 (2019)
24. Limonta, G., Oliver, I.: Analyzing trust failures in safety critical systems. In: Proceedings of the 29th European Safety and Reliability Conference (ESREL) (2019)
25. Limonta Marquez, G.: Using remote attestation of trust for computer forensics. Master's thesis, 10 December 2018
26. Mago, M., Madyira, F.F.: Ransomware software: case of wannacry. Eng. Sci. **3**(1), 258–261 (2018)
27. Matrosov, A., Rodionov, E., Bratus, S.: Rootkits and Bootkits. No Strach Press Inc., San Francisco (2019)

28. Oliver, I., et al.: Experiences in trusted cloud computing. In: Yan, Z., Molva, R., Mazurczyk, W., Kantola, R. (eds.) NSS 2017. LNCS, vol. 10394, pp. 19–30. Springer, Cham (2017). https://doi.org/10.1007/978-3-319-64701-2_2
29. Oliver, I., et al.: A testbed for trusted telecommunications systems in a safety critical environment. In: Gallina, B., Skavhaug, A., Schoitsch, E., Bitsch, F. (eds.) SAFECOMP 2018. LNCS, vol. 11094, pp. 87–98. Springer, Cham (2018). https://doi.org/10.1007/978-3-319-99229-7_9
30. Oliver, I., Lal, S., Ravidas, S., Taleb, T.: Assuring virtual network function image integrity and host sealing in telco cloud. In: IEEE ICC 2017, Paris, France, May 2017
31. Oliver, I., Ravidas, S., Hippeläinen, L., Lal, S.: Incorporating trust in NFVI: addressing the challenges. In: Proceedings of 20th Innovations in Clouds, Internet and Networks Conference, ICIN 2017, Paris, France (2017)
32. Pasquale, T., Rosaria, E., Pietro, M., Antonio, O., Ferroviario, A.S.: Hazard analysis of complex distributed railway systems. In: 2003 Proceedings of the 22nd International Symposium on Reliable Distributed Systems, pp. 283–292. IEEE (2003)
33. Proudler, G., Plaquin, D., Chen, L., Balacheff, B., Pearson, S.: Trusted Computing Platforms: TCPA Technology in Context. Prentice Hall, Upper Saddle River (2002)
34. Anthony Hidden, Q.C.: Investiation into the Clapham junction railway accident. UK Department of Transport, November 1989
35. Schindler, S., Schnor, B.: Honeypot architectures for IPv6 networks. Ph.D. thesis, Universität Potsdam, Mathematisch-Naturwissenschaftliche Fakultät (2016)
36. Schuett, C., Butts, J., Dunlap, S.: An evaluation of modification attacks on programmable logic controllers. Int. J. Crit. Infrastruct. Prot. **7**(1), 61–68 (2014)
37. Shila, D.M., Geng, P., Lovett, T.: I can detect you: using intrusion checkers to resist malicious firmware attacks. In: 2016 IEEE Symposium on Technologies for Homeland Security (HST), pp. 1–6. IEEE (2016)
38. Stumpp, K.: Draft of the security-by-design and of railway cyber security management system standards. Technical report, European Union Funding for Research and Innovation (2019)
39. Thaduri, A., Aljumaili, M., Kour, R., Karim, R.: Cybersecurity for eMaintenance in railway infrastructure: risks and consequences. Int. J. Syst. Assur. Eng. Manag. **10**(2), 149–159 (2019). https://doi.org/10.1007/s13198-019-00778-w

LoRaWAN with HSM as a Security Improvement for Agriculture Applications

Reinhard Kloibhofer[1]($\boxtimes$), Erwin Kristen[1], and Luca Davoli[2]

[1] AIT Austrian Institute of Technology GmbH, Giefinggasse 4, 1210 Vienna, Austria
{reinhard.kloibhofer,erwin.kristen}@ait.ac.at
[2] Internet of Things (IoT) Lab, Department of Engineering and Architecture,
University of Parma, Parco Area delle Scienze 181/A, 43124 Parma, Italy
luca.davoli@unipr.it

Abstract. The digital future in agriculture has started a long time ago, with Smart Farming and Agriculture 4.0 being synonyms that describe the change in this domain. Digitalization stands for the needed technology to realize the transformation from conventional to modern agriculture. The continuously monitoring of all environmental data and the recording of all work parameters enables data collections, which are used for precise decision making and the planning of in-time missions. To guarantee secure and genuine data, appropriate data security measures must be provided.

This paper will present a research work in the EU AFarCloud project. It introduces the important LoRaWAN data communication technology for the transmission of sensor data and to present a concept for improving data security and protection of sensor nodes. Data and device protection are becoming increasingly important, particularly around LoRaWAN applications in agriculture.

In the first part, a general assessment of the security situation in modern agriculture, data encryption methods, and the LoRaWAN data communication technology, will be presented.

Then, the paper explains the security improvement concept by using a Hardware Secure Module (HSM), which not only improves the data security but also prevents device manipulations. A real system implementation (Security Evaluation Demonstrator, SED) helps to validate the correctness and the correct function of the advanced security improvement.

Finally, an outlook on necessary future works declares what should be done in order to make the digital agriculture safe and secure in the same extent as Industrial Control Systems (ICSs) will be today.

Keywords: LoRaWAN · Trusted Platform Module (TPM) · Internet of Things (IoT) · Cyber-Physical Systems (CPS) · Safety & Security · Agriculture

1 Introduction

This paper aims to bring a reader closer to the importance of Long Range Wide Area Network (LoRaWAN) technology for the transmission of digital data and to present a

© Springer Nature Switzerland AG 2020
A. Casimiro et al. (Eds.): SAFECOMP 2020 Workshops, LNCS 12235, pp. 176–188, 2020.
https://doi.org/10.1007/978-3-030-55583-2_13

concept for improved data protection, which, in turn, is becoming increasingly important, particularly around LoRaWAN-based applications in agriculture.

LoRaWAN has triumphed in recent years when it comes to periodically transferring small amounts of data over long distances [1]. This type of short- and medium-range data transmissions is gaining more and more importance in data and commands' distribution for sensors and actuators at the field level and in Internet of Things (IoT)-oriented contexts [2]. A special application area will be the modern agriculture domain, where different sensors, directly installed on the field, deliver environmental data to support finding correct decisions for the exact mission planning in time.

However, the increasing digitalization in agriculture and the associated networking of machines and production systems increase the risk of cyber-attacks. Especially, by widely distributed production facilities (at field level) in agriculture and the network supported interaction with the Information Technology (IT) world, new points of attack have been disclosed. This technical progress allows an easier penetration of attackers to the production facility, manipulating it and even impairing safety (e.g., machinery safety).

A new important aspect of modern agriculture is the fact that the above-mentioned field level becomes more and more powerful. Today's field devices are highly integrated and powerful electronic processing systems, with high-performance computing capabilities, firmware updates and maintenance interfaces. The attractiveness for cyber security attacks and field device misusing is expected to rise.

IoT security deals with different types of threats. The following list summarizes the most critical vulnerabilities.

- Espionage: this vulnerability type focuses on collecting data from the cyber-attacked victim. The data is used to gain secret knowledge or to obtain information in order to prepare further attacks, e.g., theft of sensor data.
- Destruction and Exaction: the goal of this vulnerability is to perform data adulteration or produce system damage, e.g., falsification of the original sensor data.
- Sabotage: the goal of this vulnerability is to reduce or prevent correct system operations, e.g., shortening battery life by permanently activating the sensor node.
- Misuse: the goal of this vulnerability is the unauthorized use of system equipments to perform criminal actions, such as building botnets and kidnapping of foreign computers for Distributed Denial-of-Service (DDoS) attacks. An example of this kind of vulnerability is the installation of malware.

Important countermeasures are the early detection of attacks, the encryption of transmitted data and the protection against unauthorized device access by using a login procedure (e.g., with usernames and passwords, as well as based on tokens).

2   Data Encryption with Symmetric and Asymmetric Keys

The data transmission from a sender to one or multiple receivers, as well as the data storage, must be protected against eavesdropping and manipulation. Therefore, there is the need of encryption algorithms, which are a set of mathematical procedures for performing encryption tasks on data. With the use of such algorithms, data will be transformed to ciphertext through a secret key, thus requiring the use of the same or another secret key to transforming data back into its original form. Moreover, through cryptography the data is transformed so that it cannot be read or understood by an eavesdropper, while only the trusted receiver, who has permissions, can transform the ciphertext to the original data (by using the secret key). This technique is old and used from the Roman times (e.g., through the Caesar cypher).

To encrypt and decrypt, it is possible to distinguish between (i) symmetric encryption and (ii) asymmetric encryption. The symmetric encryption represents the simpler way and is characterized by the fact that keys for encryption and decryption are identical, as shown in Fig. 1. In this case, both sender and receiver must have the same secret key, which, in turn, must be generated and exchanged at least at communication channel or storage's setup time. Another problem regards the protection of this key against unauthorized read-out or distribution. Examples of symmetric encryption algorithms are Blowfish, Advanced Encryption Standard (AES), and Data Encryption Standard (DES). The most commonly used algorithms are AES-128, AES-192, and AES-256, where the number denotes the key length in bits.

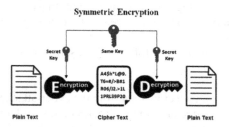

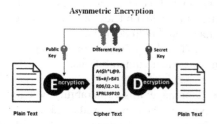

Fig. 1. Symmetric encryption (Source: https://www.ssl2buy.com/wiki/symmetric-vs-asymmetric-encryption-what-are-differences)

Fig. 2. Asymmetric encryption (Source: https://www.ssl2buy.com/wiki/symmetric-vs-asymmetric-encryption-what-are-differences)

A more complex encryption schema is represented by the usage of asymmetric encryption, which is a relatively new method. In this case, the keys for encryption and decryption are different, and denoted as private and public keys, as shown in Fig. 2. The public key, used for encryption purposes, is made freely available and can be distributed to everyone who wants to encrypt data for the receiver. Instead, the private key is known only by the receiver and will be never distributed to anyone else. A message that is encrypted using the public key can only be decrypted using its paired private key, while a message encrypted using the private key can be decrypted using the public key. Security of the public key is not required, it can be stored and sent unsecured. Asymmetric keys improve the security of information transmitted during communication.

In current Internet communications, asymmetric encryption is the most commonly used technique for securing the data transfer.

3   Overview on LoRaWAN

LoRaWAN is a Media Access Control (MAC) protocol for Wide Area Networks (WANs) [3]. A focus in the design of LoRaWAN was to allow low-power devices to communicate with a LoRaWAN server, leading to the involvement in Low-Power WANs (LPWANs). LoRaWAN is implemented on top of the LoRa modulation in the Industrial, Scientific and Medical (ISM) radio bands. The specification can be found on the LoRa Alliance website,[1] while its network architecture is shown in Fig. 3.

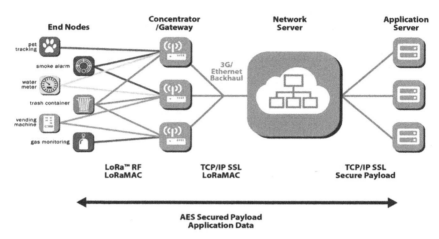

Fig. 3. LoRaWAN network architecture (Source: https://lora-alliance.org/sites/default/files/2018-04/what-is-lorawan.pdf)

Instead, LoRa represents the physical layer of a communication protocol able to support long-range communication and is based on Chirp Spread Spectrum (CSS) modulation [4], which significantly increases the communication range, if compared to Frequency Shift Keying (FSK) modulation. CSS has been used in military applications for long time, but LoRa is the first low-cost implementation available for commercial use, allowing data transmissions over distances up to 10 km.

While many existing deployed networks follow the mesh network approach, where each end-node is also used to forward messages from other nodes to extend the transmission range, LoRaWAN uses a star topology. This saves battery life of the end-nodes because they do not act as gateways (GWs). Moreover, a LoRaWAN end-node is not associated with a specific GW since, in a well-designed operating environment, uplink data from an end-device are received by multiple intermediate GWs and forwarded to the Network Server (NS). Hence, the NS can handle multiple copies of data, performs security checks, schedules acknowledgements, manages the back channel from the Application Server (AS) to the end-node, and decides over which GW the back communication will be performed.

---

[1] Source: https://lora-alliance.org/.

End-nodes can work asynchronously, meaning that they can wake-up and communicate when they have new data. For receiving downlink data from the server, the end-node opens the receiver interface at pre-defined time windows. This operating mode, defined as Class A, helps to save battery power and enables an operation time for up to 10 years with a single battery cell. Other operating modes can set the end-node to continuously open the receiver interface to react faster to commands from the server, thus consuming more battery power and therefore lowering the battery lifetime.

Regarding security and encryption, in LoRaWAN they are performed in both the network and application layers [5], as illustrated in Fig. 4. The network security enables authenticity of the end-node in the network, while the application security protects data between end-nodes and the AS. Moreover, the network layer does not have access to application data and, for both layers, AES-based symmetric encryption is used, being well-analysed, approved by the National Institute of Standards and Technology (NIST), and widely used.

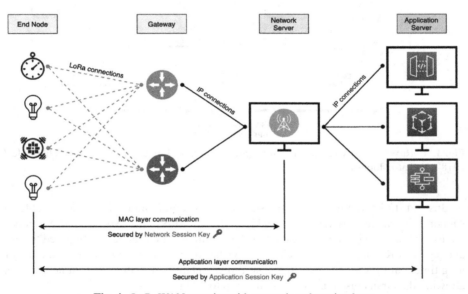

Fig. 4. LoRaWAN security with network and session keys

For data encryption and decryption, Network Session Key (NwkSKey) and Application Session Key (AppSKey) are used. These keys should be strongly protected against hacking and misuse in either end-node, NS, and AS.

For setting-up a LoRaWAN network and the application, NwkSKey and AppSKey must be generated and exchanged among the different network devices (end-node, NS, and AS) through two different techniques (defined in the LoRaWAN standard):

- Over-The-Air-Activation (OTAA): this is the preferred and most secure way, since an end-node communicates with the NS to perform the activation process, denoted as join procedure. According to the LoRaWAN specifications, the OTAA mode is used when an end-node is already deployed, or after a reset.

• Activation By Personalisation (ABP): in this mode, the session keys are pre-stored in the end-node and the servers (NS and AS). This activation might seem simpler, because the join procedure is skipped, but it has some disadvantages related to security aspects.

In both activation modes, root keys and session keys must be protected. On the server side, a Key Management (KM) system can be used [6], while on the end-node, the protection of the keys is more challenging. In order to furtherly improve the security, a periodical keys alteration is recommended, in order to prevent a successfully security key theft via brute force methods.

4   Security Module

A Trusted Platform Module (TPM, also known as ISO/IEC 11889-1:2015 [7]) is a device provided with a secure cryptographic processor, that is a dedicated microcontroller designed to secure hardware through integrated cryptographic keys. Once enabled on a system, the TPM can provide full disk encryption capabilities. Moreover, it becomes the "root of trust" for the system to provide integrity and authentication of the boot process, and keeps hard drives locked/sealed until the system completes a system verification, or authentication check. The TPM includes a unique Rivest-Shamir-Adleman (RSA)-based security key burned into it, used for asymmetric encryption. Additionally, it can generate, store, and protect other keys used in the encryption and decryption process. A TPM is normally integrated in the system hardware (HW) and cannot be removed; without the TPM, the system cannot work. A Hardware Security Module (HSM) is like a TPM, but it can also be added or connected later to the host system, by a connector, and it can perform the same security features as a TPM.

The security module adopted for the implementation purposes in this paper is an HSM called Zymkey 4i [8] and produced by Zymbit Corporation. As shown in Fig. 5, it is a small-scale module which is designed to work with Raspberry Pi (series 3 and 4) boards. However, it can also be connected to other microcontrollers or host systems.

Fig. 5. Zymkey 4i module (Source: https://community.zymbit.com/t/getting-started-with-zymkey-4i/202)

The Zymkey HSM has multiple security layers to protect against cyber and physical threats. A secure element (SE), as part of the HSM, with micro-grid protected silicon stores sensitive resources, while a security supervisor isolates the SE from the host computer and provides additional functions of multi-factor identity/authentication for devices and physical security. The key features of the Zymkey module are the following.

- Multi Device Identification and Authentication: Zymkey enables remote confirmation of the HW configuration of the host device. It has a unique Identification (ID) token that was created with several device-specific parameters. Cryptographically-derived ID tokens are never made available to customers.
- Data Integrity, Encryption & Signing: the cryptographic engine uses some of the strongest encryption functions available on the market to encrypt, sign and authenticate data. These includes Elliptic Curve Digital Signature Algorithm (ECDSA), Elliptic-Curve Diffie–Hellman (ECDH), Advanced Encryption Standard (AES-256), Secure Hash Algorithm (SHA256). It also incorporates a True Random Number Generation (TRNG).
- Key Security, Generation & Storage: the module can store key pairs in tamper-resistant silicon to support different security services. Multiple key slots can be used. There are pre-defined and user slots available. Once generated, private keys are never exposed outside of the silicon and therefore cannot be copied, or keys can be stored in the module which will be erased depending on security policy.
- Physical Tamper Detection: the module monitors the physical environment for symptoms of physical tampering (Perimeter Detection). This includes the supervision of interrupting or break of two independent wire loops. A physical intrusion into a device (like a sensor) can be monitored. Optional accelerometers detect shock or fast orientation changes. Also, the quality of the power supply can be monitored.
- Real Time Clock (RTC): the Zymkey includes a battery-backed RTC to support off-grid applications.
- Ultra-Low Power Operation: the module delivers long-term autonomous security from a built-in battery.
- Secure Element Hardware Root of Trust: the Zymkey provides different layers of hardware security, having a dual secure-processor architecture in which it is hard to penetrate.

Each module has a unique Serial Number (SN). When the Zymkey module is paired to a host system, the host platform's SN and the Secure Digital (SD) card's SN will be stored together with the unique ID in the Zymkey crypto accelerator chip. After the pairing process (binding), the module is only linked to the host system. For development purposes, a temporary binding is possible. After cutting a lock tab on the module (as shown in Fig. 6), the binding is permanent, and the module cannot be used on another host. If the host's File System (FS) is encrypted with the module through Linux Unified Key Setup (LUKS), then the FS can only be read with the module connected to the host.

Fig. 6. Lock tab of the Zymkey module

5 Implementation of HSM in a LoRaWAN End-Node

As explained in Sect. 1, security for digital data communication is a very important topic. Especially for agriculture sensor-based applications, where the physical space is not enclosed and protected as in industrial applications. Sensors are exposed in or near agriculture fields and can be stolen and then manipulated in a laboratory environment. For medium or wide agriculture environments, it is very important that both devices and data cannot be manipulated in any way, so that the whole agriculture output is not endangered.

About this, there are different types of vulnerabilities for deployed sensors, that can be improved with the use of a security element in the end-device:

1. move the sensor from the intended location;
2. physical integrity of the sensors;
3. reuse the HW for manipulation of the agriculture environment;
4. manipulate communication data.

A widely used protocol for semi-automated agriculture application is the LoRaWAN protocol, because this protocol is designed for long-range communication with small data amounts and for long-time battery use. LoRaWAN also has good security features using symmetric AES encryption and decryption on network and application layers. But, as explained in Sect. 2, encryption and decryption keys must be protected against read-out and manipulation from hackers.

5.1 Secure Evaluation Demonstrator

In the EU AFarCloud project,[2] one topic is the analysis and improvement of security in agriculture applications. Therefore, the Security Evaluation Demonstrator (SED) is under development to demonstrate how security improvements can be archived.

Figure 7 illustrates the block diagram of the SED. There are two main blocks: the "Farm" block, which represents the farm environment, and the "Cloud" block, with processing and data repository services. The Farm can be further divided in "Sensors" and "Edge" sections. The first one comprises one LoRaWAN-oriented sensor with TPM, while the second sensor only provides LoRaWAN communications. Sensor data are received by Gateway 1, a GW with integrated LoRaWAN NS and AS, and Gateway 2, a GW acting as a LoRaWAN forwarder. Gateway 1 transfers sensor data over the internal router, while an Internet Service Provider (ISP) modem, via MQTT protocol, send them to a Cloud-based MQTT broker with Data Repository. Gateway 2 performs the data transfer to the Cloud-based Data Repository via the LoRaWAN protocol. In the second case, LoRaWAN NS and AS in the Cloud are used. While by the first data transmission to the Cloud, data are ciphered with asymmetric encryption, data for the second transmission are protected with symmetric encryption. Finally, a firewall (FW) serves as an additional farm protection shield, for example commands and firmware updates.

---

[2] Source: http://www.afarcloud.eu/.

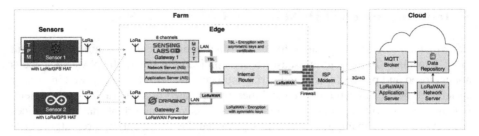

Fig. 7. Secure evaluation demonstrator

5.2 Hardware Implementation

The sensor nodes of the SED are both built-up with a Raspberry Pi [9] (Sensor 1) and an Arduino platform [10] (Sensor 2). The more powerful sensor node, Sensor 1, is built as a sandwich construction around a Raspberry Pi with a LoRa shield attached and equipped with an HSM on top. The use of two different add-on boards, sharing the same control lines, results in a problem in most cases. Thus, a physical separation of the chip select control lines on the Raspberry Pi board was necessary here, as shown in Fig. 8.

Fig. 8. Hardware implementation of the developed sensor

5.3 LoRaWAN Implementation

For the LoRaWAN software implementation, in C/C++ there are free available LoraMAC-in-C (LMIC) [11] software libraries useable for OTAA and ABP. In the proposed deployment, initially OTAA has been used, thus having three secret root keys before the activation is completed (AppKey, 64 bit; DevEUI, 64 bit; and AppKey, 128 bit) and two additional secret session keys after a successful activation of the end-node in the LoRaWAN network (NwkSKey, 128 bit; and AppSKey, 128 bit).

In the free sample software codes, the root keys are hard-coded, meaning that, if the source code is stored in the end-device, an intruder can read these keys and use them in a duplicated device. If only the compiled code is on the end-device, these root keys are still in the code and can be extracted to use them in a duplicated device.

The session keys are generated during the activation process and are stored in RAM during the execution, and could be read out, too, but a much higher technical effort is needed.

5.4 HSM Integration

With the integration of a Zymkey HSM on the Raspberry Pi, the protection of the secret keys can be considerably increased. There are two possibilities for protecting keys with this module: (i) save the keys inside the module, or (ii) encrypt the secret keys using the HSM and store the encrypted keys on the Raspberry Pi. In both cases, the HSM must be firstly paired to the Raspberry Pi.

In the proposed deployment, the second method has been adopted, meaning the encryption of the three root keys. The decryption of these keys is only possible if there is an access to the HSM. The executing software has access to the HSM and the keys, but not a hacker without authentication. For the implementation of the encryption and decryption of secret keys, the HSM provides libraries for C/C++ and Python. With the C/C++ library, the key can be encrypted (locked) and decrypted (unlocked). The session keys are not encrypted in the first version, but in an advanced version these keys should also be encrypted or stored in the HSM and not in RAM.

An additional (and higher) protection of the end-device is performed by encrypting the overall file system of the Raspberry Pi on the SD card with LUKS. With the Zymkey HSM, the key for the encryption of the file system will be stored directly inside the module and can't be read-out by an intruder.

For protection against end-device movement, the integrated GPS module of the LoRa shield has been used. In an outdoor scenario (like an agricultural environment), the GPS position will be measured at fixed time intervals. If the GPS position changed because the normally fixed sensor is moved, the software will block the wireless LoRa communication. The server should trigger an alarm if the communication of a sensor is lost for a longer time.

A physical security feature for the end-device is the module's tamper detection, implemented by using two physical wire loops which are arranged around the inner side of the sensor case. A physical manipulation of the case will interrupt one of the loops, which triggers an alert, while the software continuously monitors the status of the two wire loops.

6 Results and Expectations in Agriculture Applications

The SED is currently under construction and already well-advanced. Many implemented functions already work to full satisfaction. The following four tests are planned and in preparation, in order to verify the extended security functionalities.

1. Move the end-device from the intended location.
   In this test, the sensor is exposed outdoor with the GPS function activated. If the sensor is moved more than 100 m (location change event), or if the GPS position is not available, then the sensor triggers an alarm and interrupt the communication.
2. Physical integrity of end-nodes.
   The sensor is packed in a case together with a battery pack. Two wire loops are connected to the HSM and placed in a way that the wire loop will be destroyed if the case is opened. By cutting the tab of the HSM the device will be "armed" (thus recognizing a "close-then-open" event on one or two of the perimeter wire loops). Then, the "zymkey_perimeter_event_action" parameter will be set to "self_destruct". If the device will be opened, which is only possible by cutting one of the wire loops, the HSM will be irrevocable destroyed and the sensor cannot be used any more.
3. Reuse the hardware for manipulation of the agriculture environment.
   Once at least one of the wire loops is opened, the keys in the module are destroyed. No more access to the Raspberry Pi or the FS is possible after extracting the coin cell of the module and restarting the sensor. Then, it is not possible to read the SD card because it is encrypted with the (destroyed) keys of the HSM.
4. Manipulate the communication data.
   This test must be done before destroying the keys in the module. The LoRaWAN sensor is set-up and powered. The OTAA procedure is executed automatically and the sensor sends data to the LoRaWAN server. Without authentication to the Raspberry Pi it is not possible to read any root key or session key. The session keys are never transferred via the LoRa link but generated on the end-device and on the server side from other keys plus some parameters generated by the LoRaWAN server. It is not possible to extract the key from the communication.

Modern agriculture systems are more and more essentially software-driven automation systems, including farm management centres, data storages, powerfully edge computers for the interaction with the devices in the field domain. The field domain is in the most cases located in the open field, far away and outside of protected areas.

In the field there are several networked vehicles, which are supported by a continuously data stream of commands and control data for guidance and assistance, and a collection of different smart sensors, which register all relevant environmental parameters and data for decision finding. These smart sensors are becoming increasingly complex, supporting a great number of features. Hence, sensors not only measure the environment around, but also perform data pre-processing, data forwarding, battery monitoring, firmware update and many other functions [12]. These powerful mini-PCs in the field are very attractive for cyber-attacks in the future.

Today's field elements have already reached a high level of technical complexity and must consequently be protected in future applications, and it is hoped that security protection proposals and concepts, as described in this paper, will become more and more important.

7   Outlook

There is currently a need to define cyber-security guidelines for modern agriculture (Agriculture 4.0), such as those already developed for industrial control systems in the European Union (EU). While in the USA the United States Department of Homeland Security (DHS) has carried out research during the last years to identify potential cyber-security vulnerabilities for agriculture, in Europe, however, a similar investigation does not appear to have taken place. Authors in [13] focus on many industries to show the risks and the need of monitoring support to ensure cyber-security; but the modern agriculture domain is not included. Even in the EU publication [14] from Q4 2017, smart farming and cyber-security are not addressed.

Acknowledgments. This work has received funding from AFarCloud which is an ECSEL Joint Undertaking (JU) project under grant agreement No. 783221. The JU receives support from the European Union's Horizon 2020 research and innovation programme and Austria, Belgium, Czech Republic, Finland, Germany, Greece, Italy, Latvia, Norway, Poland, Portugal, Spain, Sweden.

Parts of this work were funded by the Austrian Research Promotion Agency (FFG) and BMK (Austrian Federal Ministry for Climate Action, Environment, Energy, Mobility, Innovation and Technology).

The work of Luca Davoli is partially funded by the University of Parma, under "Iniziative di Sostegno alla Ricerca di Ateneo" program, "Multi-interface IoT sYstems for Multi-layer Information Processing" (MIoTYMIP) project.

Federal Ministry
Republic of Austria
Climate Action, Environment,
Energy, Mobility,
Innovation and Technology

References

1. Grunwald, A., Schaarschmidt, M., Westerkamp, C.: LoRaWAN in rural context: use cases and opportunities for agricultural businesses. In: Mobile Communication - Technologies and Applications; 24. ITG-Symposium, Osnabrueck, Germany (2019). https://ieeexplore.ieee.org/abstract/document/8731787. Accessed 03 June 2020
2. Shenoy, J., Pingle, Y.: IoT in agriculture. In: 2016 3rd International Conference on Computing for Sustainable Global Development (INDIACom), New Delhi, India (2016). https://ieeexplore.ieee.org/abstract/document/7724508. Accessed 03 June 2020
3. LoRa Alliance. LoRaWAN 1.1 Specification. http://lora-alliance.org/lorawan-for-developers. Accessed 02 May 2020
4. Reynders, B., Pollin, S.: Chirp spread spectrum as a modulation technique for long range communication. In: 2016 Symposium on Communications and Vehicular Technologies (SCVT), Mons, pp. 1–5 (2016). https://doi.org/10.1109/scvt.2016.7797659
5. Eldefrawy, M., Butun, I., Pereira, N., Gidlund, M.: Formal security analysis of LoRaWAN. Comput. Netw. **148**, 328–339 (2018). https://doi.org/10.1016/j.comnet.2018.11.017
6. Naoui, S., Elhdhili, M., Saidane, L.: Trusted third party based key management for enhancing LoRaWAN security. In: 2017 IEEE/ACS 14th International Conference on Computer Systems and Applications (AICCSA), Hammamet, pp. 1306–1313 (2017). https://doi.org/10.1109/aiccsa.2017.73

7. ISO/IEC 11889. Information technology—Trusted platform module library. https://www.iso.org/standard/66510.html. Accessed 03 June 2020
8. Zymkey 4i, Hardware security module for Raspberry-Pi. https://www.zymbit.com/wp-content/uploads/2018/12/Zymbit-Data-Sheet-Zymkey-4i-DATA-SHEET-04100910A2.pdf. Accessed 03 June 2020
9. Raspberry Pi, Single Board computer, developed in the United Kingdom by the Raspberry Pi Foundation. https://www.raspberrypi.org/. Accessed 03 June 2020
10. Arduino platform, Open-source platform for single-board microcontroller kits. https://www.arduino.cc/. Accessed 03 June 2020
11. LoraMAC libraries. A LoRaWAN end-device stack implementation. https://github.com/Lora-net/LoRaMac-node. Accessed 03 June 2020
12. Codeluppi, G., et al.: LoRaFarM: A LoRaWAN-Based Smart Farming Modular IoT Architecture. Sensors, **20**(7), 2028, 1–24 (2020). https://doi.org/10.3390/s20072028
13. Nai-Fovino, I., et al.: European Cybersecurity Centres of Expertise Map - Definitions and Taxonomy. https://doi.org/10.2760/622400
14. Directorate-General for Agriculture and Rural Development (European Commission), ECO-RYS, Wageningen Economic Research. Study on risk management in EU agriculture. https://doi.org/10.2762/08778

1st International Workshop on Dependable Development-Operation Continuum Methods for Dependable Cyber-Physical System (DepDevOps 2020)

1st International Workshop on Dependable Development-Operation Continuum Methods for Dependable Cyber-Physical Systems (DepDevOps 2020)

Miren Illarramendi[1], Haris Isakovic[2], Aitor Arrieta[1], and Irune Agirre[3]

[1] Software and Systems Enginering, Mondragon Unibertsitatea,
Mondragon-Arrasate, Spain
{millarramendi,aarrieta}@mondragon.edu
[2] Computer Engineering, Cyber-Physical Systems,
Technische Univeristat Wien, Viena, Austria
haris@vmars.tuwien.ac.at
[3] Dependable Embedded Systems, Ikerlan Research Centre,
Mondragon-Arrasate, Spain
iagirre@ikerlan.es

1 Introduction

In recent years it has become evident that the use of software to perform critical functions is on the rise. As a result, dependable embedded systems are getting more intelligent and automated. For instance, the automotive industry is a clear witness of this trend, where more and more Advanced Driver-Assistance Services (ADAS) are already embedded in cars. This results in a dramatic increase of software complexity, which also requires hardware platforms with higher computing power. All these trends hinder the safety certification, as it is increasingly difficult to guarantee at design time that system errors are prevented or controlled in such a way that there will be no unreasonable risk associated to the electrical/electronic system component at operation time. These challenges are leading to the need for new development practices that reduce the overall system development time and costs without compromising safety and certification.

The rise of new connection technologies (e.g., 5G) bring new opportunities in terms of the download of frequent software updates of new (improved) releases and sending back operation-time information for fixing bugs and enhance the design. Advances done in new development practices like DevOps have shown effectiveness in software development while reducing overall development costs. The DevOps paradigm aims at having seamless methods for the Design-Operation Continuum of software systems. This paradigm has shown promising results in different domains, including web and mobile engineering. Its practices can bring several advantages to dependable CPSs, including bug fixing based on operational data, inclusion of new functionalities, etc.

However, in the context of dependable CPSs, several challenges arise, requiring DevOps paradigms to have adaptions from several perspectives: the environment in which the CPS operates needs to be considered when updating the software, dependability of software needs to be ensured to a certain level, software fault might lead to severe damages, etc. Furthermore, the safety-critical industry has well established safety-lifecycles dictated by safety standards and adopting the DevOps paradigm has several open research challenges.

The International Workshop on Dependable Development-Operation Continuum Methods for Dependable Cyber-Physical Systems (DepDevOps) is dedicated to explore new ideas on dependability challenges brought by over-the-air-software updates to the critical domain, with special focus on safety, security, availability, and platform complexity of emerging dependable autonomous systems. This is a fundamental step for the adoption of DevOps approaches in dependable embedded systems. Over the air updates can bring several benefits to dependable Cyber-Physical Systems, like solving security vulnerabilities, adding new functionalities or bug fixing and they are a key enabler for improving the design based on operation time data. In addition to this, the workshop aims to identify novel tools and architectures that enable the developers implement a streamlined and automatic workflow that makes methods and tools to be seamlessly used during design phases as well as in operation.

The first edition of DepDevOps was held as part of the 39th International Conference on Computer Safety, Reliability, & Security (SAFECOMP 2020).

2 H2020 Projects: Dependable DevOps

The DepDevOps project has been organized by researchers from two H2020 projects that are in-line with the workshop:

– Adeptness: Design-Operation Continuum Methods for Testing and Deployment under Unforeseen Conditions for Cyber-Physical Systems of Systems (https://adeptness.eu/).
– UP2DATE: New software paradigm for SAfe and SEcure (SASE) Over-the-Air software updates for Mixed-Criticality Cyber-Physical Systems (MCCPS) (https://h2020up2date.eu/).

which means that the topics of the workshop are in line with the research objectives of these projects and as both projects are in their first year, the papers presented during the workshop will be considered as inputs and inspiration for the next stages.

3 Acknowledgments

As chairpersons of the workshop, we want to thank all authors and contributors who submitted their work, Friedemann Bitsch, the SAFECOMP Publication Chair, and the members of the International Program Committee who enabled a fair evaluation through reviews and considerable improvements in many cases. We want to express our thanks to the SAFECOMP organizers, who provided us the opportunity to organize the workshop at SAFECOMP 2020. Particularly we want to thank the EC and national public funding authorities who made the work in the research projects possible. We hope that all participants will benefit from the workshop, enjoy the conference and accompanying programs and will join us again in the future!

4 International Program Committee

Erwin Schoitsch
Friedemann Bitsch
Pedro Ferreira
Shuai Wang
Jon Perez
Kim Gruettne
Leonidas Kosmidis
Shaukat Ali
Paolo Arcaini
Mikel Azkarate-Askasua
Blanca Kremer
Eduard Paul Enoiu
Francisco J. Cazorla
Aitor Agirre
Ezio Bartocci
Goiuria Sagardui
Wasif Afzal

Multilevel Runtime Security and Safety Monitoring for Cyber Physical Systems Using Model-Based Engineering

Smitha Gautham$^{(\boxtimes)}$ ⓘ, Athira V. Jayakumar, and Carl Elks

Virginia Commonwealth University, Richmond, VA, USA
gauthamsm@vcu.edu

Abstract. Cyber-Physical Systems (CPS) are heterogeneous in nature and are composed of numerous components and embedded subsystems that are interacting with each other and with the physical world. The interaction of hardware and software components at each level, expose them to attack surfaces, which need novel methods to secure against. To ensure safety and security of high integrity CPSs, we present a multilevel runtime monitor approach where there are monitors at each level of processing and integration. In the proposed multi-level monitoring framework, some monitoring properties are formally defined using Event Calculus. We then demonstrate the need for multilevel monitors for faster detection and isolation of attacks by performing data attack and fault injection on a Simulink CPS model.

Keywords: Runtime monitors · Event calculus · Model-based engineering · Cyber-physical systems

1 Introduction and Motivation

Cyber Physical Systems (CPSs) are heterogeneous architectures composed of physical, network and computational components that are tightly integrated together that allow human cyber interactions [1]. To do this, CPSs are evolving toward *software intensive systems* where functionality, integration, and operations of a given system are largely governed by its complex software interactions. Although software testing methods and practices have undergone tremendous progress over the past 20 years, the evolving nature of software intensive CPSs can create layers of unforeseen failure modes and complex attack surfaces. These can lead to safety design assurance issues at design time and become problematic for ensuring safety at runtime. Such challenges (among others) are emerging drivers for new design and development and operation practices that strive to reduce cost without compromising safety – termed as *DevOps Safety Continuum* [2].

In many safety critical application domains, runtime monitors (or runtime verification) are used to enforce operational safety and security – as a complementary defense to design assurance [3]. Runtime monitors can be thought of as means to detect and mitigate failures/attacks that design time verification may have omitted or overlooked.

© Springer Nature Switzerland AG 2020
A. Casimiro et al. (Eds.): SAFECOMP 2020 Workshops, LNCS 12235, pp. 193–204, 2020.
https://doi.org/10.1007/978-3-030-55583-2_14

In order to detect attacks and complex evolving failures across a CPS, we posit that single monitor solutions are insufficient. Rather we suggest that multiple distinct types of monitors positioned across the CPS provide more comprehensive detection and location capability [4]. This paper supports an important aspect of DevOps Continuum; namely that such multilevel monitors are a promising consideration toward ensuring operational safety in complex CPSs.

We implemented the multilevel monitoring scheme in a MathWorks Simulink Model Based Engineering tool to ascertain the benefits and challenges of evaluating multilevel monitors with respect to security and safety considerations. Model-based Design and Engineering (MBDE) approaches are widely becoming the normative methodology to design, verify and validate safety-critical Cyber Physical Systems (CPS) across various domains (e.g. automotive and aerospace). Our practical and technical contributions that help in the design of dependable CPS are:

- Development of a novel multilevel monitoring framework for runtime safety and security monitoring of CPSs.
- Evaluating the efficacy of multilevel monitoring framework in detecting faults and attacks in a distributed CPS
- Use of MBDE tools to connect design time with runtime monitoring for accessing security and safety considerations early in the design development process.

2   Related Work

With the growth in use of CPSs in numerous safety critical applications, runtime verification of such systems is becoming an essential and important topic of research. Ref. [5] presents a bus monitoring approach for COTS processors where the communication between the peripherals and the system are monitored. Ref. [3] presents a bolt-on monitor that silently receive messages over a CAN bus without affecting the system functionality. With the limited information available on the bus, the runtime monitor verifies safe system behavior. Ref. [6] present a non-intrusive monitoring approach for multi-core processors based on the execution traces received by the processors. A three layer CPS architecture is proposed in [7] comprising of transport layer, control layer and execution layer and attacks that can occur at each of these layers is surveyed but no specific example is provided. Ref. [8] provides a comprehensive survey of monitoring distributed real time systems and provides architectural frameworks to monitor processor and Bus in a CPS. Monitors have been modeled using MBDE tools in prior work, for example Ref. [9] uses Simulink to model runtime monitors. However, multilevel monitors for a CPS with specific attacks/faults has not been explored. Our paper contributes to this area by clearly demonstrating the need for multilevel monitors (data, network and functional) in a CPS to detect a wide range of attacks as well as locate their origin. We then evaluate our multilevel monitoring framework using MathWorks Simulink tools.

3   Development of a Multilevel Monitoring Framework

CPS are heterogeneous in nature encompassing many computational units and include physical interfaces to sensors and actuators. It is important to not just monitor each component in a CPS individually but also monitor the interaction of the components and the physical environment. Figure 1 depicts a common interpretation of a generalized CPS structure [9].

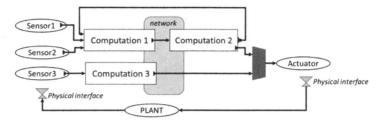

Fig. 1. Structure of a cyber physical system (Adapted from [10] but modified and redrawn).

Referring to Fig. 1, the attacks on a CPS can be broadly classified into three domains. First, attacks on low level *hardware/firmware-oriented* devices. These include sensor or actuator attacks, for example sensor spoofing, firmware attacks, replay attacks to name a few. Second, attacks on the *connection* or *network* layer (e.g. I2C, CAN, SPI) that include attack on a communication bus such as Denial of Service (DoS), packet injection, eavesdropping. Lastly, attacks on the *computational elements* such as malware injection, control flow attack, buffer overflow etc. that can affect the functionality of the processing unit. In this paper we consider attacks and faults that affect *hardware*, *network* and *computational* elements in a CPS and architect a multilevel runtime monitoring framework to effectively detect and isolate the origin of the attack/fault. We consider three levels of monitoring across a CPS. They are:

• Data monitors: They mainly monitor the *hardware/firmware-oriented* devices such as sensors and actuators that constantly interact with the outside environment. They check for integrity of the information coming from these devices through the physical interface.
• Network monitors: They mainly monitor the *connection or network* layer of the CPS. Sensors, actuators and computational units in a CPS use communication protocols such as UART, I2C and buses such as CAN. Network monitor checks for signal faults, incorrect signaling protocol, timing, configurations, etc. in these communication networks.
• Functional monitors: They mainly monitor the *computational* units of a CPS to verify the overall system behavior or functionality of a processing unit within the CPS. Safety and security properties are monitored for expected system behavior.

Having monitors at multiple levels (data, network and functional monitors) should ensure that more classes of faults/attacks can be detected and isolated early before it propagates and affects the system (Fig. 2). Attacks that fall outside the intersection, in Fig. 2 can only be detected by having a localized monitor at that particular level in the CPS. Having these local monitors at each critical level in a CPS helps cover one other's blind spot [11]. We demonstrate the benefits of multilevel monitoring scheme with the specific example of an Anti-lock Braking System (ABS). Furthermore, we show that some faults/attacks may be detected by monitors at other levels (than that of their origin). Even in such cases, monitors at multiple levels are needed to find the location of these faults/attacks.

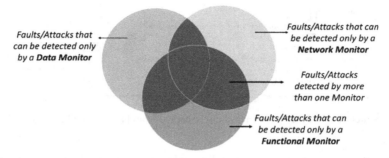

Fig. 2. Attacks/faults detected by multilevel monitors.

4   Example CPS: Anti-lock Braking System (ABS) and Event Calculus to Specify Safety and Security Properties

We use a Simulink model of an Anti-lock Braking System (ABS) from MathWorks examples as a target CPS to demonstrate multilevel monitoring framework [12]. The ABS system is summarized in the Fig. 3. ABS is a safety critical unit in a car that helps prevent the locking of brakes thereby preventing an uncontrollable skid. The slip in a car is calculated based on the wheel rotation speed and actual vehicle speed measured by sensors in the plant (modeled by the vehicle dynamics). This slip value is communicated to the ABS controller through the CAN bus. The ABS controller compares the measured slip and a pre-set threshold slip (chosen so that a slip below this threshold is acceptable for safe operation of the car) and determines if the brake has to be on or off. The brake state (on/off) output determined by the ABS controller is communicated back to the plant through the CAN bus. Some important considerations while designing the monitoring framework are:

4.1   Rationale for the Monitors Used in the ABS Controller CPS

Considering the heterogeneous nature of CPS and the attacks that can occur at various levels, we consider three monitors (Fig. 3) to detect attacks/faults: Functional monitor M1 at the ABS controller and slip calculation unit, Data monitor M2 at the wheel speed sensor, vehicle speed sensor and brake actuator and Network Monitor M3 at the CAN bus. The rationale for the choice of monitors and their placement are as follows: The data from sensors of dynamic quantities such as vehicle speed or wheel speed can be attacked or corrupted, hence a data monitor (M2) is needed there. At the ABS controller and slip calculator modules, there are various faults that can compromise the functionality of the controller/computational element, hence a functional monitor (M1) is necessary. Finally, by injecting spurious traffic into the CAN bus, genuine data being transmitted between the ABS controller and the plant can be delayed or even distorted. Therefore, it is necessary to have a network monitor (M3). ABS functionality can be monitored even from the information in the CAN bus. Although, functional monitoring on the CAN bus can offer effective bolt-on solution to existing CPS, it is important to note that the CAN bus has limited observability, all data and functionality we want to monitor may not be available of the CAN bus.

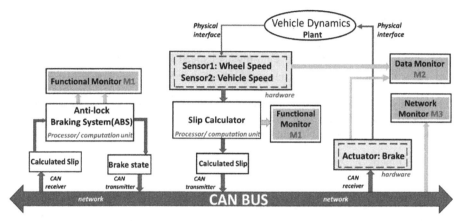

Fig. 3. Anti-lock braking system showing (a) Functional monitor M1 at the computational units (b) Data monitor M2 at the hardware sensor/actuators level (c) Network monitor M3 at the CAN bus network level.

4.2 Monitoring Properties Expressed Using Event Calculus

We define the safety and security properties to be monitored using a formal language called *Event Calculus*. All properties were derived from system level requirements for the specific ABS application. In this example, we focus on application dependent properties, but event calculus is equally expressive for application independent properties. Event calculus is a powerful logical formalism that can conveniently express the effect of events or actions in a CPS in a general way [13]. It is particularly suitable in its ability to express high level functional events as well as low level hardware events. For example, one can express the condition that the temperature of the room increases at a certain rate after a heater in turned on. Formally, in the language of event calculus, switching "on" the heater is an action or an event, that affects the temperature of the room (a fluent) at certain time points. Happens, Initiates, Terminates, HoldsAt and Clipped are the basic event calculus predicates defined in [13]. We use the Happens and HoldsAt predicates to define properties for our system. The semantics of these two predicates are as follows:

- *Happens* (α, t) means that an action or an event α happens at time t.

- *HoldsAt (f, t)* means that the fluent f holds at time t.

To keep the analysis simple, we describe only one property monitored by each of the multilevel monitors (data, network and functional) as an example to explain our framework.

Property 1 Verified by Functional Monitor M1: If the calculated *Slip* is greater than a permissible threshold of $Slip_{safe}$ at time T, then the brake should be off at time T. Here *Slip* is the event and state of the $Brake_{off}$ is the fluent.

$$\text{Happens}(Slip, \text{T}) \land \left(Slip > Slip_{safe}\right) \Rightarrow \text{HoldsAt}\left(Brake_{off}, T\right) \qquad (1)$$

Property 2 Verified by Data Monitor M2: If there is an event on wheel speed *Wheel-Speed_A* at time T_a and another event on wheel speed *WheelSpeed_B* at time T_b where $T_b = T_a + T_d$, then the rate of change of wheel speed $R_w = \frac{(WheelSpeed_B - WheelSpeed_A)}{Td}$ should be less than *Rw_safe* (rate of change of wheel speed for safe operation).

Here T_d is time elapsed between successive wheel speed measurements. *WheelSpeed_A* and *WheelSpeed_B* are the events and the rate of change of wheel speed being less than the permissible rate of change of wheel speed is the fluent:

$$\text{Happens}(WheelSpeed\_A, \text{Ta}) \land \text{Happens}(WheelSpeed\_B, \text{Tb}) \land (\text{Tb} \\ = \text{Ta} + \text{Td}) \Rightarrow \text{HoldsAt} (\text{Rw} < Rw\_safe, \text{Tb}) \qquad (2)$$

Property 3 Verified by Network Monitor M3: If there is a packet arrival in the CAN bus ($Packet_A$) at time T_a and another packet arrival ($Packet_B$) at time T_b then the rate of packet arrival $T_p = T_b - T_a$ should be less than T_{safe} which is the delay in the CAN bus when there is normal traffic for all time T.

Here Tp is time elapsed between successive packet arrivals. Arrival of $Packet_A$ and $Packet_B$ are the events and rate of packet arrival T_p is the fluent:

$$\text{Happens}(Packet_A, \text{Ta}) \land \text{Happens}(Packet_B, \text{Tb}) \\ \Rightarrow \text{HoldsAt} (\text{Tp} < Tsafe, \text{Tb}) \qquad (3)$$

The Event Calculus formalisms above combined with Simulink modeling allows designers/modelers to precisely capture monitoring properties.

5 Evaluation of Multilevel Monitors

The ABS controller, sensors and the CAN bus were injected with attacks/faults and the efficacy of the monitors in detecting these attacks/faults were evaluated. We used the data injection toolbox in [14] to inject sensor attacks on the model. Fault saboteurs were inserted in the model as explained in [15] at various points in the system. Figure 4 shows the saboteurs inserted in the ABS controller. Excessive information packets of higher priority from a malicious node flooding the CAN bus emulated a "Denial of Service" attack. The monitoring conditions were modeled using Simulink assertion verification blocks. We discuss below some examples to demonstrate that (1) there are attacks/fault scenarios that can only be detected if there are localized monitors at each level (data, functional, network) (2) Some attacks/faults may be detected by a monitor at another level (other than the level of its origin), but monitors are nevertheless needed at each level to locate the origin of the attack/fault in such scenarios. Table 1 summarizes some of the attacks/faults that were injected in the CPS to demonstrate the need for a multilevel monitoring framework.

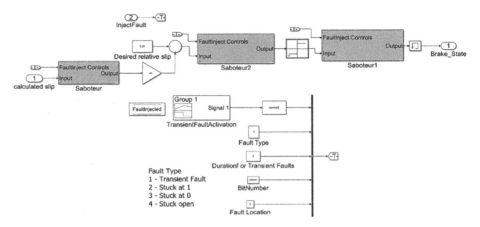

Fig. 4. Fault saboteurs injected in the ABS.

Table 1. Attacks/faults injected on the CPS.

No.	Attack/fault	Attack location	Monitors that detect
1.	Stuck-at 0 fault	ABS controller	M1 only
2.	Denial of service attack	CAN bus	M3 only
3.	Sensor measurement injection attack	Wheel speed sensor	Attack-1: M2 only Attack-2: M1 and M2

5.1 Case-1. Attacks/Faults Needing Localized Monitors at Each Level

Consider the Fig. 5 where the slip, vehicle speed and wheel rotation speed are plotted as a function of time without the attacks/faults mentioned in the Table 1.

When there is no attack/fault, the ABS is able to ensure that the vehicle speed slows down to under 15 m/s at 12 s by appropriately releasing the brake whenever the slip exceeds a threshold. In many cases, where there is an attack/fault as shown in Fig. 6, Fig. 7 and Fig. 8, the vehicle speed is ~20 m/s or higher in 12 s (thus rendering the braking ineffective). The ABS controller decides whether the brake should be on/off depending on the slip. When the slip is greater than 0.25 (a threshold value) the brake should be off and when the slip is less than 0.25, the brake should be on.

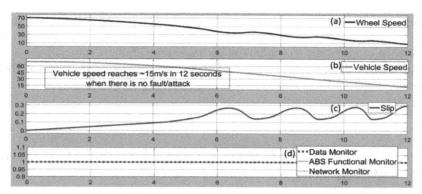

Fig. 5. (a) Wheel speed (b) vehicle speed (c) slip (d) monitor state: when there is no attack/fault on the CPS.

We first consider a fault on the ABS controller which can be critical for the system safety. A "stuck-at zero" fault was injected on the slip at about t = 5 s and hence the controller never turns the brake off and is always on. Therefore, the property, "the brake is turned off when the slip ("s") is greater than 0.25" is violated. It can be seen in Fig. 6 that around t = 6 s, the true slip communicated to the controller exceeds 0.25 and the functional monitor (M1) expects the brake to turn off. However, due to the fault (slip seen by the controller is zero) the controller still keeps the brake on. Hence, the property is violated and fault is detected by the ABS functional monitor. However, since this does not affect the signal transmission through the CAN bus or other sensor properties, the monitors at the network and data levels are unable to detect this. Hence, one specifically needs a functional monitor here to detect the fault.

Likewise, the CAN bus is prone to number of attacks: packet insertion, packet erasure, packet payload modification, to name a few [16]. These lead to Denial of Service (DoS) attack that changes the packet frequency on the CAN bus. Time interval between CAN packets is usually periodic and has a fixed delay. A malicious node can change the time interval between successive packets by injecting extra packets causing delay in the bus.

An attack on the CAN packet frequency was performed by introducing a malicious node that delays the communication to and from the ABS controller. This was not detected by either the functional monitor (M1) at the ABS or the data monitor (M2). The fixed delay for normal traffic was identified and the network monitor (M3) verifies at runtime that the time interval between subsequent packets is within bounds. When the time interval exceeds the normal levels the monitor M3 indicated an attack on the network as shown in Fig. 7. When the system has no faults/attacks, the ABS controller receives the slip value, approximately every 0.006 s through the CAN bus. However, when there is more than a certain level of network traffic due packet injection by a malicious node, the delay in the CAN bus increases, which is detected by the monitor as shown. Flooding the CAN bus with many packets can lead to huge delay as seen in Fig. 7(b) between 11th and 12th second. This affects the braking and the vehicle speed. The vehicle speed was 30 m/s instead of 15 m/s during normal conditions with no fault/attack. While we

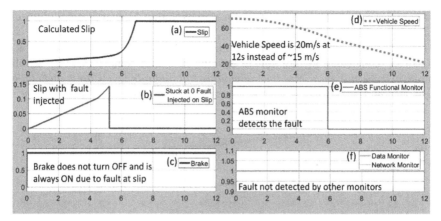

Fig. 6. For a stuck at 0 fault on the ABS controller, (a) correct slip calculated (b) slip as seen by the ABS controller due to the fault at its input (c) the brake state which is always "on" as even though the true slip exceeds 0.25, the ABS only sees the slip $= 0$ (d) vehicle speed that is affected by the ABS not correctly functioning (e) the ABS expects the brake to go "off" when slip exceeds 0.25, and thus detects a fault (f) other monitors do not detect this fault.

used this approach as a proof of concept, there are alternate ways of monitoring the bus traffic discussed in [16].

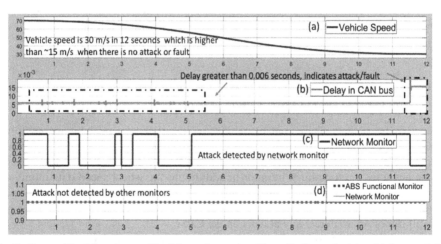

Fig. 7. Bus traffic delay detected by Network monitor For a DoS attack, (a) vehicle speed that is affected due to delay in CAN bus (b) delay in CAN bus is greater than 0.006 s (c) Network monitor detects the attack (d) all other monitors do not detect the attack.

A sensor attack, "attack-1" on the wheel speed sensor that is detected by the data monitor (M2) is showed in Fig. 8. It monitored the safety property "the absolute value of the rate of change of wheel speed should not be greater than T_w rad/s" where T_w is a threshold rate of change of wheel speed for safe operation. However, *none of the other monitors* were able to detect this attack.

Hence, in all the above cases multilevel monitors are needed as faults/attacks at one level cannot be detected by monitors at the other levels as demonstrated by the above examples. *Hence, we show that having monitors at multiple levels are beneficial (and sometimes required) to detect attacks/faults that span multiple levels and systems.*

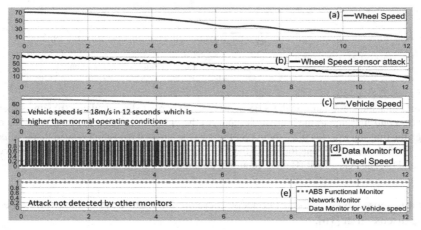

Fig. 8. For an attack on wheel speed sensor, (a) wheel speed when there is no attack/fault (b) wheel speed with an attack (c) vehicle speed affected by attack on the wheel speed sensor (d) Data monitor for wheel speed detects the attack (e) other monitors do not detect this attack.

5.2 Case-2. Attacks/Faults Detected at More Than One Level but Still Needing Multiple Levels to Find to Location of the Attack

When there is sensor measurement attack (discussed earlier) of a much higher magnitude (attack-2), it could cause the rate of wheel speed to change so drastically that it briefly affects the functional relation between the slip and break state monitored by M1. Hence it is detected by the functional monitor in addition to the wheel speed data monitor as shown in Fig. 9. Note that this example has less number of disruptions to the wheel speed and does not significantly change the eventual vehicle speed reached at 12 s. However, it is still important to detect any attacks on the CPS.

We argue *both* of these monitors are probably needed, as even though the functional monitor detects this data attack, we cannot be sure where the attack/fault originated if we *only* had one functional monitor. We would use the fact that both the wheel speed data monitor and functional monitor detected this attack to pinpoint it was at the wheel speed sensor; while if only the functional monitor had detected the attack (not the data monitor) we would probably conclude the attack was on the ABS controller.

Another issue to be considered is whether the ABS functionality (M1) and sensor data (M2) can be monitored from the information in the CAN bus. One issue is the

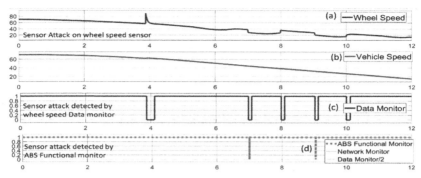

Fig. 9. Attack detected by multiple monitors (a) Wheel speed when there is sensor attack (b) vehicle speed not affected significantly by attack on the wheel speed sensor (c) Data monitor for wheel speed detects the attack (d) functional monitor detects this attack.

CAN bus has limited observability as all data and functionality we want to monitor may not be available of the CAN bus. The other issue is as follows: Suppose the slip and brake state, are available on the CAN bus, we could have implemented the same ABS functional monitor on the slip and Brake ON/OFF state from information in the CAN bus (not shown here) rather than locally as we did earlier. While such a monitor would have detected a fault in the ABS controller action, it would have also been affected by excessive network traffic. So, this monitor alone would not be able to specifically pin point the origin of the attack.

6 Conclusion and Future Work

We have developed and implemented a multilevel monitoring framework and demonstrated the need for monitors at multiple levels to detect various attacks/faults for an ABS controller CPS. We showed that existing MBE tools (Simulink) can model and evaluate such monitoring architectures and integrate safety and security considerations early in the design process. Future continuation of this work will; (1) focus on comparisons with other approaches to access the benefits and limitations, (2) further the development of a theory of multilevel monitoring for CPSs to fully characterize its assumptions and impacts. Finally, the generality and scalability of multilevel monitors deployed in diverse CPSs will be better understood by evaluating the resources needed for implementing such monitors.

References

1. Cyber physical systems and Internet of Things program. NIST, 09 March 2016. https://www.nist.gov/programs-projects/cyber-physical-systems-and-internet-things-program. Accessed 18 May 2020
2. Combemale, B., Wimmer, M.: Towards a model-based DevOps for cyber-physical systems. In: Bruel, J.-M., Mazzara, M., Meyer, B. (eds.) DEVOPS 2019. LNCS, vol. 12055, pp. 84–94. Springer, Cham (2020). https://doi.org/10.1007/978-3-030-39306-9_6

3. Kane, A.: Runtime monitoring for safety-critical embedded systems. Carnegie Mellon University (2015)
4. Gautham, S., Bakirtzis, G., Leccadito, M.T., Klenke, R.H., Elks, C.R.: A multilevel cybersecurity and safety monitor for embedded cyber-physical systems: WIP abstract. In: Proceedings of the 10th ACM/IEEE International Conference on Cyber-Physical Systems, New York, NY, USA, pp. 320–321 (2019). https://doi.org/10.1145/3302509.3313321
5. Pellizzoni, R., Meredith, P., Caccamo, M., Rosu, G.: BusMOP: a runtime monitoring framework for PCI peripherals, p. 23 (2008)
6. Convent, L., Hungerecker, S., Scheffel, T., Schmitz, M., Thoma, D., Weiss, A.: Hardware-based runtime verification with embedded tracing units and stream processing. In: Colombo, C., Leucker, M. (eds.) RV 2018. LNCS, vol. 11237, pp. 43–63. Springer, Cham (2018). https://doi.org/10.1007/978-3-030-03769-7_5
7. Lu, T., Lin, J., Zhao, L., Li, Y., Peng, Y.: A security architecture in cyber-physical systems: security theories, analysis, simulation and application fields. IJSIA 9(7), 1–16 (2015). https://doi.org/10.14257/ijsia.2015.9.7.01
8. Goodloe, A.E., Pike, L.: Monitoring distributed real-time systems: a survey and future directions, (NASA/CR-2010-216724), p. 49, July 2010
9. Whalen, M.W., Murugesan, A., Rayadurgam, S., Heimdahl, M.P.E.: Structuring simulink models for verification and reuse. In: Proceedings of the 6th International Workshop on Modeling in Software Engineering - MiSE 2014, Hyderabad, India, pp. 19–24 (2014). https://doi.org/10.1145/2593770.2593776
10. Lee, E.A., Seshia, S.A.: Introduction to Embedded Systems: A Cyber-Physical Systems Approach, 2nd edn. MIT Press, Cambridge (2017)
11. Fournaris, A.P., Komninos, A., Lalos, A.S., Kalogeras, A.P., Koulamas, C., Serpanos, D.: Design and run-time aspects of secure cyber-physical systems. In: Biffl, S., Eckhart, M., Lüder, A., Weippl, E. (eds.) Security and Quality in Cyber-Physical Systems Engineering, pp. 357–382. Springer, Cham (2019). https://doi.org/10.1007/978-3-030-25312-7_13
12. Effects of communication delays on an ABS control system - MATLAB & Simulink. https://www.mathworks.com/help/simevents/examples/effects-of-communication-delays-on-an-abs-control-system.html. Accessed 18 May 2020
13. Shanahan, M.: The event calculus explained. In: Wooldridge, M.J., Veloso, M. (eds.) Artificial Intelligence Today. LNCS (LNAI), vol. 1600, pp. 409–430. Springer, Heidelberg (1999). https://doi.org/10.1007/3-540-48317-9_17
14. Potluri, S., Diedrich, C., Roy Nanduru, S.R., Vasamshetty, K.: Development of injection attacks toolbox in MATLAB/Simulink for attacks simulation in industrial control system applications. In: 2019 IEEE 17th International Conference on Industrial Informatics (INDIN), July 2019, vol. 1, pp. 1192–1198 (2019). https://doi.org/10.1109/indin41052.2019.8972171
15. Jayakumar, A.V.: Systematic model-based design assurance and property-based fault injection for safety critical digital systems. Theses and Dissertations, January 2020. https://scholarscompass.vcu.edu/etd/6239
16. Lokman, S.-F., Othman, A.T., Abu-Bakar, M.-H.: Intrusion detection system for automotive Controller Area Network (CAN) bus system: a review. EURASIP J. Wirel. Commun. Network. 2019(1), 1–17 (2019). https://doi.org/10.1186/s13638-019-1484-3

Towards a DevOps Approach in Cyber Physical Production Systems Using Digital Twins

Miriam Ugarte Querejeta(✉)⬤, Leire Etxeberria⬤, and Goiuria Sagardui⬤

Mondragon Unibertsitatea, Goiru Kalea 2, 20150 Arrasate-Mondragon, Spain
{mugarte,letxeberria,gsagardui}@mondragon.edu

Abstract. Nowadays product manufacturing must respond to mass cus-
tomisation of products in order to meet the global market needs. This
requires an agile and dynamic production process to be competitive in
the market. Consequently, the need of factory digitalisation arises with
the introduction of Industry 4.0. One example of the digitalisation is the
digital twin. Digital twin enhances flexibility due to its adaptability and
seamless interaction between the physical system and its virtual model.
Furthermore, it bridges the gap between development and operations
through the whole product life cycle. Therefore, digital twin can be an
enabler for the DevOps application in cyber physical production systems
as DevOps aims at merging Development and Operations to provide a
continuous and an agile process. This paper analyses the use of the digital
twin to enable a DevOps approach of cyber physical production systems
(CPPS) in order to create a fully integrated and automated production
process, enabling continuous improvement.

Keywords: Digital twin · DevOps · Life cycle · Cyber physical
production system

1 Introduction

The manufacturing sector is continuously facing the rapidly changing market
needs. In fact, product manufacturing complexity is increasing as the market
requires more flexible, reconfigurable and customised systems that are capable
of adapting to changes throughout the whole product life cycle. This emerges the
need of new approaches and technologies in order to decrease the development
cost and time, improving efficiency and effectiveness. Digitalisation and Industry
4.0 are the technologies emerging to face these challenges with the transformation
of the manufacturing process into a fully digital and intelligent process where
automation plays a key role [17]. The digitalisation of the industry makes a step
forward towards the automation, integration and optimisation of the production
process and it enables operation and monitoring throughout the whole product
life cycle.

© Springer Nature Switzerland AG 2020
A. Casimiro et al. (Eds.): SAFECOMP 2020 Workshops, LNCS 12235, pp. 205–216, 2020.
https://doi.org/10.1007/978-3-030-55583-2_15

In this paper, we focus on digitisation as an enabler of the continuous improvement during the product life cycle. In this sense, digital twins are emerging as the latest trend on digital transformation. This technology links the physical asset and its virtual model in an agile and continuously evolving environment. The digital twin gives the possibility to continuously improve the model by 1) collecting real time data and analysing it in order to foresee malfunctions and 2) introducing improvements on the product and validating them in a virtual environment before deploying them into the real system. In addition, the digital twin has the ability to adapt its model seamlessly and near real time as changes are made on the system, thus facilitating the production flow. All these characteristics and capabilities of the digital twin accelerate the integration of an agile and continuous production process, principles of the so called DevOps approach.

DevOps approaches are being used widely in software development, specially for web-based applications, delivering faster applications and continuously. In fact, it has been mainly used to automate the development and deployment of web based applications from end to end [10]. DevOps is a continuation of the Agile journey [15] (often referred to continuous delivery, integration and deployment) that merges the development and operation with cross-functional collaboration process. A DevOps approach on software development brings these agile principles for continuous software development and deployment.

In other types of development, such as manufacturing systems and cyber physical production systems (CPPS), there are still some challenges that need to be addressed. These systems must deal with legacy architecture and hardware limitations in order to integrate a flexible and adaptive environment. In any case, the manufacturing sector could benefit from a DevOps approach to create a continuous production system and bring continuous improvement throught the whole product life cycle. However, adoption of DevOps in the manufacturing sector requires an agile and adaptive system where digitalisation is one of the key elements and the digital twin the main enabler.

This paper analyses the use of the digital twin for a DevOps approach on CPPS. The digital twin technology enables DevOps to develop and test the product simultaneously, reducing development costs and time to market. Moreover, the bridge between development and operations guarantees the continuous improvement in an agile environment.

The paper is structured as follows: Sect. 2 introduces briefly the background of the digital twin, DevOps and Cyber Physical Production Systems, and on the other hand, it highlights the motivation of the paper. Section 3 describes the digital twin for a DevOps approach on product manufacturing of CPPS. Finally, Sect. 4 provides the conclusions and future work.

2   Background and Motivation

2.1   Digital Twin

The digital twin has its origin in 2003, conceived by Grieves with the product life cycle management [13]. However, the term digital twin was firstly defined by NASA in 2010 [27] as follows "A digital twin is an integrated multi-physics, multi-scale, probabilistic simulation of a vehicle or system that uses the best available physical models, sensor updates, fleet history, etc., to mirror the life of its flying twin." Nowadays, there exists a wide range of definitions, therefore, it is necessary to clarify the concept. From the author's perspective on product manufacturing, the digital twin is the virtual representation of the physical asset where both counterparts are connected to each other and are dynamically updating through the whole product life cycle [21,25].

The digital twin model requires a physical entity, a virtual model and connected data [21,25]. However, Tao et al. proposed the five-dimensional Digital Twin (see Fig. 1), composed of a physical entity, virtual model, digital twin data, services and connections [26,30].

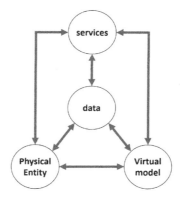

Fig. 1. Five dimensional digital twin - adapted from [30].

2.2 DevOps

DevOps aims to bridge the gap between software Development (Dev) and Operations (Ops) by combining best practices from both domains and enabling collaboration between the teams [4]. The main principles of DevOps are focused on continuous integration, continuous delivery and continuous deployment [15] as depicted in Fig. 2.

Continuous Integration: Continuous integration (CI) is a principle that puts a great emphasis on the dynamic software integration process and test automation [5] in order to detect problems easily early in the process. It is a prerequisite for continuous delivery [15].

Continuous Delivery: Continuous delivery (CD) aims at delivering new software features with greater speed and frequency [5]. This requires the software to be always ready for release [11] and promotes the automation of the release process, enabling a constant flow.

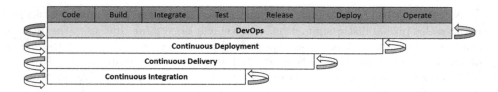

Fig. 2. DevOps principles through the software life cycle.

Continuous Deployment: Continuous deployment is usually confused with continuous delivery, however it goes a step further. Every change that is successfully committed on the previous stages is automatically deployed to production [11].

DevOps benefits from these principles to shorten time to market, reduce development costs and increase productivity with a higher quality. Moreover, it goes beyond by covering the entire life cycle, from development to operations.

2.3 Cyber Physical Production Systems

Cyber physical production systems are formed by different CPS, comprising different elements and sub-systems connected to each other autonomously and in cooperation [23]. The main objectives that a CPPS should meet are the following according to Monostori et al. [24]:

- Responsiveness to any changes in the system or environment.
- Intelligence of the components that are part of a CPPS.
- Connectivity between the elements, services, subsystems and other systems.

Therefore, the digital twin represents a fundamental prerequisite of cyber physical production systems due to its adaptive ability, real time and seamless connectivity and control of the production process.

Regarding the development of CPPS, this implies system verification and validation before releasing it into operations. System verification is often carried out in silos by each engineering discipline and thus, different interdisciplinary simulation tools are utilised for partial simulations. Consequently, the final product is not jointly validated until the system is fully integrated and interoperability issues become a major challenge. Thus, there exists the need to carry out interdisciplinary tests in a jointly environment from early stages of the development.

2.4 Motivation

DevOps practices are mostly applied to software development and little has been done on cyber physical systems. Nevertheless, Garcia and Cabot applied DevOps practices at the model level for the very first time in 2018 [11] and it has been explored to model driven engineering in cyber physical systems in the recent years [6,33].

DevOps life cycle is not only applicable to software development and its cycle changes based on the applicable environment. Implementing DevOps principles at the entire life cycle of model based approaches is the next step of cyber physical systems, enabling a continuous and dynamic life cycle of the system. However, cyber physical systems must overcome the following barriers to integrate a DevOps approach [6, 12]:

- Dealing with hardware constraints due to different communication protocols, programming environments and dedicated hardware.
- Real time communication between the physical and virtual systems.
- Obtaining feedback data from operations, customers and other systems.
- Facilitating a collaborative framework between different stakeholders and engineering disciplines.
- Supporting an agile and a flexible environment.

This paper puts forward the use of the digital twin in order to carry out a DevOps approach into CPPS. The digital twin technology facilitates a flexible environment with the dynamic adaption capability of the physical asset and its virtual counterpart. In fact, both counterparts are continuously adjusting to the changes in real time. On the other hand, this technology enables interdisciplinary collaboration so that operations and development can co-work together and get mutual feedback through the whole life cycle.

3 Digital Twin as DevOps Enabler for CPPS

The digital twin brings an agile framework for the development and operation of cyber physical systems [36]. Therefore, the authors introduce the digital twin as a DevOps accelerator where it stages a DevOps approach throughout the whole product life cycle. This way, product design, engineering, integration, operation and service activities can be performed efficiently on an agile and collaborative environment between different departments [3] and engineering disciplines such as mechanical, electrical and automation, among others.

Figure 3 represents the digital twin as the enabler of DevOps across the product life cycle of a CPPS. In this case, the digital twin is the technology to shorten the gap between the development and operations as it interchanges data seamlessly through the whole life cycle. This way, the development process benefits from the feedback obtained from the operational data and vice versa.

The following subsections describe the use of the digital twin within the development and operations of a CPPS and highlights DevOps practices in order to achieve a continuous and runtime production system.

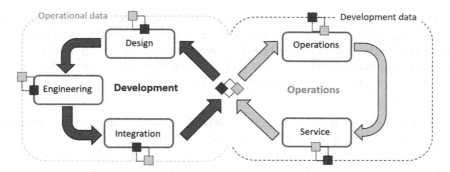

Fig. 3. Use of the digital twin for a DevOps approach across the product life cycle - inspired by [3,32].

3.1 Digital Twin in Development

The development process involves the design, engineering, and integration phases, and requires testing practices for the verification and validation of the model before being released. Model Verification and Validation, V&V, determines if the model is correct by the verification of the model, and on the other hand, it validates that the requirements are met successfully and that the model is adequate to represent the real system. Tania Tudorache proposed the V model for a mechatronic product development process in 2006 [32]. A decade later, in 2018, the use of the digital twin for V&V was introduced by Dahmen et al. as simulation based verification with experimentable digital twins [7,8].

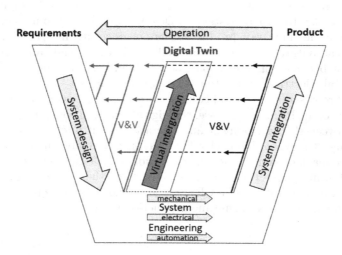

Fig. 4. V model for continuous product development process - adapted from [32].

The V-model of a traditional mechatronical system [32] verifies and validates the system during the last step of the product development process, it does not allow to perform V&V before the system is integrated. This arises system design and engineering problems during the integration stage, making its resolution difficult and increasing development costs and time to market. To confront this, there exists simulation tools that carry out partial system verification of each engineering discipline. However, carrying out simulations solely derive into interoperability issues between these interdisciplinary models during the system integration. Therefore, the V model is adjusted to integrate the digital twin practices from the experimentable digital twin [8] and thus, enable system verification and validation from the initial phase of the development process (system design) as seen in Fig. 4. The digital twin provides a new stage called virtual integration where the physical components are replaced by their virtual models before building the actual system. Moreover, a DevOps approach has been applied to the V model in order to gain insights from operations and provide a continuous product development process.

One of the applications that encompasses the whole V&V model is virtual commissioning. Virtual Commissioning is performed by the use of virtualisation and simulation technologies (such as the digital twin) in order to perform a series of collaborative verification tasks between domain specific engineering disciplines and through the whole development process (system design, system engineering, system integration or commissioning).

The main objectives of the use of the digital twin in product development process are described below [20]:

- To reduce time to market.
- To reduce development costs.
- To improve the performance of the production line.
- To reduce the failure rate and downtime of the production line.
- To solve interoperability issues between different domain tools and systems.
- To detect design and engineering errors, failures or malfunctions at earlier stages of the development process.

System Design. Designing is the first phase going down on the left side of the V model. It starts from the system requirements and describes the main physical and logical operation characteristics of the product [32]. System validation and verification must be accomplished in order to meet the requirements and this is facilitated with the digital twin as it permits testing the designed model by replacing the required physical components with their virtual models. Moreover, the digital twin provides feedback and the knowledge gained from the operational data for continuous design improvement [3].

A practical use case of the system design is the optimisation of the product. For example, Soderberg et al. applied the digital twin on design optimisation in order to obtain good geometrical quality in the final product [28].

System Engineering. System engineering is the phase following the system design up to the integration phase. An interdisciplinary approach is applied to the system design by adding domain specific engineering functionalities (mechanical, electrical, automation, etc.) to the model [32]. Traditionally, the engineering development was carried out in silos with multiple domain specific models, however, the digital twin sets up a collaborative framework where all disciplines can co-work in the same environment. Moreover, the use of the digital twin permits carrying out what-if simulations and making changes on the virtual environment before the real system is released. It also facilitates the testing of specific functionalities on a secure environment, for example Bitton et al. created a cost effective digital twin to facilitate the security evaluation of a specific industrial environment [2].

System Integration. The last phase of the V model is system integration. This is a critical phase as the engineering models, system components and interconnections are brought together [32]. Traditionally, the validation and verification of the system was carried out when the system integration was completed, thereby, unexpected errors were frequently arised due to dependency of the previous phases (design, engineering). However, the system can be tested before the real system is built with the use of the virtual models and digital twins (e.g. virtual commissioning technology). Therefore, the digital twin permits a flexible environment for continuous integration as it facilities testing the system securely on the virtual environment and it can then be automatically deployed to the real system. Another practice is the assembly commissioning process optimisation in order to improve the assembly quality and efficiency [29].

3.2 Digital Twin in Operations

Once the development process is completed, the product is realised into operations and service, closing the loop of DevOps.

Operations. The system is running on a real environment and runtime verification and validation of the system can be accomplished [14]. Operational data of the physical system can be used as input to the operational digital twin for predictions of breakdowns or failures, and vice-versa, knowledge gained on the operational digital twin can fed back to the physical asset for continuous improvement within the development process. Some of the operational applications and real use cases of the digital twin are described below:

- Optimisation of the system operation [19].
- Decision making under unexpected situations: runtime controllability verification of a control command [14], optimal state control framework [34], controllability of the physical layer [35], holistic online parallel controlling [19].
- Reconfiguration of the manufacturing system for reacting on changeover of the product order [18].

Service. Lastly, the service stage provides real time status and monitoring of the product, closing the loop of the operational cycle. In this scenario, dynamic data obtained from the physical asset (usage, wear, temperature, etc.) is mapped to the operational digital twin for real time monitoring. Furthermore, the historical data and the knowledge retrieved from the development cycle is combined with current operational data in order to carry out preventive maintenance. Thus, most of the services are related to real time monitoring, asset management and educational purposes:

- Monitoring: continuous monitoring [19,35], real time monitoring to improve the product quality and production efficiency of a welding production line, real time status warning of the production process [36].
- Real-time transmission of manufacturing updates [1].
- Tracking and updating warehouse inventory [1].
- Maximum traceability and transparency for the supply chain [22].
- Training and learning: learning environment for engineering education [31], a versatile learning environment to facilitate collaboration between industry and academia [16].

4   Conclusions and Future Work

In this paper we have discussed the use of the digital twin as the main enabler to apply a DevOps approach in Cyber Phsycal Production Systems. The digital twin is the bridge between the physical and real world, and also between the operational and development life cycles of a CPPS. Digital twin makes a step forward towards DevOps due to its agile framework for a continuous production system.

The digital twin provides current operational production data converging it with the synthetic data of the virtual model. This creates a runtime production development process as it gains insights and new requirements from operations in order to make adjustments on the go, by providing a proactive and a continuous optimisation process. A continuous production system could made a shift in virtual commissioning.

Furthermore, virtual commissioning practices are usually proceeded in silos between different domains of engineering (mechanic, electronic, automation) where seamless interaction between these interdisciplinary models is a challenge when testing the whole system. In contrary, the digital twin brings the collaboration between all these disciplines and models in the same environment, hence avoiding interoperability issues.

Beside all the benefits that the use of the digital twin and a DevOps approach would bring to the manufacturing sector, there is actually a lack a of industrial practices. One of the main challenges is the lack of standards for digital representation. In this sense, the Asset Administration Shell (AAS) is a promising standard for the digital twin representation as it holds properties, models and functionalities of all the components part of the system [9]. Nevertheless, it is still not a mature standard and its implementation into CPPS should be the way forward.

Acknowledgements. This work was accomplished by the Software and Systems Engineering research group of Mondragon Unibertsitatea (IT1326-19), supported by the Department of Education, Universities and Research of the Basque Government, and the DiManD Innovative Training Network (ITN) project. DiManD ITN is an European Training Network (ETN) programme funded by the European Union through the Marie Sktodowska-Curie Innovative Training Networks (H2020-MSCA-ITN-2018) under grant agreement number no. 814078.

References

1. Banica, L., Stefan, C.: Stepping into the industry 4.0: the digital twin approach. Ann. Univ. Dunarea de Jos Galati: Fascicle: I, Econ. Appl. Inform. **25**(3), 107–113 (2019)
2. Bitton, R., et al.: Deriving a cost-effective digital twin of an ICS to facilitate security evaluation. In: Lopez, J., Zhou, J., Soriano, M. (eds.) ESORICS 2018. LNCS, vol. 11098, pp. 533–554. Springer, Cham (2018). https://doi.org/10.1007/978-3-319-99073-6_26
3. Boschert, S., Rosen, R.: Digital twin—the simulation aspect. In: Hehenberger, P., Bradley, D. (eds.) Mechatronic Futures, pp. 59–74. Springer, Cham (2016). https://doi.org/10.1007/978-3-319-32156-1_5
4. Capizzi, A., Distefano, S., Mazzara, M.: From DevOps to DevDataOps: data management in DevOps processes. arXiv preprint arXiv:1910.03066 (2019)
5. Caprarelli, A., Di Nitto, E., Tamburri, D.A.: Fallacies and pitfalls on the road to DevOps: a longitudinal industrial study. In: Bruel, J.-M., Mazzara, M., Meyer, B. (eds.) DEVOPS 2019. LNCS, vol. 12055, pp. 200–210. Springer, Cham (2020). https://doi.org/10.1007/978-3-030-39306-9_15
6. Combemale, B., Wimmer, M.: Towards a model-based DevOps for cyber-physical systems. In: Bruel, J.-M., Mazzara, M., Meyer, B. (eds.) DEVOPS 2019. LNCS, vol. 12055, pp. 84–94. Springer, Cham (2020). https://doi.org/10.1007/978-3-030-39306-9_6
7. Dahmen, U., Rossmann, J.: Experimentable digital twins for a modeling and simulation-based engineering approach. In: 2018 IEEE International Systems Engineering Symposium (ISSE), pp. 1–8. IEEE (2018)
8. Dahmen, U., Roßmann, J.: Simulation-based verification with experimentable digital twins in virtual testbeds. Tagungsband des 3. Kongresses Montage Handhabung Industrieroboter, pp. 139–147. Springer, Heidelberg (2018). https://doi.org/10.1007/978-3-662-56714-2_16
9. Di Orio, G., Maló, P., Barata, J.: NOVAAS: a reference implementation of industrie4.0 asset administration shell with best-of-breed practices from it engineering. In: IECON 2019–45th Annual Conference of the IEEE Industrial Electronics Society, vol. 1, pp. 5505–5512. IEEE (2019)
10. Ebert, C., Gallardo, G., Hernantes, J., Serrano, N.: DevOps. IEEE Softw. **33**(3), 94–100 (2016)
11. Garcia, J., Cabot, J.: Stepwise adoption of continuous delivery in model-driven engineering. In: Bruel, J.-M., Mazzara, M., Meyer, B. (eds.) DEVOPS 2018. LNCS, vol. 11350, pp. 19–32. Springer, Cham (2019). https://doi.org/10.1007/978-3-030-06019-0_2

12. Giaimo, F., Yin, H., Berger, C., Crnkovic, I.: Continuous experimentation on cyber-physical systems: challenges and opportunities. In: Proceedings of the Scientific Workshop Proceedings of XP 2016, pp. 1–2 (2016)
13. Grieves, M.W.: Product lifecycle management: the new paradigm for enterprises. Int. J. Prod. Dev. **2**(1–2), 71–84 (2005)
14. Kang, S., Chun, I., Kim, H.S.: Design and implementation of runtime verification framework for cyber-physical production systems. J. Eng. **2019** (2019)
15. Kim, G., Humble, J., Debois, P., Willis, J.: The DevOps Handbook: How to Create World-Class Agility, Reliability, and Security in Technology Organizations. IT Revolution, Portland (2016)
16. Lanz, M., Lobov, A., Katajisto, K., Mäkelä, P.: A concept and local implementation for industry-academy collaboration and life-long learning. Procedia Manuf. **23**, 189–194 (2018)
17. Lasi, H., Fettke, P., Kemper, H.-G., Feld, T., Hoffmann, M.: Industry 4.0. Bus. Inf. Syst. Eng. **6**(4), 239–242 (2014). https://doi.org/10.1007/s12599-014-0334-4
18. Leng, J., et al.: Digital twin-driven rapid reconfiguration of the automated manufacturing system via an open architecture model. Robot. Comput.-Integr. Manuf. **63**, 101895 (2020)
19. Leng, J., Zhang, H., Yan, D., Liu, Q., Chen, X., Zhang, D.: Digital twin-driven manufacturing cyber-physical system for parallel controlling of smart workshop. J. Ambient Intell. Humaniz. Comput. **10**(3), 1155–1166 (2018). https://doi.org/10.1007/s12652-018-0881-5
20. Li, X., Du, J., Wang, X., Yang, D., Yang, B.: Research on digital twin technology for production line design and simulation. In: Xhafa, F., Patnaik, S., Tavana, M. (eds.) IISA 2019. AISC, vol. 1084, pp. 516–522. Springer, Cham (2020). https://doi.org/10.1007/978-3-030-34387-3_64
21. Lu, Y., Liu, C., Kevin, I., Wang, K., Huang, H., Xu, X.: Digital twin-driven smart manufacturing: Connotation, reference model, applications and research issues. Robot. Comput.-Integr. Manuf. **61**, 101837 (2020)
22. Mandolla, C., Petruzzelli, A.M., Percoco, G., Urbinati, A.: Building a digital twin for additive manufacturing through the exploitation of blockchain: a case analysis of the aircraft industry. Comput. Ind. **109**, 134–152 (2019)
23. Monostori, L.: Cyber-physical production systems: roots, expectations and R&D challenges. Procedia CIRP **17**, 9–13 (2014)
24. Monostori, L., et al.: Cyber-physical systems in manufacturing. CIRP Ann. **65**(2), 621–641 (2016)
25. Qi, Q., Tao, F.: Digital twin and big data towards smart manufacturing and industry 4.0: 360 degree comparison. IEEE Access **6**, 3585–3593 (2018)
26. Qi, Q., et al.: Enabling technologies and tools for digital twin. J. Manuf. Syst. (2019)
27. Shafto, M., et al.: Modeling, simulation, information technology & processing roadmap. National Aeronautics and Space Administration (2012)
28. Söderberg, R., Wärmefjord, K., Carlson, J.S., Lindkvist, L.: Toward a digital twin for real-time geometry assurance in individualized production. CIRP Ann. **66**(1), 137–140 (2017)
29. Sun, X., Bao, J., Li, J., Zhang, Y., Liu, S., Zhou, B.: A digital twin-driven approach for the assembly-commissioning of high precision products. Robot. Comput.-Integr. Manuf. **61**, 101839 (2020)
30. Tao, F., Zhang, M., Liu, Y., Nee, A.: Digital twin driven prognostics and health management for complex equipment. CIRP Ann. **67**(1), 169–172 (2018)

31. Toivonen, V., Lanz, M., Nylund, H., Nieminen, H.: The FMS Training Center-a versatile learning environment for engineering education. Procedia Manuf. **23**, 135–140 (2018)
32. Tudorache, T.: Employing ontologies for an improved development process in collaborative engineering. Doctoral thesis, Technische Universität Berlin, Fakultät IV - Elektrotechnik und Informatik, Berlin (2006). https://doi.org/10.14279/depositonce-1477
33. Wortmann, A., Barais, O., Combemale, B., Wimmer, M.: Modeling languages in industry 4.0: an extended systematic mapping study. Softw. Syst. Model. **19**(1), 67–94 (2020)
34. Zhang, K., et al.: Digital twin-based opti-state control method for a synchronized production operation system. Robot. Comput.-Integr. Manuf. **63**, 101892 (2020)
35. Zheng, P., Sivabalan, A.S.: A generic tri-model-based approach for product-level digital twin development in a smart manufacturing environment. Robot. Comput.-Integr. Manuf. **64**, 101958 (2020)
36. Zheng, Y., Yang, S., Cheng, H.: An application framework of digital twin and its case study. J. Ambient Intell. Humaniz. Comput. **10**(3), 1141–1153 (2018). https://doi.org/10.1007/s12652-018-0911-3

Leveraging Semi-formal Approaches for DepDevOps

Wanja Zaeske[1] and Umut Durak[1,2(✉)]

[1] Department of Informatics, Clausthal University of Technology,
Julius-Albert-Str. 4, 38678 Clausthal Zellerfeld, Germany
{wanja.zaeske,umut.durak}@tu-clausthal.de
[2] Institute of Flight Systems, German Aerospace Center (DLR),
Lilienthalplatz 7, 38108 Braunschweig, Germany
umut.durak@dlr.de

Abstract. While formal methods have long been praised by the dependable Cyber-Physical System community, continuous software engineering practices are now employing or promoting semi-formal approaches for achieving lean and agile processes. This paper is a discussion about using Behaviour Driven Development, particularly Gherkin and RSpec for DepDevOps, DevOps for dependable Cyber-Physical Systems.

Keywords: Semi-formal approaches · Dependable systems · Agile

1 Introduction

Software engineering is evolving towards removing disconnects among its activities with employing continuous practices to achieve agile processes. First, Test-Driven Development (TDD) bridged the gap between implementation and testing. Then, Continuous Integration (CI) and Continuous Deployment (CD) attacked the disconnect between the development and deployment. Eventually Behaviour-Driven Development (BDD) enhanced TDD with specification and continuous acceptance testing. Now DevOps is connecting development and operations.

Continuity with streamlined and automated processes has long been studied in software engineering to achieve agility. Not only iterative and incremental development life-cycles but also inevitable software evolution during operation have been asking for rapid feedback cycles between the developer and the user. DevOps is defined as the set of practices for reducing the time between committing the code and using it in normal operation [3]. It connects two worlds: the development and the operation. Accordingly it consists of two integrated cycles; one for development and the other for operation. A *Release* starts an operation cycle that is composed of *Deploy*, *Operate* and *Monitor* steps. Feedback from monitoring starts the next development cycle that is composed of *Plan*, *Design*, *Build*, *Test* and *Release* steps.

DevOps harmonizes the agile software engineering practices, from TDD and BDD to CI and CD to realize a fast forward track. It further promotes

© Springer Nature Switzerland AG 2020
A. Casimiro et al. (Eds.): SAFECOMP 2020 Workshops, LNCS 12235, pp. 217–222, 2020.
https://doi.org/10.1007/978-3-030-55583-2_16

monitoring and logging mechanism for feedback loops. As stated by Ebert et al. [8], "obviously, the achievable cycle time depends on the environmental constraints and deployment model". Inspired from the other application domains, Cyber-Physical Systems (CPS) users are now asking for on-the-fly software updates, easy problem reporting, and frequent feature enhancements. While the expectation is to have mobile-like driver-assistance or avionics applications, the dependability constraints and embedded software deployment models are preventing any cycle faster than years, deployed at the service centers by authorized personal.

This paper concentrates on dependability constraints, knowing that embedded software deployment is also an open research area for achieving full-fledged DevOps for CPS. Dependability is a system property that describes its ability to deliver services that can justifiably be trusted [1]. It is an integrated concept for availability, reliability, safety, integrity, and maintainability. Formal methods are mathematical techniques for specifying and verifying systems [7]. They have long been proposed and employed to tackle dependability challenges in general [17,19] and safety challenges in particular [2,5,12,13]. The dependable CPS community of the last decade has also praised formal methods as one of the key techniques [11,18]. While there are many research efforts that aim at integrating formal methods and agile practices, such as [4,9,21], this paper brings the semi-formal methods that are being practiced in DevOps world to the attention of dependable CPS community. The methods of interest are executable specification methods of BDD, Gherkin [22] and RSpec [6].

2   Behaviour Driven Development in DevOps

Chelimsky et al. [6] define BDD as "implementing an application by describing its behavior from the perspective of its stakeholders" It builds upon TDD, and promotes a semi-formal *ubiquitous language* for the specification of behaviours that is accessible to all the stakeholders of the system. The *ubiquitous language* idea is based on Evans [10], who stresses that the linguistic divide or the language fracture between the domain expert and the technical team leads only to vaguely described and vaguely understood requirements. The aim of BDD is to come up with executable as well as a human readable specification of the system, in a single representation [14].

BDD is structured around *features* which can be defined as the capabilities provided by the system that create a benefit to its users. A feature is usually described in BDD by a title, a brief narrative, and a number of scenarios that serve as acceptance criteria. Scenarios are concrete examples to describe the desired behaviours of the system. When the concrete examples are executable; they turn the criteria to an acceptance test. BDD calls this *automated acceptance testing*.

Gherkin is the common language to write features, particularly for the Cucumber test automation framework [22]. While it is not a Turing Complete language, it has a grammar enforced by a parser. It aims at human readability, while enabling execution in Cucumber using its grammar. The basic Gherkin keywords to specify a scenario are *Given, When* and *Then. Given* is used to describe the context of the system, the state of the system before an event. *When* is used to specify the event(s) and eventually *Then* is used to give the outcome(s).

Features that are written in Gherkin and executed in Cucumber are regarded as outer cycle. They define the behaviour of a system. RSpec is the name given to the language and the test automation framework that is used to specify the behaviour of objects [6]. It is regarded as the inner cycle. The test code is structured using *Describe, Context* and *It* keywords. *Describe* is used to define an example group. An example is a test case. *Context* is similar to *Describe*; it is used to group examples with a certain context. *It* is used to specify an example.

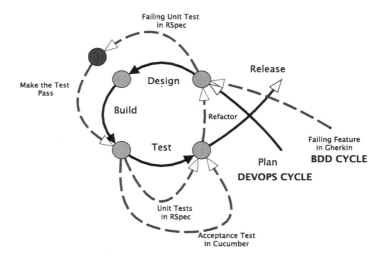

Fig. 1. Behaviour driven development in DevOps (Adapted from [23])

Figure 1 extends Yackel's ideas [23] about the integration of BDD in the development cycle of DevOps. The Plan, Design, Build, Test, and Release steps can be realized using a layered BDD approach with Cucumber and RSpec duo. Features are specified in Planning step using Gherkin. At the Design step, following a high level-design, required unit behaviour is specified using RSpec. Low-level design and implementation followed by Build step end up with a system to be tested. With every passing unit test in RSpec, system also undergoes acceptance tests in Cucumber against the feature specifications in Gherkin. The inner cycle ends when the outer cycle, namely the acceptance tests are successful and eventually leads to the Release step.

3   Gherkin and RSpec for Dependable CPS

If we take avionics as an example dependable CPS domain, the DO-178C Software Considerations in Airborne Systems and Equipment Certification [15] sets the baseline for process requirements. It necessitates high-level requirements specification that interprets the system requirements to the software item, and low-level requirements that can be directly implemented without further information. The authors would like to start a discussion about using Gherkin for the specification of high-level requirements and RSpec for low-level requirements with an example avionics application, Terrain Awareness and Warning System (TAWS).

TAWS is an airborne equipment introduced in 1990's for reducing the risk of the Controlled Flight Into Terrain (CFIT) accidents. It produces aural and visual warning for impending terrain with a forward looking capability and continued operation in landing configuration [16]. There are three classes of TAWS. Class A, being most stringent, are for large turbine powered aircraft with at least one radio altimeter; Class B for smaller turbine powered aircraft which may not have radio altimeter and Class C, being least stringent, for smaller general aviation aircraft.

Class C TAWS features include Forward Looking Terrain Avoidance (FLTA), Premature Descent Alerting (PDA), Excessive Rate of Descent (Mode 1), Negative Climb Rate or Altitude Loss After Take-Off or Go Around (Mode 3) and Five Hundred Foot Callout. The authors are prototyping a Class C TAWS, namely Open TAWS to demonstrate dependable DevOps concepts. Sample Gherkin and RSpec specifications that will be introduced in the following sections can be found at Open TAWS Git repository.[1]

DO-367 Minimum Operational Performance Standards (MOPS) for Terrain Awareness and Warning Systems (TAWS) Airborne Equipment states that during non-precision approaches Class C Equipment shall generate at least Five Hundred Foot Callout within 1.3 s of descending through 500 foot above terrain or the nearest runway, or the altitude Callout within 1.3 s of descending through the pilot selected altitude when the altitude callouts are not inhibited [16].

An excerpt from the Gherkin specification of the Five Hundred Foot Callout high-level requirement can be as follows:

```
Feature: Five Hundred Foot Callout
    DO-367 TAWS_MOPS_292
    Scenario: Aircraft less then 500 feet above the terrain
        Given Aircraft is in non-precision approach
            And Altitude callout is not inhibited
            When Aircraft descends under 500 feet above the terrain
            Then Within 1.3 seconds Five Hundred Foot Callout is given
```

Open TAWS is designed to have a terrain server, which needs to provide the terrain query interface that returns the altitude of a point at a given geographical position. Rust is selected as the programming language for Open TAWS due to its promises in safety, performance and zero-cost abstractions and growing embedded systems community [20]. An excerpt from the RSpec specification of

---

[1] https://gitlab.tu-clausthal.de/aeronautical-informatics/otaws.

the low-level requirement for the altitude query interface using Rust-RSpec[2] can be as follows:

```
rspec::describe("Altitude query", environment, |ctx| {
    ctx.specify("a position in geographical coordinates", |ctx| {
        ctx.it("should return the altitude of the terrain
        at that position", |env| {
            assert_eq!(env.sut.altitude(env.position),
            env.expected_altitude);
        });
    });
})
```

4 Outlook

The paper is a short discussion starter for employing semi-formal specification approaches of Behaviour Driven Development; namely Gherkin and RSpec for dependable CPS. The automated traceability and requirements-based test coverage analysis using test automation tools supporting Gherkin and RSpec is a promise of such an approach to support dependability and lean development. On the other side, ubiquitous specification languages, and specification-as-code approach enables both continuity and agility.

Both Cucumber and RSpec are written in the Ruby programming language, and were originally used for Ruby. While Cucumber (and Gherkin) could spread to various programming languages, RSpec is still almost exclusive to the Ruby community. There are both Cucumber and RSpec implementations for Rust. While Cucumber-Rust[3] is feature rich, Rust-RSpec is relatively limited and has not been maintained for a long time. Cucumber-Rust parses the human-readable semi-formal feature specifications and provides an API for developing test cases that implements them. However, limited API of Rust-RSpec almost fails to enable writing readable specification; they rather look like basic unit test code.

This paper reports the early experience from the example avionics application. Future work includes demonstration of a full-fledged DepDevOps with an extensive discussion about alternative tools and infrastructures.

References

1. Avizienis, A., Laprie, J.C., Randell, B., Landwehr, C.: Basic concepts and taxonomy of dependable and secure computing. IEEE Trans. Dependable Secure Comput. **1**(1), 11–33 (2004)
2. Barroca, L.M., McDermid, J.A.: Formal methods: use and relevance for the development of safety-critical systems. Comput. J. **35**(6), 579–599 (1992)

---

[2] https://github.com/rust-rspec/rspec.
[3] https://github.com/bbqsrc/cucumber-rust.

3. Bass, L., Weber, I., Zhu, L.: DevOps: A Software Architect's Perspective. Addison-Wesley Professional, Boston (2015)
4. Black, S., Boca, P.P., Bowen, J.P., Gorman, J., Hinchey, M.: Formal versus agile: survival of the fittest. Computer **42**(9), 37–45 (2009)
5. Bowen, J.P., Stavridou, V.: Formal methods and software safety. In: 1992 Safety of Computer Control Systems (SAFECOMP 1992), pp. 93–98. Elsevier (1992)
6. Chelimsky, D., Astels, D., Helmkamp, B., North, D., Dennis, Z., Hellesoy, A.: The RSpec Book: Behaviour Driven Development with Rspec. Cucumber, and Friends, Pragmatic Bookshelf **3**, 25 (2010)
7. Clarke, E.M., Wing, J.M.: Formal methods: state of the art and future directions. ACM Comput. Surv. (CSUR) **28**(4), 626–643 (1996)
8. Ebert, C., Gallardo, G., Hernantes, J., Serrano, N.: DevOps. IEEE Softw. **33**(3), 94–100 (2016)
9. Eleftherakis, G., Cowling, A.J.: An agile formal development methodology. In: Proceedings of the 1st South-East European Workshop on Formal Methods, pp. 36–47 (2003)
10. Evans, E.: Domain-Driven Design: Tackling Complexity in the Heart of Software. Addison-Wesley Professional, Boston (2004)
11. Fitzgerald, J., Gamble, C., Larsen, P.G., Pierce, K., Woodcock, J.: Cyber-Physical Systems design: formal foundations, methods and integrated tool chains. In: 2015 IEEE/ACM 3rd FME Workshop on Formal Methods in Software Engineering, pp. 40–46. IEEE (2015)
12. Gerhart, S., Craigen, D., Ralston, T.: Experience with formal methods in critical systems. IEEE Softw. **11**(1), 21–28 (1994)
13. McDermid, J.A.: Formal methods: use and relevance for the development of safety-critical systems. In: Safety Aspects of Computer Control, pp. 96–153. Elsevier (1993)
14. Okolnychyi, A., Fögen, K.: A study of tools for behavior-driven development. In: Full-Scale Software Engineering/Current Trends in Release Engineering, p. 7 (2016)
15. RTCA: DO-178C software considerations in airborne systems and equipment certification. RTCA (2011)
16. RTCA: DO-367 minimum operational performance standards (MOPS) for terrain awareness and warning systems (TAWS) airborne equipment. RTCA (2017)
17. Rushby, J., Underst, F.B.S., Stankovic, J.A.: Formal methods for dependable real-time systems (1992)
18. Seshia, S.A.: New frontiers in formal methods: learning, cyber-physical systems, education, and beyond. CSI J. Comput. **2**(4), R1 (2015)
19. Thomas, M.: The role of formal methods in achieving dependable software. Reliab. Eng. Syst. Saf. **43**(2), 129–134 (1994)
20. Uzlu, T., Şaykol, E.: On utilizing rust programming language for Internet of Things. In: 2017 9th International Conference on Computational Intelligence and Communication Networks (CICN), pp. 93–96, September 2017. https://doi.org/10.1109/CICN.2017.8319363
21. Wolff, S.: Scrum goes formal: agile methods for safety-critical systems. In: 2012 First International Workshop on Formal Methods in Software Engineering: Rigorous and Agile Approaches (FormSERA), pp. 23–29. IEEE (2012)
22. Wynne, M., Hellesoy, A., Tooke, S.: The Cucumber Book: Behaviour-Driven Development for Testers and Developers. Pragmatic Bookshelf (2017)
23. Yackel, R.: BDD in DevOps: an example of BDD in continuous integration. https://www.qasymphony.com/blog/bdd-devops-example-bdd-continuous-integration/. Accessed 20 May 2020

1st International Workshop on Underpinnings for Safe Distributed Artificial Intelligence (USDAI 2020)

1st International Workshop on Underpinnings for Safe Distributed AI (USDAI 2020)

Enabling technologies and regulatory frameworks for safe distributed AI

Morten Larsen[1], Alexandru Uta[2], and Simon Duque Anton[3]

[1] AnyWi Technologies, Leiden, the Netherlands
`Morten.Larsen@anywi.com`
[2] Leiden Institute of Advanced Computer Science, Leiden, the Netherlands
`A.Uta@liacs.leidenuniv.nl`
[3] German Research Center for AI, Kaiserslautern, Germany
`Simon.duque_anton@dfki.de`

1 Introduction

Safe distributed artificial intelligence (AI) requires a reliable and secure underpinning and Europe needs to develop its own capabilities in this area as witnessed by the increasingly frequent calls for a "European digital sovereignty". This will involve a significant effort to develop the required enabling technologies. Furthermore, to protect the investments made, it must be ensured that these technologies provide value for the involved stakeholders as well as society in general and create a lasting impact.

There are several ways in which to achieve the distribution of AI, but in all cases the right algorithms must meet the right data – and this must happen at the right moment if the application is time critical. Similarly, in order to learn from distributed "experiences", distributed learning approaches (federated, or central with redistribution of results) are needed.

The basic challenges to achieve safe distributed AI therefore include data collection, local processing and reliable transport, as well as the orchestration of distributed algorithms, all in a reliable and secure manner and in a way that respects the privacy of users, operators and the general public.

This workshop will address a wide range of enabling methods and technologies to ensure trustworthiness of data as well as the processing and use of the resulting information. Topics will range from advanced computational methods to the legal and regulatory frameworks in which they must function. There will be a session open for presenters to pitch project ideas for further work on the topics related to the workshop theme.

2   This Year's Workshop

The workshop USDAI 2020 presents discussions and insights to an interesting and relevant set of topics. The safe collection, transport, and usage of data for AI applications is discussed in four presentations and two keynote presentations.

The session starts with a keynote regarding relevance, applications and pitfalls of AI in different application scenarios. The first session **Data Collection and Processing** comprises two presentations:

1. Towards building data trust and transparency in data-driven business applications, *Annanda Rath, Wim Codenie, and Anna Hristoskova*
   In view of deriving business value from their (product) data, organisations need to adopt the right method and technology to analyse these data to infer new insights and business intelligence. This is feasible only with a certain guarantee on the completeness, trustworthiness, consistency and accuracy of the data. Thus, building trust in acquired (product) data and its analytics is pivotal if we are to realise its full benefits. To this end, we explore different technologies for building data trust, such as Blockchain, traditional distributed databases and trusted third party platforms, in combination with security algorithms. In this paper, we present a Blockchain-based solution for building data trust, based on which we designed a system prototype as a proof-of-concept.
2. Distributed AI for special-purpose vehicles, *Kevin Van Vaerenbergh, Henrique Cabral, Pierre Dagnely, and Tom Tourwé*
   In this paper, we elaborate on two issues that are crucial to consider when exploiting data across a fleet of industrial assets deployed in the field: 1) reliable storage and efficient communication of large quantities of data in the absence of continuous connectivity, and 2) the traditional centralized data analytics model which is challenged by the inherently distributed context when considering a fleet of distributed assets. We illustrate how advanced machine learning techniques can run locally at the edge, in the context of two industry-relevant use cases related to special-purpose vehicles: data compression and vehicle overload detection. These techniques exploit real-world usage data captured in the field using the I-HUMS platform provided by our industrial partner ILIAS solutions Inc.

The second session starts with a keynote as well. After that, two presentations about **AI in DevOps** are presented:

1. Cynefin Framework, DevOps and secure IoT, *Franklin Selgert*
   Cynefin does not mean tackling problems in familiar ways but with a new vocabulary. It means thinking about the world in a different way, drawing on lessons from complexity science, cognitive neuroscience and biological anthropology.
2. Creating it from SCRATCh: A Practical Approach for Enhancing the Security of IoT-Systems in a DevOps-enabled Software Development Environment, *Simon D Duque Anton, Daniel Fraunholz, Daniel Krohmer, Daniel Reti, Hans Dieter Schotten, Franklin Selgert, Marcell Marosvölgyi, Morten Larsen, Krishna Sudhakar, Tobias Koch, Till Witt and Cedric Bassem*

DevOps describes a method to reorganize the way different disciplines in software engineering work together to speed up software delivery. However, the introduction of DevOps-methods to organisations is a complex task. A successful introduction results in a set of structured process descriptions. Despite the structure, this process leaves margin for error: Especially security issues are addressed in individual stages, without consideration of the interdependence. Furthermore, applying DevOps-methods to distributed entities, such as the Internet of Things (IoT) is difficult as the architecture is tailormade for desktop and cloud resources. In this work, an overview of tooling employed in the stages of DevOps processes is introduced. Gaps in terms of security or applicability to the IoT are derived. Based on these gaps, solutions that are being developed in the course of the research project SCRATCh are presented and discussed in terms of benefit to DevOps-environments.

The aim is to unite academic research with industrial research and development in order to explore options for application-oriented uptake of new technologies in the field of safe distributed AI.

As chairpersons of the workshop, we want to thank all authors and contributors who submitted their work, the SAFECOMP Publication Chair, and the members of the International Program Committee who enabled a fair evaluation through reviews and considerable improvements in many cases. We want to express our thanks to the SAFECOMP organizers, who provided us the opportunity to organize the workshop at SAFECOMP 2020. Particularly we want to thank the EC and national public funding authorities who made the work in the research projects possible.

We hope that all participants will benefit from the workshop, enjoy the conference and accompanying programs and will join us again in the future!

Morten Larsen
Alexandru Uta

Acknowledgements. Part of the work presented in the workshop received funding from y ITEA3 through project SCRATCh (label 17005) with funding from: The Federal Ministry of Education and Research (BMBF) of the Federal Republic of Germany, within the project SCRATCh (01IS18062E, 01IS18062C), Netherlands Enterprise Agency, the regional institute for research and innovation of Brussels Belgium, Innoviris. see individual acknowledgements in papers.

International Program Committee

Morten Larsen	AnyWi Technologies (NL)
Alexandru Uta	LIACS, Leiden University (NL)
Alan Sears	Leiden Law School, Leiden University (NL)
Anna Hristokova	SIRRIS (BE)
Reda Nouacer	CEA (FR)
Ricardo Reis	Embraer (BR)
Andries Stam	Almende (NL)
Raúl Santos de la Cámara	Hi-Iberia (ES)

Valeriu Codreanu   SURFsara (NL)
Raj Thilak Rajan   TU Delft (NL)
Simon Duque Antón   DFKI (DE)
Tobias Koch   consider-it (DE)
George Dimitrakopoulos   Harokopio University (GR)

Towards Building Data Trust and Transparency in Data-Driven Business Applications

Annanda Rath$^{(\boxtimes)}$, Wim Codenie, and Anna Hristoskova

Software Engineering Department, Sirris, Brussel, Belgium
{Annanda.rath,Wim.Codenie,anna.hristoskova}@sirris.be
https://www.sirris.be

Abstract. In view of deriving business value from their (product) data, organisations need to adopt the right method and technology to analyse these data to infer new insights and business intelligence. This is feasible only with a certain guarantee on the completeness, trustworthiness, consistency and accuracy of the data. Thus, building trust in acquired (product) data and its analytics is pivotal if we are to realise its full benefits. To this end, we explore different technologies for building data trust, such as Blockchain, traditional distributed databases and trusted third party platforms, in combination with security algorithms. In this paper, we present a Blockchain-based solution for building data trust, based on which we designed a system prototype as a proof-of-concept.

Keywords: Data trust · Transparency · Data driven business · Security

1 Introduction

Companies that adopt a data-driven business model rely on (product) data to support their business operations. There are different ways companies or organisations can be driven by data. Specifically, there are those that are completely data-driven, where their business revenues are based solely on the selling data, others use data to drive a more conventional business, and still others use data to enhance or optimise their business (e.g., improve product or enhance business operation). Typically, in some service companies (e.g., sharing economy, market place, ...), large amount of data is generated, and a data-driven business model can be a powerful tool to boost the revenues, improve business efficiency, open additional business opportunities and create a positive impact on their business operation. With current competitive business environments, companies that harness the power of data to transform their businesses (e.g., offer additional services based on data) can become sustainable.

In data-driven business models, data are a critical asset and in order to sell these to business partners in the eco-system, a data provider company needs

© Springer Nature Switzerland AG 2020
A. Casimiro et al. (Eds.): SAFECOMP 2020 Workshops, LNCS 12235, pp. 229–242, 2020.
https://doi.org/10.1007/978-3-030-55583-2_17

to prove that the collected data are real, accurate and not manipulated. Companies, especially those that envision to include data-driven models in their business strategy, need to invest (in early phase) in building trust in their data and guaranteeing transparency in data analytics as a way to convince their partners. A study by Harvard Business Review[1] also highlights the importance of trust building and transparent data practices. It indicates that "in order to gain consumers' trust, transparent data practices are needed." Another report, from Sänger et al. [3], also highlights the importance of data trust and provides a roadmap for research in building trust in data.

We are currently living in the age of Big Data, where large amounts of trustworthy data can be utilised to establish innovative data-driven approaches, however, this is intrinsically tied to the trust we can put in the origins and quality of the underlying data. In this paper, we focus on building trust in data and its analytics by exploring different technological solutions from Blockchain to trusted third party platforms (e.g. Cloud), with the special focus on the Blockchain-based solutions.

The paper is organised as follows. Section 2 presents the notion of trust in data and security requirements for data trust assurance. Section 3 details the data trust solution and a high-level architecture. Section 4 is about the design of a prototype of a Blockchain-based solution. Section 5 focuses on the related work and we conclude this paper with Sect. 6.

2   Notion of Trust in Data and Security Requirements for Data Trust Assurance

In this section, we explain a notion of trust in data and highlight a list of security requirements for building trust in data.

2.1   Notion of Trust and Trust in Data

In the dictionary [6], trust refers to confidence in the honesty or integrity of a person or thing. Another definition of trust that is often cited in literature regarding trust and reputation online was proposed by Gambetta in 1988 [5] and is referred to as reliability trust: Trust is a particular level of the subjective probability with which an agent assesses that another agent or group of agents will perform a particular action, both before he can monitor such action (or independently of his capacity ever to be able to monitor it) and in a context in which it affects his own action.

In the recent decade, various trust models have been developed to establish trust. Thereby, two common ways can be distinguished, namely policy-based and reputation-based trust establishment [4]. Policy-based trust is based on the exchange of hard evidence (e.g., credentials). In general, it relies on objective "strong security" mechanisms, which are based on well defined semantics (e.g., logic programming) providing strong verification and analysis support.

---

[1] https://hbr.org/2015/10/can-your-data-be-trusted.

Reputation-based trust, in contrast, is derived from the history of interactions. Hence, it can be seen as an estimation of trustworthiness. Reputation is defined as follows: "Reputation is what is generally said or believed about a person or thing, character or standing" [4]. It is based on referrals, ratings or reviews from members of a community and can, therefore, be considered as a collective measure of trustworthiness [4, 8].

In this paper, we focus on policy-based trust establishment. We propose a solution for building trust in data and guaranteeing transparency in data analytics by means of technologies instead of using the history of interactions as a means to measure trust. The reason of focusing on policy-based trust is because we believe it is beneficial to all companies and organisations, mature or small, especially, to those that do not have long history of interactions with customers.

2.2 Security Requirements

In the following, we present security requirements for assuring that the data is tamper-proof from its creation to its storage or sharing with a third party system. These requirements cover the data source environment security, communication security, storage security and processing security.

1. Data source environment (DSE) represents the place where the data are generated. To ensure that data are not tampered with, it is pivotal to secure the DSE and make sure that the data cannot be manipulated at this level. If the data protection at this level fails, the entire eco-system fails. Various security protection techniques can be used, to achieve this security requirement, depending on the nature of the DSE (e.g. IoT-based vs Cloud-based).
2. Communication environment. To prevent possible data tampering while data are in a communication channel(s) and/or in transit, a secure communication medium must be used. Multi-layer of security (e.g. end-to-end encryption with standard security protocol) must be used in order to ensure tamper-proof data delivery.
3. Secure data processing environment and storage consists of three sub-requirements:
   - A secure data collection system must ensure that the data are collected securely from their sources and are correct and untampered.
   - Secure storage data tampering can also occur at storage level. In order to address this, we need to have a secure and tamper-proof data storage where a user can audit the data transparently.
   - Secure data auditing focuses on the validation of the data in storage. The system must allow a data client to check whether or not it has been tampered with. The auditing must be done independently, not under control/influence of a data provider.
4. The data sharing environment requires security, authenticity and correctness of data shared/sold to third party. The system must be able to prove the authenticity of data and be able to detect data tampering happened in a third party system.

It is worth mentioning that data need to be protected securely and should be tamper-proof in all of the four environments in order to meet the data trust security requirements.

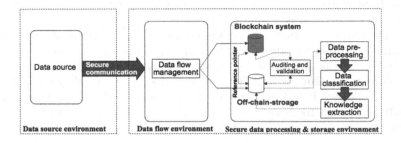

Fig. 1. High-level architecture of the blockchain-based solution

3   Data Trust Solutions and High-Level Architectures

In this section, we present our Blockchain-based solution able to guarantee data trust. Our assumption is that all entities (e.g., data provider, client, platform provider, ...) in the eco-system are untrusted, especially the data provider and there is a need to securely control and independently monitor the flow of data from creation to final destination. The proposed solution is used to ensure that the data is tamper proof and safe and if data tampering happens, it can be easily detected by means of trusted auditing tool operating independently from the data provider system.

3.1   Architecture of the Blockchain-Based Solution

As mentioned, we propose the architecture, in Fig. 1, which consists of the following modules:

1. The data source environment is where raw data are generated and sent, through secure communication, to the processing and storage facility module.
2. The Data flow management is responsible for managing the raw data. Once received, the raw data is stored in (1) the Blockchain (the immutable storage) and (2) the traditional database called "off-chain".
3. The Secure data processing and storage consists of the following three sub-modules:
    - Data storage consisting of: (1) Blockchain system, it stores a copy of data received from sources for validation purpose. The data in this storage will be used as an image to data stored in off-chain and (2) Off-chain storage stores encrypted raw data for data processing and information/knowledge extraction.

- The Data processing module is responsible for processing and extracting information and knowledge from the data set. It consists of (1) data pre-processing, (2) data classification and (3) knowledge extraction.
- The Data auditing and validation allows a data client to audit the data set, and check whether or not data tampering occurred. In case of an auditing request from a client for a given data set, the auditing module performs the operation by matching the data set stored in the off-chain and its image stored in the Blockchain. If these match, no tampering occurred. As stated earlier, the auditing module must be hosted on an independent platform not under control of the data provider to ensure transparency and trust.

This high-level architecture (see Fig. 1) provides an overview of the different modules required for securing data when they are moved to different entities/places in the system, for instance, when (product) data is moved from product installed at customer's premise to the product builder system. For the implementation of each module, it is a case-by-case study and we do not address all of them in this paper. However, in the prototype design in Sect. 4, we provide an implementation of a solution applied to a bike renting system case.

3.2   Blockchain-Based Solution- Short Description

Since there are different types of DSEs (e.g., IoT, data lake, on premise data) and each of them requires a specific security protection technique, we do not address them individually in this paper. We suppose that the DSE is secured with standard security principles (e.g., secure storage, secure access control, tamper-proof-resistance, ...) and the communication between the data source and the data flow management environment (DFM) (see Fig. 1) is secured through a standard protocol, such as TLS or SSL. Our Blockchain-based solution addresses the security between the DFM environment and the storage destination (see Fig. 1). However, in our prototype development presented in Sect. 4, we provide a solution for securing the IoT-based DSE as we take IoT as our target domain to build a proof-of-concept.

In this paper, Blockchain, with its immutable property, will be used to guarantee that the data is tamper-proof and ensure that data tampering can always be detected. As shown in Fig. 1, when the DFM module receives data from the DSE, it processes a copy of it and sends it to be stored in the Blockchain system. It is worth noting that we do not store a complete data set on the Blockchain, only a hash of it and its meta data (refer to as data image). Once, a copy of the data is successfully stored on the Blockchain, the Blockchain system returns a Unique Transaction Identification Number (UTIN) and the DFM module sends the original copy of data with this Blockchain UTIN to be stored in an off-chain storage (data resting place). A data image stored on the Blockchain is used to validate the authenticity of the original copy stored in the off-chain storage. All data stored in the off-chain needs to be encrypted and a searchable encryption algorithm [11] can be used to search for key information from the data set stored in the off-chain database without revealing the detailed information in data set. Doing so ensures integrity and confidentiality of data stored in off-chain.

If we want to check whether or not the data have been tampered with, we simply take the data stored in the off-chain and compare them to their image stored in the Blockchain. If it has been tampered with, they do not match. The communications between the DFM and the Blockchain and between the DFM and the off-chain database are secured through the TLS standard protocol.

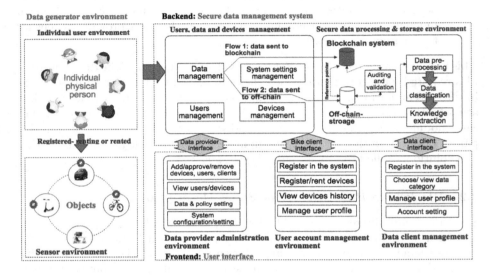

Fig. 2. Bike renting system prototype architecture

4   Prototype of Blockchain-Based Solution

In this section, we highlight the development of a system prototype of the Blockchain-based solution.

4.1   Prototype Description and Use Cases

Prototype Description. We aim at building a secure system that can provide trust in data and transparent data processing for data-driven service applications, particularly, for the sharing economy environment with the specific case of bike renting. The system is designed in a way to guarantee security, trust and reliability on data collection, knowledge extraction and data storage (e.g., tamper-evident and tamper-proof data access).

Use Case Scenarios. Suppose that a bike renting company provides a platform for users to rent bikes in a city. Each bike is attached with sensors, such as air quality and GPS, so that the company is able to collect air quality data in the area where the bike passed and also knows its GPS location. The company plans to generate revenues by selling the air quality data to partners, such as a city authority. In addition, the company also plans to make use of the GPS data for advertisement purposes since a particular time and location can be linked to an individual person (e.g., people who rent bikes) and to buildings (e.g., shops or companies). With precise GPS data and a number of bikes passing a particular location, the bike renting company can offer targeted advertisement to shops or companies that have their building in or around that location.

4.2   System Architecture and Solutions

In this section, we present in detail, the bike renting system architecture for data collection and processing. As shown in Fig. 2, there are three important modules.

1. The Data generator environment (DGE) represents the place where data are generated. It includes of two data sources: (1) bike user, his address, personal information, bike usage pattern and (2) sensor devices attached to the bike. Data in the DGE is managed and secured by a system embedded in each sensor device attached to the bike. DGE does not process data, but it forwards data to the Backend for further processing.
2. The Backend handles the data processing and additional security assurance to ensure that the data is tamper-proof in all processing states. The Backend is divided into two sub-components:
   – User, data and device management consisting of four sub-modules:
     (a) The Data management module is responsible for managing the data flow from the DGE to both storages: (1) Blockchain and (2) off-chain. This module is also responsible for assuring that the data stored in the blockchain is an exact image of the one stored in the off-chain storage.
     (b) The Users management module is responsible for managing the types of users in the system (e.g., add/remove users): (1) the bike client referring to physical users using the bike renting services; (2) the data provider or bike renting system owner referring to users who have administrative access in the system and can activate/deactivate users, add/remove devices and perform other operations necessary for assuring the well-functioning of system; (3) the data client, referring to those who purchase data from the data providers
     (c) The Device management module is responsible for managing all sensor devices in the system. Through this module, the administrator can add, deactivate or remove sensor devices and bikes from his system.
     (d) The System setting management allows the administrator to set the system parameters to their preference. For example, set the connection parameters (interfaces) between the DGE and the backend or between the backend and the frontend.
   – Secure, data processing and storage consisting of six main components:

(a) The blockchain platform (immutable storage) where an image of the data is stored permanently. The data in the immutable storage will be used to validate the data in the off-chain.

(b) The off-chain storage is responsible for managing and storing raw data received from the DGE. The off-chain can be a simple file system or a database management system.

(c) The data auditing and validation is the most critical module as it allows the data client to detect any data tampering. In case of an auditing request for a particular set of data from the data client, the auditing and validation module compares the data set in the off-chain with their images on the blockchain. If they do not match, it means that the data has been tampered with.

(d) The data pre-processing responsible for transforming the data to the desired type and format.

(e) The data classification. Once the data have been pre-processed, they are classified depending on its intended purpose. For example, create a list of bikes that passed a given GPS location.

(f) The Knowledge extraction module is responsible for extracting knowledge from a given data set. For example, an average number of bikes passed a given GPS location and time.

3. The Frontend is the interface allowing users to access the bike renting services. As shown in Fig. 2, there are three frontend interfaces for three types of user: (1) the data provider interface facilitating the data provider with the management of users, devices and system setting, (2) the bike client interface allowing the bike client to manage its bike usage history, and (3) the data client interface allowing the data client to manage its preferred set of data (bike data) selected based on their preferred GPS location.

4.3   System Development

In this section, we present the prototype development architecture, highlighting the various used technologies and programming languages. As shown in Fig. 3, there are two main parts: (1) the data structure and (2) the system components.

Data Flow Description. As shown in Fig. 3, the entire system is divided into three main components: (1) device environment, (2) backend and (3) frontend. In our prototype design, the device environment is connected wirelessly to the backend with Lora/wifi technology. The MQTT messaging protocol is used for sending sensor data to the backend. Each device publishes periodically its sensor data to the MQTT broker, installed at backend. A module for managing data from a sensor device is developed in Python and is part of the backend component. This python-based data management module acts as data flow control between the device environment and the backend. It gets sensor data by subscribing to the MQTT broker. The received data is formatted in accordance with a predefined structure in the form of the BigchainDB [16] transaction and sent to be stored/added on the BigchainDB Blockchain. After successfully stored on

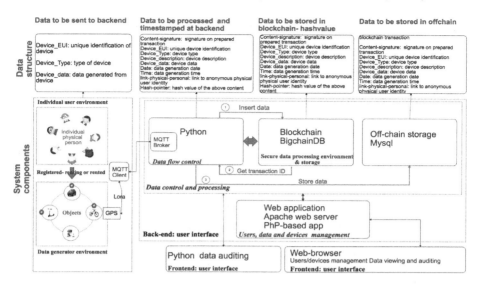

Fig. 3. Bike renting system implementation architecture

the Blockchain, BigchainDB returns a unique transaction ID. This ID combined with additional data (e.g., device and sensor data) will be sent to be stored in a Mysql database. Data stored on the Blockchain is an image of that stored in the off-chain database and is used for data auditing purposes. Two sets of frontend applications are developed to facilitate the users: (1) a web-based frontend and (2) a python-based frontend, which is used only for data auditing purposes. For the web-based frontend, php is used to develop a web application providing the following features: (1) users management, (2) devices management, (3) data viewing and (4) data auditing.

Data Structure. This part of the architecture defines the structure of data to be processed and stored on the various system locations. There are four different data structure formats for (1) devices environment, (2) data flow control, (3) BigchainDB Blockchain transaction, and (4) Mysql off-chain database (for more detail refer to Fig. 3).

System Components. In this section, we present the system components of the prototype we developed.

1. The Data generator module is responsible for retrieving sensor data and communicating it to the data flow control module. We developed micro-python library that can be deployed on pycom-Lopy [9] micro controler (MC). The developed library has two functions: (1) retrieving data from a sensor device attached to the Lopy (in our case we use Pytrack [9] GPS sensor) and (2) communicating sensor data to the data flow control module. In our implementation, we used MQTT for communicating sensor data to the data flow

control module. We also developed a MQTT pub/sub library to be installed on the Lopy MC.

2. The Data flow module hosts three important modules: (1) MQTT broker, (2) data formatter and (3) BigchainDB driver [10].

   (a) **MQTT broker.** MQTT mosquito [1] is used as the broker for the communication between the data flow control module and the device environment module. This broker is integrated with the data flow control module, which is developed in Python.

   (b) **Data formatter**, developed in Python, is responsible for formatting the data for compatibility with the BigchainDB transaction structure. This formatted data is then used as input for the BigchainDB Blockchain transaction validator, that formats the data into valid BigchainDB transaction. It is worth noting that only a valid BigchainDB transaction can be sent to the BigchainDB network to be inserted on the Blockchain.

   (c) **BigchainDB driver** is an interface connecting the data flow control module to the BigchainDB system. Through this driver, we can submit transactions to be inserted on the Blockchain or retrieve transactions from it. In our implementation, we used python-based BigchainDB driver [10], which is integrated into the data flow control module.

3. **BigchainDB.** In our prototype development, we use BigchainDB as Blockchain implementation technology. BigchainDB can reside on our backend or can be a separate external system installed on a different network or even on the Internet. It is important to note that not all Blockchain implementations fit with our proposed solution. Only Blockchain implementations with high transaction and fast data retrieval rate can be used in our case explaining why BighchainDB has been chosen.

4. **Off-chain storage** stores human-readable data from sensor devices. In our implementation, we use the Mysql database management system as off-chain storage. The Mysql database is also used to store devices' and users' information.

5. **Web backend.** The entire backend of the bike renting system is developed in two different programming languages: (1) Python and (2) PhP. The Apache web server is used as the backend system for the web content offering to the web-based frontend user while the Python backend serves as the python frontend user interface for auditing purposes.

6. **Python data auditing interface and PhP web-based auditing interface.** In our prototype, we have developed two different frontend interfaces: (1) a web-based interface for device and user management, system setting and data auditing and (2) a python frontend interface for data auditing purposes only.

4.4   Security Implementation, Experimentation and Testing

Access Control. In our implementation, we use username and password as authentication mechanism for physical users (e.g., data client, data provider and bike client) and password plus unique identification for sensor devices authentication when they onboard the system. The authentication at the MQTT broker level is done with username and password, meaning only devices with valid user and password can publish and subscribe to it.

Secure Communication Between System Components. The communication between the sensor devices and the data flow management module is secured with the TLS protocol embedded in the MQTT mosquito broker and pub/sub client module. The communications between the data flow management module and the BigchainDB Blockchain, and the Mysql system and the web server are secured with the TLS protocol. We also add another security layer to the data sent across the TLS communication by encrypting sensor data with AES before sending them through the TLS channel.

Implementation of Auditing Module. The data auditing module is one of the most important components of the system. Two auditing interfaces are developed. The first is a web-based interface allows users to audit sensor data based on the data tampering models presented below. There, a data client needs to log into the system with a username and password before being able to perform a data auditing operation. The data client needs to select data auditing periods and send the auditing request with the selected periods to the system. Once the data clients request has been received, the system performs the auditing operation and returns a detailed information if it detects data tampering activities. The second auditing interface is a python-based command-line, which allows users to audit the sensor data based on the same data tampering models.

Data Tampering Models. We implemented the solutions for the following data tampering models: (1) a data provider inserts new line(s) of data manually in the database, (2) a data provider modifies a data set manually in the database and (3) a data provider modifies a blockchain transaction identification linked to the Blockchain platform.

System Experimentation and Testing. We performed 6 different system tests based on the testing criteria defined based on the data tampering models presented above. In our test, the GPS [10] sensor data are generated randomly and sent to system through MQTT publishers. This MQTT publishers represent the GPS sensor devices in real system deployment. To simulate the data tampering activities, we manually modified the GPS data, Blockchain transaction identification and some of sensor data in off-chain Mysql database. We performed data auditing tests for both auditing interfaces: web-based and python-based command-line. Based on the results of the tests, we find that system performs correctly and its data auditing response time correlates with the length of data auditing periods, the larger auditing time interval, the larger response time. It is worth noting that the data auditing response time is largely influenced by the Blockchain transaction retrieval response time where an average data retrieval response time from Blockchain is 50, 70 ms.

5   Related Work

Several works highlight the data trust challenges [1–5, 7]. For instance, a roadmap for building data trust in big data is proposed by Sänger [3]. However, the paper does not provide solutions to the data trust challenge. In this paper, our research focuses on solutions for data-driven business applications. We limit our scope to this particular domain as we believe this use case has very high business potential and social impact. The most relevant papers to our work are:

Wang and Guo [2] focus on a Blockchain-based data trust sharing mechanism in the supply chain where they address the trust and privacy problem during the data sharing process in the supply chain. In their paper, they start with system architecture design to introduce the system framework, service process and data model for data trust sharing. Secondly, they implement the blockchain-based supply chain platform, consisting of account management module and data request processing module with open data index name extension. At last, they state a use case in supply chain to analyse their platform.

Kaaniche and Laurent [1] introduce a Blockchain-based data usage auditing architecture with enhanced privacy and availability. Towards these security and privacy challenges, they combine hierarchical identity based cryptographic mechanisms with emerging blockchain infrastructures and propose a blockchain-based data usage auditing architecture ensuring availability and accountability in a privacy-preserving fashion. The approach relies on the use of auditable contracts deployed in blockchain infrastructures. Thus, it offers transparent and controlled data access, sharing and processing, so that unauthorised users cannot process data without client authorisation. Moreover, based on cryptographic mechanisms, their solution preserves privacy of data owners and ensures secrecy for shared data with multiple service providers. It also provides auditing authorities with tamper-proof evidences for data usage compliance.

Bonatti et al. [4] work on an integration of reputation-based and policy-based trust management. The two trust management approaches address the same problem - establishing trust among interacting parties in distributed and decentralised systems. The authors analyse the differences between the two models of trust and argue that an integrated approach would improve significantly trust management systems.

The researches above focus particularly on the protection of data when they are shared between different parties in the distributed environment with the assumption that data provider is a trustworthy entity (there is no question of authenticity and origin of the data shared in the system). This opposites to what we are trying to address. In our case, we assume that all parties involving in processing data are untrusted (including data provider), hence, our solutions is designed in such a way so that it can be used in completely untrusted environment by shielding the communication and protecting data in such a way so that even data provider could not tamper them.

6   Conclusion

In this paper, we propose a system architecture that can be used as reference for building data trust in data-driven business applications. When designing systems aiming at building trust in data, we recommend a Blockchain-based solution if we want to achieve high level of data trust and if the system is planned to operate in an untrusted eco-system. However, the Blockchain-based solution does not fit in case of very load and delay intolerant/sensitive real-time applications; this is because a Blockchain transaction processing takes more time compared with a traditional database system. Given this limitation, we are currently working on other solutions for building trust in data, such as traditional distributed database and trusted third party concepts.

Acknowledgement

icity.brussels is project focused on research, development, innovation and valorization. We help Brussels emerge as the ICT Heart of Europe. Funded by the ERDF and Innoviris and as a joint initiative of ULB, VUB and SIRRIS, icity.brussels is entirely devoted to strengthening Research and Innovation in Information and Communication Technologies (ICT) in Brussels.

References

1. Kaaniche, N., Laurent, M.: A blockchain-based data usage auditing architecture with enhanced privacy and availability. In: 2017 IEEE 16th International Symposium on Network Computing and Applications (NCA), Cambridge, MA, pp. 1–5 (2017)
2. Wang, L., Guo, S.: Blockchain based data trust sharing mechanism in the supply chain. In: Yang, C.-N., Peng, S.-L., Jain, L.C. (eds.) SICBS 2018. AISC, vol. 895, pp. 43–53. Springer, Cham (2020). https://doi.org/10.1007/978-3-030-16946-6_4
3. Sänger, J., Richthammer, C., Hassan, S., Pernul, G.: Trust and big data: a roadmap for research. In: 2014 25th International Workshop on Database and Expert Systems Applications, Munich, pp. 278–282 (2014)
4. Bonatti, P., Duma, C., Olmedilla, D., Shahmehri, N.: An integration of reputation-based and policy-based trust management. Technical document, Universita di Napoli Federico II, Napoli, Italy, Linköpings universitet and L3S Research Center and University of Hannover, Hanover, Germany (2007)
5. Gambetta, D.: Can we trust trust? In: Gambetta, D. (ed.) Trust: Making and Breaking Cooperative Relations, pp. 213–237. Basil Blackwell, Oxford (1988)
6. Definition of trust. https://www.oxfordlearnersdictionaries.com/definition/english/trust_2
7. Belov, N., Schlachter, J., Buntain, C., Golbeck, J.: Computational trust assessment of open media data. In: 2013 IEEE International Conference on Multimedia and Expo Workshops (ICMEW), pp. 1–6 (2013)
8. Albanese, M.: Measuring trust in big data. In: Aversa, R., Kołodziej, J., Zhang, J., Amato, F., Fortino, G. (eds.) ICA3PP 2013. LNCS, vol. 8286, pp. 241–248. Springer, Cham (2013). https://doi.org/10.1007/978-3-319-03889-6_28

9. Pytrack Pycom. https://pycom.io/product/pytrack/
10. BigchainDB and Python BigchainDB driver. https://www.bigchaindb.com
11. Pramanick, N., Ali, S.T.: A comparative survey of searchable encryption schemes. In: 8th International Conference on Computing, Communication and Networking Technologies (ICCCNT), Delhi, pp. 1–5 (2017)

Distributed AI for Special-Purpose Vehicles

Kevin Van Vaerenbergh[(✉)], Henrique Cabral, Pierre Dagnely,
and Tom Tourwé

EluciDATALab Sirris, Boulevard A. Reyerslaan 80, 1030 Brussels, Belgium
kevin.vanvaerenbergh@sirris.be

Abstract. In this paper, we elaborate on two issues that are crucial to
consider when exploiting data across a fleet of industrial assets deployed
in the field: 1) reliable storage and efficient communication of large quantities of data in the absence of continuous connectivity, and 2) the traditional centralized data analytics model which is challenged by the inherently distributed context when considering a fleet of distributed assets.
We illustrate how advanced machine learning techniques can run locally
at the edge, in the context of two industry-relevant use cases related to
special-purpose vehicles: data compression and vehicle overload detection. These techniques exploit real-world usage data captured in the field
using the I-HUMS platform provided by our industrial partner ILIAS
solutions Inc.

Keywords: IoT · Distributed data analysis · Time series data
compression

1 Introduction

Ever more industrial assets are being instrumented and connected thanks to significant evolutions in Internet-of-Things (IoT) technology, e.g. smaller sensors
and reliable connectivity. Detailed data on how/when/where an asset is used
can be captured continuously, transferred to a central platform, where it is analysed via advanced data analytics technologies to extract useful insights. This
enables advanced health and usage monitoring applications that help to ensure
availability, reliability and safety of the equipment.

At present, such usage monitoring is mostly done at the level of the individual asset. Many companies however are operating and managing large groups
of assets, and would like to apply advanced data-driven analysis techniques to
extract insights across their entire fleet. Examples are fleets of vehicles operated
at globally-distributed sites, wind turbines arranged within parks, compressors
and pumps in industrial surroundings, etc. In that context, two issues are crucial
to consider:

This work is supported by the Brussels-capital region - Innoviris.

- reliable storage and efficient communication of large quantities of data is challenging due to the absence of continuous connectivity [8, 13]
- the traditional centralized data analytics model is challenged by the inherently distributed fleet context [5, 9]

In the next two subsections, we will explain these in more detail.

1.1 Reliable Storage and Efficient Communication of Large Quantities of Data Is Challenging Due to the Absence of Continuous Connectivity

Industrial assets can continuously gather data but are not necessarily continuously connected. Some are highly-mobile (e.g vehicles or aircraft) and sites where they are deployed can be extremely remote, hence continuous and reliable communication means are not guaranteed. In addition, different connection means are possible (e.g. fast Wi-Fi, sat-com or slower 3/4G), but each technology influences how much data can be transferred, at which speed, at what cost, etc. Finally, data offloading opportunities can be scarce and short and offloading should not interfere with normal operations. For instance, some assets need regular refuelling but this often does not take long enough to transfer all the data or does not always happen within an area with communication means.

Consequently, data needs to be stored on-asset until it can be off-loaded to a collection point. However, storage comes at a cost and explicitly managing this cost requires carefully considering the amount of data that is retained at asset-level and eventually transferred. To ensure the most relevant data is always retained, data reduction techniques need to be considered. In Sect. 3, we will detail how we consider data compression for special-purpose vehicles in such a distributed context.

1.2 The Traditional Centralized Data Analytics Model Is Challenged by the Inherently Distributed Fleet Context

Assets in a fleet are often geographically distributed and not (necessarily) continuously connected, resulting in data that is scattered over different locations. Such an inherently distributed context is in sharp contrast with the traditional centralized data analytics model, in particular the assumption of traditional AI algorithms that data needs to be available centrally for analysis.

There are good reasons to execute intelligent algorithms on the assets themselves. This can lower the communication cost and the need for bandwidth, as the model, rather than the data itself, can be transferred. It can also help to meet important privacy and security requirements, as sensitive data is processed on-asset and doesn't need to be transferred. *Edge computing*, a paradigm that empowers edge nodes within a distributed network to handle data, is currently mostly limited to relatively simple processing tasks, such as down-sampling and encryption. However, the concept of *edge intelligence*, combining edge computing and machine learning technologies, is rapidly emerging. In Sect. 4, we will illustrate how we apply AI methods at the edge for vehicle overload classification.

2   Special-Purpose Vehicle Monitoring

In the context of this work, we use vehicle usage data provided by our industrial partner ILIAS Solutions[1]. A fleet of special-purpose vehicles are instrumented by ILIAS' I-HUMS system which captures vehicle usage measurements (Fig. 1). The system consists of a smart sensor device, a collector antenna and a decentralized data processing server. The smart sensor device contains several sensors sampling at $200\,Hz$, e.g. 3-axis accelerometer and 3-axis gyroscope,

Fig. 1. ILIAS' I-HUMS sensor.

and can connect to a vehicle's CANbus for extra data collection, sampled at $1\,Hz$. The device offloads the data via the collector antenna when in the vicinity and transfers it to the data processing server.

Two relevant use cases are considered

- Data compression: compress the time series data generated by a vehicle to limit data storage requirements and speed up data transfer in such a way that relevant data is retained as much as possible.
- Vehicle overload: classify a drive as overloaded or not, in order to warn the operator, limit premature wear-and-tear and prevent warranty to become void.

3   Data Compression for Special-Purpose Vehicles

Vehicle usage data is gathered at a high frequency and to deal with this fine-grained time series data, we employ data compression. Data compression can be lossy or lossless. In contrast to most lossless techniques [12] such as [4] and [16], a much higher compression rate can be achieved using lossy techniques [14]. Many lossy compression techniques for time series have been researched [1,7] and [10] with some having trouble on compressing all data types or having a large run-time. Therefore, we looked at data compression using deep learning.

The algorithm we implemented is proposed by [3] and uses LSTM [2] for encoding and decoding time series signals. They propose a recurrent auto-encoder (RAE) [6] as base to learn the dependencies of the signal, increasing the compression of sections of the signal that have low informativeness/variance. A detailed description of the algorithm can be found in the next section.

---

[1] https://www.ilias-solutions.com.

3.1   Methodology

The intuition behind the methodology is that all data points are not equally relevant. Many assets have "stable" periods where they are barely active, and periods with higher activity. For instance, a vehicle can be waiting at a traffic light, generating a stable period of mostly irrelevant data. Later on, the vehicle can be driving off-road in mountainous terrain, generating a period with relevant data to better understand/monitor it's behaviour. The methodology intends to detect the irrelevant periods and send the related data with a lower resolution, e.g. 1 min granularity, while keeping the periods with relevant data at a higher resolution, e.g. 1 s granularity.

The methodology follows these three steps:

- Train a model to characterize the data input, i.e. model the stable and active behaviours
- Use the model to detect the stable and active periods in the signal to compress
- Down-sample the stable periods or up-sample the active periods

The model used is a recurrent auto-encoder (RAE). RAEs are a specific kind of recurrent neural nets (RNN) [15] dedicated to reconstruct an input signal using time-dependent features. It is composed of two long short-term memory nets (LSTM), one encoder and one decoder. The encoder compresses the input signal, which the decoder receives and from which it tries to reconstruct the input signal as closely as possible. Some limitations are given to the decoder in order to avoid a perfect reconstruction of the signal. These limitations ensure that the decoder focuses on the main characteristics of the input signal and discards unnecessary information.

The methodology relies on two parameters; standard deviation (STD) threshold and error margin. The STD threshold is used to segment the training data into segments with similar variance. Training data can be acquired from the asset itself or from a similar one. The data is greedily partitioned into segments given that the total variance for all the data points within the same segment is close to the STD threshold (depending of the data characteristics). The RAE is trained to be able to reconstruct these segments. When the RAE is successfully trained, it can be used to compress the time series input signals.

The error margin parameter influences the amount of compression reached by the algorithm. The trained RAE is the basis to identify the to-compress segments in the signal, i.e. to detect the boundaries of the segments that can be accurately reconstructed given the allowed error. The compression relies on the down sampling of these segments. The algorithm loops over the data to identify the segments to compress. Stable periods in the signal can be better reconstructed by the RAE and therefore have a larger compression rate. The resulting signal is a compressed version of the original signal which consists of several segments of the RAE input size.

3.2 Results

We applied the methodology on the signal received from the x-axis of the acceleration from a driving vehicle, sampled at 200 Hz.

To train the RAE, we segment the signal given a STD threshold, calculated in an automatic way by bootstrapping a set of segments of distinct sizes from the original signal and averaging their STD. The original segmentation method scans the signal sequentially and defines the periods where the STD threshold is not surpassed. Unfortunately, this approach does not take into account the change in variability of the signal. In some situations, this can lead to a segment that is a combination of a period with high variability, followed by a period of low variability. This is avoided by simply scanning the signal first to define the indexes where there is a sudden change in STD over a rolling window. The indexes identified by the first scan, together with the fixed STD thresholds are used to segment the signal properly, as can be seen in Fig. 2.

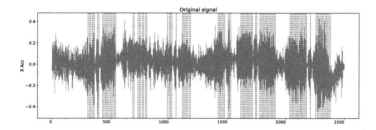

Fig. 2. Example of the segments found in the signal using the two-step segmentation process.

We trained the RAE using the segments defined above offline. We use an auto-encoder consisting of two LSTM layers for encoding and decoding, with 128 and 64 as input size for encoding, and the reverse for decoding. The network was trained using 500 epoch, a batch size of 64 and an input size of 30. When the RAE is trained, we run the compressing algorithm on the original signal. When the trained network is validated, it can be used on the edge device to compress in real time.

We compress the original signal given a series of allowed error margins (0.1 to 0.5 with 0.1 step size) and two different minimum segment sizes for constructing the training data (15 and 30). The STD threshold is calculated automatically using a bootstrapping methodology but this can be defined manually by a domain expert. The minimum segment size of the training data is chosen to be half and the same as the RAE input size. This influences the amount of detail that the RAE can reconstruct, as a minimum of half of the input size results in a up-sampling of the segments to twice their original size for training, increasing the details of the segments. Using a minimum size equivalent to the RAE input size will not increase the details of the original segments.

Figure 3 shows the results of a compression given a low error margin (0.1) and a varying minimum segment size. The segments size influences the RAE's ability to learn more details, as can be seen when comparing the left plot (minimum size 15) and middle plot (minimum size 30) resulting compressed signal. The smaller segment size compression reconstructs the original signal in more details without increasing in signal size (see the comparison plot on the right side). While we have a more detailed reconstruction of the original signal using a smaller segments size, the training of the RAE does take significantly more time due to the larger size of training data.

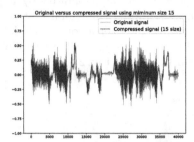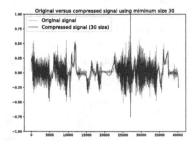

Fig. 3. Comparison of a piece of the compressed signal versus the original signal, given error margin 0.1 and minimum segment size 15 (left) or 30 (right).

In Fig. 4, we compare the signal sizes with respect to a varying error margin, the original signal size and the theoretical compression size using Huffman encoding [11]. There is a clear correlation between the allowed error margin and the resulting compresses signal size. Since the compression is based on the same trained RAE, one can simply apply a small error margin when a small compression is needed, e.g. when the asset still has a large amount of storage space left but no connection to a data sink

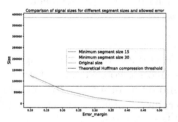

Fig. 4. Comparison of sizes for different parameter settings.

has been found in days, or use a large error margin if storage space is becoming scarce.

4   Overload Indication for Special-Purpose Vehicles

In this section, we illustrate how we apply AI methods at the edge for vehicle overload classification. Detecting overload is particularly challenging, as the behavior of a vehicle is tied to the road it is driving on, as well as to the driving style in question. Furthermore, not all moments of driving are likely to be good indicators of vehicle load: a heavily loaded vehicle driving at constant speed on a high-way is not in the same "effort" state as the same vehicle going uphill.

We compare two approaches that draw on vehicle measurements to predict the load of a vehicle at any given time during driving. The first approach uses a machine learning classifier built on features derived from sliding windows of the time series measurements, which reflect the dynamics of the vehicle over a short period of time. The second approach uses a Long Short Term Memory (LSTM) neural network on the raw measurement data to make the classification.

4.1 Data

The full dataset contains 10 h of driving from 3 different vehicles of the same type. To ensure that the models developed are sufficiently robust to cover different contexts and situations, and to eliminate the driver behavior as factor influencing the load estimation, all drives were performed by different drivers on routes incorporating on-road and off-road terrain, normal roads and highways, and characteristics that allowed accelerating, breaking and turns.

To limit the overload detection to moments when the vehicle was in motion, only periods when vehicle speed was above 0 km/h was used. This resulted in a dataset with 7 h of driving, split among the different vehicle load classes - normal load (3100 kg) and low (3640 kg), medium (3940 kg) and heavy overload (4380 kg).

The dataset contains a total of 9 drives with an average duration of 39 min (standard deviation: 3.2 min; normal and low overload classes are represented in 4 and 3 drives, respectively. Medium and heavy overload classes occur in a single drive).

4.2 Machine Learning Classifier

As a first approach, we train a machine learning classifier based on features derived from the recorded measurements.

Feature Definition. To capture the dynamics of the vehicle during driving with different loads, a rolling window of 10 s was slid through the dataset and used to calculate features based on the driving attributes. These features, listed in Table 1, were normalized with a standard score.

To control for highly correlated pairs of features, the Pearson correlation was calculated for all combinations and a threshold of 0.9 was set. This revealed that flow rate features (mean and std) were highly correlated with engine RPM. The former ones were excluded from the model dataset.

Table 1. Features used to build the classifier.

Attribute name	Description	Features derived
Engine RPM	Rotations per minute (RPM)	mean and std
Acceleration	Speed range over window duration (km/h)	
Speed	Vehicle speed (km/h)	min, max and mean
Accelerometer	3-axis acceleration values (g)	sum
Engine load	Load of the engine (%)	mean and std
Throttle position	Position of the throttle (%)	mean and std
Pressure	Absolute pressure (kPa)	mean and std
Flow rate	Flow rate (g/s)	mean and std

Dataset Preparation. The time-dependent nature of the data poses an added challenge in the building of a classifier, because train and test dataset cannot be simply defined using a random split of the data, to avoid that neighbouring time points fall in both train and test datasets, as these are likely to be heavily correlated, given the rolling window nature of the dataset. The limited number of drives, however, does not allow splitting the dataset along individual drives. To tackle this issue, the drives in the dataset were segmented to create *synthetic* drives. This segmentation was performed as follows: 1) Identify moments when vehicle speed dropped to below 1 km/h (putative vehicle stop); 2) Split drives along those speed drop moments; 3) Divide each drive split into 5 min.

Furthermore, to avoid spill-over of one synthetic drive to the next one, the first 9 samples in each synthetic drives are excluded (because we're using 10 s rolling windows, which correspond to 10 samples). This procedure generated 112 synthetic drives distributed along the different load classes as follows: normal: 29, low: 66, medium: 9, heavy: 8.

To reduce the class imbalancement, which hampers the modelling performance, the two major classes (normal and low load) were undersampled. This was achieved by defining as maximum number of drives three times the number of drives of the least represented class. This resulted in a dataset, which consisted of 23 5-min drives for the normal load and low overload classes and 9 and 8 drives for the medium and heavy overload classes, respectively.

The splitting of the dataset into train and test datasets was done using a (load) balanced 3:1 ratio.

Results. The goal of the solution presented here is to predict the load category of a vehicle at any given point in time. Furthermore, based on this individual frame predictions, we calculate the overall load class for each drive by means of a majority vote.

Different classification algorithms were tested with a 10-fold cross-validation using an accuracy score. The k-nearest neighbour (KNN) and random forest (RF) both showed a high prediction accuracy. The RF classifier had, in addition, a very short standard deviation, showing a high degree of consistency across the

10 iterations of the cross-validation and was, therefore, chosen for the vehicle overload classification.

The random forest classifier parameters were fine-tuned using a random search cross-validation approach, where a number of possible parameters were randomly selected within a defined range. To compensate for the unbalanced load classes (normal and low load classes occur 3 to 4 times more than the medium and heavy classes), the proportion of time points in each class was used as class weights for the classifier to reduce the impact of having an unbalanced dataset.

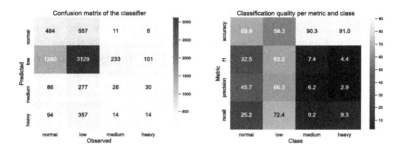

Fig. 5. Confusion matrix of the RF classifier (left) and prediction quality for different metrics and per load class (right).

The results of the random forest prediction on individual time frames of the test dataset are summarized in Fig. 5. The left plot shows the confusion matrix, where the values on the matrix diagonal correspond to matches between the predicted and observed values. These account for 55% of all observations (prediction accuracy). The plot on the right shows the value of 4 classification quality metrics for each of the overload cases: accuracy, precision (the percentage of "positive" predictions that are correct, a positive being each class), recall (the percentage of correctly predicted "positives") and f1 score (the harmonic mean of precision and recall). Accuracy was generally very high across all four classes. A closer look, however, shows that precision and recall were fairly low, except for the low load class (the most represented one), indicating a bias of the classifier towards this class. The f1 score, which offers a better interpretation of the classifier's performance since it balances both precision and recall metrics, shows a low percentage across the normal, medium and heavy load classes.

In addition to determining the class of any given time frame, the accuracy of the model in determining the correct load class for a given drive was taken by comparing the most common class for each drive with the correct load class. The model could correctly identify the low load class in 83.3% of the synthetic drives and the normal load case in 50% of the cases. It failed at identifying any of the medium or heavy load drives.

These results indicate that a random forest classifier was not robust enough to yield accurate predictions, as a consequence of the limited size of the dataset and the unbalanced load classes. We, hence, tested a different approach based on an LSTM network.

4.3   LSTM Approach

An alternative approach to the classification of overload driving consists in the use of deep learning algorithms that considers the full (or a large portion) of the available measurements using their "raw" values. This bypasses the need to infer features, leaving it up to the algorithm to identify underlying patterns in the data that are capable of distinguishing between the two classes.

Neural networks are a popular option and probably the most robust technique in the field. Within neural networks, recurrent neural networks are particularly suited for the problem we are tackling, as they make predictions along a temporal sequence. Long Short Term Memory (LSTM) is a type of recurrent neural network which considers temporal sequences and allows the input of the previous event to be fed into the decision making procedure of the current one. It is ideally placed to tackle the prediction of load class over time and will be tested here.

Dataset Preparation. The same segmentation of the vehicle drives in the dataset, as described for the random forest classifier, was used for the LSTM network.

Results. The LSTM network was allowed to learn over 50 epochs, with its performance increasing rapidly for both train and test dataset stabilizing at around 97% and 85% f1 score, respectively. Overall prediction accuracy on the test dataset was 84%. We can visualize the confusion matrix and the performance of the four classification quality metrics per load class using the same visualization as previously shown (Fig. 6). The LSTM network proved more robust than the random forest classifier across most load classes, with the exception of the heavy load class, which failed completely. The remaining three classes had a recall rate that ranged from 79.7% for the medium load class (the least represented one) to 97.2% for the normal load class.

In terms of accuracy in predicting the load class for the entirety of a drive, the LSTM network predicted the low load class in all cases and the normal load class in 50% of the cases. Notably, it was capable of predicting 2 out of the 3 medium load classes correctly, a marked improvement compared to the random forest classifier.

The results for the LSTM model show that it is more robust in face of the limitations of the current dataset already mentioned. They suggest that with more sampling, notably for the least represented load classes, a high degree of model performance is possible.

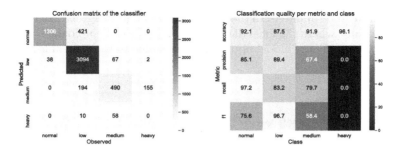

Fig. 6. Confusion matrix of the LSTM network (left) and prediction quality for different metrics and per load class (right).

5   Conclusion

In this paper, we have explained first that two issues are crucial to consider when exploiting data across a fleet of industrial assets deployed in the field:

- reliable storage and efficient communication of large quantities of data is challenging due to the absence of continuous connectivity
- the traditional centralized data analytics model is challenged by the inherently distributed fleet context

In the context of two industry-relevant use cases related to special-purpose vehicles, we have illustrated how advanced machine learning techniques can be applied at the edge.

For the first use case, we adapted a state of the art data compression technique to apply on the edge device that can realise a high compression of time series measurements. The proposed approach can achieve a compression rate up to more then 100 when defining a large margin of error on the compressed signal. Since the algorithm is highly parameterisable, the user can easily start with a set of parameters that results in a low compression but a high reconstruction rate of the original signal.

For the second use case, we evaluated two approaches for vehicle overload detection that classify a drive within its first few seconds. Given a limited amount of vehicle overload drives from different vehicles in diverse road conditions, we extracted a set of dynamic features from the vehicle usage data that represent the dynamics of the vehicle. A random forest model that uses these features had low predicting power, but the feature-free LSTM-based approach showed promising results, with even the least represented classes attaining a fair prediction accuracy.

For both use cases, the approaches are designed to run locally on a vehicle, so that it can operate in situations of no or unstable connectivity. The edge computations require only the model parameters and the streaming vehicle measurements to compute their results, while the training of the global model using historical data can take place in a central location. Whenever the vehicle is connected, its local model is updated and data stored on the vehicle is uploaded, so that the global model can be updated. In the future, we intend to integrate federated learning mechanisms, where the local data no longer needs to be uploaded, models are trained locally, and only model updates are uploaded to the central location.

References

1. Elmeleegy, H., Elmagarmid, A., Cecchet, E., Aref, W., Zwaenepoel, W.: Online piece-wise linear approximation of numerical streams with precision guarantees. Proc. VLDB Endow. **2**(1), 145–156 (2009)
2. Hochreiter, S., Schmidhuber, J.: Long short-term memory. Neural Comput. **9**, 1735–1780 (1997)
3. Hsu, D.: Time series compression based on adaptive piecewise recurrent autoencoder. arXiv:1707.07961 [cs], August 2017
4. Huffman, D.A.: A method for the construction of minimum-redundancy codes. Proc. IRE **40**(9), 1098–1101 (1952)
5. Jin, C., et al.: A comprehensive framework of factory-to-factory dynamic fleet-level prognostics and operation management for geographically distributed assets. In: 2015 IEEE International Conference on Automation Science and Engineering (CASE), pp. 225–230 (2015)
6. Kingma, D.P., Welling, M.: Auto-encoding variational bayes (2013)
7. Lazaridis, I., Mehrotra, S.: Capturing sensor-generated time series with quality guarantees. In: Proceedings of the 19th International Conference on Data Engineering (Cat. No.03CH37405), pp. 429–440 (2003)
8. Ma, T., Hempel, M., Peng, D., Sharif, H.: A survey of energy-efficient compression and communication techniques for multimedia in resource constrained systems. IEEE Commun. Surv. Tutor. **15**(3), 963–972 (2013)
9. Oda, T., Tachibana, Y.: Distributed fleet control with maximum entropy deep reinforcement learning (2018)
10. Papaioannou, T.G., Riahi, M., Aberer, K.: Towards online multi-model approximation of time series. In: 2011 IEEE 12th International Conference on Mobile Data Management, vol. 1, pp. 33–38 (2011)
11. Rao, J., Niu, X., Lin, J.: Compressing and decoding term statistics time series. In: Ferro, N., et al. (eds.) ECIR 2016. LNCS, vol. 9626, pp. 675–681. Springer, Cham (2016). https://doi.org/10.1007/978-3-319-30671-1_52
12. Ringwelski, M., Renner, C., Reinhardt, A., Weigel, A., Turau, V.: The hitchhiker's guide to choosing the compression algorithm for your smart meter data. In: Proceedings of the 2nd IEEE ENERGYCON Conference and Exhibition/ICT for Energy Symposium (ENERGYCON), pp. 998–1003 (2012)
13. Sadler, C.M., Martonosi, M.: Data compression algorithms for energy-constrained devices in delay tolerant networks. In: Proceedings of the 4th International Conference on Embedded Networked Sensor Systems, SenSys 2006, p. 265–278. Association for Computing Machinery, New York (2006)
14. Salomon, D.: A Concise Introduction to Data Compression. Undergraduate Topics in Computer Science (2008)
15. Sherstinsky, A.: Fundamentals of recurrent neural network (RNN) and long short-term memory (LSTM) network. Phys. D **404**, 132306 (2020)
16. Ziv, J., Lempel, A.: A universal algorithm for sequential data compression. IEEE Trans. Inf. Theory **23**(3), 337–343 (1977)

Cynefin Framework, DevOps and Secure IoT

Understanding the Nature of IoT Systems and Exploring Where in the DevOps Cycle Easy Gains Can Be Made to Increase Their Security

Franklin Selgert^(✉)

AnyWi, 3e Binnenvestgracht 23, 2312 NR Leiden, The Netherlands
franklin.selgert@anywi.com

Abstract. In the relatively new domain of the Internet of Things (IoT), startups and small companies thrive in and stride in bringing new products to the market. Many of them experience problems and fail to profit from their IoT innovation. A lot of those problems are security related. In IoT development, security issues are often overlooked or underestimated.

This article explores, from a holistic viewpoint, how security in IoT systems can be prevented or mitigated with a minimal effort. Concepts examined are: The Cynefin framework, Business DevOps, and the role of constraints and requirements in the design phase.

Keywords: DevOps · Cynefin · IoT · SCRATCh · Security

1 Introduction

Cynefin (Sense of Place) is a sense making framework: it guides decision makers by providing a simple yet powerful classification of systems in general. Business DevOps is often considered as the "holy grail" of all software development approaches, whose purpose is to increase control over the whole software lifecycle and to speed up software delivery. The role of constraints and requirements in the sense of how to include security aspects in the design Phase. The Paper examines, based on these three concepts, where to focus one effort to maximize security of the IoT system. This article is written as part of the SCRATCh project that explores tools and methods to improve on security in IoT based infrastructures.

1.1 Cynefin Framework

The Cynefin framework, "sense of Place" (Fig. 1). Cynefin framework [1] is meant as a guidance what type of action or behavior fits best in a certain context or state of the system (domain). In this way Cynefin is a classification model where each of the five domains is a class. Based on this classification model patterns of counter measures can be recognized to control the system.

© Springer Nature Switzerland AG 2020
A. Casimiro et al. (Eds.): SAFECOMP 2020 Workshops, LNCS 12235, pp. 255–265, 2020.
https://doi.org/10.1007/978-3-030-55583-2_19

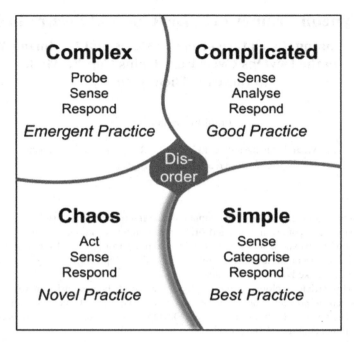

Fig. 1. Cynefin framework [1]

Cynefin is a framework that is designed to help us make sense of what confronts us, to give us a better understanding of our situation and the approaches that we should take [2]. The framework has five domains [3]:

Simple, in which the relationship between cause and effect is obvious to all, the approach is to Sense – Categorize – Respond and we can apply best practice. An example would be a simple heat control system. Central unit few sensors and a straight forward control based on temperature readings.

Complicated, in which the relationship between cause and effect requires analysis or some other form of investigation and/or the application of expert knowledge, the approach is to Sense – Analyze – Respond and we can apply good practice. A heat and ventilation control system with multiple sensors, and an algorithm that controls the system actuators.

Complex, in which the relationship between cause and effect can only be perceived in retrospect, but not in advance, the approach is to Probe – Sense – Respond and we can sense emergent practice. Multiple building control systems connected to weather forecast information and company planning systems, control based on an Artificial intelligence algorithm that uses feedback information from different building systems.

Chaos, in which there is no relationship between cause and effect at systems level, the approach is to Act – Sense – Respond and we can discover novel practice. Any of the above where an unknown source disrupts part of the system.

Disorder, which is the state of not knowing what type of causality exists, in which state people will revert to their own comfort zone in making a decision. this domain is not discussed in this paper.

In full use, the Cynefin framework has sub-domains, and the boundary between simple and chaotic is seen as a catastrophic one: complacency leads to failure. In conclusion, chaos is always transitional and dynamics are a key aspect.

Although the Cynefin framework is not specifically designed for the classification of IoT systems, it is possible to position both IoT systems and their development processes in one of the five domains. Positioning is however not static and multiple factors can cause a system to cross one of the domain boundaries. According to [4] there are a few main patterns of movement through the domains: "Moving through domains, As knowledge increases, there is a "clockwise drift from chaotic through complex and complicated to simple. Similarly, a "buildup of biases", complacency or lack of maintenance can cause a "catastrophic failure": a clockwise movement from simple to chaotic, represented by the "fold" between those domains. There can be counter-clockwise movement as people die and knowledge is forgotten, or as new generations question the rules; and a counter-clockwise push from chaotic to simple can occur when a lack of order causes rules to be imposed suddenly."

1.2 Business DevOps

Business DevOps is meant as a movement in the market that aims to integrate the business, development and operations functions in small teams that translate business demand into secure IT solutions in an extreme short time-to-market. Main drivers are transparency and reducing waste by automating the complete pipeline from requirements unto the solution working in the production environment. Security is a property that emerges in every domain. Regulation is an action as a result of the emergence of a significant risk in any given sector.

Business DevOps is a movement in the market to reorganize processes and the way different disciplines work together to speed up software delivery and stabilize operations. Applying this approach in any organization is seen as a complex endeavor - different disciplines, social context, enterprise organizations a total of variables makes the system complex.

1.3 Design Constraints and Requirements

As most development cycles start with some form of constraints and requirements, investigating how these can contribute to a more secure system makes sense. An example would be to look at the role of regulation, seen here as a public effort to counteract emerged negative effects of new technology by forcing compliance to design constraints and rules. In many cases, this role is performed only after the fact, lack of security, has led to a unacceptable risk exposure.

1.4 Structure of the Document

The structure of this paper is as follows. In Sect. 2, we will compare IoT systems in regards their position in the Cynefin Framework, specifically large IoT systems. This positioning sketches a bit of the behavior of large IoT systems and what methods Cynefin offers to interact and steer this behavior. In Sect. 3, we combine DevOps and Cynefin and suggest where in the DevOps process efforts can be optimized in regards to increasing the security, based on four assumptions. In Sect. 4, we explain in more detail how the four assumptions play out in each phase of the DevOps, combining Cynefin, DevOps, design constraints and requirements into a more holistic view on Security. In Sect. 5, we conclude.

2   Large IoT Systems Versus Cynefin

The question addressed in this section is how to classify an IoT system in the respective domains (the five states) of the Cynefin classification model.

Given that any IoT system is designed to fulfil a design Goal (stakeholder needs), it should be predictable to some extent. In the Cynefin framework it can therefore be classified in one of the ordered domains: Simple or Complicated. The system is considered Simple if causality is obvious, and Complicated if causality is present but of a more complex nature, for example if an IoT system uses artificial intelligence or machine learning algorithms.

Security issues in an IoT system can push a system into the Cynefin framework classes Chaotic or Complex. The Complex class is applicable in case the causality becomes unpredictable for the system owner, for example in case of unauthorized manipulation of data. This state is difficult to detect, as the output of the system can still be perceived as valid. The class Chaotic is applicable if parts of the system fail as a result of manipulation of other parts. There is also a center part in the Cynefin network "Disorder", meaning not knowing where you are –this part of the framework is not discussed in this paper (Table 1).

Table 1. Mapping IoT systems onto the Cynefin framework

Complex Causality becomes unpredictable	Complicated Causality of issues of the IoT is analyzed based on Artificial Intelligence or machine learning algorithm
Chaotic IoT The System or Parts of the system fail with potential increasing damage to the environment it is operating in	Simple IoT Causality is straightforward

3   Combining Cynefin, Business DevOps and Security

How does security come into play in the two models Cynefin and Business DevOps? Security in itself is not a single property but an invisible attribute of a product or piece of software. The "security attribute" of an IoT system is an outcome of a risk assessment process. What happens if device XY is compromised, is it severe, is it easy to mitigate? Depending on the application, the result will be different. It's about creating narratives or scenarios for security. Narratives are often used to explore the boundaries and place of a system in relation to the Cynefin framework [4]. A specific boundary to explore is between the Simple and Chaos domain, also referred to as a cliff [1], because it is seen as a catastrophic failure of a system. A security breach can push a simple system over this edge.

Business DevOps can be classified as a software development process in the Complicated domain and the development part often part of the Complex domain [2, 5]. The business DevOps pipeline includes multiple stages where potential security issues can be injected into the artefacts of the IoT system. Rather than ignoring the boundary between Simple and Chaotic, we recommend: acknowledge it and design a build in failure mode. Conclusion for the Design Phase of DevOps is:

1. Design Phase: Any system will cross over to the Chaotic domain sometime. Design any system to prevent to reach the Chaotic domain or mitigation the consequences of a system in chaos.

The other boundaries are less catastrophic and require a different type of mitigation. A system will move through the domain crossing boundaries deliberately or unintended [4]. In this case the focus is less on recovery and more on prevention of security related issues, detecting and stopping the unintended movement of a system counterclockwise in the Cynefin framework, e.g. from Complicated to Chaos. Conclusion for the DevOps phases Code and Build, and Monitor:

2. Code and Build Phase: as most systems start in the Simple domain, "as designed" checking for the obvious threats and vulnerabilities is step one for prevention.
3. Monitor Phase: as a system grows it may become Complicated by design or Complex by error. Fingerprinting accepted behavior and monitoring change is a way to control the movement of a system through the domains.

Conclusion 2 is about tooling and discipline in the design phase, conclusion 3 is more complicated and involves Ai or Machine learning, Sense (monitoring), analyze (Ai & ML), Response (intervene).

4 A Holistic View on Security Within Business DevOps

There is no standard DevOps process. Therefore, an arbitrary choice is made for this article by using the following order: Plan, code, build, test, release, deploy operate monitor, see Fig. 2. Business DevOps [6].

4.1 Development

Plan/design, Code, Build and Test is development. In business DevOps Terms it is referred to as continuous integration. Development itself is a container of lots of different activities that should lead to a magnificent product/service. As pointed out by [5],

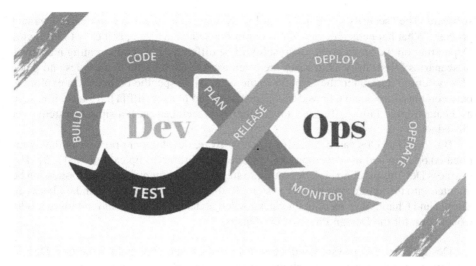

Fig. 2. Business DevOps [6]

"The Cynefin framework can be used to identify the best suited software development methodology and practices for each of the identified situation". In this sense, researching a potential new product is often a trial and error exercise based on a problem statement with requirements with little procedural constraints an environment that maps to the complex part of the Cynefin framework. Why: any development process consists of some requirements gathering, stakeholder needs etc., interpretation, translation into features and stories a more social process in which new insights and requirements emerge during the development itself. Indicating a Probe-Sense-Respond type of behavior. Typical agile methods like Agile Scrum can be applied here. However, in the world of Business DevOps Kanban is used often too.

Many innovative companies working on IoT have software development methods adapted that fit in the Cynefin complex domain. Main focus is often functionality and fit to the market demands. And yet, in this part most of the security aspects of the product are determined [7]. Success or failure is tightly correlated with behavior and skills of the team members [1]. Improving on security is not only about using the right tooling - it is also about improving the skillset of the team and increasing the presence of Security related requirements in the design phase.

A typical toolset used in this phase to increase security is the combination of threat modeling, static code analysis, code review and vulnerability checking. Some tooling can be easily injected in the DevOps pipeline, but a tool like threat modeling needs a team approach. It is effective if it used to increase the awareness regarding security of the whole team, [7]. [5, p. 100] talks about team empowerment.

Is this enough? Assuming any (IoT) system eventually will fall into the Chaotic domain, the key question is: what is needed to recover from chaos. According to Cynefin "act, sense, response" can bring the system back under control or into an isolated state. Looking at IoT, act, sense response means one can interact, measure the system and do something. Exactly those are the things that are missing in many IoT systems [8]: sensors cannot be updated, a limited set of measurements is possible, there are no means for direct interaction, etc. Yet, a security breach can push a whole system into chaos. It is in the design phase that system attributes are programmed and it is in this phase where we can improve on "continuous security" by simply making the system more controllable, without the need of knowing for what type of event or requirement we do this.

Thus, the question arises: how to achieve "continuous security" Inserting the right set of features into the development process forces a team to think about security and risk. In mature markets this is what certification does, although certification is mostly performed only after the product is ready for release. The constraints to pass for certification, e.g., based on best and good practices, should already inserted in the design phase.

Certification should be considered as a good practice in Complex and Complicated domains. The translation of the requirements that are implied by the certification like ISO 27001:2013 can be designed in multiple viable solutions. The good practices gathered by ENISA (European Agency for Cyber Security) can be seen as an example of recommendations to be interpreted by designers to increase security.

STRIDE[1], as a method for threat analysis, done in cooperation with the whole design team at the start of development, is identified in the 2019-state-of-devops-report-puppet-circleci-splunk survey [7] as an important good practice to enhance overall security, and a way to design an architecture that enables a build in failure mode or a dynamic failure mode. As an example of a build in failure mode would be automatic recovery of a failed firmware update. Dynamic failure mode would be a continuous monitoring system with algorithms that interact with the system to counteract certain security events.

Conclusion: development and design phase belong in most situation to the Complex domain, a domain where Agile is a good practice to be applied [9]. Increasing security awareness, inject requirements and use of tooling are a key step in improving overall security of an IoT systems. Focus in this stage is:

1. Assure that the system has control points that allow for Probe-Sense-respond and Act-Sense-Response, Build in failure modes and dynamic failure modes. A way to do this is to use a set of recommended requirements, test scenario's and design practices e.g. STRIDE.
2. Do the obvious: code review, static analysis, and specifically also vulnerability checking.

4.2 Test

It aint what you don't know that gets you in trouble, its what you know for sure that just ain't so (Mark Twain).

Although represented as a separate phase in Fig. 2. Business DevOps [6], testing is an activity that occurs in all stages and preferably before coding (test driven development). At this point before release testing it is about confidence in the software/product.

---

[1] The STRIDE acronym stands for Spoofing, Tampering, Repudiation, Information disclosure, Denial of Service, Elevation of privilege. Naming the 6 most common security categories.

There is no universal answer as how to increase the confidence to a level that is acceptable. The simple answer is that "it depends" in what sector the product is deployed or whether it is mission critical. At this point the risk analysis performed in the design phase using STRIDE and e.g. DREAD [2] (a Risk Assessment Model) will guide testing and depict the level of automation achievable. Instruments are penetration testing, compliance validation, and again, vulnerability checking.

The IoT system we test is by definition Simple or Complicated by design, as it is an effort to comply with predefined rules, needs and requirements. That implies that testing is in line with that expectation. But what if all systems eventually cross over to Complex or Chaotic how to test system behavior in those situations? According to [2, p. part 2]: *"An increasing challenge for testers will be to look for information about how systems fail, and test for resilience rather than robustness. Tolerance for failure becomes more important than a vain attempt to prevent failure"*

Testing for the failure modes of the system becomes important to be confident on the system resilience when entering the unordered domains of the Cynefin framework.

For large IoT systems, testing is complex due to the impossibility of a complete simulation of a real environment and the coverage of all imaginable scenario's. A typical tool of use could be unit test prioritization: if not all tests can be performed, only the most relevant should. One could, e.g., test if the system has enough control points that allow for probe-sense-respond and act-sense-response to restore a system from a failed state. Failure mode testing is a method to ensure resilience of the IoT systems in the operate phase.

Automation of this phase means in DevOps terms "continuous testing" - an important goal, as it would speed up releases and allow for swift deploy of smaller changes. In current practice, automation also means that a system can be setup automatically and mimic the operate phase. For IoT systems, this is not always possible.

4.3 Release

Release is more a decision phase; in the Simple domain it can be automated, while in the Complex domain, e.g., if the system is heavily regulated, there are probably multiple compliancy checks and QA processes to complete. With IoT, an additional problem is the presence of hardware constraints that cannot be grasped in terms of emulating software: setting up instant staging environments cannot be automated as is done with a lot of cloud environments.

4.4 Deploy

Deploy is perceived as an activity in the Simple domain: in DevOps, deployment is tested, its main rule based and repeatable and often automated. Large distributed IoT systems do not always comply with the term Simple. The number and variety of devices cannot be extensively tested and minor variation and errors in the design can push the whole system over the edge into chaos. A typical example is a firmware update of a

---

[2] The DREAD acronym stands for Reproducibility, Exploitability, Affected users, Discoverability, naming 5 risk catagories.

set of end nodes: failure of this deployment renders a number of IoT nodes without a connection. Depending on the role of these nodes the complete system can become unreliable. A good design and proper failure mode testing are a way to mitigate these risks. Focus in this phase is recovery after failure: resilience.

4.5 Operate

The system is deployed functioning and acting on data, stable and reliable according to preset rules: the system is in the Simple domain. In this phase the system is vulnerable to events that causes a catastrophic push from Simple into the Chaotic domain, e.g. by a security breach. Or to a more gradual counterclockwise movement [4], caused by degrading of components or loss of knowledge in the support and design team [1].

What the Cynefin framework teaches here is that the best action pattern in case of a disruption is: act-sense-response. As design constraint one could insert:

1. It should be possible that a system allows for, act to sense and respond type of interaction, e.g. allow for firmware updates, shutting down parts of the system, etc.
2. Means to detect this unauthorized manipulation of sensor data or other anomaly, e.g. logfile analysis, machine learning algorithms, predefined behavior patterns.
3. Default fall back options to stabilize a system "failure modes".

Relevant constraints are all those constraints that help a design team to incorporate methods to influence the system, bring it back to order or isolate it, as well as constraints that open the mindset of designer to think about means to detect deviation of allowed behavior patterns.

4.6 Monitor

Monitoring has two aspects:

1. Systemic: collecting data from a life system and in the complete CI/CD pipeline
2. Organizational: collecting data from the organization responsible for the system

Organization monitoring is about maintaining processes, expertise and knowledge within the teams responsible for a certain system, in this paper it is left out of the discussion. Item 1 Data collection is needed to prevent chaos and provide feedback (act sense/analyze respond). Many systems are complicated, specifically IoT stems, because they contain many smaller parts with a variety of behavior patterns. Simple response actions cannot always be applied in this realm. Machine Learning (ML) and Artificial Intelligence (AI) can be used to analyze a system behavior and make detection of anomaly simpler. A drawback is that ML and AI as mechanism are in itself systems that can drift through the domain as a consequence of small changes.

Focus in this Phase is sense-categorize-and-respond: monitoring is the most important part of keeping a system safe and to know when to act if a system tends to cross a domain boundary.

5 Conclusion

We can conclude that security is involved in all phases of the DevOps process, but there are two particular phases, namely Design and Monitor, that need special attention if one is to produce secure IoT systems and to intend to keep those systems secure. Improving security in IoT is accepting the situation that your IoT system will fail and fall in to what the Cynefin framework calls the Chaotic domain. Knowing this, only two questions remain:

1. How can I detect failure, chaos?
2. How can I restore the system from failure?

Detection is the domain of monitoring, restoring from failure, e.g. when crossing the boundary between Simple and chaos, is a design constraint to achieve a fail-safe mode.

Having concluded this, it should be noted that it is not the intention of this paper to neglect security in other DevOps Phases. Merely, it is the intent of this paper to provide the easy gains towards more secure IoT systems (Table 2).

Table 2. Summary of the IoT and Cynefin

Complex IoT	Complicated IoT
• Complicated systems may cross over to this domain by: additional functionality, subtle unauthorized manipulation of data, failures of system parts	• ML/AI involved in the system • Operate phase of multiple systems • A simple system may cross over to this domain by: expansion, increase of functionality
Chaotic IoT	Simple IoT
• A place to leave quickly • systems may cross over to this domain by: additional but bad tested functionality, unauthorized manipulation of data, failures of essential system parts, security breaches	• Straight forward IoT system, e.g. some automated control systems • Sudden unexpected Events can push a system over to Chaotic

Acknowledgements. This work has been supported by several organizations: - The ITEA3 17005 project SCRATCh.

References

1. Puik, E., Ceglarek, D.: The quality of a design will not exceed the knowledge of its designer; an analysis based on axiomatic information and the cynefin framework. In: 9th International Conference on Axiomatic Design (ICAD 2015) (2015)
2. Christie, J.: cynefin-and-software-testing-part-1, June 2017. https://www.associationforsoft waretesting.org/2017/06/11/cynefin-and-software-testing-part-1-james-christie/

3. Snowden: cognitive-edge.com. https://cognitive-edge.com/resources/glossary/
4. Kurtz, C.F., Snowden, D.J.: The new dynamics of strategy: sense-making in a complex and complicated world. BM Syst. J. **42**(3), 462–483 (2003)
5. O'Connor, R.V., Lepmets, M.: Exploring the use of the cynefin framework to inform software development approach decisions. In: ICSSP 2015: Proceedings of the 2015 International Conference on Software and System Process, August 2015 (2015)
6. DevOps. [Art]
7. Mann, A., Stahnke, M., Brown, A., Kersten, N.: 2019-state-of-devops-report.html. Circle Internet Services, Inc., Puppet, Splunk (2019). https://puppet.com/resources/report/state-of-devops-report/
8. C.S. (EBOS): D1.4 CHARIOT design method and support tools (ver.1), Chariot (2019)
9. Pelrine, J.: On understanding software agility – a social complexity point of view. Emerg.: Complex. Organ. **13**(1), 26–37 (2011)
10. Babar, Z., Lapouchnian, A., Yu, E.: Modeling DevOps deployment choices using process architecture design dimensions. In: Ralyté, J., España, S., Pastor, Ó. (eds.) PoEM 2015. LNBIP, vol. 235, pp. 322–337. Springer, Cham (2015). https://doi.org/10.1007/978-3-319-25897-3_21
11. Joosten, A.: Unorder and the applicablity of agile. University of Amsterdam Faculty of Science, Amsterdam (2018)
12. Schmidt, T., Mathiassen, L.: Agility in a small software firm: a sense-and-respond analysis. Int. J. Bus. Inf. Syst. (IJBIS) **4**(1), 85–104 (2009)
13. Snowden, D.: Cynefin, a sense of time and place: an ecological approach to sense making and learning in formal and informal communities (2011)
14. Winteringham, M.: atdd-vc-bdd. https://www.hindsightsoftware.com/blog/atdd-vs-bdd

Creating It from SCRATCh: A Practical Approach for Enhancing the Security of IoT-Systems in a DevOps-Enabled Software Development Environment

Simon D. Duque Anton[1(✉)], Daniel Fraunholz[1], Daniel Krohmer[1],
Daniel Reti[1], Hans D. Schotten[1], Franklin Selgert[2], Marcell Marosvölgyi[2],
Morten Larsen[2], Krishna Sudhakar[3], Tobias Koch[3], Till Witt[3],
and Cédric Bassem[4]

[1] German Research Center for Artificial Intelligence (DFKI),
Kaiserslautern, Germany
{simon.duqueanton,daniel.fraunholz,daniel.krohmer,
daniel.reti,hans.schotten}@dfki.de
[2] AnyWi, Leiden, The Netherlands
{franklin.selgert,marcell.marosvolgyi,morten.larsen}@anywi.com
[3] consider it GmbH, Wedel, Germany
{sudhakar,koch,witt}@consider-it.de
[4] NVISO, Brussels, Belgium
cbassem@nviso.eu

Abstract. DevOps describes a method to reorganize the way different disciplines in software engineering work together to speed up software delivery. However, the introduction of DevOps-methods to organisations is a complex task. A successful introduction results in a set of structured process descriptions. Despite the structure, this process leaves margin for error: Especially security issues are addressed in individual stages, without consideration of the interdependence. Furthermore, applying DevOps-methods to distributed entities, such as the Internet of Things (IoT) is difficult as the architecture is tailormade for desktop and cloud resources. In this work, an overview of tooling employed in the stages of DevOps processes is introduced. Gaps in terms of security or applicability to the IoT are derived. Based on these gaps, solutions that are being developed in the course of the research project SCRATCh are presented and discussed in terms of benefit to DevOps-environments.

Keywords: DevOps · IoT · Cyber security

1 Introduction

Several studies, e.g. from *Gartner* [8,12], continue to predict drastic numbers of Internet of Things (IoT) devices in use. Some are dedicated to certain specialised

© Springer Nature Switzerland AG 2020
A. Casimiro et al. (Eds.): SAFECOMP 2020 Workshops, LNCS 12235, pp. 266–281, 2020.
https://doi.org/10.1007/978-3-030-55583-2_20

environments, such as industrial applications, creating the Industrial Internet of Things (IIoT), or automotive scenarios. However, these IoT and IIoT devices contain severe vulnerabilities, often due to the fact that security solutions are not suited or not applied to IoT environments. *Mirai* and other botnets were capable of infecting up to 500 000 devices with dictionary attacks and consequently use those devices to perform Denial of Service (DoS) attacks that heavily impacted the internet [1,9]. In IIoT environments, where devices are linked with Cyber-Physical Systems (CPSs), attacks in the digital domain are capable of influencing the physical domain. Thus, vulnerabilities in the IoT can not only cause monetary loss, but also physical harm to persons and assets. At the same time, the DevOps-method has been well-established in software life-cycle management. A typical DevOps-life-cycle with the respective tasks mapped to the phases is shown in Fig. 1. The DevOps methodology is well described and intro-

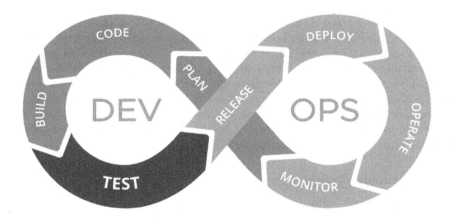

Fig. 1. The DevOps-Life-Cycle

duced in many companies. There are multiple ways to implement the process depending on type of organisation and maturity of the organisation. In general, three continuous phases can be distinguished in to which the eight steps of a DevOps-cycle are mapped as follows:

1. Continuous Integration (CI): Code and build steps
2. Continuous Deployment (CD): Test, release, and deploy steps
3. Continuous Feedback (CF): Operate, monitor, and plan steps

This terminology is generally accepted in industry. DevOps as method is mainly used in controlled environments where connections are stable and infrastructure can be used by software to set up adhoc staging areas. However, most tooling specific for cloud or enterprise environments cannot be used for large deployed IoT systems. Distributed deployment and feedback is difficult to achieve with the tools at hand. Furthermore, several studies show an unacceptable number of security related issues that pass undetected to deployment without the means for a quick recovery [17, page 32].

This work presents a state of the of art regarding the area of DevOps, with a focus on gaps in security as well as IoT-applicability in Sect. 2. It is used as a framework for investigating these gaps and developing improvements to be implemented in the course of research project SeCuRe and Agile Connected Things (SCRATCh) in Sect. 3.

2   Tooling for the DevOps-Cycle

DevOps is currently implemented by many companies, in different levels of maturity. Proof of this is the abundance of available tooling and consultancy. An overview by XebiaLabs [18] illustrates this. This overview of the different tools and the phase in which the are employed is shown in the periodic table of DevOps-tools, provided by XebiaLabs see Fig. 2 [18] in the appendix. However, tooling is not per definition applicable in the IoT domain and the main advantage of DevOps, quickly implement updates and mitigate security breaches, is lost. The increasing issue of creating secure IoT systems puts an additional focus into the DevOps cycle. There are tools readily available to build a DevOps Chain, however, specific IoT security objectives are not tackled by these tools. DevOps does not provide sufficiently holistic solutions yet. This section presents an overview of the three main phases of DevOps, tools that can be used, their shortcomings and recommendations to improve working methods and tools for a more secure DevOps life-cycle in the IoT-domain.

2.1   Continuous Integration (CI)

THe plan, code and build phases of DevOps are referred to as CI or continuous integration. This is where the DevOps process initially starts and a product or piece of software is created. Scrum and other agile methods are used and teams do incremental code development (sprints) until a certain release or minimal viable product is created. Code is regularly checked in to the main branch, called integration and builds of the code are made often on regular basis, e.g daily. Important aspects in this phase related to IoT and security are [15]:

1. Specific security related design constraints
2. System design or architecture
3. Security awareness agile team [11]
4. Code and vulnerability checking.

Most companies are at this level and apply some type of continuous integration, however, not every organisation applies all of the 4 points mentioned.

Recommendations: The Design-Phase is a bit of a chaotic stage [15] where agile working methods are common practice. Security by design is not a hollow phrase. It is important because most security features and future behaviour of a system is set in the design phase. Yet it is not common practice. A few simple methods and tools to improve the implementation of Security are:

1. Inject security design constraints as non functional requirements or stories into the process:
   - In the design phase specific security features are not always injected by the customer or product owner, using the outcome of some good practice research e.g. from European Union Agency for Cybersecurity (ENISA), will increase security awareness and contribute to a more robust architecture. Some good practices are listed in the knowledge base of SCRATCh.
2. Design resilient architecture:
   - If design constraints are reflected in the architecture or system design, it is likely that the system is better equipped in the operate phase to recover from security breaches.
   - IoT solution architectures can play an important role in keeping a system safe. If in the architecture methods are defined that increase the resilience of a system e.g. methods to securely interact with the system.
3. Introduce a simple security analysis exercise for the team, e.g. using STRIDE:
   - Number one on the list of practices that improve Security in the survey [11] is collaboration between security and development teams on threat models. A simple template developed in SCRATCh can be used for this purpose.
4. Pick an appropriate threat checking tool:
   - Integrate security tools into the CI pipeline ensure that developers can be confident they're not inadvertently introducing known, security problems into their code-bases [11]. It is recommended to extend threat checking through out the DevOps cycle, e.g at release to check for changes in used libraries, at operate to check for new introduction of security issues.

2.2 Continuous Deployment (CD)

For CD it is assumed that staging areas can be setup instantaneously, the potential to be released software can undergo automatic testing in this staging area, results of these "final" test lead to deployment or not. It is clear that a gap exist here for IoT systems, as it is impossible to setup adhoc IoT environments that mimic the real implementation [15].

The deployment software stack itself is complex. Common tools to operate software are containers (Docker), local virtual machines (VMware, VirtualBox) and cloud systems (AWS, Azure). For orchestration, Vagarant and Kubernetes are well-established options. The automated configuration is frequently realized with Ansibl, Puppet, Saltstack and Chef.

Transport (TLS) or application (HTTPS, SSH) layer security can be considered standard for communication in the deployment phase, Sect. 3.4 discusses methods for pre- and late provisioning, thus confidentiality, integrity and authenticity are provided. Several tools also include support for enterprise authentication, such as LDAP. Security in the deployment phase is significantly based on (default) configuration, best practices and linting. Sect. 3.4 discusses methods for pre- and late provisioning to cover the authenticity of a IoT device. It is important to avoid insecure default configurations. Vagrant, for example, used default credentials and a default key pair for SSH communication in the past. It is also imperative to include linting tools to verify configurations during the deployment. An example of such a tool is hadolint or kubesec.io. Hadolint checks configuration files of docker containers for compliance with security best practices, whereas kubesec.io conducts an automated risk assessment of the configuration. Furthermore, the choice and procurement of base systems may affect security. Several environments allow to share base systems among their users. Using base systems from untrusted sources imposes a security risk. Additionally, the integrity should be validated to ensure a secure basis for further deployment. An example for integrity protection is the container signing tool Portieris by IBM and Notary by Docker. Compromised systems cannot be avoided completely by complying to best practices. There have been, for example, 75 vulnerabilities be reported for Ansible between 2013 and 2020. To increase resiliency defense-in-depth strategies may be applied and container firewalls as provided by vArmour may be set up. Distributing firmware or configuration to a life IoT system ads to the complexity of these containers and the underlying design of the IoT hardware, as a interrupted update can cause a loss of connection without immediate means to recover.

In the recent past, the severity of insecure deployment stacks was showcase in the Tesla Hack in 2018. Tesla used a Kubernetes console that was not password protected. Criminals found it and gained access to the orchestrated containers. One of these containers included credentials for an AWS cluster, which was compromised subsequently.

2.3 Continuous Feedback (CF)

The operate, monitor, and plan-phase of the DevOps-cycle are referred to as CF. In these phases, the system is operated in the intended fashion and its operation is monitored.

An IoT system in operation generates feedback (monitoring) information, some part of this feedback can lead to automatic adaptation or change in the IoT environment as a preventive act to mitigate an identified risk, Other feedback is fed back into development to improve on the system, and some feedback will be analysed by operation. The whole system of data collection and actions is a constant learning curve that if successfully implemented leads to a more stable system.

Among other Key Performance Indicators (KPIs), such as application performance and throughput, the operate and monitor-phases are analysing the systems for security-related incidents. In general, if the vulnerabilities have not been discovered in the code- or build-phase based on source code analysis or functional testing, they can be detected in the operate- and monitor-phases by either host- or network-based intrusion detection systems. A strong focus of security tools for DevOps lies on data management and the ensurance of privacy, e.g. by companies such as SignalSciences, HashiCorp, and CyberArk. CyberArk provides account management for privileged accounts aiming at the reduction of information leakage and misconfiguration. HashiCorp enables provisioning and securing cloud environments and SignalSciences provides Web Application Firewalls (WAFs). Their focus lies on the ensurance of data security. However, as no complete security can be guaranteed for any system, it is desireable to detect attacks and intrusion if they occur. Snort performs network-based intrusion detection with a wide set of rules based on network packets. Tripwire provides a similar approach by creating snapshots of a given system's state and alerting the user in case of a change. Thus, intrusions and changes in behaviour can be detected.

There are, however, several disadvantages or drawbacks to such solutions. Since classic Intrusion Detection Systems (IDSs), such as Snort and Tripwire, do not take into consideration the architecture of the systems, the rules for detecting intrusions are generic. Furthermore, the extent of an attackers influence, as well as their goals and methods, cannot be derived from such information. Getting insight about the intention and approach of an attacker would allow to better prepare for future attacks. Finally, rule-based IDSs can only protect against attacks of which the signatures are known, meaning that unknown or stealthy attacks cannot be detected.

Within SCRATCh two tools are under development that improve Security in the Operate Phase, Deception in IoT (Sect. 3.2) and Anomaly Detection (Sect. 3.3).

3   Solution Concepts

This section presents individual solution concepts, addressing challenges in the DevOps-cycle brought up by security risks as well as the adaption of DevOps into IoT-environments. A summary mapping the solutions to the respective phases is shown in Table 1. Since project SCRATCh addresses singular challenges in IoT-based DevOps environments, not every phase is covered by individual solutions. Instead, concerns that were raised due to distributed DevOps applications as well as their implications on security, are the main focus of SCRATCh. The table shows that CI is not addressed in the context of SCRATCh since most issues in terms of security integration and IoT applicability are in the CD and CF phases. Generally, consideration of security issues, security by design, could provide a more seamless integration and coverage of security objectives. This would require systems and software to be developed in a fashion that integrates security integration as early as the design phase. If tooling for security is applied in later stages, the risks are realised in the CD or CF phase.

3.1   Pentesting IoT Devices

During a penetration test (or pentest for short), an application's overall security posture is measured against simulated cyber attacks. The result of a pentest are potential security vulnerabilities that could impact the application's security posture in terms of confidentiality, integrity and availability. Historically, pentests are performed before a new application or application's feature is released

Table 1. Mapping of Solutions to DevOps-phases

Solution	CI	CD	CF
Pentesting IoT Devices (Sect. 3.1)	✓		
Deception in IoT (Sect. 3.2)			✓
Anomaly Detection (Sect. 3.3)			✓
ID for the End Node (Sect. 3.4)		✓	
Software/Firmware Updates (Sect. 3.5)	✓		

so that there is less chance of potential vulnerabilities making it to production. The tests performed during a pentest, are often performed manually by a pentester and with the support of tools. These tools can take many forms, ranging from tools that scan for security vulnerabilities fully automatic, to tools that allow manual interaction with an application component, in a way that it was not intended by the developers. Sometimes, and depending on the tooling available, a pentester might even write its own tools to allow testing of very specific cases. Within the context of SecDevOps, performing a pentest before deployment would thus not fit the continuous deployment practice as a pentest is not fully automatic and would therefore not allow fully automatic deployments.

Within the context of testing IoT devices, tools that automatically test security are scarce. This can be attributed to a couple of key properties that differentiate IoT devices from more traditional applications such as web or mobile applications:

- Diverse and embedded nature – IoT devices are often designed to have a single use (smart light bulbs, smoke detectors) and are often developed on hardware and software platforms tailored specifically for that use. As a result, there is not one but a highly diverse set of hardware and software platforms to take into account;
- Use of different physical layer communication technologies: IoT devices are connected to networks via a wide range of wireless links, such as Bluetooth Low Energy (BLE), 802.11, GSM/UMTS, LoRaWAN;
- Use of different application layer communication technologies: IoT devices tend to make use of machine to machine communication technologies such as MQTT and AMQP;
- Large attack surface: IoT devices are part of a large and complex ecosystem. For example, a home alarm will be receiving input from motion detection, cloud and even mobile applications.

Due to the above-mentioned characteristics, fully relying on automated tools for IoT device testing is not yet feasible today. As such, validating security requirements through manual pentesting still remains a crucial part of securing an IoT device. There are a couple of challenges in pentesting of IoT devices.

First of all, there is a lack of security verification requirements and testing guides for IoT devices. For example, for pentesting traditional application such as web and mobile applications, OWASP provides security verification standards and testing guides that provide details on generic security verification requirements and how these can be validated through testing. For IoT devices, consolidated guides such as these do not yet exist.

Second, there is a lack of tooling to support pentesting activities of IoT devices. For example, for testing the security of web applications, tools such as Burp Suite and OWASP Zap exist. These tools provide features such as inspection and manipulation of HTTP request sent between client and server and automatic vulnerability scanning through fuzzing HTTP requests. While these tools can also be used if the IoT device makes use of HTTP, unfortunately, for many specific IoT technologies as mentioned above, there is a lack of tooling. Interesting to note is that for many of the traditional pentest tools today more and more being automated as well. For example, Burp Suite Enterprise Edition and OWASP ZAP's Docker containers allow for an easy integration of these tool's automatic vulnerability scanning features in a deployment pipeline.

SCRATCh aims to assist the community in establishing the foundations for validation security requirements of IoT devices through pentesting. In the short term, this will enable verifying the overall security posture of IoT devices, albeit through a laborious and mostly manual testing endeavor. However, by providing solid foundations for efficient pentesting SCRATCh hopes more and more tools will be able to provide automatic testing. SCRATCh aims to achieve this by focusing on the following three steps:

- First, SCRATCh aim to create a repository of security verification requirements for IoT devices;
- Second, based on these requirements we aim to start with the creation of a testing guide that documents how these verification requirements be tested for specific technologies;
- Third, we invest in the creation of tooling that supports these testing activities.

3.2   Deception in the IoT

The earliest form of deception in the field of computers were honeypots, which were network port functioning as canaries to detect interaction. As no legitimate service was using this network port, every connection to the port would be illegitimate. Later the field of deception technology has been extended to different computer domains such as databases, memory stacks and network topology. A database could have canary tables or entries which raise alerts when accessed and computer memory could have canary entries on different stack locations, which, when being overwritten, indicate buffer overflow attacks. The network topology could change over time, utilizing Moving Target Defense (MTD), to confuse potential attackers and reduce the attack surface. In classical security operations an asymmetry between attackers and defenders exist, where defenders cannot afford to make any mistake, whereas the attacker has unlimited time and attempts to find a mistake. Deception may help to give the defender the advantage of detecting malicious attempts, while causing uncertainty and precaution for the attacker. Bell and Whaley coined a taxonomy for deception, where they distinguish two modes of deception, simulation or showing the false and dissimulation or hiding the truth. Further, according to this taxonomy, simulation can be described as either mimicking, inventing or decoying and dissimulation as either masking, repackaging or dazzling. In SCRATCh, deception strategies are researched for the IoT security domain. A large focus of IoT security lies on firmware security and update distribution, which could be improved using canaries for reverse engineering detection, canaries for memory corruption detection and feint patches in firmware updates to distract from the actual vulnerabilities the security update patches. Similarly, special pins on a hardware chip could be used as a tampering detection and disable the chip. How such deception and canary tokens could be planted into the firmware as part of the CI-pipeline is in scope of the SCRATCh research. Another focus of IoT security is the network security, where the application of the previously introduced MTD is being researched. One possible strategy could be that the addresses of each IoT device change in short time intervals.

3.3 Anomaly-Based Intrusion Detection

Methods and tools for intrusion detection are well-established for end user devices. Such tools encompass anti-virus software and firewalls, furthermore network segmentation is a commonly applied method to secure systems. Generally, there are two methods to detect and prevent attacks: signature-based and anomaly-based. Signature-based intrusion detection is founded on the assumption that a given attack is characterised by a certain behaviour, e.g. a pattern of network packets. A signature-based IDS can scan for this pattern and consequently detect this kind of attack. Such systems are robust for known attacks, however, obfuscation techniques can make it hard for an IDS to detect the attack. Furthermore, novel attacks cannot be detected as no signature is known of them. Most common tools are signature-based.

Anomaly-based IDS learn models of a system's normal behaviour and discovery deviations from the normal behaviour. This allows them to detect formerly unknown attacks for which no signature is available. However, this commonly comes at the cost of a higher false positive rate, i.e. events that are incorrectly classified as an attack, compared to signature-based IDS.

These approaches work well for known attacks and regular system behaviour. In the domain of the IoT, a heterogeneous landscape of devices, many of which work without user interaction, these preconditions are not met. Due to the variety of use cases, it is difficult to derive system models for anomaly-based IDS. Additionally, several devices contain several vulnerabilities so that signature management becomes difficult. Especially if attacks solely make use of valid commands and packets attacks are difficult to detect based on their signature. In order to tackle this issue, two dimensions are evaluated in an automated fashion: Timing and spatial distribution. Previous research has shown that in the IIoT, most behaviour is periodic or at least reoccurring [10]. An algorithm called

Matrix Profiles [19] can be used to extract sequences of characteristic behaviour, e.g. number of packets in and out, open connections, and detect anomalies. Since this algorithm is efficient in terms of computational time, this can be done for each device in a network, so that despite the heterogeneous systems, each device has an anomaly score to detect intrusions. The sequences are extracted by the *Matrix Profile* algorithm in a sliding window fashion. Then a distance metric is calculated and the minimum of all distances for a given sequence is kept. A low minimal distance indicates the presence of a similar sequence in the time series, a high minimal distance indicates an outlier that can be an attack. Apart from regular behaviour in terms of timing, IoT networks often contain regular patterns of communication. These patterns can be extracted by considering the amount of in- and outbound connections, e.g. based on TCP sessions. If this value is taken in a periodic fashion, a time series is created that can be analysed for anomalies with the *Matrix Profile* algorithm.

As previous research shows, *Matrix Profiles* are capable of perfectly, i.e. with neither false positives nor false negatives, detect attacks in novel industrial environments, such as the IIoT [4, 6]. Since IoT environments are similar in important characteristics, this approach in combination with the integration of relationships between devices is expected to detect attacks that are formerly unknown with a high accuracy.

In addition, machine learning methods have proven to successfully learn a normal model behaviour, despite irregular human interaction, and reliably detect attacks in network traffic data. Especially Support Vector Machines (SVMs) and Random Forests perform well with perfect or near perfect accuracy [5].

3.4 Secure Deployment ID for IoT Components

Deploying new software to a IoT device has several challenges, with secure identification being the first that needs to be addressed.

IoT Identity Provisioning. It sounds simple, but is an essential question in the digital world: how do you prove ownership of a physical device? Consider you want to bring in some new IoT device into your home or office network. Leaving aside the challenge of connecting it to WiFi, by assuming you just plugged it into your router, how do you connect to it? And how do you make sure nobody else connects to it or, even worse, completely high-jacks the device? Most of the times there is a centralised web platform where you register yourself and your devices. But likely you are not the only user connecting a new device at the moment - how do you know which device belongs to which user? There are a few ways to do this - and some compromise security more than others. Within SCRATCh we intend to look implementing a feasible solution for SMEs out of:

- Late Stage Parameter Configuration [13]
- Pre-Provisioning Keys

There are large similarities within the usual identity processes. The device needs to hold a secret which is only known to the rightful owner. When claiming ownership towards a management platform, both the user and the device are linked upon matching that secret.

Late-Stage Parameter Configuration. If the device is as sophisticated as a laptop and provides some means of either input or output, the identity process can be achieved by multiple means like

(a) entering a secret on the device which then is also entered on the management platform
(b) displaying a random key generated on the device and send to the platform which is entered again on the management platform by the user

If the device does not have such means of interaction

(c) using an additional device like a mobile phone which connects locally to the IoT device and acts as input/output provider is an option.

As a variation of process the user could attach storage to the device holding such secret key. All these processes share a commonality - they can be performed post-distribution when the devices is within the target network. There are many other approaches and deviations to connect new devices, especially if already authenticated devices exist within the target network. They are not considered as they still cause the initial challenge of getting one device registered, which mostly happens by using one of the processes described above. The benefit of this process is to avoid the logistical challenges laid out in the Pre-Provisioned Keys section below.

Pre-Provisioned Keys. Some IoT devices come with pre-provisioned key. The onboarding process is similar to a) - a secret already exists on the device (ideally some kind of secure element) and is provided either physically (e.g. printed on the box of the IoT device) or digitally (like USB sticks) to the user. While this process is quite intuitive and, depending on the target audience, simpler to perform the logistical process of matching the digital secret within the device and the externally available secret should not be underestimated.

Identities Can Be Stolen. It is important to consider that identities can be stolen. It happens to devices [3] as it happens to people [3]. The same way you don't let your wallet with your credit card laying around in a cafe, you need to protect the device identity from being stolen. A simple text file on an SD card will likely not be enough. Considering you plan to use this to provide the next level of Netflix, Hulu or Amazon prime - you can be sure that this text file will be shared on the Internet quickly and people will abuse and consume your services free of charge. As a general rule its good to remember that the attack on the identity (and thus affiliated services) should be more expensive than purchasing the services legally. Secure elements are a proven solution here - at the costs of cents they protect already today high value assets from credit cards to passports and ID cards.

Additional Challenges to Consider. Having an architectural approach for your IoT identity provisioning solving the previously mentioned challenges is good. But usually it is only a part of the entire life cycle and environment to consider.

For the **life cycle** it must be assumed that devices are being de-provisioned (due to being broken, stolen, sold, hacked, etc.). Some of those devices will be re-provisioned by a different user. Some devices need to be able to rollback to a trusted state and re-provisioned while considering that this can be an attack vector as well. The chosen identity solution needs to consider this. From a security point it must be possible to blacklist devices and not just trust anything.

Some **environmental challenges** come from the device and the enclosing network itself. Starting with the available bandwidth: Not every device is connected to broad band allowing Mega or even Gigabytes to be transferred. E.g. a Sigfox payload size is as little as 12 bytes [16]. This imposes limits on ciphers to be used for secure transmission of the shared secrets.

Being **on- or off-grid** with regards to the power connection will impact the latency of communication (e.g. the device may not be always on due to power saving requirements), the computational power you can put into your provisioning may be limited due to the same reason as well.

The device may be behind **NAT or other firewall** setups not allowing direct communication as intended. A proxy may be required to ensure secure communication to the managing entity.

In general it is challenging to ensure not just secure identity provisioning, but maintaining the devices security through the entire life cycle. Another challenge the SCRATCh project is looking at, is to provide easy means of updating the device in the field. Re-reading the previously mentioned challenges may make you aware of the further challenges out there when managing IoT infrastructures.

Solution Direction. The solution direction SCRATCh aims at is to provide a easy and usable method for SMEs to get their IoT devices out to the customer without worrying about the logistical aspect pre-provisioned processes allowing a late-stage parameter configuration. For this the device will actively seek a connection to a pre-configured proxy server which then established a secured connection via a unique address. Once this connection is in place the centralized IoT server can negotiate the identity with the device and register it to the rightful owner. The credentials will be encrypted during transfer and at rest and where possible be stored in a secure element, given this is available.

3.5 Software/Firmware Updates for IoT

Keeping an IoT system safe throughout its life cycle needs some methods of interacting and updating the infrastructure [15,17]. In the SCRATCh project we see secure identification as discussed in Sect. 3.4 as a first step to solve. Apart from the ownership of the device, the device also needs to know for sure that the firmware updates are provided by the intended source, a requirement addressed by update authorization. In this section this problem is addressed.

Large Scale IoT deployment poses difficulties on software update security. Partially caused by the many different use cases, huge variety in actual devices and their capabilities and architectures. There are devices running advanced operating systems, having microprocessor units (MPU's), some run on powerful microcontroller units (MCU's) yet others have very restricted resources. And there are devices with combinations of powerful MPU's and MCU's, each running their own firmware. This leads to many combinations where specific risks arise or where requirements or objectives compete or even become mutually exclusive [2].

Platforms or tool kits can help manage these problems, but might be limited in that they only cover some security aspects or only applicable to a limited set of device types. It's pointed out by the ENISA [7] that several issues arise in firmware/software updates of IoT devices, e.g.: Complex ecosystems, fragmentation of standards and regulations and security integration.

A cryptography system which can be tailored to the specific use case, addresses these issues. Redwax [14] which provides a modular and decentralized approach, is demonstrated here with a very simple example. The principles of the Redwax architecture are appealing in our context because they aim for flexibility yet hide handles which require cryptography experts.

In this scenario a new firmware is being sent to an IoT device and the goal is to check the authenticity of the time stamp (which may include a firmware sum) and whether the update is newer than the active firmware or not. This happens on the IoTdevice. If the check fails the device can take appropriate actions, e.g. go to a specific fail state, refuse the new firmware and keep the current etc.

As an example we consider a Redwax time stamp server, which is located on premise where the firmware development takes place. Access is under company control. The server is a hardware device equipped with a secure element (SE). The server is being setup with timestamp front-end module, signing back-end module which uses a OpenSSL engine with the SE to provide signing with a private key. The server generates (root) certificates which are to be installed on the IoT devices.

The time stamping is used to protect against the out-of-date firmware problem, where firmware could be provided with expiration date through manifest, and rollback attacks. This is even more advantageous in a setting where regular software updates are part of a strategy. The secret key, being kept in the time stamp server, suffers minimal exposure and provides trust for the source. A next step is to extend this with public key infrastructure (PKI) and implement it in e.g. an small and medium-sized enterprise (SME) setting. Emphasis is then on "the integration and deployment of their own cryptography system"[14] (architecture).

In a next phase research will be done on how to cope with the specific IoT issues like non continuous connections, low bandwidth and hardware limitations.

It is not given that we will reach the end goal of secure deployment of software containers and at the same time having a fail safe mode implemented in all IoT devices. However, the goal is clear and for any gap identified alternative solutions might provide a mitigation.

4   Conclusion

The DevOps-cycle has been successfully established for the application in IT- and cloud-based environments. Such environments are easy to manage in a centralised fashion, creation, roll-out, and management of code can be performed with established tools. However, the de-centralised nature of IoT environments makes it difficult to apply the standard tools presented in this work. Furthermore, it opens up security issues, in the roll-out of identities and software, but also in monitoring the networks for intrusions. Such gaps in available tooling are addressed by the research project SCRATCh, which focuses on selected demands not yet met by standard tooling. Such tools include connecting to edge nodes and uploading identities to them,securely updating software to non-classic IT-devices as well as intrusion detection methods for novel threats and threat intelligence. In a next step, these solution approaches are integrated into test case environments and evaluated with realistic scenarios.

Acknowledgements. This work has been supported by ITEA3 through project SCRATCh (label 17005) with funding from:
  – The Federal Ministry of Education and Research (BMBF) of the Federal Republic of Germany, within the project SCRATCh (01IS18062E, 01IS18062C).
  – Netherlands Enterprise Agency
  – The regional institute for research and innovation of Brussels Belgium, Innoviris.
The authors alone are responsible for the content of the paper.

A   Appendix

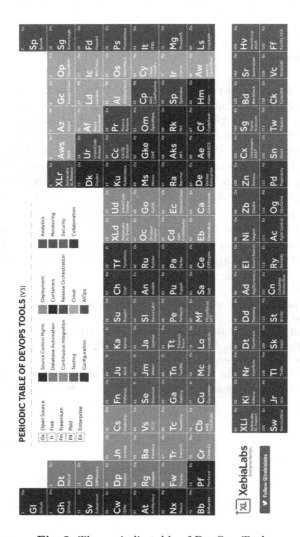

Fig. 2. The periodic table of DevOps-Tools

References

1. Antonakakis, M., et al.: Understanding the mirai botnet. In: 26th USENIX Security Symposium Security 17), pp. 1093–1110 (2017)

2. Asokan, N., Nyman, T., Rattanavipanon, N., Sadeghi, A.R., Tsudik, G.: Assured: architecture for secure software update of realistic embedded devices, October 2018. https://arxiv.org/pdf/1807.05002.pdf
3. Bradford, V.: Why device id may not be enough to stop fraud
4. Duque Anton, S., Ahrens, L., Fraunholz, D., Schotten, H.D.: Time is of the essence: machine learning-based intrusion detection in industrial time series data. In: 2018 IEEE International Conference on Data Mining Workshops (ICDMW), pp. 1–6. IEEE (2018)
5. Duque Anton, S., Kanoor, S., Fraunholz, D., Schotten, H.D.: Evaluation of machine learning-based anomaly detection algorithms on an industrial Modbus/TCP data set. In: Proceedings of the 13th International Conference on Availability, Reliability and Security, pp. 1–9 (2018)
6. Duque Anton, S.D., Fraunholz, D., Schotten, H.D.: Using temporal and topological features for intrusion detection in operational networks. In: Proceedings of the 14th International Conference on Availability, Reliability and Security (ARES), pp. 1–9 (2019)
7. Enisa: Baseline security recommendations for IoT, November 2017. https://www.enisa.europa.eu/publications/baseline-security-recommendations-for-iot
8. Goasduff, L.: Gartner says 5.8 billion enterprise and automotive IoT endpoints will be in use in 2020, August 2019. https://www.gartner.com/en/newsroom/press-releases/2019-08-29-gartner-says-5-8-billion-enterprise-and-automotive-io
9. Kolias, C., Kambourakis, G., Stavrou, A., Voas, J.: DDoS in the IoT: mirai and other botnets. Computer 50(7), 80–84 (2017)
10. Lohfink, A.P., Duque Anton, S.D., Schotten, H.D., Leitte, H., Garth, C.: Security in process: visually supported triage analysis in industrial process data. IEEE Trans. Vis. Comput. Graph. 26(4), 1638–1649 (2020)
11. Mann, A., Stahnke, M., Brown, A., Kersten, N.: 2019 state of the art DevOps report (2019). https://puppet.com/resources/report/state-of-devops-report/
12. van der Meulen, R.: Gartner says 8.4 billion connected "things" will be in use in 2017, up 31 percent from 2016, February 2017. https://www.gartner.com/en/newsroom/press-releases/2017-02-07-gartner-says-8-billion-connected-things-will-be-in-use-in-2017-up-31-percent-from-2016
13. NXP: Late stage parameter configuration
14. Redwax: Redwax project. https://redwax.eu
15. Selgert, F.: Cynefin framework, devops and secure IoT. In: Proceedings of the 39th International Conference on Computer Safety, Reliability and Security (2020)
16. Sigfox: Sigfox technical overview, May 2017. https://api.build.sigfox.com/files/59c211c69d14790001fbe9a2
17. Skoufis, C.: D1.4 chariot design method and support tools (ver.1) (2019). https://www.chariotproject.eu/uploadfiles/D1.4.pdf
18. XebiaLabs: Periodic table of DevOps tools (v3) (2020). https://xebialabs.com/periodic-table-of-devops-tools/
19. Yeh, C.C.M., et al.: Matrix profile i: all pairs similarity joins for time series: a unifying view that includes motifs, discords and shapelets. In: 2016 IEEE 16th International Conference on Data Mining (ICDM), pp. 1317–1322, December 2016. https://doi.org/10.1109/ICDM.2016.0179

3rd International Workshop on Artificial Intelligence Safety Engineering (WAISE 2020)

3rd International Workshop on Artificial Intelligence Safety Engineering (WAISE 2020)

Orlando Avila-García[1], Mauricio Castillo-Effen[2], Chih-Hong Cheng[3],
Zakaria Chihani[4], and Simos Gerasimou[5]

[1] Research and Innovation, Atos Spain, Spain
`orlando.avila@atos.net`
[2] Lockheed Martin Corporation, USA
`mauricio.castillo-effen@lmco.com`
[3] DENSO AUTOMOTIVE Deutschland GmbH, Germany
`c.cheng@denso-auto.de`
[4] CEA LIST, CEA Saclay Nano-INNO, France
`zakaria.chihani@cea.fr`
[5] Department of Computer Science, University of York, UK
`simos.gerasimou@york.ac.uk`

1 Introduction

The *International Workshop on Artificial Intelligence Safety Engineering (WAISE)* is dedicated to exploring new ideas on AI safety, ethically aligned design, regulations, and standards for AI-based systems. WAISE aims at bringing together experts, researchers, and practitioners from diverse communities, such as AI, safety engineering, ethics, standardization, certification, robotics, cyber-physical systems, safety-critical systems, and industries such as automotive, healthcare, manufacturing, agriculture, aerospace, and critical infrastructure. The third edition of WAISE was held on September 15, 2020 as part of the 39th International Conference on Computer Safety, Reliability, & Security (SAFECOMP 2020).

2 Programme

The Programme Committee (PC) received 23 submissions in the following categories:

- Full scientific contributions – 15 submissions
- Short position papers – 5 submissions
- Proposals of technical talk/sessions – 3 submissions

Each paper was peer-reviewed by at least three PC members, following a single-blind review process. The workshop organizers also selected technical talks/sessions to be presented at the workshop. The committee decided to accept 11 papers for oral presentation, eight full scientific papers and three short position papers, which are included in the final proceedings; resulting in an acceptance rate of 55%. Two proposals for technical talks were accepted for presentation but not included in the final proceedings.

Due to COVID-19, WAISE 2020 was held online and organised into thematic sessions following a highly interactive format comprising recorded videos and live Q&A sessions between authors and workshop audience. We selected the following three topics to distribute the presentations into three thematic sessions:

Thematic Session 1: Machine Learning Uncertainty and Reliability

- Revisiting Neuron Coverage and its Application to Test Generation. Matthias Woehrle, Stephanie Abrecht, Maram Akila, Sujan Sai Gannamaneni, Konrad Groh, Christian Heinzemann and Sebastian Houben
- A Principal Component Analysis approach for embedding local symmetries into Deep Learning algorithms. Pierre-Yves Lagrave
- A Framework for Building Uncertainty Wrappers for AI/ML-based Data-Driven Components. Michael Kläs and Lisa Jöckel

Thematic Session 2: Machine Learning Safety

- Rule-based Safety Evidence for Neural Networks. Tewodros A. Beyene and Amit Sahu
- Safety Concerns and Mitigation Approaches Regarding the Use of Deep Learning in Safety-Critical Perception Tasks. Oliver Willers, Sebastian Sudholt, Shervin Raafatnia and Stephanie Abrecht
- Positive Trust Balance for Self-Driving Car Deployment. Philip Koopman and Michael Wagner
- Integration of Formal Safety Models on System Level using the Example of Responsibility Sensitive Safety and CARLA Driving Simulator. Bernd Gassmann, Frederik Pasch, Fabian Oboril and Kay-Ulrich Scholl

Thematic Session 3: Assurances for Autonomous Systems

- A Safety Case Pattern for Systems with Machine Learning Components. Ernest Wozniak, Carmen Carlan, Esra Acar-Celik and Henrik J. Putzer
- Structuring the Safety Argumentation for Deep Neural Network Based Perception in Automotive Applications. Gesina Schwalbe, Bernhard Knie, Timo Sämann, Timo Dobberphul, Lydia Gauerhof, Shervin Raafatnia and Vittorio Rocco
- An Assurance Case Pattern for the Interpretability of Machine Learning in Safety-Critical Systems. Francis Rhys Ward and Ibrahim Habli
- A Structured Argument for Assuring Safety of the Intended Functionality (SOTIF). John Birch, David Blackburn, John Botham, Ibrahim Habli, David Higham, Helen Monkhouse, Gareth Price, Norina Ratiu and Roger Rivett

The following technical talks were accepted for presentation:

- Applying Heinrich's Triangle to Autonomous Vehicles: Analyzing the Long Tail of Human and Artificial Intelligence Failures. Amitai Bin-Nun, Anthony Panasci and Radboud Duintjer Tebbens
- Solving AI Certification in SAE G-34/EUROCAE WG-114. Mark Roboff

3 Acknowledgements

We thank all authors of submitted papers to WAISE 2020 and congratulate the authors whose papers were selected for inclusion into the workshop programme and proceedings. We also thank the Steering Committee (SC) for their support and advice in organizing WAISE 2020. We especially thank our distinguished PC members, for reviewing the submissions and providing high-quality feedback to the authors:

- Rob Alexander, University of York, UK
- Vincent Aravantinos, Argo AI, USA
- Rob Ashmore, Defence Science and Technology Laboratory, UK
- Alec Banks, Defence Science and Technology Laboratory, UK
- Markus Borg, RISE SICS, Sweden
- Lionel Briand, University of Ottawa, Canada
- Simon Burton, Bosch, Germany
- Guillaume Charpiat, Inria, France
- Raja Chatila, ISIR/UPMC-CNRS, France
- Huascar Espinoza, CEA LIST, France
- Jose Faria, Safe Perspective Ldt, UK
- John Favaro, INTECS, Italy
- Michael Fisher, University of Liverpool, UK
- Jelena Frtunikj, Argo AI, USA
- Simon Fuerst, BMW, Germany
- Mario Gleirscher, University of York, UK
- Stéphane Graham-Lengrand, SRI International, USA
- Jérémie Guiochet, LAAS-CNRS, France
- José Hernández-Orallo, Universitat Politècnica de València, Spain
- Nico Hochgeschwende, Bonn-Rhein-Sieg University, Germany
- Xiaowei Huang, University of Liverpool, UK
- Bernhard Kaiser, Assystem GmbH, Germany
- Guy Katz, Hebrew University of Jerusalem, Israel
- Philip Koopman, Carnegie Mellon University, USA
- Timo Latvala, Huld Oy, Finland
- Chokri Mraidha, CEA LIST, France
- Jonas Nilsson, Nvidia, Sweden
- Sebastiano Panichella, University of Zurich, Switzerland
- Davy Pissoort, Katholieke Universiteit Leuven, Belgium
- Philippa Konmy, Adelard, UK
- Mehrdad Saadatmand, RISE SICS, Sweden
- Rick Salay, University of Waterloo, Canada
- Mario Trapp, Fraunhofer ESK, Germany
- Ilse Verdiesen, TU Delft, Netherlands

We also thank the following additional reviewers:

- Morayo Adedjouma, CEA LIST, France
- Patrik Hoyer, University of Helsinki, Finland
- Deebul Nair, Bonn-Rhein-Sieg University, Germany
- Xingyu Zhao, Heriot-Watt University, Scotland

Revisiting Neuron Coverage
and Its Application to Test Generation

Stephanie Abrecht[1], Maram Akila[2], Sujan Sai Gannamaneni[2], Konrad Groh[1],
Christian Heinzemann[1], Sebastian Houben[2(✉)], and Matthias Woehrle[1]

[1] Robert Bosch GmbH, 70465 Stuttgart, Germany
{stephanie.abrecht,konrad.groh,
christian.heinzemann,matthias.woehrle}@de.bosch.com
[2] Fraunhofer IAIS, Schloss Birlinghoven, 53757 Sankt Augustin, Germany
{maram.akila,sujansai.gannamaneni,sebastian.houben}@iais.fraunhofer.de

Abstract. The use of neural networks in perception pipelines of
autonomous systems such as autonomous driving is indispensable due
to their outstanding performance. But, at the same time their complexity poses a challenge with respect to safety. An important question in
this regard is how to substantiate test sufficiency for such a function.
One approach from software testing literature is that of coverage metrics. Similar notions of coverage, called neuron coverage, have been proposed for deep neural networks and try to assess to what extent test
input activates neurons in a network. Still, the correspondence between
high neuron coverage and safety-related network qualities remains elu-
sive. Potentially, a high coverage could imply sufficiency of test data. In
this paper, we argue that the coverage metrics as discussed in the current literature do not satisfy these high expectations and present a line
of experiments from the field of computer vision to prove this claim.

1 Introduction

Recently, deep neural networks (DNNs) have started to outperform most other
machine learning (ML) techniques in the analysis and prediction of complex data
including voice and image recognition [2]. Particularly in image classification,
DNNs routinely surpass human performance [7], which makes them attractive
for an increasing number of (industrial) tasks. One example are computer vision
tasks in automated driving applications where DNNs are used to interpret sensor
data (*e.g.* from cameras). These tasks may be safety-critical if the system needs
to rely on predictions for safe movement and, therefore, pose a high demand for
extensive verification and validation (V&V) (see [21] for a recent survey).

The increasing importance of V&V shifted the initial focus on performance-
centered metrics for the evaluation of DNN models towards measures of interpretability [1] and robustness, *e.g.* under image perturbations [5,20]. From a
practitioner's point of view, however, a fundamental question is how to decide
whether a DNN has been sufficiently tested for a given task. In software testing,
this is usually assisted by use of coverage metrics [15] that provide a measurable

A. Casimiro et al. (Eds.): SAFECOMP 2020 Workshops, LNCS 12235, pp. 289–301, 2020.
https://doi.org/10.1007/978-3-030-55583-2_21

criterion when to stop testing and allow for inferring additional tests improving coverage. The idea of coverage has been transferred to coverage metrics on DNNs that measure which parts of a DNN are "active" during inference. Such ideas sparked several approaches to test networks and generate new test cases designed to either break the model or make it more robust [8,12,14,19].

In this paper, we review these coverage metrics and discuss how they can be used for V&V in an image recognition task. First, we focus on the underlying definition of coverage, which plays a critical role when determining whether full coverage is reached. Second, our experiments show that full coverage can be reached without exploring the full semantic input space of a DNN, even if limited to only correct predictions. And last, we benchmark previous approaches to increase coverage by generating new test cases [14] with simple augmentation techniques like translation and rotation. Furthermore, we find that neuron coverage is highly dependent on the chosen layer within the DNN.

Structure of the Paper: Next we provide more details on coverage metrics. Section 3 defines our research questions and experimental setup before we describe the results of our experiments in Sect. 4. Section 5 concludes the paper.

2   Fundamentals

We first review the definition of coverage from software testing (Sect. 2.1). Then, we discuss different definitions of neurons and activations from the literature that form the basis of neuron coverage for DNNs (Sect. 2.2).

2.1   Coverage

Coverage is a widely-used metric in software testing. Most well-known are structural coverage metrics based on source code such as Branch and Modified Condition/Decision Coverage (MC/DC) used for white-box testing of small software units [15]. However, coverage criteria are not restricted to code and can be selected based on the corresponding test level. Additional examples include coverage of requirements and respective equivalence classes on an embedded software level. Hence on a lower level, there are white-box coverage metrics in which we measure based on internals of an implementation, while black-box coverage based on the software's purpose is used on a high functional level. In summary, a coverage metric supports the testing process by providing a quantitative measure that must be adequate for the test level and purpose.

From an academic perspective, Bron *et al.* [3] discuss properties that a coverage metric should: (*i*) have an underlying static **model**, (*ii*) be (practically) **coverable**, *i.e.* we can achieve full coverage, (*iii*) be **actionable**, *i.e.* we know how to continue, and (*iv*) have an **exit** strategy when reaching full coverage.

For a statement coverage goal, it is quite apparent how these properties are useful. We can build a coverage model upon the given source code. As long as we find a non-covered statement, we either formulate a corresponding new test or verify via analysis that a given statement is not reachable. If statement coverage is reached, we may stop testing on code/unit level for this coverage goal.

2.2 Neuron Definition and Activations

Neuron Definition. Neurons are the basis for defining coverage in the context of DNNs. However, there are different possibilities for defining what a neuron is.

The *biologically inspired view* considers a neuron an element that receives input signals, aggregates them, and depending on some threshold fires a signal to other neurons. Translated to ML, a neuron comprises an element in a convolutional or linear layer including the subsequent ReLU. Other layers, such as pooling layers, may not be considered.

The *(software) architecture inspired view* considers a neuron any switching element that affects the computation paths of the function (*i.e.* of the DNN). This would include any layer that comprises switching elements, such as fully-connected layers, non-differentiable activation functions like ReLUs as well as max pooling layers (but not average pooling layers). Some non-linear, but differentiable activation functions, *e.g.* ReLU, may also be split into a finite number of equivalence classes to account for non-linearities. Conceptually, the switching elements divide the huge input space into local linear halfspaces that (*i*) could be individually tested but (*ii*) increase combinatorially with model depth.

Regretfully, there are different definition of neurons from literature that do not follow clearly along the above view and this results in different numbers of coverage items to be considered. The differences mainly present themselves in two respects: (*i*) How to handle spatial layers such as convolutional layers and (*ii*) which layers to include. The earliest related work is DeepXplore [14] whose neuron definition is further used in DeepGauge [12], Dissector [19], and the work by Kim *et al.* [8]. This definition reduces convolutional layers to a single neuron per filter, *i.e.* all elements in a single filter are reduced to their mean activation which removes fine-granular information about spatial coverage. Other works also consider the spatial distribution of convolutional layers such as Sun *et al.* [17]. In their neuron definition, pooling layers and final predictions are excluded. For reasons of practical feasibility, we restrict ourselves to a notion of neuron coverage in which we inspect neurons individually. For an approach that considers combinations of activations, we refer to DeepCT [11].

In this work, we use a definition inspired by approaches in interpretability and visualization, *e.g.* [13] focused on a software architecture inspired view:

Definition 1 (Layer and element-wise coverage (LWC)). *A neuron is an individual output element of a layer. All layers are considered separately, except for activations that are always considered part of the previous layer.*

The main difference between the LWC definition and the one from the related work above is how to handle convolutional layers, since in the definition of LWC each patch multiplied by the kernel counts as an individual output as shown in Fig. 1. Figure 2 compares coverage based on the DeepXplore definition (DXC) [12,14] and LWC for an initial convolutional layer deploying a simple CNN for MNIST (*cf.* "Simple" in Table 2 for the architecture). For both cases, we use the activation/coverage definition in Definition 2.

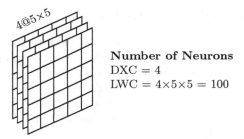

Number of Neurons
DXC = 4
LWC = 4×5×5 = 100

Fig. 1. The difference between neuron counts in DXC and LWC for convolutional layers: For DXC a whole channel is aggregated to a single neuron by averaging. In contrast, LWC considers each element individually, *cf.* [13].

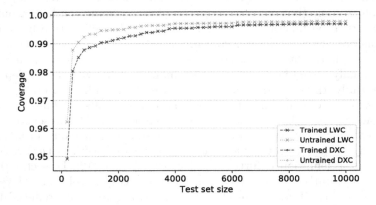

Fig. 2. Comparison of neuron coverage according to the definition of a neuron for an initial convolutional layer `cre11` of Simple CNN (Table 2): The trained and untrained DXC cannot be distinguished as they show very similar behavior and reach full coverage with small test set size.

We see a clear difference in coverage values for the first convolutional layer due to the discrepancy in neuron definitions. This can mainly be attributed to the fact that in the MNIST dataset, outer pixels are rarely set, such that neurons corresponding to outer edges are typically not covered. While this can be remedied with augmentation as shown below, the standard MNIST test set does not feature this out-of-the-box. A DXC approach removes this information and shows perfect coverage for any test set size, which we deem unwanted for an application in testing that should uncover such issues.

Another main difference is the resulting number of neurons, which represents the number of coverage items for testing. We compare the resulting neurons for each definition in Table 1. For DXC approaches, we recompute the number of neurons as they differ from the ones reported in the literature. As we see for both LWC and the approach by Sun *et al.* [17] a detailed study of convolutional layers increases the number of coverage items by one order of magnitude, even for small DNNs. LWC and Sun *et al.* only differ in handling pooling and prediction layers. Sun *et al.* [17] additionally discuss the coverage of the number of interactions. Such an approach further increases the number of neurons to be considered in particular for fully connected layers. In summary, there currently is no consistent neuron definition in the literature, yet the competing definitions have a considerable impact on the number of coverage items.

Table 1. Neuron counts for different definitions and several architectures

Architecture	DXC	Sun *et al.* [17]	LWC
MLP 784 × 128 × 64 × 10	986	976	986
MNIST CNN in [17]	258	14,208	17,738
LeNet-5	258	6,508	8,094
VGG-19	16,168	14,861,288	16,391,656

We follow Definition 1 in this work. When aggregating coverage across layers as shown in Table 1, each definition inherently emphasizes different layer types (*e.g.* DXC emphasizes fully connected layers, Sun *et al.* [17] excludes pooling layers). In order to avoid bias in interpretation of aggregated coverage, we study layer-wise coverage in the following. Intuitively, as layers perform different functions in a network, we follow the approach used in software testing in which we separate coverage into individual units (here layers) in order to receive actionable feedback as described above (*cf.* Sect. 2.1).

Neuron Activation. In classical software testing, it is easy to define whether a line of code has been covered, namely if it has been executed. In DNNs, things are more difficult as all neurons are executed in every inference. Therefore, approaches for DNN coverage use notions of activation of neurons for checking whether they are covered. The actual coverage may thus be defined differently based on the activation value $v(n)$ of a neuron n given an input datum. From an architectural viewpoint, comparing a neuron activation to one (or more) thresholds (*e.g.* a threshold of 0 for ReLU and Max Pooling layers) is most suitable. From a biologically-inspired perspective, several definitions are plausible, *e.g.* different thresholds may be selected (also adapted dynamically based on the current run and input data), or concepts of most activated neurons (*e.g.* Top-k Neuron Coverage in [12]) can be used. There are also definitions of activation that are tuned to a training set [12], which seems dangerously subjective counteracting the typical verification perspective that testing procedures should be independent from software construction. Burkov *et al.* argue that only correct predictions should be used for coverage [4], however, that may depend on the application and the kind of insight one hopes to achieve with the testing setup.

A common definition is based on a single threshold t, *i.e.* $v(n) \bowtie t$, *where* $\bowtie \in \{\geq, >\}$ and $t \in \mathbb{R}$, [14]. Some works suggest to normalize $v(n)$ based on all activations in a layer, such that $v_{norm} \in [0, 1]$. In practice, this does not make a difference for ReLU layers and $v(n) > 0$, however, for other choices a normalization may be more suitable. Since our view is software architecture inspired, we simply use unnormalized activations and a threshold of 0, which has the advantage that (i) there is no additional cost and no test dependency due to normalization, and (ii) a natural fit to layers with ReLU activation as studied in this work, see *e.g.* [4].[1] Coverage on the prediction layer should be handled differently due to its unique activation functions as described in [4] and is excluded from the analysis in the remainder.

Definition 2 (Covered neuron). *A neuron n is covered, when its activation is larger than zero, i.e. $v(n) > 0$ for at least one test datum.*

Intuition: Let us revisit Fig. 2 and study the resulting coverage in detail for a convolutional layer, *i.e.* `cre11` of the Simple network as defined in Table 2. The figure plots coverage over the test set size. It is expected that the coverage increases monotonically with the test set size. This is motivated by looking at the extreme cases: zero coverage for zero tests and full coverage for an infinite test set. Note that 100% coverage may still not be achieved due to dead neurons, which are intuitively similar to unreachable code in code coverage. However, the mere size of the test set does not necessarily correspond to novel test cases and by extension to an increase in coverage. As an example, a simple copy of a test set doubles its size, but the coverage remains the same. Therefore, in such coverage plots, we see a high level of coverage for small test set sizes and a small increase as more tests activate the same neurons again.

Let us compare the coverage of a trained filter, say an edge detector, with a random filter (untrained) in the first layer. The coverage of the trained filter measures how often the edge is observed in the test data at all locations. In contrast the coverage of the random filter measures how often the test data correlates with the random filter. Thus, it may be expected that for a smaller number of features in the first layer the coverage of the random filter is close to that of the trained filter as can be seen in Fig. 2.

3   Research Questions and Experimental Setup

A high coverage means that the test data was sufficient to activate all neurons. Potentially, we can infer two things from this. A high coverage metric could be used as a proxy that the test data contains all relevant cases. This would be particular appealing for verification. Additionally, we check whether a coverage based test generation generally facilitates efficient testing, here comparing to standard data augmentation. The experimental section reflects on both points.

---

[1] In a software architecture inspired view, both activation and non-activation should be included for coverage (*cf.* branch coverage). Since non-activation is the standard case and typically achieved with few tests, we focus on the activation part.

Effectively, we answer the following **research questions**:

- What impact does augmentation have on coverage in initial layers?
- Is the structural coverage metric dependent on classes?
- Does neuron coverage-based differential test generation suggest better tests than test time augmentation techniques?

Table 2. Architectures used: Simple CNN and LeNet5 [9], Abbreviations used: CV = Conv2D, MP = MaxPool2d, L = Linear, R = ReLU, S = Softmax

Simple	crel1	max1	crel2	max2	frel1	preds	
	CV(1, 20, 5) + R	MP(2)	CV(20, 50, 5) + R	MP(2)	L(800, 500) + R	L(500, 10) + S	
LeNet5	crel1	max1	crel2	max2	frel1	frel2	preds
	CV(1, 6, 5) + R	MP(2)	CV(6, 16, 5) + R	MP(2)	L(400, 120) + R	L(120, 84) + R	L(84, 10) + S

All experiments are either performed on MNIST or Fashion-MNIST. The networks, defined in Table 2, are trained using SGD optimizer with a learning rate of 0.01 and momentum of 0.5. We use Pytorch for all the experiments. The complete test data is used for the experiments unless stated otherwise. We use the architectures in Table 2 in the experiments for both datasets. We perform augmentation with translation and rotation in standard pytorch and use the following parametrizations: (i) **Weak augmentation:** For weak augmentation, we set the translation bound to $\pm 10\%$ and a rotation bound of $\pm 5°$ for random sampling. (ii) **Strong augmentation:** For strong augmentation, we set the translation bound to $\pm 20\%$ and a rotation bound of $\pm 10°$.

4 Experiments

4.1 Impact of Augmentation on Coverage in Initial Layers

In Fig. 2, we see that achieving full coverage, in particular LWC, in initial convolutional layers is not possible on the MNIST test set. Our assumption is that this is due to the data setup of MNIST, with centered images and considerable (non-informative) boundaries.

Experiment: We study in detail the effect of input diversity on coverage of the first convolutional layer crel1 in the simple CNN in Table 2. In particular, we analyze the impact of test time augmentation in order to strengthen a test set. (For actual testing, we would need to verify that augmentation does not invalidate labels. We refrain from reviewing augmented samples for this study as we focus on coverage, not performance.) We use augmentations as described in Sect. 3. We also train models using both types of augmentation to a similar

Table 3. Performance on different MNIST test sets for the Simple CNN models trained with weak or strong augmentation (aug.), tested with standard MNIST test set and test set augmentations of size 10000, except for Strong-500 with size 500

Train on	Test on			
	Standard	Weak aug.	Strong aug.	Strong-500
Weak aug.	0.9910	0.9826	0.8765	0.892
Strong aug.	0.9905	0.9890	0.9795	0.982

performance as shown in Table 3 in order to investigate potential impacts from training.[2]

Result: We see in Table 4 that coverage results are consistent across different training regimes, *i.e.* the uncovered neurons do not result from training, but from the choice of test set. Given the same test set size, weak augmentation during test time can already cover most of the neurons in `crel1` which the standard MNIST test set misses. With strong augmentation, we obtain full coverage, even with a very small test set of size 500 (Strong-500). Our conclusion is that augmentations can be very helpful to achieve coverage in early convolutional layers. As discussed above, this is based on a fine-granular notion of coverage for convolutions since an approach such as DeepXplore already achieves full neuron coverage for the standard MNIST test set (*cf.* Fig. 2).

Table 4. Neuron coverage for `crel1` (number of uncovered neurons in parentheses) on different MNIST test sets for models described in Table 3, tested with standard MNIST test set and test set augmentations of size 10000, except for Strong-500 with size 500

Train on	Test on			
	Standard	Weak	Strong	Strong-500
Weak augment	0.9968 (37)	0.9999 (1)	1.0 (0)	1.0 (0)
Strong augment	0.9950 (58)	0.9997 (3)	1.0 (0)	1.0 (0)

4.2 Class Dependency of Structural Coverage Metrics

A common belief in deep learning is that the later layers encode some semantic concept of the data. With this we have in mind that the presence or absence of specific features encoded in a later layer are combined in the final layer to come to the network's prediction. For the data sets considered in this work, these concepts should be independent of the location, scale and rotation of the input

---

[2] Obviously, the performance of the weakly trained model, does not generalize to strong augmentation.

data. In other words they should be independent of the augmentation process chosen for our experiments. Thus we would expect that the coverage of the later layers is largely unaffected by augmentation. If these semantic concepts correlate with the output class and coverage is a good metric for these concepts, we should see an effect of the output class on the coverage of the later layers.

We have seen above that input diversity through augmentation helps with coverage in the initial convolutional layer. Similarly, we can investigate whether diversity on outputs, *i.e.* using data from different classes, supports coverage on the final feature layer (the penultimate layer, before the output layer).

Experiment: Concretely, in the following we study coverage in layer `fre11` (*cf.* "Simple" in Table 2). Note that Sun et al. [17] indicate that even with a single MNIST digit, one can achieve high coverage on a test set, indicating that thus coverage is a "bad proxy for functional coverage". We investigate this more deeply using experiments in which we construct test sets that contain only subsets of digits and check if coverage on `fre11` is affected by this reduction (as a proxy for "output diversity"). The intuition is that each digit correlates with specific signal paths in the network and if these signal paths are decoupled for later layers, coverage should drop considerably when sub-sampling digits.

The networks are the ones from above in Sect. 4.1, *i.e.* trained with all digits and strong augmentation. Again, we use two variants of test time augmentation with a base test set size of 10000. Sub-selecting one digit results in approximately 1000 samples, *i.e.* for a single test digit the test set has size ≈ 1000, for 3 digits ≈ 3000.

Table 5. Coverage results for layer `fre11` if we select specific digits from an MNIST test set (standard or augmented): In the second column, the coverage for all digits is shown. Bold numbers indicate that the subset of digits has the same coverage as All.

Test set	All	Only 0	Only 9	Only 5	0,1	8,9	4,5
Standard	0.9900	0.9260	0.8960	0.9460	0.9680	0.9480	0.9780
Weak aug.	0.9900	0.9580	0.9620	0.9740	**0.9900**	0.9840	**0.9900**
Strong aug.	1.0000	0.9920	0.9920	0.9940	0.9991	0.9940	0.9997
Test set	All	0,1,2	7,8,9	4,5,6	0,1,2,3	6,7,8,9	3,4,5,6
Standard	0.9900	0.9880	0.9740	0.9840	0.9880	0.9840	0.9900
Weak aug.	0.9900	**0.9900**	**0.9900**	**0.9900**	**0.9900**	**0.9900**	**0.9900**
Strong aug.	1.0000	**1.0000**	0.9980	0.9997	**1.0000**	0.9994	**1.0000**

Results: Table 5 summarizes our results. We see that with a full test set we obtain (almost) perfect coverage for different test set variants. Strong augmentation also helps with achieving full coverage for `fre11`. We also see that even if we select just a single digit, coverage on `fre11` is only marginally reduced. Moreover, we only need data from a small subset of the digits to achieve the same coverage as for the full test set. Even for the penultimate layer, input diversity through augmentation helps with coverage. This shows that for MNIST there is no direct dependency between output diversity in the form of digits in the test set and the feature diversity needed for coverage of `frel1`. Note that we obtained similar results for the same architecture using the Fashion-MNIST dataset. We hypothesize that coverage based on mere activation of a neuron is not sufficient to capture semantic concepts for the following reasons: (i) Even with a single digit, augmentation provides a strong boost in coverage (without any change on the output class) and (ii) for augmented test sets when adding additional digits, we see almost no improvement in coverage anymore which suggests that comparable diversity is already achieved although additional digits should stimulate new features. We leave the further exploration of this question as future work.

4.3 Coverage-Guided Differential Testing vs. Augmentations

Several gradient-based approaches [12,14,18] have been proposed to generate realistic and novel test samples with an explicit aim of maximizing coverage. Do such approaches generally perform better w.r.t. coverage compared to simple test time augmentations discussed above? We study this research question based on DeepXplore [14]. DeepXplore uses gradient ascent to generate novel test cases from existing data, *i.e.* in a sense in the same class of "local modifications" of existing data as data augmentation. Gradients are generated using a loss function optimizing for two goals: (i) finding samples that exist on the decision boundary by maximizing differential output of multiple DNNs (*differential goal*) and (ii) maximizing activation of inactive neurons (*coverage goal*). We evaluate whether the DeepXplore approach performs better than weak and strong augmentations discussed in Sect. 3 on both architectures described in Table 2, especially for deeper layers. We perform experiments, with (i) a dataset containing all classes and (ii) focusing on one class and studying coverage on this subset.

Table 6. Overview of raw coverage (baseline) and coverage from different test generation methods: Columns 4 and 5 show the coverage when using DeepXplore[14] and are compared to results using weak and strong augmentations (largest coverage bold).

Network	Layers	Raw	DeepXplore Full	DeepXplore Layer	Weak Aug	Strong Aug
CNN	`crel2`	.9763	.9918	.9928	.9847	**.9935**
	`frel1`	.9975	.9975	.9986	.998	**1.0**
LeNet5	`crel1`	.9921	.9926	.9929	.9974	**.9987**
	`crel2`	.9848	.9969	**.9974**	.9924	.9966
	`max2`	.9960	**1.0**	**1.0**	.9994	**1.0**

Experiment: We use DeepXplore with hyper-parameters $\lambda 1 = 1, \lambda 2 = 2, s = 0.5$. Experiments are conducted using two architectures, the Simple CNN used earlier and a LeNet5 (Table 2) on Fashion-MNIST. As s basis for differential output using multiple DNNs, we train three models of each network with different initial seeds that achieve $\approx 91\%$ accuracy on the Fashion-MNIST test set. As described, in DeepXplore, the coverage goal of the joint loss is to increase the activation of inactive neurons. In our experiments, we consider two different versions: DeepXplore Full and DeepXplore Layer. In DeepXplore Full, inactive neurons from the entire network are randomly chosen and considered in the loss. In DeepXplore Layer, we only consider inactive neurons from the specific layer to see whether such a focused sampling strategy provides additional benefits. As discussed, we perform two experiments with (i) the full class diversity of Fashion-MNIST (*cf.* Table 6) in which the experiment is conducted using 500 random samples from test dataset and (ii) focus on a subset containing only the class "AnkleBoot" (*cf.* Table 7), featuring its 1000 samples. All experiments are performed five times with different random seeds.

Results: Table 6 shows results for **all classes** for both architectures that the coverage increases across all layers for the generated images. The increase in coverage for DeepXplore is higher than the one achieved via weak augmentation. DeepXplore Layer is slightly and consistently better than DeepXplore Full. As we see from the table, the largest coverage gain is however obtained by strong augmentation for most layers including deeper layers. The results for a test dataset of a **single class** in Table 7 are similar. The gain in coverage due to augmentations in early layers is higher than the one obtained via generated images. For deeper layers, coverage gain for generated images is higher than for weak augmentation, but strong augmentation generally provides the largest increase in coverage. DeepXplore Layer does not show benefits over sampling the full network (DeepXplore Full) in this case.

Table 7. Overview of raw coverage (baseline) and coverage from different test generation methods on Simple CNN: Coverage for DeepXplore variants are compared to results using weak and strong augmentations (largest coverage bold).

Layers	Raw	DeepXplore Full	DeepXplore Layer	Weak Aug	Strong Aug
crel1	.9917	.9744	.9764	.9845	**.9947**
crel2	.8909	.9633	.9622	.9481	**.9843**
frel1	.8459	.9373	.9333	.9199	**.9696**

4.4   Experiments Summary and Discussion

In addition to the results presented, we also studied effects of training, different thresholds for neuron activation and other data sets and their impact on coverage. We found the results to be consistent with the ones presented here, but omitted them for the sake of brevity. All results indicate that augmentation performs favorably on DNNs for an MNIST-like task, especially if taking into account that coverage-guided test data generation is also computationally more costly than performing augmentation. However, for deeper DNNs in which late layers learn high-level features, a coverage-guided test generation with semantic concept changes may fare differently. Nevertheless, Li *et al.* [10] discuss similar concerns w.r.t. the fault detection capabilities of the k-multisection criterion described in DeepGauge [12] with MNIST and LeNet as well as with ImageNet and pre-trained VGG-19 and ResNet-50 networks. While we performed our experiments on image classification tasks, the coverage metric is general and can be applied to more complex tasks in computer vision and other application domains.

5   Conclusion

In this paper, we evaluated different coverage definitions for DNNs and analyzed how they can be used for analyzing coverage and for test generation. Our results indicate that the specifics of neuron definition matter and that different kinds of layers behave very differently with respect to coverage. From our experiments, we further see that (*i*) augmentation is useful for coverage, (*ii*) full coverage can be reached while using only a subset of the classes and (*iii*) test time augmentation can beat coverage-guided test generation on MNIST-like tasks.

In conclusion, our experimental results show that structural coverage metrics are not sufficient for arguing that a DNN has been sufficiently tested. This, in turn, raises the need for additional coverage measures, e.g. considering also the semantic features of the input space that the DNN shall be able to detect. To this end, future research should investigate how input coverage [6] or coverage of latent space features [16] can improve the argumentation.

Acknowledgment. The research leading to the results presented above are funded by the German Federal Ministry for Economic Affairs and Energy within the project *KI Absicherung—Safe AI for automated driving.*

References

1. Adadi, A., Berrada, M.: Peeking inside the black-box: a survey on explainable artificial intelligence (XAI). IEEE Access **6**, 52138–52160 (2018)
2. Alam, M., Samad, M.D., Vidyaratne, L., Glandon, A., Iftekharuddin, K.M.: Survey on deep neural networks in speech and vision systems. arXiv:1908.07656 (2019)
3. Bron, A., Farchi, E., Magid, Y., Nir, Y., Ur, S.: Applications of synchronization coverage. In: Symposium on Principles and Practice of Parallel Programming, pp. 206–212 (2005)
4. Burkov, A.: Machine Learning Engineering (2020). http://www.mlebook.com/wiki/doku.phps
5. Geirhos, R., Temme, C.R., Rauber, J., Schütt, H.H., Bethge, M., Wichmann, F.A.: Generalisation in humans and deep neural networks. In: Advances in Neural Information Processing Systems, pp. 7538–7550 (2018)

6. Gladisch, C., Heinzemann, C., Herrmann, M., Woehrle, M.: Leveraging combinatorial testing for safety-critical computer vision datasets. In: Workshop on Safe Artificial Intelligence for Automated Driving (2020)
7. He, K., Zhang, X., Ren, S., Sun, J.: Delving deep into rectifiers: surpassing human-level performance on imagenet classification. In: IEEE International Conference on Computer Vision, pp. 1026–1034 (2015)
8. Kim, J., Feldt, R., Yoo, S.: Guiding deep learning system testing using surprise adequacy. In: International Conference on Software Engineering (2019)
9. LeCun, Y., Bottou, L., Bengio, Y., Haffner, P.: Gradient-based learning applied to document recognition. Proc. IEEE **86**(11), 2278–2324 (1998)
10. Li, Z., Ma, X., Xu, C., Cao, C.: Structural coverage criteria for neural networks could be misleading. In: 41st International Conference on Software Engineering: New Ideas and Emerging Results, pp. 89–92. IEEE Press (2019)
11. Ma, L., et al.: Deepct: tomographic combinatorial testing for deep learning systems. In: 26th International Conference on Software Analysis, Evolution and Reengineering, pp. 614–618. IEEE (2019)
12. Ma, L., et al.: Deepgauge: multi-granularity testing criteria for deep learning systems. In: International Conference on Automated Software Engineering (2018)
13. Olah, C., et al.: The building blocks of interpretability. Distill **3**, e10 (2018). https://doi.org/10.23915/distill.00010
14. Pei, K., Cao, Y., Yang, J., Jana, S.: DeepXplore: automated whitebox testing of deep learning systems. In: Symposium on Operating Systems Principles, pp. 1–18 (2017)
15. Pezzè, M., Young, M.: Software Testing and Analysis: Process, Principles, and Techniques. Wiley, Hoboken (2008)
16. Schwalbe, G., Schels, M.: A survey on methods for the safety assurance of machine learning based systems. In: European Congress Embedded Real Time Software and Systems (2020)
17. Sun, Y., Huang, X., Kroening, D., Sharp, J., Hill, M., Ashmore, R.: Structural test coverage criteria for deep neural networks. ACM Trans. Embed. Comput. Syst. **18**(5s), 1–23 (2019)
18. Tian, Y., Pei, K., Jana, S., Ray, B.: DeepTest: automated testing of deep-neural-network-driven autonomous cars. arXiv:1708.08559 (2017)
19. Wang, H., Xu, J., Xu, C., Ma, X., Lu, J.: Dissector: input validation for deep learning applications by crossing-layer dissection. In: International Conference on Software Engineering (2020)
20. Woods, W., Chen, J., Teuscher, C.: Adversarial explanations for understanding image classification decisions and improved neural network robustness. Nat. Mach. Intell. **1**(11), 508–516 (2019)
21. Zhang, J., Li, J.: Testing and verification of neural-network-based safety-critical control software: a systematic literature review. Inf. Softw. Technol. **123**, 106296 (2020)

A Principal Component Analysis Approach for Embedding Local Symmetries into Deep Learning Algorithms

Pierre-Yves Lagrave[(✉)] [ID]

Thales Research and Technology, Palaiseau, France
pierre-yves.lagrave@thalesgroup.com

Abstract. Building robust-by-design Machine Learning algorithms is key for critical tasks such as safety or military applications. By leveraging on the ideas developed in the context of building invariant Support Vectors Machines, this paper introduces a convenient methodology for embedding local Lie groups symmetries into Deep Learning algorithms by performing a Principal Component Analysis on the corresponding Tangent Covariance Matrix. The projection of the input data onto the principal directions leads to a new data representation which allows singling out the components conveying the semantic information useful to the considered algorithmic task while reducing the dimension of the input manifold. Besides, our numerical testing emphasizes that, although less efficient than using Group-Convolutional Neural Networks as only dealing with local symmetries, our approach does improve accuracy and robustness without introducing significant computational overhead. Performance improvements up to 5% were obtained for low capacity algorithms, making this approach of particular interest for the engineering of safe embedded Artificial Intelligence systems.

Keywords: Safe machine learning · Robustness-by-design · Model-based engineering · Lie groups · Data representation

1 Introduction

Real world data embed structural symmetries, and incorporating those into the design of Machine Learning models appears very natural (e.g., translation/rotation invariance for image classification, tone invariance for voice to text translation). In this context, Convolutional Neural Networks (CNN) [12], which ensure equivariance to translations, have been shown to be very efficient architectures for image processing tasks.

A simplified way of dealing with the generic notion of symmetry is to consider Lie groups theory [16], so that we can represent the transformations of the input data as the action of a Lie group on the set to which the inputs belong to.

© Springer Nature Switzerland AG 2020
A. Casimiro et al. (Eds.): SAFECOMP 2020 Workshops, LNCS 12235, pp. 302–314, 2020.
https://doi.org/10.1007/978-3-030-55583-2_22

According to this formalism, CNN used for image processing tasks therefore appear to be equivariant to the action of the Lie group of translations on the set of 2-dimensional images.

From a safety standpoint, data symmetries usually translate into requirements with respect to the behavior of the trained algorithms and taking those into account in the algorithms design could provide a basis for the specification of efficient post-hoc formal verification methods. Indeed, for critical tasks such as safety or military applications (e.g., autonomous trains, drones flight trajectory planning, etc.), proving the robustness of an algorithm is mandatory to its deployment and robust-by-design algorithms are in this sense quite useful. With respect to translations, CNN are examples of robust-by-design algorithms, as the translation symmetry is directly encoded into the convolution layers.

Besides, other approaches for embedding symmetries into Machine Learning algorithms exist, including the use of data augmentation techniques, the specification of penalized loss functions [14] or the use of transformed input data [9,18]. As exogenous to the core algorithms design, they are particularly convenient from a practical standpoint since they allow to leverage on existing efficient implementations of these. However, the performance results stemming from their coupling with classical Machine Learning algorithms are unfortunately not always supported by a sound theory. Consequently, conducting some extensive robustness testing is in this case a strong prerequisite to any operational deployment.

The purpose of this paper is to investigate a methodology relying on the Principal Component Analysis (PCA) technique for embedding local Lie group symmetries into Deep Learning algorithms. More precisely, by building and diagonalizing a Tangent Covariance Matrix (TCM), we propose leveraging on the ideas introduced in [18] for Support Vector Machines (SVM) [22]. As shown by our numerical results for the MNIST [13] and ROT-MNIST [11] datasets, feed forward Neural Networks (NN) benefit from our proposed representation of the input data obtained by projection onto the eigenvectors of the TCM. Indeed, our results emphasize that the dimension of the input manifold can be significantly reduced and that, for the same number of trainable parameters, better performances are obtained with our PCA-based approach than with the classical method, improving accuracy and robustness by up to 5% for low capacity algorithms. As our approach only aims at dealing with local symmetries, our performance results are below those of state-of-the-art Group-Convolutional Neural Networks (G-CNN), as expected. However, for a comparable number of parameters, our approach leads to algorithms which are significantly faster for both training and making predictions. It therefore appears to be well suited to practical cases where clean input data may be scarce and computational resources limited, as it is the case for embedded Machine Learning systems.

Although finding a rigorous justification to our results is not an easy task as it is closely linked to the problem of specifying a rigorous Deep Learning theory, we do provide some rational supporting our approach by using a data representation formalism anchored in algebraic topology, as introduced in [2].

2   Related Work and Contributions

The development of Deep Learning algorithms embedding symmetries represented as group actions is an active area of research. Using group theory, several attempts have been made to generalize the CNN structure to achieve equivariance to more general actions, leading to algorithms known as G-CNN.

The G-CNN structure was first introduced in [4] and it was further shown in [10] that, for compact groups, the use of equivariant layers is a necessary and sufficient condition for building equivariant Neural Networks. Although their proposed methodology has the advantage of being amenable to an efficient implementation, it has the drawbacks of requiring a discretization of continuous groups (which is not always possible) and having a linear time complexity in the cardinality of the discretized group.

Some work specifically focuses on Lie group symmetries and proposes to build corresponding G-CNN. In [1], a B-splines approach is proposed but the methodology is only applicable to homogeneous inputs spaces for the considered group actions. Building on the same ideas, [21] proposes an architecture using partial derivative equations to build equivariant layers to Lie group actions, provided that these actions are transitive. The work [7] generalizes the above approaches to general Lie group actions and to arbitrary continuous data. In some less recent work focusing on pattern recognition in images [20], the usual back-propagation algorithm is generalized to train Neural Networks with layers preserving local invariance.

Embedding symmetries into the design of Machine Learning models has also been investigated for other algorithms than NN, and in particular for SVM algorithms [17]. In [18], it is shown that, for linear kernels, it is possible to build SVM which are locally invariant to one-parameter Lie groups by whitening the input data by multiplication with an appropriate matrix. Following the link established with the PCA technique, this approach has been further generalized to general kernels in [3].

The purpose of our work is to investigate the applicability of the PCA approach derived in the context of building invariant SVM to Deep Learning algorithms. More precisely, following the algebraic topological formalism introduced in [2], our goal is to study the impact of data representation on the performance on Neural Networks, focusing on representations emphasizing Lie group symmetries.

We therefore see the contribution of this work as it follows:

- We generalize the PCA approach introduced for SVM to Deep Learning algorithms operating on arbitrary inputs and subject to generic Lie group actions.
- We instantiate our framework for image classification tasks and we provide some numerical results obtained when working with the reference MNIST and ROT-MNIST digits datasets, together with a discussion with respect to the performance of state-of-the-art G-CNN.
- To substantiate the rational of our approach, we analyze the PCA implied data representation using a rigorous formalism, anchored in algebraic topology theory.

3   Background

In the following, symmetries will be represented as actions of the elements of Lie groups on the input data, and we give below some corresponding background.

3.1   Lie Groups

A group is a set G, together with a multiplication map $\star : G \times G \to G$ which is required to be associative and to have a neutral element $e \in G$. Furthermore, each element $g \in G$ is required to be invertible in G, meaning that there exists a unique element denoted g^{-1} such that $g \star g^{-1} = g^{-1} \star g = e$.

A Lie group is a group for which the elements form a smooth manifold and for which the multiplication and inversion maps operate smoothly on this manifold. The Lie algebra $\mathfrak{g}$ of the Lie group G is the tangent space at the identity element and is a vector space of dimension n equal to the dimension of G seen as a manifold. The Lie algebra can therefore be represented by a basis $\zeta_1, ..., \zeta_n \in \mathfrak{g}$ of infinitesimal generators, so that any transformation $g \in G$ can be associated with an infinitesimal generator ζ_g, which can be expressed as a linear combination of the $\zeta_i \in \mathfrak{g}$.

3.2   Group Action and Equivariance

A group G is acting on a set S if there exists a map $\circ : G \times S \to S$ which is compatible with group law in the sense that $h \circ (g \circ S) = (h \star g) \circ S, \forall g, h \in G$.

For two sets X and Y on which a group G acts respectively with $\circ_X$ and $\circ_Y$, a function $f : X \to Y$ is said to be G-equivariant if $\forall x \in X$ and $\forall g \in G$, $f(g \circ_X x) = g \circ_Y f(x)$.

Similarly, $f : X \to Y$ is said to be G-invariant if $f(g \circ_X x) = f(x), \forall x \in X$ and $\forall g \in G$.

Hence, G-invariance is therefore a special case of G−equivariance, for which the group action $\circ_Y$ is trivial.

3.3   Some Examples

We consider the set I_2 of 2−dimensional gray scale images that we represent, as in [20] using convolution techniques, by continuous functions $f : \mathbb{R}^2 \to [-1, 1]$, where $f(x, y)$ represents the value of the renormalized pixel at position (x, y).

Examples of Lie groups acting on the set I_2 include the translation group $\mathbb{R}^2$, the rotation group $SO(2)$ and the special euclidean group $SE(2)$.

For $t = (t_1, t_2) \in \mathbb{R}^2$, its action on $f \in I_2$ is defined by:

$$(t \circ f)(x, y) = f(x + t_1, y + t_2) \tag{1}$$

For $R_\theta \in SO(2)$, its action on $f \in I_2$ is defined by:

$$(R_\theta \circ f)(x, y) = f(x \cos \theta - y \sin \theta, x \sin \theta + y \cos \theta) \tag{2}$$

For $T_{t,\theta} \in SE(2)$, its action on $f \in I_2$ is defined by:

$$(T_{t,\theta} \circ f)(x, y) = f(t_1 + x \cos \theta - y \sin \theta, t_2 + x \sin \theta + y \cos \theta) \tag{3}$$

4   Tangent PCA Implied Data Representation

After having introduced some mathematical tools for manipulating data representations, we specify our PCA-based approach for Deep Learning algorithms and we make a link with the data augmentation techniques.

4.1   Mathematical Framework for Data Representation

Following the ideas from [2], we see the input data as functions spaces, i.e. as sets of real-valued functions on some topological space V. More formally, denoting by $\mathscr{X}$ the input space, a data point $x \in \mathscr{X}$ will be associated with a set $\mathscr{F}_x$ of functions f_x operating on the topological space V. We denote by $\sim$ this association, so that $x \sim \{f_x(V), f_x \in \mathscr{F}_x\}$. In the following, we call a function $f_x \in \mathscr{F}_x$ a representation of x.

Coming back to the gray scale image example, we have $V = \mathbb{R}^2$ and the set $\mathscr{F}_I$ for a given image I in particular includes f_I^0, the function associating each position to its pixel value in a default observation setting, all the translations and rotations of f_I^0, the Fourier Transform of f_I^0, etc.

More generally, if a data point $x \in \mathscr{X}$ is represented by a function $f_x^0 \in \mathscr{F}_x$ and is subject to the action of a Lie group G, then its functional space contains all the functions $g \circ f_x^0$, for all $g \in G$. In the following, we consider a discrete measurement, meaning that a data point x represented by f_x will be written as $x = (f_x(v_1), ..., f_x(v_N))$, for $v_i \in V$ and $N \in \mathbb{N}^*$.

4.2   Deep Learning and TCM Based PCA Transformations

We remind here that [18] proposes training SVM which are (locally) invariant to a one parameter Lie group by minimizing the expected ℓ^2 norm of the associated infinitesimal generator applied to the decision boundary function. For linear kernels, the authors show that this optimization problem can actually be solved by training a SVM on whitened inputs and they also provide a PCA interpretation of their approach. In [3], the same approach is applied to non-linear kernels by building an appropriate Kernel-PCA map. In the following, we propose leveraging on the PCA interpretation of these approaches for embedding invariance properties into Deep-Learning algorithms.

To do so, we start from a training data set $(x_1, y_1),...,(x_l, y_l)$, with $x_i \in \mathbb{R}^N$ and $y_i \in \mathbb{R}$, and consider that each input x_i is represented by a corresponding function f_{x_i}, i.e. that we have $x_i = \left(f_{x_i}\left(v_k^i\right) \right)_{k=1}^N$. We further assume that we are interested in building a Deep Learning algorithm targeting the invariance to the transformations arising with the action on $\mathbb{R}^N$ of a n-dimensional Lie group G, with Lie algebra $\mathfrak{g}$ represented by its basis $\zeta_1, ..., \zeta_n$. Following the approach described in [18] for linear SVM, we define the corresponding TCM C_G as it follows,

$$C_G = \frac{1}{n} \sum_{i=1}^n \left\{ \frac{1}{l} \sum_{j=1}^l \zeta_i(x_j) \zeta_i(x_j)^T \right\} \tag{4}$$

where $u \to u^T$ refers to the transpose operator.

By diagonalizing C_G, we obtain the decomposition $C_G = S_G D_G S_G^T$, where S_G is an orthogonal matrix of eigenvectors and D_G a diagonal matrix of eigenvalues. We then propose building new representations $f_{x_i}^G$ of the inputs by projecting the original data onto the eigenvectors of the TCM C_G. More precisely, we define:

$$f_{x_i}^G \left(v_k^i \right) = \langle S_G x_i, e_k \rangle_{\mathbb{R}^N} \tag{5}$$

where $(e_1, ..., e_N)$ is the canonical basis of $\mathbb{R}^N$ and $\langle ., . \rangle_{\mathbb{R}^N}$ the canonical scalar product. To ease the exposition, we have only detailed here the formalism corresponding to the linear PCA approach. However, non-linear transformations of the original data could also be obtained by using the Kernel-PCA projection technique [19] in which the tangent vectors are embedded into some high dimensional space.

By using the representations $f_{x_i}^G$ as inputs to Deep Learning algorithms, we aim at separating the components which are G-invariant from those which are less semantically meaningful for the considered task. For instance, coming back to the example given in [18] in the context of image classification, this approach allows separating the component corresponding to the relative value of the pixels from that corresponding to their absolute position.

In some sense, this approach externalizes some logic from the algorithms, as relevant features are directly passed as inputs instead of being learned through the networks. By doing so, the algorithms could get faster to a meaningful internal representation of the data for the considered task, which would be possibly of smaller dimension than in the original set-up by using less trainable parameters, as illustrated on Fig. 1. Besides, as for the usual PCA approach, the dimension of the input manifold could be reduced in some cases, keeping in mind that we are however interested in removing components with a high relative variance, as they are those conveying the less useful information. Coming back to the example of Fig. 1 where the reduction dimension of the input space is not represented, if the contribution of $f_x (v_1)$ to the outputs is low enough, it can simply be removed.

When working with the linear approach, a link with the initialization strategy of the weights Ω of the first layer of the NN can also be established. Indeed, the first activation function is applied component-wise to the vector $\Omega S_G x$ and the PCA transform would be made statistically void if the weights were to be sampled according to a spherical distribution (e.g., i.i.d Gaussian random variables). We therefore propose sampling these weights uniformly in a hypercube.

The above discussion is quite heuristic and does not aim at giving a rigorous proof for the validity of our approach. This is indeed a challenging task as deeply related to the specification of a generic Deep Learning theory, which is in itself a very active domain of research as illustrated by [5,6,15]. We have rather tried to formalize the underlying intuitions.

4.3   Link with Data Augmentation Techniques

Another approach for embedding symmetries into a Deep Learning algorithm consists in augmenting the training dataset with symmetrized inputs, hoping

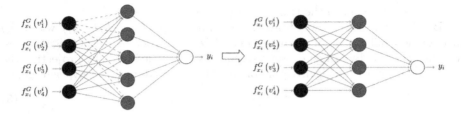

Fig. 1. On the left, a Neural Network tailored for the representation f_{x_i} is operating on the PCA implied representation $f_{x_i}^G$. We assume that the value of the first component $f_{x_i}(v_1^i)$ has a high variance with respect to the action of G and has a low relative impact, though not negligible, on the learned features and on the output value y_i. On the right, a Neural Network with fewer parameters and operating on the representation $f_{x_i}^G$ should lead to similar performance results.

for the algorithm to learn the corresponding invariance directly from the data during its training.

More precisely, data augmentation techniques consist in adding more training inputs of the form $(g \circ x_i, y_i)$, for some $g \in H$, with $H \subseteq G$. Hence, by seeing $g_1 \circ x_i$, $g_2 \circ x_i$, etc., corresponding to a same output y_i, the algorithm is somehow able to learn the invariance property. It means that part of the algorithm logic is dedicated to this task. In our approach, we directly encode the local invariance property into the PCA-transformed inputs, leading to a more compact representation of the useful information and allowing to a faster training of the algorithm. However, as our approach only deals with local invariance, it can still benefit from data augmentation, as illustrated by our numerical results shown in Sect. 5.

To illustrate the above discussion, let's consider $N = 2$, $G = SO(2)$, $g_1 = R_\theta$ and $g_2 = R_{\theta+d\theta}$. By operating on the augmented training dataset, an algorithm can therefore access the infinitesimal generator ζ_θ and imply the corresponding invariant features, to be used in deeper layers. In our approach, these features embedding the information about the group action are directly given as inputs.

5 Numerical Experiments

We give in this section the numerical results obtained when testing our approach in the context of image classification, using both MNIST and ROT-MNIST datasets. In this context, we denote $\mathcal{N}^{n_h,n_l}$ the fully connected NN with n_l layers of n_h neurons with ReLu activation functions and with one output layer of 10 neurons, on the top of which a softmax function is applied. With respect to the initialization of the NN, the weights are sampled uniformly following [8] and the bias are set to zero.

When the algorithm $\mathcal{N}^{n_h,n_l}$ operates on data transformed according to the linear PCA approach corresponding to a group G, it will be denoted $\mathcal{N}_G^{n_h,n_l}$. While performing our testing, we have been interested in several dimensions, including in particular the generalization accuracy and the robustness of the considered algorithms. All our tests and timing estimations have been performed by running the algorithms using 8 Intel cores of type i7-8705G CPU @ 3.10 GHz.

The testing we have performed is subject to the statistical noise stemming from several randomness components, including in particular the NN weights initialization and the generation of the evaluation scenarios. In order to better appreciate the statistical relevance of the reported results, each experiment has been conducted 10 times and we report the corresponding average result A, together with the associated standard deviation σ, by using the notation $A_{(\sigma)}$.

5.1   MNIST Dataset

When working with the MNIST dataset, all the considered algorithms have been trained on the original training set of 60,000 samples. Their accuracy and robustness have then been measured on the original testing set of 10,000 samples, and on the following additional testing scenarios:

- hvt: a random translation of (t_h, t_v) pixels, where $t_h \sim \mathcal{U}(-2, 2)$ and $t_v \sim \mathcal{U}(-2, 2)$, is applied to each of the original 10,000 testing samples.
- rot: a random rotation of θ degrees, where $\theta \sim \mathcal{U}(-30, 30)$, is applied to each of the original 10,000 testing samples.
- iso: a random isometry, i.e. a combination of a random translation of (t_h, t_v) pixels and a random rotation of θ degrees, where $t_h \sim \mathcal{U}(-2, 2)$, $t_v \sim \mathcal{U}(-2, 2)$, and $\theta \sim \mathcal{U}(-30, 30)$, is applied to each of the original 10,000 testing samples.

The three above scenarios, for which $\mathcal{U}(a, b)$ refers to the uniform distribution on the interval $[a, b]$, respectively correspond to the action of a local Lie subgroup of the translation group $\mathbb{R}^2$, the rotation group $SO(2)$ and the special euclidean group $SE(2)$, which have been introduced in Sect. 3.

From the results shown in Table 1, we see that our PCA-based approach allows achieving better accuracy results than the classical approach. The networks $\mathcal{N}_G^{n_h, 1}$ also appear to be more robust than $\mathcal{N}^{n_h, 1}$, even for scenarios which do not necessarily correspond to the underlying Lie group G - for instance, $\mathcal{N}_{SO(2)}^{n_h, 1}$ consistently achieves better performance results than $\mathcal{N}_{\mathbb{R}^2}^{n_h, 1}$ in the hvt scenario.

As discussed in Sect. 4, our PCA approach could be used to reduce the size of the input layer by removing the components with a high relative variance. This point is illustrated by the results shown on Fig. 2, where we in particular observe that $\mathcal{N}_{SO(2)}^{32, 1}$ remains quite efficient when compared to $\mathcal{N}^{32, 1}$, even after having removed 200 components out of the original 784. Although the slope of the accuracy decrease is also quite small for other groups, the benefit of the dimension reduction is however less pronounced than for the $SO(2)$ case. Despite the fact that these results are promising with respect to the design of embedded algorithms operating with memory constraints, we have however not observed any accuracy improvement when removing the components.

Table 1. MNIST dataset accuracy results for fully connected Neural Networks, trained with 50 epochs. From left to right and top to bottom: original testing set, `hvt`, `rot` and `iso` scenarios

n_h	$\mathcal{N}^{n_h,1}$	$\mathcal{N}_{\mathbb{R}^2}^{n_h,1}$	$\mathcal{N}_{SO(2)}^{n_h,1}$	$\mathcal{N}_{SE(2)}^{n_h,1}$	$\mathcal{N}^{n_h,1}$	$\mathcal{N}_{\mathbb{R}^2}^{n_h,1}$	$\mathcal{N}_{SO(2)}^{n_h,1}$	$\mathcal{N}_{SE(2)}^{n_h,1}$
32	$95.5_{(0.5)}$	$96.3_{(0.1)}$	$96.5_{(0.2)}$	$96.3_{(0.2)}$	$82.0_{(1.9)}$	$84.9_{(0.8)}$	$86.1_{(0.8)}$	$84.7_{(0.5)}$
64	$96.9_{(0.2)}$	$97.3_{(0.1)}$	$97.3_{(0.2)}$	$97.2_{(0.1)}$	$86.9_{(0.6)}$	$88.2_{(0.7)}$	$88.8_{(0.7)}$	$88.0_{(0.4)}$
128	$97.3_{(0.3)}$	$97.7_{(0.2)}$	$97.7_{(0.2)}$	$97.7_{(0.1)}$	$88.6_{(0.4)}$	$89.6_{(0.3)}$	$90.1_{(0.6)}$	$89.5_{(0.6)}$
256	$97.7_{(0.2)}$	$97,8_{(0.1)}$	$97.9_{(0.1)}$	$97.9_{(0.1)}$	$89.4_{(0.8)}$	$90.3_{(0.8)}$	$90.9_{(0.4)}$	$90.0_{(0.7)}$
512	$97.7_{(0.1)}$	$97.9_{(0.2)}$	$98.1_{(0.1)}$	$98.0_{(0.2)}$	$89.7_{(0.7)}$	$90.3_{(0.5)}$	$91.5_{(0.4)}$	$90.5_{(0.4)}$

n_h	$\mathcal{N}^{n_h,1}$	$\mathcal{N}_{\mathbb{R}^2}^{n_h,1}$	$\mathcal{N}_{SO(2)}^{n_h,1}$	$\mathcal{N}_{SE(2)}^{n_h,1}$	$\mathcal{N}^{n_h,1}$	$\mathcal{N}_{\mathbb{R}^2}^{n_h,1}$	$\mathcal{N}_{SO(2)}^{n_h,1}$	$\mathcal{N}_{SE(2)}^{n_h,1}$
32	$86.1_{(1.3)}$	$87.7_{(0.7)}$	$88.1_{(0.6)}$	$87.4_{(0.3)}$	$71.6_{(2.3)}$	$74.3_{(0.9)}$	$75.7_{(0.5)}$	$74.0_{(0.5)}$
64	$89.1_{(0.4)}$	$89.7_{(0.3)}$	$90.0_{(0.5)}$	$89.8_{(0.5)}$	$76.8_{(0.8)}$	$78.2_{(0.7)}$	$79.0_{(0.8)}$	$78.0_{(1.1)}$
128	$90.3_{(0.8)}$	$91.0_{(0.3)}$	$91.0_{(0.5)}$	$91.0_{(0.4)}$	$79.1_{(1.1)}$	$80.1_{(0.7)}$	$81.0_{(0.5)}$	$80.0_{(0.8)}$
256	$91.1_{(0.5)}$	$91.2_{(0.3)}$	$91.6_{(0.5)}$	$91.3_{(0.4)}$	$80.3_{(1.1)}$	$80.9_{(0.8)}$	$82.2_{(0.8)}$	$80.7_{(0.6)}$
512	$91.4_{(0.8)}$	$91.4_{(0.7)}$	$92.0_{(0.4)}$	$91.8_{(0.6)}$	$80.5_{(1.3)}$	$81.1_{(0.9)}$	$83.1_{(0.6)}$	$81.6_{(0.4)}$

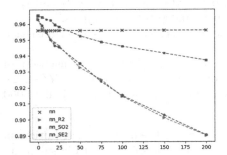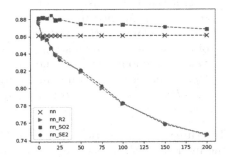

Fig. 2. Accuracy of the several algorithms $\mathcal{N}_G^{32,1}$ measured as a function of the removed PCA components on the testing set (left) and on the `rot` scenario (right) for the MNIST dataset, with the markers size being proportional to the associated standard deviation

5.2   ROT-MNIST Dataset

To draw a comparison with state-of-the art results for G-CNN algorithms, we have conducted some testing using the ROT-MNIST dataset for which the algorithms are trained on the 12,000 samples of the original training set. Their accuracy is then measured on the 50,000 samples of the testing set, without any further processing. The corresponding results include the cases of training without and with data augmentation. In [4,7] the data augmentation is done by randomly rotating each element during the optimization process. To be able to apply our approach without having to develop specific optimization routines, we have proceeded differently by defining an augmentation factor κ so that, for each sample (x_i, y_i) in the original training set, we have added $\kappa - 1$ new samples $(g_j \circ x_i, y_i)$, for $g_1, ..., g_{\kappa-1}$ drawn uniformly from the rotation group $SO(2)$.

The Table 2 shows that, for the testing set, our PCA-based methodology allows to obtain better results than the original structure $\mathcal{N}^{n_h,2}$ and that better results are obtained with our approach by using less parameters, consistently with the MNIST dataset results. We can also see that our approach seems to be compatible with the data augmentation technique, as we still get some improvements even for large augmentation factors such as $\kappa = 32$. Besides, when considering the iso scenario, we see that working with $SO(2)$ leads to lower accuracy results than those obtained when considering $\mathbb{R}^2$ and $SE(2)$. This result is expected as, with this dataset, the rotation invariance is actually embedded during the training in all the considered algorithms, as opposed to the translation one. The fact that $\mathcal{N}^{n_h,2}_{SO(2)}$ underperforms $\mathcal{N}^{n_h,2}$ in the iso scenario for $n_h \geq 128$ may be due to some overfitting with respect to the rotation component.

Also, similar experiments as those corresponding to the results of Fig. 2 have shown that $\mathcal{N}^{32,2}_{SO(2)}$ outperforms $\mathcal{N}^{32,2}$ on the testing set even after the removal of 200 components. Moreover, $\mathcal{N}^{32,2}_{\mathbb{R}^2}$ and $\mathcal{N}^{32,2}_{SE(2)}$ outperform $\mathcal{N}^{32,2}$ and $\mathcal{N}^{32,2}_{SO(2)}$ in the hvt scenario up to the removal of 25 components. However, when removing additional components, $\mathcal{N}^{32,2}_{SO(2)}$ outperforms the two algorithms embedding a translation invariance, consistently with the results obtained for the MNIST dataset.

With respect to the comparison with state-of-the-art algorithms and in particular, with the LieConv approach [7], the Table 3 gives the results obtained using the implementation of the authors and their ImgLieResnet architecture. We can see that the ImgLieResnet algorithm allows reaching consistently better performance than those reported by our approach in Table 2. This result is expected because their architecture allows embedding the entire Lie group symmetries within the network, while our approach only deals with local symmetries. Moreover, the topology of the ImgLieResnet is quite different to that of fully connected NN, including in particular several convolutional layers which have been proven very efficient for image processing tasks.

These performance differences have also to be put in perspective of the timings associated with the two approaches. When comparing the ImgLieResnet with the parameters described in [7] ($\approx 600k$ parameters) with $\mathcal{N}^{512,2}_{G}$ ($\approx 650k$ parameters), we observed that the training time was approximately 900 sec/epoch for the former and of 0.9 sec/epoch for the latter. With respect to prediction timing, the ImgLieResnet is also much slower than $\mathcal{N}^{512,2}_{G}$, taking approximately 4.2×10^{-2} sec/sample to be compared with 2.7×10^{-5} sec/sample.

Table 2. ROT-MNIST testing set (top) and `iso` scenario (bottom) accuracy results for fully connected Neural Networks, trained with 50 epochs without (left) and with (right) data augmentation ($\kappa = 32$)

n_h	$\mathcal{N}^{n_h \cdot 2}$	$\mathcal{N}^{n_h \cdot 2}_{\mathbb{R}^2}$	$\mathcal{N}^{n_h \cdot 2}_{SO(2)}$	$\mathcal{N}^{n_h \cdot 2}_{SE(2)}$	$\mathcal{N}^{n_h \cdot 2}$	$\mathcal{N}^{n_h \cdot 2}_{\mathbb{R}^2}$	$\mathcal{N}^{n_h \cdot 2}_{SO(2)}$	$\mathcal{N}^{n_h \cdot 2}_{SE(2)}$
32	$69.3_{(1.9)}$	$73.1_{(0.6)}$	$75.8_{(0.8)}$	$71.6_{(1.1)}$	$82.2_{(4.6)}$	$89.1_{(0.3)}$	$89.4_{(0.3)}$	$88.9_{(0.4)}$
64	$79.3_{(0.9)}$	$80.6_{(1.2)}$	$82.4_{(1.0)}$	$80.2_{(0.4)}$	$90.8_{(0.7)}$	$92.5_{(0.2)}$	$92.2_{(0.2)}$	$92.5_{(0.2)}$
128	$83.8_{(1.1)}$	$85.1_{(1.1)}$	$86.0_{(0.7)}$	$85.0_{(0.1)}$	$93.2_{(0.4)}$	$94.7_{(0.1)}$	$94.5_{(0.2)}$	$94.7_{(0.1)}$
256	$85.7_{(1.3)}$	$85.9_{(0.9)}$	$87.2_{(0.9)}$	$86.5_{(1.4)}$	$94.7_{(0.1)}$	$96.0_{(0.1)}$	$95.7_{(0.1)}$	$95.9_{(0.1)}$
512	$86.7_{(0.9)}$	$87.2_{(1.2)}$	$87.4_{(0.5)}$	$86.8_{(0.5)}$	$94.8_{(0.3)}$	$96.3_{(0.1)}$	$96.2_{(0.1)}$	$96.2_{(0.2)}$

n_h	$\mathcal{N}^{n_h \cdot 2}$	$\mathcal{N}^{n_h \cdot 2}_{\mathbb{R}^2}$	$\mathcal{N}^{n_h \cdot 2}_{SO(2)}$	$\mathcal{N}^{n_h \cdot 2}_{SE(2)}$	$\mathcal{N}^{n_h \cdot 2}$	$\mathcal{N}^{n_h \cdot 2}_{\mathbb{R}^2}$	$\mathcal{N}^{n_h \cdot 2}_{SO(2)}$	$\mathcal{N}^{n_h \cdot 2}_{SE(2)}$
32	$46.5_{(1.9)}$	$49.2_{(0.8)}$	$46.9_{(0.9)}$	$49.8_{(0.7)}$	$49.9_{(2.7)}$	$55.5_{(1.2)}$	$54.8_{(0.5)}$	$55.7_{(0.7)}$
64	$52.5_{(0.8)}$	$55.1_{(0.9)}$	$52.0_{(1.1)}$	$56.3_{(0.6)}$	$57.1_{(1.3)}$	$61.3_{(0.8)}$	$60.0_{(0.6)}$	$62.2_{(0.7)}$
128	$57.7_{(0.9)}$	$60.0_{(0.6)}$	$56.3_{(0.5)}$	$60.8_{(0.5)}$	$63.5_{(1.1)}$	$66.8_{(0.3)}$	$62.7_{(0.9)}$	$66.7_{(1.13)}$
256	$60.6_{(1.3)}$	$61.5_{(1.0)}$	$58.9_{(0.7)}$	$62.7_{(1.5)}$	$66.9_{(0.6)}$	$69.8_{(0.5)}$	$65.7_{(0.6)}$	$70.1_{(0.40)}$
512	$61.7_{(1.5)}$	$62.7_{(1.4)}$	$59.6_{(0.5)}$	$63.8_{(1.0)}$	$67.5_{(0.8)}$	$71.0_{(0.9)}$	$67.4_{(0.5)}$	$71.7_{(0.41)}$

Table 3. ImgLieResnet results for the ROT-MNIST dataset, with and without data augmentation

DataAug/G	$\mathbb{R}^2$	$SO(2)$	$SE(2)$
With	98.50	98.60	98.61
Without	95.32	97.82	95.96

6 Conclusions and Further Work

By leveraging on the ideas developed in the context of building locally invariant SVM algorithms, we have specified a PCA-based approach for embedding Lie groups symmetries into Deep Learning algorithms. We have motivated the rational of our approach by using a data representation formalism anchored in algebraic topology and have shown some numerical results for two reference datasets.

The conducted testing shows that, although our approach is not as efficient as G-CNN algorithms, it does allow obtaining some improvements with respect to standard fully connected Neural Networks for both accuracy and robustness dimensions. We have also highlighted that, for the considered datasets, working with $SO(2)$ allows to significantly reduce the dimension of the input manifold.

Besides, our approach is also quite convenient as it does not induce any material computational overhead compared to the standard one, except for the diagonalization of the TCM (PCA step for linear kernels) which can be performed offline on a standalone basis. The timings for G-CNN obtained using the LieConv implementation are however significantly higher, for both training and prediction.

The testing we performed only covered image classification tasks for quite simple datasets and it will be interesting to evaluate our methodology for other inputs types, with more complex structures. In this context, we will investigate its applicability to real-world examples involving structured datasets such as radar signals analysis and to real-world perception pipelines operating at a high frequency, with limited computational resources. This will constitute the opportunity to consider the use of non-linear kernels into more details, to better link the NN weights initialization strategy with our approach, and to better quantify the robustness of the approach with respect to several degrees of transformation of the training data.

Finally, the scope of this paper is limited to Lie groups based transformations, but we believe that the approach consisting in using informed data representations could be extended to more generic transformations by using projection techniques onto appropriate Lie algebras. The corresponding results could then be used to increase the robustness with respect to adversarial attacks, should the corresponding perturbations exhibit enough structure.

References

1. Bekkers, E.J.: B-spline CNNs on lie groups. In: International Conference on Learning Representations (2020). https://openreview.net/forum?id=H1gBhkBFDH
2. Bergomi, M., Frosini, P., Giorgi, D., et al.: Towards a topological-geometrical theory of group equivariant non-expansive operators for data analysis and machine learning. Nat. Mach. Intell. **1**, 423–433 (2002). https://doi.org/10.1038/s42256-019-0087-3
3. Chapelle, O., Schölkopf, B.: Incorporating invariances in nonlinear support vector machines. In: Proceedings of the 14th International Conference on Neural Information Processing Systems: Natural and Synthetic, NIPS 2001, pp. 609–616. MIT Press, Cambridge (2001)
4. Cohen, T., Welling, M.: Group equivariant convolutional networks. In: Balcan, M.F., Weinberger, K.Q. (eds.) Proceedings of The 33rd International Conference on Machine Learning. Proceedings of Machine Learning Research, PMLR, New York, 20–22 June 2016, vol. 48, pp. 2990–2999 (2016). http://proceedings.mlr.press/v48/cohenc16.html
5. Cohen, U., Chung, S., Lee, D., et al.: Separability and geometry of object manifolds in deep neural networks. Nat. Commun. **11**(746), 1–13 (2020). https://doi.org/10.1038/s41467-020-14578-53
6. Ensign, D., et al.: The complexity of explaining neural networks through (group) invariants. In: Hanneke, S., Reyzin, L. (eds.) Proceedings of the 28th International Conference on Algorithmic Learning Theory. Proceedings of Machine Learning Research, PMLR, Kyoto University, Kyoto, Japan, 15–17 Oct 2017, vol. 76, pp. 341–359 (2017). http://proceedings.mlr.press/v76/ensign17a.html
7. Finzi, M., Stanton, S., Izmailov, P., Wilson, A.G.: Generalizing convolutional neural networks for equivariance to lie groups on arbitrary continuous data. arXiv preprint arXiv:2002.12880 (2020)

8. Glorot, X., Bengio, Y.: Understanding the difficulty of training deep feedforward neural networks. In: Teh, Y.W., Titterington, M. (eds.) Proceedings of the Thirteenth International Conference on Artificial Intelligence and Statistics. Proceedings of Machine Learning Research, PMLR, Chia Laguna Resort, Sardinia, Italy, 13–15 May 2010, vol. 9, pp. 249–256 (2010). http://proceedings.mlr.press/v9/glorot10a.html
9. Kondor, R.: Group theoretical methods in machine learning. Ph.D. thesis (2008)
10. Kondor, R., Trivedi, S.: On the generalization of equivariance and convolution in neural networks to the action of compact groups. In: Dy, J.G., Krause, A. (eds.) Proceedings of the 35th International Conference on Machine Learning, ICML 2018, Stockholmsmässan, Stockholm, Sweden, 10–15 July 2018, Proceedings of Machine Learning Research, vol. 80, pp. 2752–2760. PMLR (2018). http://proceedings.mlr.press/v80/kondor18a.html
11. Larochelle, H., Erhan, D., Courville, A., Bergstra, J., Bengio, Y.: An empirical evaluation of deep architectures on problems with many factors of variation. In: Proceedings of the 24th International Conference on Machine Learning. ICML 2007, pp. 473–480. Association for Computing Machinery, New York (2007). https://doi.org/10.1145/1273496.1273556
12. LeCun, Y., Bengio, Y.: Convolutional Networks for Images, Speech, and Time Series, pp. 255–258. MIT Press, Cambridge (1998)
13. LeCun, Y., Cortes, C., Burges, C.: Mnist handwritten digit database. ATT Labs (2010). http://yann.lecun.com/exdb/mnist
14. Leen, T.K.: From data distributions to regularization in invariant learning. Neural Comput. 7(5), 974–981 (1995). https://doi.org/10.1162/neco.1995.7.5.974
15. Mallat, S.: Understanding deep convolutional networks. Philos. Trans. R. Soc. A: Math. Phys. Eng. Sci. 374(2065) (2016). https://doi.org/10.1098/rsta.2015.0203
16. Olver, P.: Applications of Lie Groups to Differential Equations. Springer, New York (1993)
17. Schölkopf, B., Burges, C., Vapnik, V.: Incorporating invariances in support vector learning machines. In: von der Malsburg, C., von Seelen, W., Vorbrüggen, J.C., Sendhoff, B. (eds.) ICANN 1996. LNCS, vol. 1112, pp. 47–52. Springer, Heidelberg (1996). https://doi.org/10.1007/3-540-61510-5_12
18. Schölkopf, B., Simard, P., Smola, A., Vapnik, V.: Prior knowledge in support vector kernels. In: Proceedings of the 1997 Conference on Advances in Neural Information Processing Systems, NIPS 1997, vol. 10, pp. 640–646. MIT Press, Cambridge (1998)
19. Schölkopf, B., Smola, A., Müller, K.-R.: Kernel principal component analysis. In: Gerstner, W., Germond, A., Hasler, M., Nicoud, J.-D. (eds.) ICANN 1997. LNCS, vol. 1327, pp. 583–588. Springer, Heidelberg (1997). https://doi.org/10.1007/BFb0020217
20. Simard, P.Y., LeCun, Y.A., Denker, J.S., Victorri, B.: Transformation invariance in pattern recognition — tangent distance and tangent propagation. In: Orr, G.B., Müller, K.-R. (eds.) Neural Networks: Tricks of the Trade. LNCS, vol. 1524, pp. 239–274. Springer, Heidelberg (1998). https://doi.org/10.1007/3-540-49430-8_13
21. Smets, B., Portegies, J., Bekkers, E., Duits, R.: PDE-based group equivariant convolutional neural networks (2020)
22. Vapnik, V.: The Nature of Statistical Learning Theory. Statistics for Engineering and Information Science. Springer, Heidelberg (2000). https://doi.org/10.1007/978-1-4757-3264-1

A Framework for Building Uncertainty Wrappers for AI/ML-Based Data-Driven Components

Michael Kläs[(✉)] and Lisa Jöckel[(✉)]

Fraunhofer Institute for Experimental Software Engineering IESE,
Fraunhofer-Platz 1, 67663 Kaiserslautern, Germany
`{michael.klaes,lisa.joeckel}@iese.fraunhofer.de`

Abstract. More and more software-intensive systems include components that are data-driven in the sense that they use models based on artificial intelligence (AI) or machine learning (ML). Since the outcomes of such models cannot be assumed to always be correct, related uncertainties must be understood and taken into account when decisions are made using these outcomes. This applies, in particular, if such decisions affect the safety of the system. To date, however, hardly any AI-/ML-based model provides dependable estimates of the uncertainty remaining in its outcomes. In order to address this limitation, we present a framework for encapsulating existing models applied in data-driven components with an uncertainty wrapper in order to enrich the model outcome with a situation-aware and dependable uncertainty statement. The presented framework is founded on existing work on the concept and mathematical foundation of uncertainty wrappers. The application of the framework is illustrated using pedestrian detection as an example, which is a particularly safety-critical feature in the context of autonomous driving. The Brier score and its components are used to investigate how the key aspects of the framework (scoping, clustering, calibration, and confidence limits) can influence the quality of uncertainty estimates.

Keywords: Artificial intelligence · Machine learning · Safety engineering · Data quality · Operational design domain · Out-of-distribution · Dependability

1 Introduction

Components based on machine learning and other AI methods are increasingly finding their way into software-intensive systems. In this context, we talk about data-driven components (DDCs) if the functionality provided by the component is not explicitly specified and implemented by developers, but is automatically generated by algorithms based on data. Such data-driven components play an important role, particularly in areas such as autonomous driving or Industry 4.0, because they provide opportunities for perception that cannot yet be reasonably realized with conventional software. Well-known tasks are the recognition of people, traffic signs, or other objects and structures in camera images, but also speech recognition and natural language processing.

© Springer Nature Switzerland AG 2020
A. Casimiro et al. (Eds.): SAFECOMP 2020 Workshops, LNCS 12235, pp. 315–327, 2020.
https://doi.org/10.1007/978-3-030-55583-2_23

Especially when applied in the context of safety-critical systems, there is, however, the challenge that – in contrast to traditional software – we can neither assume nor demonstrate that data-driven components will provide the intended output for any input. For example, we cannot assume that a person recognition component will really recognize all types of people in any operating condition. The outputs of data-driven components are thus always subject to uncertainty. Therefore, it seems essential to quantify the degree of uncertainty, which is usually also situation-dependent, and consider it in subsequent decision-making. For example, when the outcome of a pedestrian being detected at a distance of 40 m has a moderate uncertainty, this could lead to a precautionary reduction in speed, whereas when the outcome is highly uncertain, i.e., if there is probably no pedestrian, the current speed may be maintained as long as sufficient time remains for a braking maneuver at short notice.

Existing data-driven models (DDMs) and modeling approaches, however, usually do not explicitly consider uncertainty in their outcomes, or provide uncertainty estimates that are not dependable from a statistical point of view [1]. To address this limitation, which we discuss further in the background section of this paper, Kläs and Sembach introduced the mathematical foundations for 'uncertainty wrappers', which enclose an existing data-driven model and enrich its outcomes with dependable uncertainty estimates [2]. The concept considers the three different kinds of common sources of uncertainty introduced in the onion shell model: limitations regarding the *model fit*, *data quality*, and *scope compliance* [3].

Contribution: To make uncertainty wrappers applicable in practice, we developed a framework, which we present in this paper. The framework underpins the previously published mathematical concepts with specific methods and provides a reference architecture as well as tooling support for building and applying uncertainty wrappers. In order to show its applicability and potential benefits, we illustrate the application on an existing DDM for pedestrian detection and investigate how the key elements of the framework (scoping, clustering, calibration, and confidence limits) influence the quality of uncertainty estimates as measured by the Brier score and its components.

Structure: Section 2 motivates the relevance of the proposed framework, positioning it in the context of related work and introduces the Brier score measure. Section 3 presents the framework and illustrates its use on a simplified example of pedestrian detection. Section 4 investigates which parts of estimation quality as measured by the Brier score are addressed by the key aspects of the framework. Finally, Sect. 5 concludes the paper with previous application experience and an outlook on future work.

2 Background

In this section, we will first provide a short summary on uncertainty estimates and observed limitations in their calculations (see [1] for a more elaborate discussion). Next, we will briefly introduce the foundations of the uncertainty wrapper concept that we use and elaborate in this paper. Finally, we will introduce the Brier score as a measure for evaluating uncertainty estimates.

Uncertainty Estimates: Uncertainty estimates for categorical outcomes, which are commonly provided as probabilities, can be obtained by different means. There are, for example, specific kinds of DDMs that implicitly provide uncertainty estimates, such as decision trees, which provide not only the selected category, but also its probability. Several ML approaches have also been extended to provide DDMs with uncertainty estimates (e.g., various Neural Networks [4, 5]). For example, Henne et al. [6] and Snoek, et al. [7] provide benchmarking for a selection of such approaches. However, uncertainty estimates directly provided by DDMs are usually not dependable, i.e., there is no statistical guarantee for these values. Sometimes the provided values are not even probabilities in a probabilistic sense, such as in the case of Naïve Bayes and Support Vector Machines. Moreover, DDMs usually focus on providing accurate prediction results, not uncertainty estimates. Therefore, they ignore uncertainty-relevant features that do not contribute to the accuracy of the model. Finally, their estimates are usually calculated based on data used during model training, which increases the risk of overfitting and thus of overconfident estimates [1].

There are approaches that can be applied to calibrate improper probability estimates using an independent representative calibration dataset [8]. Scikit-learn, e.g., provides algorithms for *sigmoid* (parametric) and *isotonic* (nonparametric) calibration [9]. However, the use of calibration methods does not solve the problem that the provided uncertainty estimates are usually received from a black box; e.g., domain experts cannot semantically validate the criteria based on which the model decides whether a certain result has a higher or lower attributed uncertainty. Moreover, the calibration methods of which we are aware provide no upper boundary for the estimated uncertainty given a requested level of statistical confidence, which limits their usefulness in a safety argument. Finally, existing approaches largely ignore the fact that a DDM might also be applied outside the scope for which it was calibrated and that the provision of realistic uncertainty estimates and of accurate outcomes does not necessarily require the same inputs and features, which is, however, an implicit assumption when integrating the calculation of uncertainty estimates directly into a DDM [1].

Uncertainty Wrapper: The model-agnostic concept of an uncertainty wrapper proposed by Kläs & Sembach [2] addresses these limitations. It defines uncertainty as the likelihood that the outcome of a DDM is not correct considering a given definition of correctness. Based on this definition, Kläs & Sembach show that uncertainty can be mathematically decomposed into the three classes of an onion shell model [3]: (1) Model-fit-related uncertainty occurs due to the inherent modeling limitations when creating a DDM. (2) Quality-related uncertainty results from applying a DDM on input data with quality limitations, which is a common phenomenon in practice. (3) Finally, scope-compliance-related uncertainty addresses circumstances where a DDM is applied for cases outside the application scope for which it was built and tested.

Where model-fit-related uncertainty can be determined with traditional model testing approaches, the likelihood of scope compliance is determined by '*scoping*'. Scoping checks the adherence of a specific case to a number of scope factors that should all be valid for each case within the intended application scope. Quality-related uncertainty is addressed by *clustering* the cases in the application scope into areas with similar uncertainty considering relevant quality factors. The estimates for individual clusters need to be *calibrated* on a dataset representative for the intended application scope. Finally, considering a requested level of *confidence*, statistics are proposed for estimating an upper boundary for the uncertainty in each cluster.

Although the concept of uncertainty wrappers appears promising, a framework operationalizing the concept has been missing to date, along with a reference architecture for the wrapper, specific methods that can be applied for clustering and scoping, as well as tooling support.

The work most closely related to the framework proposed in this paper may be the framework proposed by Czarnecki and Salay for managing perceptual uncertainty [10], which, however, remains on a more descriptive level. Whereas the uncertainty wrapper focuses on situation-aware estimates at runtime, known tooling support usually focuses on dealing with uncertainty at design time. For example, Matsuno et al. [11] provide a tool that investigates how uncertainty in ML affects safety arguments, and the *nn-dependability-kit* examines the robustness of data-driven components against known perturbations during testing [12].

Evaluating Uncertainty Estimates: Defining uncertainty as the probability that the DDM outcome is not correct, we can consider uncertainty estimation as a (binary) probabilistic classification task. With scoring rules, decision theory provides a means for evaluating the utility of such estimates. We generally request certain properties for scoring rules to be reasonable; the most relevant one is that they should be strictly proper. Strictly proper scoring rules assure that the scoring result only depends on the probability to be estimated and is optimized exclusively by estimating the correct probability.

Theoretically, the number of strictly proper scoring rules is infinite. However, there are some popular rules such as negative log-likelihood and especially ***Brier score (bs)***, which was introduced by Brier in 1950 [13] and is, e.g., applied by Snoek, et al. [7]. It measures the mean squared difference between the predicted probability of an outcome and the actual outcome. Applied to uncertainty, this means that if the estimated uncertainty is 80% and the actual outcome is wrong (e.g. '1'), $bs = (1 - 0.8)^2 = 0.04$. So it can be considered as a cost function with a minimum of 0, where lower values mean more accurate uncertainty estimates. Choosing the Brier score as a cost function is especially appealing if we do not know how the estimates are planned to be used further, since it does not emphasize particular decision thresholds but assumes a uniform distribution.

Murphy was able to show that the Brier score can be further detailed by decomposing it into three additive components, which he named uncertainty, resolution, and reliability [14]. Deviating from this designation, we speak of variance instead of uncertainty to avoid confusion, and of unreliability instead of reliability since counterintuitively, low reliability values would mean high reliability. Besides Brier score, we consider its three components since they provide a more detailed picture of the specific limitations affecting uncertainty estimates, which are also addressed by different elements of the uncertainty wrapper framework:

$$bs = var - res + unr \qquad (1)$$

Variance (var) describes the empirically observed variation in the correctness of the DDM outcomes (i.e., Bernoulli variance). This means DDMs with a high average error rate provide a high average uncertainty and thus a high variance.

$$var \; = \; E(P(correct)) \, E \, (P(wrong)) \tag{2}$$

Resolution (res) describes how much the case-specific uncertainty estimates differ from the empirically observed average error rate of the DDM (i.e., the case-independent average uncertainty).

$$res \; = \; E(P(wrong \mid uncertainy) \; - \; E(P(wrong)))^2 \tag{3}$$

Unreliability (unr) describes how much, given an estimated uncertainty, the empirically observed uncertainty (i.e., the error rate) differs. If we have, for example, ten cases with an estimated uncertainty of 30%, *unr* is 0 if we empirically observe that the DDM outcome for three of them is wrong.

$$unr \; = \; E(uncertainy \; - \; P(wrong \mid uncertainty))^2 \tag{4}$$

3   Framework and Application Example

This section introduces a framework for building uncertainty wrappers for arbitrary data-driven models, assuming the availability of a labeled dataset that is representative of the model's *target application scope* (TAS), i.e., its intended application settings. TAS as a concept is thus comparable to the operational design domain as defined by SAE J3016 for automated driving. A dataset or sample is considered as *representative* if it "ensures external validity in relationship to the population of interest the sample is meant to represent" [15], e.g., by using a random selection approach. Besides the *input* of the data-driven component, the dataset also needs to comprise the *intended outcome* for each case (e.g., the location of a pedestrian in a given input image). Given a definition of *correctness*, we can apply the DDM for each case in the dataset and derive whether the outcome is correct or not.

Figure 1 illustrates how the uncertainty wrapper architecture complements the DDM with a *quality model* and a *quality impact model* to determine quality-related uncertainties and a *scope model* and a *scope compliance model* to determine the likelihood of scope incompliance. Finally, the wrapper combines both results into an overall uncertainty statement considering the requested level of *confidence*.

In this setting, *uncertainty* is defined by the likelihood that outcomes of the DDM are not correct, and a *dependable uncertainty estimate* is a justified upper boundary on this for a given level of confidence [2]. In our application, we get as an outcome a bounding box with, e.g., the corners (34, 352) and (51, 359) that could potentially contain a pedestrian, extended with the dependable uncertainty estimate that the probability of providing a wrong box is less than 4%, considering a confidence level of .9999 and the definition of correctness.

The tooling that is part of the framework supports the creation and validation of each uncertainty wrapper element in a separate module developed in Python, the de-facto

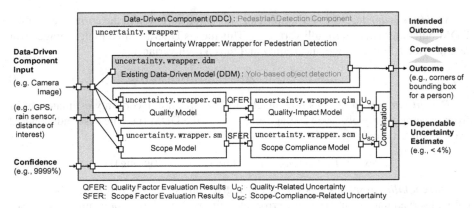

QFER: Quality Factor Evaluation Results U_Q: Quality-Related Uncertainty
SFER: Scope Factor Evaluation Results U_{SC}: Scope-Compliance-Related Uncertainty

Fig. 1. Wrapper architecture including the dataflow between the data-processing models

standard language for data science in most companies (cf. [16]). The elements realizing the overall wrapper as well as elements provided in submodules have been validated to be compliant with the estimator interface of the popular open-source machine learning package 'scikit-learn' [9]. As a result, the elements are intuitive to use for most data scientists, can simply reuse existing models and metrics from scikit-learn, and can be easily integrated into larger data analysis pipelines or ensembles of models.

The sections below illustrate each element using a simplified example application of pedestrian detection on a dataset containing approx. one million images. Although the framework was also applied and validated in an industry setting with field data, we decided to illustrate its usage on YOLOv3 as a publicly available DDM [17] and with data generated using the driving simulator CARLA [18], which allows us to publish concrete numbers as well as raw data (upon request). The given example primarily serves to illustrate the framework; it does not claim high external validity.

Scope Models contain all elements required to process the inputs of a DDC in order to provide case-specific information on 'scope compliance'-related causes for uncertainty considering a set of scope factors. Each scope factor is quantified by one or more scope measures, which provide measurement results that are then evaluated with a scope factor evaluation. For example, if the TAS of the DDC is limited to Germany, we need to find out whether the model is applied outside Germany, since the data we used to test the model and calibrate the uncertainty estimates might not be representative for usage outside of Germany. Therefore, we would need to define measures that extract the geo-location from the DDC input and a factor that applies an evaluation returning the likelihood that the geolocation is within Germany.

```
sm = ScopeModel(List[ScopeFactor(List[ScopeMeasure], ScopeFactorEval)]).fit(...)
scope_factor_eval_results = sm.predict(ddc_input)
```

The framework mainly distinguishes three kinds of scope factors (Fig. 2). *Boundary-based* factors define a valid range for specific DDC inputs. These boundaries can be explicitly stated in the TAS definition, such as requesting a geolocation within Germany, or implicitly derived from empirical data, such as a valid range for temperatures.

Condition-based factors model multivariate concepts like location-specific temperature ranges. Finally, *novelty-detecting factors* try to detect cases that are outside the TAS but still satisfy boundary- and condition-based scope factors. This is important since we would usually need an infinite number of scope factors to describe a TAS perfectly.

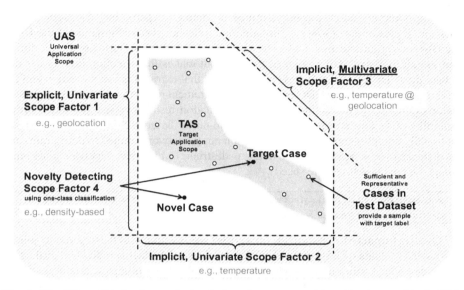

Fig. 2. The different kinds of scope factors help to detect a potential application outside the TAS.

In order to detect such novel cases, the framework relies on *one-class classification*, considering the cases of the test dataset as representations taken from the TAS. The framework supports the creation of novelty-detecting factors based on one-class support vector machines, kernel-density estimation, and percentile-based boundaries [19]. Moreover, the framework calculates performance statistics for the novelty-detecting factors using cross-validation. The *false alarm rate* is calculated by the ratio of cases that are predicted as novel in hold-out parts of the test data. Since, as for any one-class classification task, we do not have a representative set of cases labeled as novel, the framework supports sampling cases from the input space defined through boundary- and condition-based scope factors (i.e., the white area in Fig. 2) assuming a given, e.g., equal, distribution. The obtained *overall alarm rate* (incl. correct as well as false alarms, which cannot be distinguished due to missing labels) can then be related to the false alarm rate in order to select the most appropriate novelty-detecting factor.

Scope Compliance Models provide for a given case an estimate of the uncertainty jointly introduced by 'scope compliance'-related causes considering the factor-individual evaluation results provided by the scope model. The implementation applies the multiplicative combination proposed in [2] and finally returns an estimate for the likelihood that the model will be used outside its intended application scope TAS.

```
scm = ScopeComplianceModel(ScopeModel,MultiplicativeCombinationModel(epsilon)).fit(...)
scope_rel_uncert = scm.predict(scope_factor_eval_results)
```

Quality Models contain all elements required to process the inputs of a given DDC in order to provide case-specific information on 'data quality'-related causes of uncertainty. A quality model thus represents the counterpart to the scope model and follows the same structure. Quality factors can be identified by domain experts, but also through data analysis. For example, a low sun altitude may influence the performance of the DDM used for pedestrian detection. Unlike the use of the DDM outside Germany, the use during low sun altitude may still be part of the TAS but makes the detection task harder due to backlight. Therefore, measures can be defined that extract the sun's location and the driving direction from the DDC input. The measurement results are then evaluated using factor evaluation to determine the binary evaluation result low_sun_altitude. Further examples of factors are the amount of precipitation based on the rain sensor signal (optionally complimented with a convolution neural network trained to detect rain) and the distance over which we want to detect pedestrians (which may depend, among other things, on the current vehicle speed).

```
qm = QualityModel(List[QualityFactor(List[QualityMeasure], QualityFactorEval)]).fit(...)
quality_factor_eval_results = qm.predict(ddc_input)
```

Quality Impact Models provide for a given case an estimate of the uncertainty jointly introduced by 'data quality'-related causes considering the factor-individual evaluation results provided by the quality model. In order to make the resulting uncertainty estimate not only statistically sound but understandable and traceable for safety engineers and domain experts, we train an information-gain-based decision tree structure to identify clusters with similar uncertainties (cf. Fig. 3). The dependent variable is the correctness of the DDM outcome and the independent variables are the quality factor evaluation results of the quality model. In order to provide statistically sound results, the clusters (i.e., the tree nodes) are identified using a training dataset and then calibrated with a separate calibration dataset representative of the TAS. Moreover, the given confidence level is considered when the uncertainty estimates are calculated.

```
qim = QualityImpactModel(QualityModel,DecisionTreeAlg,confidence).fit(...).calibrate(...)
quality_rel_uncert = qim.predict(quality_factor_eval_results)
```

The results can be evaluated semantically based on the decision tree structure; e.g., the distance to the pedestrian increases the uncertainty. Moreover, the appropriateness of the refinement can be evaluated comparing the base rate (dashed line in Fig. 3) against the degree of separation provided by the identified clusters measured as loss of certainty (cl). Given a disjoint test dataset, the Brier score results can also be considered.

Finally, the calibration can be checked using a calibration curve [20]. The calibration curves in Fig. 4 show that applying a confidence level during calibration pushes the calibration line above the perfect line, making the uncertainty estimates more conservative but also more reliable when tested on new datasets not used for calibration. For example, the uncertainty of the cases in cluster #14 is no longer underestimated.

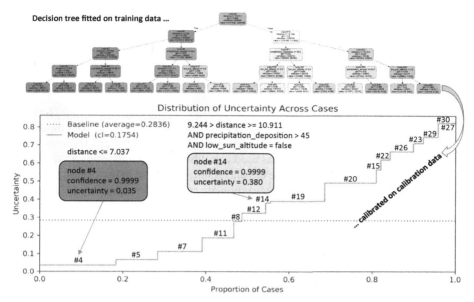

Fig. 3. A calibrated decision-tree-based quality impact model with confidence = .9999 and its evaluation, visualizing uncertainty estimates and certainty loss (cl) in comparison to DDM baseline.

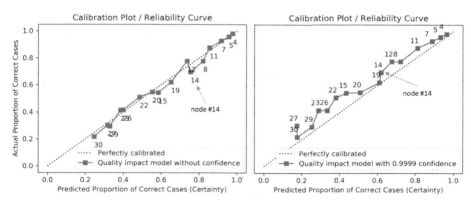

Fig. 4. The calibration curves illustrate the differences between a quality impact model calibrated without a confidence level (left) and one calibrated with a confidence level of .9999 (right).

Wrappers provide a transparent option for enriching existing DDMs with uncertainty estimates, taking the inputs of the DDC and providing uncertainty estimates with a requested level of confidence as a second output. Internally, they delegate the task to the encapsulated DDM and the introduced wrapper elements.

```
wrapper = Wrapper(DataDrivenModel, QualityImpactModel, ScopeComplianceModel)
ddm_outcome, uncertainty = wrapper.predict(ddm_input, confidence)
```

4   Brier-Score-Based Investigation

In order to investigate the influence of the key aspects of an uncertainty wrapper –
scoping, clustering, calibration, and *confidence limits* – on the quality of the provided
uncertainty estimates, we proceeded as follow:

(1)   We prepared three separate datasets using the driving simulator CARLA. The *train-ing dataset* was used to identify clusters based on the quality impact model and
provide naïve baseline estimates based on the average error rate. The *calibration
dataset* representing the TAS was used to calibrate the quality impact model. The
test dataset was used to evaluate the uncertainty estimates by calculating the Brier
score and its components. In order to simulate common issues observed in practice,
we modified the distribution of the different kinds of pedestrians between the train-ing and the calibration dataset (e.g., more children). We also kept some unintended
cases from the simulation results that were not compliant with our TAS definition
in the test dataset, such as pedestrians detected beyond the maximum intended
application distance.

(2)   Next, we used the framework to create five (partial) wrapper instances A to E:

A addresses *none* of the key aspects. The provided uncertainty estimates are case-independent using the average error rate determined on the training dataset.

B addresses *scoping*, which means that it uses a scope compliance model (cf.
Figure 3) to detect cases that are outside the TAS and rejects them. Estimates
are still case-independent using the average error rate determined on the training
dataset.

C addresses not only scoping, but also *clustering*, meaning it uses a quality impact
model based on a decision tree, which was learned on the training dataset using
information gain and a maximum depth of 4. Estimates are now case-aware con-sidering quality factors such as the amount of precipitation measured by the rain
sensor to determine the appropriate cluster (i.e., leaf in the decision tree).

D addresses not only scoping and clustering, but also *calibration*, meaning the
uncertainty-related values in the leaves of the decision tree (i.e., our clusters) are
updated based on the calibration dataset.

E finally addresses all key aspects, which adds *confidence limits*. This means for
our example that an upper boundary for the uncertainty estimate is determined for
each cluster. The calculations consider not only the specific uncertainty, but also
the requested confidence level of .9999 and the number of cases in the cluster.

(3)   Finally we applied the wrapper instances A to E to our test dataset with 291,584 data
points. On the results, we calculated the Brier score and its components, which we
introduced in Sect. 2. Moreover, the proportion of clusters providing overconfident
uncertainty estimates (o/confident) were determined as a measure of dependability.
The uncertainty estimates of a cluster are considered as overconfident if the observed
rate of wrong DDM outcomes exceeds the cluster-adjusted uncertainty estimate.

Table 1 summarizes the investigation results. Metrics that change from the preceding
wrapper instance to the current one are printed in bold. At this point, we would like
to point out once again that the reported results were obtained for data based on

images generated by a driving simulator and the application of a general-purpose object detection DDM. Thus, the absolute numbers should be interpreted with care. However, the general effects and tendencies we report are confirmed by our experience when we applied the framework on real-world datasets in an industry setting.

Table 1. Characteristics and performance of several (partial) wrapper instances

	Instance A	Instance B	Instance C	Instance D	Instance E
Scoping	–	✓	✓	✓	✓
Clustering	–	–	✓	✓	✓
Calibration	–	–	–	✓	✓
Confidence	–	–	–	–	✓
#outcomes	291584	242576[*]	242576[*]	242576[*]	242576[*]
#clusters	1	1	16	16	16
Brier score	0.28339	0.23995	0.18319	0.15485	0.15502
+ Variance	0.23924	**0.22009**	0.22009	0.22009	0.22009
− Resolution	0.00000	0.00000	**0.06526**	0.06526	0.06526
+ Unreliability	0.04416	**0.01986**	**0.02836**	**0.00002**	**0.00019**
o/confident	100%	100%	100%	**56%**	**0%**

*Further cases (cf. Instance A) were identified by the wrapper as being outside the TAS

Discussion: Instances without clustering have only one cluster comprising all cases, whereas instances C-E are based on the same 16 clusters identified during clustering. Scoping, which detects and indicates situations for which the DDC was not intended, is considered in instances B-E, which is reflected by the reduced number of valid DDM outcomes. Scoping influences variance and unreliability (cf. Instance A vs. B). Variance is reduced since applications outside the TAS are more likely to lead to higher error rates, and unreliability is reduced since situations outside the TAS are usually not well represented in the training data. Clustering increases the resolution by providing uncertainty estimates based on the 16 different clusters identified (cf. Instance B vs. C). The separation into individual clusters, however, can also increase overall unreliability to some extent. Calibration then addresses unreliability, with a representative calibration dataset able to reduce unreliability even to close to zero (cf. Instance D). Usually, ~50% of the clusters will now provide overconfident estimates. Depending on the chosen confidence level, the ratio of clusters with overconfident estimates can be reduced to zero or at least to close to zero (cf. Instance E). Depending on the number of clusters and calibration data points, this can, however, increase unreliability, since the estimate now has to consider some 'safety' margin. In total, brier score is reduced from 0.28339 to 0.15502 by the uncertainty wrapper.

5 Conclusion

The uncertainty wrapper framework differs from existing solutions for dealing with uncertainty in AI/ML-based components. It makes the sources contributing to uncertainty transparent, enabling them to be evaluated by experts instead of being hidden in the algorithms of the DDM or its extensions (cf., e.g., approaches benchmarked in [6]). Moreover, unlike in existing solutions, a requested confidence level, which can even change at runtime depending on the integrity level needs, is considered when providing the uncertainty estimates, which makes them justifiable and more dependable. Compared to naïve approaches, the wrapper also makes uncertainty estimates situation-aware, thereby providing separation between cases with high and low uncertainty (cf. Fig. 3). Finally, the framework is model-agnostic as well as holistic in terms of model fit, quality, and uncertainty related to scope compliance.

Based on the Brier score and its components, which we applied to investigate the quality of uncertainty estimates, we showed that an uncertainty wrapper can contribute to estimation quality by improving all the components of the Brier score, i.e., variance, resolution, and unreliability. Specifically, *clustering* cases with a quality impact model as part of an uncertainty wrapper addresses its resolution as well as its *calibration* unreliability. Moreover, a *scope compliance* model, which is also part of the uncertainty wrapper, can help to reduce variance and unreliability by detecting and excluding cases outside the target application scope. In contrast, using a *confidence limit* increases unreliability. However, it also makes overconfident estimates much more unlikely and thus contributes to the overall dependability of uncertainty estimates (cf. Fig. 4).

Although the presented framework was applied and validated in an industry setting with field data, we cannot provide these results in this paper. Instead, we used a publicly available DDM and data generated using a driving simulator. In the next step, however, we plan to provide a more detailed evaluation of the approach on publicly available traffic sign images augmented with typical quality deficits [21] and compare the results with the results of probabilistically extended DDMs.

Acknowledgments. Parts of this work have been funded by the Ministry of Science, Education, and Culture of the German State of Rhineland-Palatinate in the context of the project MInD and the Observatory for Artificial Intelligence in Work and Society (KIO) of the Denkfabrik Digitale Arbeitsgesellschaft in the project "KI Testing & Auditing". We would like to thank especially Naveed Akram and Pascal Gerber for providing the dataset we used to illustrate the framework application, and Jan Reich and Sonnhild Namingha for the initial review of the paper.

References

1. Kläs, M.: Towards Identifying and Managing Sources of Uncertainty in AI and Machine Learning Models - An Overview. arXiv:1811.11669 (2018)
2. Kläs, M., Sembach, L.: Uncertainty wrappers for data-driven models – increase the transparency of AI/ML-based models through enrichment with dependable situation-aware uncertainty estimates. In: WAISE 2019, Turku, Finland (2019)
3. Kläs, M., Vollmer, A.M.: Uncertainty in machine learning applications – a practice-driven classification of uncertainty. In: WAISE 2018, Västerås, Sweden (2018)

4. Phan, B., Khan, S., Salay, R., Czarnecki, K.: Bayesian uncertainty quantification with synthetic data. In: WAISE 2019, Turku, Finland (2019)
5. Gal, Y.: Uncertainty in Deep Learning. University of Cambridge, Cambridge (2016)
6. Henne, M., Schwaiger, A., Roscher, K., Weiss, G.: Benchmarking uncertainty estimation methods for deep learning with safety-related metrics. In: SafeAI 2020, New York, USA (2020)
7. Snoek, J., et al.: Can you trust your model's uncertainty? Evaluating predictive uncertainty under dataset shift. In: Advances in Neural Information Processing Systems (2019)
8. Niculescu-Mizil, A., Caruana, R.: Predicting good probabilities with supervised learning. In: 22nd International Conference on Machine Learning (2005)
9. Pedregosa, F., Varoquaux, G., Gramfort, A., Michel, V., et al.: Scikit-learn: machine learning in Python. J. Mach. Learn. Res. **12**, 2825–2830 (2011)
10. Czarnecki, K., Salay, R.: Towards a framework to manage perceptual uncertainty for safe automated driving. In: WAISE 2018, Västerås, Sweden (2018)
11. Matsuno, Y., Ishikawa, F., Tokumoto, S.: Tackling uncertainty in safety assurance for machine learning: continuous argument engineering with attributed tests. In: WAISE 2019, Turku, Finland (2019)
12. Cheng, C.-H., Huang, C.-H., Nührenberg, G.: nn-dependability-kit: engineering neural networks for safety-critical systems. https://arxiv.org/abs/1811.06746 (2018)
13. Brier, G.W.: Verification of forecasts expressed in terms of probability. Mon. Weather Rev. **78**(1), 1–3 (1950)
14. Murphy, A.H.: A new vector partition of the probability score. J. Appl. Meteorol. **12**(4), 595–600 (1973)
15. Dumicic, K.: Representative samples. In: Lovric, M. (ed.) International Encyclopedia of Statistical Science. Springer, Heidelberg (2011). https://doi.org/10.1007/978-3-642-04898-2
16. Developer Survey Results. https://insights.stackoverflow.com/survey/2019 (2019)
17. Redmond, J., Farhadi, A.: YOLOv3: An Incremental Improvement. arXiv:1804.02767
18. Dosovitskiy, A., Ros, G., Codevilla, F., Lopez, A., Koltun, V.: CARLA: an open urban driving simulator. In: 1st Annual Conference on Robot Learning (2017)
19. Pimentel, M., Clifton, D., Clifton, L., Tarassenko, L.: A review of novelty detection. Sig. Process. **99**, 215–249 (2014)
20. Kumar, A., Liang, P.S., Ma, T.: Verified uncertainty calibration. In: NIPS 2019 (2019)
21. Jöckel, L., Kläs, M.: Increasing trust in data-driven model validation. In: Romanovsky, A., Troubitsyna, E., Bitsch, F. (eds.) SAFECOMP 2019. LNCS, vol. 11698, pp. 155–164. Springer, Cham (2019). https://doi.org/10.1007/978-3-030-26601-1_11

Rule-Based Safety Evidence for Neural Networks

Tewodros A. Beyene[✉] and Amit Sahu

fortiss - Research Institute of the Free State of Bavaria,
Guerickestraße 25, 80805 München, Germany
{beyene,sahu}@fortiss.org

Abstract. Neural networks have many applications in safety and mission critical systems. As industrial standards in various safety-critical domains require developers of critical systems to provide safety assurance, tools and techniques must be developed that enable effective creation of safety evidence for AI systems. In this position paper, we propose the use of rules extracted from neural networks as artefacts for safety evidence. We discuss the rationale behind the use of rules and illustrate it using the MNIST dataset.

Keywords: Neural network · Safety · Evidence · Certification

1 Introduction

The complexity of embedded software and increasing demands on dependability, safety, and security has already outpaced the capabilities of current verification and certification methods. Unless these methods advance quickly to ensure the highest dependability requirements demanded by safety-critical software, new and exciting capabilities such as AI may never reach the market. Safety-critical systems are often subject to a rigorous safety certification process. The process is aimed at providing assurance that the system can be safely used in a specific environment under specific conditions [1,5]. The system can also be deemed safe by a regulatory body only after such assurance is established for the system. The certification process is typically guided by domain-specific safety standards such as DO-178C for avionics and ISO26262 for the automotive domains. Demonstrating compliance with a safety standard involves gathering convincing evidence during the development of the system.

Safety cases are commonly used forms of evidence that are created to convince inspectors that a system is safe. A safety case communicates a clear, comprehensive and defensible argument that a system is acceptably safe in its operating context [2]. The argument should make it clear that it is reasonable to assume the system can be operated safely. In general, we define evidence for safety certification as *"information or artefacts that contribute to developing confidence in the safe operation of a system"* [3]. Safety evidence can be supported by argumentation. Safety arguments are a set of inferences between claims and evidence

© Springer Nature Switzerland AG 2020
A. Casimiro et al. (Eds.): SAFECOMP 2020 Workshops, LNCS 12235, pp. 328–335, 2020.
https://doi.org/10.1007/978-3-030-55583-2_24

that leads from the evidence forming the basis of the argument to a top-level safety claim, which typically claims that the system is safe to operate in its intended environment.

The advent of new capabilities such as AI is currently demanding tools, methods and techniques for assuring safety and dependability of these systems. In response to this demand, there have also been recent efforts to extend safety assurance approaches for traditional software to AI-based systems, such as self-driving cars and other autonomous systems. There are two main challenges to extending existing safety assurance approaches to AI systems. The first challenge is finding efficient analysis, testing, and verification methods that are used to create safety evidence and build the safety argument on. The second challenge is finding *"information or artefacts that contribute to developing confidence in the safe operation of the AI system"*, i.e., artefacts for AI systems that can serve as a piece of evidence [4]. Among other things, a candidate evidence artefact needs to be verifiable, auditable, and maintainable and could come from diverse methods.

In this position paper, we take on the second challenge and propose the use of rule extraction methods to create safety evidence for neural networks, and the use of extracted rules as safety evidence. We discuss in detail the features of extracted rules that make them good candidates to be used as evidence artefacts in safety cases.

2   Rule Extraction

Rule extraction is a procedure that takes a trained neural network together with the data on which the network was trained, and produces a description of the network's hypothesis that is comprehensible yet closely approximates the network's predictive behavior [6]. The procedure can greatly help experts in explaining the network as well as arguing about safety and dependability of the network. There are different types of rule extraction algorithms, and which are defined by two important factors, namely, the employed rule extraction approach and the type of generated rules.

Rule Extraction Approaches. In general, rule extraction techniques explicitly or implicitly make an assumption on their perceived view of the underlying NN architecture. Based on this view, there are two main approaches. The first approach, called *pedagogical approach*, aims at finding the corresponding output for the input to an NN by treating the network as a black-box. The weights and parameters of the internal structure of the network are not considered by the approach [11]. The second approach, called *decompositional approach*, works by splitting the network at neuron level, obtaining rules for each neuron, and aggregating the results to generate rules representing the entire network. While it was a common practice to perform training and rule extraction sequentially, some decompositional algorithms perform both the network training and rule generation simultaneously [12]. These algorithms take less time, but they do not work for all NN architectures. Some algorithms can also extract both continuous and discrete rules by using a decision tree from pre-trained neural networks [13].

Types of Extracted Rules. Depending on the task, different types of rules can be used. For feedforward NNs, relevant rules include (1) *If-then*: boolean conditional statement; (2) *M-of-N*: M of N conditions are satisfied; (3) *Decision Tree*: conditions organized in a hierarchical binary tree fashion; (4) *fuzzy rules*: conditional statements with approximation for partial truths; and (5) *first-order rules*: conditions with quantifiers and variables.

Rule Extraction for DNNs. Rule extraction techniques for DNN employ a divide and conquer mechanism, where rules are generated layer-by-layer [14]. As such techniques demand high memory usage and computational time, they need special methods to enable efficiency. The most common techniques applied are rule pruning and network pruning [15], where less important components of extracted rules and the input neural network are pruned, respectively.

3   Rule-Based Safety Evidence

Given a safety claim, its corresponding evidence should be generated during the establishment of the claim by chaining together smaller pieces of safety evidence on all data and functions involved during the claim establishment. Moreover, the structure of the evidence artefact should encourage incremental maintenance of evidence when a piece of evidence becomes obsolete. In this section, we present the rationale behind the use of rules as evidence artefacts for safety. We also discuss the complexity of rules extraction techniques.

3.1   Rules as Evidence Artefacts

Rules and rule extraction techniques possess characteristic features that provide the basis for the use of rules as artefacts of safety evidence for NNs. We summarise below some of these features.

Diverse Perception/View of Rules. Some properties of an NN can only be established by having a detailed view of its underlying inner units. For example, the coverage property in autonomous vehicles requires the coverage of all features (e.g., not only lane marking but also other vehicles) in the given image classification datasets. Decompositional rule extraction techniques can generate rules that can be used as evidence for such properties. There are also properties that can be established by viewing the NN as a black-box. An example is correctness of a network with simple noise, such as fog, in the empirical image dataset.

Applicability of Extraction Techniques in Diverse Architectures. There exists a class of rule extracting techniques where the network is trained specifically to facilitate efficient rule extraction. Such techniques are often specific to particular network architecture. Such rules can be useful in federated learning, where a shared global model is trained across many participating clients that keep their training data locally [18]. As each client may have a distinct platform and network architecture, the diverse nature of rule extraction techniques enables rules to be employed as evidence for each client. The safety evidence for the entire learning comprises pieces of evidence for each client.

Amenability of Rules for Quality Assessment. Safety evidence that uses rules will have a characteristic feature of amenability for quality assessment. The set of criteria for evaluating rules includes *accuracy*, *fidelity*, and *consistency* [16]. Properties of the NN such as coverage with respect to a given dataset and absence of blind spot can be established by assessing the extracted rules.

Diverse Expressive Power of Rules. Depending on the specific type of safety claims, evidence with different expressiveness are needed. For example, while *decision trees* can provide the required expressiveness for hierarchical properties of an NN, *if-then* are not expressive enough for such properties.

3.2 Algorithmic Complexity of Rule Extraction

Another consideration for using rules as evidence artefacts is the availability of efficient algorithms for rule extractions. Most early decompositional rule extraction approaches employed a search process for subsets of rules at each hidden and output units of the NN, which is exponential in the number of inputs to the node [17]. This factor has been the Achilles heel for using rule extractions for analyzing, validating, testing, and interpreting neural networks. However, various heuristics can be applied to limit space exploration [10] and achieve tractability for real-world problems. In addition, for some NN architectures, crisp symbolic rules can be extracted in polynomial time [7]. The complexity of extracted rules, which is defined as a factor of number of extracted rules and number of antecedents per rule, is another problem. However, there exist methods such as *network pruning* and *rule pruning, rule abstraction, distillation approach* that are aimed at reducing the size of the generated rulesets. Approaches like *partial order reductions* and *priority synthesis* from the formal methods community can also be considered for reducing the extracted rules to a manageable size.

4   Illustration

In this section, we illustrate our proposed approach of using extracted rules as safety evidence for the MNIST dataset using a complex NN LeNet (includes CNN and fully connected layers). Extracting decision trees from datasets with semantic features makes the NN models easier to understand. However, as safety-critical applications like autonomous driving and medical imaging consist of images, we have considered the MNIST image dataset of handwritten digit classification. Another reason for MNIST dataset is that its commonly used as a baseline for adversarial noise property, which is essential for safety critical applications. Extracting a decision tree from pixels of an image does not add enough interpretability information about the NN. For this reason, we have selected the last fully connected layer of the model as a feature layer and built the surrogate decision tree over this feature-output combination.

The first step in obtaining rule-based evidences from NNs is to extract rules with a high fidelity score. Therefore, we applied two pedagogical rule extraction techniques:

- TREPAN [10]: The algorithm uses an Oracle that can query and sample examples from the dataset. Each node is split based on the best fit that generates the highest fidelity with the NN model. In contrast to the M-of-N rules of the original algorithm, here we have used If-then rules.
- Surrogate Random Forest Model: In this algorithm, the NN model was taken as a black-box model generating feature-output combination. This combination is used to train a separate Random Forest Model from scratch.

The second step is to identify safety properties for which a rule can be used as an evidence artefact. We have used adversarial noise, which is a critical issue in applying NNs for real-world problems. There have been many training methods developed to handle adversarial noise including augmenting training datasets with adversarial images [9] and provably bound the model (avoid misclassification) against fixed noise [8]. As a basis of our approach, we have selected models that are trained to have robustness against adversarial perturbation. The models are trained with the following methods [8]:

1. Plain: trained with basic backpropagation algorithm.
2. Adversarial Training (AT): trained with adversarial images to make the model robust to adversarial perturbation.
3. Maximization of Linear Regions (MMR): trained with MMR regularizer to increase the provable bound on effective adversarial noise.
4. MMR+AT: a hybrid approach that uses both MMR and AT approaches.

We have found that plain and AT models have their rules closer towards the median. The models also have more rules with features containing negative minimum values than the other models. The properties of these models with respect to the adversarial noise of $\epsilon = 0.3$ from [8], and fidelity scores for surrogate models are shown in Table 1. To have the rules be justified as evidence, both the safety property (robustness to noise) and the correctness (and completion) of the secondary model need to be accessed. Following two measures provide the respective initial analysis: (1) L2 robust error is a term defined in [19], which is a measure of the percentage over the input dataset which do not have a guaranteed safety against the given ϵ noise. (2) Fidelity score quantify the approximation provided by the secondary model as a substitute for the primary NN model. Since NNs approximate the true function that defines the classification and the

Table 1. Fidelity with different surrogate models and adversarial robustness

Model	Decision tree fidelity (%)	Random forest fidelity (%)	L2 robust error Lower Bound (%)	L2 robust error Upper Bound (%)
Plain	94	98.67	3.1	100
AT	91.34	98.5	1.8	100
MMR	87.12	96.37	5.8	11.6
MMR+AT	90	97.08	4.6	9.7

decision tree is approximating the NNs, we need high fidelity for the secondary model and low robust error bound for the NN to use them as evidence. As can be observed, the surrogate Random Forest model had better fidelity scores than the surrogate Decision Tree. We attributed this effect to the higher complexity of the Random Forest model because it can provide a better approximation of the complex function represented by the NN model. Also, looking at the individual features, we observe that decision trees that include nodes with higher scoring (measured using Random Forest model) features have better fidelity than the decision trees with lower scoring features.

We observe that simple decision trees have lower fidelity scores than the more complex models (Random Forest). In addition, the models with robustness against adversarial property achieved lower fidelity than plain or simpler models. Looking at the rules extracted for the MNIST dataset, we assessed classes of properties for which the rules can be used as evidence. The following properties can use rules as evidence artefacts:

1. Interpretability of the decision process: this can be done by analysing the trace of a decision tree for each data point. In the example, we observed the trace in the form of rules on features applied to reach the classification. For a particular datapoint, the set of applied rules can serve as an evidence artefact of the decision process.
2. Robustness to noise: it can be checked by observing the effect of noise on individual rules. In the example, threshold value of the feature w.r.t. the range of observed values could act like a robustness measure.
3. Feature coverage: coverage of the decision tree is more tractable as compared to coverage over neuron activations, which results in an exponential blow-up. In the example, coverage over 100 neurons requires exponential combination of activations, i.e., 2^{100}. However, hierarchical distribution of rules results in tractable coverage over the features.
4. Input coverage: In our example, input coverage boils down to coverage over the image pixels. In this regard, NNs are better as CNNs cover the whole image for features but needs to be checked for the decision trees.

5   Conclusion

In this paper, we proposed the use of rules extracted from NN as evidence artefact for a given safety claim over the NN. We have also argued and illustrated different types of safety evidence can be defined using extracted rules. While rules have been widely used for NN interpretability, their usage as evidence artefacts has not been yet explored to the best of our knowledge. This work is a first step towards the goal of using rules as safety evidences. One direction of future work could be to explore the relation between types of extracted rules and the corresponding classes of safety properties. Another direction could be the soundness and completeness arguments for rule extraction methods. Such arguments help in assuring the validity and sufficiency of the extracted rules as evidence artefacts for safety certification.

References

1. Ericson, C.A.: Concise Encyclopedia of System Safety: Definition of Terms and Concepts. Wiley, New York (2011)
2. Ministry of Defence (MoD) UK: Defence Stanandard 00–56 Issue 4: Safety Management Requirements for Defence Systems (2007)
3. de la Vara, J.L., et al.: Towards a model-based evolutionary chain of evidence for compliance with safety standards. In: Ortmeier, F., Daniel, P. (eds.) SAFECOMP 2012. LNCS, vol. 7613, pp. 64–78. Springer, Heidelberg (2012). https://doi.org/10.1007/978-3-642-33675-1_6
4. de la Vara, J., Nair, S., Walawege, R.P.: On the use of artefacts as safety evidence: a conceptual model. Technical report (2013)
5. Kornecki, A., Janusz, Z.: Certification of software for real-time safety critical systems: state of the art. Innov. Syst. Softw. Eng. 5, 149–161 (2009). https://doi.org/10.1007/s11334-009-0088-1
6. Craven, M.W.: Extracting comprehensible models from trained neural networks. Ph.D dissertation, University of Wisconsin-Madison (1996)
7. Bologna, G.: A model for single and multiple knowledge based networks. Artif. Intell. Med. 28, 141–163 (2003)
8. Croce, F., Andriushchenko, M., Hein, M.: Provable robustness of ReLU networks via maximization of linear regions. In: AISTATS (2019)
9. Goodfellow, I.J., Shlens, J., Szegedy, C.: Explaining and harnessing adversarial examples. In: ICLR (2015)
10. Craven, M., Shavlik, J.: Using sampling and queries to extract rules from trained neural networks. In Machine Learning: Proceedings of the 11th International Conference, San Francisco, CA (1994)
11. KumarSethi, K., Kumar Mishra, D., Mishra, B.: Extended taxonomy of rule extraction techniques and assessment of KDRuleEx. Int. J. Comput. Appl. 50(21), 25–31 (2012)
12. Ozbakır, L., Baykasoglu, A., Kulluk, S.: A soft computing-based approach for integrated training and rule extraction from artificial neural networks: DIFACONN-miner. Appl. Soft Comput. 10, 304–317 (2010)
13. Sato, M., Tsukimoto, H.: Rule extraction from neural networks via decision tree induction. In: International Joint Conference On Neural Network (2001)

14. Zilke, J.: Extracting rules from deep neural networks. M.S. thesis, Computer Science Department, Technische Universitaet Darmstadt (2015)
15. Setiono, R., Leow, W.K.: FERNN: an algorithm for fast extraction of rules from neural networks. Appl. Intell. **12**, 12–25 (2000). https://doi.org/10.1023/A:1008307919726
16. Andrews, R., et al.: An evaluation and comparison of techniques for extracting and refining rules from artificial neural networks. QUT NRC, February 1996
17. Fu, L.M.: Rule generation from neural networks. IEEE Trans. Syst. Man Cybern. **28**(8), 1114–1124 (1994)
18. Yang, Q., Liu, Y., Chen, T., Tong, Y.: Federated machine learning: concept and applications. ACM Trans. Intell. Syst. Technol. **10**, 1–19 (2019)
19. Wong, E., Kolter, J.Z.: Provable defenses against adversarial examples via the convex outer adversarial polytope. In: ICML (2018)

Safety Concerns and Mitigation Approaches Regarding the Use of Deep Learning in Safety-Critical Perception Tasks

Oliver Willers, Sebastian Sudholt, Shervin Raafatnia[✉],
and Stephanie Abrecht

Robert Bosch GmbH, Chassis Systems Control, Automated Driving,
70499 Stuttgart-Weilimdorf, Germany
{Sebastian.Sudholt,Shervin.Raafatnia,Stephanie.Abrecht}@de.bosch.com

Abstract. Deep learning methods are widely regarded as indispensable when it comes to designing perception pipelines for autonomous agents such as robots, drones or automated vehicles. The main reasons, however, for deep learning not being used for autonomous agents at large scale already are safety concerns. Deep learning approaches typically exhibit a black-box behavior which makes it hard for them to be evaluated with respect to safety-critical aspects. While there have been some work on safety in deep learning, most papers typically focus on high-level safety concerns. In this work, we seek to dive into the safety concerns of deep learning methods on a deeply technical level. Additionally, we present extensive discussions on possible mitigation methods and give an outlook regarding what mitigation methods are still missing in order to facilitate an argumentation for the safety of a deep learning method.

1 Introduction

During the last years new applications were enabled by machine learning (ML) and especially, by deep learning (DL) methods. Their capability of solving problems which cannot be fully specified makes DL a key enabler in many applications, especially in the field of Advanced Driver Assistance Systems (ADAS) and Automated Driving (AD). Therefore, DL is also of fundamental importance for the fast growing field of ADAS and AD as it is not possible to specify an open context in every detail (e.g., the data representation of a pedestrian in all varieties cannot be specified such that it could always be recognized by a rule-based algorithm).

Parts of the research leading to the presented results are funded by the German Federal Ministry for Economic Affairs and Energy within the project "KI Absicherung – Safe AI for automated driving". We would like to thank the consortium for the successful cooperation, in particular Matthias Woehrle, Peter Schlicht and Christian Hellert for reviewing our work and their thoughtful comments.

© Springer Nature Switzerland AG 2020
A. Casimiro et al. (Eds.): SAFECOMP 2020 Workshops, LNCS 12235, pp. 336–350, 2020.
https://doi.org/10.1007/978-3-030-55583-2_25

Different from humans, current DL algorithms do not learn semantic or causal relationships but simply correlations in data they are presented with. For example, a DL algorithm used for detecting objects in camera images learns correlations between the pixels of the image and object representations, e.g., bounding boxes. While DL algorithms provide state-of-the-art performance, it is difficult to understand how they arrive at their predictions, which poses a problem from a safety point of view.

While safety-related aspects in the automotive area are usually handled through approaches defined in ISO 26262 [19], the usage of DL methods introduces a number of additional safety-related aspects not covered in this norm. Most notably, DL algorithms may predict incorrect results, e.g., an object detector may miss to predict an object. These kinds of limitations are not covered in ISO 26262 but rather in the recently published ISO PAS 21448 also known as Safety of the Intended Functionality (SOTIF) [20].

SOTIF is the absence of unreasonable risk due to hazards resulting from functional insufficiencies of the intended functionality. A prerequisite for achieving SOTIF is a proper understanding of the system, its limitations as well as the conditions which may unveil these limitations. This is a difficult task for systems incorporating DL components because the learning process of DL algorithms is entirely different from a human one. Humans analyze systems and their weaknesses on a semantic level, e.g., interpreting a difficult scene as a composition of things like lightning conditions, type and position of objects, behavior of actors, etc. However, in DL the problem space shifts from a semantic level to the level of data representations (e.g., pixel values of an image). Thus, DL-specific insufficiencies and failure causes are not necessarily intuitive for humans, making it difficult to understand such methods and their limitations. Hence, arguing the safety of a system that relies on the correctness of DL outputs requires a dedicated safety consideration of such algorithms.

In this paper, we give a concise overview of safety concerns and their underlying problems regarding the use of DL algorithms focusing on Deep Neural Networks (DNNs)[1]. In particular, we will consider DNN used in the perception pipeline of an ADAS or AD system. Typical use cases for such components are DNN-based object detection or semantic segmentation of the input data. The information obtained from these DNN-components are then further used in an ADAS or AD system which may incorporate additional information such as parallel sensing paths or post processing of the DNN's output. The goal of the system is to enable one or multiple functions, e.g., an automated emergency brake or a highway pilot. Furthermore, we present potential mitigation approaches along with a deep technical discussion. It needs to be noted that we have no claim on completeness of the list of safety concerns and their mitigation. Theses are just the possible problems we could identify according to our experiences and knowledge, together with some promising approaches for their alleviation.

---

[1] Please note that while we focus on DNNs, a large amount of the safety concerns discussed in this paper may also be valid for other types of ML-based methods.

While these issues and the methods suggested here for their mitigation are known, the categorization and mapping presented here is to the best of our knowledge novel.

2   Related Work

During the last years the question how one can use NL in safety critical tasks has attracted a considerable amount of research over a broad range of applications (medical diagnosis, avionics, automotive, etc.). For example, [30] provides an overview an overview about safety assurance for neural networks in avionics.

As pointed out in [13], currently, there exists no agreed-upon way to verify and validate ML components used in ADAS or AD systems. In particular, the foundational statistical ML principles of empirical risk minimization and average losses are not fully applicable when considering safety, as discussed in [33]. However, several works exist which define requirements or safety criteria such a component needs to fulfill.

In [23], the authors derive safety criteria for neural networks from an abstract top-level goal. Thereby, the posed goals and criteria are on a purely functional level outlined in a Goal Structuring Notation (GSN). Following this line of work, Burton et al. [6] and Gauerhof et al. [12] propose a systematic approach using GSN in order to argue the safety of ML-based components. In their work, they formulate requirements for an ML model derived from the discussed safety concerns. In a further work, Burton et al. [7] propose an approach for constructing an argumentation for the safety of an ML model which they term *performance evidence confidence*. The approach is based on a design-by-contract principle of the safety argumentation which in turn uses safety contracts.

Another work that deals with this topic is given by Adler et al. [1]. Here, the authors extract areas of activity by a systematic literature search. Based on this, challenges regarding the use of DNNs in safety critical applications are listed and methods which might help to overcome them are mapped. However, the validity of the list as well as the effectiveness of the mapped methods remains to be shown.

In this work, we seek to expand the discussion about safety concerns with regard to the usage of DNNs in safety-critical perception tasks. We concretize these concerns and discuss potentials as well as limitations of possible mitigation approaches.

3   Background

A Deep Neural Network (DNN) is a machine learning model which in most use cases for ADAS and AD is tasked to predict the posterior probability for a dependent random variable Y (e.g., class probabilities) based on an independent random variable X (e.g., input images). For this, one needs to specify the expected type of distribution of Y. This is important as the DNN needs to be equipped with a link function which maps to the correct range of Y. In case of a classification task, Y is typically expected to follow a multinomial distribution and the link function of choice is the well-known softmax. As X and Y are unknown, the typical approach for obtaining a good DNN model is to record a dataset $D = \{(x_i, y_i)\}_{i=1}^{N}$ with realizations of X and Y and perform maximum-likelihood estimation of the parameters with respect to the data. Here, x_i is a data sample (e.g., camera image) and y_i the corresponding annotation(s) (e.g., bounding boxes of objects). In practice, optimization is typically achieved by minimizing a loss function using (stochastic) gradient descent.

According to ISO PAS 21448, *functional insufficiencies* are insufficiencies inherent in the system possibly leading to hazards. Such an insufficiency can appear, e.g., in form of a performance limitation leading to an incomplete or wrong perception of the environment. A functional insufficiency can be unveiled under some conditions. A set of such conditions is referred to as a *triggering event*. In particular, considering a DNN module in the perception pipeline of an ADAS or AD system, such an event can provoke an erroneous output possibly causing a hazardous behavior of the system.

4 Safety Concerns

We define safety concerns (SCs) as underlying issues which may negatively affect the safety of a system. They are either (i) the direct root of a functional insufficiency or (ii) describe a black-box-like characteristic of the system which in turn makes it hard to assess safety. SCs are usually tied to subcomponents of the system. In particular, there exist specific concerns when deploying a DL algorithm in an ADAS or AD vehicle.

(i) The concerns which turn into functional insufficiencies originate from the inherent design of DL methods. In general, a supervised DL algorithm approximates the unknown probability distribution $p(X, Y)$ using a dataset D of samples of p [4]. The algorithm produces incorrect results, if its approximation of the underlying distribution p is not good enough at a given data point.

(ii) The concerns relating to black-box-characteristics originate from DL-specific properties. DL algorithms usually project the input data into high-dimensional spaces which cannot be entirely interpreted by a human anymore. While it is, for example, well known that classification-based DL methods partition their input space into non-convex subspaces, giving semantic meaning to these subspaces is largely impossible.

In the following, we will describe the safety concerns of DL algorithms in an AD perception pipeline in detail. As mentioned in the introduction, these issues were identified in line with the ISO PAS 21448 approach for achieving SOTIF and according to our experiences and knowledge of DNNs.

Data Distribution Is Not a Good Approximation of Real World (SC-1). The first overarching concern is that the distribution of the data used in development might not be a good approximation to the one of the real open world which is *a priori* unknown. As mentioned before, the distribution meant here is on the level of data representations, which are high-dimensional and counterintuitive. Therefore, we can only approach them from (or estimate them on) a semantic level by analyzing influencing factors such as daylight, object appearance and weather conditions. This is prone to incompleteness since not all aspects important for the data representation may be covered this way. Besides, the data collection can have other shortcomings which are independent of the level at which it is represented. Examples of such problems are bias (e.g. over- or under-representation of certain factors) or disregarding effects related to different physical deployments (e.g. varying sensor position and angle due to different system variants or manufacturing tolerances). Training and testing a DNN with data which do not sufficiently cover the Operational Design Domain (ODD) will very likely lead to an insufficient performance or robustness later in the field.

Distributional Shift Over Time (SC-2). A DNN is trained and tested at a certain point in time, e.g., during development. However, our world is changing continuously. This means that even if we would train a "perfect" algorithm, the probability distribution of the input data will change over time (e.g., new vehicles with a different appearance will be released). Since such a change will occur naturally, this concern needs to be addressed by appropriate measures being effective over the product's lifetime.

Incomprehensible Behavior (SC-3). One of the main difficulties in arguing safety of DNNs is our inability to explain exactly how they come to a decision. In other words, the non-linearity and complexity of DNNs is a double-edged sword; on the one hand, it enables them to automatically extract features and relate those to outputs via non-linear activation functions, which, in turn, makes them so suitable for solving problems that cannot be specified in detail. On the other hand, those features and their connection to the outputs are counterintuitive and incomprehensible for us. Hence, unlike in the case of rule-based functions, it is hardly possible to derive a causal relation between the data representation and network predictions. Consequently, identifying weaknesses and failure causes of DNNs is difficult and sometimes infeasible, impeding the applicability of common safety engineering methods (e.g., fault tree analysis, common cause analysis).

Unknown Behavior in Rare Critical Situations (SC-4). This concern is directly related to the long-tail problem in the AD context which describes the fact that there exists an enormous amount of scenarios with a low occurrence probability. These scenarios may however be safety-critical. For testing, it would require a practically impossible amount of driving hours to capture them by chance. Regarding this issue, two important aspects need to be mentioned: first, note that according to statistical learning theory, the performance of a ML model evaluated on a test dataset can only be generalized if training and test data are independent and identically distributed (i.i.d.) samples out of the same probability distribution as the one faced later in the open world [4]. Thus, it might be problematic to artificially insert rare scenarios into the test data used to estimate the generalization capabilities of DNN's performance. Second, even though one could define a separate dataset in order to test the function with respect to such data, it is hardly possible to identify a rare critical situation from the perspective of a DNN *a priori*. This is due to the fact that DNNs do not look at semantic content but rather the data itself making it very difficult to define appropriate test cases in advance.

Unreliable Confidence Information (SC-5). In practice, DNNs will be faced with input data for which they cannot make an accurate prediction. This may either stem from an insufficient amount or representativeness of training data or an inherent uncertainty in the data itself (e.g., motion blur). Ideally, the DNN should reliably indicate if its prediction can be trusted or not. This behavior would allow for a number of established safety approaches to be used for a DNN component such as giving more weight to parallel information paths, initiating an emergency maneuver or a driver handover. Most DNN algorithms used in practice output some form of posterior probability (e.g., class probabilities) and one may be tempted to use the value of the highest probability or the information entropy as a measure of confidence. This may, however, be highly critical if the probabilities are not well calibrated. In particular, it has been shown that DNNs using the standard multinomial cross entropy loss in combination with the softmax as link function tend to be overconfident in their predictions [15]. Even worse, it can be shown that if these DNNs use Rectified Linear Units (ReLUs) as activation functions they can produce arbitrarily high posterior probabilities when dealing with data far away from the training data [17]. While confidence information may not benefit the solution of the problem itself, it serves as an enabler of a safety argument in a safety case.

Brittleness of DNNs (SC-6). As shown by many works, the brittleness of DNNs is a major safety concern. This includes the robustness against common perturbations such as noise or certain weather conditions (e.g., [18]), translations/rotations (e.g., [2]), as well as targeted perturbations known as adversarial examples (e.g., [14,32]). Note that regarding adversarial examples, adversarial patches are of special interest in the context of ADAS and AD (e.g., [10,25,28]). This is due to the fact that a would-be attacker can simply change the operation environment of a vehicle instead of hacking into the vehicle itself. Physical adversarial patch-based attacks do thus scale considerably better than those based on overlaying the raw sensor data recorded in a vehicle with noise.

Inadequate Separation of Test and Training Data (SC-7). For training and testing DNNs, data is usually divided into training, validation and test datasets. For not overestimating the DNN's performance, the test dataset needs to be (sufficiently) uncorrelated to the other ones. However, in practice, highly correlated data is usually acquired since, e.g., data is recorded in sequences (i.e. consecutive frames are rather similar) or data is recorded at same locations several times. Another aspect is that developers tend to optimize on test datasets during training because they strive for the highest possible performance. Therefore, a training process is continued until performance goals of a network are met on the test dataset. Although good and labeled data is expensive and thus, rare in practice, using a test dataset several times means also an optimization with respect to the test data leading to an overestimation of a DNN's performance.

Dependence on Labeling Quality (SC-8). For supervised learning, labeled datasets are required for developing a DNN. Labeling is typically done manually and its quality directly affects the resulting function and thus, the obtained test results [16]. If the label quality is not sufficient, the test results may be misleading. As a result, the function could have an insufficient performance later in the field. Hence, the labeling quality needs to be ensured in order to argue the safety of such a learning function.

Insufficient Consideration of Safety in Metrics (SC-9). Using state-of-the-art metrics such as mean average precision and false positive/negative rate, only the *average* performance of DNNs is evaluated. Consequently, when assessing the performance of a DNN, typically all elements of a test dataset influence the performance metric. There may, however, be elements which the DNN predicted incorrectly but would not impact the system itself. For example, consider the case of a DNN used for pedestrian detection which serves the function of an automated emergency brake. If the car is driving at 30 km/h and fails to detect a pedestrian at 500 m distance, this will in all likelihood not have an impact on the safety of the system. However, in common metrics, such a person will be counted in the same way as a person standing directly in front of the car. This will inevitably lead to giving the DNN a worse safety rating than is actually the case.

5   Potential Mitigation Approaches

Releasing an ADAS or AD system requires a comprehensive argumentation to show that all concerns related to the system's safety are identified, understood and mitigated. After having discussed the safety concerns regarding the use of DNNs within such systems in Sect. 4, we present several promising mitigation approaches (MAs) which could be used in order to provide supporting arguments and evidences for a safety case. We do not provide a complete list of possible methods/solutions within the mitigation approaches and those presented might be interchangeable.

Well-Justified Data Acquisition Strategy (MA-1). The basis for testing ML functions is an appropriate dataset reflecting the context in which the function is supposed to work. In particular, one needs to argue that the dataset used is a suitable representation of the data which the DNN will face within the ODD ((SC-1), (SC-4)). As pointed out before, the distribution which is relevant here is on the level of the data representations (e.g., pixel-level distribution). Finding suitable random samples from this distribution is - in most cases - highly non-trivial, mainly due to the dimensionality of the data. Thus, we propose to follow a two-step approach here. The first step is to specify the data content, as well as the data acquisition and selection process, in a structured and thorough manner. For this, essential ODD factors such as weather conditions, road types, occurring objects and their variations in the ODD need to be determined, see e.g., [22]. Additional factors such as mounting tolerances of the sensors and predictable changes over the product's lifetime (e.g. sensor aging) should be considered as well. Finally, the existence of specified variations and their frequencies in the acquired data need to be verified. The aforementioned analysis happens on a semantic level and may not fully cover the specifics of the data at hand (e.g., certain biases in the pixel distribution of an image). Thus, the second step is to analyze the raw data and find suitable datapoints which are missing from the first step. This can, for example, be achieved by finding a latent representation of the data using a variational autoencoder and sampling the latent space in a suitable manner.

Providing Reliable Confidence Information (MA-2). As explained before, the posterior probability predicted by a DNN tends to be overconfident even for inputs close to the training data [15] and may be arbitrarily high when moving away from the training data [17]. In order to be able to output reliable confidence information and thus mitigate (SC-5) amongst others, a number of approaches have been proposed. In [15], a number of heuristic approaches are evaluated. Besides heuristics, other approaches have made use of Bayesian methods in order to extract uncertainties. In [11], the authors use dropout during inference which turns their neural network into a Bayesian model. This approach is known as *Monte Carlo Dropout*. Another Bayesian approach is presented by Blundell *et al.* [3]. Here, the authors model the weights of the neural network using Gaussian distributions and minimize the ELBO loss. Besides the actual method itself, it is still an open question how one can determine if a measure of confidence is reliable or not in the context of AD. In [29], the use of expected calibration error (ECE) and maximum calibration error (MCE) is proposed. Both metrics operate on the probabilities predicted from the neural network. First, the maximum posterior probability is quantized into a desired number of bins for a test dataset. Then, the accuracy is computed for each. Generally, the outputs are well-calibrated if the accuracy of each bin is equal to the average probability in this bin. The difference in these two values is called calibration error. While for ECE the calibration error is averaged over all bins, MCE simply returns the largest calibration error. However, a main drawback of both metrics is that they both depend on a parameter, namely the number of bins, which heavily influences the obtained result.

Using Gray-Box Methods (MA-3). A major impediment to the safety argumentation of DNNs is their black-box character SC-3. Even though turning the black-box to a white-box will be scarcely possible in the foreseeable future, several methods were introduced recently to gain understanding of the root causes for DNN's predictions by visualizing decisive parts of the input (e.g., gradient-weighted class activation mapping [31]) or by forcing the DNN to provide more interpretable outputs (e.g., object attributes [24]). While these methods cannot enable an analytical safety evaluation, they still can contribute to a safety case, e.g., by making the analysis of a test result more meaningful or by supporting the extraction of uncertainties for DNN's prediction (e.g., by analyzing the distribution of decisive parts of an image with respect to certain object classes). Note that the trustworthiness of such methods needs to be shown which is non-trivial.

Specification of Adversarial Threat Models and Incorporation of Defense Methods (MA-4). Defending against adversarial examples is part of SC-6 mitigation and requires determining a threat model first, which in essence represents an assumption on what a possible attacker can perform as an attack. Typical models in computer-vision-based problems include changing the pixel values in an image at arbitrary locations with a certain budget (e.g., [27]). Other data-level threat models include adversarial patches [5] or affine transformation-based attacks [9]. Allowing data-level changes may oftentimes be an unrealistic or highly improbable threat model. For example, in the case of autonomous vehicles, an attacker would need access to the camera memory, which stores the pixels of a recorded image. This form of attack does not scale well and is thus probably neglectable. There are a number of other techniques, known as physical adversarial examples, that do scale well. Here, the environment in which a datum is recorded is altered instead of the datum itself. Common techniques for this include sticker-based attacks (e.g., [25,26]). Many other existing threat models are not listed here[2]. In general, no threat model can be assumed by default. In the future, there might be standards and norms which define an appropriate threat model for a given domain. In the meantime this choice must be made on a per-case basis and argued accordingly.

Having chosen and argued for a specific threat model, one has to deploy defense mechanisms to protect against it. The main problem with most known mechanisms is that they may have given good results initially but were quickly exposed after having been published (see, e.g., [8]). As of writing this paper, there are only two defense approaches which are effective to at least a certain degree and are somewhat accepted in the ML community[3]. First, an empirical approach known as adversarial training with PGD adversaries [27], which tries to optimize a DNN to predict the correct class for a given sample's strongest adversarial example. While this approach is not able to guarantee that it actually finds the strongest adversary under a given threat model, it is very flexible with respect to choosing this model. The second approach uses a convex outer approximation of reachable activations of the ReLU units of a DNN to defend against adversarial examples [34]. It gives guaranteed lower bounds on the loss values of adversarial examples. A drawback of this analytic method is that the training procedure takes considerably longer than standard SGD training.

Testing (MA-5). Naturally, a key component of a safety argumentation is testing, usually including verification and validation activities. While verification rather addresses issues which are already known or foreseeable, validation focuses on identifying unknown issues. In the following, we will refer to mitigation approaches that address these issues as MA-5a and MA-5b, respectively.

MA-5a: Known or predictable critical cases can be assessed via targeted testing. This approach supports mitigating SC-1, SC-4, SC-5, and SC-6. The selection

---

[2] For a concise overview of common threat models see, e.g., [35].

[3] Defending against adversarial examples is currently a heavily researched topic and there may exist other effective methods.

of test data is key for a thorough analysis of DNNs. A method for identifying targeted test cases is HAZOP (Hazard & Operability, [21]), a standard safety procedure to systematically identify malfunctions and risks of a complex system. In [36], the authors adapt HAZOP to computer vision systems and provide a catalog containing an extensive set of known critical situations for computer vision tasks as a basis for assessing the quality and thoroughness of test data. Of special interest is the stability of DL algorithms with respect to certain effects in the input space (e.g. blur, windscreen smudges or exposure related effects). As highlighted by Zendel *et al.* [37], the evaluation of robustness requires a targeted addition of difficult samples into a test dataset. A benchmark for robustness against known corruptions and perturbations is introduced in [18]. Another approach for effectively testing DNN algorithms is search-based-testing [38]. This technique aims at exploring the input space in a targeted manner enabling, e.g., a sensitivity analysis with respect to certain ODD factors or different combinations of them. Note that while some of the approaches mentioned can make use of real data (recorded on public roads or test tracks) others require artificially generated data. However, for obtaining reliable test results on synthetic data, the validity of this data with respect to real data has to be shown, which is a highly non-trivial problem.[4]

MA-5b: The unknown and unpredictable problems associated with deploying DNNs in a safety-critical open-world context can only be identified *by chance*. For this purpose, field test data need to be collected randomly in accordance to the guidelines mentioned in MA-1. Such a testing mainly addresses SC-4, but also supports the mitigation of SC-6, by providing means for finding previously unknown safety-critical situations[5] Note that the open-context nature of the operational domain, renders the coverage of the entire problem space via brute-force approaches practically infeasible. Instead, one needs to combine field testing with other methods, as pointed out in this paper, to enable the release of such systems.

Deep Analysis of Test Results Obtained in an Iterative Development Process (MA-6). As is known, DL is a data-driven approach and its development should be pursued in an iterative way. Discovered weaknesses of the DL component are continuously mitigated by optimizing architectures and hyperparameters or by adding new data that covers previously missing aspects. Hence, a fundamental part of this process is analyzing the intermediate results, ideally leading to a continuous improvement. In order to extract as much information as possible from these results, the analysis should be performed in a structured and if possible, automated manner (e.g., by extracting systematic weaknesses from comprehensive metadata by which the data should be enriched beforehand). In addition to cases where the DL component makes wrong predictions, cases associated with high uncertainty should be considered in order to gain insights about

---

[4] Even though synthetic data may look "realistic" to a human, the data-level distribution may be significantly different leading to non-meaningful test results.

[5] For reasons described in SC-7, the test set used for the ultimate performance evaluation needs to remain unseen until final testing.

conditions that could lead to wrong predictions. This approach can contribute to the mitigation of SC-4 and SC-6.

Data Partitioning Guidelines (MA-7). In order to address SC-7 and estimate a DNN's performance correctly, guidelines regarding partitioning the data into training, validation and test datasets are necessary. In particular, test data must not be correlated with training data since otherwise the generalization capability of the ML algorithm will be overestimated. This means that, e.g., consecutive frames of a video sequence may not be assigned to different partitions. Further measures could be that test data needs to be acquired at different days and locations as training data. Such guidelines need to be well-justified and the partitioning needs to be subsequently reviewed.

Labeling Guidelines (MA-8). The dependence of supervised learning methods on well-labeled data (see SC-8) requires strict labeling guidelines and checks. The guidelines should be defined with respect to the specific task (e.g. semantic segmentation or object detection) and should ideally contain additional application-specific annotations in order to enable an automated evaluation, e.g., of the relative frequencies of ODD factors such as weather conditions, object-specific metadata, etc. Guidelines compilation has to be justified and the adherence to them needs to be reviewed. Appropriately performed, this mitigates SC-8 and supports the argumentation with respect to SC-1.

Evaluating Performance with Respect to Safety (MA-9). As pointed out above, current state-of-the-art performance metrics in machine learning calculate average values not considering safety with respect to a certain function (e.g., automated emergency brake) (SC-9). Realizing that it will not be possible to reach 100% performance, it is obvious that a safety argumentation is hardly possible based on these metrics. However, considering an object detection component in the perception pipeline of an AD vehicle, it is actually not necessary to assure that all objects are detected but all the objects which are *relevant* with respect to system safety. Additionally, one could further refine that all *relevant* objects need to be detected *or* a low confidence value needs to indicate that the DNN might be wrong such that the system can manage the situation safely (e.g., by relying more on other information paths). Another important aspect is the analysis of errors over time. If one considers, for example, an object detection network, missing an object in one single frame might not be problematic at all because this can be compensated, e.g., by state-of-the-art object tracking methods or by plausibility checks (e.g., a pedestrian will probably not disappear within a few milliseconds). But if an object is not detected in several consecutive frames, the severity of the error is much higher. Therefore, tailored evaluation metrics are necessary in order to meaningfully assess DNNs from a safety perspective.

Continuous Learning and Updating (MA-10). In order to maintain the safety of a DNN-based component, the open context and distributional shift over time problems (SC-4, SC-2) need to be addressed in the product's life cycle. In particular, the DNN could face novel inputs in which the parameter distribution

Table 1. Overview of safety concerns and associated mitigation approaches.

Safety concern	Mitigation approaches
Data distribution is not a good approximation of real world (SC-1)	Well-justified data acquisition strategy (MA-1), enabling the output of reliable confidence information (MA-2), testing (MA-5), deep analysis of test results obtained in an iterative development process (MA-6), labeling guidelines (MA-8)
Distributional shift over time (SC-2)	Enabling the output of reliable confidence information (MA-2), continuous learning and updating (MA-10)
Incomprehensible behavior (SC-3)	Using gray-box methods (MA-3)
Unknown behavior in rare critical situations (SC-4)	Well-justified data acquisition strategy (MA-1), enabling the output of reliable confidence information (MA-2), testing (MA-5), deep analysis of test results obtained in an iterative development process (MA-6), continuous learning and updating (MA-10)
Unreliable confidence information (SC-5)	Enabling the output of reliable confidence information (MA-2), using gray-box methods (MA-3), testing (MA-5)
Brittleness of DNNs (SC-6)	Enabling the output of reliable confidence information (MA-2), specification of adversarial threat models and incorporation of defense methods (MA-4), testing (MA-5), deep analysis of test results obtained in an iterative development process (MA-6), continuous learning and updating (MA-10)
Inadequate separation of test and training data (SC-7)	Data partitioning guidelines (MA-7)
Dependence on labeling quality (SC-8)	Labeling guidelines (MA-8)
Insufficient consideration of safety in metrics (SC-9)	Evaluating performance with respect to safety (MA-9)

(e.g. pixel values in an image) differ from that of the data seen during development. This can occur either because the difference oversteps the generalization abilities of the network (long-tailed open context) or the input includes something completely new (e.g. a new type of vehicle) which the network has not seen during training. Therefore, it may be necessary to continually develop the network. Note that continuous learning does not necessarily mean online learning of the DNN already in use. While this approach is generally possible, it comes with its own specific problems, namely continuous validation of the newly learned model in the vehicle with only minimal computation power as well as weak to no human supervision. Continuous learning as proposed here includes an offline development step. New and useful data is recognized by a DNN or some other mechanism and send to a development center where a new version of the DNN is trained and validated. Finally, the old DNN in the ADAS or AD vehicle is replaced with the new one, either through software-over-the-air solutions or in a workshop. This process ensures the in-use DNN to be up-to-date while still having the ability to make use of large scale computation power for validation.

6 Conclusion

In this work, we have presented a concise list of safety concerns regarding deep learning methods used in perception pipelines of autonomous agents, especially highly automated vehicles. We also presented an extensive discussion on possible mitigation approaches addressing those safety concerns. A summary of the concerns and their possible mitigation approaches are provided in Table 1. It is important to note that the discussed approaches have very different maturity and complexity. Furthermore, while all of the approaches can definitely contribute to a safety case, for the time being it remains an open question when a specific safety concern is sufficiently mitigated. In particular, many of the mitigation methods involve parameters for which there does not exist a single *correct* value. For example, some methods supply a key performance indicator (KPI) telling the user how well the DNN under test performed with respect to this KPI. However, the threshold for this KPI used to determine whether the deep learning algorithm is safe cannot be obtained analytically in many cases. Therefore, it is essential to collect knowledge and consolidate this in standardization activities in order to define suitable processes, practices and thresholds. Extensive discussions with experts working in this field would be of great help and importance for this purpose.

References

1. Adler, R., et al.: Hardening of artificial neural networks for use in safety-critical applications - a mapping study. arXiv (2019)
2. Alcorn, M.A., et al.: Strike (with) a pose: neural networks are easily fooled by strange poses of familiar objects. arXiv (2018)
3. Blundell, C., Cornebise, J., Kavukcuoglu, K., Wierstra, D.: Weight uncertainty in neural networks. In: ICML (2015)

4. Bousquet, O., Boucheron, S., Lugosi, G.: Introduction to statistical learning theory. In: Bousquet, O., von Luxburg, U., Rätsch, G. (eds.) ML -2003. LNCS (LNAI), vol. 3176, pp. 169–207. Springer, Heidelberg (2004). https://doi.org/10.1007/978-3-540-28650-9_8

5. Brown, T.B., Mané, D., Roy, A., Abadi, M., Gilmer, J.: Adversarial Patch. arXiv (2017)

6. Burton, S., Gauerhof, L., Heinzemann, C.: Making the case for safety of machine learning in highly automated driving. In: Tonetta, S., Schoitsch, E., Bitsch, F. (eds.) SAFECOMP 2017. LNCS, vol. 10489, pp. 5–16. Springer, Cham (2017). https://doi.org/10.1007/978-3-319-66284-8_1

7. Burton, S., Gauerhof, L., Sethy, B.B., Habli, I., Hawkins, R.: Confidence arguments for evidence of performance in machine learning for highly automated driving functions. In: Romanovsky, A., Troubitsyna, E., Gashi, I., Schoitsch, E., Bitsch, F. (eds.) SAFECOMP 2019. LNCS, vol. 11699, pp. 365–377. Springer, Cham (2019). https://doi.org/10.1007/978-3-030-26250-1_30

8. Carlini, N., Wagner, D.A.: Towards evaluating the robustness of neural networks. In: IEEE Symposium on Security and Privacy (2017)

9. Engstrom, L., Tran, B., Tsipras, D., Schmidt, L., Madry, A.: Exploring the landscape of spatial robustness. In: ICML (2019)

10. Eykholt, K., et al.: Physical Adversarial Examples for Object Detectors. arXiv (2018)

11. Gal, Y., Ghahramani, Z.: Dropout as a Bayesian approximation: representing model uncertainty in deep learning. In: ICML (2016)

12. Gauerhof, L., Munk, P., Burton, S.: Structuring validation targets of a machine learning function applied to automated driving. In: Gallina, B., Skavhaug, A., Bitsch, F. (eds.) SAFECOMP 2018. LNCS, vol. 11093, pp. 45–58. Springer, Cham (2018). https://doi.org/10.1007/978-3-319-99130-6_4

13. Gharib, M., Lollini, P., Botta, M., Amparore, E., Donatelli, S., Bondavalli, A.: On the safety of automotive systems incorporating machine learning based components: a position paper. In: DSN (2018)

14. Goodfellow, I., Shlens, J., Szegedy, C.: Explaining and harnessing adversarial examples. In: ICLR (2015)

15. Guo, C., Pleiss, G., Sun, Y., Weinberger, K.Q.: On Calibration of Modern Neural Networks. arXiv (2017)

16. Haase-Schütz, C., Hertlein, H., Wiesbeck, W.: Estimating labeling quality with deep object detectors. In: IEEE IV (2019)

17. Hein, M., Andriushchenko, M., Bitterwolf, J.: Why ReLU networks yield high-confidence predictions far away from the training data and how to mitigate the problem. In: CVPR (2019)

18. Hendrycks, D., Dietterich, T.: Benchmarking neural network robustness to common corruptions and perturbations. In: ICLR (2019)

19. ISO: Road vehicles - functional safety (ISO 26262) (2018)

20. ISO: Road vehicles - safety of the intended functionality (ISO/PAS 21448) (2019)

21. Kletz, T.A.: HAZOP & HAZAN: Notes on the Identification and Assessment of Hazards. Hazard Workshop Modules, Institution of Chemical Engineers (1986)

22. Koopman, P., Fratrik, F.: How many operational design domains, objects, and events? In: Workshop on AI Safety (2019)

23. Kurd, Z., Kelly, T.: Establishing safety criteria for artificial neural networks. In: Knowledge-Based Intelligent Information and Engineering Systems (2003)

24. Lampert, C.H., Nickisch, H., Harmeling, S.: Attribute-based classification for zero-shot visual object categorization. In: TPAMI (2014)

25. Lee, M., Kolter, J.Z.: On Physical Adversarial Patches for Object Detection. arXiv (2019)
26. Li, J., Schmidt, F.R., Kolter, J.Z.: Adversarial camera stickers: a physical camera-based attack on deep learning systems. arXiv (2019)
27. Madry, A., Makelov, A., Schmidt, L., Tsipras, D., Vladu, A.: Towards deep learning models resistant to adversarial attacks. In: ICLR (2018)
28. Morgulis, N., Kreines, A., Mendelowitz, S., Weisglass, Y.: Fooling a Real Car with Adversarial Traffic Signs. arXiv (2019)
29. Pakdaman Naeini, M., Cooper, G., Hauskrecht, M.: Obtaining well calibrated probabilities using Bayesian binning. In: AAAI (2015)
30. Schumann, J., Gupta, P., Liu, Y.: Application of neural networks in high assurance systems: a survey. In: Schumann, J., Liu, Y. (eds.) Applications of Neural Networks in High Assurance Systems. Studies in Computational Intelligence, vol. 268, pp. 1–19. Springer, Heidelberg (2010). https://doi.org/10.1007/978-3-642-10690-3_1
31. Selvaraju, R.R., Cogswell, M., Das, A., Vedantam, R., Parikh, D., Batra, D.: Grad-CAM: visual explanations from deep networks via gradient-based localization. In: ICCV (2017)
32. Szegedy, C., et al.: Intriguing properties of neural networks. In: ICLR (2014)
33. Varshney, K.R.: Engineering safety in machine learning. In: Information Theory and Applications Workshop (2016)
34. Wong, E., Kolter, J.Z.: Provable defenses against adversarial examples via the convex outer adversarial polytope. In: ICML (2018)
35. Yuan, X., He, P., Zhu, Q., Li, X.: Adversarial examples: attacks and defenses for deep learning. In: TNNLS (2019)
36. Zendel, O., Murschitz, M., Humenberger, M., Herzner, W.: CV-HAZOP: introducing test data validation for computer vision. In: ICCV (2015)
37. Zendel, O., Honauer, K., Murschitz, M., Steininger, D., Domínguez, G.F.: Wild-Dash - creating hazard-aware benchmarks. In: Ferrari, V., Hebert, M., Sminchisescu, C., Weiss, Y. (eds.) ECCV 2018. LNCS, vol. 11210, pp. 407–421. Springer, Cham (2018). https://doi.org/10.1007/978-3-030-01231-1_25
38. Zhang, J.M., Harman, M., Ma, L., Liu, Y.: Machine Learning Testing: Survey, Landscapes and Horizons. arXiv (2019)

Positive Trust Balance for Self-driving Car Deployment

Philip Koopman[1,2]([email]) and Michael Wagner[1]

[1] Edge Case Research, Pittsburgh, PA 15201, USA
mwagner@ecr.ai
[2] Carnegie Mellon University, Pittsburgh, PA 15213, USA
koopman@cmu.edu

Abstract. The crucial decision about when self-driving cars are ready to deploy is likely to be made with insufficient lagging metric data to provide high confidence in an acceptable safety outcome. A Positive Trust Balance approach can help with making a responsible deployment decision despite this uncertainty. With this approach, a reasonable initial expectation of safety is based on a combination of a practicable amount of testing, engineering rigor, safety culture, and a strong commitment to use post-deployment operational feedback to further reduce uncertainty. This can enable faster deployment than would be required by more traditional safety approaches by reducing the confidence necessary at time of deployment in exchange for a more stringent requirement for Safety Performance Indicator (SPI) field feedback in the context of a strong safety culture.

Keywords: Self-driving cars · Autonomous vehicles · System safety · Deployment

1 Introduction

At some point, developers must make a decision that it is time to deploy a Self-Driving Car (SDC) design. Ultimately, all the testing and safety engineering efforts come down to a binary go/no-go decision: is the vehicle ready to operate on public roads with sufficiently safe outcomes? This paper proposes an approach to living with the uncertainty that will be inherent in making this decision.

At the time of deployment, the SDC design team must be able to show that ***expected operational safety will be acceptable***. However, with the still-maturing state of SDC technology, it is likely that there will be significant uncertainty surrounding any such expectation. Moreover, due to practical limits on simulation and human-supervised testing, the scale of operations required to establish confidence that the error bars on the expectation also fall within acceptable safety outcomes will be too large to achieve in any way other than collecting data from actual at-scale deployment. (We use the term "confidence" in a general mathematical sense of a confidence interval and the like, and not in the sense of the strength of an individual's subjective belief.)

© Springer Nature Switzerland AG 2020
A. Casimiro et al. (Eds.): SAFECOMP 2020 Workshops, LNCS 12235, pp. 351–357, 2020.
https://doi.org/10.1007/978-3-030-55583-2_26

This results in a cyclic dependency: the only way to resolve uncertainty is to deploy, but deployment cannot be justified based on a high confidence expectation of acceptable safety due to excessive uncertainty. We propose a framework to ensure a responsible deployment decision based on Positive Trust Balance (PTB), involving a combination of validation, engineering rigor, post-deployment feedback, and safety culture.

A key observation is that traditional safety engineering is based on the premise that the first deployed unit is safe enough to be part of an at-scale production run and that – potential product recalls notwithstanding – no further changes will need to be made after deployment to achieve the desired lifecycle safety target. Such a claim might be unsupportable via practicable validation efforts for salient aspects of SDC technology such as the use of machine learning based systems. However, rather than saying that it is hopeless to assure safety at deployment, we instead propose an approach in which the *expected* level of safety is shown to be acceptable, but there is a non-negligible potential for higher than desired operational risk exposure due to *uncertainty*. This might still result in net tolerable risk if post-deployment feedback can be relied upon to aggressively reduce uncertainty over the system lifecycle.

In a related work, [8] assumed that safety was perfectly characterized when deploying, and explored the implications of uncertainty of in potential safety improvements after deployment. In contrast, we deal with uncertainty of the expected safety at the time of deployment.

2   Current Approaches to Deployment Decisions

2.1   Positive Risk Balance

A decision to deploy should include a decision as to whether the system is expected to be "safe enough." While there is no universally accepted criterion, a common approach is that SDCs should be at least as safe as a human-driven car. If the SDC is safer than a human, it is said to have Positive Risk Balance (PRB) [4].

Typically, PRB is stated in terms of the SDC having a lower fatality rate than otherwise comparable human-driven vehicles. A more nuanced view should also encompass major injury rates, minor injury rates, and perhaps property damage events. Setting a credible risk target is not trivial, and should take into account comparable loss event rates for the target Operational Design Domain (ODD), risk distribution profile (e.g., whether vulnerable road users are put at increased risk), and numerous other considerations (e.g., according to Section 16 of [1]) rather than simply using a generic national-level statistic for fatality rates. Other safety postures are possible, such as comparison only with unimpaired human drivers, or even a goal of zero at-fault loss events.

For present purposes we assume some reasonable definition of PRB is the goal. That assumption having been made, the question is how to decide whether PRB will be achieved before deploying.

2.2   Driver Test

A commonly proposed deployment criterion is passing some sort of simulated and/or real-world driving road test, potentially drawing upon elements of human-equivalent road tests and a scenario catalog (e.g., [3]).

An operational test is essential to confirm the validity of simulation and analysis. However, any predetermined test will struggle to assess analogues to some real-world human driving skills such as the ability to handle novel unstructured situations and "common sense" contextual interpretation. While such attributes are not stressed in human driver test procedures, traditional driver licensing addresses them indirectly via minimum age, supervised instruction, and brief observation of behavior by a human driver test official. Such an approach is deemed sufficient based upon significant experience with human abilities and cognitive development plus mandatory insurance. There is no analogous testing-only approach to evaluate judgment maturity for SDC technology for licensing and insurance risk evaluation purposes.

2.3 Testing Metrics

Administering a comprehensive SDC driving test requires significant resources, so a common alternative approach has been to use metrics that reflect on-road testing experience. Example metrics are number of miles driven, automation disengagements [2], and crashes per mile. (It is important to note that physical testing on public roads presents potentially significant risk that must be mitigated [9].) More sophisticated approaches combine simulation results with actual road miles.

While it is difficult to justify a deployment decision for a vehicle that lacks substantial real-world testing, large-scale testing campaigns don't necessarily ensure safety. Potential threats to validity for a road testing safety campaign must also be addressed, including changes to underlying vehicle software mid-campaign, driving only "easy" miles, and in general driving in conditions that do not cover risky portions of the ODD.

Even if road testing addresses all experimental concerns, the sheer number of miles required (likely billions of miles [8]) is infeasible to conduct using physical road tests before deployment.

2.4 SOTIF Approaches

The need for billions of miles of testing can, in principle, be reduced by identifying scenarios based on real-world operation and ensuring that the vehicle performs properly for all scenarios possible within the ODD. A methodical iterative improvement approach to this is used for Safety of the Intended Function (SOTIF) based workflows [6, 13]. The general idea is to iteratively identify and mitigate so-called triggering events that expose requirements gaps or other functional insufficiencies, resulting in ever-expanding scenario catalog. It is generally assumed that the deployment decision will be based on having high confidence that risk is not unreasonable. However, if a heavy tail distribution of triggering events is present, it might be that it is economically infeasible to discover enough of the "unknown hazardous" scenarios to achieve such high confidence, even if all available evidence based on mitigation of known hazards supports a conclusion of being safe enough to deploy.

The 2019 revision of ISO/PAS 21448 describing a SOTIF approach includes both iterative improvement during development and a newly added field monitoring section. Both activities are essential to achieve practical safety, and are aligned with the approach described in this paper. However, it is beneficial to also define a more explicit relationship between initial deployment safety and the role of field feedback in making the initial deployment decision, especially in the presence of substantial uncertainty.

3   The Positive Trust Balance Approach

It seems likely that a combination of the approaches discussed will be required, including analysis, simulation, testing, scenario catalogs, and iterative improvement. But, even doing all these things together is likely to result in an unacceptable level of uncertainty about whether a PRB has actually been achieved before deployment. The proposed four-prong Positive Trust Balance (PTB) approach addresses this uncertainty.

The issue is that design validation techniques are based on leading metrics that *predict* a PRB, rather than lagging metrics that confirm a PRB has been achieved in practice [12]. And, even if pre-deployment on-road PRB lagging metrics could be gathered (at great expense), it would likely be unaffordable to repeat full-scale on-road evidence collection before deploying each periodic software update.

A prime motivation for quick SDC deployment is to mitigate losses attributed to human drivers. However, a key deployment risk is uncertainty as to whether PRB will actually be achieved, or if instead losses will be worse than with human drivers due to premature deployment. Fundamental sources of uncertainty (and therefore lack of confidence) that complicate understanding of advanced SDC technology risk include:

- Lack of a human-comprehensible design for tracing tests back to design intent as is typically done with a V-model development cycle.
- Still-maturing best practices for developing machine learning-based systems.
- Addressing the problem of how an SDC can know that it is operating (or about to operate) outside its ODD when it encounters an unforeseen edge case.

Resolving this uncertainty requires more than yet another testing or simulation tool. Rather, it requires a fundamental re-thinking of the goal of having conclusive evidence that a safety target has been reached before deploying a system.

We suggest considering a PTB approach that involves an ***initial practicable, evidence-based expectation that a safety target will be achieved, and then uses operational data to improve the confidence of that expectation over time***. It is essential to have a robust safety culture for this approach to be viable.

3.1   Pre-deployment Validation

Pre-deployment validation, including analysis, simulation, and testing, should be carried out to the maximum extent reasonably practicable. That having been said, it has long been known that brute force testing is impracticable for establishing the safety of high criticality systems (e.g., [10]). Therefore, we should accept that a testing-only approach will leave substantial uncertainty as to safety.

Consider a hypothetical validation strategy:

- 10,000 million mile simulation campaign
- 100 million miles of collected road data used to feed those simulations
- 10 million miles of actual road testing used to validate simulation results

Even if the road testing proceeds with no incidents whatsoever, there will be uncertainty as to how well the SDC can handle infrequent events that arrive too seldom to be thoroughly characterized by the road data and road test campaign. As a simple illustration, a substantial fraction of rare events that happen once every 100 million miles won't have been seen at all in that data collection, let along be seen in road testing. But some of those same comparatively rare events will in aggregate occur more frequently than every 100 million miles during deployment. That will in turn potentially invalidate any PRB validation claim of a 100 million mile or longer average fatal mishap arrival rate. This is in addition to residual concerns about simulation accuracy that will further increase uncertainty.

Consider a developer claim that road testing and simulation has been done to the limits of economic practicality. The outcome of such a successful limited testing campaign will be that developers believe the system is safe – *as far as they know*. But, that knowledge of safety will have low confidence if it is not based on more data collection and testing than the expected fatality interarrival rate, which is generally impractical. Put another way, the developer will have an expectation of reasonable safety, but the error bars will be too big for comfort due to economic constraints.

Something will need to be done about the error bars.

3.2 Engineering Rigor

Functional safety standards require not only testing, but also evidence that a sufficiently rigorous engineering process has been applied. In particular, the conventional software features of the SDC should be designed according to established safety standards, such as ISO 26262 [7] for functional safety.

While engineering practices for some aspects of SDC technology such as machine learning are still evolving, there are known bad practices to be avoided, and the use of best practices should be confirmed. For example, training machine learning-based systems on safety validation data is clearly undesirable, but in practice corners might inadvertently be cut or data management mistakes might be made. Best practices are not a panacea, but it should be established that they have been followed. Moreover, it is difficult to justify that questionable engineering practices will result in a safe SDC. Conformance to SDC-specific safety standards and guidelines can help with this (e.g., [1, 6, 13]).

3.3 Feedback and Continuous Improvement

Even though validation and engineering rigor have been used to attain an acceptable *expected* safety outcome, confidence will likely be low enough that an unacceptable outcome might yet occur (e.g., the mean risk outcome is acceptable, but figurative error bars also encompass unacceptable outcomes). To address this concern, feedback from actual operations should be used to improve confidence as well as fix any problems.

A traditional recall approach that waits for unambiguous trends in mishaps and only then issues reactive fixes is insufficient here. No developer should deploy an SDC suspected or known to be unacceptably safe and then wait for multiple fatal crashes to accumulate before taking corrective action. *The degree of safety uncertainty inherent to novel SDC technology incurs an obligation to proactively monitor operations and to respond to all incidents, including near misses.*

A specific approach to feedback is the use of Safety Performance Indicators (SPIs) as defined in ANSI/UL 4600 [1]. SPIs are operational metrics that cover not only lagging indicators, but also leading indicators. SPIs are tied directly to an SDC's safety case. Near miss reporting [14] is an essential part of this approach. The aviation industry uses SPIs to improve after near misses and process breakdowns without waiting for actual loss events to drive lessons learned [5].

While it is always possible to get unlucky, in general if near misses are much more common than loss events, monitoring and correcting root causes of near misses can increase confidence faster than losses occur. Safe failure fraction SPIs are useful, such as the ratio of road testing near misses to operator-prevented mishaps.

This approach also encompasses the notion of small scale SDC pilot deployments. These still require a decision that the SDC is expected to be safe enough to deploy at pilot scale followed by feedback and improvement to build confidence over time.

3.4 Safety Culture

As with the design of any safety critical system, a robust safety culture [11] is essential to providing acceptably safe SDCs. Some particularly important issues are:

- Avoiding setting unreasonably low initial quality and validation goals based on an argument that post-deployment updates will fix bugs. Such an argument is not aligned with the PTB approach.
- Using the lack of maturity in accepted practices in some areas (e.g., still evolving best practices for safe machine learning) as an excuse for not following well known best practices for more traditional aspects of the system, such as functional safety.

The need for a robust, transparent robust safety culture should not be news to anyone involved in safety critical system design. *With a PTB approach it is absolutely essential to have a strong safety culture* both to ensure good technical outcomes as well as enable public trust to be built over time.

4 Conclusions

A Positive Trust Balance approach to self-driving car deployment includes all of: testing, employing engineering rigor, using field feedback for continuous improvement, and building a transparent, robust safety culture. Rather than requiring likely unattainable conclusive proof that a risk target has been met on day one, instead the deployment decision is made based on practicable evidence collection that supports a reasonable expectation that risk will be sufficiently low. This must be coupled with a firm commitment to improve confidence in that expectation using post-deployment feedback. A robust and transparent safety culture is essential to ensure that the developer is committed to making acceptable safety decisions over the system lifecycle.

In the end, what will matter the most is whether stakeholders trust the safety of SDCs at least as much as they trust the safety of human-driven vehicles (i.e., Positive Trust Balance). We believe that strong tool support for a PTB approach embodied in a safety case will be crucial for combining these elements in practice and developing stakeholder trust.

References

1. ANSI/UL 4600 Standard for Safety for the Evaluation of Autonomous Products, April 2020
2. Banerjee, S., et al.: Hands off the wheel in autonomous vehicles? In: DSN (2018)
3. Cerf, V.: A comprehensive self-driving car test. CACM **61**(2), 7 (2018)
4. Di Fabio, U., Broy, M., Brüngger, R.J., et al.: Ethics commission automated and connected driving. Federal Ministry of Transport and Digital Infrastructure of the Federal Republic of Germany (2017)
5. ICAO: Safety Management Manual (SMM), Doc 9859 AN/474, 2nd ed. (2009)
6. ISO: Road Vehicles – Safety of the Intended Function. ISO/PAS 21448:2019
7. ISO: Road Vehicles – Functional Safety. ISO 26262:2018
8. Kalra, N., Groves, D.: The enemy of good: estimating the cost of waiting for nearly perfect automated vehicles. Rand Corporation, RR-2150-RC (2017)
9. Koopman, P., Osyk, B.: Safety argument considerations for public road testing of autonomous vehicles, SAE WXC, 2019-01-0123, April 2019
10. Littlewood, B., Strigini, L.: Validation of ultra-high dependability for software-based systems. C ACM **36**(11), 69–80 (1993)
11. NASA: NASA Safety Culture Handbook, NASA-HDBK-8709.24 (2015)
12. Fraade-Blanar, L., et al.: Measuring automated vehicle safety, RAND Technical Report RR2662 (2018)
13. SaFAD working group: Safety First for Automated Driving, Technical Report
14. Williamsen, M.: Near-miss reporting: a missing link in safety culture. Prof. Saf. **58**, 46–50 (2013)

Integration of Formal Safety Models on System Level Using the Example of Responsibility Sensitive Safety and CARLA Driving Simulator

Bernd Gassmann$^{(\boxtimes)}$ ⓘ, Frederik Pasch ⓘ, Fabian Oboril ⓘ,
and Kay-Ulrich Scholl ⓘ

Intel Corporation, Intel Labs, Karlsruhe, Germany
{bernd.gassmann,frederik.pasch,fabian.oboril,
kay-ulrich.scholl}@intel.com

Abstract. Automated Driving (AD) is about to transform our daily life. However, on the way towards mass deployment, some challenges have to be resolved. Among these, the safety assurance problem is a key issue. Therefore, Intel/Mobileye proposed a formal, mathematical model called Responsibility Sensitive Safety (*RSS*) to digitize reasonable boundaries on the behavior of other road users by establishing clear mathematically proven rules. While the concept of *RSS* and a first reference implementation are already known to the community, a remaining question is the integration of *RSS* into a complete AD system. In this paper, we address this gap and describe the integration of *RSS* into the CARLA driving simulator as practical example.

1 Introduction

The transportation industry is currently undergoing one of its biggest transformation ever. In particular, the increasing amount of automation is a major factor in this process. While great progress was made in the last years on the functional side, assuring safety under all operating conditions, and all environment conditions is still an open research question.

Classical functional safety standards address possible hazards caused by malfunctioning behavior (ISO 26262 [7]) and consider intended functionality (ISO/PAS 21448 [8]) with focus on specified design process together with the imposition of specific technical requirements and validation methods. The ANSI/UL 4600 standard [1] addresses safety principles and processes especially for the evaluation of automated vehicles focusing on the creation of a valid safety case with its goals, argumentation, and evidence. NHTSA [10] envisions that validation methods are applied to appropriately mitigate the safety risks associated with Automated Driving Systems (ADS). Therefore, significant investments in operational safety of ADS are required, in particular in the areas of scenario development and formal verification, testing and validation tools [2,18].

© Springer Nature Switzerland AG 2020
A. Casimiro et al. (Eds.): SAFECOMP 2020 Workshops, LNCS 12235, pp. 358–369, 2020.
https://doi.org/10.1007/978-3-030-55583-2_27

As a possible solution to the problem of safety assurance, Intel/Mobileye proposed the "Responsibility Sensitive Safety" (*RSS*) safety model [16]. *RSS* is a technology-neutral formal mathematical approach of a safety concept for the decision making component of an ADS. *RSS* formalizes human notions of driving safely like *"Do not hit someone from behind"*, *"Do not cut in recklessly"*, *"Right-of-Way is given, not taken"*... *RSS* continuously monitors the current state of the environment and the state of the ADS itself, calculates the safety envelope (i.e. the longitudinal and lateral safety distances), and performs a proper response in case of violation of the safety envelope.

The longitudinal safety distance defined by *RSS* in a vehicle following scenario depends, for example, on the velocities of the front (v_f) and rear (v_r) car, the maximum braking β_{max}^f the front car can or will apply, the amount of braking β_{min}^r the rear car can or will apply and the reaction time ρ, or the amount of time it takes the rear car to perceive the danger and act accordingly. In addition, the possibility of the rear car accelerating with up to α_{max}^r during the reaction time is taken into account. The positive minimum safety distance evaluates to ([16] Definition 1):

$$d_{min} = \left[v_r\rho + \frac{1}{2}\alpha_{max}^r\rho^2 + \frac{(v_r + \rho\alpha_{max}^r)^2}{2\beta_{min}^r} - \frac{v_f^2}{2\beta_{max}^f} \right]_+ \qquad (1)$$

In a similar way, the lateral safety distance (see [16] Definition 6) is defined by *RSS*. If both, the longitudinal and lateral safety distance are violated, the situation is considered to be dangerous and *RSS* provides a proper reaction that will bring the car back into a safe state. Therefore, it will impose proper restrictions for the longitudinal ($accel_{max}^{lon}$) and lateral ($accel_{max}^{lat}$) accelerations of the driving command that is sent to the vehicle.

As driving simulators like the *CARLA* AD simulator [5] provide the possibility to simulate a large variety of safety critical scenarios with full access to ground truth data [18], these can support the test and validation of ADS to a certain degree. Integrating formal safety models with a driving simulator allows to perform safety assessment of parts of the ADS as well as an in-depth analysis of the safety models themselves, i.e. their behavior in corner-cases which are hard to cover by testing in reality.

In this paper we will briefly describe how safety models in general fit into an ADS architecture. Then, we show how road topology can be considered for situation modeling for AD safety models in general and demonstrate the integration of the formal safety model "Responsibility Sensitive Safety" (*RSS*) [16] on system level into the *CARLA* driving simulator to support the safety assessment of ADS. Finally, we present a demonstrator setup which enables human test persons to experience AD safety concepts.

2   Integration of Safety Models on System Level

Koopman et al. [9] describe a layered residual risk approach for automated vehicle safety validation which includes phased simulation and testing to mitigate residual validation risks, human-interpretable observability points to ensure the system is doing the right thing for the right reason, checking for gaps in the requirements and design faults and finally a run-time monitoring approach, a safety checker functional block, to manage identified risks, catch assumption violations and "unknown unknowns". More general, safety checkers are also referred as ethical governors or safety monitors [3].

A general functional reference architecture of an ADS is sketched in the upcoming SAE J3131 [15] recommended practice. Therein, the reflexive layer on top of the basic control layer contains a safety checker/monitor, that indirectly prevents the system from violating one or more safety goals by flagging safety-relevant anomalies (see Fig. 1). Based on safety-grade map and environment information the checker validates the planned trajectory of the ADS.

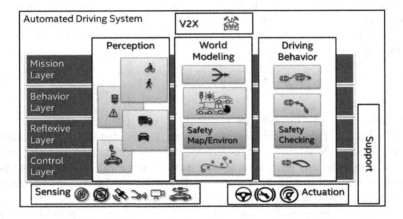

Fig. 1. The integration of safety models as a monitor/checker component into an ADS architecture, loosely based on upcoming SAE J3131. On the bottom left the sensing system of the ADS including cameras, LIDAR, RADAR, GPS, etc. is sketched. The perception system processes and fuses the sensor data to create information on a higher level of abstraction to build up an internal model of the world, the ADS is operating on. Vehicle to vehicle or vehicle to infrastructure communication can support the creation of the environment model with its traffic participants, the map of the road network, its regulations as well as other static and dynamic entities. Based on this, the driving behavior creates and executes a plan to operate within the world and sends control commands to the actuation system of the vehicle (bottom right). The horizontal layers indicate the time hierarchy of the ADS functions from mission layer at the top for strategic functions beyond the sensor range, behavior layer for tactical functions, reflexive layer to produce motion control requests and the control layer at the bottom for closed-loop motion control functions. The reflexive layer includes checks for drivability and potential hazards.

The proposed framework for online verification of motion planning of ADS in [14] mainly follows that kind of separate stand-alone formal safety checker. In addition to the trajectories proposed by the planner, the framework generates fail-safe trajectory extensions which allows to check multiple trajectories and select a verified one among these. The independence from the actual planner enables the argumentation with classical functional safety standards; even the input to the safety checker can be based on an independent perception chain if required.

Another possibility is to embed safety checkers directly into the planning function as part of the behavior layer of the driving behavior (see Fig. 1). The tactical planner considers safety metrics already while creating the trajectories. This also supports Machine Learning approaches, e.g. by punishing unsafe plans and rewarding safe plans within the learning process. Cheng et al. [4] incorporate safety checks as control barrier functions in a reinforcement learning framework. Like this, the planner itself becomes aware of the safety metrics and enables optimal and safe planning at once. The drawback of this approach is that the safety envelope around the planner is not obvious anymore.

Finally, the safety checker functionality can be deployed outside the actual ADS and used as an external assessment tool. This allows black-box testing of the of ADS functions by applying the safety metrics to validate the behavior safety. Any of these integration methods require map and environment information as input to the safety checker.

3   Road Topology and Situation Modeling Considerations for AD Safety Models

A safety checker has to consider all potential constellations of the vehicles to ensure no critical one is missed when performing the situation analysis. The *RSS* safety model mainly distinguishes the following main constellations of two vehicles [16]:

- the vehicles drive in the same direction on the same road
- the vehicles drive in opposite direction on the same road
- the vehicles drive on different roads that overlap in certain areas having to respect priority rules (intersection)
- areas with no actual road geometries like parking lots (unstructured)

There are different map data formats available like *OpenStreetMap* [13] or *OpenDRIVE* [11] representing geometric and semantic road data. The analysis required for safety models like *RSS*, e.g. on intersection level, demands knowledge on priority rules and sophisticated operations on the map data. For this, we introduce the open source *AD map access* library[1] providing a C++ implementation for accessing and operating on AD map data. *AD map access* supports reading the standardized *OpenDRIVE* file format and provides high-level operations required for automated driving like map matching, route planning, prediction, and i.e. right-of-way handling within intersections.

---

[1] https://github.com/carla-simulator/map.

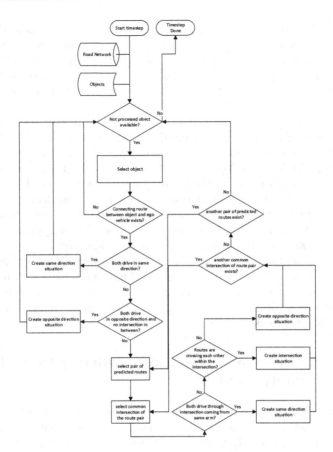

Fig. 2. Flow diagram of the considerations to be done to determine possible constellations of two vehicles

Having AD map data and a list of objects from the environment model at hand the type of constellation of two vehicles can be determined as sketched in Fig. 2: Using the road network data, the shortest connecting route between two vehicles is calculated. If both vehicles are driving in the same direction with respect to the connecting route a same-direction-constellation is created. This is done, regardless if intersections between the two vehicles are present, because one vehicle just follows the other, potentially through the intersection (see Fig. 3). If both vehicles drive in opposite directions and there is no intersection in between an opposite-direction-constellation is created (see Fig. 4 (left)). Otherwise, the planned route of the ego-vehicle has to be analyzed pairwise with all possible routes of the other vehicle as the others' planned route is not known. Every intersection crossed by both routes might result in a new constellation to be considered: If both drive through the intersection coming from different intersection arms with routes not crossing, the vehicles pass each other and an opposite-direction-constellation is created (see Fig. 4 (right)).

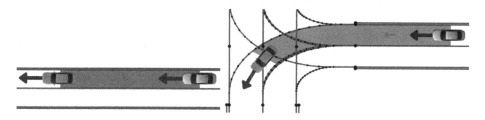

Fig. 3. One vehicle is following the other on the same road, driving in the same direction: (left) either on the same lane or on another parallel lane. (right) Same direction: Both vehicles drive through the intersection from the same arm: ego (bright) vehicle is following the other (dark) vehicle.

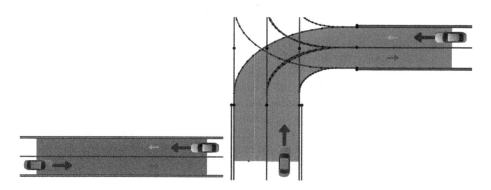

Fig. 4. Both vehicle are approaching each other, driving in the opposite direction: (left) on the same road either on the same or on parallel lane. (right) Both vehicles approach the intersection and will exit the intersection at the arm that the respective other is entering.

Other cases lead to the creation of an intersection-constellation where the routes are crossing each other (see Fig. 5). To determine if one route has priority over the other as per traffic rules the capabilities of the *AD map access* are used. In case of traffic light intersections, the kind and status of the relevant traffic light determines the current priorities.

This map based approach covers the main connecting routes following the road network definitions but isn't claiming completeness. In reality, a wide variety of road layouts exist which have to be considered. In addition, this method is limited to structured constellations. For completeness extensions towards unstructured constellations where e.g. other vehicles enter/exit the road or drive on larger areas with no defined traffic direction are required.

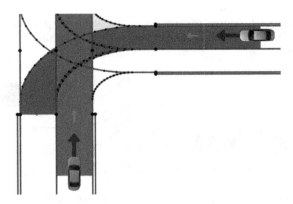

Fig. 5. Intersection: Both vehicles approach the intersection with routes crossing within the intersection: ego (bright) vehicle is turning left; the other (dark) vehicle is driving straight.

4   Applying *RSS* Within *CARLA* Simulator

In this section, we describe how *RSS* is integrated into the overall *CARLA* architecture. This follows the integration of a safety checker as external assessment tool as described in Sect. 2. We decided to split the integration in two main parts: the *RSS Sensor* and the *RSS Restrictor*. Like this, the *RSS Sensor* can be attached as virtual sensor to any of the vehicles providing *RSS* safety metrics without influencing the vehicle behavior. If a *RSS* conform vehicle behavior is required, the *RSS Restrictor* functionality can be called to restrict the control commands before forwarding them to the respective vehicle (see Fig. 6).

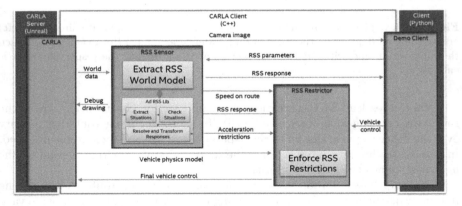

Fig. 6. Integration of *RSS* safety model into *CARLA* architecture with *RSS Sensor*, *RSS Restrictor* and Demo Client Interface

4.1 RSS Sensor

The *RSS Sensor* is a client-side sensor. It implements the 'Extract RSS World Model' and the *RSS* checker functionality as part of the 'Ad RSS Lib' sketched in Fig. 6. When attached to a vehicle, the *RSS Sensor* 'ticks' as every other *CARLA* sensor. Every 'tick' all vehicles are analyzed according to *RSS*:

1. Perform map matching of the ego-vehicle.
2. Update the ego-vehicle route on which the *RSS* calculations are based.
3. Calculate the ego dynamics on the route:
    - Determine the heading of the route θ^{route}
    - Calculate speed components $v_{\text{route}}^{\text{lat}}, v_{\text{route}}^{\text{lon}}$
    - Keep track of accelerations $a_{\text{route}}^{\text{lat}}, a_{\text{route}}^{\text{lon}}$
4. Create the relevant vehicle constellations required as input to the *RSS* as described in Sect. 3.
5. Perform the safety check calling into the *RSS Open Library*[2] [6].
6. Analyze and report the check results including the proper response provided by the *RSS* safety model.
7. (optional) Trigger debug visualization

4.2 RSS Restrictor

If an additional *RSS Restrictor* is instantiated, the output from the *RSS Sensor* can be used to make the vehicle behave in a *RSS* conform manner. The *RSS Restrictor* implements the 'Enforce RSS Restrictions' functionality sketched in Fig. 6.

Regardless of the incoming control commands—either by an AD stack, a simple *CARLA* control client or even a manual control client—a vehicle equipped with a *RSS Restrictor* will consider the proper response calculated by the *RSS Sensor* and behave *RSS* conform; limited to the extend of the feature set supported by the *RSS Sensor* and on the accuracy that can be achieved by the simple implementation.

Limitations. In general, providing *RSS* conform restrictions of the future vehicle trajectory is not trivial. While enforcing longitudinal restrictions is mainly achieved by braking, the nature of lateral restrictions is far more complex. Restricting the lateral movement within the lane requires to control the vehicle steering where counter steering is the analogy of longitudinal braking. While braking longitudinally ultimately ends up in standing still, counter steering might easily lead to a movement to the other side within the lane, which is not the desired behavior. *RSS* requests to stop the movement in the respective lateral direction in the first place, not to move to the opposite (the longitudinal analogy of the latter would be driving backwards to increase the distance between the two vehicles again).

---

[2] https://github.com/intel/ad-rss-lib.

RSS leaves enough lateral space towards the other traffic participant, that, by applying the braking force β_{min}^{lat} within the reaction time, both vehicles will be able to stop their lateral movement towards each other (reaching laterally μ-velocity of 0 as defined in [16] Definition 6) and avoid a collision with each other. After μ-lateral-zero velocity is reached, the lateral acceleration is again restricted to $[0; \alpha_{max}^{lat}]$ or $[-\alpha_{max}^{lat}; 0]$ respectively.

The *RSS Restrictor* and the *RSS Sensor* are running within *CARLA* usually at a frequency that is rather too slow for performing a closed loop control. This doesn't allow the actual control of the accelerations like it would be possible by a real vehicle controller. Furthermore, we cannot afford the effort to tune the *RSS Restrictor* to every kind of vehicle possible to be spawned within *CARLA* in respect to concrete control parameters. Therefore, we decided to go for a simple implementation of the restrictor that intervenes only if a dangerous situation is reported.

Longitudinal Restriction. In case the acceleration restrictions reported by the *RSS Sensor* trigger a brake in longitudinal direction by a negative result ($\text{accel}_{max}^{lon} < 0$), the throttle is set to zero and the brake control value ($\text{brake}^{ctrl} \in [0.0; 1.0]$) is calculated based on the simulated vehicles maximum wheel torques ($\text{brake}_{wheel,max}^{torque}$), the wheel radius ($\text{radius}_{wheel}$) and the vehicle mass:

$$\text{brake}_{max}^{torque} = \sum_{wheel} \text{brake}_{wheel,max}^{torque} \tag{2}$$

$$\text{brake}_{desired}^{torque} = \text{mass} \left| \text{accel}_{max}^{lon} \right| \text{radius}_{wheel} \tag{3}$$

$$\text{brake}^{ctrl} = \frac{\text{brake}_{desired}^{torque}}{\text{brake}_{max}^{torque}} \tag{4}$$

Lateral Restriction. The means of choice to respond on a lateral restriction is to counter steer into route direction θ^{route}, the steer output control value ($\text{steer}_{out}^{ctrl} \in [-1.0; 1.0]$) is calculated based on the steer control input (steer_{in}^{ctrl}), the ego heading (θ^{ego}), the simulated vehicles maximum wheel steering angle ($\text{steer}_{wheel,max}^{angle}$):

$$\text{steer}_{max}^{angle} = \max_{wheel} \text{steer}_{wheel,max}^{angle} \tag{5}$$

$$\text{steer}_{restr} = \frac{\arctan(\theta^{route} - \theta^{ego})}{\text{steer}_{max}^{angle}} \tag{6}$$

$$\text{steer}_{out}^{ctrl} = \begin{cases} \max(\text{steer}_{in}^{ctrl}, \text{steer}_{restr}), & \text{if } v_{route}^{lat} < 0, \\ \min(\text{steer}_{in}^{ctrl}, \text{steer}_{restr}), & \text{if } v_{route}^{lat} > 0. \end{cases} \tag{7}$$

5   RSS CARLA Demonstrator

While integrating *RSS* into *CARLA* and driving around with the keyboard control, very soon the idea of using steering wheel and pedals to control the ego-vehicle came up. Then, the idea was growing quickly towards a demonstrator providing the opportunity for people experiencing *RSS* without the need to know on the details of the safety model.

The demonstrator hardware setup consists of a PC, a display, a steering wheel and pedals for throttle and brake. To provide an immersive user experience, the steering wheel supports force feedback, i.e. it can be controlled by the application (see Fig. 7).

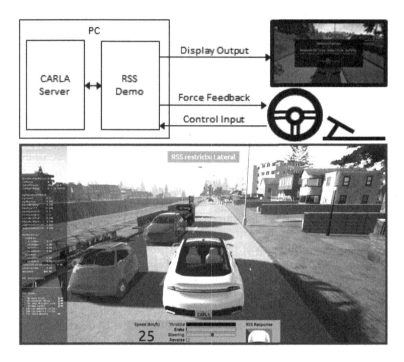

Fig. 7. Demonstrator setup: The ego vehicle is trying to steer to the left and provoke a collision. The *RSS Restrictor* is preventing the collision by overriding the throttle and steering control values.

On the PC a *RSS* demo application connects to a *CARLA* server instance. It's based on the reference manual_control_steeringwheel.py and instantiates and attaches a *RSS Sensor* to the ego vehicle. In case the *RSS Sensor* reports a dangerous situation, the values of the steering wheel get overridden by the ones provided by the *RSS Restrictor* and a physical force is applied to the steering wheel. In case of lateral restrictions, the steering wheel gets pushed back to a safe angle. For longitudinal restrictions the steering wheel vibrates. Additionally, the unsafe situation is displayed and a red frame is drawn into the display. These effects enable a test person to haptically experience the effects of RSS.

Two demo modes are available. The first one is an open world approach, where the test person drives along a predefined route through a world with random traffic. While this allows experiencing many different situations, it's also easy to miss them, leading to varying user reception. After this main feedback from a set of about 20–30 independent test persons, a second mode was implemented which guides the test person through a prepared scenario where the features of RSS are explained in more detail.

The scenario follows a route and is divided into different situations that showcase the RSS rules one by one. It's defined as *OpenSCENARIO* [12] and executed by ScenarioRunner[3]. The test person drives along the route (supported by navigation hints) and the behavior of the other traffic participants and the traffic lights is triggered by the location of the ego vehicle. That allows, for example, to create a situation, where another traffic participant cuts the right of way.

6   Outlook

In this paper we presented how safety models are integrated on system level using the example of *RSS* safety model and *CARLA* driving simulator as a first public available reference on how *RSS* can be integrated while supporting complex road networks. The integration into an open source driving simulator like *CARLA* can help gain the public trust for the deployment of ADS when equipped with a safety model like *RSS*, or the Automatic Preventive Braking, *APB*, model [17] in future. In this way, one can experience and investigate the safety benefits of *RSS* independent from the actual automated driving technology implemented below. In addition, these enhancements open the possibility for using *CARLA* to test AD stacks for their conformance to *RSS* or some other future *RSS*-like standard.

After the initial step is taken, the implementation will be extended by further use-cases. A big field not yet covered by the presented open source implementation are pedestrians and behavior in unstructured environments, which play a major role especially in urban environments. Furthermore, the *RSS Sensor* in its current form takes the ideal object data from the *CARLA* internal world. Therefore, also hidden objects around the corner are currently considered as if they were known to the ego vehicle: Handling of occlusions on the side of the *RSS Sensor* as well as in other components like *RSS map integration* and *RSS Open Library* will be integrated.

One limitation of the simulation setup is the general question on how much of the reality can be covered by the simulated scenarios. Simulation cannot replace on-road testing, it only can supplement it. By using only simulated vehicles one can never be sure to have covered the behavior of real vehicles on the road, especially if these are controlled by human operators. Nevertheless, applying different scenarios which were derived from real world data will support the analysis of various aspects of safety checkers like *RSS*. In future, we intend to

---

[3] https://github.com/carla-simulator/scenario_runner.

apply the implementation to real traffic scenarios and evaluate the behavior of the traffic participants in respect to the safety metrics.

References

1. ANSI/UL 4600 - Standard for Safety for Evaluation of Autonomous Products (2020). https://standardscatalog.ul.com/standards/en/standard_4600_1
2. Aptiv, Audi, Baidu, BMW, Continental, Daimler, Fiat Chrysler Automobiles, HERE, Infineon, Intel, Volkswagen: Safety first for automated driving. White Paper, July 2019
3. Charisi, V., et al.: Towards moral autonomous systems. CoRR abs/1703.04741 (2017). http://arxiv.org/abs/1703.04741
4. Cheng, R., Orosz, G., Murray, R., Burdick, J.: End-to-end safe reinforcement learning through barrier functions for safety-critical continuous control tasks. In: Proceedings of the AAAI Conference on Artificial Intelligence, vol. 33, pp. 3387–3395, July 2019. https://doi.org/10.1609/aaai.v33i01.33013387
5. Dosovitskiy, A., Ros, G., Codevilla, F., Lopez, A., Koltun, V.: CARLA: an open urban driving simulator. In: Proceedings of the 1st Annual Conference on Robot Learning, pp. 1–16 (2017)
6. Gassmann, B., et al.: Towards standardization of AV safety: C++ library for responsibility sensitive safety. In: 2019 IEEE Intelligent Vehicles Symposium (IV) (2019)
7. ISO: ISO 26262 - Road vehicles - Functional safety (2018)
8. ISO: ISO 21448 - Road vehicles - Safety of the intended functionality (2019)
9. Koopman, P., Wagner, M.: Toward a framework for highly automated vehicle safety validation. SAE Technical Paper (2018). https://doi.org/10.4271/2018-01-1071
10. NHTSA - US Department of Transportation: Automated Driving Systems: a vision for safety (2017)
11. OpenDRIVE (2020). https://www.asam.net/standards/detail/opendrive/
12. OpenSCENARIO (2020). https://www.asam.net/standards/detail/openscenario/
13. Open Street Map (2020). https://www.openstreetmap.org
14. Pek, C., Koschi, M., Althoff, M.: An online verification framework for motion planning of self-driving vehicles with safety guarantees. In: AAET 2019 - Automatisiertes und vernetztes Fahren, pp. 260–274 (2019)
15. SAE - Society of Automotive Engineers: SAE J3131 - Automated Driving Reference Architecture
16. Shalev-Shwartz, S., Shammah, S., Shashua, A.: On a formal model of safe and scalable self-driving cars. arXiv preprint arXiv:1708.06374v6 (2017)
17. Shalev-Shwartz, S., Shammah, S., Shashua, A.: Vision zero: on a provable method for eliminating roadway accidents without compromising traffic throughput. arXiv preprint arXiv:1901.05022v2 (2018)
18. Takács, Á., Drexler, D.A., Galambos, P., Rudas, I.J., Haidegger, T.: Assessment and standardization of autonomous vehicles. In: 2018 IEEE 22nd International Conference on Intelligent Engineering Systems (INES), pp. 000185–000192. IEEE (2018). https://doi.org/10.1109/INES.2018.8523899

A Safety Case Pattern for Systems with Machine Learning Components

Ernest Wozniak, Carmen Cârlan$^{(\boxtimes)}$, Esra Acar-Celik, and Henrik J. Putzer

fortiss GmbH, Guerickestraße 25, 80805 Munich, Germany
{wozniak,carlan,acarcelik,putzer}@fortiss.org

Abstract. Several standards from the domain of safety critical systems, in order to support the argumentation of the safety assurance of a system under development, recommend the construction of a safety case. This activity is guided by the objectives to be met, recommended or required by the standards along the safety lifecycle. Ongoing attempts to use Machine Learning (ML) for safety critical functionality revealed certain deficits. For instance, the widely recognized standard for functional safety of automotive systems, ISO 26262, which can be used as a basis to construct a safety case, does not reason about ML. To this end, the goal of this work is to provide a pattern for arguing about the correct implementation of safety requirements in system components based on ML. The pattern is integrated within an overall encompassing approach for safety case generation for automotive systems and its applicability is showcased on a pedestrian avoidance system.

Keywords: Machine learning · Safety case · ISO 26262 · GSN

1 Introduction

Industry is quite reserved in introducing Machine Learning (ML) to implement safety critical functionality for the market products. This is due to the poor confidence in the correct behavior of functionality implemented by ML components [1]. As such, there is a stringent need for improvements not only in the area of ML-based algorithms design and implementation, but also in validation and verification approaches, possibly relying on new metrics. Nevertheless, even with a proper set of methods and metrics, there would still be a need for guidelines for reasoning about the safety assurance of the ML components. Safety assurance is usually guided by standardized documents. ISO 26262 is a well known, and prominent standard for functional safety in the automotive domain [2]. The document recommends the execution of a safety lifecycle, along the system development lifecycle. During the safety lifecycle, technical safety requirements are elicitated and then refined during the product development at hardware and software level. For the development of hardware and software, ISO 26262 recommends the execution of two separate processes, specified as V-models. The current shortcoming of ISO 26262 is that it does not reason about ML as it does

© Springer Nature Switzerland AG 2020
A. Casimiro et al. (Eds.): SAFECOMP 2020 Workshops, LNCS 12235, pp. 370–382, 2020.
https://doi.org/10.1007/978-3-030-55583-2_28

for technologies like software (SW, see part 6 of ISO 26262) or hardware (HW, see part 5 of ISO 26262). Another relevant standard for automotive, i.e. ISO/PAS 21448 [3] makes only few references to ML, and only in the context of level 1 and 2 automation. In general ISO/PAS 21448 (also called SOTIF - Safety Of The Intended Functionality) abstracts from specific technology (whether this is SW, HW or ML) and their limitations. It focuses on hazardous behaviour caused by the intended functionality or performance limitations of a system that is free from the faults addressed in the ISO 26262 series.

In order to enable the usage of ML for the implementation of safety-critical functionality in automotive systems, this work proposes a pattern to construct a safety case – a clear, comprehensive and defensible argument, supported by diverse evidence, guaranteeing safety of an item [4]. The pattern is specified in the Goal Structuring Notation (GSN), which is one of the most prominent notations used for modeling safety cases [5]. The proposed pattern scopes at guiding the reasoning about the safety assurance of systems that have parts of their functionality implemented with ML. The argumentation structure described by the pattern is aligned with the reasoning about safety assurance ISO 26262 recommends for software and hardware components, and aims at completing the set of argumentation patterns for building the safety case of systems compliant with ISO 26262 that we propose in [6]. The last, in an implicit fashion, supports also consideration of ISO/PAS 21448 in a construction of a safety case. Further, the pattern may then serve not only to build a safety case for a specific use-case from the automotive domain, but also acts as a suggestion on how to ultimately extend ISO 26262 with ML related concerns.

The paper is structured as follows. Section 2 presents the state of the art in arguing about the safety of ML-based systems. Next, Sect. 3 introduces fundamental concepts on which this work builds up. Section 4 provides a GSN-based pattern for arguing the satisfaction of safety requirements at the ML component level. Its evaluation is conveyed in Sect. 5 where it is used to construct a safety case for a pedestrian detection component. Finally, the paper is concluded in Sect. 6, together with a discussion on possible future work.

2   Related Work

Currently intensified efforts in exceeding the boundaries of using machine learning, even for the implementation of safety-critical functionality, result in many works which elaborate on the safety aspects of ML. However, to our knowledge, none of these works provides an overview of how to integrate the safety argumentation fragment related to machine learning in an overall safety case of a system compliant with ISO 26262.

McDermid et al. [1] propose a framework that allows the dynamic update of the system safety case as the behavior of the system evolves. They claim that the safety case shall argue about the coverage of gaps between the "real world" and the "world as imagined". These could, for instance, be caused by the limitations of the data used to train an ML model. Nevertheless, authors do not indicate how to argue against these insufficiencies, unlike we do in this work.

372 E. Wozniak et al.

Picardi et al. [7] propose GSN-based pattern for arguing about the satisfaction of performance properties by ML components from within the domain of medical systems. Similarly to our proposed pattern, the satisfaction of performance properties is argued based on a specific operating context, performance benchmark, usage of a particular machine learning model and training/validation/test data sets. In addition to this argumentation, we also consider an argument over the correct decomposition of ML safety requirements into sub-requirements. Further, authors discuss also aspects that shall be defended, in order to demonstrate confidence in the behavior of a machine learning component. For instance training, validation and test data sets shall be evidenced to be representative of the intended operational environment. In a consecutive and very recent work, Picardi et al. [8] provides more details on how to argue about these confidence aspects. For that they propose a general pattern. Our work is complementary to the work of Picardi et al. [8], as the pattern that we provide acts as an instantiations of their confidence argument pattern.

The earlier work of Picardi et al. [7] is also extended by Burton et al. [9]. The latter proposes an approach for constructing confidence arguments for the performance evaluation techniques, and reveals the limitations of current approaches for evaluating the performance of ML. However, their discussion focuses on the employment of ML for a specific use-case of pedestrian detection. Gauerhof et al. [10] elaborate on the same use case with the goal to construct a safety argumentation. Both these works introduce relevant goals, strategies and evidences, that were generalized by our pattern, so that they can be applied to ML based components of various functionality.

Salay and Czarnecki [11] provide certain guidelines for reasoning about the safety assurance of ML-components in the automotive domain, while adapting the software safety lifecycle proposed in ISO 26262 (Part 6). To some extent, our pattern mirrors their reasoning. Rudolph et al. [12] provide support for arguing about the appropriate usage of a neural network for the implementation of safety-critical functionality of an automotive system. In contrast to their work, we provide a complete approach for the safety argumentation of ML-systems in automotive applications. However, we could use the results of the work of Rudolph et al. [12] to guide the instantiation of the pattern we propose.

3 Foundations

Machine Learning in Safety-Critical Domains. ML is considered in this work as a 3rd kind of technology, next to SW and HW. This is the principle advertised in [13] and the main driving force to extend ISO 26262 by introducing, yet unpublished, VDE-AR-E 2842-61 from DKE-/AK 801.0.8 standard [14]. The lifecycle offered by the standard is aligned with the safety lifecycle of ISO 26262 (to ease its adaptation by the industry) and further extends it to frame ML concerns. To this end it defines a V-model like process (see Fig. 1) to develop a component based on ML - *ML component*. The first phase of the left branch this is initiation, where the main activity concerns refinement of system level requirements into ML requirements. It is currently debatable how and even if such refinement will be feasible, mainly due to complexity of the problem that ML-based solutions deal with. This work assumes that certain form of requirements at the ML component level will be necessary. Second phase concerns data acquisition, i.e. gathering and labeling of data used for training, validation and testing. Next is design phase which outputs *ML model design*. The last phase concerns implementation and training activities. The implementation is an artifact expressed in a programming language such as Python, or preferably in a strongly typed language such as C++. This is then used as an input to execute a training procedure which outputs *ML model*. The right side of the process follows the common principle of a V-model, i.e. its phases object in verifying outcomes of activities executed within the phases of the left branch. An ultimate artifact obtained after traversal through all the phases of the V-model this is *ML component*. It contains *ML model* and provides interfaces to communicate with other, ML, SW, or HW-based components.

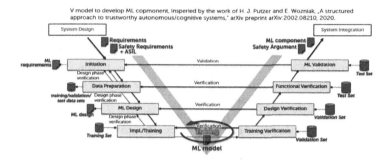

Fig. 1. V model process to develop ML component

Safety Case Patterns for ISO 26262 Compliant Systems. In [6], we propose a catalogue of GSN-based patterns for modeling safety argumentation based on evidence generated during the execution of the safety lifecycle recommended by ISO 26262. Each pattern follows a similar structure entailing four lines of argumentation, while each argumentation line is inspired by the types of artefacts (work products) generated during the ISO 26262 safety lifecycle. First, a system property may be decomposed in sub-properties at the same development tier. Second, the property may be refined into properties specified at the next development tier. Third, the satisfaction of a system property (goal or requirement) is argued by referencing the system design at different levels of abstraction. Further, the correctness of the system architecture and the SW and HW implementation is argued based on verification and validation evidence. ISO/PAS 21448 aligns with the safety lifecycle of ISO 26262 (see Figure 10 of the SOTIF standard [3]). Therefore pattern of Carlan et al. [6] may also implicitly consider SOTIF related concerns within the safety case constructed using the pattern.

4 GSN-Based Pattern to Argue Safety of ML Components

Currently, ISO 26262 does not provide any recommendation for the safety assurance of ML-based systems. ISO/PAS 21448 makes only few references to ML which do not provide sufficient information to reason about limitations of this technology. This hinders the usage of ML in automotive systems for the implementation of safety-critical functionality. In previous work [6], we proposed a set of patterns for arguing about the safety assurance of systems compliant with ISO 26262. In the same work, we presented a general structure for arguing the satisfaction of a safety requirement (see Sect. 3), structure that has been derived from the assurance objectives specified in ISO 26262 at hardware and software level. Based on this argumentation structure, in this section, complementing the set of patterns proposed in [6], we propose a pattern that tailors the rationale for arguing the satisfaction of ML safety requirements. The pattern may be used for arguing the correct implementation of ML safety requirements by an ML component, while considering the context in which the system shall operate.

Following the structure for arguing about the satisfaction of safety requirements by HW or SW components (see Sect. 3), the claim regarding the correct implementation of machine learning requirements is supported by four lines of argumentation (see Fig. 2). Similarly to software or hardware safety requirements, machine learning safety requirements may be further decomposed into sub-requirements, case in which the safety argumentation shall consider both the correct decomposition of the requirement and the satisfaction of each sub-requirement. Also similar with the safety argumentation at hardware and software level, the appropriateness of the chosen design of the ML-based solution shall be argued about. Further, mirroring the argumentation regarding the correct hardware or software implementation of safety requirements, for ML solutions, one shall argue about the correct training of the ML model, having as an input adequate training data and an appropriate ML design. The last argumentation line concerns the appropriate data acquisition. This objective is characteristic to ML-based approaches, where data plays crucial role.

Next, we present how we further develop these lines of argumentation. The goals within the argumentation patterns we present next can be classified into two groups, depending on whether they argue about the satisfaction of a specific ML safety requirement or they are general safety assurance goals. The second group is independent of ML safety requirement. Their inclusion in the system safety case is conditional, e.g. it may depend on an assigned ASIL (Automotive Safety Integrity Level). Please note that numbering of identifiers for goals and strategies does not start from 1 as it is a continuation of patterns from [6].

One characteristic activity when developing ML-based solution is the preparation of data sets (consisting of samples and labeling) used for training, validation and evaluation (see Fig. 3). The training data set serves the purpose of training an ML model, the validation set is used to choose the hyperparameters of the model in order to avoid overfitting, whereas the test data is used to verify

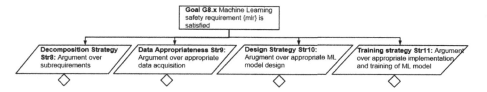

Fig. 2. Top level of GSN based pattern for safety case construction for ML component

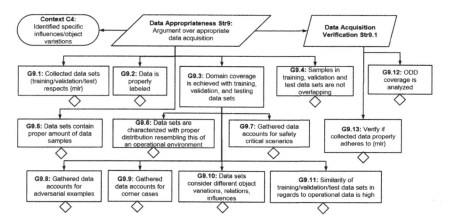

Fig. 3. Refinement of data appropriateness strategy

properties of a trained model. The following goals support the claim regarding data appropriateness:

– **G9.1: Collected data (training/validation/test) satisfies {mlr}.** Certain ML safety requirements can be explicit requirements on data sets, e.g. {*test set shall contain scenario with five pedestrians simultaneously crossing a road*} or implicit, e.g. {*ML model shall handle images blurred up to 25%*} that implies that the data sets shall contain blurred images.
– **G9.2: Data is properly labeled.** This goal aims at proper labeling of collected data samples. This may refer not only to the problem of labeling the right objects, but also the proper size of the bounding boxes, etc.
– **G9.3: Domain coverage is achieved with training, validation, and testing data sets.** This goal strives for collecting representative data samples and is further refined into several sub-goals. Goal G9.6 requests that data sets are characterized with proper distribution comparable to an operational environment. This means that ODD attributes considered by the system of interest, such as weather conditions, contrast, etc., shall be properly reflected in data sets. Next, *G9.7* urges for collection of safety critical scenarios within data sets. An example could be highly occluded pedestrians on a crosswalk. Goals *G9.8* and *G9.9* request to enhance data sets with correspondingly, adversarial examples, and corner cases. Next, *G9.10* requests to consider

different object variations, relations, influences. For instance, a valid relation between objects, in case of pedestrian detection, is a pedestrian which carries another pedestrian, e.g. mother and a small child. Last, *G9.11* raises the relevance of collecting data sets which properly represent operational environment. For example if an autonomous car is intended to operate on European roads, collected data sets shall come from that region.

– **G9.4: Samples in training, validation and test data sets are not overlapping.** For example, the same image or three different images but showing the same situation, shall not appear in these three data sets.
– **G9.5: Data sets contain proper amount of data samples.** Numbers of data samples for training shall be sufficient in order to properly train the model. Also the ratio between amount of data samples in each set shall be taken into consideration. A common approach is to provide the ratio of 60/20/20.

The *Data Acquisition Verification* strategy guides the assurance of data appropriateness by analysing the ODD (Operational Design Domain) coverage, i.e. whether indeed, collected data sets are representative (*G9.12*), and by assessing whether the collected data adheres to ML safety requirement (*G9.13*).

Figure 4 presents the refinement of *Design* strategy of the ML safety argumentation pattern. Certain safety requirements may determine the choice of a certain design of the used ML component. For example, the {*objects within 10 meters, classified as pedestrians with uncertainty 0.2 and higher, shall be ultimately considered as pedestrians*} requirement would have implications on design because it implicitly requests calculation of uncertainties. In order to achieve that, a possible design choice is to consider BNN (Bayesian Neural Network) or use MC dropout. The main goals that shall be achieved by the design of an ML component are presented in the following:

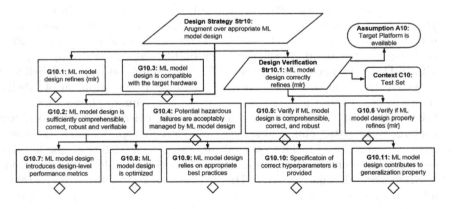

Fig. 4. Refinement of design strategy

- **G10.1: ML model design refines {mlr}.** The design shall respond to the needs that explicitly or implicitly result from ML safety requirement. An example of that was discussed few lines before, and can also be found in the use case section.
- **G10.2: ML model design is sufficiently comprehensible, correct, robust and verifiable.** *Comprehensibility* minimizes the risks of ambiguous interpretations by different ML experts, while *correctness* contributes to proper training of an ML model. *Robustness* enforces solution that is able to cope with erroneous input. Further, the *verifiability* allows to verify design for example by including additional layers in an NN for the sake of learning NN patterns. This goal is further refined into several subgoals. *G10.7* refers to an introduction of performance metrics (formerly known as KPIs - Key Performance Indicators) in a design. Next, *G10.8* strives for optimization, regarding properties of ML design such as performance, availability or reliability. Further, goal *G10.9* advocates reliance on well known, proven designs/ML algorithms, to solve specific problem. *G10.10* concerns the most important aspect of design, i.e. hyperparameters. The last subgoal *G10.11* refers to generalization aspect which is highly influenced by a proper design.
- **G10.3: ML model design is compatible with the target hardware.** The component design shall be executable on a target hardware platform. For instance, the target hardware shall sustain computational requirements that are induced by a certain design choice.
- **G10.4: Potential hazardous failures are acceptably managed by ML model design.** Detection and mitigation mechanisms for ensuring the operation in case of failures shall be provided in the design.

Figure 5 presents the argumentation about the safety of an ML component by referring to implementation and training activities. An ultimate artifact of these two is an ML model. Following the standard-mandated objectives for HW and software implementation, the ML model implementation shall integrate good practices (see *G11.2*). For example, the ML model should be implemented in Python or in a strongly typed language such as C++. Further, the usage of qualified/certified tools is highly advised. Another good practice, targeted by *G11.4*, is the usage of an appropriate training platform to assure that functional and non-functional properties of a trained model will sustain on a target platform. Next, we present the goals supporting the claim about the verification of the trained model:

- **G11.5: ML model is robust.** First, the ML model shall be evaluated against predefined performance metrics (see *G11.10* goal). There exist numerous performance metrics that may be used to reason about robustness of ML model. The purpose of this goal is to find those relevant and use them. Similarly to when software is developed, *G11.11* requests that corner cases shall be considered during training. Corner case involves variables or situations at extreme levels and gives high probability to result in error behavior, and a defect of the ML model under test. Additionally to corner cases, one has

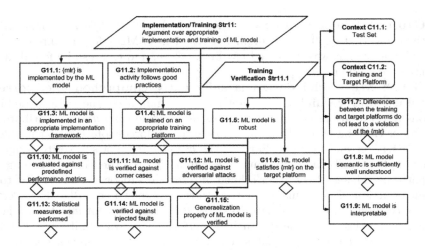

Fig. 5. Refinement of training strategy

to consider adversarial attacks (Goal *G11.12*), which pose another threat to robustness of ML models. Adding an imperceptible non-random perturbation to a source test can fool the ML model under test. Further, the usage of statistical measures and the execution of fault injection shall be argued. Fault injection may concern different aspects, e.g. erroneous input data, or sudden interrupt during ML model operation.

- **G11.6: ML model satisfies {mlr} on the target platform.** The ML model executed on target platform delivers the desired output.
- **G11.7: Differences between the training and target platforms do not lead to a violation of the {mlr}.** Similarly to *G11.4*, this goal leverages awareness of possible issues due to usage of different platforms for training and execution of an ML model.
- **G11.8: ML model semantic is sufficiently well understood.** The semantics of an ML model supports the reasoning about its performance.
- **G11.9: ML is interpretable.** Apart from ML model semantics, it is also desirable to be able to interpret its decision making process. In case of rule-based approaches or neural symbolic integration, this task is easier. However, when NNs are used, the problem becomes more challenging. There are however ongoing works, which for instance try to find intermediate representation of NN model, to be able to interpret it.

5   Evaluation

The objective of this section is to showcase how the proposed GSN pattern can be used for the construction of an argumentation fragment addressing the fulfillment of safety requirements by an ML-based component. In this work, we consider as the system of interest (SoI) a pedestrian avoidance system. This system is built with several components, software or hardware based, among which there is also a machine learning component responsible for pedestrian detection. The top most safety goal assigned to the SoI is that *"pedestrian avoidance system is safe in a given context"*. Starting from this goal, we model the safety case of the system by using the patterns proposed by Carlan and Gallina [6], whereas for the ML component we use the pattern presented in this paper. Subsection 5.1 provides more details about the considered pedestrian avoidance system and in particular about the ML component for pedestrian detection, whereas the application of the pattern is shown in Subsect. 5.2. The safety case for pedestrian avoidance system in a form of a GSN model made in D-Case tool[1] (together with images of the model diagrams), developed using complete set of patterns introduced in [6] and the pattern provided in this work, can be viewed under the link provided in the footnote[2]. This shows how the complete pattern may be used, but also feasibility of finding evidences for claims defined within the pattern.

5.1 Description of Pedestrian Detection Component

The main functionality of the ML component is to detect pedestrians (i.e., 2D bounding box detection of pedestrians) based on the analysis of video data acquired from a single camera. In Fig. 6, an illustration of the perception pipeline with its main building blocks and intermediate interfaces is provided.

Fig. 6. Perception pipeline with its main building blocks including the ML component

The aim of the perception pipeline is to match the 2D ground-truth bounding boxes "as well as possible". This means that ideally a single bounding box for each visible pedestrian is returned, with accurately estimated coordinates and dimensions. The steps of the pipeline are presented in Fig. 6.

The ML component is realized by the Single Shot MultiBox Detector (SSD) [15], which is a Convolutional Neural Network (CNN) and which was shown to have a high potential for classification tasks [15]. SSD enables multiclass classification of various objects with a localization of objects within a given

---

[1] https://www.jst.go.jp/crest/crest-os/tech/D-CaseEditor/index-e.html.
[2] https://download.fortiss.org/public/pedestrian-avoidance-safety-case.zip.

380   E. Wozniak et al.

frame. The network receives pre-processed raw image data and feeds the image into the network. In the end, the network performs both classification and localization (i.e., providing a bounding box for a detected pedestrian) in one forward pass.

5.2 Safety Argumentation of ML for Pedestrian Detection

The initial safety goal assigned to pedestrian avoidance system results in subgoals which emerge by applying the GSN patterns from Carlan and Gallina [6]. At the technology level, [6] provides a pattern for arguing about the refinement of technical safety requirements (i.e. requirements at the system level) into SW or HW safety requirements. This work, according to the principle of perceiving ML as a 3rd kind of technology, extends this strategy by considering also ML safety requirements (i.e. requirements allocated to ML component). A possible such ML safety requirement could be *MLR_001*: *"having as an input raw image data, pedestrians detection component returns a bounding box for each perceived pedestrian within the 20 m range, with accurately estimated coordinates and dimensions"*.

Figure 7 represents an instantiation of the GSN pattern proposed in this paper. For the sake of simplicity and to avoid redundant information, parts of the GSN model (represented with the dashed box) were removed from the figure. The removed parts contain goals from the GSN pattern, which are not specific to the ML safety requirement. As our system of interest has ASIL D assigned, all the safety goals specified in our pattern shall be demonstrated to be satisfied. In case of different ASIL assignment, it has to be decided what would be the

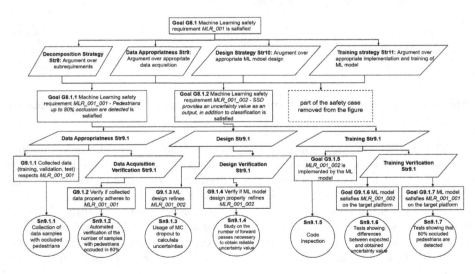

Fig. 7. Partial instantiation of the proposed safety case pattern for the Pedestrian Detection component

sufficient subset of goals to achieve, while each goal shall be supported by at least one evidence. For instance, *G9.2* may be argued by comparing outcome of automated labeling to human-specified labels.

Due to space restrictions, in Fig. 7 we only present two subrequirements of *MLR_001*. Requirement *MLR_001_001* implicitly states that the gathered data shall consider cases with occluded pedestrians. Later, it is important to verify whether indeed, the trained model can properly classify occluded pedestrians. *MLR_001_002* has primarily implications on the design, and hence it is supported by the *Design Str.*, but also *Impl/Training Str.* as it has to be verified if the feature of calculating uncertainty was indeed implemented, and whether it works, i.e. ML model provides correct values.

6   Conclusions and Future Work

This paper presented a GSN-based pattern for arguing about the correct implementation of safety-critical functionality by an ML component. The patterns proposed in [6], together with the pattern presented in this work, provide a complete framework to build a safety case for automotive systems, even if parts of their functionality rely on ML technology.

One limitation of this work is that, similarly to related works, it does not reason about the completeness of an argumentation provided by the proposed pattern. Neither does it make a claim that proposed set of goals and strategies is ultimate. Completeness in this case is non-quantifiable and can be achieved by an overall consensus of stakeholders interested in safety of ML-based solutions. Such consensus may result in standardization as it was achieved for SW and HW-based systems within ISO 26262. Consequently this pattern draws from related works and projects from the domain of AI safety, such as KI Absicherung[3], to form goals and strategies.

To this end, in order to provide further support in the construction of a safety case, future work shall address the following aspects. First, the manner how different ASIL levels influence an ultimate selection of the goals defined within the proposed pattern should be examined. For instance, verification of an ML model against corner cases may no longer be necessary if the ML model delivers functionality of lower criticality, e.g. gestures recognition to control the radio. Second, further possible types of evidence to support claims shall be investigated due to the constant advances in the area of ML. Finally, the elicitation of safety requirements for ML-based components remains a challenge that still needs to be addressed.

---

[3] Bundesministerium für Wirtschaft und Energie, Project KI Absicherung (eng. AI Safety) https://www.ki-absicherung.vdali.de/.

References

1. McDermid, J., Jia, Y., Habli, I.: Towards a framework for safety assurance of autonomous systems. In: Proceedings of the Workshop on Artificial Intelligence Safety, vol. 2419. CEUR-WS.org (2019)
2. ISO 26262: Road vehicles - Functional safety (2011)
3. ISO/PAS 21448: Road vehicles - Safety of the intended functionality (2019)
4. Bloomfield, R., Bishop, P.: Safety and assurance cases: past, present and possible future – an Adelard perspective. In: Dale, C., Anderson, T. (eds.) Making Systems Safer, pp. 51–67. Springer, London (2010). https://doi.org/10.1007/978-1-84996-086-1_4
5. The Assurance Case Working Group (ACWG) - Goal Structuring Notation Community Standard Version 2, January 2018
6. Carlan, C., Gallina, B.: Enhancing state-of-the-art safety case patterns to support change impact analysis. In: 30th European Safety and Reliability Conference, November 2020. http://www.es.mdh.se/publications/5789-
7. Picardi, C., Hawkins, R., Paterson, C., Habli, I.: A pattern for arguing the assurance of machine learning in medical diagnosis systems. In: Romanovsky, A., Troubitsyna, E., Bitsch, F. (eds.) SAFECOMP 2019. LNCS, vol. 11698, pp. 165–179. Springer, Cham (2019). https://doi.org/10.1007/978-3-030-26601-1_12
8. Picardi, C., Paterson, C., Hawkins, R., Calinescu, R., Habli, I.: Assurance argument patterns and processes for machine learning in safety-related systems. In: Proceedings of the Workshop on Artificial Intelligence Safety, Series CEUR Workshop Proceedings, vol. 2560, pp. 23–30. CEUR-WS.org (2020)
9. Burton, S., Gauerhof, L., Sethy, B.B., Habli, I., Hawkins, R.: Confidence arguments for evidence of performance in machine learning for highly automated driving functions. In: Romanovsky, A., Troubitsyna, E., Gashi, I., Schoitsch, E., Bitsch, F. (eds.) SAFECOMP 2019. LNCS, vol. 11699, pp. 365–377. Springer, Cham (2019). https://doi.org/10.1007/978-3-030-26250-1_30
10. Gauerhof, L., Munk, P., Burton, S.: Structuring validation targets of a machine learning function applied to automated driving. In: Gallina, B., Skavhaug, A., Bitsch, F. (eds.) SAFECOMP 2018. LNCS, vol. 11093, pp. 45–58. Springer, Cham (2018). https://doi.org/10.1007/978-3-319-99130-6_4
11. Salay, R., Czarnecki, K.: Using machine learning safely in automotive software: an assessment and adaption of software process requirements in ISO 26262. CoRR, abs/1808.01614 (2018). http://arxiv.org/abs/1808.01614
12. Rudolph, A., Voget, S., Mottok, J.: A consistent safety case argumentation for artificial intelligence in safety related automotive systems. In: ERTS 2018, Series Proceedings of 9th European Congress on Embedded Real Time Software and Systems, ERTS 2018, January 2018
13. Putzer, H.J., Wozniak, E.: A structured approach to trustworthy autonomous/cognitive systems. arXiv preprint arXiv:2002.08210 (2020)
14. DKE: Dke deutsche kommission elektrotechnik elektronik informationstechnik in din und vde - "dke/ak 801.0.8 spezifikation und entwurf autonomer/kognitiver systeme" (2020)
15. Liu, W., et al.: SSD: single shot multibox detector. In: Leibe, B., Matas, J., Sebe, N., Welling, M. (eds.) ECCV 2016. LNCS, vol. 9905, pp. 21–37. Springer, Cham (2016). https://doi.org/10.1007/978-3-319-46448-0_2

Structuring the Safety Argumentation for Deep Neural Network Based Perception in Automotive Applications

Gesina Schwalbe[1]([⊠]) [ID], Bernhard Knie[2,7], Timo Sämann[3], Timo Dobberphul[4], Lydia Gauerhof[5], Shervin Raafatnia[6], and Vittorio Rocco[7]

[1] Continental AG, Regensburg, Germany
`gesina.schwalbe@continental-corporation.com`
[2] Automotive Safety Technologies GmbH, Wolfsburg, Germany
[3] Valeo Schalter und Sensoren GmbH, Kronach, Germany
[4] Volkswagen AG, Wolfsburg, Germany
[5] Corporate Research Robert Bosch GmbH, Renningen, Germany
[6] Robert Bosch GmbH, Stuttgart-Weilimdorf, Germany
[7] Università di Roma Tor Vergata, Rome, Italy

Abstract. Deep neural networks (DNNs) are widely considered as a key technology for perception in high and full driving automation. However, their safety assessment remains challenging, as they exhibit specific insufficiencies: *black-box nature, simple performance issues, incorrect internal logic,* and *instability.* These are not sufficiently considered in existing standards on safety argumentation. In this paper, we systematically establish and break down safety requirements to argue the sufficient absence of risk arising from such insufficiencies. We furthermore argue why diverse evidence is highly relevant for a safety argument involving DNNs, and classify available sources of evidence. Together, this yields a generic approach and template to thoroughly respect DNN specifics within a safety argumentation structure. Its applicability is shown by providing examples of methods and measures following an example use case based on pedestrian detection.

Keywords: Automated driving · Safety case · Deep neural networks

1 Introduction

Deep neural networks can solve tasks which cannot be easily specified, involving high dimensional input spaces. They promise to be an alternative to rule-based algorithms for environment perception in autonomous driving, like pedestrian detection. However, their safety assessment in the automotive context remains challenging: DNNs exhibit specific *insufficiencies*, that can lead to hazardous failures not covered by existing safety standards [15, B.2, p. 34] (see discussion in Sect. 2). For completeness, a safety case must cover the known, technology specific insufficiencies, which might involve specialized sources of evidence. A

© Springer Nature Switzerland AG 2020
A. Casimiro et al. (Eds.): SAFECOMP 2020 Workshops, LNCS 12235, pp. 383–394, 2020.
https://doi.org/10.1007/978-3-030-55583-2_29

structured, two-fold approach towards this challenge for the use of DNNs is presented in this work. Section 3 features the top-down part: *DNN insufficiencies* known from literature are structured (*black-box property, simple lack of generalization, incorrect internal logic*, and *instability*), to derive DNN specific safety requirements, which then are broken down into sub-requirements (see Fig. 1). Section 4 provides the bottom-up part: The influence of DNN insufficiencies on the different types of evidence (development, system level, and V&V) is investigated. According to this, a structure for DNN related evidence is suggested (see Fig. 2). Our concrete contributions towards safety critical DNN applications are as follows:

- A template to structure the safety argumentation part specific to DNNs is developed in the form of safety requirements and evidence categories. The structured approach facilitates coverage not only of known sources of evidence but also of known DNN specific insufficiencies.
- For the suggested evidence classes, typical examples of methods and measures are given. As a running example, the automated driving use case pedestrian detection is used.

Scope. As a running example use case, an automotive pedestrian perception and successive control function for an emergency braking automation is assumed, with perception realized by a DNN. With the architectural concept inspired by the STAMP/STPA model [18], hazards could be caused by a late, early, or misdetection of pedestrians by the DNN. We here want to focus on misdetections. The failures of hardware and software implementations, as well as non-DNN-specific SOTIF aspects are not considered (see e.g. [8] on how to structure the validity of assumptions). Concentrating on a first structure, the evaluation of the contribution of specific evidence methods is reserved for future work. This also holds for system architectural aspects like redundancy.

2 Related Work

Completeness of a safety argument requires that all insufficiencies of the used technology that might lead to malfunctioning are considered. However, established safety standards do not yet sufficiently cover DNN specific aspects. The automotive functional safety standard [13] focuses on failures emerging from hardware and traditional software, and few of the suggested methods are applicable to DNNs [21]. The standard on safety of the intended functionality (SOTIF) [15] extends this towards failures caused by foreseeable misuse, environment, and performance limitations of complex sensoric systems [15, Table 1]—as of today not considering DNN specific limitations in detail. The same holds for the available domain specific draft standards that collect best-practice methods for design as well as verification and validation (V&V). Examples for driving automation are the white paper [31], and the UL4600 [28]; for aviation the report [5]; and national activities are e.g. the German DIN SPEC 13266 [6] on computer vision systems. We would like to amend the above bottom-up, evidence-driven approaches with a top-down, insufficiency-oriented perspective. For this we unify following previous diverse work of the authors. DNN specific safety concerns and insufficiencies were collected in [22] and [30]. The product argumentation aspects handled here are built upon [24]. A collection of evidences was provided in [25]. And our evidence structuring can be considered a refinement of [3], who identified six types of evidence required for confidence in a safety requirement.

3 Respecting DNN Insufficiencies in Safety Requirements

The moment any safety load rests upon the functionality of a DNN, it is required to either function accurately or provide reliable failure indication for mitigation measures (see Sect. 4). Hazardous misbehavior could e.g. be overlooking a pedestrian (false negative) leading to a crash, or ghost detections (false positive) leading to unnecessary braking and rear crash. Usual assessment investigates DNN behavior (i.e. generalization ability) according to human "understanding" of the task, which includes expected decision boundaries, corner cases, and continuity of the solution. This introduces a human bias to the assessment: e.g. , an assessor will expect an algorithm to react similar on examples that he or she assumes similar or identical. DNNs—other than manually designed algorithms—are not tied to such assumptions, as will be discussed in the lack of explainability in Sect. 3.1. For the sake of completeness of a safety argument, such assumptions must be validated and avoided. To achieve this, we suggest to derive DNN related safety requirements from types of DNN specific generalization issues. This will include issues both on the semantic level, i.e. describable in natural language; and on the non-semantic level. In Sect. 3.1 we summarize and categorize known DNN insufficiencies from literature, from which generic safety requirements are derived in Sect. 3.2 (see Fig. 1).

3.1 DNN Insufficiencies

DNN insufficiencies are properties of trained DNN models inherent to their technology, and with negative impacts for the use in safety-critical systems [22]. Structured overviews of DNN insufficiencies can be found e.g. in [22] and [30]. For the sake of our arguments, we consider two super-categories of DNN insufficiencies: The *black-box property* of DNNs indirectly infringing the safety case, and generalization issues which can directly cause hazardous failures. Lack of operational efficiency [22] concerning hardware and implementation dependent aspects (inference time, memory consumption) are not considered.

The black-box property of DNNs refers to their *lack of explainability*. DNNs use learned features to derive their predictions. These are extracted from data representations rather than the semantic content of the input. This flexibility is one of their major benefits for hard-to-specify perception applications: For example, the representation of a pedestrian in all its varieties cannot be completely semantically specified such that it could always be recognized by a rule-based

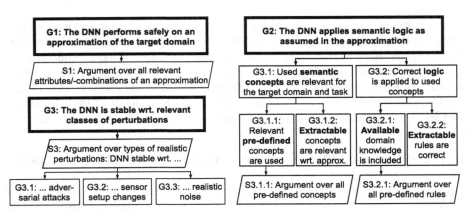

Fig. 1. Safety requirements (**goals** G) and decomposition **strategies** (S) derived in Sect. 3.2 in goal structuring notation [26].

algorithm. The flexibility comes at a cost: The learned features and their correlations are not necessarily comprehensible for humans, or even counterintuitive [9,30]. The high-dimensional internal structures of DNNs further hinder interpretable representations, which are be needed for traditional inspection and test case selection.

Lack of generalization ability summarizes *performance limitations* [15, 3.9] which can cause erroneous output. Generalization here means the performance on an unseen test set relative to that of the training set, as an estimate for the performance in the field. We suggest the following categorization: simple generalization issues, logical issues, and stability issues. The *simple generalization ability* refers to the performance on input data which is *semantically close* to the training data. This means the distributions of few semantic attributes like weather condition are changed compared to the training data. Reasons for a simple lack of generalization can be manifold, e.g. memorization of the training data, underfitting, or a underrepresentation of attributes in the training data. For example, if only few training samples feature rain, the DNN performance in rainy conditions may be very low. Another issue can be a *lack of internal logic*: The internal representation and reasoning a DNN applies originate from correlations in the training data, and may be wrong. This leads to errors that generalize according to semantic rules. For example, due to a bias in the data, a DNN may predict pedestrians not based on physiological features, but below all traffic lights. This *lack of reasoning* may already be obvious from a *lack of the internal representation* if no indicative features of pedestrians are included. Lastly, DNNs suffer from a *lack of stability* against *(slight) perturbations*—possibly imperceptible slight changes to an image that do not change the semantic information. Fairly easy-to-find perturbations may change the output of a DNN drastically and unpredictably [1]. Perturbation types and sources are manifold, e.g. : permanent or temporary sensor setup changes [3]; adversarial attacks applied in the real world or at pixel level (see taxonomy in [1]); and noise from domain (fog), sensor (dust, dirt), or intrinsic noise (faulty pixels, transmission error).

3.2 Derived Safety Requirements

We suggest to associate to each lack of generalization ability a safety requirement to mitigate it. The first is mitigation of the lack of simple generalization ability: The DNN should perform safely on a semantic approximation of the input domain, i.e. on a subset that that covers relevant semantic aspects (Fig. 1, G1). This means both a sufficient (weighted) overall performance, and sufficient performance on *each* safety critical subset (S1). Especially, one needs to argue separately over all relevant attributes and attribute combinations. In the case of pedestrian detection, such attributes could be age, occlusion, weather etc. The challenge of this semantic input space coverage is discussed later in Sect. 4.3.

When testing, the behavior of a function is interpolated from test samples. Here, implicit assumptions are made, like a certain stability or invariance of the function. For example, if the DNN detects a pedestrian, it should still do so if a non-related object like a far traffic light is changed. On a semantic level, this requires that the DNN applies semantic logic as assumed in the semantic approximation specified before (Fig. 1, G2). Sub-requirements are that relevant features or concepts are internally represented (G3.1), and that the logic/reasoning applied to them is correct (G3.2). In the case of both reasoning and concepts, one can either formally verify specified ones (G & S3.x.1), or manually inspect extracted ones (G3.x.2, see verification in Sect. 4.3). Interpolation assumptions may not only fail on a semantic level, but also due to instabilities. Therefore, the last goal is that the DNN behavior is stable in the input domain with respect to relevant slight perturbations (Fig. 1, G3). It remains a challenge to identify all safety relevant, i.e. realistic, perturbations (S3 and G3.1–3).

4 Respecting DNN Insufficiencies in Evidences

We categorize and will further structure two major types of evidence for sufficient safety: *Detection and measurement*, which is obtained via V&V; and *prevention and mitigation*, which can be subdivided into best-practice measures for item creation, and reduction of the safety load via system level mechanisms (see Fig. 2). In the following, this structure is detailed, and example methods are provided. Furthermore, we will discuss the challenges imposed by DNN insufficiencies with the result that V&V alone cannot provide sufficient confidence about safety. Best-practice cannot fully compensate this, due to the lack of field experience with DNNs in automated driving. Thus, our conclusion is that all types of evidence should be considered (compare [3]).

4.1 Mechanisms During Creation

The example use case is based on a DNN that is trained offline. For this kind of artificial intelligence component a creation process can be followed that consists

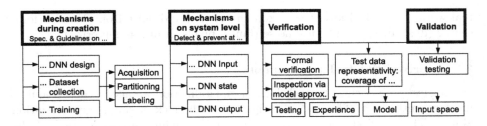

Fig. 2. Hierarchical overview of evidence categories identified in Sect. 4.

of three phases: *design of the network*, *data collection* and *training*. The corresponding intermediates are the raw network with initial values; labeled datasets for training, verification and validation; and the trained network.

Today's state of the art software engineering is requirement-based with design, implementation and verification steps following appropriate sets of rules and strategies to prove fulfillment of requirements and predefined goals (see the ISO/IEC 330xx family of standards, and [12]). Applying these general principles to the creation process of offline trained DNNs means: One has to define requirements and goals for intermediates in a design step, implement them, and prove their achievement by a verification step. Defining and complying to strategies and guidelines for certain activities supports the systematic achievement of goals and requirements where applicable.

This section structures types of requirements, goals, guidelines or strategies for the different creation phases and their intermediates, which were extracted from relevant and current references about reliable DNNs [3, 12, 22, 29–31]. Evidencing their fulfillment helps to argue the mitigation of DNN insufficiencies during its creation process. The examples aim to show the diversity of aspects, for details consult the referenced literature.

Design of the Network. The DNN design implicitly makes prior assumptions about the application, e.g. convolutional DNNs introduce translation invariance. A DNN respecting the following aspects helps to create a reliable and robust raw network as a stable starting point for the further phases.

DNN specification [31] containing requirements for: robustness of the algorithm [31]; the architectural design (including layer parameters) [22]; the DNN class [22]; the interfaces [12] with definition of the output space and input resolution [29] to enable the output of reliable confidence information [30]; weight initialization [25].

Design guidelines defining the unified language for the specification [29] and using best practices from established design approaches.

Data Collection. High quality datasets are essential to maximize the performance of trained networks, as they are the source for the learned features.

Dataset specification [31]*:* Considering the following aspects will minimize the insufficiencies arising from incomplete datasets: dataset quality, coverage and relevance [31]; dataset representativity [3,25]; sample classification and the corresponding equivalence classes [31]; corner cases and other boundaries [31]; dataset robustification and necessary perturbations [25]; dataset augmentation including adversarial examples and attribute randomization [22].

Data acquisition strategy [30] defining an adequate choice for data sources.

Data partitioning guidelines [30] giving rules how to divide the dataset into training, verification and validation data.

Labeling specification [31] High quality labeling is essential to maximize the quality of datasets. At least the following requirements should be considered to minimize insufficiencies from weak labeling: choice and boundaries of label classes [22]; labeling accuracy and quality [31]; adversarial examples [22].

Labeling guidelines [30] to ensure unified and exact labeling and to avoid labeling errors.

Training. The training practically decides on whether the available data (and further knowledge) is processed efficiently. This includes preventing e.g. over- and underfitting. Especially, training quality directly influences the DNN quality.

Training specification: Considering the following types of goals increases the probability of getting the intended output of the training phase: hyperparameters (batch size, regularization, loss function, etc.) [31]; active learning [22]; domain randomization [22]; robustness; constraints for internal logic [25]; well-calibrated uncertainties [22]; accuracy and failure rates [3].

Training strategy defining the procedure of adjustments of training parameters and the training sequence and iterations.

Hyperparameters tuning guidelines [31] to systematically adjust the parameters to achieve the training goals.

Configuration management strategy [12] to establish training baselines [31]. This enables analyzing the training steps, setting termination points, and recovering optimal stages.

Further modification activities for deploying, optimization, compression or quantization have not the goal to increase the reliability of a DNN and therefore, no arguments for mitigation of insufficiencies are derived conducting these activities. The challenge is to prove that all assumptions and safety arguments are still valid after these further modifications.

4.2 Mechanisms on Component and System Level

Besides the mechanisms during DNN creation, other mechanisms, such as detection of causes for performance limitations, can be applied to decrease the safety load on the DNN and increase the overall safety. While detection mechanisms are the first measure to be aware of an potential error, they can be used for further handling, such as prevention, mitigation or even forecast. Examples are to filter the output, switch to alternative predictors, or increase caution, e.g. the controller initiates a gentle slow down if the prediction quality is unsure. We suggest to structure the mechanisms with respect to their intervening point: input, DNN and output of DNN. Some methods make use of their combination.

Input Before providing the input to DNN, *modification* of the input can decrease the chance for an error, e.g. by normalization, denoising, filtering, or removal of non-semantic features causing adversarial examples [25]. Furthermore, the input of DNN might be *monitored* for causes of performance limitations. For example, detection of adversarial examples [4] causing instability errors, or out-of-distribution samples, i.e. samples very different from the training data, can indicate a to-be-expected error within the pedestrian detection.

DNN Error *detection* and *mitigation* methods can be applied on the DNN itself. If the exact error is known, e.g. from input monitoring and estimation, the *DNN output might be corrected* by an additional output [23]. Uncertainty measures of the DNN, indicating the current inherent uncertainty state of the function [11,17], are treated as promising safety mechanisms. For example, the output of the DNN can be dropped in the case of high uncertainty. Otherwise, the uncertainty level should be forwarded to the next component [25].

Output The output and the behavior of the DNN can be *monitored* to detect errors. In general, anomaly detection [7] as well as plausibility checks might be applied to the DNN output to detect errors, e.g. pedestrians cannot vanish in clear sight. For doing so, the processing information of the input within the DNN is compared to the behavior for clean data. An example method is ODIN [19]: By using temperature scaling (calibration of the DNN confidence output) and exploring the behavior for small perturbations around the input, ODIN can detect samples to which the network might not be capable to generalize. Another method, GraN [20], is introduced for detecting misclassified data samples in general, and adversarial examples. It investigates the norm of the gradient of the DNN function on the current input-output combination. Other than monitoring, the DNN output might be *modified*, e.g. further processed and fused with other signals. For example, when fusing with outputs of different DNNs as part of an *ensemble*, the final output might increase the performance and reduce errors, even though ensuring sufficient model diversity for the latter may be hard [25]. A *fusion* with signals gathered from other sensors also result in redundancies that might have different limitations.

4.3   Verification and Validation

Verification activity should determine whether the specified requirements are met [13, 3.180]. and focuses on known insufficiencies [15, 3.18]. Validation tries to identify new insufficiencies affecting safety, and provides assurance, that the safety requirements are adequate [13, 3.148] in the sense of correctness and completeness. In the following, attention is concentrated on DNN-specific requirements as derived in Sect. 3.2, other than e.g. requirements on the system-level safety mechanisms.

In practice, the terms verification and validation are hard to distinguish and share the following common challenges. One is the *open-world* domain typical for DNNs, which exhibits many rare scenes and may change over time. Being high-dimensional, partly non-semantic, and complex, open world domains cannot be explored or specified thoroughly using human interpretable attributes [30].

The goal of test data is to effectively reveal inconsistencies between expected and DNN output that indicate DNN insufficiencies. Near misses are less valuable for this than implausible errors, imposing a challenge for defining *performance indicators*. For effectivity, high *test data representativity* is required, which is another V&V challenge. We propose to handle this as a coverage problem and suggest as coverage criteria both the semantic features of the input space, and the DNN-specific ones, meaning coverage of DNN state-space. The latter is hard to achieve formally due to the enormous size of the state-space and since the sub-space of valid samples is unknown. Thus, semi-formal exploration of the state-space should further aim for coverage of DNN-specific weaknesses: coverage of instability sources, and of previous counterexamples. For *semantic input space coverage*, all relevant semantic aspects of the objective need to be statistically covered, especially cases defining the true decision boundary (e.g. high occlusion). Ontologies such as [2] are a good starting point to find such aspects. Challenges remain: the real distribution of values may be hard to approximate due to the open-world context or a lack of real samples; and validating realism of synthetic samples is an unsolved problem [30]. The model decision boundaries and decision-relevant features not necessarily agree with those assumed by humans. To reveal related weaknesses, a high *coverage of the model state space* is required. This can be done globally, e.g. via coverage of neuron activation patterns [27]; or locally by estimating the expected distance to the decision boundaries (see verification). A lack of instability imposes a major challenge for the *validity range* of test samples: Due to the black-box property of correlations, we may not be able to retrace their cause, wherefore the behavior out of the validity range cannot be guaranteed or even estimated. The validity range of a sample includes how far and how stable the nearest sample with significantly different behavior is. A distance metric can be L2-distance, as used in the formal verification example in [16]. Lastly, DNNs are prone to regression as long as the effect of parameter adaptions on the global behavior cannot be controlled. Hence, *previous counterexamples* should be tested. Prominent sources are e.g. earlier test phases also from similar tasks, and operation experience like (near) failure reports and accident databases.

Verification. The types of verification activities from ISO 26262[13, 3.180] that are in principle applicable to DNNs are [21]: *walk-through or inspection* of the algorithm, *testing and semi-formal verification*, and *formal verification* requiring a formal notation that is linked to intermediate outputs of the considered model. A main verification specific challenge is to provide methods applicable to DNNs. For current formal verification methods, requirements must be formulated as range constraints on neuron outputs which is seldom possible due to the black-box property. Provers, e.g. solvers like Reluplex [16], are mostly limited in architecture types and speed due to DNN sizes. By definition, inspection and walk-through require interpretable approximations of the model. A standard but less expressive example is to indicate the attention of the DNN on selected samples via heatmapping. Alternatively, the internal logic can be assessed using local or global rule extraction, but methods that can deal with up-to-date DNN complexity are scarce [10]. For details on the example methods see [25].

Validation. Ensuring that all safety-relevant factors have been taken into account is already a non-trivial task for non-AI-based functions due to the open-world context. The state-of-the-art validation approach in automotive is to evaluate the function on a large, randomly collected amount of real-world data ([14, 8.4.3.4], [31, Sect. 3.3.2]). The goal is to test the problem space for safety-relevant factors. However, the effectivity of explorative testing decreases with increasing autonomy level, function and environment complexity: Statistical coverage is harder to achieve; given validity range problems, it is difficult to decide when enough variations of the same semantic content have been considered; and lastly, exploring features used by the DNN is infringed by the black-box problematic, which makes it impossible to specify, and thus cover, all decision-relevant features. The central activity for validating DNNs remains the collection of a (large and) representative test dataset, with emphasis on model state-space coverage.

The discussion above shows: V&V for DNNs cannot be separated clearly, and are challenged by the complexity coming along with DNNs. Especially due to the representativity and validity range problems, one cannot expect to gain sufficient confidence in safety only via V&V. One needs to address V&V at all development stages and even beyond.

5   Conclusion

Generic safety requirements and an evidence structure were suggested to include DNN specifics into a safety argument with a focus on completeness. Nevertheless, the structure revealed several open challenges and difficulties for a complete safety case for DNNs. Further research will refine the suggested argumentation on the proposed use case, fill the method gaps, and evaluate the contributions of the different methods to the overall risk reduction.

Acknowledgements. The research leading to the results presented above is funded by the German Federal Ministry for Economic Affairs and Energy within the project "KI Absicherung – Safe AI for automated driving". The authors would like to thank the consortium for the successful cooperation. Special thanks to Simon Burton, Horst Michael Groß (Ilmenau University of Technology, Neuroinformatics and Cognitive Robotics Lab), Christian Hellert, Fabian Hüger, Peter Schlicht, and Oliver Willers.

References

1. Assion, F., et al.: The attack generator: a systematic approach towards constructing adversarial attacks. In: Proceedings of the 2019 IEEE Conference on Computer Vision and Pattern Recognition Workshops (2019)
2. Bagschik, G., Menzel, T., Maurer, M.: Ontology based scene creation for the development of automated vehicles. In: Proceedings of the 2018 IEEE Intelligent Vehicles Symposium, pp. 1813–1820. IEEE (2018). https://doi.org/10.1109/IVS.2018.8500632
3. Burton, S., Gauerhof, L., Sethy, B.B., Habli, I., Hawkins, R.: Confidence arguments for evidence of performance in machine learning for highly automated driving functions. In: Romanovsky, A., Troubitsyna, E., Gashi, I., Schoitsch, E., Bitsch, F. (eds.) SAFECOMP 2019. LNCS, vol. 11699, pp. 365–377. Springer, Cham (2019). https://doi.org/10.1007/978-3-030-26250-1_30
4. Carlini, N., Wagner, D.: Adversarial examples are not easily detected: bypassing ten detection methods. In: Proceedings of the 10th ACM Workshop on Artificial Intelligence and Security, AISec 2017, pp. 3–14. Association for Computing Machinery (2017). https://doi.org/10.1145/3128572.3140444
5. Cluzeau, J.M., Henriquel, X., Rebender, G., et al.: Concepts of design assurance for neural networks. Technical report, European Union Aviation Safety Agency (EASA) (2020)
6. Deutsches Institut für Normung e.V.: DIN SPEC 13266:2020-04: Guideline for the development of deep learning image recognition systems. Beuth Verlag, 2020-04 edn, April 2020. https://doi.org/10.31030/3134557
7. Gauerhof, L., Gu, N.: Reverse variational autoencoder for visual attribute manipulation and anomaly detection. In: Winter Application Conference on Applications of Computer Vision (2020)
8. Gauerhof, L., Munk, P., Burton, S.: Structuring validation targets of a machine learning function applied to automated driving. In: Gallina, B., Skavhaug, A., Bitsch, F. (eds.) SAFECOMP 2018. LNCS, vol. 11093, pp. 45–58. Springer, Cham (2018). https://doi.org/10.1007/978-3-319-99130-6_4
9. Geirhos, R., Rubisch, P., Michaelis, C., Bethge, M., Wichmann, F.A., Brendel, W.: ImageNet-trained CNNs are biased towards texture; increasing shape bias improves accuracy and robustness. In: Proceedings of the 7th International Conference on Learning Representations (2018)
10. Hailesilassie, T.: Rule extraction algorithm for deep neural networks: a review. CoRR abs/1610.05267 (2016)
11. Henne, M., Schwaiger, A., Roscher, K., Weiss, G.: Benchmarking uncertainty estimation methods for deep learning with safety-related metrics. In: Proceedings of the Workshop on Artificial Intelligence Safety, vol. 2560, pp. 83–90. CEUR-WS.org (2020)
12. ISO/IEC JTC 1/SC 7: ISO/IEC/IEEE 12207:2017: Systems and Software Engineering—Software Life Cycle Processes, 1 edn. (2017)
13. ISO/TC 22/SC 32: ISO 26262-1:2018(En): Road Vehicles—Functional Safety—Part 1: Vocabulary, ISO 26262:2018(En), vol. 1. 2 edn. (2018)
14. ISO/TC 22/SC 32: ISO 26262-4:2018(En): Road Vehicles—Functional Safety—Part 4: Product Development at the System Level, ISO 26262:2018(En), vol. 4. 2 edn. (2018)
15. ISO/TC 22/SC 32: ISO/PAS 21448:2019(En): Road Vehicles—Safety of the Intended Functionality (2019)

16. Katz, G., Barrett, C., Dill, D.L., Julian, K., Kochenderfer, M.J.: Reluplex: an efficient SMT solver for verifying deep neural networks. In: Majumdar, R., Kunčak, V. (eds.) CAV 2017. LNCS, vol. 10426, pp. 97–117. Springer, Cham (2017). https://doi.org/10.1007/978-3-319-63387-9_5

17. Kendall, A., Gal, Y.: What uncertainties do we need in Bayesian deep learning for computer vision? In: Advances in Neural Information Processing Systems, vol. 30, pp. 5580–5590 (2017)

18. Leveson, N.: Engineering a Safer World: Systems Thinking Applied to Safety. Engineering Systems. MIT Press, Cambridge (2012)

19. Liang, S., Li, Y., Srikant, R.: Principled detection of out-of-distribution examples in neural networks. CoRR abs/1706.02690 (2017)

20. Lust, J., Condurache, A.: GraN: an efficient gradient-norm based detector for adversarial and misclassified examples. In: ESANN (2020). http://www.esann.org/node/8

21. Salay, R., Queiroz, R., Czarnecki, K.: An analysis of ISO 26262: using machine learning safely in automotive software. CoRR abs/1709.02435 (2017)

22. Sämann, T., Schlicht, P., Hüger, F.: Strategy to increase the safety of a dnn-based perception for HAD systems. CoRR abs/2002.08935 (2020)

23. Schorn, C., Guntoro, A., Ascheid, G.: Efficient on-line error detection and mitigation for deep neural network accelerators. In: Gallina, B., Skavhaug, A., Bitsch, F. (eds.) SAFECOMP 2018. LNCS, vol. 11093, pp. 205–219. Springer, Cham (2018). https://doi.org/10.1007/978-3-319-99130-6_14

24. Schwalbe, G., Schels, M.: Strategies for safety goal decomposition for neural networks. In: Abstracts 3rd ACM Computer Science in Cars Symposium (2019)

25. Schwalbe, G., Schels, M.: A survey on methods for the safety assurance of machine learning based systems. In: Proceedings of the 10th European Congress on Embedded Real Time Systems (2020)

26. SCSC Assurance Case Working Group: SCSC-141B: Goal Structuring Notation Community Standard (2018). https://scsc.uk/scsc-141B

27. Sun, Y., Wu, M., Ruan, W., Huang, X., Kwiatkowska, M., Kroening, D.: Concolic testing for deep neural networks. In: Proceedings of the 33rd ACM/IEEE International Conference on Automated Software Engineering, pp. 109–119. ACM (2018). https://doi.org/10.1145/3238147.3238172

28. Underwriters Laboratories, Edge Case Research: UL4600: Standard for Safety of Autonomous Products. Edge Case Research (2019)

29. Voget, S., Rudolph, A., Mottok, J.: A consistent safety case argumentation for artificial intelligence in safety related automotive systems. In: Proceedings of the 9th European Congress Embedded Real Time Systems (2018)

30. Willers, O., Sudholt, S., Raafatnia, S., Stephanie, A.: Safety concerns and mitigation approaches regarding the use of deep learning in safety-critical perception tasks. CoRR abs/2001.08001 (2020)

31. Wood, M., Robbel, P., Wittmann, D., et al.: Safety First for Automated Driving (2019). http://www.daimler.com/documents/innovation/other/safety-first-for-automated-driving.pdf

An Assurance Case Pattern
for the Interpretability of Machine
Learning in Safety-Critical Systems

Francis Rhys Ward$^{(\boxtimes)}$ and Ibrahim Habli

Assuring Autonomy International Programme, The University of York, York, UK
{Rhys.Ward,Ibrahim.Habli}@york.ac.uk

Abstract. Machine Learning (ML) has the potential to become widespread in safety-critical applications. It is therefore important that we have sufficient confidence in the safe behaviour of the ML-based functionality. One key consideration is whether the ML being used is interpretable. In this paper, we present an argument pattern, i.e. reusable structure, that can be used for justifying the sufficient interpretability of ML within a wider assurance case. The pattern can be used to assess whether the right interpretability method and format are used in the right context (time, setting and audience). This argument structure provides a basis for developing and assessing focused requirements for the interpretability of ML in safety-critical domains.

Keywords: Interpretability · Explainability · Machine learning · Artificial intelligence · Assurance · Safety · Safety-case

1 Introduction

Machine Learning (ML) algorithms are powerful tools and have applications in domains in which safety is a concern. One potential weakness of these algorithms is that they are often too complicated to understand - they may relate thousands of variables into patterns which cannot be understood by a human. This property is often referred to as the black-box problem. How can we accept these algorithms into safety-critical decision-making roles if we cannot understand how their decisions are made? [5,13] This problem has limited the growth of ML algorithms in areas such as healthcare [20,31].

A solution to this issue is to use ML algorithms which are more interpretable, or to try to explain their behaviour. In some sense an algorithm is interpretable if we can understand how it works and/or why it makes the decisions that it does make. [8] defines interpretability in the context of ML as 'the ability to explain or to present in understandable terms to a human' but notes that what constitutes an explanation is not well-defined. In practice, the term interpretability is used to refer to a number of distinct concepts [21]. A ML model may be said to be interpretable if the algorithm is simple enough for us to understand, otherwise there may be some post-hoc methods which can be used to interpret a black-box.

© Springer Nature Switzerland AG 2020
A. Casimiro et al. (Eds.): SAFECOMP 2020 Workshops, LNCS 12235, pp. 395–407, 2020.
https://doi.org/10.1007/978-3-030-55583-2_30

From a safety perspective, interpretability may help us to (1) understand the system retrospectively, i.e. to understand, with respect to a harm-causing action or decision, what went wrong, and why and (2) understand the system prospectively, i.e. to predict, mitigate, and prevent future harm-causing actions or decisions. But to what extent does machine learning need to be interpretable to provide assurance? To answer this question, we must decide on who needs to understand the system, what they need to understand, what types of interpretations are appropriate, and when do these interpretations need to be provided.

To this end, we present an argument pattern, i.e. reusable structure, that can be used for justifying the sufficient interpretability of ML within a wider assurance case. Structured argumentation is well-established in the safety-critical domain as a means for communicating, justifying and assessing confidence in properties of interest (e.g. risk reduction and acceptability). The pattern presents an explicit argument that can be used to assess whether the right interpretability method and format are used in the right context (time, setting and audience). We show how our pattern can be instantiated for assuring the interpretability of a system of neural networks intended for retinal disease diagnosis.

The following section provides a background to ML interpretability. In Sect. 3 we present an argument pattern for assuring that ML systems are interpretable. Then in Sect. 4 we motivate the need for interpretability in safety-critical ML systems.

2   A Brief Overview of Interpretability

There is a wealth of literature on interpretability of ML and AI [21], covering a wide range of philosophical and psychological perspectives [1,12,23,26]; the legal implications of (un)interpretable ML [4,11,30]; technical methods for interpreting different types of ML models [3,14,15,17,19,22,27,28]; and further discussions which try to bring some clarity to the field [7,20,21,29].

Lipton in [21] seeks to clarify the myriad different notions of interpretability of ML models in the literature - what interpretability means and why it is important. It is noted that interpretability is not a monolithic concept and relates to distinct ideas. The distinction is often made between methods which are intrinsically *transparent* and post-hoc methods that attempt to *explain* a model. We identify the following types of interpretability. A model/system is:

- **Transparent** if we understand **how it genuinely works** (mechanistically, at some level, for some part of the process). A transparent model is one which is inherently simple enough for humans to understand. For example, for a learned model, could a human take the inputs and generate the same outputs as the model (in reasonable time)?
- **Explainable** if we can understand **why** it makes the decisions that it does make by using some post-hoc analysis and/or *approximation*, covering:
  - **Global explainability** techniques which approximate the model with a simpler more transparent one. This simple approximate model is an explanation.

- **Local explainability** techniques which map inputs to outputs and identify important inputs. These help us to answer the question 'what were the important factors in this decision?'

We can categorize some of the features of these different types of interpretability. Transparency provides faithful representations of the model, whereas explainable methods are often approximations, or incomplete explanations. Hence, there is a spectrum which captures the level of fidelity of different types of interpretability. Some methods interpret the whole model (global) whereas some interpret individual decisions (local). Transparency can be seen as an intrinsic property of a model (it is either easy to understand or not, or some degree in between), whereas explainability techniques are post-hoc methods which require some extra effort to implement.

It may be impossible for some systems/models to be fully and completely interpretable. For instance, a neural network may have some local explainability in that we can map certain inputs to outputs. But this does not provide a complete picture of how the model works globally and it is not transparent. We are interested in sufficient levels of interpretability needed to assure safety in different contexts.

Table 1. Phased safety-argument development alongside ML life-cycle

Safety-argument phase	ML life-cycle stage	Interpretability needs
Preliminary	Data Management	Global/Local: Identify Weaknesses in Data
Interim 1	Model Learning	Global: Aid Model Design
Interim 2	Model Verification	Global/Local: Identify Weaknesses in Model
Operational	Model Deployment	Local: Understand Decisions

3   An Argument Structure for the Interpretability of ML

Safety arguments, or "safety cases", are a well-established method used to assure system properties in the field of safety engineering. [16] advocates a phased safety argument approach wherein a number of safety case versions are issued alongside the developing technology, enabling an evolving safety argument. This phased safety argument will inform, and be informed by, the development process. This can be combined with the ML life-cycle from [2], which discusses the assurance of the complex, iterative process starting with the collection of data used to train an ML model, and ending with the deployment of that model. A safety argument should evolve with the ML life-cycle, as in Table 1. Because of the cyclical nature of the ML life-cycle, interpretability at a later stage may bring to light flaws which can then be accounted for on the next iteration.

In Fig. 2, we define an argument pattern that explicitly addresses the interpretability assurance considerations, i.e. primary claims, argument strategies and evidence. The argument is represented using the pattern language of the Goal Structuring Notation (GSN) [16]. GSN is a graphical argumentation notation which explicitly represents the individual elements of a safety argument (claims, evidence, and context) and the relationships that exist between these elements. When the elements of GSN are linked together in a network they are described as a "goal structure". We draw heavily from [6] which presents a pattern for arguing the assurance of machine learning, with a focus on clinical diagnosis. The first step is to ask why the project needs interpretability and set the desired requirements that the project should satisfy (e.g. being able to investigate accidents see Sect. 4.1). Figure 1 shows a key for GSN.

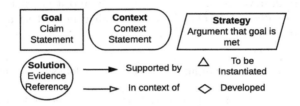

Fig. 1. GSN key

- **Goal** - these are the claims being made in the argument.
- **Context** - the relevant additional information to the argument.
- **Strategy** - the argument approach for the support of a claim.
- **Solution** - evidence reference that claims have been met.
- **Supported by** - (solid arrows) indicates inferential/evidential relationships.
- **In context of** - (hollow arrows) declares contextual relationships.
- **To be instantiated** attached to an element indicates that some part of the element's content is a variable that requires instantiation. Variables are declared using curled braces, such as {ML Model}.

3.1 Interpretability Claim

In Fig. 2, the starting point is the claim that the ML Model is sufficiently interpretable in the intended context. 'ML model', 'interpretable', and 'context' are variables in this claim to be instantiated As discussed in the previous section, the term 'interpretable' may refer to different types of interpretability. The substantiation of the 'ML model' will be the actual ML model being used, or a component of it, or the system as a whole - whatever needs to be interpreted. The context refers to the setting, time, and audience of the interpretation.

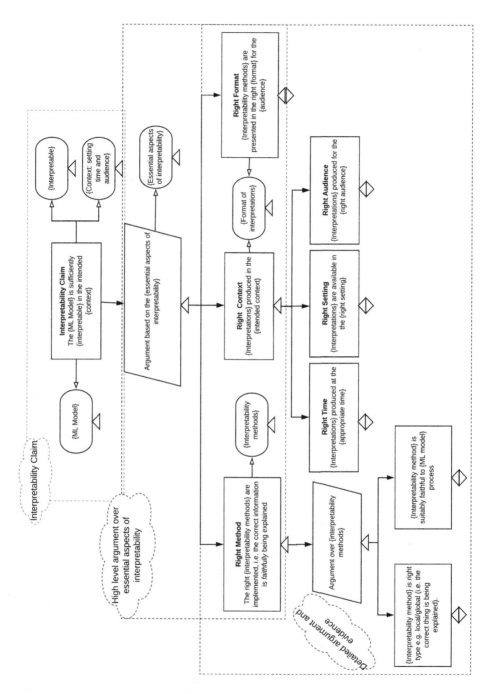

Fig. 2. General argument structure

3.2   High Level Argument

We identify three essential aspects of the interpretability argument, building on past work on context-aware systems [10]:

- Right Method - The right interpretability methods are implemented, i.e. the correct information is faithfully being explained.
- Right Context:
    - Time - Interpretations produced at the appropriate times.
    - Setting - Interpretations are available in the right setting.
    - Audience - Interpretations produced for the right audience.
- Right Format - The interpretability methods are presented in the right format for the audience.

A detailed argument over these essential aspects is presented in the next subsections.

3.3   Argument over Interpretability Methods

This is the argument that suitable interpretability methods have been implemented, a method may simply be choosing a transparent model, or employing some post-hoc explainability techniques. There are two parts to this argument, first that the methods provide the type of interpretability required to satisfy the high level interpretability claim (e.g. if the claim is that the ML model is locally explainable in the context of accidents then the methods must provide this local explainability). Secondly the interpretability methods must be suitably faithful to the model process; these methods may be approximations to the model and may therefore not be accurate interpretations in all cases [29]. The interpretability methods must satisfy some desired level of fidelity in the given context. Both of these being satisfied equates to the correct information being explained.

Once a set of interpretability methods has been proposed, evidence that these methods are sufficient for purpose must be gathered. There are at least three different things which must be evaluated with regard to interpretability: how satisfying and appropriate produced interpretations are to stakeholders; how faithful interpretations are to the actual model workings; and the relevance of the interpretation being given. There is some initial research on how to evaluate the interpretability of ML models. [25] outlines how levels of explainability can be measured with respect to different user groups. [8] proposes an evidence-based taxonomy of evaluation approaches for interpretability. These are ways in which interpretations can be evaluated with respect to how effective they are at *convincing users*. Whilst it is important that stakeholders are satisfied with interpretations, these interpretations also need to be an accurate depiction of how the system actually works.

Especially in safety-critical systems, it is important that interpretations, or explanations, of how a system works are not only convincing and satisfying but also reliably a faithful account of how the model is actually working. [28]

presents a technical method for evaluating the faithfulness of a certain kind of local explanation technique. These types of evaluation help users to understand how a model is genuinely working, even so far as the explanations can help users to gain enough insight to improve the model. [19] evaluates *fidelity* (faithfulness to the model) of explanations vs interpretability (how easy it is to understand) finding there are trade-offs between the two.

Recent work has highlighted the capacity of even high-fidelity explanations to mislead users [18]. Three key issues with current post-hoc methods, when optimised for fidelity, are described: i) they do not capture causal relationships; ii) they cannot choose between multiple (qualitatively different) high-fidelity explanations; iii) they can vary significantly with small perturbations of the input data. These problems lead to the possibility that current explainability techniques can actually mislead users. Importantly, explanations must also provide the most relevant information.

3.4   Argument over Context

For simplicity we split context into time, setting, and audience.

- **Right Time:** Interpretations must be provided at the right time to avoid being intrusive or confusing. Not every decision may need to be explained and some interpretations may be needed in real time whereas others may only need to be produced under specific circumstances. For example, a diagnostic system may need to provide local explanations to clinicians alongside every diagnosis prediction, whereas an autonomous vehicle may only need to provide an explanation when an incident has occurred.
- **Right Setting:** It is important that interpretations are usefully available to the audience in the correct setting. Consider again a diagnostic tool, interpretations must be available to doctors in the clinical setting alongside diagnosis predictions. It is not useful for engineers to be able to produce interpretations if the audience do not have access to them in the relevant setting.
- **Right Audience:** Interpretations must clearly be provided to the right people to satisfy the interpretability claim and to satisfy the motivations for interpretability, e.g. policy makers vs developers vs users.

3.5   Argument over the Format of Interpretations

The format of the interpretations is key. Once suitable methods for interpreting the system have been chosen, they must be presented in a format which is comprehensible and relevant to the audience. Section 3.3 discusses how to evaluate the extent to which interpretations are appropriate and satisfying to stakeholders and Sect. 4.4 outlines the needs of different stakeholders.

3.6   Example: Deep Learning for Diagnosis in Retinal Disease

We now examine a paper by DeepMind [9] that presents a system of two Neural Networks (NNs) working to predict retinal disease from scans of the eye. The paper purports to address the "black-box problem" by producing a midpoint result in the system. The first model takes as input a scan of the retina and produces a tissue-segmentation map. The second neural network takes the segmentation map and outputs a diagnosis and referral (with confidence levels). This process supplies some system-level transparency. We can instantiate this example in our argument structure as follows (Fig. 3):

Interpretability Claim: The desired type of interpretability is transparency at the level of the system logic, the system being the combination of the two NNs. The context is defined by: the setting - the retinal diagnosis pathway; the time that interpretations are produced - alongside the system diagnosis prediction; the audience - the retinal clinicians.

Argument Over Method: The method by which interpretability is produced is that the system structure, including the production of the segmentation map, closely resembles the normal decision-process used by clinicians. This means that the system logic is inherently comprehensible, i.e. transparent, to the retinal clinicians. Note that this is true even though the individual NNs being used are not interpreted in any way. This is clearly a faithful method of interpreting the system logic, as transparency of the system is by definition faithful (the interpretation of the system logic is the system logic itself).

Argument Over Context: The audience are the retinal clinicians, and they need interpretations of system behaviour in the clinical setting and alongside each system diagnosis prediction.

Argument Over Format: The format of the interpretation is the transparent system logic, including the segmentation map. Presumably, the same prediction accuracy results could have been achieved without including the mid-point output of the segmentation map. Including this step allows clinicians to understand the system logic, since the production and use of the segmentation map are part of the normal clinical process and are understood by the retinal clinicians.

In summary, the healthcare setting here is clearly safety-critical and the designers of this system have identified interpretability as a requirement of the system in order that clinicians are able to understand and verify the system's predictions. Even though the individual NNs used were not interpreted, the method still provided some transparency of the system logic to the retinal clinicians, increasing their understanding of, and trust in, the ML system.

4   Discussion: Key Safety Interpretability Questions

4.1   Why Do We Need Interpretability in Safety-Critical Domains?

There are many reasons why we should want our ML systems to be interpretable. Interpretability may:

- Increase **insight** into model behaviour (and into the operational domain).
- Identify **weaknesses** of the model, cases where the model under-performs.
- Enable the increase of **robustness** - i.e. assurance that the system will behave as intended in new environments/situations.

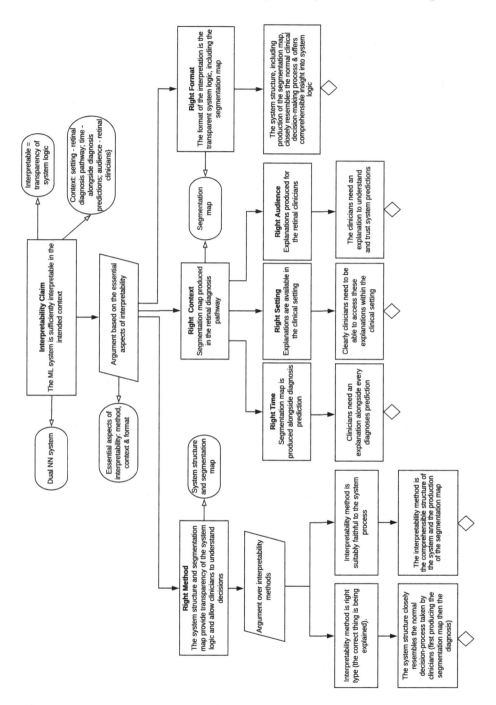

Fig. 3. DeepMind example

- Inform effective **improvements**/corrections.
- Protect against **unfair** models helping to avoid discrimination.
- Improve **trust** in the model and allow informed consent [31].

These advantages are beneficial in any domain of ML use. With regards to safety, interpretability is of interest for two key reasons:

- To understand the system retrospectively: to understand, with respect to a harm-causing action or decision, what went wrong, and why. This is important for post-hoc system diagnostics, establishing **accountability**, and accident inquiries.
- To understand the system prospectively: to **predict**, mitigate, and **prevent** future harm-causing actions or decisions.

Furthermore, the right to an intelligible explanation is supposedly required by law under the well-known 2018 GDPR regulation [11]. However, [24] argues that a right to explanation of automated decision-making does not exist in the GDPR due to the fact that the GDPR lacks precise language as well as explicit and well-defined rights and safeguards against automated decision-making. This closely relates to the lack of a precise language in the technical field of ML interpretability [21].

4.2 What Needs to Be Interpreted?

The different types of interpretability identified in Sect. 2 result in the interpretation of a set of distinct objects or processes. Transparency may refer to: the transparency of the whole model, wherein the entire global logic of the model can be explained and understood by a human; the transparency of the learning algorithm, we may understand that some algorithms converge to a solution in reasonable time (e.g. linear models), whereas we may not know whether another algorithm finds an optima at all (e.g. neural networks) [21]; transparency of parameters and model structures, do we understand what these are referring to and do they even map to human-understandable concepts? Similarly post-hoc explainability methods may try to explain and interpret these processes, e.g. through approximating the global logic of a model, or they may explain local decisions. Global interpretability methods generate evidence that applies to a whole model (or system), and can be used to support safety assurance by allowing reasoning about all possible future outcomes. Local methods generate explanations for an individual system decision, and may be used to 1) predict how the system will behave in specific situations and 2) analyse why a particular problem occurred, and to improve the model so future events of this type are avoided.

4.3 When Are Interpretations Needed?

Interpretations will be needed for different reasons during development and operation (Fig. 4). ML developers may seek global explanations to better understand the model to aid design; stakeholders will need different types of interpretations during operation (local explanations may be more important during operation to explain individual cases - e.g. when explaining why an accident occurred). During development interpretations will be needed for:

- **Data Management -** interpreting the model may identify imbalances/gaps in the data.
- **Model Selection -** the interpretability of a model should influence this.
- **Model Learning -** being able to interpret the model will inform the model learning stage, e.g. in aiding hyper-parameter selection, data augmentation, etc.
- **Model Verification -** being able to interpret model decisions will aid verification and help to identify the cause of model weaknesses.

And during operation:

- **Normal operation -** e.g. for advisory systems such as diagnostic tools explanations may be compulsory.
- **In cases where the model is known to underperform -** which will aid contestability or identifying when to hand over control to a human.
- **Accident or incident Investigation -** Local explainability (e.g. counterfactual) to discover why particular decisions were made.
- **Model Run-time Improvement/Learning -** To improve models as new data and situations are encountered.

4.4   Who Needs an Interpretation?

Different stakeholders need different types of interpretations, consider lay users, expert users, designers, etc. Developers need explanations and transparency to understand how the model works in order to predict when undesirable model behaviour will occur and make corrections and improvements. Whilst developers may need some local explainability to understand and account for edge cases, in general they will need global interpretability to aid design. End-users will need local explanations to satisfy understanding of individual decisions. Figure 4 lists some potential stakeholders and the explanation needs for each.

5   Summary

In this paper, we built on previous work, which developed an assurance argument pattern for reasoning about ML in safety-critical domains. We extended this argument pattern by identifying interpretability as a key consideration. The extended argument pattern can be used to guide developers of ML systems as part of a wider safety or assurance case. It identifies how to create a structured assurance argument for the interpretability of ML models to support a decision over the deployment of the models in safety-critical applications. The key points in the argument are the essential aspects: right method, right context, and right

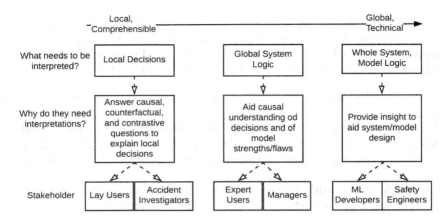

Fig. 4. Interpretation needs for different stakeholders

format. These are claims that we have identified as necessary to form an explicit argument over interpretability; importantly these claims must also be supported by appropriate evidence.

The focus of future work should be to evaluate the applicability of the argument structure which should be presented to ML practitioners, their feedback should be used to make any necessary improvements. Further work may expand our argument structure to address different cases, for instance by drawing a more concrete link between relevant assurance properties and clear interpretability needs in a particular system. We hope that this argument structure will provide a clear basis for developing and assessing requirements for the interpretability of ML in safety-critical domains.

References

1. Achinstein, P.: The Nature of Explanation. Oxford University Press, Oxford (1983)
2. Ashmore, R., Calinescu, R., Paterson, C.: Assuring the machine learning lifecycle: desiderata, methods, and challenges (2019)
3. Avati, A., Jung, K., Harman, S., Downing, L., Ng, A., Shah, N.H.: Improving palliative care with deep learning. BMC Med. Inform. Decis. Making **18**, 122 (2017). https://doi.org/10.1186/s12911-018-0677-8
4. Budish, R., et al.: Accountability of AI under the law: the role of explanation (2017)
5. Burton, S., Habli, I., Lawton, T., McDermid, J., Morgan, P., Porter, Z.: Mind the gaps: assuring the safety of autonomous systems from an engineering, ethical, and legal perspective (2020)
6. Picardi, C., Hawkins, R., Paterson, C., Habli, I.: A pattern for arguing the assurance of machine learning in medical diagnosis systems. In: Romanovsky, A., Troubitsyna, E., Bitsch, F. (eds.) SAFECOMP 2019. LNCS, vol. 11698, pp. 165–179. Springer, Cham (2019). https://doi.org/10.1007/978-3-030-26601-1_12

7. Doran, D., Schulz, S., Besold, T.R.: What does explainable AI really mean? A new conceptualization of perspectives (2017)
8. Doshi-Velez, F., Kim, B.: Towards a rigorous science of interpretable machine learning (2017)
9. Fauw, J.D., et al.: Clinically applicable deep learning for diagnosis and referral in retinal disease (2018)
10. Fischer, G.: Context-aware systems: the 'right' information, at the 'right' time, in the 'right' place, in the 'right' way, to the 'right' person (2012)
11. Goodman, B., Flaxman, S.: European union regulations on algorithmic decision-making and a "right to explanation" (2016)
12. Grimm: The goal of explanation (2010)
13. Habli, I., Lawton, T., Porter, Z.: Artificial intelligence in health care: accountability and safety. Bull. World Health Organiz. **98**(4), 251 (2020)
14. Hendricks, L.A., Akata, Z., Rohrbach, M., Donahue, J., Schiele, B., Darrell, T.: Generating visual explanations. In: Leibe, B., Matas, J., Sebe, N., Welling, M. (eds.) ECCV 2016. LNCS, vol. 9908, pp. 3–19. Springer, Cham (2016). https://doi.org/10.1007/978-3-319-46493-0_1
15. Higgins, I., et al.: Learning basic visual concepts with a constrained variational framework (2017)
16. Kelly, T.: A systematic approach to safety case management (2003)
17. Koh, P.W., Liang, P.: Understanding black-box predictions via influence functions (2017)
18. Lakkaraju, H., Bastani, O.: How do i fool you?: Manipulating user trust via misleading black box explanations (2019)
19. Lakkaraju, H., Kamar, E., Caruana, R., Leskovec, J.: Interpretable & explorable approximations of black box models (2017)
20. Lipton, Z.: The doctor just won't accept that! (2015)
21. Lipton, Z.C.: The Mythos of model interpretability (2017)
22. Lundberg, S.M., Lee, S.I.: A unified approach to interpreting model predictions (2017)
23. Miller, T.: Explanation in artificial intelligence: insights from the social sciences (2018)
24. Mittelstadt, B., Russell, C., Wachter, S.: Explaining explanations in AI (2018)
25. Mohseni, S., Zarei, N., Ragan, E.D.: A survey of evaluation methods and measures for interpretable machine learning (2018)
26. Mueller, S.T.: Explanation in human-AI systems: a literature meta-review synopsis of key ideas and publications and bibliography for explainable AI (2019)
27. Olah, C., Schubert, L., Mordvintsev, A.: Feature visualization how neural networks build up their understanding of images (2017)
28. Ribeiro, M.T., Singh, S., Guestrin, C.: "why should i trust you?" Explaining the predictions of any classifier (2016)
29. Rudin, C.: Please stop explaining black box models for high-stakes decisions (2018)
30. Wachter, S., Mittelstadt, B., Floridi, L.: Why a right to explanation of automated decision-making does not exist in the general data protection regulation (2017)
31. Watson, D., et al.: Clinical applications of machine learning algorithms: beyond the black box (2019)

A Structured Argument for Assuring Safety of the Intended Functionality (SOTIF)

John Birch[1]([⊠]), David Blackburn[2], John Botham[3], Ibrahim Habli[4], David Higham[5], Helen Monkhouse[1], Gareth Price[6], Norina Ratiu[7], and Roger Rivett[1,2,3,4,5,6,7]

[1] HORIBA MIRA Ltd., Nuneaton, UK
john.birch@horiba-mira.com
[2] Bentley Motors Ltd., Crewe, UK
[3] Ricardo UK Ltd., Cambridge, UK
[4] University of York, York, UK
[5] Imagination Technologies, Kings Langley, UK
[6] McLaren Applied, Woking, UK
[7] Aston Martin Lagonda, Gaydon, UK

Abstract. Current safety standards for automated driving recommend the development of a safety case. This case aims to justify and critically evaluate, by means of an explicit argument and evidence, how the safety claims concerning the intended functionality of an automated driving feature are supported. However, little guidance exists on how such an argument could be developed. In this paper, the MISRA consortium proposes a state machine on which an argument concerning the safety of the intended functionality could be structured. By systematically covering the activation status of the automated driving feature within and outside the operational design domain, this state machine helps in exploring the conditions, and asserting the corresponding safety claims, under which hazardous events could be caused by the intended functionality. MISRA uses a Traffic Jam Drive feature to illustrate the application of this approach.

Keywords: Safety assurance · Safety case · SOTIF · ODD · Automated driving

1 Problem

1.1 Safety Assurance of Automated Driving

Automated Driving (AD) promises to revolutionize the future of road transportation. However, the challenge of assuring its safety is significant and is subject to ongoing discussion and research. There are a variety of emerging standards such as ISO/PAS 21448 [1], UL 4600 [2] and ISO/TR 4804 [3] that relate to the safety of AD. These standards leave freedom for developers to reason about the safety of their systems by calling for the achievement of high-level goals or objectives, rather than conformance to prescriptive requirements, and by avoiding a declaration of what level of residual risk is reasonable or otherwise.

© Springer Nature Switzerland AG 2020
A. Casimiro et al. (Eds.): SAFECOMP 2020 Workshops, LNCS 12235, pp. 408–414, 2020.
https://doi.org/10.1007/978-3-030-55583-2_31

It is therefore not considered appropriate, nor feasible, to attempt to generate a compliance argument of the form "The Automated Driving System (ADS) is safe because its development complies with the requirements of standard X". Instead there is a professional responsibility placed on engineers to creatively justify, based on clear and rigorous evidence, why they believe their ADS is free from unreasonable risk. It is proposed that this justification should be communicated in the form of a safety argument, as part of a safety case [4], that will feature claims, assumptions and evidence related to a variety of standards, as acknowledged in [2]. This will help to ensure greater transparency in the development of ADS by enabling safety assessors and other stakeholders to critically evaluate the basis on which the system might be deployed.

1.2 Role of the Operational Design Domain

It is often the case that the Intended Functionality (IF), [1], of the ADS can only be achieved for a restricted set of vehicle, and external environmental, conditions referred to as the Operational Design Domain (ODD), [5], and defined as the "Operating conditions under which a given driving automation system or feature thereof is specifically designed to function (...)" [6]. This limitation may arise from known performance limitations or specification insufficiencies. To justify that the ADS is free from unreasonable risk it is necessary to reason about its IF when the vehicle is within the ODD, but also when the vehicle is transitioning into and out of the ODD.

The aim of this paper is to propose an approach to assuring ADS safety, initially aligned to ISO/PAS 21448, which is based on the central role played by the ODD and its transitions. It is illustrated with some example safety assurance considerations for a generic "Traffic Jam Drive" (TJD) feature.

2 Proposed Approach

2.1 ODD Transitions in an Example TJD Drive Cycle

Consider a typical drive cycle in which the generic TJD feature described in [7] may be used:

- The driver starts their journey by initializing the vehicle outside of the ODD before driving it into the ODD (e.g. onto a highway in clear weather with a lead vehicle etc.);
- TJD availability is indicated to the driver and the driver chooses to enable the feature, handing responsibility for the Dynamic Driving Task (DDT) [6] to the TJD feature;
- The TJD feature continues to control the DDT until either:

  - The driver chooses to deactivate the feature and resume control, or
  - The TJD hands control back to the driver without driver request;

- The driver leaves the highway (exiting the ODD), completes their journey and parks and secures the vehicle.

If the TJD feature were to be activated before entry to the ODD, or if the vehicle were to leave the ODD with the TJD still in control, the TJD feature would be responsible for controlling the DDT under conditions for which it was not designed. However, unless the driver is ready to resume control it may be unsafe for the TJD feature to relinquish DDT responsibility on exiting the ODD.

2.2 Presence of the Vehicle in the ODD and Activation Status of the Intended Functionality

The two key parameters identified in the above drive cycle, whose combination is critical for considering safe control of the DDT, are:

1. The presence of the vehicle in the ODD, or otherwise;
2. The activation status of the (TJD) feature.

MISRA expresses the combination of these parameters in the form of a state termed the "ODD-Activation State" which can take one of four values:

- State 1 – The IF is active whilst the vehicle is within the ODD
- State 2 – The IF is active whilst the vehicle is outside of the ODD
- State 3 – The IF is inactive whilst the vehicle is within the ODD
- State 4 – The IF is inactive whilst the vehicle is outside of the ODD

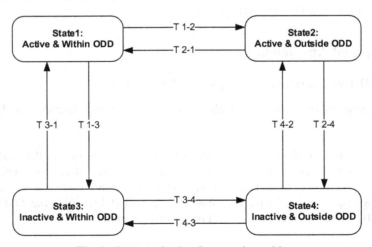

Fig. 1. ODD-Activation States and transitions

These states and the possible transitions between them are depicted as a state machine in Fig. 1. It might be argued that transitions could occur directly between State 1 and State 4 and also between State 2 and State 3. This would require the IF activation status to change at exactly the same time as the vehicle presence in the ODD changes. In practice this is very unlikely to occur, although it is recognized that the time spent in some of the states could be very short.

2.3 Example TJD Safety Claims

By explicitly defining the states and transitions in Fig. 1 the corresponding safety implications and possible safety claims can be systematically identified. Let us illustrate this by returning to the TJD drive cycle example. Using the ODD-Activation state machine

Table 1. Example TJD ODD-Activation States and transitions and corresponding safety claims

ODD-Activation State or transition	TJD drive cycle step	Example informal safety claims
State 4	Driver initialises vehicle outside of the ODD as the vehicle has not yet entered a highway with a lead vehicle, even though visibility is good	The TJD feature will detect when the vehicle is outside of the ODD Activation of the TJD is prevented until the vehicle enters the ODD
T 4-3	Vehicle enters the highway behind a lead vehicle. Visibility remains good and so the vehicle has entered the ODD. The driver is still in control of the DDT	–
T 3-1	TJD availability is indicated to the driver and the driver chooses to activate the feature, handing across control of the DDT	The handover of DDT control to the TJD is as anticipated by the driver - it is intuitive and predictable and does not occur unless it is requested by the driver who is ready for it
State 1	The TJD feature continues to control the DDT until…	The TJD controls the DDT within the ODD in a safe manner (e.g. successfully performing Object and Event Detection and Response (OEDR) [6] by keeping the vehicle in lane and at a safe distance to the lead vehicle, avoiding obstacle collision etc.)
T 1-3	…the driver chooses to deactivate the feature, taking back control of the DDT …	The hand-back of control to the driver by the TJD is as anticipated by the driver - it is intuitive and predictable and does not occur until the driver is ready
T 1-2 *State 2* *T 2-4*	…or the TJD hands DDT control back to the driver because, for example, visibility suddenly drops due to a change in the weather Note: this would ultimately cause entry into State 4, via State 2	The TJD will never make an active decision to leave the ODD (e.g. by causing the vehicle to leave the highway whilst it is responsible for the DDT) The TJD will detect the vehicle leaving the ODD (e.g. due to a sudden change of weather conditions, outside of its control) in a timely manner If the vehicle leaves the ODD whilst the TJD is in control of the DDT the TJD feature will take an appropriate and timely safe action, such as handing back control of the DDT to an alert driver or reaching a Minimal Risk Condition (MRC) [6] The TJD feature will not regularly have to hand-back responsibility for the DDT to the driver because of the inability of the feature to cope with commonly occurring conditions (such as a change in weather)

(continued)

Table 1. (*continued*)

ODD-Activation State or transition	TJD drive cycle step	Example informal safety claims
State 4	The driver completes the drive cycle, bringing the vehicle to rest	–

(Fig. 1), Table 1 expands the steps previously outlined with some example informal claims that one may wish to make about the corresponding ADS behaviour.

The example claims presented in Table 1 may be challenging to substantiate in practice but that only serves to highlight their necessity. For example, it may be that the driver and the TJD feature have a conflicting view under certain conditions of whether the vehicle is present in the ODD. These views may not only conflict with each other but also with the "true" status of ODD presence. Such a discrepancy may serve as a potential source of harm. This would prevent the claim "The TJD feature will detect when the vehicle is outside of the ODD" from being substantiated, which would cause the issue to be highlighted, and hopefully addressed, as a weakness within the safety case.

Another challenging issue highlighted by the state machine in Fig. 1 and the example claims in Table 1 is the risk associated with being in State 2 (the IF being active whilst the vehicle is outside of the ODD). By its nature this is clearly an undesirable state to be in, but acknowledging its conceptual existence provides the ADS developer with the opportunity to explain their strategy to limit the corresponding risk. One example strategy might be to make use of "defensive regions" that lie on the boundary of "μODDs" in which "best effort" behaviours are specified, as proposed in [8].

2.4 MISRA SOTIF Argument Structure

From the example claims in Table 1, and by considering the states and transitions in Fig. 1, we can extract some general high-level claims that one may wish to make about any ADS. These have been collated in a single argument structure expressed in Goal Structuring Notation (GSN) [9], the top level of which is shown in Fig. 2.

For completeness, the argument structure incorporates reference to the consideration of post-release SOTIF issues. Whilst this is an important topic it is not one considered to be central to the ideas presented in this paper and is thus not explored further.

3 Discussion and Further Work

The four-state model and corresponding safety argument represents MISRA's initial insight into an approach that highlights the central role played by the ODD in assuring ADS safety. The argument in Fig. 2 represents an initial structure for a series of subsequent claims and items of evidence that will relate to a variety of topics in [1]. It is anticipated that these claims will be categorized according to the following MISRA argument themes related to those introduced in [10]:

- The rationale for the SOTIF requirements used to specify the IF;
- The satisfaction of these requirements by the implemented IF;

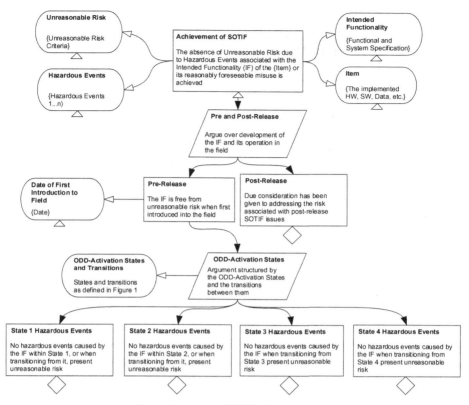

Fig. 2. Top-level SOTIF safety argument

- The means used to perform the various SOTIF-related activities;
- The development environment in which they have been performed.

Work is ongoing to further develop the argument structure and to recommend supporting claims. This will include broadening the argument scope (beyond [1]) to incorporate causes of hazardous events relating to malfunctions (functional safety) and vulnerabilities (cybersecurity). It is anticipated that this work will form a basis for a subsequent MISRA publication that follows on from [10].

References

1. ISO/PAS 21448:2019 Road Vehicles – Safety of the intended functionality
2. UL 4600 UL Standard for Safety for Evaluation of Autonomous Products. First Edition, April 2020
3. ISO/CD TR 4804 Road Vehicles – Safety and security for automated driving systems – Design, verification and validation methods
4. Hawkins, R., Kelly, T., Knight, J., Graydon, P.: A new approach to creating clear safety arguments. In: Dale, C., Anderson, T. (eds.) Advances in Systems Safety, pp. 3–23. Springer, London (2011). https://doi.org/10.1007/978-0-85729-133-2_1

5. Gyllenhammar, M., et al.: Towards an operational design domain that supports the safety argumentation of an automated driving system, January 2020
6. SAE J3016: Taxonomy and Definitions for Terms Related to Driving Automation Systems for On-Road Motor Vehicles, June 2018
7. NHTSA DOT HS 812 623: A Framework for Automated Driving System Testable Cases and Scenarios, September 2018
8. Koopman, P., Osyk, B., Weast, J.: Autonomous vehicles meet the physical world: RSS, variability, uncertainty, and proving safety. In: Romanovsky, A., Troubitsyna, E., Bitsch, F. (eds.) SAFECOMP 2019. LNCS, vol. 11698, pp. 245–253. Springer, Cham (2019). https://doi.org/10.1007/978-3-030-26601-1_17
9. Goal Structuring Notation Community Standard Version 2, January 2018
10. MISRA Guidelines for Automotive Safety Arguments, ISBN 978-1-906400-24-8, September 2019

Author Index

Abrecht, Stephanie 289, 336
Acar-Celik, Esra 370
Akila, Maram 289

Bäckman, Ronny 161
Balbis, Abel 54
Bassem, Cédric 266
Beyene, Tewodros A. 328
Birch, John 408
Blackburn, David 408
Bonitz, Arndt 148
Botham, John 408
Brenner, Eugen 123

Cabral, Henrique 243
Cârlan, Carmen 370
Cleaveland, Matthew 82
Codenie, Wim 229
Cullmann, Christoph 98

Dagnely, Pierre 243
Dan, György 69
Davoli, Luca 176
Dobberphul, Timo 383
Duque Anton, Simon D. 266
Durak, Umut 217

Elks, Carl 193
Etxeberria, Leire 205

Fabian, Martin 9
Fei, Zhennan 9
Ferdinand, Christian 98
Filho, Ênio 136
Fraunholz, Daniel 266

Gannamaneni, Sujan Sai 289
Gassmann, Bernd 358
Gauerhof, Lydia 383
Gautham, Smitha 193
Gebhard, Gernot 98
Godot, Jean 54
Groh, Konrad 289

Habli, Ibrahim 395, 408
Hahn, Sebastian 98
Heinzemann, Christian 289
Higham, David 408
Houben, Sebastian 289
Hristoskova, Anna 229

Ivanov, Radoslav 82

Jayakumar, Athira V. 193
Jöckel, Lisa 315

Karos, Thomas 98
Kästner, Daniel 98
Kaur, Ramneet 82
Kläs, Michael 315
Kloibhofer, Reinhard 176
Knie, Bernhard 383
Koch, Tobias 266
Koopman, Philip 351
Kristen, Erwin 176
Krohmer, Daniel 266
Kurunathan, Harrison 136

Lagrave, Pierre-Yves 302
Langer, Lucie 148
Larsen, Morten 266
Lee, Insup 82
Limonta, Gabriela 161

Macher, Georg 123
Marko, Nadja 36
Marosvölgyi, Marcell 266
Martinez, Jabier 54
Mauborgne, Laurent 98
Monkhouse, Helen 408

Oboril, Fabian 358
Ogawa, Kiyoshi 23
Oliver, Ian 161

Pasch, Frederik   358
Platzer, Michael   111
Poorhadi, Ehsan   69
Price, Gareth   408
Puschner, Peter   111
Putzer, Henrik J.   370

Raafatnia, Shervin   336, 383
Rath, Annanda   229
Ratiu, Norina   408
Reti, Daniel   266
Rivett, Roger   408
Rocco, Vittorio   383
Ruehrup, Stefan   148
Ruiz, Alejandra   54
Ruiz Nolasco, Ricardo   54

Sagardui, Goiuria   205
Sahu, Amit   328
Sämann, Timo   383
Schmittner, Christoph   123, 148
Scholl, Kay-Ulrich   358
Schotten, Hans D.   266
Schwalbe, Gesina   383
Selgert, Franklin   255, 266
Selvaraj, Yuvaraj   9
Severino, Ricardo   136
Sokolsky, Oleg   82

Striecks, Christoph   36
Sudhakar, Krishna   266
Sudholt, Sebastian   336

Tanaka, Nobuaki   23
Tourwé, Tom   243
Tovar, Eduardo   136
Troubitysna, Elena   69

Ugarte Querejeta, Miriam   205

Van Vaerenbergh, Kevin   243
Vasenev, Alexandr   36
Veledar, Omar   123

Wagner, Michael   351
Ward, Francis Rhys   395
Wilhelm, Stephan   98
Willers, Oliver   336
Witt, Till   266
Woehrle, Matthias   289
Wozniak, Ernest   370

Yomiya, Hisashi   23

Zaeske, Wanja   217